Advances in Cybernetics and Systems

Advances in CYBERNETICS *and* SYSTEMS

Volume 2

Edited by

J. ROSE

Blackburn College of Technology and Design
Director-General, World Organization of
General Systems and Cybernetics (W.O.G.S.C.)

GORDON AND BREACH SCIENCE PUBLISHERS

London New York Paris

Gordon and Breach Science Publishers, Ltd.
42 William IV Street
London W.C. 2

Editorial office for the United States of America

Gordon and Breach, Science Publishers Inc.
1, Park Ave.
New York, N.Y. 10016

Editorial office for France

Gordon & Breach
7-9 rue Emile Dubois
Paris 75014

Library of Congress catalog card number 74-76604.
ISBN 0 677 15670 7.
Printed in Great Britain.

PREFACE

The contents of these three volumes record the International Congress of Cybernetics and Systems held at the University of Oxford from 28th August to 1st September, 1972, under the aegis of the World Organisation of General Systems and Cybernetics (W.O.G.S.C.). Delegates from 26 countries of all the continents attended the event and 132 papers were presented.

The aims of this event were as follows:

1) To afford an international forum for an exchange of ideas and up-to-date information in the field of cybernetics and general systems.

2) To investigate the areas common to both cybernetics and general systems.

3) To strengthen the scientific basis of the interdisciplinary science of cybernetics with special emphasis on general systems theory.

4) To point the way to future development in this field.

5) To reinforce the organisational structure in order to further the cause of cybernetics and general systems.

The Congress consisted of two plenary sessions, two symposia ("Cybernetics and Health"; "Cybernetics and Automation") and meetings of six sections (Artificial Intelligence; Neuro- and Bio-Cybernetics; Engineering Cybernetics; Social and Economic Systems; Cybernetics, Modeling and Computer Simulation; Cybernetics, Education and Communication).

The papers presented at the plenary session and the symposia deal with fundamental topics of wide significance, viz. "intelligent" machines, system growth dynamics, progress in neurocybernetics, some general aspects of automation, the application of cybernetics to medical problems, systems causality in nature and problems of the environment.

Various aspects of artificial intelligence are discussed in Section One including computer games, heuristics, pattern recognition and theorem proving, while Section Two deals with a large number of topics pertaining to neuro- and bio-cybernetics, viz. the C.N.S., disease, visual systems and medical practice.

Problems of automata are considered in Section Three, e.g. threshold, finite, fuzzy and mobile types, as well as optimisation procedures. The expanding subject of social and economic systems is considered in Section Four; this includes a discussion of some management problems.

Section Five contains papers or models and computer simulation, including several references to environmental problems. A wide variety of topics are considered, including systems dynamics, human population, hydrological and biological systems, psychosynthesis, and visual images.

The last session (Six) surveys recent developments in the field of education and communication as related to cybernetics. Among the topics considered are teaching and program language processing systems, and learning and human cybernetics.

The scope of papers presented at this Congress is much wider than that at the London Congress in 1969, while the standard is also superior. No doubt, this reflects the considerable advances made by cybernetics and systems in the last few years. Some of the papers are truly pioneering and of fundamental importance to science and technology. Because of space limitations most of the papers had to be greatly abridged. It is hoped that expanded versions of these papers brought up-to-date will appear in due course in "Kybernetes".

Ours is the age not only of an information explosion but also of a proliferation of sciences. A catalogue published in 1959 by J.T. Thykouner listed 1150 sciences then in existence; by now this list has grown, the number exceeding 1200. In addition, each science is subdivided into sections, leading to excessive specialisation and to the situation when the expert "knows more and more about less and less", while the once common "language" has now disintegrated into groups of terms to such an extent that scientists in various fields find it difficult to understand each other's contributions. A common "language" of science is thus of importance, this term extending not only to semantic aspects but also to the very background of the pool of knowledge. Perhaps the synthesis of Cybernetics with General Systems Theory could fill this vacuum and meet an urgent need.

In 1931 A. Einstein asked in an address at the C.I.T. "Why does this magnificent applied science which saves work and makes life easier bring us so little happiness? The simple answer runs:

'Because we have not yet learned to make suitable use of it'". Perhaps one way out of this difficulty may be one of Wiener's theses that cracks in the complex edifices of contemporary life were caused not by inconsistencies in our use of science, but by simple failures of meaning, by mistaken identities and by avoidable breakdowns in communications; in other words, danger signs are misread and the resulting information goes unchecked.

I wish to thank the Council and the Liaison Committee of the W.O.G.S.C., for their encouragement and assistance in organising this Congress. My thanks are due to Dr. J.A. Cade for his valuable help in editing part of the proceedings, a most demanding task. I am grateful to Queen's College, Oxford and the Examinations Schools of the University of Oxford for the facilities offered. I wish to express my gratitude to the Lord Mayor of Oxford and distinguished speakers, Dr. W. Perry (Vice-Chancellor of the Open University in the United Kingdom), Professor Kan Chen (President-designate of the S.M.C. Group of the I.E.E.E.) and Dr. A.M. Hilton for gracing the official banquet with their presence and delivering the speeches. My thanks are also due to my secretary, the indefatigable Miss R.R. Black, for her valuable assistance in organising the Congress and preparing the proceedings. Finally, I would like to thank the Chairman of the sessions and authors of papers for their willing co-operation. In particular, I wish to record my thanks to Professor T.C. Helvey, the Director of External Affairs of the W.O.G.S.C., for his splendid and tireless help at the Congress. It is hoped that the goodwill of all concerned will be extended to the W.O.G.S.C. and to the next Congress to be held (hopefully) in 1975.

J. ROSE
Editor and Congress Organiser

CONTENTS: VOLUME II

SECTION III: ENGINEERING CYBERNETICS (AUTOMATION)

SECTION IV

CONTENTS: VOLUME I

SYMPOSIUM: CYBERNETICS AND HEALTH

SECTION I: ARTIFICIAL INTELLIGENCE

CONTENTS: VOLUME III

SECTION VI

SECTION II

COMPUTERS IN PROBLEM ORIENTED MEDICINE

F.W. DONALDSON

Prof. of Computer Science, University of Tennessee Space Institute, Tullahoma, Tennessee 37388, U.S.A.

SUMMARY

Though problem oriented practice has been in existence for at least the past twenty years, the digital computer with its massive memory and rapid access for storage and retrieval of problem oriented medical records has been and will continue to be the driving force in the spread of the concept of problem oriented medicine. This paper will review the concept of POM and the PROMIS computer system that makes the concept more palatable to more physicians, and will review the progress of problem oriented practice to date in the United States.

INTRODUCTION

The practical and economical use of computers in any field has depended to a very large extent on the ability to establish standards in that field. Anyone in the computing field will recognize the value of standards for programming languages, file formats, character sets, hardware, and even program documentation.

A major hindrance in the use of computers in medicine has been the lack of standards and the nearly impossible task of establishing them. It has been extremely difficult to get two hospitals or two insurance companies to agree on a standard insurance claim form and you can see why it has been difficult to establish standard patient record formats. Where standards have been established it is because computers have forced them.

It would appear that a majority of doctors in the past, having completed their internship and possibly their residency, were forevermore on their own. This has been especially true of the small town doctor who immediately became overloaded the day he opened his office. At last there is a cure in sight for this illness.

THE PROBLEM ORIENTED RECORD (POR)

The development of the problem oriented record system was pioneered by Dr. Lawrence L. Weed of the University of Vermont. Though there is some flexibility in POR, it holds promise of becoming the widest used standard in the medical field fitting equally well the doctor in solo practice, in the clinical environment, the hospital out-patient clinic, the hospital ward, the public health service clinic, the prevention clinic, and especially the teaching hospital where we expect POR to be taught, or anywhere that medical records must be kept on well or sick people. There are definite signs that POR and problem oriented medicine (POM) are catching on rapidly in the United States. Wherever Dr. Weed speaks to medical societies, medical school staffs and students, and to groups of doctors, he is met with enthusiastic acceptance. There are exceptions, of course. Dr. Weed tells it like it is today, and one can tell by the reactions of his student and faculty audiences that what he says is truth. His book on Medical Records, Medical Education, and Patient Care [1] must be a best-seller in the medical world judging by my personal sampling. Investigations of Dr. J. Willard Hurst of Emory University in Atlanta, Georgia show that an estimated 25% of the medical schools in the United States are teaching (POM) with the number increasing constantly. POR as a standard, forms the very foundation for POM. It establishes the basis for the guidance system for the practice of POM. Together they form the foundation of the first real systems approach to medical care.

Though POM has been practiced for a number of years on paper, it is the computer, with its fast manipulation capability, that makes it really practical from the standpoint of greater efficiency and greater patient throughput. However, if a physician established the system in his office in preparation for going on-line to a computer system and never got around to the computer, he would still be far ahead as far as quality medical care is concerned.

We will discuss each phase briefly from the standpoint of automation. Information under all items of Phase I can be input directly into the computer where the computer system puts the information into proper format. The patient can use a computer terminal with computer controlled branching questionnaire or he can use a machine readable marked sensed form for his medical history. This is the beginning of his data base

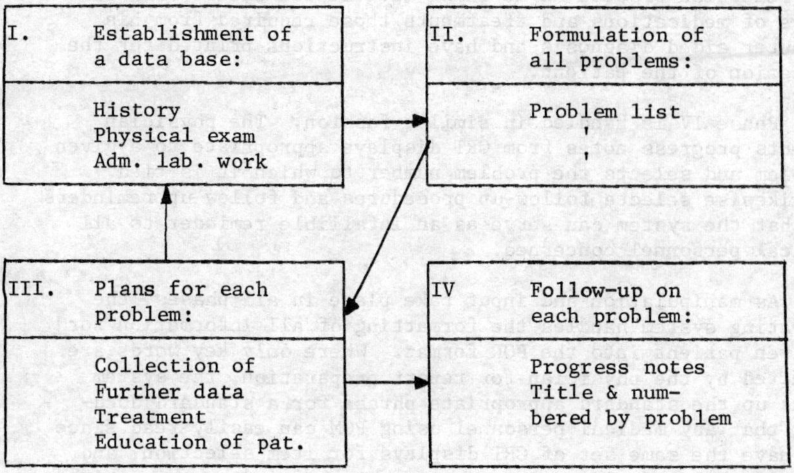

The four phases of POR

and this might have been input considerably in advance of his visit to the physician. The physical exam and laboratory results can be input directly into the computer by paramedics handling this phase of data base collection which will be supplemented later by request of the examining physician from his terminal as he discusses today's problem with the patient. The physical exam might have been of the multiphasic health screening variety with most test results entered directly into the computer by the instrument used. This should be done for population masses in a given region as a foundation for data bases for the beginning of POM.

From the data base, we see in Phase II the physician will formulate all of the patient's problems into a problem list or add to the problem list if such a list already exists. This is the key to POM. Each problem is assigned a number by which all plans, treatment, progress notes, etc., are referenced. Hence the term Problem Oriented. The physician need *not* key in the names of these problems or their numbers since he can select these from prepared lists which he can readily call up as displays on his Cathode Ray Tube (CRT). He simply points to the items he wants or pushes a key corresponding to any item. The computer system handles all housekeeping for him through the CRT display and selection process.

In Phase III the physician can call for further tests or further information from the patient. He orders his tests by the selection process as in Phase II. He can select from displays of medications and treatments those required from his computer aided diagnosis and have instructions printed for the education of the patient.

Phase IV is handled in similar fashion. The physician selects progress notes from CRT displays appropriate to a given problem and selects the problem number to which it is tied. He likewise selects follow-up procedures and follow-up reminders so that the system can serve as an infallible reminder to all medical personnel concerned.

As manipulation and input take place in all phases, the operating system handles the formatting of all information for a given patient into the POR format. Where only key words are selected by the physician for report preparation, the system looks up the standard appropriate phrase for a standard document that any medical personnel using POM can easily read since all have the same set of CRT displays for item selection, and the same holds for documents that are to be read by the patient and other non-medical personnel.

The system serves as a guidance system to medical care. Dr. Weed and his staff have developed some 20,000 CRT display frames with data processing specialists writing the guidance control programs [2]. These frames serve as diagnostic, medication, and treatment aids and are likewise used for medical orders and the composition of summary reports and indeed for composing medical prescriptions for the pharmacy. The hospital wing where Dr. Weed uses the system in a medical school teaching environment doesn't have a pencil in the place. All medical personnel including students and nurses manipulate the system through the CRT. The system serves as a powerful teaching device. This is truly an automated POM system.

Drs. Harold D. Cross and John C. Bjorn are using the system in a private practice environment in a town of 5,000 people in Maine. These two doctors have pioneered in manual or non-automated POM for a number of years. They have found this logical or systems approach to medical care valuable even without automation. They are presently tied into Dr. Weed's system by telephone line hookup. Their book, Problem Oriented Practice [3], is highly recommended reading.

POM shows great promise of becoming the standard required to establish a network of automated regional medical information systems. Dr. Weed continues his work of expanding his display frames, and we look upon his effort as the start of a centralized National Library of Displays maintained by the best medical personnel of the country having at their disposal the best medical libraries of the country. We expect that as frames are modified or new information added, such as new medications and treatments, these will be transmitted out over the regional network to automatically up-date all frames of the network. The new information is there whenever the physician needs it. It is not hard to see this as a device for continuing education for all medical personnel of the country. It certainly is a dream worth pursuing and I am working madly on what I hope will be the first major region to implement the POM system in a five county, five city region of Central Tennessee with a total population of 120,000 people.

HOW POM WORKS

We have already reviewed the four phases of the POR and how it is maintained by the physician-paramedic-computer combination. Let us take a look at how the physician uses the system in his day-to-day office practice.

He has a master CRT with all temporary storage and controls possibly at his reception desk. He has in addition relatively inexpensive CRTs, no more expensive than a small TV, in each of his examination rooms since he will want to manipulate the system as he talks to his patients.

Assume that he sees a patient for 7.5 minutes. With his library of displays and patient records stored on high speed disks, he can retrieve one frame in less than one second. With a little practice he can manipulate the system and never stop talking to the patient thus consuming no patient time. Assuming that he looks at one frame for two seconds (normally it will be less), he can access 140 frames during one patient visit. However, he should average no more than 50. With his own and his patient's identities input, he retrieves the patient's problem list. In the meantime he is checking the patient's problem of today and quickly checks to see if it is a new or old problem. If new, he adds it to the list by selection from the appropriate frame for the body system involved. He assigns it a number also by selection from a frame. He calls up the results of tests and vital signs already input today before he sees the patient. He numbers these results that are to be retained with the proper problem number. If more tests are needed for proper diagnosis, he orders them through the system by calling for the appropriate frames and pointing to the tests desired. These are typed out on the hard copy terminal in his laboratory and he leaves this patient to paramedics to run these tests and proceeds to visit with his next patient while they are being run. If they cannot be done in his own laboratory, he orders the tests from an outside laboratory and has instructions printed out for his patient by the system to take along to the laboratory, or they are automatically printed at a terminal at that laboratory.

If the physician has sufficient information, he will start his sequence of frames to aid in diagnosis. Having arrived at the most likely possibilities, he uses his past experience to make his final choice.

He is now ready to call upon the appropriate displays of the best medications and treatments. As he makes his selections, these are being accumulated by the system to add to the patient's record under the appropriate problem number and instructions are being accumulated for printout for the patient. With a bit of practice, the physician can do all of this manipulation without diverting his attention from his patient.

The question might be asked, what happens if the system goes down or he is out somewhere with an emergency where the system is not available. The answer is that with day to day use of the system with its updating capability for the physician, the physician is in a position to treat any emergency case more intelligently in such an emergency as a result of his continued updating by the system. I would like to emphasize that the real key to POM is the POR. To be most effective, an automated system is necessary for the retrieval and manipulation of massive record systems. I would also like to emphasize that the POR and the computer control program serve as the guidance system in POM that will take much of the guesswork out of medical practice in the future. To quote one physician in one of my audiences, "this system will make a specialist of the worst 'klunkhead' doctor in the country".

The benefits of automated POM are so great that neither time nor space permit me to even list them without comment. Thus I will have to stop at this point. If you would like to corner me sometime during the remaining sessions, I would be glad to go into detail.

Does automated POM offer better medical care and is it cost-effective if used on a large scale? The object of my work in Middle-Tennessee is to show that the answer to both of these questions is "yes" [4].

REFERENCES

1. L.L. WEED, *Medical Records, Medical Education, and Patient Care* (Year Book Medical Publishers, Inc., 35 East Wacker Drive, Chicago, Ill., U.S.A., 1969).

2. J.R. SCHULTZ, S.V. CANTRILL and K.G. MORGAN, "An initial operational problem oriented medical record system — for storage, manipulation, and retrieval of medical data" *AFIPS Conf. Proc. 38* (AFIPS Press, Montvale, N.J., U.S.A., 1971).

3. J.C. BJORN and H.D. CROSS, "Problem oriented practice" (Modern Hospital Press, Chicago, Ill., U.S.A., 1971).

4. F.W. DONALDSON, "On-line computing in the medical profession" *Proc. Second International Symposium on Computers in Medicine* (John Wright & Sons Ltd., London, 1971).

INFLUENCE OF VISUAL ATTENTION ON BACKGROUND ACTIVITY IN SINGLE CELLS OF MONKEY VISUAL CORTEX*

B. BRIDGEMAN

Dept. of Psychology, Stanford University, Stanford, Calif. 94305, U.S.A.

SUMMARY

For 39 neurons in the visual cortex of 3 monkeys, background firing rate was compared in attention and non-attention conditions. Attention in this context is defined in terms of reinforcement contingencies; the attention condition required the animal to perform a continuous visual tracking task for reinforcement, while during the non-attention period no visual activity was reinforced and the monkey viewed a field to which he had been habituated for at least 50 hours. Attention and non-attention periods, each lasting 2.5 seconds, were interlaced to prevent any long-term activity changes from biasing the results. The cells fell into two qualitatively different classes: 34 showed only small changes with visual attention, while five showed dramatic and long-lasting inhibitions. In the first group the activity during the attention condition was lower than that during non-attention (t-test for matched pairs, sig. at 2% level). The second group showed a strong attention-induced inhibition which eliminated background activity altogether and became stronger with each successive tracking period. Activity gradually returned during rest, requiring up to one minute to reach the previous background level. The length of this inhibited period suggests that a tonic influence from another brain area rather than a simple recurrent inhibition is responsible for the phenomenon.

Though attention plays an important role in perception, both its general neuronal mechanisms and its specific effects on single cells in sensory systems are poorly understood. In this paper a neuronal mechanism for the brain's control of its input will be based on data from background activities of single

*Supported by NIH Grant MH 12970 to Dr. Karl H. Pribram. I thank Dr. Pribram, D.N. Spinelli, and R.W. Phelps for advice and assistance.

neurons in the monkey visual cortex while visual attention is manipulated: a period during which a monkey performs a continuous visual task for reinforcement is defined as a period of high visual attention, while a period of passive wakefulness is defined as a period of relatively less attention. Behaviorally, this manipulation is better defined than in previous studies which have used non-visual sensory arousal [1] or reticular stimulation [2,3,4] to change the state of visual cortex.

METHOD

Training, surgical, and electrophysiological techniques have been described previously [5]. Three immature rhesus monkeys implanted for chronic microelectrode recording tracked a small spot moving slowly across a tangent screen. During each trial the target spot moved up and down over 25° at 10°/sec and monkeys were rewarded for visually tracking the return part of the scan without saccadic eye movements. During the inter-trial intervals no visual activity was reinforced, and the animal viewed an environment to which he had been accustomed during at least 50 hours of training. The monkeys generally did not fixate or track the target as it moved upward.

Background activity of a cell, recorded from an extra-cellular microelectrode, was collected during each trial and divided into 50 msec bins. Neuronal activity records were based on at least 50 sec, but usually several minutes, of data, and a cell was included in the sample only if no excitation or inhibition due to visual receptive field properties appeared during at least one set of 10 or more consecutive trials. Activity during the upward movement of the target (not tracked) was included in the non-tracking condition, while activity during the tracked return scan was summed and labeled the tracking condition. Thus data for the two conditions were collected in alternating 2.5 sec epochs. Target movement during the non-tracking epochs made distal stimulus conditions as similar as possible under the two experimental conditions, while the alternation controlled for any long-term activity changes. Trials in which tracking was unsuccessful were discarded.

RESULTS

From a total of 84 neurons in three monkeys from which some data were obtained, the 39 which were analyzed yielded records of a minimum duration and showed no visual responses under the conditions used (many of the cells in the analyzed sample did show visual responses under other stimulus conditions). Twenty-three of the analyzed cells (59%) were suppressed by visual tracking, 12 cells (31%) were excited, and the activity of 4 cells (10%) changed less than 5%.

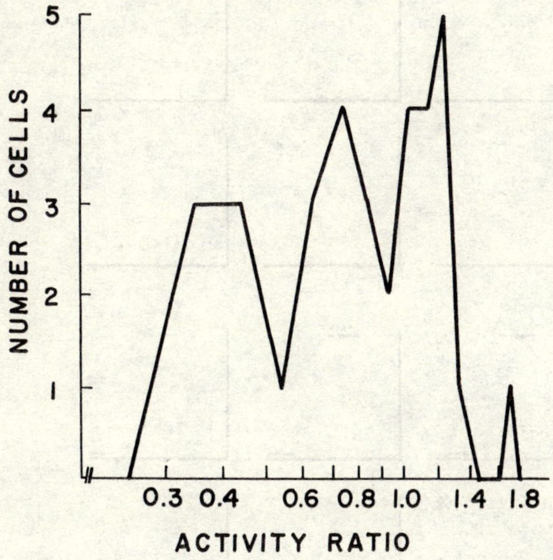

Fig. 1. Ratio of total number of spikes during visual tracking to total number of spikes at rest for 34 cells. A log plot normalizes the ratio distribution. Each point is centered in a domain 0.1 ratio units wide.

The ratios of activity in the tracking and non-tracking conditions for 34 of these neurons (group I) fell into the distribution shown in Fig. 1. Strong decrease in activity was more frequent during tracking than was strong increase in this group: six neurons had activities of half the resting level or less during tracking, while none had double or more its normal background level. A t-test for matched pairs performed on the background activities in the tracking and non-tracking conditions is significant at the .02 level ($t=2.59$; $t_{.02(30)}=2.46$). No consistent changes in firing rate as a function of the duration of visual tracking were observed, either within or between trials.

Five other neurons (group II) showed a qualitatively different effect, in which the tracking condition yielded a strong and long-lasting inhibition of background activity. After a few

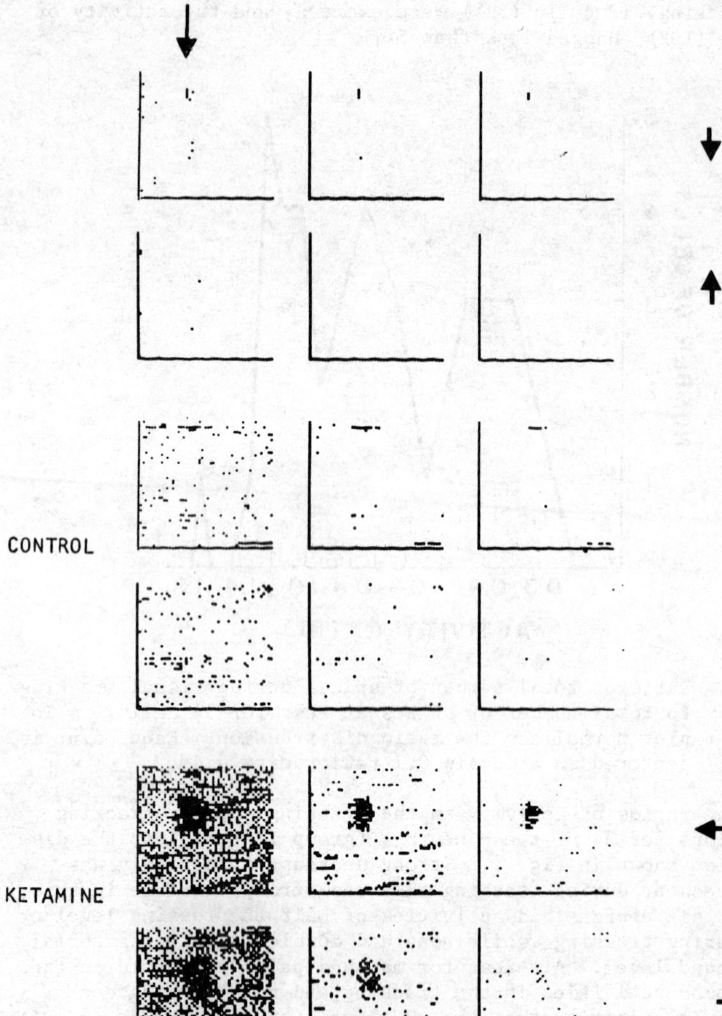

Fig. 2.

Explanation to Fig. 2.

Fig. 2. Change in activity with attention. A dot appears in the first column (level 1) if the cell fired once or more during a 50 msec period. For levels 2 and 3 a dot appears only if the cell fired at least 2 or 3 times respectively during the same period. The heavy arrows (right) indicate the movement of the fixation target, which was tracked only in the down direction. Within a display each vertical column of dots represents a separate trial, with the first trial at the left. Top: a group II cell whose activity was suppressed by tracking. After several minutes of rest (arrow) activity reappeared but was quickly suppressed by more tracking. Row 2 shows that the suppression was effective even between tracking trials. Center: Two control maps also collected in alternating fashion, but without a stimulus. Data appear in horizontal lines beginning at the bottom. Bottom: Records made during horizontal scans of the moving stimulus, beginning at the bottom, with the eyes immobilized by anesthesia. Activity is further increased and a receptive field appears. The tracking condition, resting level, and background under anesthesia represent a continuum of decreasing visual attention, with background increasing at every stage.

---

trials of visual tracking the background activity disappeared completely (Fig. 2.), the inhibition carrying over from trial to trial and summating. The temporal pattern of recovery after a series of visual-tracking trials is shown in Fig. 3: there was no firing for 28 sec after the end of the tracking period, after which activity gradually increased to normal. Another similar neuron showed its first action potential 21 sec after the last tracking.

The distribution of group II cells was not random, for three of the five cells in this group were found in a single pass through a column of cortex in one monkey. These three cells had somewhat shorter time constants of recovery than the two cells reported above, so that some background activity could be recorded between trials (Fig. 4, top). After a rest period, however, an increase in background activity always occurred (Fig. 4, bottom).

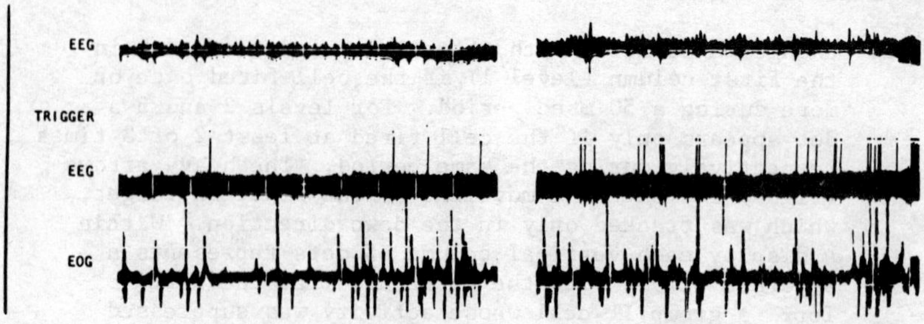

Fig. 3. Recovery of activity after suppression by visual tracking. The first and last channels show low-pass filtered AC records from the microelectrode and a vertical electro-oculogram respectively: neither shows consistent changes over the recovery period. The second channel shows a Schmitt trigger response obtained from the third channel, a high-pass filtered record from the microelectrode. The last trial of visual tracking ended at the vertical line at the left. Each data block is 50 sec long. Spikes retouched.

DISCUSSION

The results of this experiment, a reduction of background activity in most cells and a strong, long-lasting suppression in a few, are consistent with earlier work on background activity in single cells of visual cortex. The excitability of the visual system has been manipulated indirectly both in the rabbit [2,3,4] and in the cat [1,6], where visual activation usually resulted in suppression in some neurons and excitation in others, the suppression predominating, though the effect has never been quantified as in Fig. 1.

Because tracking can yield long-lasting inhibitory changes in visual cortex, it is likely that the changes which accompany tracking do not originate in the visual cortex itself but are mediated by afferents from other areas. Inhibition cannot maintain itself by circulating in neuronal loops, and the tracking-excited cells which form part of group I have responses which are too short-lasting to mediate a post-synaptic inhibition of group II cells.

These results can be interpreted in terms of Pribram's theory [7] that information processing in primary sensory channels is modified by influences from intrinsic cortex, in

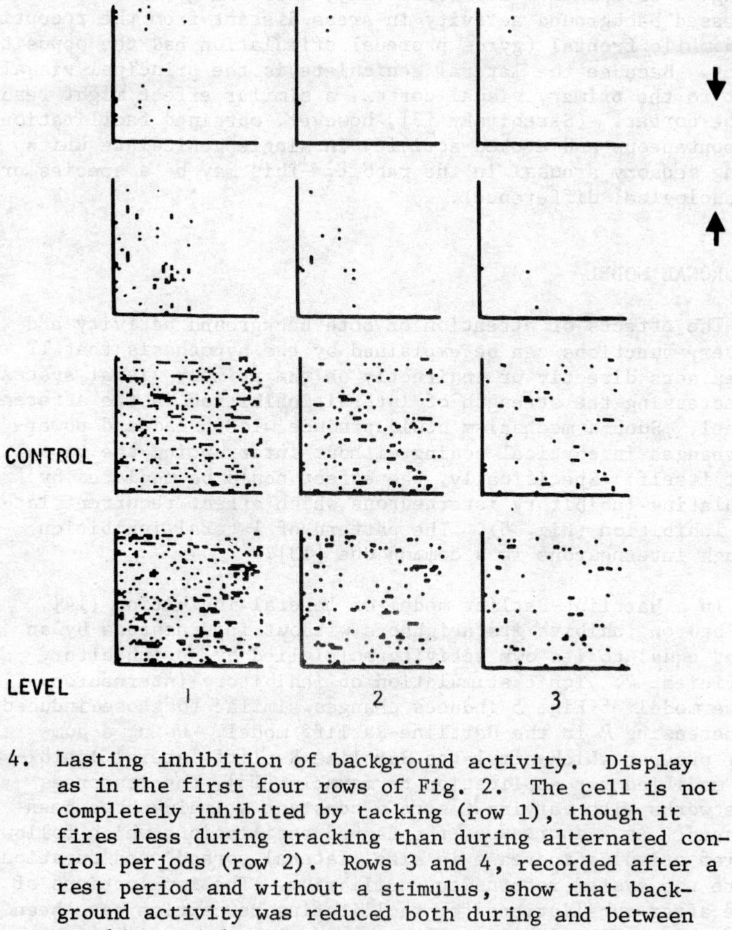

Fig. 4. Lasting inhibition of background activity. Display as in the first four rows of Fig. 2. The cell is not completely inhibited by tacking (row 1), though it fires less during tracking than during alternated control periods (row 2). Rows 3 and 4, recorded after a rest period and without a stimulus, show that background activity was reduced both during and between tracking trials. Tracking was halted at 28 trials.

the case of vision by lateral frontal and infero-temporal (IT) areas. While IT ablation in monkeys yields deficits in difficult visual discriminations [8,9], IT stimulation increases the period during which the gross evoked response to the second of two light flashes is depressed [10]. IT stimulation also has the effect of increasing visual attention [11].

Stimulation of the hippocampal fusiform gyrus in cats, thought to be homologous to primate IT cortex [12], can modify lateral geniculate receptive fields. In the cell illustrated in Fig. 2 of Spinelli & Pribram [12], fusiform gyrus stimulation decreased background activity in areas distant from the receptive field while frontal (gyrus proreus) stimulation had the opposite effect. Because the lateral geniculate is the principal visual input to the primary visual cortex, a similar effect might result in the cortex. (Skrebitsky [3], however, obtained facilitation of spontaneous and evoked activity in single geniculate units during sensory arousal in the rabbit. This may be a species or methodological difference).

A NEURONAL MODEL

The effects of attention on both background activity and recovery functions can be explained by the hypothesis that IT cortex acts directly or indirectly on the primary visual system by increasing the strength of lateral inhibition in the afferent channel. Such a mechanism could produce widespread and powerful changes in cortical coding without interrupting the visual input itself. Specifically, the effect could be mediated by stimulating inhibitory interneurons which affect recurrent lateral inhibition (Fig. 5). The pattern of lateral inhibition through interneurons is a common one [13].

In a Hartline-Ratliff model of lateral inhibition [14], each neuron inhibits its neighbors without interneurons by an amount equal to its own activity multiplied by an inhibitory coefficient k. Tonic stimulation of inhibitory interneurons in the model of Fig. 5 induces changes similar to those induced by increasing k in the Hartline-Ratliff model. Using a computer program which simulates Hartline-Ratliff lateral inhibition modified for application to mammals [15], the responses of networks with varying k's to a constant stimulus have been compared. As k increases, the damped oscillations which follow a brief stimulus increase in size, lateral spread, and duration before the system returns to equilibrium. The implications of these after-oscillations for facilitating perception have been discussed previously [15]. Longer and stronger oscillations mean that a second stimulus will have a weaker effect on the total activity of the network, yielding a longer recovery function. At the same time, larger k's decrease background activity in the simulation, reflecting the results of the experiment reported here. Cells whose background firing levels are more or less strongly affected by attention might be influenced more or less strongly by the interneurons (because the hypothesis requires very few interneurons, the chances of recording from one are unfortunately slight).

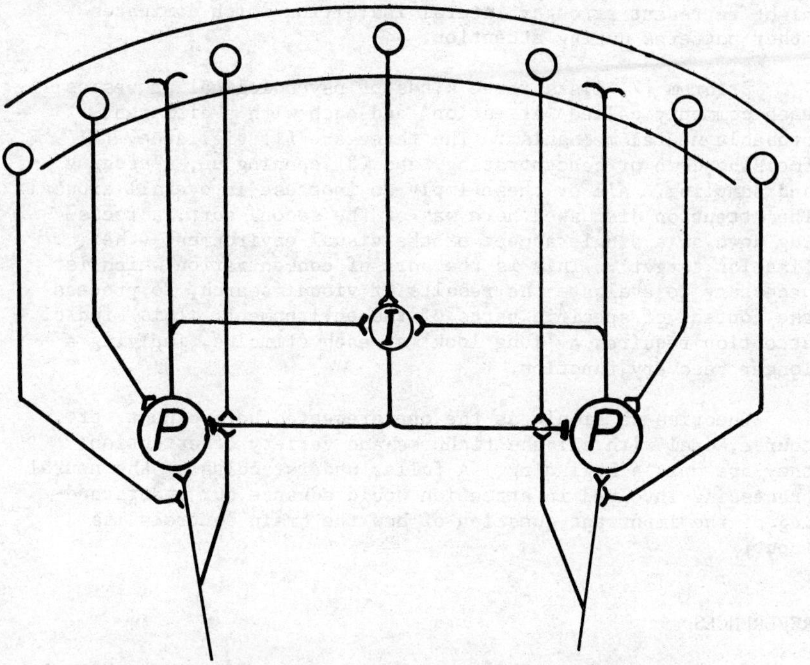

Fig. 5. A model for efferent modification of information flow in sensory systems. All connections not within the cortex are in the Lateral Geniculate in this illustration, though similar networks exist elsewhere in the brain. I: inhibitory interneuron. P: principal cell. V-shaped synapses are excitatory and bar-shaped ones inhibitory. Efferent signals from the center cortical cell in the figure can increase the inhibition of the principal cells through the interneuron, modifying visual information flowing from optic tract fibres (bottom) to the visual cortex (top).

The relation of attention to damped sinusoidal oscillations elicited by brief electrical stimuli has been investigated directly [16], using a conditioning technique to manipulae attention as defined in this paper. In prepyriform cortex of the cat, gross evoked responses took the form of damped oscillations only during attention periods. In terms of the lateral inhibitory hypothesis presented here, the damped oscillations might represent stronger lateral inhibition which dominates other patterns during attention.

Pribram [7] lists three kinds of psychological processes each commonly called 'attention' and each with a different probable neural mechanism. The three are (1) vigilance, (2) focusing down or concentrating, and (3) opening up, searching and sampling. All of these imply an increase in overall arousal. The attention discussed here was of the second sort, a focusing down on a single aspect of the visual environment (the fixation target). This is the sort of concentration which is necessary to evaluate the results of visual search, to process the content of specific parts of the environment. This kind of attention requires a 'long look' at each stimulus, implying a longer recovery function.

Theories as simple as the one presented here cannot, of course, deal with all the richness and variety of attention; they are only a beginning. A fuller understanding of the neural processing involved in attention would advance our understanding of the important question of how the brain controls its input.

REFERENCES

1. Y. SAITO, K. MAEKAWA, S. TAKENAKA and S. KASAMATSU, "Single cortical unit activity during EEG arousal" *Electroenceph. Clin. Neurophysiol. Suppl. 9*, 95-98 (1958).

2. J.M. FUSTER, "Excitation and inhibition of neuronal firing in visual cortex by reticular stimulation" *Science 133*, 2011-2012 (1961).

3. V.G. SKREBITSKY, "Nonspecific influences on neuronal firing in the central pathway" *Exp. Brain Res. 9*, 269-283 (1969).

4. T. LÖMO and A. MOLLICA, "Activity of single units in the primary optic cortex in the unanesthetized rabbit during visual, acoustic, olfactory and painful stimulation" *Arch. Ital. Biol. 100*, 86-120 (1962).

5. B. BRIDGEMAN, "A simple system for extracellular microelectrode recording from awake animals" *Electroenceph. Clin. Neurophysiol. 33*, 116-118 (1972).

6. D.H. HUBEL, "Single unit activity in striate cortex of unrestrained cats" *J. Physiol. 147*, 226-238 (1959).

7. K.H. PRIBRAM "Looking to see: some experiments on the brain mechanisms of attention in perception" In: *Perception and its Disorders XLVIII* (The Assn. for Research in Nervous and Mental Disease, New York, 1970).

8. K.L. CHOW, "Further studies on selective ablation of associative cortex in relation to visually mediated behavior" *J. Comp. Physiol. Psychol. 45*, 109-118 (1952).

9. M. MISHIN and K.H. PRIBRAM, "Visual discrimination performance following partial ablations of the temporal lobe I. Ventral vs. Lateral" *J. Comp. Physiol. Psychol. 47*, 14-20 (1954).

10. D.N. SPINELLI and K.H. PRIBRAM, "Changes in visual recovery functions produced by temporal lobe stimulation in monkeys" *Electroenceph. Clin. Neurophysiol. 20*, 44-49 (1966).

11. L.K. GERBRANDT, D.N. SPINELLI and K.H. PRIBRAM, "The interaction of visual attention and temporal cortex stimulation on electrical activity evoked in the striate cortex" *Electroenceph. Clin. Neurophysiol. 29*, 146-155 (1970).

12. D.N. SPINELLI and K.H. PRIBRAM, "Changes in visual recovery functions and unit activity produced by frontal and temporal cortex stimulation" *Electroenceph. Clin. Neurophysiol. 22*, 143-149 (1967).

13. W. BURKE and A. SEFTON, "Recovery of responsiveness of cells of the lateral geniculate nucleus" *J. Physiol. 187*, 213-229 (1966).

14. F. RATLIFF, *Mach Bands: Quantitative Studies on Neural Networks in the Retina* (Holden-Day, San Francisco, 1965).

15. B. BRIDGEMAN, "Metacontrast and lateral inhibition" *Psychol. Rev. 78*, 528-539 (1971).

16. W. FREEMAN, "Harmonic oscillation as a model for cortical excitability changes with attention in cats" *Science 133*, 2058-2059 (1961).

FUNCTION OF THE ELECTRONIC SIMULATION OF DIFFERENT PERCEPTIVE UNITS IN THE VERTEBRATE RETINA*

R. ECKMILLER

Institute of Physiology, Freie Universität Berlin, Germany

SUMMARY

Perceptive units (PU) are neural networks with receptive fields as input area and one single neuron at the output (here, a ganglion cell). An analog model was developed for the electronic simulation of a part of the vertebrate retina. This model consists of various simulation circuits for 115 photoreceptors, 25 horizontal cells, 115 bipolar cells, 25 amacrine cells and 25 ganglion cells, and is designed as a kind of special purpose analog computer. Several different PU's were simulated and their functions were studied by means of various light stimuli. The excitability distribution which was measured for an ON-unit fits neurophysiological data well. The summation properties of different ON- and OFF-units were measured with intermittent light spot stimuli with variable diameter at 0.5 and 10 Hz. The maximal impulse rate was then related to the spot diameter. With various measurements it is attempted to separate the different structured PU's by their function. The influence of horizontal cells on the overall functions was especially tested.

INTRODUCTION

In studying the function of the vertebrate retina it is of fundamental interest to determine which structures of the retinal network are responsible for the network's various functions. A neuronal network with a receptive field (RF) as its input area, which consists of a group of photoreceptors and one single output neuron (here, a ganglion cell), will be defined as *perceptive unit (PU)*. The ganglion cell changes its instantaneous impulse rate by evaluating the excitatory and inhibitory signals at its input. At present there are many results available

*This work was supported by a grant from the Stiftung Volkswagenwerk.

from extracellular ganglion cell recordings during the presentation of various light stimuli but little data from single cell recordings within the retina. Therefore, the contribution of the various types of retinal neurons (photoreceptors, horizontal cells, bipolar cells, amacrine cells, ganglion cells) to the signal processing of single PU's is still largely unknown, although several groups are working on this problem [1,8,10,11,13,14]. In the present paper some features of various PU's are discussed which were simulated with a hardware model.

THE ELECTRONIC ANALOG MODEL

A special-purpose analog computer was designed [3,4,5,6] to simulate parts of various vertebrate retinae (Fig. 1). The computer design is based on histological and electrophysiological

Fig. 1. The entire model with the light-sensitive area on the moveable "receptor head" at right on the table.

data from vertebrate retinae. Special electronic circuits on printed cards simulate 115 photoreceptors (mounted in a moveable head), 25 horizontal cells, 115 bipolar cells, 25 amacrine cells and 25 ganglion cells. These cells are interconnectable by means of patchboards. The 25 ganglion cells belong to 25 different PU's with overlapping antagonistic receptive fields (RF) and with on-centers and off-peripheries or vice versa. The horizontal and amacrine cells are interconnected with neighbouring cells of the same type so that membrane potential changes in these cells can spread laterally with a spatial decrement.

A block diagram is shown in Fig. 2. A RF-center consists of 7 receptors and a RF-periphery consists of 30 surrounding receptors in this case.

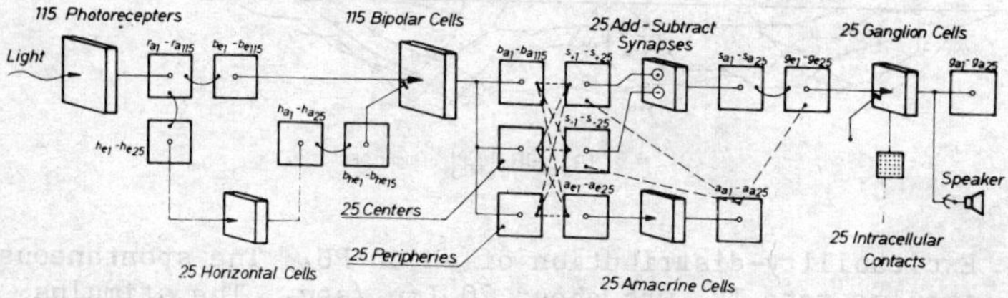

Fig. 2. Block diagram of the entire model. The patchboards for interconnections are drawn as squares and the cell layers as 3-dimensional blocks. The Add-Subtract-Synapses (ASS) belong to the ganglion cells and can be chosen as either type of synapse.

SIMULATION RESULTS

The excitability-distribution was measured for a PU with on-center (on-PU). The stimulus was a light spot as large as the RF-center which was switched on or off each sec and moved to several locations within the RF (Fig. 3). The excitability condition inverts at the border between RF-center and RF-periphery, i.e. the maximum impulse rate IR_{max} is reached at "light-on" in the center and at "light-off" in the periphery. This is demonstrated in Fig. 3 and fits the corresponding electrophysiological findings.

The simulated on-PU consists of 37 receptors in a 1:1 connection to 37 bipolars whose input signals are evaluated as excitatory or inhibitory by one ganglion cell and then converted into an impulse train at the cell-output.

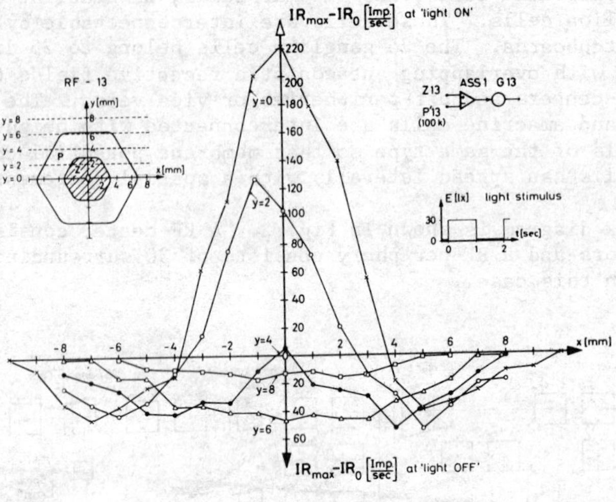

Fig. 3. Excitability-distribution of an on-PU. The spontaneous impulse rate IR_0 was about 20 Imp./sec. The stimulus had a diameter of 6 mm. IR_{max} is the average value of the inverse shortest impulse intervals for three stimulus periods.

The measured asymmetries in the excitability-distribution result in part from differences in the direction-sensitivity of the photo-transistors used for the simulation of the photoreceptor outer segments. The weighting factor w_c for the seven center channels was $w_c = 1/7$, and that for the 30 periphery channels $w_p = 1/10$. Accordingly, with diffuse illumination the ganglion cell would show an off-reaction because of the choice of the weighting factors for the different signal channels from the receptors to the ganglion cell ($7 \cdot 1/7 - 30 \cdot 1/10 = -2$).

For the examination of the summation properties [2,7,9] of different retinal PU's a circular light spot was centered in the RF-center and was varied in the diameter at varying frequencies of intermittent illumination. In Fig. 4a the results are plotted for an on-PU which differed from that discussed above only in the weighting factors, which were $w_c = 1/5.6$ and $w_p = 1/30$.

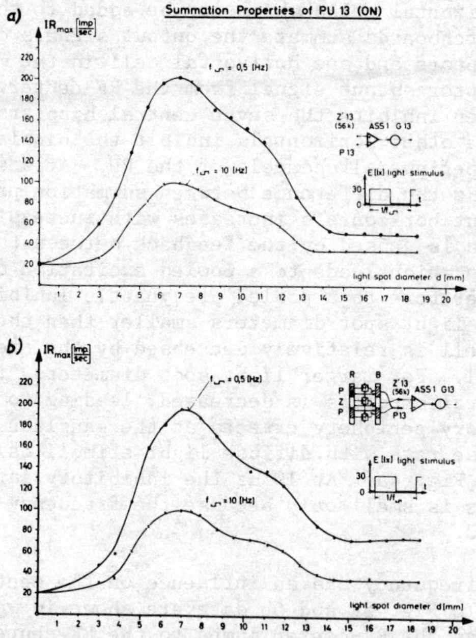

Fig. 4. Maximal impulse rate IR_{max} as function of the light spot diameter d for two different on-PU's (a) and (b) and two stimulus frequencies. (IR_{max} and IR_0 defined as for Fig. 3).

To estimate the frequency-dependence of the summation properties, the response to the diameter variation was measured at two frequencies of intermittent light stimulation. For light spots smaller than the RF-center the value of IR_{max} increases proportional to d^2 as expected for linear summation. The inhibitory influence from the RF-periphery leads to a decrease in IR_{max} as the spot diameter increases further. With stimulation of the total RF including center and periphery the neuronal excitation remains above the spontaneous level because of the mentioned choice of the weighting factors w_c and w_p: $7 \cdot 1/5.6 - 30 \cdot 1/30 > 0$.

If horizontal cells which are connected with each other inhibit the bipolars presynaptically, the summation properties of the PU change. This is shown in Fig. 4b.

Eight horizontal cells which can be added to the simulated network via patchboards summate the output signals of the 30 periphery receptors and one horizontal cell in the middle summates the receptor output signal from the RF-center. This horizontal cell then inhibits the seven central bipolars presynaptically while the other horizontals inhibit the bipolars which belong to the peripheral channels of the PU. At a stimulus frequency of 0.5 Hz the difference between summation properties with and without horizontals increases with increasing light spot diameter. This is caused by the feedback between the neighboring horizontals which leads to a pooled excitation of the horizontals and therefore to a pooled presynaptic inhibition of the bipolars. For light spot diameters smaller than the RF-center, the ganglion cell is relatively decreased by the one central horizontal cell. For larger light spot diameters, the excitation of the peripheral bipolars is decreased, leading to a diminution of the inhibitory periphery effects at the ganglion cell. Therefore the impulse rate with diffuse light stimuli is significantly higher than in Fig. 4a. At 10 Hz the inhibitory influence of the horizontals is small only because the frequency-dependent gain is reduced.

Stimulus frequency has an influence on the center-periphery interaction. In Fig. 5a and 5b data are shown in which a light spot as large as the RF-center jumps to the RF-center for the first half of a stimulus period and to either the RF-periphery or outside the RF for the second half of the period. As before, two PU's with and without horizontal cell inhibition are compared. The difference between the curves in each diagram results from the postinhibitory excitation mediated via the peripheral channels of the PU's, i.e if the light spot jumps from the RF-periphery to the RF-center then the maximal impulse rate of the ganglion cell is caused not only by "light-on" in the RF-center but also by "light-off" in the RF-periphery at the same time. (Note that at 0.5 and 10 Hz the lower curves of Fig. 5a and 5b cross those of Fig. 4a and 4b at a stimulus diameter of 6 mm). A feature common to all four curves is a rising phase above 0.1 Hz and a maximum at 0.6 Hz. This can be explained by the fact that the neuron models, especially the receptors, fail to reach their "steady state" during the light and the dark phases above 0.1 Hz. This leads to an increase of the average membrane depolarization of the ganglion cell and therefore to an elevation of the maximal impulse rate. At higher jumping frequencies of the stimulus the curves drop off because of the low-pass properties of the neuronal channels. The change in the difference between the curves with frequency can be interpreted as the changing time correlation of center-excitation and postinhibitory periphery-excitation. Another reason might be a different frequency dependence of the two excitation components.

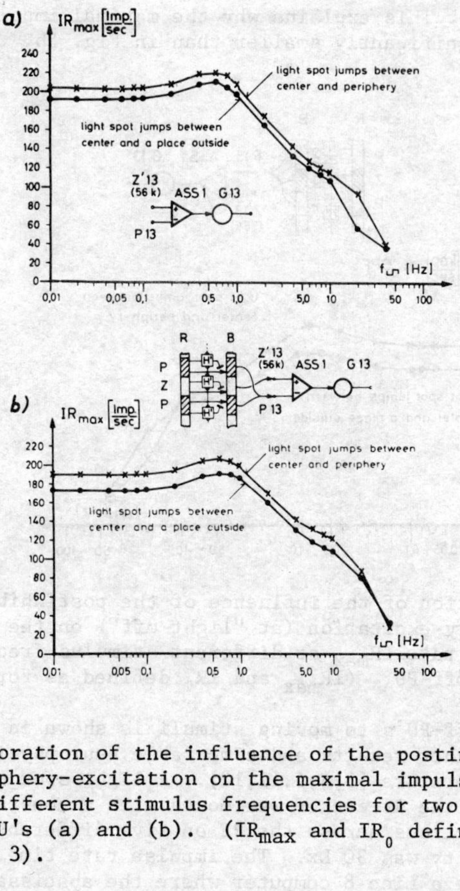

Fig. 5. Exploration of the influence of the postinhibitory periphery-excitation on the maximal impulse rate IR_{max} at different stimulus frequencies for two different on-PU's (a) and (b). (IR_{max} and IR_0 defined as for Fig. 3).

An analogous explanation applies to Fig. 6 which shows the results for an off-PU with inhibitory interacting horizontals. The maximal impulse rate at "light-off" is plotted versus the jumping frequency.

The difference between this off-PU and the on-PU discussed in Fig. 5b lies only in the fact that now the signals from the center channels are inverted, i.e. hyperpolarization of the center-bipolars leads to depolarization and therefore to an increase of the impulse rate at the ganglion cell. The signals from the peripheral channels remain non-inverted by feeding them into the (+)-input of the ASS. Because of the non-linear function of the receptors which is known from neurophysiological findings, the dynamic reaction to "light-off" is not as strong as to "light-on". This explains why the maximal impulse rates in Fig. 6 are significantly smaller than in Fig. 5b. The response

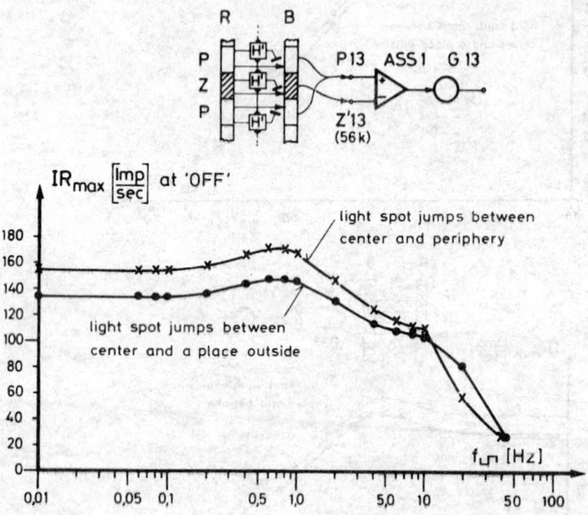

Fig. 6. Exploration of the influence of the postinhibitory periphery-excitation (at "light-off") on the maximal' impulse rate IR_{max} at different stimulus frequencies for an off-PU. (IR_{max} and IR_0 defined as for Fig. 3).

of on-PU's and off-PU's to moving stimuli is shown in Fig. 7a and 7b. For further results and comparable neurophysiological findings see literature [3,4,6,11,12]. A light spot of the same diameter as the RF-center was moved with a constant velocity in both directions across the RF on five different tracks. The spot luminosity was 30 Lx. The impulse rate time functions were processed by a Linc 8 computer where the abscissa of each point marks the middle of an interval between two spikes and the ordinate gives the inverse of this interval as instantaneous impulse rate. The data are from single trials. With increasing excentricity of the tracks from the RF-center the excitation peak decreases for the on-PU (Fig. 7a). This PU responds to a stimulus on a track at y = 6 mm as an unsensitive off-PU rather than as an on-PU. Fig. 7b shows the results of the same experiment with an off-PU. At the track y = 0 mm, the ganglion cell shows the strongest excitation when the stimulus reaches the periphery coming from the center. This finding results in the fact that the excitation of the peripheral channels coincides with the post-inhibitory excitation of the central channels. The same asymmetry occurs for on-PU's where the inhibition is maximal for the stimulus leaving the center and entering the periphery. The off-PU responds to a stimulus on a track at y = 6 mm as an on-PU. The time courses of the impulse rate are very similar to comparable neurophysiological findings [12].

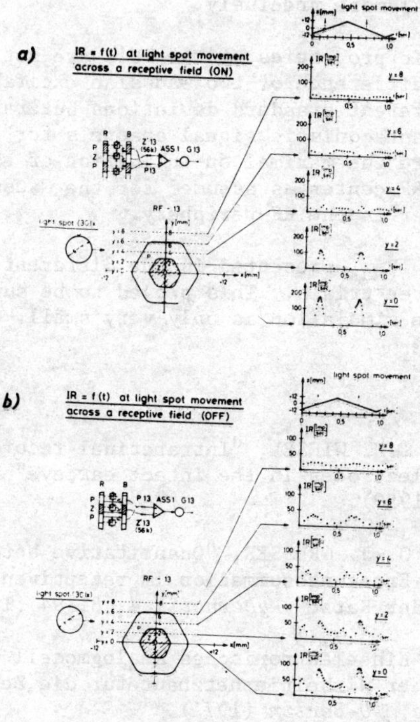

Fig. 7. Impulse rate time-functions of an on-PU (a) and an off-PU (b) in response to a light spot which is moving on different tracks across the RF. IR_0 = 20 Imp./sec.

DISCUSSION

The simulation results show that many features of perceptive units in the vertebrate retina can be studied with the described special analog computer. The influence of horizontals on signal processing in single PU's can also be simulated to act postsynaptically. The amacrines can also be involved [4]. Further neurophysiological and histological findings on the vertebrate retina will have to clarify the contributions of the horizontals and the amacrines [13,14] more precisely.

The antagonistic properties of the PU's are not simulated to result from the difference of two Gaussian excitability distributions with different standard deviations but rather from the interaction of antagonistic signal channels for center and periphery. Therefore the maximal on-inhibition of an on-PU is not present in the RF-center as assumed for the Gaussian curve hypothesis but rather in the RF-periphery.

The values for IR_{max} presented in the different diagrams result from only three trials. This proved to be sufficient because noise in the simulation is only very small.

REFERENCES

1. K.T. BROWN and T.N. WIESEL, "Intraretinal recording with micropipette electrodes in the intact cat eye" *J. Physiol.* *149*, 537-562 (1959).

2. U. BÜTTNER and O.-J. GRÜSSER, "Quantitative Untersuchungen der räumlichen Erregungssummation im rezeptiven Feld retinaler Neurone der Katze" *Kybernetik 4*, 81-94 (1968).

3. R. ECKMILLER, "Ein elektronisches Analogmodell zum Studium der Bedeutung der Wirbeltiernetzhaut für die Zeichenerkennung" *Dr.-Thesis, TU-Berlin* (1971).

4. R. ECKMILLER, "Electronic simulation of retinal receptive fields in vertebrates" In: *Biocybernetics*, *4*, 109-114 (G. Fischer, Jena 1972).

5. R. ECKMILLER and O.-J. GRÜSSER, "Electronic simulation of the vertebrate retina" (In preparation).

6. R. ECKMILLER and O.-J. GRÜSSER, "Electronic simulation of the velocity function of movement-detecting neurons" *Bibl. Ophthal.* *82*, 274-279 (Karger, Basel 1972).

7. H.-J. FREUND and G. GRÜNEWALD, "Räumliche Summation und Hemmungsvorgänge im rezeptiven Feldzentrum von Retina-Neuronen der Katze" *Exp. Brain Res. 8*, 37-52 (1969).

8. O.-J. GRÜSSER, "A quantitative analysis of spatial summation of excitation and inhibition within the receptive field of retinal ganglion cells of cats" *Vision Res. Suppl. 3*, 103-127 (1971).

9. O.-J. GRÜSSER, D. SCHAIBLE and J. VIERKANT-GLATHE, "A quantitative analysis of the spatial summation of excitation within the receptive field centers of retinal neurons" *Pflügers Arch. 319*, 101-121 (1970).

10. A KANEKO, "Physiological and morphological identification of horizontal, bipolar and amacrine cells in goldfish retina" *J. Physiol. 207*, 623-633 (1970).

11. A.L. NORTON, H. SPEKREIJSE, H.G. WAGNER and M.L. WOLBARSHT, "Responses to directional stimuli in retinal preganglionic units" *J. Physiol. 206*, 93-107 (1970).

12. R.W. RODIECK and J. STONE, "Response of cat retinal ganglion cells to moving visual patterns" *J. Neurophysiol. 28*, 819-832 (1965).

13. F. WERBLIN, "Lateral interactions at inner plexiform layer of verebrate retina: antagonistic responses to change" *Science 175*, 1008-1010 (1972).

14. F. WERBLIN and J. DOWLING, "Organization of the retina of the mudpuppy, Necuturs maculosus. II. Intracellular recording" *J. Neurophysiol. 32*, 339-355 (1969).

MODEL OF THE BINOCULAR VS. MONOCULAR SCOTOPIC VISION

A. ARIGONI

Instituto di Fisica, Università di Ferrara, Italy

SUMMARY

The dark-adapted observer is presented with two faint point sources, placed at a given distance, well above the stereoscopic threshold. He is instructed to look at them, binocularly, for a given inspection time t_i. Then, one eye is abruptly closed. The sensation of depth is found to decay slowly. An homomophic model is suggested to simulate the process operated by the visual system in the above said situation. The system is compared to an autobalancing sequence of stages. The time needed to attain the steady state condition, as far as the sensation of relative depth is concerned, depends on the amount of information gained through the binocular inspection time t_i on the relative depth d.

PRELIMINARY CONSIDERATIONS

Firstly, it may be mentioned that stereoscopic depth perception involves both brief and long-term temporal aspects. The first one, known for a long time and emphasized by Julesz [1], is related to the fact that "surprisingly" sensation of space can rapidly develop; the second aspect, which concerns our experiments on stereoscopic depth, refers to the temporal transformation of the depth sensation after the closing of one eye [2,3].

Our experiments consist in measuring the delay time, t_d, with which the subjects (young normal individuals, highly motivated and skilled, and further, experienced in tests on the specific matter) realize the disappearing of the depth which had before been sesed (binocularly), after one eye is abruptly closed.

It is finally noted that even after prolonged monocular inspection the two sources do not reach the "no apparent depth" condition. This residual effect [2] seems to be due to the tri-dimensionality of monocular images predicted by Heinrich [4] in 1909. This may be ascribed to eye aberrations, particularly effective in this respect in our low scotopic conditions, where the depth-of-field of the eye attains its minimum value [5].

APPARATUS, METHOD AND EXPERIMENTAL FINDINGS

The dark-adapted observer is seated in a dark cage. His head is kept in position with the aid of a chin rest. Head movements are carefully avoided. Two point sources are placed at a viewing distance of 2.5 m. One of them, the right one, is fixed and the subject is instructed to look at it; the other one is varied in depth within wide limits. Eye movements from the source to the other are avoided. Target separation is about 3°; test-spot illumination is about 100 times the absolute threshold.

The experiments are of two kinds: A and B. The observer is presented by two sources at time t_0. Hence in experiments A after a relative depth d_j (j = -30 cm. (distally), 25,..,0, ..,+25,30 (proximally)), which determines a corresponding degree of disparity η is fixed [1], the time t_d is measured by keeping t_i as a parameter (i = 10 sec.). In experiments B, on the other hand, d_j is assumed to be a parameter, measuring t_d as a function of the dependent variable t_i (i = 1,2,..,30 sec.). Every experiment is repeated after a suitable rest period, until three responses for each value either d_j or t_i are recorded. It has to be stated that it is the observer himself who closes his lect eye at time t_i, by manipulating an electromechanical device.

In Figs. 1 and 2, t_d is plotted vs. d_j, the binocular inspection time t_i being kept constant (10 sec.). Data recorded from different subjects are collected. In the majority of cases, t_d increases as d_j increases.

Figures 3 and 4 show t_d vs. t_i; in particular, the latter of the two is relative to a single observer and shows a typical behaviour of t_d vs. t_i; it is used as reference in discussion to follow. The said behaviour, when t_i is relatively small, is t_i-dependent; as t_i itself exceeds 15 seconds, t_d becomes negligible.

In Fig. 4 it is noticeable that for d_j there also exists a "saturation" value; the different diagrams, which appear in the figure, approach each other as η increases.

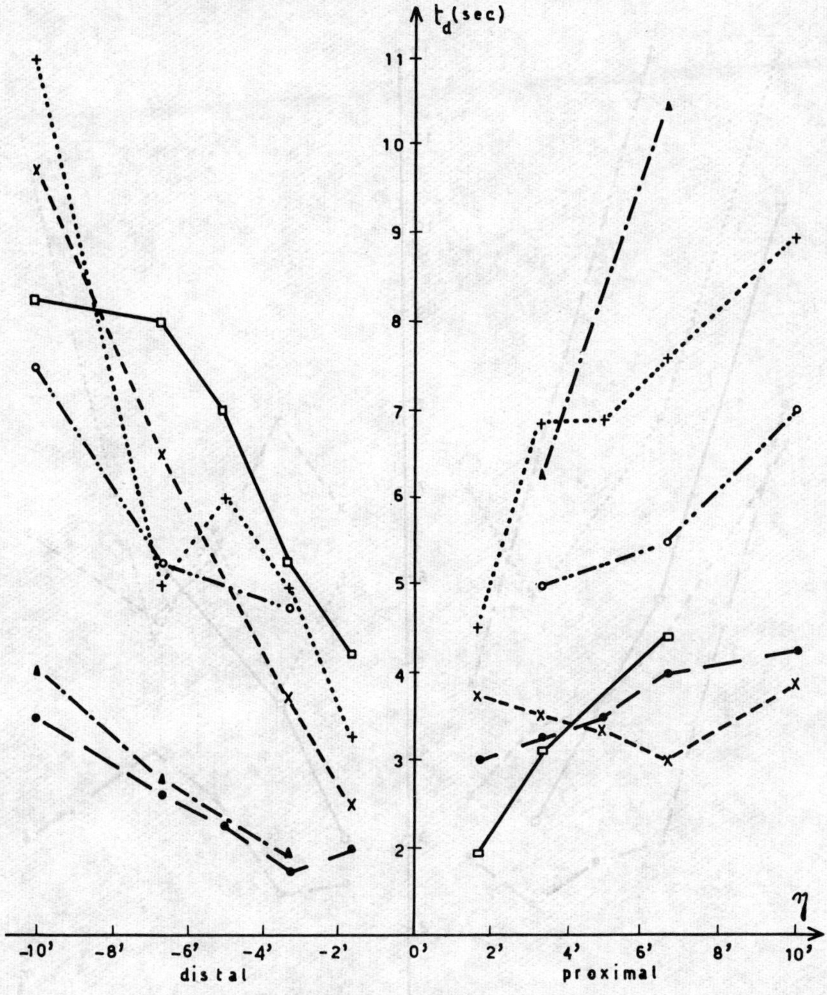

Fig. 1.

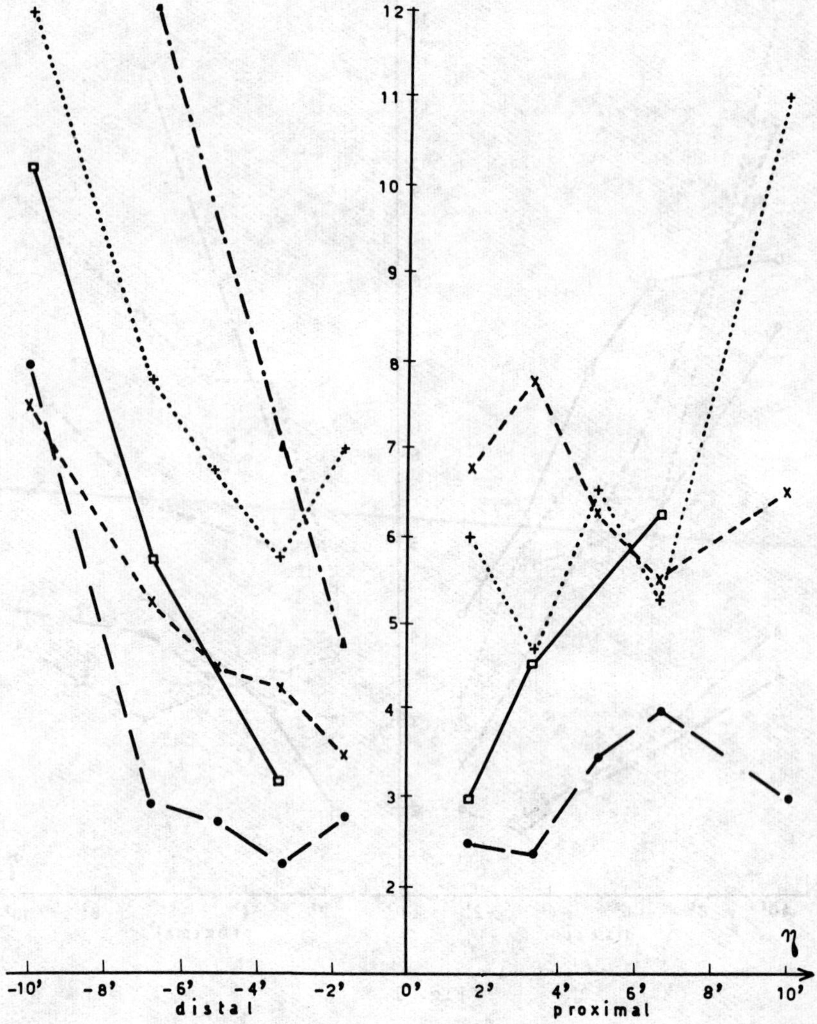

Fig. 2.

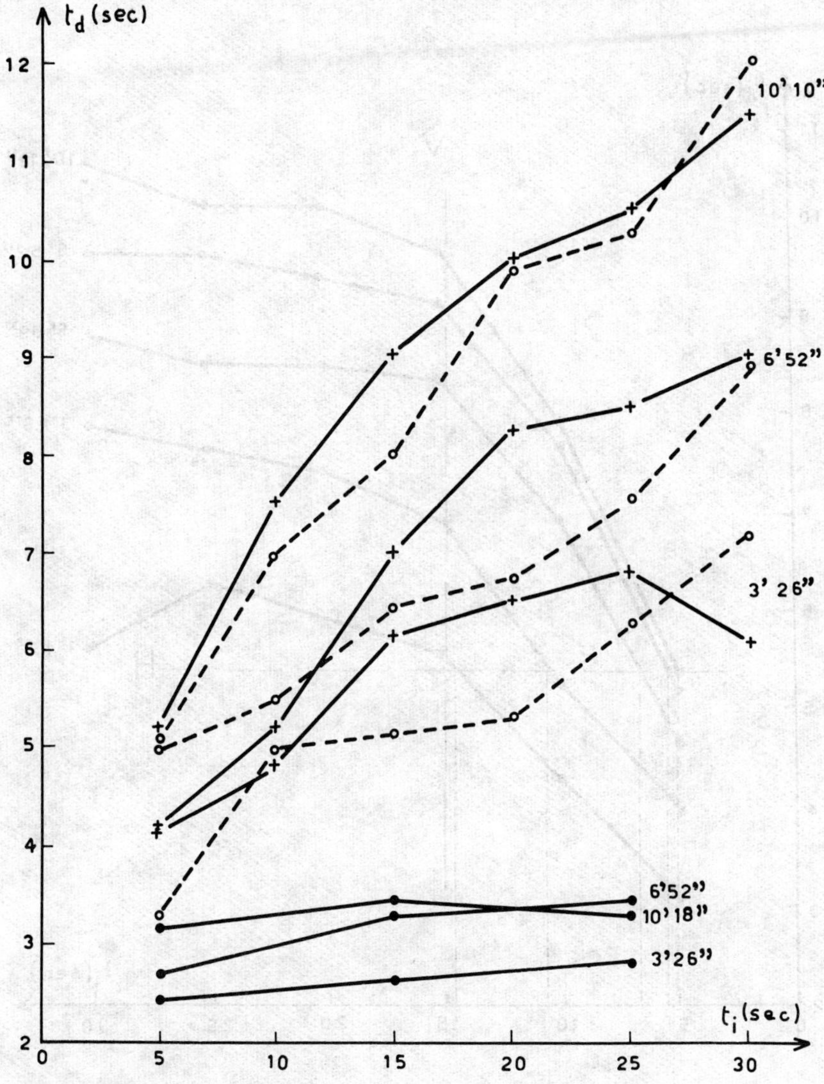

t_d (sec)
12
11
10
9
8
7
6
5
4
3
2
0
5
10
15
20
25
30
t_i (sec)
10'10"
6'52"
3' 26"
6'52"
10'18"
3'26"

Fig. 3.

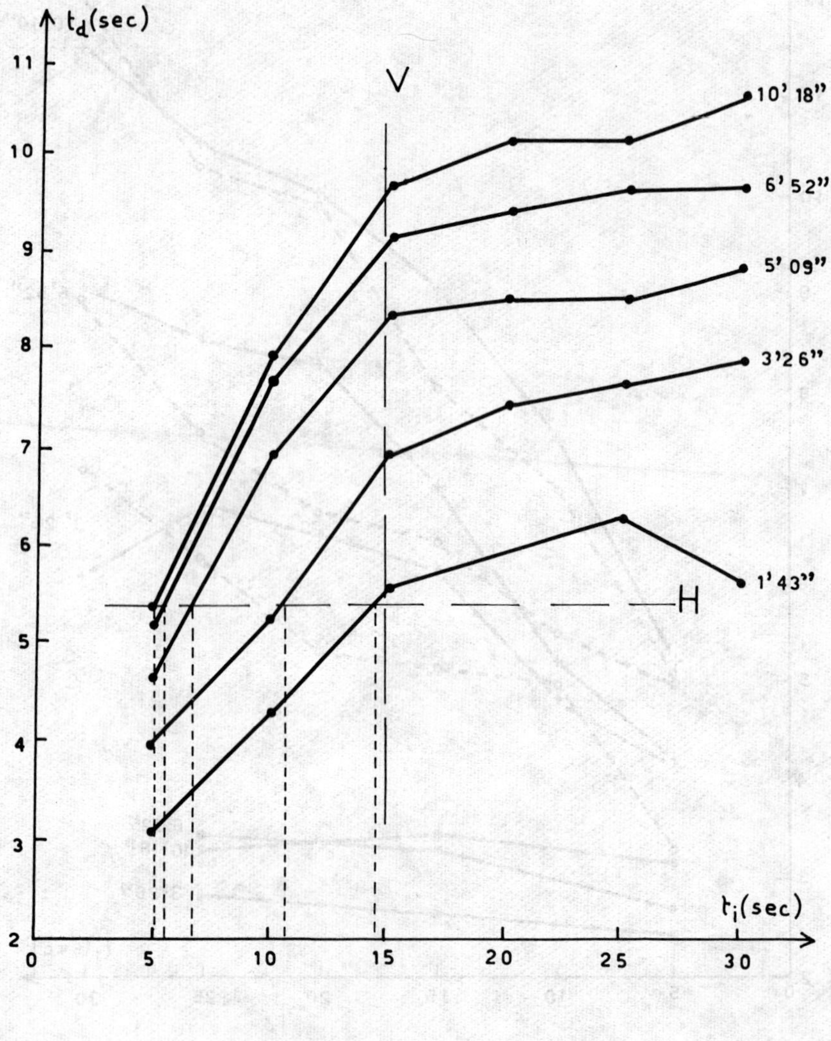
t_d(sec)
11
10
9
8
7
6
5
4
3
2
0
5
10
15
20
25
30
t_i(sec)
V
H
10' 18"
6' 52"
5' 09"
3'26"
1'43"

Fig. 4.

DISCUSSION OF THE FINDINGS

The fact that the depth sensation can develop in a surprisingly rapid way [1] indicates that fading times could be much shorter than those t_ds measured in our experiments, if the "non-apparent depth" were realistically transmitted by the organs, which are involved in the process of scotopic binocular vs. monocular vision; particularly in considering that it is the subject (observer), who coses one of his eyes. It may be shown that the neural nets composing these organs are responsible for t_d.

After the discussion of the above problems an analysis of the behaviour of t_d versus t_i and d_j can suggest some functional details and aid in proving our hypothesis. According to this, t_d would be directly dependent on the "unobserved variable" — a variable that in the specific process can not be directly measured [6] — which expresses the quantity of information integrated and memorized by the above-mentioned organs during t_i.

The delay with which the observer realizes the fading of the two point sources relative depth depends on t_i until the latter is below around 15 seconds; inspection times above which t_d are not appreciably affected by it, as it appears in Figs. 3 and 4. Since, as already noted, the magnitude of t_d is much greater than the time required for developing a sensation of depth, it may be noted that a kind* of "statistical aspection" takes place, if a prolonged inspection time t_i is maintained, a process whose continuation occurs during the inspection though reasonably limited to a certain value of t_i. The evidence of such a process is shown by the considerable dependency of t_d on t_i. In other words, the small quantity of information, by which the relative depth can be "refereed", can be assumed by the observer as a short time (few milliseconds) for either familiar or simple images [8]; observing the point sources for a longer t_i, the subject** "perceives" [9] the information

*Disparity: $\eta = \frac{(a \cdot \delta}{R^2)}$ (a = interpupillar distance; δ = relative depth of the two point sources; R = distance between eye and the observed object).

**The process of statistical expectation is caused by the tendency of the perceptive organs to facilitate messages recognition on the basis of statistical characteristics of those which had been previously received. The type of process is often developed in any kind of perceptive organs (see for example, C. Benedetti [7]).

contained in more inspection phases, or "present thickness" [11]. These are decreasing quantities of information because of the successively decreasing uncertainty about the situation, which tends to zero* for the already occurred perception [12].

The contribution to the proof of the hypothesis, which is given by experiments type B, concerns the complexity of the situations, i.e. the relative displacement of the point sources, which increases as the relative depths increase. It supports the same hypothesis, because it can be shown that the complexity of the observed situations is a direct function of d_j.

The last argument is given by considering once again the findings relative to experiments A. Looking at Fig. 4, it can be shown — with reference to the horizontal line H — that particularly on the left side of the line V in order that t_d be constant relatively to the different prefixed values of η (10'18", 6'52", 5'09", 3'25", 1'43"), the corresponding t_is must be considerably different.

THE MODEL

Having proved the above hypothesis, it is now possible to draw the iconic model which simulates the process, i.e. a model which by a largely homomorphe block diagram "represents" the psychophysiological constitution of the aggregate of organs and the information exchanges among them. This is shown in Fig. 5.

The model and the discussion above lead to the following:

1) The quantities of time t_ds depend on the corresponding quantities of information the observer in some way perceives during the periods t_i.

2) The present belief that intelligent activity is wholly dependent on central organs is also being studied and it is not exact; the model claims, in fact, that an amount of intelligent operating is delegated to those peripheric organs which are connected with those particularly sensitive, e.g. the retina.

---

*By "perception" one indicates an intelligent process happening in each inspection phase by which messages are recognized, integrated and memorized, with the aid of mnemonic contents gathered in the previous phases. The use of "perception" has been introduced by Leibniz and used again by J.F. Herbert; it, even if it has fallen into desuetude in philosophy, it is at present largely used in the technique of models, information theory, psychology, and elsewhere [10,11]. In the place of it other terms are also used; Benedetti, for instance, uses "conscious perception" [7].

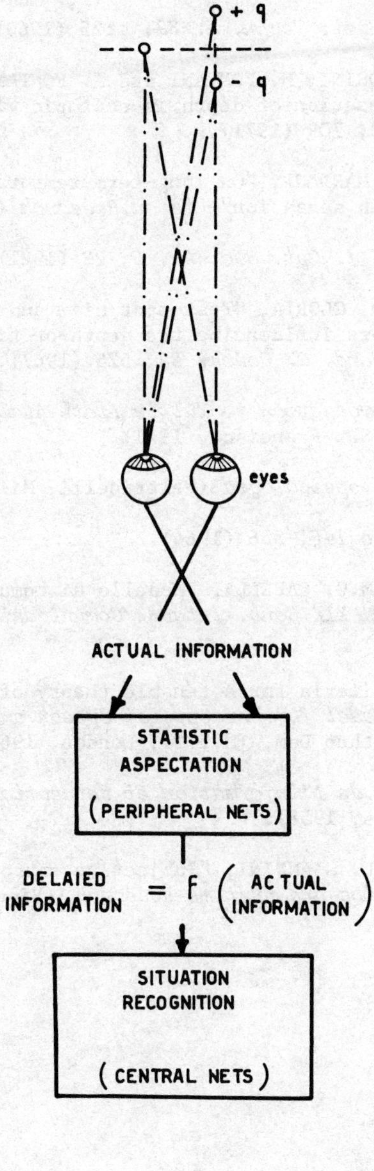
+ q
- q
eyes
ACTUAL INFORMATION
STATISTIC
ASPECTATION
(PERIPHERAL NETS)
DELAIED
INFORMATION
= f
ACTUAL
INFORMATION
SITUATION
RECOGNITION
(CENTRAL NETS)

Fig. 5.

REFERENCES

1. B. JULESZ, *Bell Syst. Techn. J. 39*, 1125 (1960).

2. L. RONCHI, R. FROSINI, M. FONTANI and A. FONTANA, "Binocular vs. monocular sensation of depth in scotopic vision" *Atti Fond. G. Ronchi 5*, 709 (1971).

3. L. RONCHI and A. MARIANI, "On long-term temporal aspect of stereoscopic depth sensation" *Vision Research* (in press).

4. AMES and PROCTOR, *J. Opt. Soc. Am. 5*, 22 (1921).

5. L. RONCHI and E.M. GLORIA, "Test-spot size and fixation distance as factors influencing the depth-of-field of the human eye" *Atti Fond. G. Ronchi 22*, 525 (1967).

6. VAN DER GEER, *Introduction to Multivariate Analysis* (W.H. Freeman and Co., San Francisco, 1971).

7. G. BENEDETTI, *Neuropsicologia* (Feltrinelli, Milano, 1969).

8. B. JULESZ, *Science 145*, 356 (1964).

9. A.O. ARIGONI and M.G. CAPELLA, "Modello di comunicazione nell'appercezione" *XIX Conv. Intern. Comunicazioni, Genova* (1971).

10. F. ATTENEAVE, "Criteria for a tenable theory of forms perception" In: *Model for Percept. of Speech and Visual Forms*, Wienant Wathen Dum, (M.I.T., London, 1967).

11. A. MOLES, *Theorie de l'information et perception esthetique* (Flammarion, Paris, 1958).

12. A.O. ARIGONI and L. GIANNINI, "Subjective entropy" *Eur. Meet. on Cybernetics and Systems Research*, (Vinna, 1972).

AN ON-LINE EIGHT PATIENT HEART RHYTHM MONITOR

C.L. FELDMAN*, P.J. SINGER** and M. HUBELBANK***

SUMMARY

It has been accepted for a number of years that the recognition and rapid treatment of certain subtle changes in the heart rhythm of patients recovering from acute myocardial infarction ("heart attack") can essentially eliminate sudden death within the cardiac intensive care unit and reduce overall in-hospital mortality among these patients by about one-third. The obvious difficulty in effecting such care is the burden it places on the attending staff to continuously monitor every beat of many patients simultaneously and unfailingly detect that single abnormal beat which may herald sudden death. This paper describes a real-time monitoring system built about a minicomputer which analyzes each beat in the electrocardiogram of eight patients, recognizes those which are abnormal, and either alerts the attending staff immediately or provides a record of the event for later examination, depending on how immediately life threatening the event may be.

MEDICAL BACKGROUND

In the early 1960's, a variety of physicians more or less independently conceived of and implemented the concept of a coronary care unit (CCU) [1,2,3]. In the intervening decade the coronary care unit has received unprecedented acceptance because of the dramatic reduction in hospital mortality from myocardial infarction that it affords — estimated variously at between 1/3 and 1/2 [3,4,5]. Today, nearly 50% of the 7,000 hospitals in the United States claim to have coronary care units although the lack of trained personnel available to many of these facilities opens such optimistic statistics to serious questions.

Worcester Polytechnic Institute, Worcester, Mass. 01609, U.S.A.

**Electronics for Medicine, Inc., 80 Union Ave., Sudbury, Mass. 01776, U.S.A.*

***Electronics for Medicine, Inc., 80 Union Ave., Sudbury, Mass. 01776, U.S.A.*

The essential subject of this communication is a computer system for use in the CCU. This system is capable of monitoring each beat of the electrocardiogram of eight patients simultaneously and communicating the relevant information to the attending staff. Since this development has meaning only within the context of current concepts of coronary care and since these concepts come as something of a surprise to their progenitors as well as the public at large, the first few paragraphs will develop the background essentials.

The heart, as schematically depicted in Fig. 1, consists of four chambers. The upper chambers, or atria, serve primarily as booster pumps to insure filling of the lower chambers, the ventricles. The ventricles, sources of the major pumping effort, beat in synchrony with each other, each supplying its own portion of the total circulation. The right ventricle affords circulation to the lungs while the left ventricle affords circulation of oxygenated blood to the rest of the body including the heart itself. Because of the great demands placed upon it the left ventricle has substantially the thickest muscle wall of the four chambers, requires the largest portion of the blood supplied to the myocardium (heart muscle) and is the side of the majority of acquired heart disease.

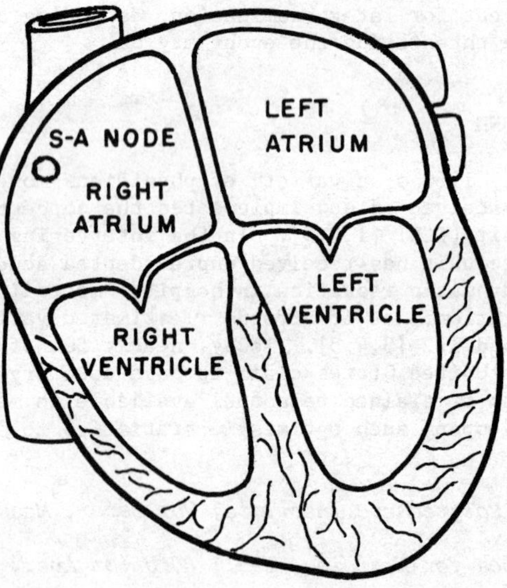

Fig. 1. The heart.

In the normal heart, enervation is supplied by the S-A node pacemaker located in the right atrium. A wave of depolarization spreads over the atria causing them to contract. This depolarization wave excites special conduction fibers in the ventricles which in turn cause the spread of depolarization with accompanying contraction throughout the ventricles. Although the details of this conduction mechanism are not especially important at this time it is essential to remember that all portions of the heart have a degree of automaticity and can, without stimulation, depolarize spontaneously. In the normal heart the sinus pacemaker controls, because its inherent rate is greater than the inherent rate of the various inferior (anatomically speaking) fibers.

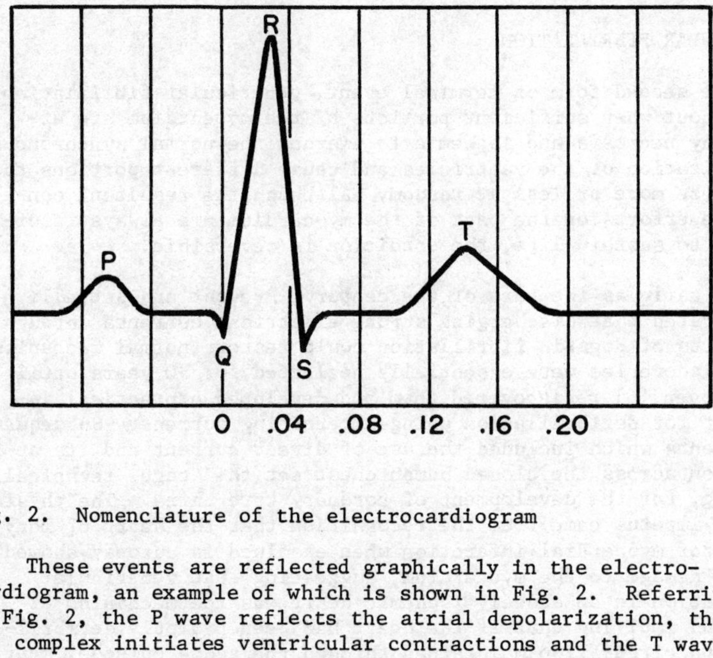

Fig. 2. Nomenclature of the electrocardiogram

These events are reflected graphically in the electrocardiogram, an example of which is shown in Fig. 2. Referring to Fig. 2, the P wave reflects the atrial depolarization, the QRS complex initiates ventricular contractions and the T wave occurs with ventricular repolarization.

In the arteriosclerotic heart the extensive vascular network which supplies blood to the myocardium is subject to fatty deposits which, to a greater or lesser degree, restrict blood flow and consequent oxygenation reaching various portions of the myocardium. In ischemia there is inadequate oxygenation of a portion of the myocardium (accompanied by pain, this syndrome is known as angina pectoris) while in myocardial infarction there is blockage of a coronary artery, depriving the myocardium of oxygen and causing a portion of the myocardium to die.

Early in the history of cardiology, it was recognized that living functions of the heart could terminate in one of two ways — asystole and ventricular fibrillation. The more obvious of these two mechanisms, asystole, occurs when the sinus pacemaker fails or the ventricles do not receive or respond to pacemaker stimuli while, simultaneously, there is insufficient automaticity in the ventricles themselves to provide a life-sustaining heart rate. Of course, if the ventricles are reasonably healthy, life can be sustained despite the existence of pathology that might lead to asystole, by use of an electronic pacemaker.

VENTRICULAR FIBRILLATION

The second form of terminal event, ventricular fibrillation, comes about when sufficient portions of the myocardium are affected by necrosis and ischemia to disrupt the normal synchronous depolarization of the ventricles and cause different portions to depolarize more or less at random. Although the resultant contractile efforts on the part of the myocardium are always insufficient to sustain life, the condition is reversible.

As early as the turn of the century, Prevost and Bettelli demonstrated that discharging strong electrical currents through the hearts of dogs in fibrillation could restore normal mechanism. These discoveries were essentially neglected for 30 years until Kouwenhoven [6] rediscovered them and developed a practical instrument for defibrillation using alternating current. Subsequent refinements which included the use of direct current and its application across the closed human chest set the stage, technically speaking, for the development of coronary care units. The physiological impetus came from the recognition that the heart of many victims of myocardial infarction when examined in autopsy showed minimal damage to the myocardium, suggesting that ventricular fibrillation in an acutely ischemic heart was the mechanism of death and implying that if the heart had been promptly defibrillated and circulation maintained through the acute episode, many lives might have been saved.

CORONARY CARE UNITS

With the stage thus set, prototype coronary care units were set up primarily with the intent of grouping together those patients most likely to experience ventricular fibrillation and a trained team with appropriate equipment to perform timely resuscitation.

The key technical element in these coronary care units was a high-gain amplifier for the electrocardiogram and a cathode-ray oscilloscope for its continuous display. In these early units the nurses were instructed to watch the oscilloscope for ventricular fibrillation (assisted by rate meters in many cases) and perform resuscitation as indicated. In practice, it was soon observed that ventricular fibrillation was almost inevitably preceded by other, less dramatic, signs of ventricular instability. Further, it was demonstrated that drug therapy aimed at reducing the irritability of diseased ventricles was nearly 100% effective in eliminating "primary" ventricular fibrillation (i.e., ventricular fibrillation in the presence of minimal myocardial damage). Of course, such treatment did not in any way reverse myocardial damage resulting from infarction of the vessels. In a number of different coronary care units in the mid-1960's it was demonstrated that careful attention to the premonitory signs of ventricular irritability resulted in mortality rates of approximately 15% or 20% — the lower limit set by the number who come to hospitals with such serious myocardial damage that they cannot, even under optimum circumstances, maintain circulation consistent with life. This was in contrast to mortality rates of 30% or 35% in unmonitored hospital beds.

VENTRICULAR PREMATURE BEATS

The best defined sign of potentially lethal instability in the ischemic heart is the ventricular premature beat (VPB) (also called premature ventricular contraction (PVC) or extrasystole). Classically, it is a ventricular contraction which occurs spontaneously with minimal effect to the normal sinus

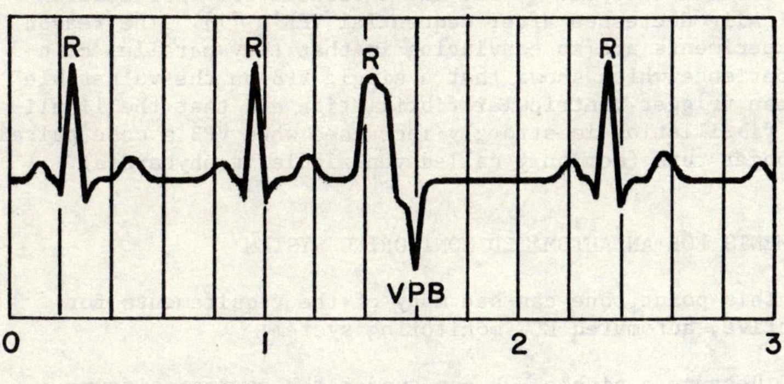

Fig. 3. A ventricular premature beat

pacemaker and is readily recognized by man or machines in accordance with the following characteristics (see Fig. 3):

1) Prematurity — the VPB must necessarily occur before (in the limit, at the same time) the sinus-originated ventricular contraction, otherwise its raison d'être ceases.

2) Compensatory Pause — usually the VPB does not interfere with the normal sinus pacemaker. It ordinarily replaces one sinus originated systole and has no effect on the succeeding beat. Thus, the interval between the extrasystole and the next sinus beat is long by an amount exactly sufficient to compensate for the prematurity of the extrasystole.

3) Bizarre Morphology — Since the extrasystole originates at some arbitrary location in the ventricles its morphology is almost always quite different from the morphology of the normal systole. In practice, more often than not, it appears quite broad compared to a normal systole.

To the cardiologist of the 60's some of this seemed out of keeping with what was then common knowledge. It has been said that VPB's, like gray hair, are a sign of advancing age; this is indeed true. It would appear, however, that although most VPB's are benign they have malignant potential when they appear together with ischemia. This conclusion, suggested by mortality experience in the coronary care unit, is further reinforced by a plethora of experimental evidence. The most convincing of these experiments probably has been the demonstration of a vulnerable zone of about approximately .04 seconds prior to the apex of a T wave in which extremely small electric shocks applied to the myocardium can precipitate fibrillation; and related experiments which have shown that the threshold for fibrillation monotonically decreases after sequential VPB's [1]. The reason these experiments are so convincing is that they parallel clinical experience which shows that a single VPB on the vulnerable period can trigger ventricular fibrillation and that the likelihood of fibrillation is strongly increased when VPB's come paired or in longer runs (commonly called ventricular tachycardia).

REQUIREMENTS FOR AN AUTOMATED MONITORING SYSTEM

At this point, one can see many of the requirements for an effective, automated ECG monitoring system:

1) Because a single VPB can, under the correct circumstances, trigger ventricular fibrillation, the system should exercise constant vigilance, monitoring each beat of every

patient under surveillance.

2) The system should be capable of a graded response, signalling the occurrence of a single VPB in patients whose VPB's are rare, drawing attention selectively to the more malignant events such as VPB's in the vulnerable period of the T wave or runs of VPB's for patients producing showers of ordinary VPB's and sounding an immediate alarm should asystole or ventricular fibrillation occur.

3) The system should indicate trends in the arrhythmic cardiac behavior so that the efficacy of therapy can be quickly and accurately assessed.

Of course, there are a variety of other requirements that a coronary monitoring system shares with all other monitoring systems, including: economy, reliability, ease of use, immunity to artifact (and consequent low rate of false positives) and capability for verification of computer judgments.

Finally, there is the requirement that the system be able to handle an extremely wide range of atypical situations with minimal degradation and system performance. Typical of these variants are the following:

1) Interpolated VPB's — true extrasystoles which interpolate themselves between two sinus beats without disrupting the normal sinus rhythm.

2) Late VPB's — VPB's which occur very late in the cardiac cycle and may not even be premature.

3) Occasional highly irregular rates such as in atrial fibrillation or severe sinus arrhythmia.

SYSTEM HARDWARE

After several iterative passes the hardware shown in Fig. 4 finally evolved. The primary component in the system is a Digital Equipment Corporation PDP-11 with 8k of core memory. To the basic computer (and inside the main frame cabinet) have been added a variety of devices including a two-microsecond eight-bit multiplier, a crystal clock, analog-to-digital converter with eight multiplex channels and controllers for the other peripherals.

The most essential of the peripherals is a video display with character generator, solid state store, and keyboard. The video terminal provides the primary man/machine interface — commands are communicated to the machine through the keyboard while the machine communicates with the staff by way of the video display.

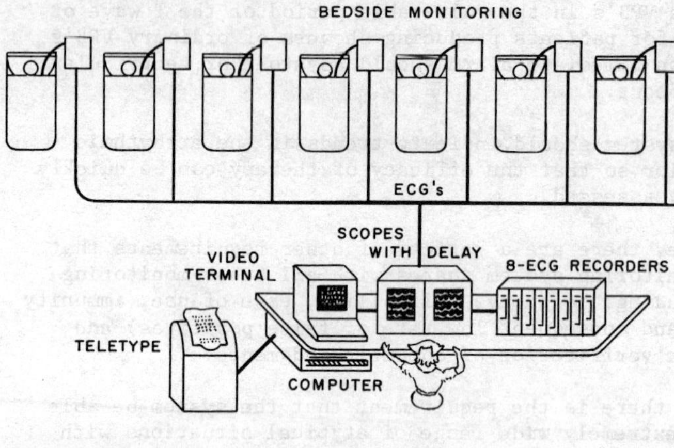

Fig. 4. Computer-assisted monitoring system

Normally, a teleprinter is fitted so that the machine-monitored reports can be reduced to hard copy and included in the patient's chart.

Subsequent to initial amplification (to a level of approximately two volts) in the bedside monitor the electrocardiogram of all eight patients is received by the computer in parallel with an electronic ECG delay line and a conventional central station containing a visual monitoring screen and ECG writers. This conventional equipment is utilized by the computer which contains drivers to turn on the ECG writers connected to the output of the electronic delay line whenever the computer has detected any of those anomalies which have been specified for verification. This write-out, made possible by the delay line, includes approximately two seconds prior to the anomaly and a like amount after its conclusion.

SOFTWARE — SYSTEM ORGANIZATION

The program should be looked upon in two levels — the supervisory algorithm and the VPB detection algorithm. The supervisory algorithm is shown schematically in Fig. 5. At the highest level are two routines — a clock handling routine and a routine which will either receive a character from the keyboard or output a character to the screen. Although neither of these routines can be interrupted, the character output routine takes only 20 to 30 microseconds and thus causes no appreciable delay for the clock handler. The clock interrupt occurs every five milliseconds and the character handling routine can be called no more often than every 600 microseconds because of the terminal limitation.

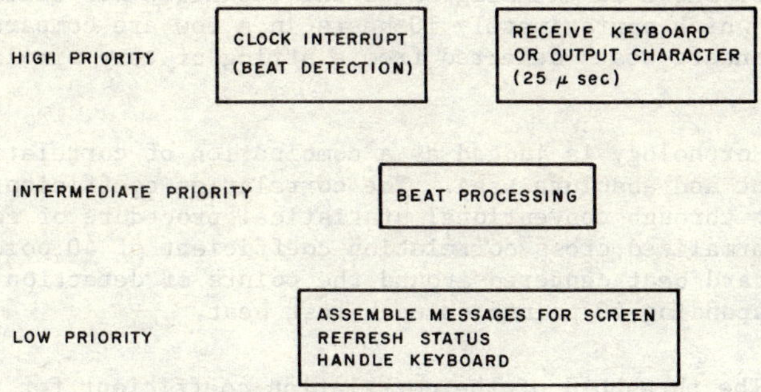

Fig. 5. Overall program organization

The clock interrupt routine which must be executed for each patient at each clock cycle does the A/D conversions, automatic gain control, filtering, and QRS detection. It is this routine which uses the majority of computer time.

The second level of priority includes those calculations which must be performed subsequent to detection of each beat for each patient. On the bottom level is a set of algorithms which assemble the messages to be written on the screen, services the keyboard, etc.

SOFTWARE — VPB DETECTION

The VPB detection algorithm is itself shown in Fig. 6. Hopefully, Fig. 6 is largely self-explanatory; however, there are a few items which deserve comment:

1) The adaptive filter/inhibitor is driven by what is essentially a filtered absolute value of the signal first derivative. To allow this value to average over minor excursions of the signal yet operate sufficiently rapidly to change the filter or cause inhibition of detection, it operates at the

front end of a delay line while the detection takes place at the back end, approximately one-half second later.

2) After each detection there is a refractory period of approximately .1 seconds in which another QRS cannot be detected. This is short enough to accommodate maximum rates found yet sufficiently long as to make very rare more than a single detect on a QRS complex.

3) Not shown in the diagram is the technique for initialization in which approximately 10 beats in a row are compared and a "standard beat" selected from a string of very similar beats.

4) Morphology is judged as a combination of correlation coefficient and absolute area. The correlation coefficient is arrived at through conventional statistical procedure of computing the normalized cross correlation coefficient of 40 points of a standard beat centered around the points of detection with the corresponding 40 points on each test beat.

5) The threshold of the correlation coefficient for judging the morphology abnormal is approximately 0.75; however, it is adjusted by means of an adaptive algorithm [7] so that for people with highly variable morphology the threshold is actually at a lower value of correlation coefficient. The area (absolute value) must be approximately 50% greater than the normal area for judging morphology abnormal and the two criteria (correlation and area) are inclusive ored.

6) The prematurity is typically set to 10% of the average R-R interval (the average is an exponentially weighted average recursively calculated with a time constant of about five beats) but should be set to zero in the event of atrial fibrillation (in the event that the rate algorithm has detected irregular rates the prematurity criterion is automatically, temporarily set to zero).

7) Because of requirement for detecting compensatory pause the algorithm is always one beat behind in addition to the delay for filtering.

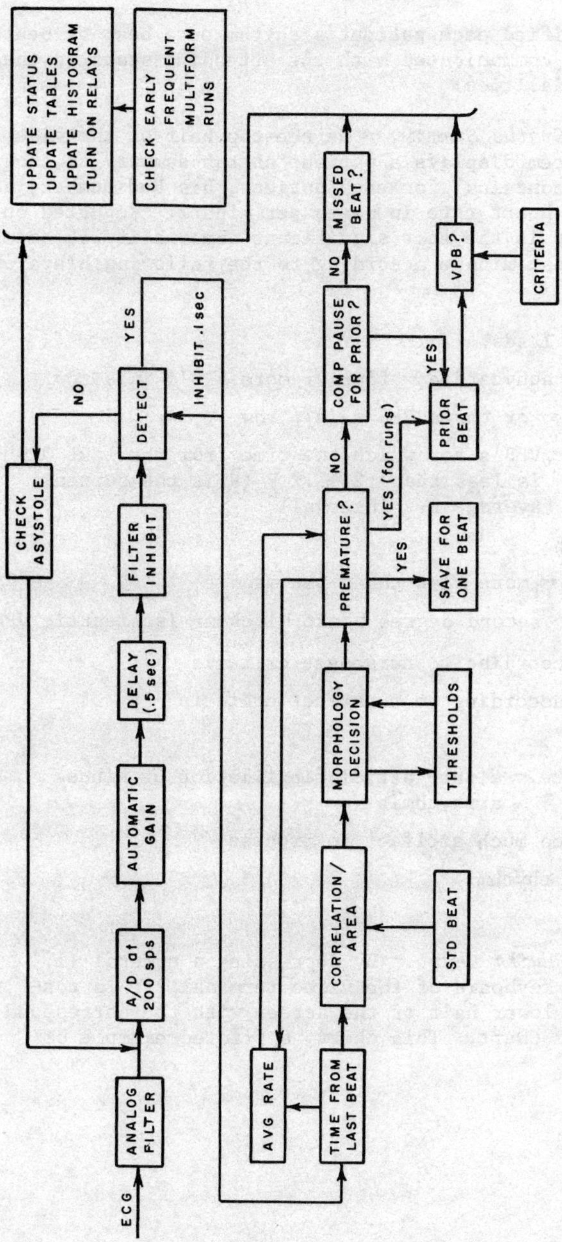

Fig. 6. VPB detection algorithm

COMPUTER — NURSE COMMUNICATIONS

Having classified each patient's rhythm on a beat-by-beat basis, the system communicates with the attending staff in the following four modalities:

1) *Patient Status Summary* — On the top half of the video terminal, the system displays a patient status summary as shown in Fig. 7. This contains, for each patient, his bed number, name, rhythm status and heart rate in beats per minute. Reported on the status summary is the most significant abnormality to have occurred in the last minute according to the following hierarchal list:

Asystole/(no leads)

Ventricular tachycardia — four or more VPB's in a row

Runs VPB — two or three VPB's in a row

Early VPB's — VPB's for which the time from the last QRS is less than .2 + .2 $\bar{R}$ ($\bar{R}$ is the current average R-R interval)

Multiform VPB

Frequent VPB — more than three per minute

Missed beat — second degree heart block or isoelectric VPB

Low rate — according to nurse-set criteria

High rate — according to nurse-set criteria

VPB

Irregular rate — either atrial fibrillation or sinus arrhythmia

Artifact — too much artifact to process

Normal sinus rhythm

2) *Patient Rhythm Chart* — By depressing a numeral (1 through 8) on the keyboard of the video terminal, it is possible to fill the lower half of the screen with the corresponding Patient Rhythm Chart. This chart, a printed example of

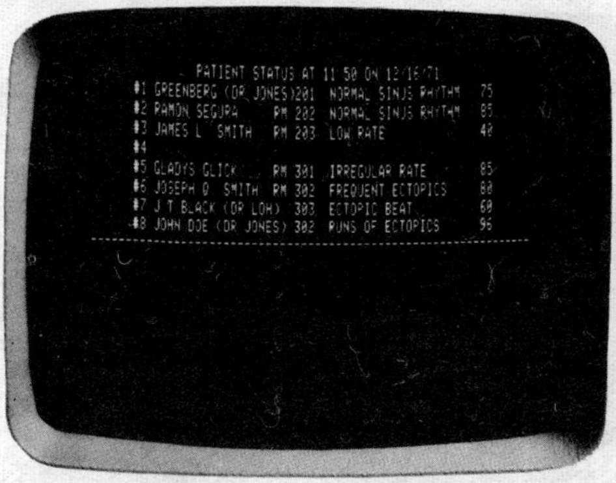

Fig. 7. Patient status summary on video terminal

which is shown in Fig. 8, summarizes all rhythm abnormalities observed in that patient. By adding a teletype to the basic system, it is also possible to print out, either automatically or upon keyboard command, each patient's rhythm chart.

3) *Recorder Actuation Lines* — As part of the basic system, the recorder actuation lines are provided to turn on an ECG recorder and write out, from a delayed ECG, abnormal events. Through keyboard commands, it is possible to do this for VPB's and/or missed beats. If the patient has many VPB's it is possible to specify that only early and/or runs of VPB's be printed out rather than all VPB's.

4) *Cardiac Rhythm Histogram* — This histogram (Fig. 9) shows the number of VPB's a patient has had in each minute of the past hour. It may be shown on the video terminal (displacing the patient status temporarily) and/or printed on the teleprinter.

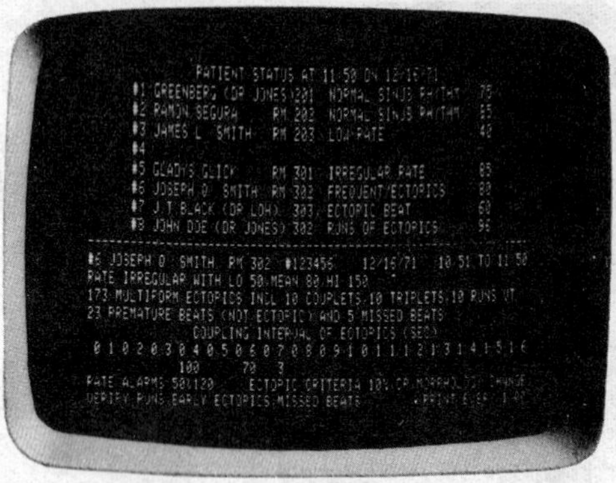

Fig. 8. Patient status summary and patient rhythm chart

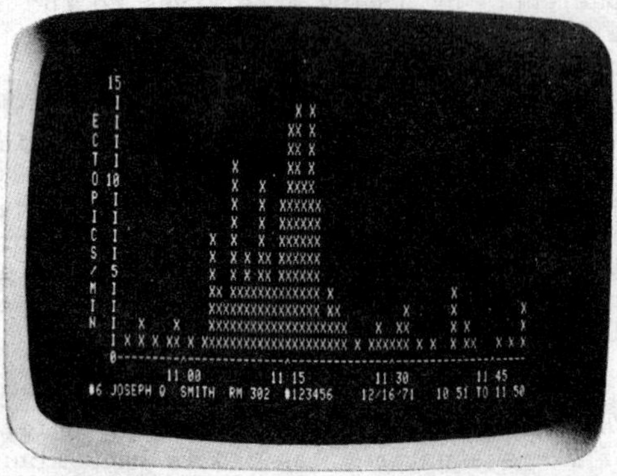

Fig. 9. VPB histogram

NURSE — COMPUTER COMMUNICATION

The nurse communicates with the computer by means of the keyboard on the video terminal. By depressing the specially marked keys on the keyboard, the nurse can give the computer any of the following instructions:

1) Start or stop monitoring of a particular bed

2) Set VPB criteria (any combination of prematurity, compensatory pause, and morphology changes)

3) Set rate alarms

4) Specify which abnormalities should be automatically printed on the ECG recorder (any combination of all VPB's, runs of VPB's, early VPB's, missed beats — asystole or VT will be written out automatically)

5) Specify the patient's name and room number

6) Reset the clock if the computer has been turned off (a rare event)

7) Call up histogram

8) Print on teleprinter

If more than one command is required to complete a given instruction, the nurse will be directed through simple statements on the video screen in what to do. For entering a patient's name (or other comments in the space provided with the patient's name) the original lettering of the standard typewriter keyboard has been retained along with the special markings.

EXPERIENCE WITH THE SYSTEM

The earliest implementation of this system was on a PDP-7 at Worcester Polytechnic Institute [7]. It was shown that the system detected 80% to 90% of VPB's (depending upon prematurity setting) with a false positive rate of about one per hour. However, this system operated only on taped material, handling a single patient, and with no feed-back to attending staff.

The next version of the system, using essentially the detection algorithms described above but with different interactive capabilities, was installed at the Peter Bent Brigham Hospital in Boston in February, 1971, and operated for approximately six months under the overall supervision of Dr. Bernard Lown, Director of the Levine Cardiac Center. During this period, a number of minor changes were made in the basic algorithms and a good deal of experience with requirements of the nursing staff was gathered. Probably the most important lesson was that the amount of information presented (basically that described in Reference 7) was excessive, creating more questions for the attending staff than it answered. The other important lesson of that trial was the enormous diversity of physiologic conditions with which the system would have to cope.

The latest version of the system was installed approximately June 1 in the cardiac care unit of University Hospital in Boston under the supervision of Dr. Michael Klein. It incorporated changes suggested by the Peter Bent Brigham experience. The system was turned over to the nurses for use early in July and remains in use at the time this paper is being presented. The Cardiac Care Center at University Hospital resembles closely the environment of a community hospital with a large diverse group of patients (perhaps 50% myocardial infarction) referred by a variety of attending physicians.

Interestingly, lessons derived from this experience have been essentially those derived from the experience at Peter Bent Brigham — only more so. In this situation with eight patients rather than four and a somewhat more harassed group of nurses, the importance of the computer succinctly presenting important information is very much in evidence. Further, since there are a few surgical patients, a number of patients with pacemakers, and many patients referred purely for rhythm abnormalities, the range of the response of the system must be extended even further than before.

To date, it has been found that the primary tool for coping with the set of problems consists of training and motivating the nurses. It appears that the system's inherent flexibility suffices to meet the needs of approximately 90% of the patients if the nurses are meticulous in setting parameters for each patient (VPB criteria and ECG writer requirements) and in examining the output of the computer. Current protocol assigns a block of patients (two to four) to each nurse. At hourly intervals, the nurse examines the computer output for each of her patients, making note of rate variations and ectopic activity and adjusting parameters as needed. The higher level unusual events are brought to the nurse's attention automatically by the machine. Further, each nurse is required to maintain the leads on her patients in a condition suitable for monitoring. Generally, this requires daily changing of the leads and some experimentation during initial set-up to assure that the leads are optimally placed to find large QRS complexes relative to P and T waves.

Finally, there is currently underway a detailed investigation of the computer's accuracy. Fifty patient hours of ECG have been recorded on a hot stylus recorder at two and one-half millimeters per second parallel with computer analysis of this data. At the time this paper is written these efforts are being examined visually and compared with the computer output. Hopefully, at the time this paper is presented, this analysis will be completed.

REFERENCES

1. B. LOWN, "Intensive heart care" *Sci. Amer. 219* (1968).

2. D.M. LOWRIE, T.W. GREENWOOD, M. GODDARD, A.C. HARVEY, K.W. DONALD, D.G. JULIAN and M.F. OLIVER, "A coronary care unit in the routine management of acute myocardial infarction" *Lancet 2*,109 (1967).

3. B. LOWN, M.D. KLEIN and P.J. HERSHBERG, "Coronary and pre-coronary care" *Amer. J. Med. 46*,705 (1969).

4. J.F. PANTRIDGE and J.S. GEDDES, "A mobile intensive care unit in the management of myocardial infarction" *Lancet 2*,271 (1967).

5. R.L. MacMILLAN ET AL., "Changing perspectives in coronary care. A five year study" *Amer. J. Cardiol. 20*,451 (1967).

6. J.R. JUDE, W.B. KOUWENHOVEN and G.G. KNICKERBOCKER, "Experimental and clinical study of portable external cardiac defibrillator" *Surg. Forum 13*,185 (1962).

7. C.L. FELDMAN, P.G. AMAZEEN, M.D. KLEIN and B. LOWN, "Computer detection of ventricular ectopic beats" *Comp. and Biomed. Rsch. 3*,666 (1970).

A PRELIMINARY STUDY OF THE USE OF A DIGITAL COMPUTER MODEL OF THE HEART, CIRCULATION, BODY FLUID COMPARTMENTS AND KIDNEYS TO DETERMINE THE CHANGES IN INTRINSIC CARDIAC CONTRACTILITY AFTER A HEART ATTACK

D. INGRAM and C.J. DICKINSON

Department of Medicine, University College Hospital Medical School, University Street, London WC1E 6JJ, U.K.

SUMMARY

The heart pumps out blood delivered to it at a rate determined by the filling pressure. "Contractility" might be defined as the change in output resulting from a change in filling pressure. This property can easily be measured in an isolated system, but in the whole body with intact nervous and chemical stabilizing systems intrinsic contractility cannot be measured by any present technique, since at least ten different negative feedback systems operate to minimise changes in output pressure of an delivery of blood by the heart. A good measure of contractile function would be very desirable, and we have modelled the human system on a digital computer, optimising the values of time constants, loop gains and other variables until the model could not be faulted in its behaviour in any clinical situation. We have devised another computer analysis which takes into account clinical measurements of heart rate, blood pressure, 24 hours excretion of electrolytes, urea and water by the kidney, and uses them to arrive at that estimate of "cardiac contractility" which most accurately matches the behaviour of the model. Initial results from application of this technique to the study of data from ten patients indicate a reasonable accord with clinical expectation.

SUMMARY

The heart pumps out blood delivered to it at a rate determined by the filling pressure. "Contractility" might be defined as the change in output resulting from a change in filling pressure. This property can easily be measured in an isolated system, but in the whole body with intact nervous and chemical stabilizing systems intrinsic contractility cannot be measured by any present technique, since at least ten different negative feedback systems operate to minimise changes in output pressure of and delivery of blood by the heart. A good measure of contractile function would be very desirable, and we have modelled the human system on a digital computer, optimising the values of time constants, loop gains and other variables until the model could not be faulted in its behaviour in any clinical situation. We have devised another computer analysis which takes into account clinical measurements of heart rate, blood pressure, 24 hours excretion of electrolytes, urea and water by the kidney, and uses them to arrive at that estimate of "cardiac contractility" which most accurately matches the behaviour of the model. Initial results from application of this technique to the study of data from ten patients indicate a reasonable accord with clinical expectation.

QUANTIFICATION OF CARDIAC FUNCTION

Nervous and hormonal control systems in the body alter cardiac performance by changing the physiological state of the myocardium. They are said to alter "myocardial contractility". The pumping action of the heart may be quantified in the form of families of function curves relating the cardiac output (l/min) to the mean filling pressure of blood from the veins (mm Hg). The rising limb of the function curve may be approximated by a straight line (Fig. 1). The slope of this line varies with the contractile state of the heart and may be taken as an index of cardiac contractility. Intrinsic contractility is the slope obtaining when the heart is isolated (e.g. by drugs) from external control [1]. Contractility is a generic concept encompassing many mechanisms which together affect overall cardiac functions. Many indices of contractile function have been proposed based on measurement of tension, length and load in isolated muscles or of pressure, volume and flow of blood in the aorta or within the left ventricle. Such indices have provided a practical means of quantifying changes in isolated muscle experiments. Reproducible results have also been achieved in controlled heart-lung preparations in spite of experimental difficulties arising from the limited types and

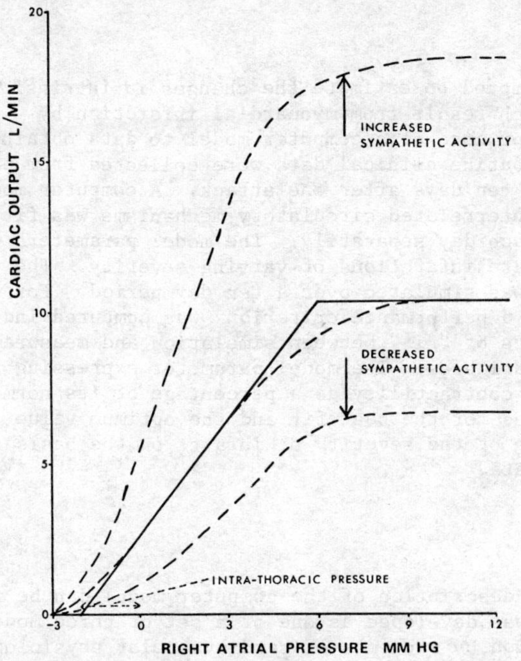

Fig. 1. Typical 'cardiac function' curves (interrupted lines). Solid line shows a linear approximation.

accuracy of measurements available. Normally the heart operates with continually changing input and output load characteristics of the vascular beds under the adaptive control of the autonomic and hormonal nervous systems. Contractility indices measured in this situation have shown great lability.

HEART ATTACK

In acute myocardial infarction a segment of muscle tissue in the heart wall becomes starved of blood and ceases to contract. Thus the total intrinsic contractility falls acutely and a sequence of homeostatic regulatory mechanisms is brought into play to compensate for the fall in cardiac output and blood pressure which occurs. These include constriction of blood vessels, stimulation of the heart, mobilisation of extra vascular fluid reserves, and retention of salt and water by the kidney. Tissue reparation is also initiated.

METHODS

We have attempted to estimate the changes in intrinsic contractility which result from myocardial infarction by matching the performance of a computer model to data obtained from patients. Routine clinical data were collected from patients during the ten days after the attack. A computer model of the relevant interrelated circulatory mechanisms was fitted to the data for each day separately. The model parameters were adjusted to simulate infarctions of varying severity. The course of events was simulated over a ten day period. For each simulation or run a performance criterion was computed indicating the goodness of "fit" between simulation and measurement of the clinical variables. The model parameter expressing the intrinsic cardiac contractility as a percentage of its normal value was optimised for the best fit and the optimum value taken as a measure of the severity of infarct on the basis of successive days data.

COMPUTER MODEL

Only a brief description of the computer model can be included here. It was developed as one of a set of three models for self instruction by students of cardiovascular physiology. It has been demonstrated to the Physiological Society and details published in the Proceedings [2]. Designed originally to simulate typical circulatory phenomena for a 70kg man it was adapted to exhibit blood pressure, cardiac output and weight appropriate to the known age, sex weight and height of a particular patient according to formulae published in the literature.

The *heart and lungs* are represented by a single cardiac function curve [3] with characteristics determined both by four preset parameters (including intrinsic contractility as a percentage of normal) and dynamically by sympathetic nervous activity and the loading effect of high arterial blood pressure.

The *systemic vascular bed* is modelled by a single hydrodynamic circuut split into arterial and venous compartments at the mid point of the capillary bed. The arterial compartment is resistive whereas the venous compartment has capacitance (volume distensibility) and resistance [4].

Control of blood pressure is incorporated as a baroreceptor feedback loop. The effect on cardiac function and vascular parameters being based on extrapolation to the human from animal experimentation and on clinical data accumulated in the literature [4]. Equations interrelating pressure, volume and flow within this idealised circuit are solved by an iterative method which adjusts the index of sympathetic activity until the stable operating point is reached at which cardiac output and return of blood to the heart are in balance.

Three *body fluid compartments* - intracellular, interstitial and plasma are described by their volumes and content of sodium, potassium and urea. Albumen is synthesised and remains within the plasma compartment. Plasma and red cell volume together make up the circulating blood volume in equilibrium with the interstitial fluid across the capillary walls. The equations here follow the work of Starling [5] on the balance of hydrostatic and colloid osmotic pressures and of Guyton [6] on the compliance characteristic of the interstitial compartment. The fluxes between the interstitial and intracellular compartments are based on active transport tending to conserve intracellular potassium, osmotic movement of water and some passive diffusion of sodium and potassium. *Dietary intake of salt, potassium and protein* are based on the average British diet. The protein supports anabolic mechanisms building up lean body mass. Urea and some water result from intracellular catabolic processes. Urea is assumed freely permeable within the body fluids.

Thirst is estimated on the basis of osmotic and volemic stimuli and determines the simulation of water intake.

A semi-empirical approach was taken in the modelling of *renal function*. It is based on such consensus as exists on mode of action and relative activity of glomerular filtration, the renin angiotensin system, aldosterone and vasopressin on the excretion of water, salt, potassium and urea.

Inevitably such a model embraces many simplifications and approximations. As previously reported the model has shown the potential for realistic simulation of a very wide variety of clinical conditions. It is designed to provide output of variables in the forms customary in clinical practice.

PERFORMANCE CRITERION

The model may be considered a mathematical process which receives as input a set of parameter values and generates as output a set of data simulating the time course of variables representing the clinical status of a patient. Some of these output variables are measurable and on the basis of these the simulation may be compared to actual patient data. A normalised weighted square error criterion, F_j, is used as the measure of "fit" between clinical measurement and corresponding process variables.

$$F_j = \sum_{i=1}^{n} \left(\frac{X_{ij} - P_{ij}}{P_{ij}} \right)^2 \times W_i$$

where X_{ij} is the value of process variable i for day j after the infarction

P_{ij} is the clinical measurement of variable i for day j after the infarction

W_i is the weighing factor applied to the fitting of variable i

j = 1,2.3...1.0 is the day number

n is the number of variables included in the criterion.

OPTIMISATION OF PARAMETERS

We required in general terms to find the set of input parameter values (parameters of optimisation) which minimises F_j. The many non-linear relationships represented in the model preclide precise analytical solution. Linearisation and analysis of small perturbations in the system would be unrealistic since it would impair the clinical realism of the simulation. Many approaches have been developed in recent years to such optimisation problems. These involves approximations of varying sophistication to the topology of the performance surface in the multidimensional space defined by the parameters of optimisation [7]. The search strategies are to some extent empirical and a "try it and see" approach still prevails.

Particular attention was paid to the convergence of solutions to the mathematical equations of the model since imprecise solution sometimes caused spurious optimisation. Local optima have also been observed though it was possible in the straight forward optimisation to detect these without resort to general stochastic search techniques. It was also necessary to constrain parameter ranges since with certain performance criteria the best fit occurred at a physiologically unrealistic state. The problem could be overcome either by mapping to a constrained parameter space or by introducing a penalty function into the computation of performance criterion based on some measure of the deviation from a physiological condition.

Whilst the program suite developed for this project is designed to encompass multi-parameter optimisation the clinical situation under analysis (myocardial infarction) involves a primary change in only one parameter. Clinical changes following infarction are well represented on the basis of a decrease in the intrinsic slope of the cardiac function curve. In certain situations myocardial infarction may occur in the presence of or may precipitate renal failure. Analysis of data collected in this situation would provide a greater scope for these techniques.

PATIENT DATA

Patients aged under 70 years suspected of suffering their first heart attack were admitted to the series. To date ten patients have been studied - nine men and one woman.

The following standard clinical and laboratory data was recorded:

i) 6 hourly blood pressure and heart rate

ii) 24 hour fluid balance

iii) The occurrence of pain

iv) Body weight (if possible)

v) Plasma concentrations of sodium, potassium and urea (10am samples on days 1,2,3,5,10)

vi) 24 hour excretion of urine sodium, potassium and urea was measured on days 1,2,3,5,10

(temperature and respiration rate were recorded but not used in this study).

Other clinical and laboratory data were recorded including age, sex, weight and height, previous medical history, drug treatment, routine E.C.G.'s, serum enzyme concentrations (SGOT, HBD), clinical signs, symptoms, X-ray indications.

Details of the patient and data to be compared with the computer simulation were coded onto punched cards (header card plus 3 cards per day of data).

PROGRAM STRUCTURE

A suite of computer programs was written to handle the matching of data to the computer model. The structure of programs allowed flexibility in:

(i) The model used

(ii) The fitting procedures (optimisation technique)

(iii) The basis for quantification of "degree of fit"

(iv) Specification and control of output from optimisation and simulation programs

Each optimisation was termed a task and several tasks were submitted as a batch. A typical task procedure was as follows:

i) The model was initialised to a state typical of an average 70kg man aged about 40 years. The patient data cards were then read and used

(a) To set the model to an initial state characteristic of a healthy man or woman of the age, weight and height specified

(b) To form a file of data for this patient on the disc backing store.

ii) The variables and weighting factors (X_{ij},W_i) to be incorporated in the performance criterion were specified.

iii) Parameters controlling the length of simulation and iteration interval of the model were set.

iv) Desired graphical and other output was specified (during each separate simulation the variables X_{ij} used in computation of the performance criterion were stored automatically).

v) Details of the simulation program and routine for calculating the performance criterion were then passed as parameters to the optimisation sub-program. Through successive steps of parameter perturbation, simulation and performance criterion evaluation the optimum parameters were derived. Output was in the form of graphs and numerical information tracing the approach to the optimum. Alternatively graphs of sections of the performance surface were plotted.

The most interesting output so far has been a set of graphs showing the variation of performance criterion with contractility for data from each successive day.

RESULTS

Figure 2 shows the typical performance profiles by day number relating performance criterion to initial intrinsic contractility. All the measured data specified above were included in this performance criterion. Optima at values above 200% of normal often occurred on several of the later days. This is not a physiologically realistic result. In such a situation venous pressure would be abnormally low running counter to clinical expectation and inference from the observation of the jugular venous pressure. To counter this a penalty function was introduced into F_j whenever simulated right atrial pressure fell below normal. This adjustment leads to changes shown in Fig. 3. Taking the optimum contractility values from these

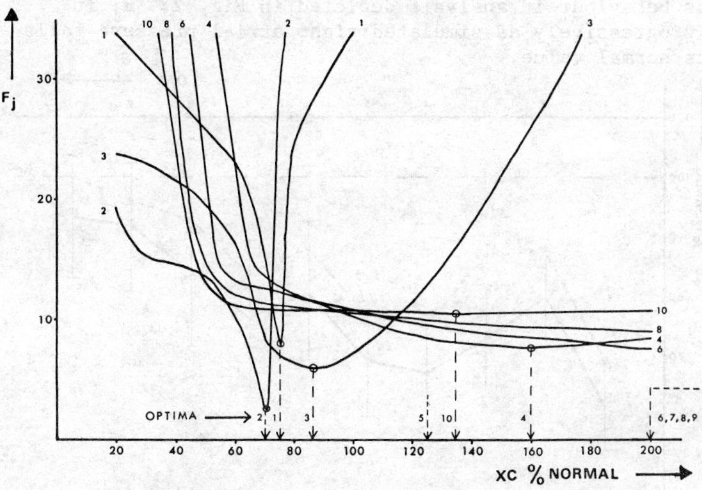

Fig. 2. Set of curves for one patient relating performance criterion, F_j, to intrinsic contractility, XC% of normal. The number of days after the heart attack and the optimum contractility values are indicated for each curve. Optima above twice normal contractility (days 6,7,89) are inconsistent with other clinical observations (see Fig. 3).

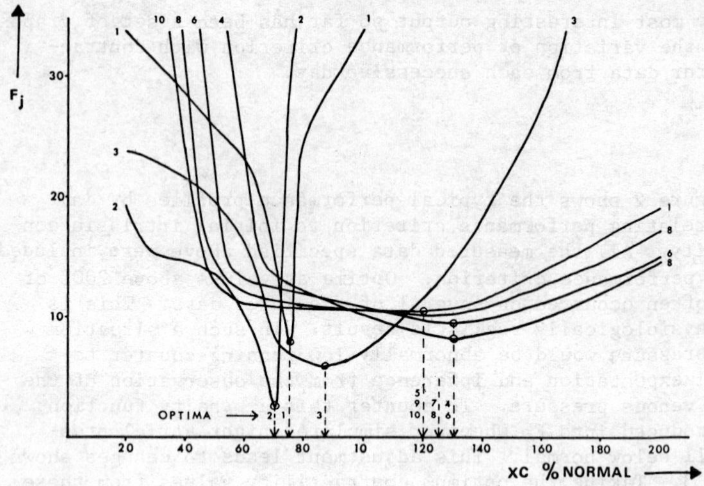

Fig. 3. Effect of introducing a penalty function to correct anomalous behaviour in analysis depicted in Fig. 2. F_j increases progressively as simulated right atrial pressure falls below its normal value.

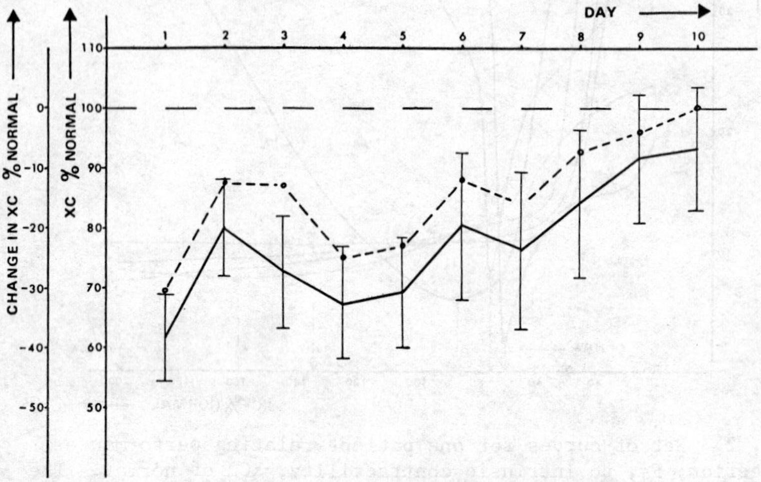

Fig. 4. Summary of analysis of data from ten patients. Average intrinsic contractility, XC (solid line with S.E. of mean) falls by about one third on the first day and appears to recover progressively to a near normal value at the end of ten days. The time course of change in intrinsic contractility is also shown (interrupted line). Changes are calculated relative to the average of estimates for days nine and tem for each patient. The trend of results is the same.

curves and computing averages for all 10 patients we arrive at results summarised in Fig. 4.

This shows the average time course of change in intrinsic contractility for the first 10 patients studied. The intrinsic contractility drops on average about 30% in days 1-2 and appears to recover progressively during days 3-10 although at present we have no measure of the normal value to which it will ultimately return.

DISCUSSION

These are early results and full assessment has not yet been made. Some "anomalous" behaviour has been detected in individual results - notably in one case associated with intensive drug treatment, but the average trend depicted in Fig. 4 seems to accord reasonably with clinical expectation. The quantitative indices of intrinsic contractility will be correlated with enzyme levels and other indicators of the severity of infarct (e.g. based on assessment of the E.C.G.). It is also intended to investigate the sensitivity of the result to accuracy in measurement of the different variables.

REFERENCES

1. A.D. JOSÉ, "Effect of combined sympathetic and parasympathetic blockade on heart rate and cardiac function in man" *Amer. J. Cardiol. 18* (3), 476-478 (1966).

2. C.J. DICKINSON, and P. SHEPARD, "A digital computer model of the systemic circulation and kidney for studying renal and circulatory interractions involving electrolytes and body fluid compartments ("MacPee")" *J. Physiol. 210*, 10-12 (1971).

3. E.H. STARLING, *The Linacre Lecture on the Law of the Heart* (Longmans, Green and Co., London, 1918).

4. A.C. GUYTON, *Circulatory Physiology: Cardia Output its regulation and control* (W.B. Saunders and Co., London, 1963).

5. E.H. STARLING, "On the absorption of fluids from the connective tissue spaces" *J. Physiol. 19*, 312-326 (1865).

6. A.C. GUYTON, H.J. GRANGER, and A.E. TAYLOR, "Interstitial fluid pressure" *Phys. Rev.* *51* (3), 521-563 (1971).

7. J. KOWALIK, and M.R. OSBORNE, *Methods for Unconstrained Optimisation Problems* (American Elsevier Publishing Company, New York, 1968).

A COMPREHENSIVE SYSTEM FOR AUTOMATED ECG INTERPRETATION

P.W. MACFARLANE, T.P. TAYLOR, H.T. CAWOOD,
C. TAYLOR, and T.D.V. LAWRIE

University Department of Medical Cardiology,
Royal Infirmary, Glasgow C 4, U.K.

SUMMARY

This paper discusses the use of digital computers for interpretation of ECGs. In particular a low cost system is described which undertakes a complete ECG interpretation including arrhythmia analysis and a comparison of serial tracings for detection of sequential changes. This is achieved by storing up to two interpretations in digital form on disc. Previous diagnoses are retained in Boolean form and a few selected measurements are stored in numerical format. This technique for comparison of tracings is thought to be new, and should have considerable influence in furthering the use of a digital computer for ECG interpretation. The paper also suggests that the cost of adopting automated techniques should not add significantly to the running costs of a cardiology department and the overall conclusion was that this method of ECG interpretation will be the one of choice in the near future.

INTRODUCTION

One of the branches of medicine which is most suited to the application of computer techniques is cardiology. In particular the automation of electrocardiogram (ECG) interpretation has received considerable attention over the past years. As a result there is now an increasing number of hospitals using computing systems, sometimes on a bureau basis, for ECG analysis although the total is not excessive. This is due both to economic reasons and the fact that many cardiologists and physicians are not yet satisfied that the methods currently available are clinically satisfactory [1].

This paper describes a system which it is thought meets many of the shortcomings of other software packages currently being offered by commercial interests. In particular the total cost of the computing hardware required is approximately £15,000 while the facilities offered by the program such as arrhythmia analysis and a comparison of successive tracings for detection of sequential changes are among the most recent advances.

METHODS

The computing systems used in the development of this ECG interpretation program have been in the PDP8 series. The facilities required for running the program are 8K core store, an analogue to digital converter, 1.6 million words of disc storage and an output printer. The system on which the program is currently being developed has additional equipment including a further 12K core store, high speed paper tape input/output, digital magnetic tapes etc. but these are not essential to the program operation.

The program has been written to interpret 3 lead ECGs as derived from the modified axial lead system. In summary three simultaneously recorded ECG wave forms are obtained from a patient and these represent different components, in three mutually perpendicular directions along the natural axes of the body, of the total cardiac electrical activity. A more complete description of the lead system used can be found elsewhere [2].

The ECG is obtained at the bedside using a data acquisition trolley which contains the ECG amplifiers, a monitoring oscilloscope and a four channel magnetic tape recorder. Thus the computer program accepts input in the form of analogue signals which are provided from the magnetic tape. Approximately 20 seconds of ECG are obtained from each patient and normally a technician will record about 15 patients in one morning or afternoon recording session. In our hospital four data acquisition units are available for daily use and a fifth is in use at a peripheral hospital (Law Hospital) 20 miles distant. In the latter case used magnetic tapes are sent by van each day to Glasgow Royal Infirmary and the computer interpretations are returned within 24 hours by the same method.

The methods used for replaying the ECGs to the computer and for the analysis have been described previously [3,4]. In summary 7½ seconds of ECG are chosen by the computer operator and input to the PDP8E system for the analysis, which takes 27 seconds with the latest disc based version of the program.

In summary a typical interpretation consists of a set of wave measurements over which the ECG tracing is later mounted by hand, an arrhythmia interpretation and the diagnostic interpretation which includes a comparison with a previous report if one is available. A typical interpretation excluding the wave measurements has been retyped for illustrative purposes as in Fig. 1. The facility for comparison of ECGs is the most recent addition to the program and one which is believed to be unique. This will therefore be discussed in more detail.

SINUS RHYTHM AND VENTRICULAR EXTRASYSTOLES

Q WAVES IN THE ANTEROLATERAL LEAD

T WAVE INVERSION ALSO NOTED

SEQUENTIAL CHANGES OF ANTEROLATERAL
MYOCARDIAL INFARCTION

Fig. 1. A typical ECG interpretation retyped for illustrative purposes.

ANALYSIS OF SEQUENTIAL CHANGES

In order to compare day to day variations in the electrocardiogram a system has been devised whereby the diagnostic interpretation of an ECG is retained in digital form on a computer disc. This has been achieved by storing a series of Boolean variables which indicate the presence or absence of various ECG abnormalities and by saving in addition a few important wave measurements (such as the angle of the maximum T wave vector in various planes).

In order to determine criteria for a significant daily variation in appearances, a group of normal patients and a group of patients who have suffered a myocardial infarction was studied. In this way it was possible to examine the variation of ECG measurements from day to day so that normal ranges could be established. It was then shown that patients with a myocardial infarction in most cases exhibit changes in serial measurements in excess of the normal variation.

It was decided to save a maximum of two records for each patient, namely the primary record which is the first ECG obtained on admission or outpatient visit to hospital and the secondary record which is the most recent ECG interpretation. This means that if a patient has had four ECGs recorded prior to a fifth being input for interpretation, the first ECG and the fourth ECG in the series will have been stored in the computer for comparison with the fifth ECG. This technique was adopted since it could well be that the variation in a particular parameter on successive days was within normal limits over the series while the variation between the first and fourth was frankly outwith normal. It would therefore have been of little use to store only the most recent ECG interpretation.

The primary record for each patient consists basically of the patient's unique hospital identification number together with his age, sex, date of first ECG recording, a clinical classification number and a count of the total number of ECGs recorded during an inpatient's stay or an outpatient's visits. The record also contains the various Boolean parameters together with some measurements as previously discussed and a pointer to the secondary record. The latter contains basically the date of the ECG recording and the ECG interpretation in a form similar to the primary record.

At each stage in the interpretation and particularly if myocardial infarction or ischaemia is detected a comparison is made with the previous ECG reports. For example if myocardial infarction is found to be present, the program compares T wave measurements with the previous one or two ECGs and alternative outputs can be printed depending on the findings. An example of the logic used is shown in Fig. 2. It is thought that these methods will prove very flexible for further development of automated ECG interpretation.

DISCUSSION

The basic ECG interpretation program has been in operation routinely for 18 months. The additional logic for analysis of sequential changes has just recently been completed and is therefore in the experimental stages. This means that extensive testing of the new subroutines will be undertaken before they are used for routine purposes.

There are several advantages in using an analysis involving a comparison with a previous tracing. With older methods, for example on one occasion the computer interpretation might report myocardial infarction while with a later ECG from the same patient it may state only myocardial ischaemia. With the new methods, it would be possible to influence the interpretation of the second ECG by the fact that myocardial infarction has previously been detected. Therefore the T wave abnormalities can be reoprted as being due to the previously detected myocardial infarction rather than as being

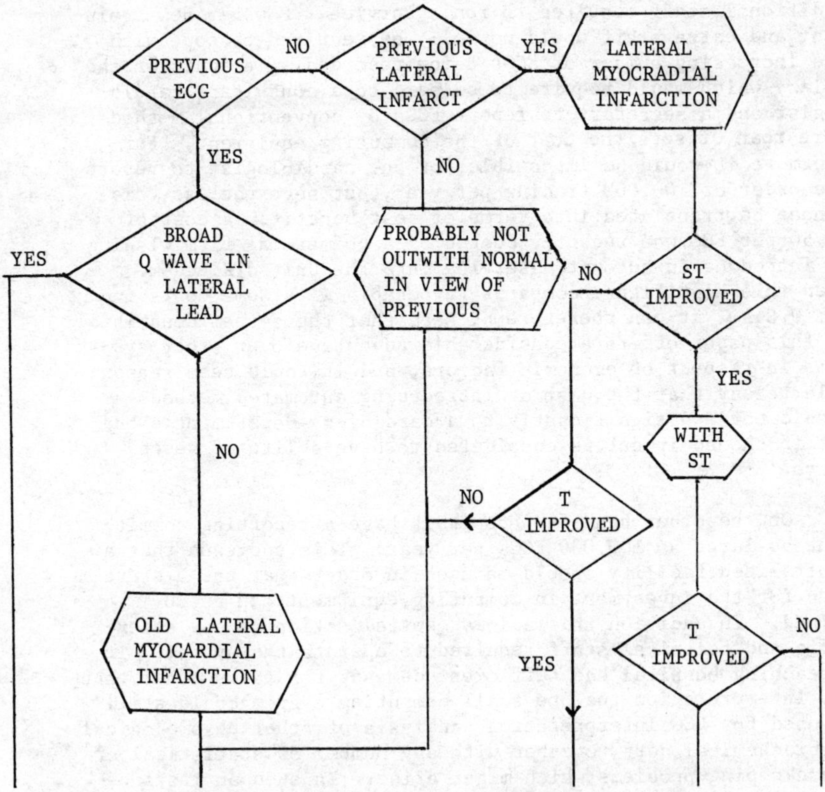

Fig. 2. A section of the logic used for analysis of serial tracings. At this point in the analysis a significant Q wave but no ST-T abnormalities have been found in the antero-lateral lead. The hexagonal frame encloses a printout statement and the diamond shaped frame encloses a question.

---

due to myocardial ischaemia. This is in keeping with the methods used by a cardiologist making his own interpretation.

With the system described above it is not unreasonable to consider that over 100,000 ECGs per year could be interpreted, assuming that the machine were available for this purpose all of the working day. This would mean that with equipment costing approximately £15,000 and allowing for depreciation over seven years with maintenance of £1,000 per annum that the contribution in respect of computer hardware to the cost of interpreting one ECG would be about 3p. There remains to be taken into consideration the cost of ECG data acquisition units, and any additional staff required to run a service. However new equipment and extra staff would normally be required to cope with the increasing number of ECGs being recorded. In addition the salary which would require to be paid to a consultant cardiologist and a secretary to report ECGs by conventional methods more than offsets the cost of the computing equipment. Furthermore it would be impossible for one cardiologist to report the order of 100,000 tracing per year, but nevertheless this cannot be translated into terms of cost benefit. A cost of £2.50 per ECG was recently quoted by a commercial firm wishing to introduce an automated service into the United Kingdom. Even this high figure compares favourably with some costs in the U.S.A. It can therefore be seen that the system described in this paper offers a considerable advantage over other systems in respect of economic factors, and it would seem reasonable to say that the cost of introducing automated methods should not add significantly to a cardiology department's budget if the equipment is considered to have a life of seven years.

On the other hand few hospitals have a reporting commitment as large as 100,000 ECGs per year. This suggests that a centralised facility should be used in order that the best return for the investment in computing equipment can be obtained. In addition this allows centralisation of the scientific and technical staff required to operate the system. If a teaching hospital had sufficient demands for tasks other than ECG interpretation the one small computing system could still be used for ECG interpretation, analysis of other physiological or biochemical data together with any number of statistical or housekeeping problems which might arise. In such an instance it is more difficult to assess the cost benefit of installing the equipment but at £15,000, the cost compares exceptionally favourably with installing radiological apparatus which most hospitals have.

CONCLUSION

The number of ECGs being recorded annually is increasing not only in our own hospital but in many other cities and countries. It would seem realistic that with the anticipated price reduction in the cost of automated ECG interpretation systems, the most suitable way to keep pace with the increasing demand for ECG interpretation would be for this technique to become the method of choice in the near future.

REFERENCES

1. P.W. MACFARLANE, and T.D.V. LAWRIE, "Reflections on the Introduction of Automated ECG Interpretation" *Kybernetes* *1*, 157 (1972).

2. P.W. MACFARLANE, "A Modified Axial Lead System for Orthogonal Lead Electrocardiography" *Cardiovascular Research 3*, 510 (1969).

3. P.W. MACFARLANE, "ECG Waveform Identification by Digital Computer" *Cardiovascular Research* 5, 141 (1971).

4. P.W. MACFARLANE, H. CAWOOD, T.P. TAYLOR, and T.D.V. LAWRIE, "Routine Automated Electrocardiogram Interpretation" *Bio-medical Engineering 7*, 176 (1972).

EVALUATING THE PERFORMANCE OF ELECTROCARDIOGRAPHIC R-WAVE DETECTORS*

J.D. ANDERSEN and E.D. ANDERSEN

Medical Department B, (head: A. Tybjaerg Hansen), Rigshospitalet, University Hospital, Copenhagen, Denmark

SUMMARY

Reliable QRS-detectors are needed for several applications, and in recent years detectors using new principles have appeared, but none have reached the capabilities of the skilled human observer. To select the optimum detector for a given application or to predict the effects of circuit redesign or change in critical parameters it is important to characterize objectively the performance of each detector.

Statistical decision concepts long used in communication engineering and detection problems were applied to develop a standardized method for the evaluation of performance of R-wave detectors. The method makes allowance for the relative importance of classification errors (false positive or missed QRS's) by calculation of the average risk in the particular application. This method makes it possible for the designer to estimate the degree of accuracy of R-wave detection of the unit under given circumstances.

This method has been used to evaluate performance of three QRS-detectors using 52 segments of tape recorded ECG signals of a total duration of nearly 9 hours. Two sets of signals from the coronary care unit, Medical Department B, Rigshospitalet, were used; one consisted of specially selected 'difficult' arrhythmias and artifacts, the other comprised randomly selected representative signals

*This work has been supported in part by the Rask-Ørsted Foundation, Danish Ministry of Education (Research Grant no. 8442-415). We wish to thank Mr. H.H. Konstantin-Hansen and Mr. K. Stolberg-Christensen for valuable technical assistance.

INTRODUCTION

In recent years complicated automatic signal categorizers or pattern recognizers have appeared in the medical field intended for helping or replacing the human observer in tedious routine tasks. A good example of such an automated system is the electrocardiographic arrhythmia detector, mainly developed for the automatic detection of arrhythmias (disturbances in the heart rhythm) in patients admitted to coronary care units. Such systems have been introduced to secure immediate treatment of cardiac arrest and to lighten the administration of drugs given to prevent cardiac emergencies.

An arrhythmia detector continuously classifies a received electrocardiogram (ECG) recorded by means of electrodes from a patient's chest into an "arrhythmic" or "non-arrhythmic" type. This classification is entirely dependent on proper localization in time of a characteristic waveform in the ECG signal, the QRS complex or R-wave, which electrically reflects the depolarization of the ventricles of the heart (Fig. 1). Owing to biological variation, different leads etc., there is a great variation in the morphology of ECG's, especially in the diseased patient whom physicians want to monitor. Thus a reliable R-wave detector is a prerequisite for the proper performance of

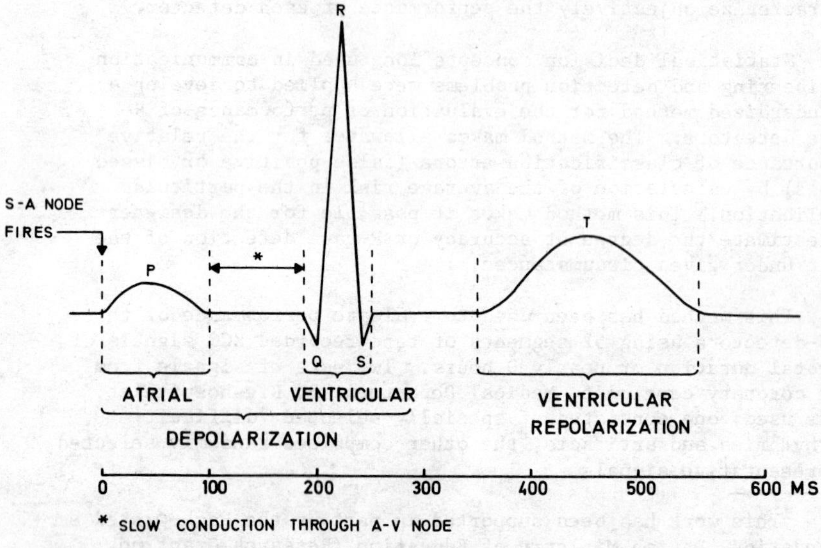

Fig. 1. The normal electrocardiogram (monitoring lead). The ventricular depolarization phase correspomds to the QRS interval. Detection of an R-wave requires that the detector indication falls within this interval.

an arrhythmia detector. A reliable detector can also be used as a front-end pre-processor for a computer analyzing ECG on line, in demand pacemakers and telemetry, in trigger circuits for synchronized DC-shock or X-ray contrast media injections etc.

Because of the complexity of detectors and the wide range of variation of the ECG signal it is no simple matter to predict the performance of a detector circuit in a given environment. Consequently, a statistical description yielding a quantitative measure of performance can serve a twofold purpose. First, for a given unit, it can indicate what changes in circuit design or parameters could lead to improvement for a particular application. Second, by allowing direct comparison between a number of detectors it facilitates selection of the optimum one in a definite situation.

STATEMENT OF THE DETECTION PROBLEM

In order to develop a standardized method for the evaluation of performance of R-wave detectors, statistical decision concepts long used in communication engineering and detection problems were applied [1,2].

The principal errors in the function of QRS detectors are, from the user's point of view, inaccurate timing and misclassification errors. Inaccurate timing makes it difficult to establish a fiducial point for further signal handling like averaging and waveform measurements. Establishing an exact reference point with respect to the QRS cycle in terms of the statistical communication theory means making parameter estimation, the parameter being for instance the exact time for the beginning of the QRS interval (labelled "ventricular depolarization" in Fig. 1).

The second type of error is that of misclassification, which in the case of a QRS detector can be either to declare QRS present, when it is actually absent (false alarm or false positive type of error), or to fail to declare QRS present, when it actually is present (false negative or miss type of error). This decision situation involving two alternatives is an example of hypothesis testing (signal detection) in the statistical communication theory. The purpose of the QRS detector is to test the hypothesis that at a given moment a QRS is present or it is not, and to make a decision that will result in optimum performance based on what is received, distorted as it may be by noise.

THE STATISTICAL MODEL

Based on these considerations we have adopted the following decision theoretical model to represent the detection situation (Fig. 2). The ECG observed is assumed to be composed of "signal" and "noise". Signal has the value x_1="QRS present" when we are in the QRS interval (depolarization phase in Fig. 1), otherwise the value x_2="QRS absent". Noise is defined as the residue obtained by subtracting the "true" signal from the ECG actually received after transmission. The detection model is shown in Fig. 3. Since it is impossible in practice to decide whether the heart is physically in the

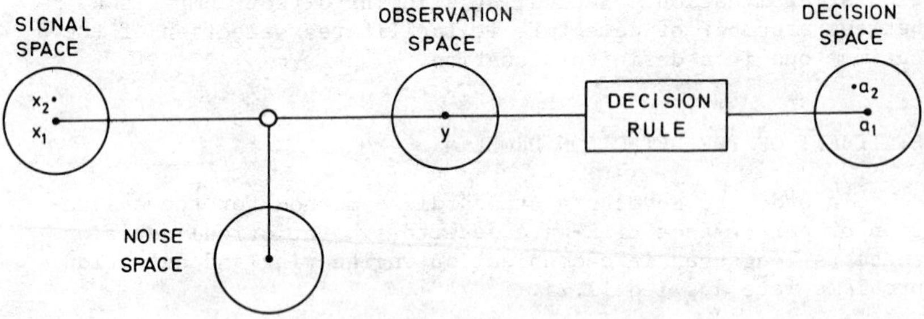

Fig. 2. The detection situation in general terms. A decision a is to be made about a condition x based on some data y according to a decision rule.

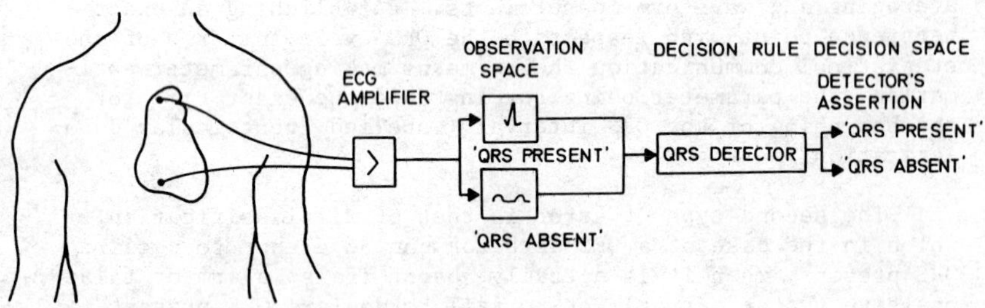

Fig. 3. A diagram to illustrate the decision theoretical model employed. The ECG amplifier represents the total transmission path from the patient's heart to the input signal of the detector. The observed signal can be the input signal of the QRS detector or a voltage in the detecor, for example the filtered and rectified input.

depolarization phase or not (with the non-invasive techniques used here), the human observer decides from the electrocardiogram whether this is the case. This does not add much inaccuracy to the description, since in practical clinical use the skilled ECG interpreter is the standard in which the performance of detectors are being compared. However, he can be in doubt whether a spike in the ECG is a QRS complex or not. In these rare cases, the decision of the individual detector has been taken to represent the true situation. Let x represent the true state of affairs that we are trying to guess (presence or absence of an R-wave at a given moment, represented by x_1, respectively x_2). Each of the two possible physical states may be expected to occur with the a priori probability P, respectively Q.

In a similar manner take y to represent the signal observed somewhere in the transmission path from the heart to the final decision circuit. Here, y is the input signal of the detector but it might also represent the filtered and rectified signal or the input of a comparator in the detector or a set of voltages and logical levels in the detector. The value of y is assumed in some way to determine the decision of the detector.

If a particular sequence of x's occur, the received y's may vary because noise has introduced errors. Assuming a continuum of states for a single parameter y, we can express its probability density function on the condition that the true physical state is x_1 or x_2 respectively. These functions are two conditional probability density functions. In Fig. 4, $p(y|x_2)$ for example expresses the probability of receiving a particular y on the assumption that x_2=QRS absent" is the true physical state. Here it is convenient to introduce misclassification costs which can be adapted to each particular application of a detector. Let the cost incurred in case of a false alarm be the amount C_f, in case of a missed beat the amount C_m. Given a description of the decision situation, the decision problem is to find the rule by which a decision a_i (a_1=the assertion "QRS present", a_2="QRS absent") based on the observation y is to be made if, on the average over an imaginary ensemble of identical situations, the error cost is to be minimized. Such considerations lead to detector design using optimum filtering techniques as indicated by Braun [3].

Based on this model a reasonable measure of performance is the average risk or expected cost of misclassification errors per time unit $R = Pr_1 + Qr_2$

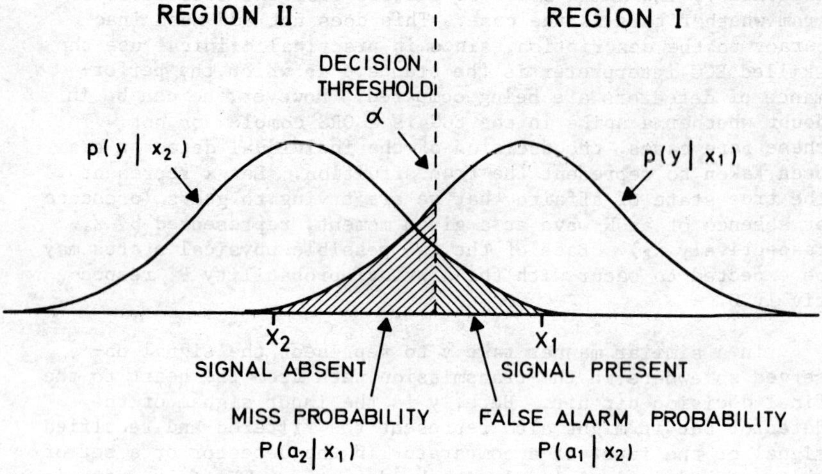

Fig. 4. Condition probability density functions for an observed signal y. $p(y|x_2)$ is the conditional probability function for y, provided that QRS complex is absent, $p(y|x_1)$ when a QRS complex is present.

where $r_1 = C_m P(a_2|x_1)$

and $r_2 = C_f P(a_1|x_2)$.

$P(a_2|x_1)$ is the probability of a miss error and $P(a_1|x_2)$ the probability of a false alarm error. The performance index PI could then be defined as PI = -R. Other measures of performance could of course have been chosen. A discussion of these can be found in the thesis by Becker [4].

In the present evaluation the fraction, which is the sum of all QRS complexes in the segment ("QRS time") made up of the total observation time, was used as an estimate for the a priori probability of the occurrence of a QRS complex for each type of ECG. Similarly, the fraction "non-QRS time"/total observation time was used for estimating Q, the number of false positives/total number of QRS's for estimating $P(a_1|x_2)$ and the number of false negatives/total number of QRS's as an estimate for $P(a_2|x_1)$.

EVALUATION OF PERFORMANCE

The method outlined above was used to determine an index of performance for three R-wave detectors by estimating the average risk per time unit. The first instrument, designated the CR detector, is a laboratory model designed and built by Christian Rovsing Ltd. It consists of an analogue third order band pass filter, a numerical rectifier and a peakfinder circuit, which continuously tracks peaks exceeding 25% of the peak value of the previously detected QRS complex. Such peaks are examined with respect to trailing edge slope and compared to an adjustable threshold. If this threshold is exceeded during a 20 msec time interval, the peak is considered to be an R-wave. If no better alternative is found within the next 200 msec, it is declared to be an R-wave, unless two or more peaks exceeding it by more than 30% occurs in that period. In that case the waveform is regarded as noise.

The second unit, named the HP detector, is a commercially available arrhythmia detector, the Hewlett-Packard 7822A. It consists of an automatic gain control to normalize system gain which is set by depressing a button on the front, a filter with a passband centered at 8 Hz and an amplitude comparator. Detection of a QRS complex is followed by an inhibition period of about 280 msec. After detection of a widened QRS, this refractory period is extended by a further 280 msec to prevent triggering by the T-wave [5].

The third QRS detector, designated SW, is part of a commercially available device developed by Simonsen & Weel Ltd., the ECG Arrhythmia Computer EAC 804. This also consists of a band pass filter, an automatic gain controlled amplifier, the gain being controlled by the previously detected peaks (exponentially weighted in time), a differentiator and a rectifier. This is followed by a peak detector, giving an output pulse if the peak exceeds one third of the previously detected peak amplitude. A discriminator starts comparing how long the signal exceeds the threshold, and the peak is accepted as QRS if both circuits accept the wave. Acceptance is followed by a refractory period of 300 msec. The refractory period after QRS detection, found in all three detectors, should prevent subsequent false positive detection of large T-waves. All three detectors have artefact rejection circuits, which are slightly different in construction.

In the present study the test data were drawn from patients admitted to the coronary care unit of a university hospital. The ECG's have been recorded on a ½ inch FM magnetic tape at the speed of 15/16 inch/sec on a seven-track Lyrec instrumentation recorder. Half-hour segments of ECG's were selected from continuous 12-hour recordings from each of 51 patients. Twenty-three of the segments were chosen to represent as many different arrhythmias and waveforms as possible. The remaining 28 segments were selected at random, one segment from each new patient admitted to the coronary unit during a period of some weeks. One segment consisted exclusively of noise.

The test setup is seen in Fig. 5. The tape was mounted on a FM recorder*, replayed at a speed of 15/16 inch/sec and the signal distributed to the inputs of the three detectors and directly to one channel of the ink recorder**. The indication of occurrence of a QRS complex was picked up, multiplexed and recorded on a second channel of the recorder. For each test ECG segment an identified 10-minute period was evaluated and recorded at a paper speed of 10 mm/sec (some difficult

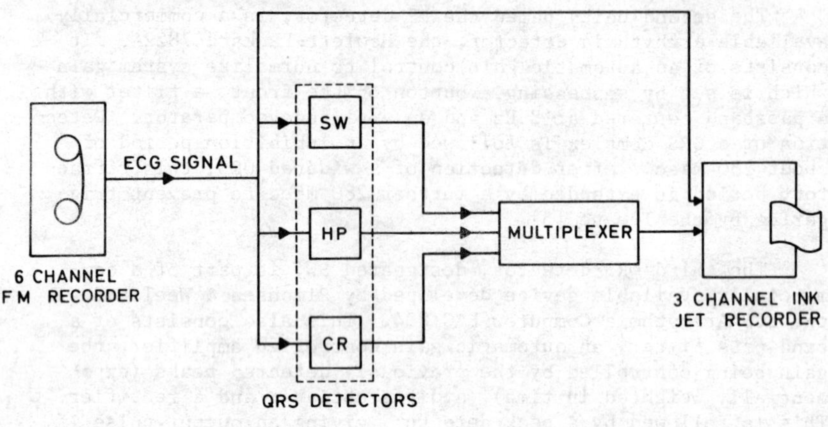

Fig. 5. Experimental setup. The ECG signal from the tape recorder is distributed to the three detectors. Their responses are recorded with the ECG.

---

*Lyrec TR81 FM recorder (center frequency 1.688 kHz, upper frequency limit 313 Hz at 15/16 inch/sec).

**Elema-Schönander 3 channel ink jet recorder Mingograf-34. Frequency range approximately 0 - 700 Hz.

arrhythmias at a speed of 25 mm/sec). Each ECG as well as the response of the three detectors were reviewed by skilled ECG interpreters. Figure 6 shows an example of such a recording.

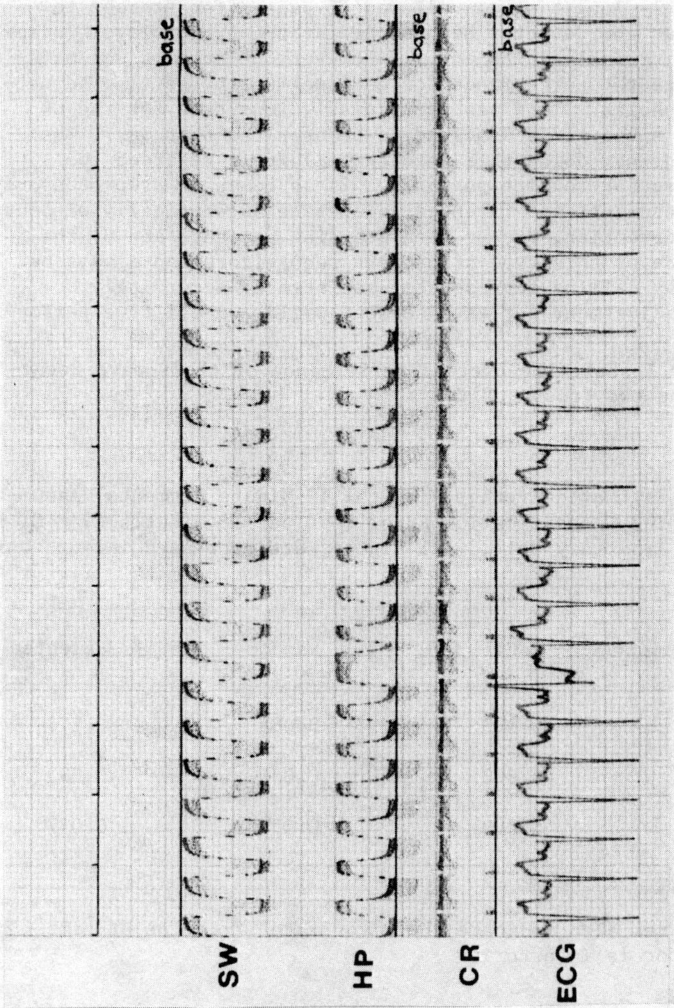

Fig. 6. Typical tracing recorded at a paper speed of 10 mm/sec. The CR detector detection is delayed 150 msec. Upper scale shows time in seconds.

RESULTS AND DISCUSSION

Two of the detectors required storage of a short ECG segment regarded as "typical" at the onset of each test period. Sufficiently long time was allowed to pass after storage to assure that the detector had settled at the proper level (adaptation of variable gains etc.). However, no attempt was made to optimize the performance for each segment by setting adjustable thresholds. This was particularly important for the CR detector, since it is designed to be operated that way. The reasons for not doing this were that 1) it is regarded too troublesome for routine purposes, 2) as computer preprocessors these instruments are intended to operate automatically without human intervention, except when changing patient, and 3) the performance of this type of pattern recognizers can always be improved by calling for operator assistance; accordingly, operator adjustment for each segment would conceal true performance.

Table I shows the overall performance of the R-wave detectors on the two groups of ECG's.*

TABLE I. Estimated Average Risk (51 10-Minute Segments) Assuming Classification Error Cost per 10 Minutes $C_f = C_m = 1$ Arbitrary Unit. All Figures are expressed in such Units.

Detector	Total	Random	Selected
CR	0.123	0.084	0.173
HP	0.072	0.051	0.093
SW	0.082	0.087	0.077

These figures also indicate the error rate (fraction of time the detector is in error).

*Details can be obtained from the authors.

The CR detector performed better on random than on selected ECG's because the latter group contained more ECG's with rapid heart rate. As the refractory period of the detector had been adjusted to about 500 msec, it could not cope with instantaneous heart rates above 120/min. However, its capability of recognizing small complexes among larger ones was superior to that of the other detectors.

This is illustrated in Fig. 7 which shows the performance (average risk) for each of the 28 ECG's chosen at random. The highest risk for the CR detector was found in group 8 (rapid heart rate), whereas the risk in group 4 was rather low.

The HP and SW had about the same risk, but the tracings showed that HP had a tendency to miss R-waves; the errors of the SW detector were often of the false alarm type. This is also reflected in calculations of average risk: if one assumes a cost ratio C_f/C_m of 1:10 (by decreasing C_f to 1/10), a much

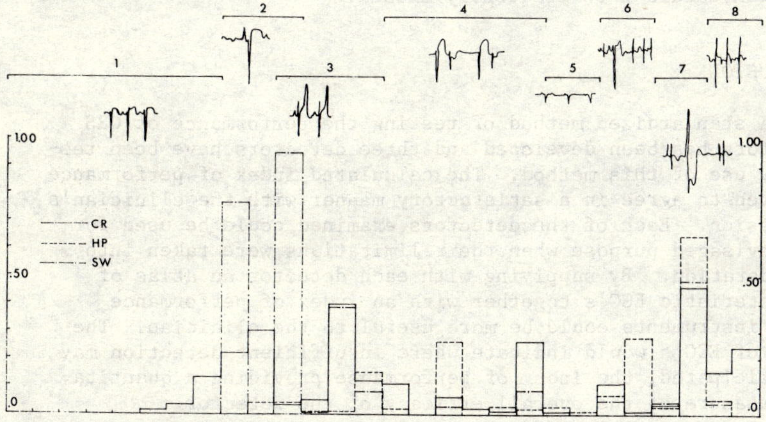

Fig 7. 'Risk profile'. The figure shows the performance of the three detectors on 28 randomly selected ECG's. Each bar indicated the estimated expected cost (with $C_f = C_m = 1$, corresponding to the estimated error rate). The bars have been grouped together according to the predominant morphological characteristics of the ECG's which are outlined above each group. 1 = normal, 2 = tall P-wave, 3 = tall T-wave, 4 = amplitude variations, 5 = low amplitude, 6 = rapid changes in the heart rate, 7 = ectopic beats, 8 = rapid heart rate.

better performance index is obtained for the SW detector compared to the others. This clearly indicates that the most advantageous use of the SW detector is for purposes where it is important to catch every QRS complex, whereas false positives are less serious. Accordingly, the detector is more suited for the application as a computer front-end preprocessor than for instance as a trigger for DC-shocks.

Since the very high risks were associated with triggering on P-waves or T-waves, it might be desirable to improve design by not letting the detector accept a new wave until after a delay period of about 350 msec. During this period it should examine whether better alternatives are given.

The HP detector performed well on the average, and its high risk was found to be associated with missed R-waves after large beats, for example after grossly differing ectopics. Because of the T-wave rejection mechanism (prolongation of refractory period to 480 msec after a widened QRS) beats in ventricular tachycardia were frequently missed.

CONCLUSION

A standardized method of testing the performance of QRS detectors has been developed and three detectors have been tested by use of this method. The calculated index of performance appeared to agree in a satisfactory manner with the clinician's impression. Each of the detectors examined could be used for the envisaged purpose when their limitations were taken into consideration. By supplying with each detector an atlas of characteristic ECG's together with an index of performance these instruments could be more useful to the clinician. The atlas of ECG's would indicate where insufficient detection may be anticipated, the index of performance providing a quantitative measure of the overall efficacy of the detector.

However, it must be strongly emphasized that such a measure does not take into account that in patient monitoring some ECG changes are much more serious than others, because they are fatal or potentially fatal and consequently require immediate intervention from the medical or nursing staff. Such situations not only include the onset of ventricular tachycardia or fibrillation, extreme bradycardia or asystole, but also ventricular ectopics, especially multifocal or R-on-T ectopics, both of which may be premonitory of the more serious ventricular arrhythmias. It is self-evident that if QRS-detectors are to be helpful in these cases, a very high degree of reliability is mandatory. Otherwise, they will only provide a false security or even do more harm than good.

The present investigation has not been directed specifically towards this problem, so a general conclusion regarding this point cannot be given. However we have included in our recordings some examples of the arrhythmias mentioned above. It appeared that the three detectors were far from correct in their decisions because of the abrupt changes from one stationary type of ECG to another. This may to some extent be remedied by proper presetting of alarm limits. However, these particular problems require further investigation.

REFERENCES

1. W.W. HARMAN, *Principles of the Statistical Theory of Communication* (McGraw-Hill Book Company, Inc., New York, 1963) chapter 10.

2. D. MIDDLETON, *An Introduction to Statistical Communication Theory* (McGraw-Hill Book Company, In., New York, 1960).

3. C.A. BRAUN, F.X. BOSTICK, P.C. RICHARDSON, A.J. WELCH and F.B. VOGT, "Real time matched filter detection of the QRS complex by replica correlation" *U.S. Government Report* AD 718124 (1970).

4. P.W. BECKER, *Recognition of Patterns, Using the Frequencies of Occurrence of Binary Words* (Polyteknisk Forlag, Copenhagen, 1968).

5. T.C. HORTH, "Premonitory heartbeat patterns recognized by electronic monitor" *Hewlett-Packard J. 21*, 12 (October 1969).

CYBERNETIC SIMULATION OF THE DYNAMICS OF THE CARDIOVASCULAR SYSTEM AND THE EFFECTS OF HYPERTENSION AND PASSIVE TILTING

F.J. RICCI

Defense Communications Agency (DCA),
1860 Wiehle Avenue, Reston, Virginia 22070, U.S.A.

SUMMARY

The work presented in this paper is a complement to work done by Grodins, Rideout, Mc Adams, Dickinson, Hamilton and others. The paper considers a digital computer simulation of the complete cardiovascular system and thus is an extension of the work done on Hybrid and Analog Computers. At this particular time, a complete mathematical description of the *human* cardiovascular system including the effects of tilting has been developed. An integrated CVS model has been simulated and both the short and long term pressure regulatory effects have been examined on the digital computer.

THE MODEL OF THE CARDIOVASCULAR SYSTEM

There has been much previous research conducted in the area of both *modeling* and *simulating* the *cardiovascular* system. Numerous investigators have studied parts of the cardiovascular system such as flow in the veins and arteries as well as ventricular action. As an example, Rideout [7-10] and Dick [16,17) at the University of Wisconsin have made extensive studies of major transients in the canine cardiovascular system utilizing a hybrid computer. Grodins [4-6] has done extensive work in developing equations and control system models of the cardiovascular system and McAdam [11], has developed an analog simulation of the Mammallian Cardiovascular system and investigation of the system arterial pressure regulator. Other investigators such as Beneken [18], Guyton [19,20], Hara [36], Katona [37], Katra [8], McLeod [12-15], and Defares [15], as well as Sagawa [21,22], and Warner [23,24] have developed control system and computer models of parts of the cardiovascular system. Gianunzio [25] has tried to refine a great deal of the cardiovascular modeling and develop a hybrid computer model of cardiac dynamics. Many other investigators have developed models and simulations of parts of the cardiovascular system. For example, Dickinson [26] has developed a digital computer model of the effects of gravitational stress upon the heart and venous system.

The list of investigators and investigations having to do with the cardiovascular system is certainly very extensive. A comprehensive survey would be voluminous. It seems clear, however, after making an extensive search of the literature, that a need exists for a comprehensive model of the human cardiovascular system using cybernetic principles that can be utilized on a popular digital computer. If this model can be developed and simulated and then tested to examine the differences between normal humans and pathological cases, some significant new contributions will arise. This is especially true since various changes in the model can be made to simulate effects such as spinal cord injury, heart injury, etc. All of this can be done without obtaining patients with this disorder or affecting normal human beings. The aim of this paper is to develop a cybernetic model that has been simulated on a digital computer.

The Effects of Passive Tilting (An Example of a Pathological Case)

In the rehabilitation of disabled persons such as quadriplegics and paraplegics a need arises for reconditioning the patient using a tilt board. Many investigations with regard to the effects on the heart due to tilting and the use of patients physiological responses to control the degree and duration of tilting have been done. Hamilton [27] has done an extensive analysis of the cardiovascular dynamics during passive tilting while many other investigators such as Guyton [19,20], Samueloff [28], Nall [29], Tuckman and Shillingford [30], as well as Kottke, Kubicek [31], Vallbona [32], Guttman [33], Bevegard [34], and Hellebrandt [35], have studied the effects of tilting on the heart. However, many of the effects still have to be investigated and verified.

Much of the work done to examine the effects of tilting has been done on a limited number of patients and acute cases have only been studied when the subjects were available. Work done by Kottke, Kubicek, Olson, and Hastings [31], whose studies were performed on the parameters of cardiovascular performance of quadriplegic patients, is an example of a study done on a limited number of subjects.

Although there is nothing like actual laboratory analysis for experimental testing, a simulation model will enable more extensive testing to be done. Once the model has been developed the effects of tilting will be considered by including the mathematical effect of changing the position of a person.

An extensive analysis is not performed in this paper. The emphasis is on developing a model adequate for digital computation and including the effects of tilting. It is left to the digital simulation to determine the complicated effects of this pathological phenomena.

In order to develop an adequate model of the cardiovascular system the *heart*, *systemic* and *pulmonary* system are modeled separately. Following Grodin's work [4-6] where he considered a steady-state, non-pulsatile flow without feedback and linear Starling curves with zero y-intercept; a mechanical analog of the heart is utilized. An extension of considering flow is implemented using Poiseuilles flow equations. Feedback is incorporated in the model by considering short term heart rate feedback and long term control of the kidneys.

Compartmentalization of both the venous and arterial systems are undertaken so that the full effect of the distensibility and non-linearity of these systems may be considered. The compartmentalization of both the venous and arterial systems is undertaken by segmenting both systems in terms of pressure differentials and fluid flow obeying Poiseuille's flow equations. The system simulated is depicted in Figs. 1 and 2. The system consists of a finite number lineal segments representing the systemic arterial tree extending from the head to the foot; a similar number of segments for the venous tree paralleling the arteries. Cross-linkages serve to model the major blood flow controlling regions: head, arms, abdomen, and legs.

The feedback mechanism of the kidney for long term control, as well as short term rate feedback from the aortic arch and carotid sinus are considered. Enough sections are used such that the effects of tilting (gravity) and the non-linear behavior of the system may be considered.

The simulation itself is not on a beat for beat basis but is rather oriented to a steady-state solution which considers the effects of tilting and hypertension of humans with and without feedback.

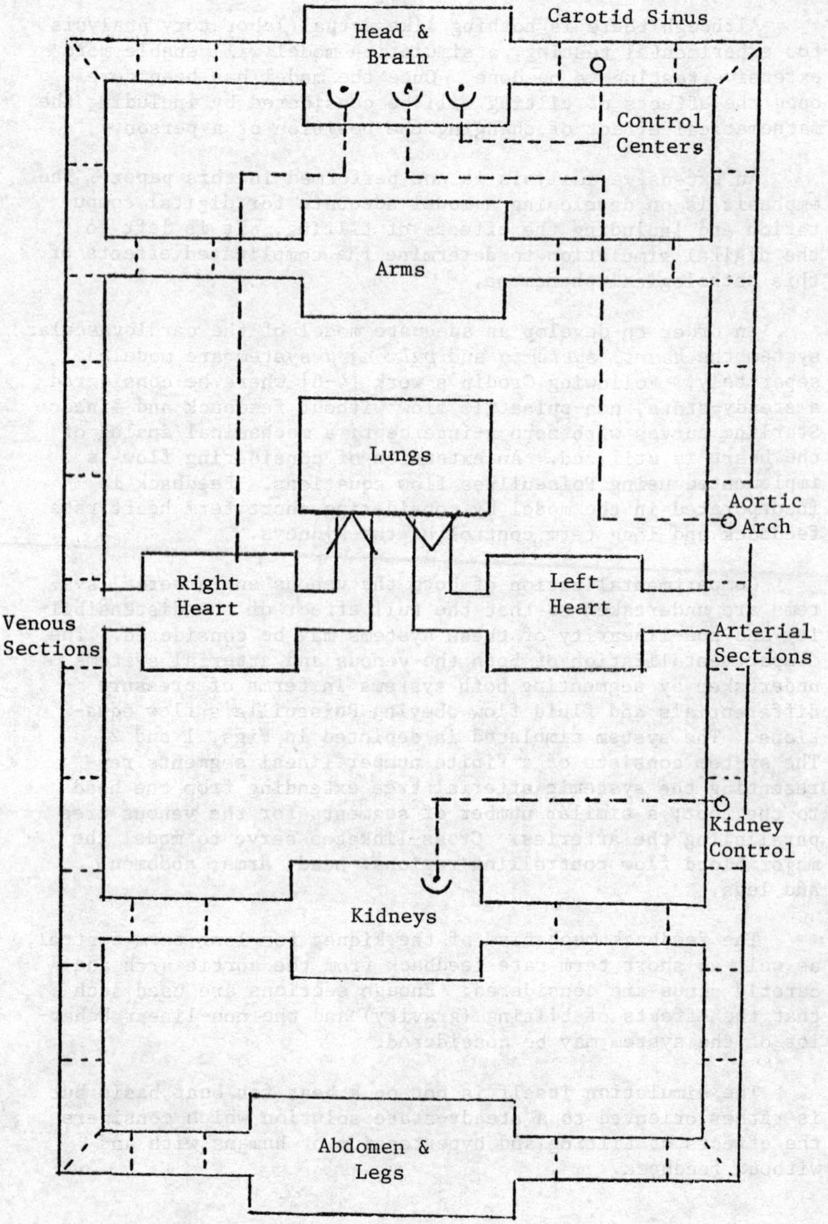

Fig. 1. Model of a cardiovascular system.

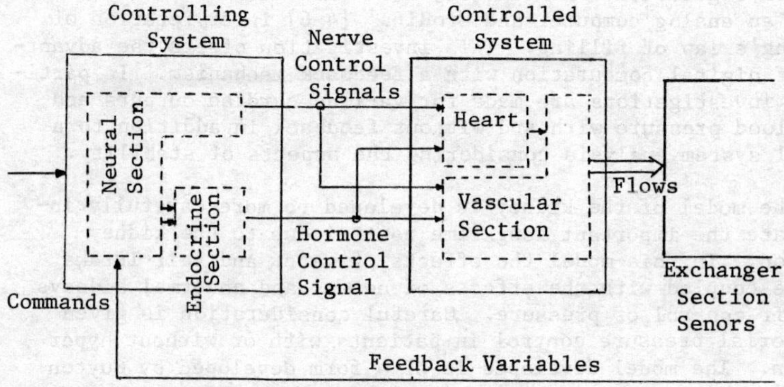

Fig. 2. The cardiovascular regulator.

Thus the specific model developed is oriented toward simulations that enable one to investigate spatial pressure and volume distributions, the effects of the heart rate feedback control (short term control) and kidney control (long term control). The spatial distribution model allows one to examine the effects of tilting as well as hypertension, while the autoregulation model is used to investigate the effects of pressure control; and the kidney model is utilized to investigate the effects of hypertension on normal and abnormal kidneys.

The important aspects of this model is that one can investigate pathological phenomena without having to use patients. For example, in the spatial blood pressure and volume distribution model, distributions for both the venous and arterial circulatory systems for different head up, recumbent and head down tilting positions are presented. The response of the system to sinusoidal as well as step input tilt angles are investigated. The model developed is not able to simulate various cervical damages that are prevalent in quadripelegics and paraplegics, but abnormalities of blood flow, blood volume and cardiac output are considered.

In utilizing the model for investigating regulation of pressure, the effects of system behavior with and without feedback is considered. This technique of investigating the operation of the cardiovascular system as a regulator has been considered before using analog and hybrid computers but this is one of the few models that have been developed on a digital computer. Although the model is very intricate, certain pathological cases can be investigated as well as various degrees of feedback regulation. McAdam [11] has done extensive analysis utilizing an analog computer and Grodins' [4-6] interpretation of Starling's law of filling. This investigation offers the advantages of digital computation with a feedback mechanism. In particular, investigations are made for various cardiac outputs and high blood pressure with and without feedback in addition to a control system analysis considering the aspects of stability.

The model of the kidney is developed to more carefully investigate the important long time control due to the kidney function. In this model the effects of water and salt intake will be coupled with the effects of normal and abnormal kidneys in their control of pressure. Careful consideration is given to arterial pressure control in patients with or without hypertension. The model developed is of a form developed by Guyton [19,20] to investigate water and salt intake regulation but will be used in this paper for the investigation of hypertension.

The coupling of the three basic models

- Spatial distribution of blood pressure and volume
- Cardiovascular regulation
- Kidney regulation

give a comprehensive total model of the behavior of the cardiovascular system in relation to passive tilting and hypertension that will be valuable for this investigation as well as for future investigations.

Although both analog and hybrid computer simulation of these same models can and probably will be done, it is felt that a digital computer simulation has the advantage that the model will be useable for more investigations in the future.

CONCLUSION

It is the intent of this paper to provide a brief description of an integrated CVS model developed on a digital computer. The complete results are shown in more extensive papers which the author has published. This paper has presented the background for the research and the general model itself.

The resulting computer simulation and experimentations in the area of tilting and hypertension are intended to be a contribution to the medical engineering field.

The experimentation has shown that there is definitely an inverse relation between heart rate and blood pressure. Long term high pressures are attributed to faulty control of blood volume and urine output.

REFERENCES

1. N. WIENER, *Cybernetics, or Control and Communication in the Animal and the Machine* (M.I.T. Press, Cambridge, Mass., 1965.

2. NATIONAL ACADEMY OF ENGINEERING, Engineering and Medicine, (Washington, D.C., 1970).

3. H.T. MILHORN, "The Application of Control Theory to Physiological Systems", W.B. Saunders, 1966.

4. F.S. GRODINS, "Integrative Cardiovascular Physiology: A Mathematical Synthesis of Cardiac and Blood Vessel Hemodynamics" *Quart. Rev. Biol. 34*, No. 2, 93-116 (June 1959).

5. F.S. GRODINS, "The Cardiovascular Regulator" Chapter 8, *Control Theory and Biological Systems* (Columbia University Press, New York).

6. F.S. GRODINS, "Computer Simulation of Cybernetic Systems", reprinted from Computers in *Biomedical Res. 1* (Academic Press Inc., New York).

7. V.C. RIDEOUT, and D.E. DICK, "Difference - Differential Equations for Fluid Flow in Distensible Tubes" *IEEE Transactions on Biomedical Engineering BME-14*, No. 3 (July 1967).

8. V.C. RIDEOUT, and J.A. KATRA, "Computer Simulation Study of the Pulmonary Circulation"*Simulation 12*, No. 5 (May 1969).

9. V.C. RIDEOUT, and M.F. SNYDER, "Computer Modeling of the Human Systemic Trec" *J. Biomech. 1*, 341-353 (1968).

10. V.C. RIDEOUT, and M.F. SNYDER, "Computer Simulation Studies of the Venous Circulation" *IEEE Transactions on Bio-Medical Engineering BME-16*, No. 4 (October 1969).

11. W.E. McADAM, "An Analog Simulation of the Mamalian Cardiovascular System and Investigation of the Systemic Arterial Pressure Regulator" *Master Thesis, Northwestern University* 1961).

12. J. McLEOD, "Physbe-A Physiological Simulation Benchmark Experiment" *Simulation* (December 1966).

13. J. McLEOD, "Physbe-A Year Later" *Simulation 10*, No. 2 (January 1968).

14. J. McLEOD, "Toward Uniform Documentation - Physbe and 1130 CSMP" *Simulation* (May 1970).

15. J. McLEOD, and G.J. DEFARES, Analog, "Computer Simulation of Heart" *AIEE* (January 1963).

16. D.E. DICK, "A Hybrid Computer Study of Major Transients in the Canine Cardiovascular System" *PhD Thesis, University of Wisconsin* (1968).

17. D.E. DICK, G.L. KENDRICK, B.S. MATSON, and V.C. RIDEOUT, "Measurement of Nonlinearity in the Arterial System of the Dog by a New Method" *Circ. Res. XXII* (February 1968).

18. E.W. BENEKEN, and V.C. RIDEOUT, "The Use of Multiple Models in Cardiovascular System Studies: Transport and Perturbation Methods" *IEEE Transactions on Bio-Medical Engineering BME-15*, No. 4 (October 1968).

19. A.C. GUYTON, T.G. COLEMAN, J.C. FOURCADE, and L.G. NAVOM, "Physiological Control of Arterial Pressure" *Bull. N.Y., Acad. Med. 45*, No. 9 (September 1969).

20. A.C. GUYTON, T.H. MILHORN, and T.G. COLEMAN, "Simulation of Physiological Mechanisms - Parts I and II" *Simulation 8-9* (July and August 1967).

21. K. SAGAWA, E.A. TAYLOR, and C.G. GUYTON, "Dynamic Performance and Stability of Cerebral Ischemic Pressor Response" *Amer. J. Physiol.*, 141-196 (1962).

22. K. SAGAWA, O. CARRIER, and A.C. GUYTON, "Elicitation of Theoretically Predicted Feedback Oscillation in Arterial Pressure" *ibid.*, 141-196 (1962).

23. R.H. WARNER, "Simulation as a Tool for Biological Research" *Simulation* (October 1964).

24. R.H. WARNER, and A. COX, "A Mathematical Model of Heart Rate Control by Sympathetic and Vagus Efferent Information" *J. Appl. Physiol. 17* (1962).

25. J.W. GIANUNZIO, "Hybrid Computer Simulation of Cardiac Dynamics" *Master Thesis, University of Wisconsin* (1967).

26. C.J. DICKINSON, "A Digital Computer Model of the Effects of Gravitational Stress Upon the Heart and Venous System" *Medical and Biological Engineering 7*, 267-275 (Pergamon Press, Oxford, 1969).

27. L.L. HAMILTON, "Study of the Cardiovascular Dynamics During Passive Tilting in Relation to a Servo Controlled Tiltboard" *PhD Thesis, Case Western Reserve University Medical School*, Cleveland, Ohio (1967).

28. S.L. SAMUELOFF, F.C., N.L. BROWSE, and J.T. SHEPHARD, "Response of Capacity Vessels in Human Limbs to Head-Up Tilt and Suction on Lower Body" *J. Appl. Physiol. 21*, 47-54 (1966).

29. M.L. NALL, and F.C. FERGUSON, "Physiology of the Circulation of the Brain" *Physiol. Rev. Suppl.* No. 3 (1956).

30. J. TUCKMAN, and J. SHILLINGFORD, "Effect of Different Degrees of Tilt on Cardiac Output, Heart Rate, and Blood Pressure in Normal Man" *Brit. Heart J. 28*, 32-39 (1966).

31. F.J. KOTTKE, W.G. KUBICEK, M.E. OLSON, and R.H. HASTINGS, "Studies on the Parameters of Cardiovascular Performance of Quadriplegic Patients" *Archives of Physical Medicine and Rehabilitation* (December 1963).

32. C. VALLBONA, W.A. SPENCER, D. CORDUS, and J.W. DALE, "Control of Orthostatic Hypotension of Quadriplegic Patients with a Pressure Suit" *Ibid.* (January 1963).

33. L. GUTTMNA, A.F. MUNRO, R. ROBINSON, and J.J. WALSH, "Effect of Tilting on the Cardiovascular Responses and Plasma Catecholamine Levels in Spinal Man" *Paraplegia 1* (1963).

34. S. BEVEGARD, "The Effect of Body Position on the Circulation at Rest and During Exercise, with Special Reference to the Influence on the Strike Volume" *Acta Physiological Scandinava 49*, 2790298 (1960).

35. F.A. HELLEBRANDT, and E.B. FRANSEEN, "Physiological Study of the Vertical Stance of Man" *Physiol. Rev. 23*, 220-55 (1943).

36. H.H. HARA, "Analog Simulation of Human Blood Circulation" *Proceedings of the San Diego Symposium for Biomedical Engineering* (1962).

37. P.G. KATONA, W.D. JACKSON, and G.O. BARNETT, "Computer Simulation of the Blood Pressure Control of Heart Period" *Proc. 18th ACEMB 7*, 109 (1965).

38. F.J. RICCI, *Analog/Logic Computer Program and Simulation*, (Spartan Books, Subsidiary of Hayden Publishers, New Jersey, 1972).

ECG/LAB: ON A TANDEM COMPUTER COMPLEX

PERRY A. SCHEINOK*

Division of Biometrics and Computing, Department of Physiology and Biophysics, Hahnemann Medical College, 231 North Sixteen St., Philadelphia, Pennsylvania, 19102, U.S.A.

PAUL SHRAGER

Computer Center, Hahnemann Hospital, Philadelphia, Penn., U.S.A.

SUMMARY

Hardware, software and systems considerations are examined for the linking up of two major on-line systems, ECG and Clinical Chemistry. This has been done on a tandem computer system, using the IBM-1800 as a computing and filing device, and the IBM-System/7 for data acquisition and as a communications concentrator.

Previously, this author, leading a team of programmers, and in association with the Electrocardiologist, Leonard Dreifus described the hardware, software and systems components of a Clinical Research ECG Station using an IBM-1800 computer [1]. The success of this endeavor led the Department of Laboratories at our institution to desire computerization of all facets of information handling in its clinical laboratories, starting with Clinical Chemistry.

Recently, Clinical Laboratories on both sides of the Atlantic have begun the task of on-line computerization with mixed, but mostly successful results [2-9]. Institutions can choose to either lease or purchase a turnkey operation, or to hire a programming staff; rent, lease or buy appropriate computers; and construct the system from scratch. In 1971, J. Lloyd Johnson Associates of Northbrook, Illinois, at the behest of the College of American Pathologists, published a review of computerized systems operating at 77 clinical laboratories throughout the United States, including both turnkey operations and self-programmed systems [10]. The authors recommended that most medium-sized to large laboratories would benefit greatly from on-line computerization, and that a

---

*Presently Executive Director, Delaware Health Services Authority, Inc., 5 Reed St., Dover, De. 19901, U.S.A.

turnkey operation would be the road to follow. They also detailed the parallel daily activity between computerized and non-computerized laboratory systems and flow-charted the elements existing in a "Simple Laboratory Information System". In interpreting this flow chart, the most obvious flaw existing in a manual laboratory system relates to the proliferation of errors, such as wrong patient admission numbers, lost orders, missed specimen collection, possible lost specimens, etc., abounding in such a system. Clearly, such errors raise the cost of hospital care by 1) extending the patient's stay due to the delay in diagnosis and treatment, 2) leading to temporary erroneous diagnoses necessitating repeated laboratory determinations without charge. Although some of these errors are not under laboratory control, many of them can be eliminated with a well-conceived computerized system.

Transcription errors, in particular, struck a responsive chord at Hahnemann where the manual system in Clinical Chemistry utilized four transcriptions for each test. If we assume that for highly motivated personnel a 3% error rate in manual transcription is not an overestimate, then excluding all other sources of error, the probability of a test being reported back correctly to the nursing station is, at most, $(1-.03)^4 = (.97)^4 = .885$, or, at least one out of every nine tests would be reported in error.

Another force militating for laboratory computerization was a 6% compound growth in the number of tests done. At several stations, laboratory personnel and equipment were close to full capacity, necessitating either overtime work, or additional equipment and personnel. Assuming that 25% of each technician's time is spent with calculations, transcriptions, and specimen handling, we estimated that computerizations would allow a 20% increase in workload with constant personnel size and laboratory equipment. This goal would then be accomplished with fewer errors and better service.

Although the Johnson study recommended that a Laboratory Director's best strategy was to procure a turnkey operation, the presence of a successful internally developed IBM-1800 ECG operation with a sophisticated programming staff, expert in the development of on-line systems, prompted Hahnemann's decision to develop its own laboratory system. This decision was bolstered by the computer being temporally underutilized, in spite of all the batch-mode biomedical and data processing jobs plus the on-line ECG's which were using the system.

MATERIALS AND METHODS

Hardware

A. Computer equipment:

As is usual with such projects, the decisions made in the initial planning stage establish the boundary values for the final system configuration. This can be a two-edged sword, but in some areas we were extremely fortunate. For example, after visiting several existing IBM-1800 Laboratory installations, we decided not to lease the IBM file management software package (CLMS). Instead, Hahnemann exchanged its ECG software for the Laboratory file software created at St. Vincent's Hospital in New York. We concluded that CLMS was so general and burdensome, besides being grossly overpriced, that a colossal effort was necessary to parametrize it properly to be locally usable. This was subsequently corroborated by the Johnson report (cf. 9, p. 402).

One of our earliest system concepts was to project the work-list on a video display unit at each work station, allowing the laboratory technician to notify the computer of such changes as cup switching, washouts, overruns, etc., via remote terminals. This concept led to the ultimate hardware configuration, consisting of a complete remote communications network, utilizing a mini-computer as a communications concentrator and controller. Concomitantly, it was adjudged economically and systemically desirable to place the ADC on the mini-computer, and thus obviate the need for it on the 1800. This relegated the 1800 to functioning as a computing and filing device.

The IBM-System/7 was chosen as the mini-computer because of its extremely fast memory cycle time (400 to 800 nanoseconds), and the purported existence of an efficient cross-assembler (MSP-7), which would assemble S/7 programs on the 1800.

The present computer configuration consists of the following:

1) an IBM-1800 computer with 32,768 16-bit word of core memory with 2 μsec memory cycle time. Its peripherals consist of a 240 line/min printer; a card reader/card punch; 2 IBM-2311 disk drivers, each containing 7.25 million words of random access storage; 2 tape units; and a Digital-to-Analog Converter (DAC) which is used for the ECG microfilming system.

2) an IBM-System/7 mini-computer with 8192 16-bit words of semi-conductor core memory. For peripherals, it has:

a) an IBM-5028 teletype 33 console with paper tape input-output which reads/writes at 30 cps.

b) 4 groups of 16-bit Digital Output (DO) (64 points)

c) 5 groups of 16-bit Digital Input (DI) (80 points)

d) 2 groups of 16-bit Analog Input (AI) (32 points)

The following peripheral hardware has also been added to the system.

1) Seven Telterm II video display terminals, manufactured by Delta Data Systems Corporation of Cornwell Heights, Pennsylvania.

2) A 120 cps impact printer and interface, supplied by Delta Data and used in conjunction with one of the Telterms for hard copy.

3) A Calcomp-565 drum plotter to test various data acquisition functions of the system.

Other hardware equipment tieing the system together is discussed below.

B. The IBM 1800-System/7 communication link

To use the DMA channel of the 1800 at its indicated capacity (10^5wds/sec), we obtained matching groups (16-bit) of Process Interrupt (PI), Digital Input (DI), and Digital Output (DO) for both the 1800 and the S/7 plus one additional set of DO for the S/7. The resulting system used the DMA channel on the 1800 and a Direct Control Channel (DCC), software controlled, on the S/7.

1) S/7 to 1800: A specified bit on the DO (S/7) fires a bit on the PI (1800) through an Asynchronous Communications Control Interface (ACCI), built to specifications by Computer Systems Associates of Swarthmore, Pennsylvania. The bit firing on the 1800 PI interrupts the 1800 and enters the 1800 program activating the DMA channel. The DMA then takes control and sends a Digital Input Ready (DIR) signal to the S/7 PI. This interrupt causes the S/7 program to load the word to be transmitted into its DO, which automatically transfers it via the ACCI into the 1800 DI. The stand-alone DO on the S/7 then sends a pulse, Digital Input Sync. (DIS), to the DMA channel

which activates the 1800 to read the word from its DI into core over the DMA channel. This DIS pulse clears DIR and reads DI. As soon as the word is read, the DMA activates a new DIR and the entire process repeats. On the last word, the DMA shuts down automatically on hardware command.

2) 1800 to S/7: the 1800 program activates the DMA, sending a Digital Output Ready (DOR) pulse to the PI on the S/7. Simultaneously, the word appears on the 1800 DO and thus via the ACCI on the DI of the S/7. The DOR interrupts the S/7 which services the interrupt by reading the DI into core. Immediately, the S/7 sends a Digital Output Sync. (DOS) pulse to the DMA, which loads another word into the 1800 DO and sends a DOR to the S/7 PI, to repeat the process. As the last word, the DMA sees the nth DOS pulse and shuts down.

C. The multiplexer/CRT hardware:

The multiplexing has two stages: a) Buffered Asynchronous (BA) and b) Direct Synchronous (DS). The BA multiplexer contains 16-bit buffers for each I/O channel, which can be multiplexed on a one-word cycle. The DS multiplexer has no buffering and must receive at the internal rate (9600 BAUD, maximally) of the CRT terminals while it can transmit at DMA channel rate. Therefore, once the I/O path is established to the CRT, the software must "lock on" to the device until all channel transmission is complete. Data is transferred from the S/7 *to* the asynchronous multiplexer through the *DO* process hardware, and *from* the asynchronous multiplexer back to the S/7 through the *DI* process hardware. The S/7 does not communicate directly to the CRT's, but instead communicates with the asynchronous multiplexer. The latter's five channels are connected to the 1) Lab Master Console CRT, 2) ECG editing CRT, 3) printer, and 4) synchronous multiplexer. Presently one channel is unused. The synchronous multiplexer operates all Laboratory CRT's via the standard polling methods. The schematic appears in Fig. 1.

The details of the hardware and methodology for laboratory data acquisition from the autoanalyzers and ECG data acquisition in the IBM-System/7 are discussed fully in our parallel publication, and will not be discussed here [11].

The S/7 will serve as the controller for up to 20 devices, all independent of one another in terms of types of transmission (send or receive) and speed. It buffers the messages, monitors the status of the devices, initiates transmission from the 1800 when more data is required, sends data to the 1800 when the buffers are full, and converts data from binary to ASCII, and vice versa. The abovementioned tasks in the S/7 all run concurrently and none infringes upon the other (Fig. 1).

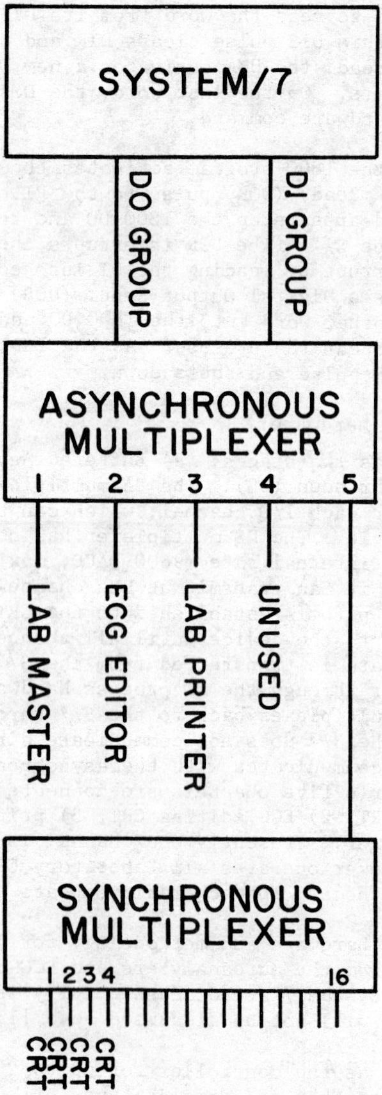

Fig. 1. The S/7-Multiplexer-CRT Scheme

Software

A. 1800 MPX

The IBM-1800 operates under the Multi-programming Executive Operating System (MPX), described fully in the appropriate IBM manuals. MPX produces software support for the IBM-2311 disks, and allows for time-sharing on the 1800 so that background data processing or scientific computation can be done when the real-time foreground task relinquishes control of the processor controller.

B. System/7 Operating System (S/7OS)

The S/7OS, written totally at Hahnemann, consists of a master scheduler and the following modules:

1) loader
2) system queue
3) scheduler communication area
4) operator console driver and extended EBCDIC debugger
5) digital input driver and process interrupt handler
6) digital output driver
7) analog input driver
8) asynchronous multiplexer driver
9) roll-in/roll-out handler
10) time-sharing system

The primary advantage of this modular design is that each I/O handler is independent. This allows for the addition or removal of the driver to correspond to the appropriate process hardware. The names of the programming modules describe their functions fully, but a detailed description of these modules is given in our parallel publication [11].

A unique approach has been taken to maximize the S/7 semiconductor memory utilization using the roll-in/roll-out handler. Since the function of the S/7 varies continuously, the initiator queue controlling the roll operations constantly monitors the communication area to ascertain external hardware activity. This handler loads process hardware drivers when the appropriate channel becomes active. Thus, the portion of memory allocated to the driver can be used as a buffer when such driver is not needed. To avoid loss of data, the handler rolls the buffer out across the DMA channel and requests MPX to load the hardware driver and to dump the rolled buffer to a 2311 input queue file. Also, software has been written which allows the S/7 to unload itself onto a 1800 disk file every five minutes. Thus, at most, five minutes of data could be lost on a sudden power drop.

C. Laboratory file software

A General Supervisory File System (GSFS) has been developed for the IBM-1800-S/7 tandem system which subsumes both the existing ECG queue and file system and St. Vincent's Laboratory file system.

The latter consists of a master data file containing basic patient identification and linkages to:

1) Daily Result Files; volatile transaction files, created, used and destroyed daily; for both in-patients and out-patients.

2) Cumulative Result Files; contain cumulative test data on in-patients only.

3) Procedure Files; contain standardized data such as all statistics pertinent to each laboratory procedure.

4) Scratch Files; used for intermediate storage of results.

GSFS is modular and functionally independent of the two sub-systems data file structures (ECG and Lab). Thus, new data files can be added to the system without interfering with existing files.

GSFS utilizes standard IBM-360 DOS partitioned data sets rather than the standard MPX method of file structure. This minimizes 2311 head seek time, and locks out batch processing users under MPX, from accessing these data files.

D. System/7-1800 communications software

The S/7 controls all bidirectional data transfers as follows:

1) 1800 to System/7 data transfers: The user program in the 1800 can write in standard FORTRAN format to the 1800 communications file. This is converted to ASCII code and spooled to a buffer from which it is transmitted to the S/7. The S/7 interprets this word as either a "request" or a "message pending" command. In the latter case, the device number, i.e., the specific S/7 peripheral, is also transmitted in this ID word. The S/7 enters this "message pending" into its input queue and when the device is ready, the S/7 sends a "clear to send" message to the 1800. The 1800 then transmits via its DO channel a fixed number of words (device-dependent). This transfer is externally synchronized by the S/7 DO.

2) System/7 to 1800 data transfers: Since the S/7 transfers of data cannot be internally spooled, the 1800 must

accept data on a demand basis. When a message is ready for transmission, the S/7 transfers a one-word ID to the 1800 specifying the device that initiated the S/7 output. The 1800 then starts its DI channel, synchronized by the S/7, accepting and spooling the latter's output. This spool file is then accessible from a user program in standard FORTRAN format.

The Computerized Laboratory System

The highlights of the system, as presently conceived, are as follows:

The patient test data is typed from the requisition forms into a CRT terminal connected to the S/7 computer. This allows the typist to visually check the input on the screen. Only after the visual check is satisfactory, is the data transmitted to the computer. This is the *only* manual transcription in the entire system. The computer formulates the individual work lists for each station from the CRT input, and projects them on the CRT screens at the individual work stations. For washouts and retests, the technician can communicate with the computer whatever changes are made in the work list (deletions, insertions, etc.). The computer keeps a daily running log of all changes to function as an audit trial.

Presently, only the SMA-12/60 is on-line, but within six months, all the autoanalyzers will have been connected to the 1800-S/7 by cable wiring. All test data will then flow into the computer in the order of the numbers on the work sheets for each station, as presently occurs for the SMA-12/60. The computer will monitor each piece of equipment, printing error messages on the IBM-5028 relating to system status. The S/7 could take an autoanalyzer off-line if it were faulty, but this is optional and needs further study. The CRT's (one for each work station) will be hardwired into the multiplexing device described above and thus connected into the S/7.

In addition to S/7OS which handles traffic problems for all analog and communications data, software has been written locally for the S/7 for:

1) Data Acquisition
2) A-to-D Conversion
3) Plateau averaging for the SMA-12/60
4) Peak-spotting for the individual one and two channel autoanalyzers.

The IBM-1800 calculates all test results, eliminating the need for the present charts, tables, and manual calculations.

GSFS then posts the data in the proper files, and sorts them out by patient name or number. The patient files reside on disk, and every two hours, the 1800 prints out a summary sheet containing all test results for the last five lab/active days for each patient whose required tests are completed by that time. These sheets are immediately sent to the Nursing Stations to be placed on the charts. The entire file on a patient's stay is resident in the cumulative data file disk, and a week after the patient's discharge, is dumped onto magnetic tape for permanent storage. For interim results requested by physicians, the Laboratory Coordinator can query the computer via the Laboratory Master Console.

DISCUSSION

As the Johnson study pointed out, a Clinical Laboratory Data System interfaces to almost all the other hospital information sub-systems, such as Billing, Nursing, Medical Records, etc. Thus, it can be considered as a focal point for starting a locally based Hospital Information System. Indeed, Hahnemann intends to tie the Admissions Office via CRT's into the system, once the Laboratory System is set up. Also, card output for every test will be provided to the Billing section, so that a one to one correspondence will exist between tests and patient bills; a matter usually lacking in manual systems. Once the individual autoanalyzers with their attendant CRT's are functioning, it should then also be possible to place CRT printers at all Nursing Stations for communicating test results.

A major problem in such systems relates to down time. As is well-known, redundant hardware components will improve the reliability of a system drastically. Unfortunately, the expense of totally redundant elements would be prohibitive to most medical research facilities. Thus, any major hardware breakdown reduces our individual ECG and Lab systems to their pristine manual state, with the attendant concern of the associated staff. This is ironic, since many physicians and paramedical personnel have traditionally resisted the advent of computers in their areas of competence. However, once the system functions satisfactorily, computer down time is generally considered to be a major tragedy. Granted that the mean time between failures for computer mainframes and even some peripherals is increasing greatly, nevertheless, time losses due to mechanical failures on disk drives, tape units, ECG carts, etc. have remained essentially constant. Until hardware costs are sufficiently low to allow for complete redundancy, even the best designed systems will be plagued by the vagaries of hardware failure, and will provide a less than optimal way of treating the patient. For, in the last analysis, that is what computerized systems in a hospital are all about; powerful tools to aid in the medical handling of the patient, whether directly or indirectly.

ACKNOWLEDGEMENTS

The authors would like to thank Mr. Kurt Thum, Mr. Robert Chiang, Mr. Martin Reich, Mrs. Kathie Kaib Shrager, Miss Mary Anne Mc Connell and Mrs. Kathy Morris for their contributions to this project. Special thanks are due to Mr. John Moore of St. Vincent's Hospital for the use of their Laboratory File Software, and to Miss Linda Anderson and Mrs. Elissa Wudarski for their liaison work and the latter's editorial help with the manuscript.

REFERENCES

1. P.A. SCHEINOK, K.W. THUM, M.B. REICH, A. KRAZESKY, and L.S. DREIFUS, "Developing a computer ECG research station" *Kybernetes 1*, 221-229 (1972).

2. A. FLECK, and D. REEKIE, "The computer in the clinical biochemistry laboratory: *Int. J. Bio-Med. Computing 1*, 41 (1970).

3. D. SIMPSON, G.E. SIMS, M.I. HARRISON, and L.G. WHITBY, "Equipment for linking the autoanalyzer on-line to a computer" *J. Clin. Path. 24*, 170 (1971).

4. C.S. KLASS, "Use of the Lufotronics CRS-7S S/12 analog-to-digital data conversion system" *Amer. J. Clin. Path. 55*, 475 (1971).

5. G. BRECHER, and H.F. LOKEN, "The laboratory computer - is it worth the price?" *Amer. J. Clin. Path. 55*, 527 (1971).

6. J. POLETTI, J.F. Jr. ZACK, and T.J. MUELLER, "Computer control in the clinical laboratory" *Amer. J. Clin. Path 53*, 731 (1970).

7. A.E. RAPPOPORT, and E.N. RAPPOPORT, "Laboratory automation, Hospitals" *44*, 114 (August 16, 1970).

8. G.H. MURPHY, and C.S. NAPPS, "Automated test reports, Hospitals" *45*, 60 (May 16, 1971).

9. N.W. CARTER, and P.D. GRIFFITHS, "On-line acquisition of the output of a multi-channel analyzer (SMA-12/60) by means of an Elliott computer system" *J. Clin. Path. 24*, 661 (1971).

10. J. LLOYD JOHNSON ASSOCIATES, "Clinical laboratory computer systems" *A comprehensive evaluation, Northbrook, Illinois* (1971).

11. P.A. SCHEINOK, and P. SHRAGER, "ECG/Lab: a merger of two systems on a mini-midi computer complex" *Kybernetes 2*, (1973).

INTERACTIVE-COMPUTER SUPPORT IN DECISION MAKING IN MANAGEMENT OF PATIENTS WITH CANCER

A.S. GLICKSMAN*, J. HAHN, R. LEVINE, L. LIDOFSKY and J.B. NICKSON

The Department of Radiotherapy and the Laboratory of Computer Science of the Mount Sinai School of Medicine of the City University, New York, U.S.A.

SUMMARY

In the development of a rational approach to treatment of patients with cancer the experience of the past is a major input into the decision-making process. A computer stored data base can be a powerful tool in deciding between surgery, chemotherapy, and radiotherapy or some combination of these. Modestly priced interactive computer-systems now have the capability and speed so that they can be significant components in this decision making loop. The system to be described consists of a series of feedback loops; it is based on a computer with a mass storage device.

INTRODUCTION

In the development of a rational approach to treatment of patients with cancer the experience of the past is a major input into the decision-making process. The great clinicians of earlier generations utilized their own experience to decide on the most appropriate form of therapy. The number of suitable alternatives available were severely limited. Fairly standard approaches to a particular disease entity were maintained. This is no longer so.

In the last quarter century significant advances in the physiological support of the patient and technical improvements have extended the frontiers of surgery to its anatomical limits. Organ transplantation continues to push this frontier even further forward. Following World War II radiotherapy became heir to major technical advances. Radioactive isotopes, the by-product of

---

*Present Address: *Chairman, Dept. of Radiation Oncology. Rhode Island Hospital, Eddy Street, Providence, Rhode Island, 02903, U.S.A.*

nuclear fission, became available for therapeutic use. Cobalt-60, a fairly inexpensive material, now makes it possible for megavoltage radiations to be available in even remote parts of the world where technical support for more intricate apparatus might not be readily obtained. Furthermore, microwaves research and particle accelerators have laid the foundation for the development of high energy linear accelerators which can be used to irradiate deep seated tumors with precision and a minimum of untoward effects. Perhaps the most spectacular development of the last quarter century has been the introduction and successful application of chemotherapeutic agents for the management of cancer. This, again, was a product of World War II research directly derived from the study of mustard gas. Nitrogen mustard was the progenitor of a long line of alkylating agents. This was soon followed by oncolytic antibiotics, antimetabolites, and so on.

The second major change over the last quarter century has been the rate at which the practice of medicine is changing. It has been pointed out that 90% of the medications used today did not exist a quarter century ago; life support techniques in surgery not only are becoming much more sophisticated but more readily available. Intricate radiotherapeutic equipment and the techniques with which these can be employed have increased as never before in this discipline. These new procedures, techniques and drugs which have become available for the control of cancer have introduced appreciable alternatives.

Today, no matter how diligently the practitioner attempts to remain well informed, the so-called information explosion contributes to his ignorance explosion. The rate at which he can continue to acquire, assimilate and utilize information does not approach the rate at which new information is being generated. Therefore, his position relative to the total information in his own field of endeavor becomes less and less comprehensive, and therefore by default he becomes more and more ignorant of the total body of information, even in his own field. It is in this setting that a computer stored data base can be a powerful tool in deciding upon appropriate treatment.

COMPUTING PROCEDURE

At Mount Sinai Hospital in New York City we are developing a computer system which incorporates both an on-line tumor registry and an interactive, graphically oriented treatment-planning capability. The oncologist now has a large file of tumors, their treatments and subsequent outcomes available to him. He may evaluate these to supplement his own experience. When he has selected a course of action, he enters patient characteristics and treatment plan to the system graphically and proceeds to compute and evaluate that plan.

The hardware configuration used consists of a Digital Equipment Corporation PDP II computer with 28K words of memory, a 256K word fixed head disk and dual DECtape drives. For graphical input a 20 × 20 inch GRAFPEN sonic digitizer is used. For graphic output a Tektronix 611 display is available as well as a Hazeltine 2000 alpha-numeric CRT display. A 17 inch refresh display, with local refresh memory and light pen interaction will be added in September of 1972. For hardcopy output a high speed electrostatic printer plotter manufactured by VERSATEC is used. The plotter prints up to 1024 points on .01 inch centers simultaneously at a rate of up to approximately 125,000 points per second. For high speed program input and tumor registry data input a 300 cpm card reader is available.

Information stored in the tumor registry includes 5 basic categories. The first category is the identification of the patient, the second category is information concerning the patient's diagnosis, the third category concerns the present treatment, the fourth category is follow-up information, and finally, the fifth category concerns special study information.

In the first category the patient's name, identification number, age and sex are included. Since it may be necessary at some time in the future to locate the patient or his family, the patient's address and that of the next of kin can prove very useful. One in five Americans will change his address every single year. Sometimes this becomes an extremely complicated matter. However, not all of the identification information need be stored in the tumor registry files *per se* since much of the information necessary to locate the patient is already incorporated in the permanent record of the patient in the files of the hospital. This file can be queried when sufficient information in the tumor registry does not exist to locate a particular patient.

The patient's diagnosis in terms of the site and pathology is the next category. The systematized nomenclature of pathology developed by the American College of Pathology has become the standard code for the department of pathology, the medical records librarian, as well as the tumor registry. The extent of the disease is described by a system developed by the International Union Against Cancer and the American Cancer Society. Three basic pieces of information are required: A description of the specific tumor in terms of its size, stage fixation, invasion of regional lymph nodes and thirdly if distant spread has occurred. This is utilized in a standard TN & M ("T" for the description of the tumor, "N" for the nodal involvement and "M" for the presence or absence of metastases). These can be combined to express specific stages — e.g., $T_1N_0M_0$ = stage 1. There are a number of diseases for which an internationally accepted staging system exists without TNM descriptions, for instance, carcinoma of the cervix, carcinoma of the ovary, Hodgkin's disease. For these the extent of disease is recorded by this means, e.g., stage 1, 2, etc. For those tumors for which neither an accepted TN & M system or an internationally accepted staging system exists the disease is described in categories describing local, regional status and the presence or absence of distant spread. Previous treatment, its type, where performed and date are entered into the file, and finally, information concerning concurrent or past illnesses of import to the disease process, particularly previous history of cancer, are included in the patient's data file.

The description of the treatment of the disease utilizes current procedure terminology of the American Medical Association for the surgical procedure. However, this formidable code is hopelessly inadequate for the details of radiotherapy or the developing techniques in the chemotherapy. Special forms and codes have been developed so that this data can be entered into the tumor registry precisely and completely.

The next major category of information records the course of the patient's illness, the length of time that he remains free of disease, the time when first recurrence appears, either locally or distantly, all necessary pieces of information to understand the response to treatment. The initiation of new courses of treatment by chemotherapy, surgery, radiation are also included in the file at the point.

There are an increasing number of patients whose treatment policy is part of an ongoing research project. These patients need to be specifically identified so that inadvertently treatment does not vary from the prescribed course.

The tumor registry data will be punched on cards from data generated by the admissions office, attending physician and house staff. It will be stored initially on small rolls of magnetic tape capable of storing in excess of 250,000 characters of storage. To facilitate retrieval, a tape is transferred to the fixed head disk which has a worst case access time of 33 milliseconds. In the future we hope to have the entire data base stored on a larger disk so that the transfer from tape to disk will be unnecessary.

The user interacts with the data base principally through an alpha-numeric cathode ray tube terminal. In addition he has available to him other input and output devices including a high speed printer for generating printed records.

The retrieval system — which is still being developed — has considerable generality. Each item in a patient's record may be used as a "key" for retrieval. That is, the system may be queried to identify, for example, all patients who are female, whose age at first treatment was 37, whose diagnosis was breast cancer, whose treatment was surgery and radiotherapy, whose physician was Dr. Jones, and who live in Albany, New York, etc. Thus, the logical complexity of the retrieval criteria may include any, and in fact *all* of the "keyed" data common to all of the patient records. When this mode of retrieval is utilized, each patient's record is transferred to the core memory of the computer and each relevant key is examined to determine whether the patient meets the retrieval criteria. While this technique has maximum generality, the fact that each record must be read into core can make retrieval slower than desired, especially when the number of patients stored in the registry increases in number. To deal with this aspect of the retrieval problem, we have resorted to another mode of operation.

We recognize that certain keys have a higher probability than others of being used for retrieval. For example, in determining a treatment procedure, we would probably never desire to retrieve on patient address or name of next of kin. We would, however, be highly likely to desire to retrieve on TNM or SNOP and perhaps in addition age, sex or physician's name. For a number of critical keys of this type we will keep separate lists or directories broken down into the significant elements which constitute the inclusive set associated with this key. For example, the inclusive set associated with age might be 0 to 2 years old, 3 to 8 years old, 9 to 15, etc. This inclusive set associated with sex is, of course, male or female, and the set associated with physician is one whose size is equal to the total number of physicians whose patients have been entered into the registry.

As we indicated earlier, a list or directory is generated for each set having a high probability of being used as a retrieval key. To identify a group of patients who meet the retrieval criteria the computer program is required only to search the desired lists — not the total registry — and find those patients meeting the search or retrieval criteria. What can then be obtained is a simple listing of patient identification and/or name; or a report may be obtained summarizing other data describing those patients whose characteristics satisfy the search criteria.

To date we have not yet reached this stage, but we anticipate that a cathode ray tube generated display might appear as shown in Fig. 1. The retrieval was for breast, inflitrating duct cancer $T_2N_0M_0$. In the first and second columns are the identification of the patient. Age, sex and race are then shown and in the next column the treatment categories (not specific techniques) are given and finally the outcome.

SITE - 174X BREAST
SNOP - 8503
TNM - 200

PAT. ID.	PATIENT NAME	AGE	SEX	RACE	TREATMENT	OUTCOME
154789654	PAPPAS, LENORA	36	F	W	S	NED/7YR
854051404	KORNFIELD, ROSE	49	F	B	S	DEAD/6YR
476935909	PINZE, SHELLEY	71	F	W	S+R	DEAD/6YR
326870426	MANDELL, MARTINE	52	F	W	S	AWD/5YR
105533204	BURLINGHAM, ALICE	63	F	W	S	NED/5YR
050667267	DIAZ, MARIA	48	F	W	S+R	NED/5YR
655089187	JIJI, LATIVIA	39	F	B	S+R	DEAD/4YR
596853315	POOLE, CHARLOTTE K.	66	F	W	S	AWD/4YR
313105364	WASHINGTON, DELILAH	62	F	W	S+R	NED/4YR
915946444	RUGGIERIO, JOSEPH	57	M	W	S	NED/4YR
635973216	MORIKAWA, SARAH K.	53	F	B	S+R	NED/3YR

Fig. 1. Retrieval for breast carcinoma, T2NOMO, displaying patient data, treatment and outcome

When a new patient arrives, before assigned to a particular treatment, the tumor registry can be queried to determine the optimum treatment for this patient. Given the site of the disease and specific details, such as the TN&M or staging, the information can be displayed on a CRT or a print-out can be had for a permanent record. In essence, this is suggesting that the responsible physician can have available to him the details of that treatment policy which were successful in the past in managing patients with like disease and that he then stick with the winning technique. Where insufficient number of successes exist in the file, the responsible physician may well want to consider the introduction of a new technique or a whole new approach to the disease. In fact, it is incumbent upon the practicing physicians to match their results against the most successful techniques available at his own institution, those available in his local region and, as a matter of fact, those available throughout the world. If his results are not comparable to the best available throughout the world, he has the responsibility to move on to those that will give his patients a better chance of survival.

Between half and two-thirds of all patients with cancer will require radiotherapy either as a curative or palliative measure. Thus, if on the basis of the first analysis, radiotherapy is indicated as the treatment of choice for the patient, the radiotherapy treatment planning system can be used in an interactive mode to develop optimum treatment for the patient. This treatment can take the form of external beam therapy utilizing a linear accelerator or a Cobalt-60 apparatus or a radioactive implant using radium or another radionuclide. Approximately 90% of all treatment by radiotherapy is by external beam. The radiotherapy treatment planning programs which have been developed at Mount Sinai Hospital can handle both implant and external beam therapy.

RADIOTHERAPY TREATMENT PLANNING

The basic programs were originally developed by Dr. Jack Cunningham of the Ontario Cancer Clinic for use on a timesharing computer system. We are continuing to modify and extend the original programs to take advantage of the full range of input and output capabilities which Sinai has or is in the process of acquiring. Furthermore, we are attempting to improve some of the computational procedures previously used. Finally, they are also being modified to run more efficiently on the PDP 11.

One of the programs developed at Mount Sinai permits the user to input implant positions and size information directly from the X-ray plates using the GRAFPEN (Fig. 2). This slide shows the user at the GRAFPEN table in the process of inputting such data. The

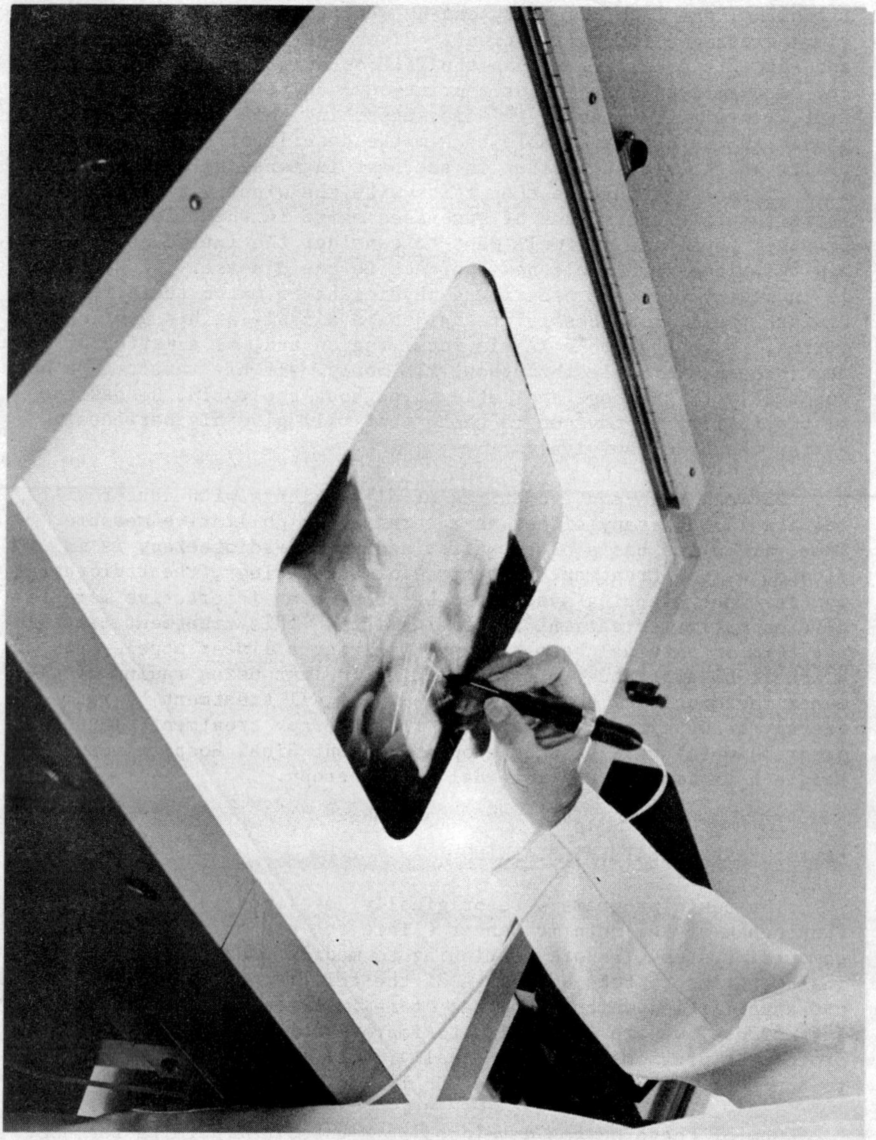

Fig. 2. Sonic digitization of implanted needle endpoints for dose strength analysis

GRAFPEN shown here has a 20 × 20 inch drawing surface enabling X-rays up to this size to be utilized. Once the size and position data has been input, the user enters the physical and radiological specifications of the radioactive needles using the CRT keyboard. The dose delivered will be calculated by the PDP 11 program.

A choice of output will ultimately be available using one of three cathode ray tube terminals. At present only two CRT terminals are in use, namely, the alpha-numeric and the storage oscilloscope display. Figure 3 illustrates the use of the alpha-numeric display for dose distribution output. A menu then offers the user a number of options, such as, removing a needle, adding a needle or changing the plane of observation (Fig. 4). A further option is included which allows the user to remove the individual needles at different times so that a homogeneous dose distribution throughout the volume or any other pattern of distribution desired can be developed. Ultimately, we hope to produce a program which will take the desired distribution and inform the user which needles should be moved and at which time each of the needles should be completely removed to produce the desired dose distribution.

The storage oscilloscope displays output formats, such as a 3-dimensional representation of a treatment plan (Fig. 5). The axes and isodose value labels will be added shortly. A 2-dimensional contour plan is shown in Fig. 6. Any of the graphic displays drawn on the oscilloscope can be output for future reference using the high speed point plotter (Fig. 7). Since the plotter is a matrix plotter, i.e., plots a complete horizontal line at one time, the plotting time is independent of the data density. A typical display of the type shown in the previous figures, which may be 10 inches square, can be plotted in approximately 8 seconds.

Programs are currently being tested for the external beam treatment planning and they should be operational by August, 1972. These will be for multiple external portal therapy capable of calculating doses with wedges and compensators as well as accounting for inhomogeneity of the tissues traversed by the radiation beams. When a refresh oscilloscope is added to the system, it will be possible to have a larger display. The user will be able to interact with the system through the use of a light pen. Moving displays may also be available. Furthermore, a brighter picture will be obtained.

THERAPY

Having decided that a lesion is suitable for radiotherapy, it is necessary to decide upon the proper treatment technique. In current practice, one calls upon the experience of the individual

```
SOURCE    SOURCE    ACTIVE    TOTAL     END
 NUMBER   STRENGTH   LENGTH    LENGTH    POINTS
   1        2.0       3.0       4.0     2.0,  0.,  0.; 2.0, 4.0,  0.
   2        2.0       3.0       4.0      0., 2.0,  0.; 4.0, 2.0,  0.

 HORIZONTAL AXIS = X       0. 4.000
 VERTICAL AXIS =   Y       0. 4.000
 PERPENDICULAR CO-ORD Z =     0.

 SCALE=   3 TO 1

 A=   80.0 RADS/HR
 B=   40.0 RADS/HR
 C=   20.0 RADS/HR
 D=   10.0 RADS/HR
 E=    5.0 RADS/HR

 ACCURACY = +/- 5.0 PERCENT

+     EEEE                   DD                    EEEE
    EEE              DDD     11       DD              EEE
   EEE            DD        B11BC        DD             EEE
 EEE            DD       C   11   C        DD            EEE
EE            DD       C     11     C        DD            EE
            DD        C      11      C         DD
          DD         C   B   11   B    C         DD
        DD         CC        11         CC         DD
      DD          C     B    11     B     C          DD
     D          C       B    11             C          D
   DD         C        B     11      B        C         DD
  D        CC         B      11      B           C        D
 DD     CC         BB     A  11  A      BB          C      D
 D    C     BBB          A   11   A           BBB     C    D
 D               AAAA        11         AAAA               D
D                            11                             D
D222222222222222222222222222211222222222222222222222222222222
 D     B   A     A           11             A    A   B     D
 D    C     B            A   11   A             B     C    D
 D      C          BB     A  11  A      BB          C      D
  D        C          B      11       B          CC       D
   DD        CC        B     11     B         CC         D
    DD          C            11             CC         DD
      DD         CC     B    11    B      CC         DD
        DD         C         11          C         DD
         DD          C   B   11   B     C         DD
           DD         C      11      C          DD
E            DD        C     11     C         DD            E
EEE            DD            11             DD            EEE
  EEE             DD       C 11          DD             EEE
    EEE             DDD      11      DDD              EEE
      EEE                 DDD11DDD                  EEE
```

Fig. 3. CRT display of implant dose strength on the selected plane

```
PLEASE ENTER A DIGIT(FORMAT I2).
1... CHANGE PLOT OPTION.
2...DELETE A NEEDLE.
3...ADD A NEEDLE.
4...CHANGE THE PLOT CO-ORD.
5...SWITCH TO PRINT.
6...RUN.
7...TERMINATE.
8...SWITCH TO DISPLAY.
9...DELETE ALL NEEDLES.

AXIS NO.1  PERP LABEL=Z  LOW LIMIT=  0.  HIGH LIMIT=  0.
AXIS NO.2  VERT LABEL=Y  LOW LIMIT=  0.  HIGH LIMIT= 4.0
AXIS NO.3  HORZ LABEL=X  LOW LIMIT=  0.  HIGH LIMIT= 4.0

A-P MAGNIFICATION= 1.00
LAT MAGNIFICATION= 1.00
SCALE = 2
NO.DOSE LEVELS= 5
DOSE LEVELS . . .
80.00.40.00.20.00.10.00, 5.00.
1...AXIS LABELS.
2...LOW LIMITS
3...HIGH LIMITS.
4...MAGNIFICATIONS.
5...DOSE LEVELS.
6...SCALE.
7...MENU.
8...EXIT.
```

Fig. 4. Display of user options for selection of the next step in dose strength

radiotherapist or the department for a suitable treatment technique. Major departments with well trained radiotherapists will have sophisticated approaches. In departments with less adequately trained individuals, more pedestrian approaches will be the rule. Not infrequently, this ends up woth single field or parallel opposed techniques for the vast majority of cases. With computer implemented treatment planning it is possible to make available, even to the remotest radiotherapy department, more elegant techniques, eminently more suited to achieve the aims of the therapist (Fig. 8).

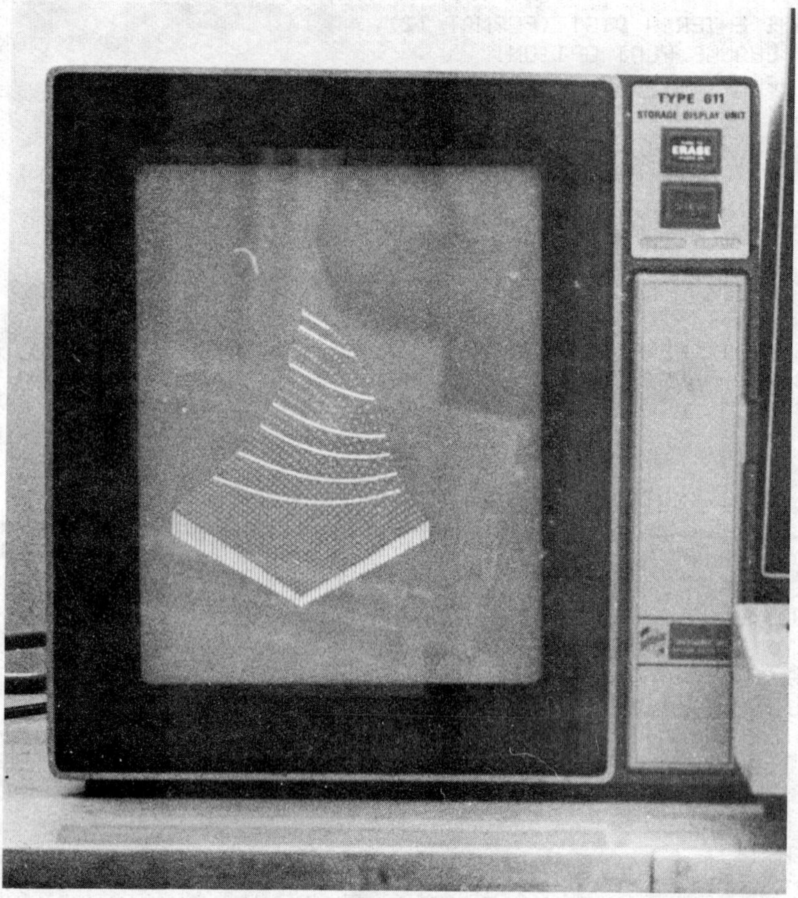

Fig. 5. Three dimensional representation of dose strength

The use of a planning simulator permits decisions as to the best arrangements of the portals or irradiation. If multiple fields are to be used, their size, shape and relationship to each other may be accurately described. Many more possibilities for such inter-relationships may be tested with a simulator than is practical with a treating unit. The use of an image intensifier system with the planning simulator for continuous readout of the area of the body traversed by the X-ray beams appears at this time to be the optimal system, provided that the area visualized by the image intensifier is larger than the largest treatment field available on the apparatus used for treatment.

Fig. 6. Two dimensional representation of dose strength

Once an apparently suitable treatment technique by external beam has been arrived at, an isodose distribution needs to be computed. Preparation of isodoses by hand involved delays and places a repetitive task upon the radiological physicist and dosimetrist. The ability to develop and display quickly and accurately isodose distributions throughout the tumor volume is related directly to computer applications in radiotherapy taken directly from simulator movements. Even the best dosimetrist can produce only a limited number of alternative treatment plans for a particular case. Rarely is it possible to develop a 3-dimensional view of the isodose distribution in the target volume for more than one particular treatment technique.

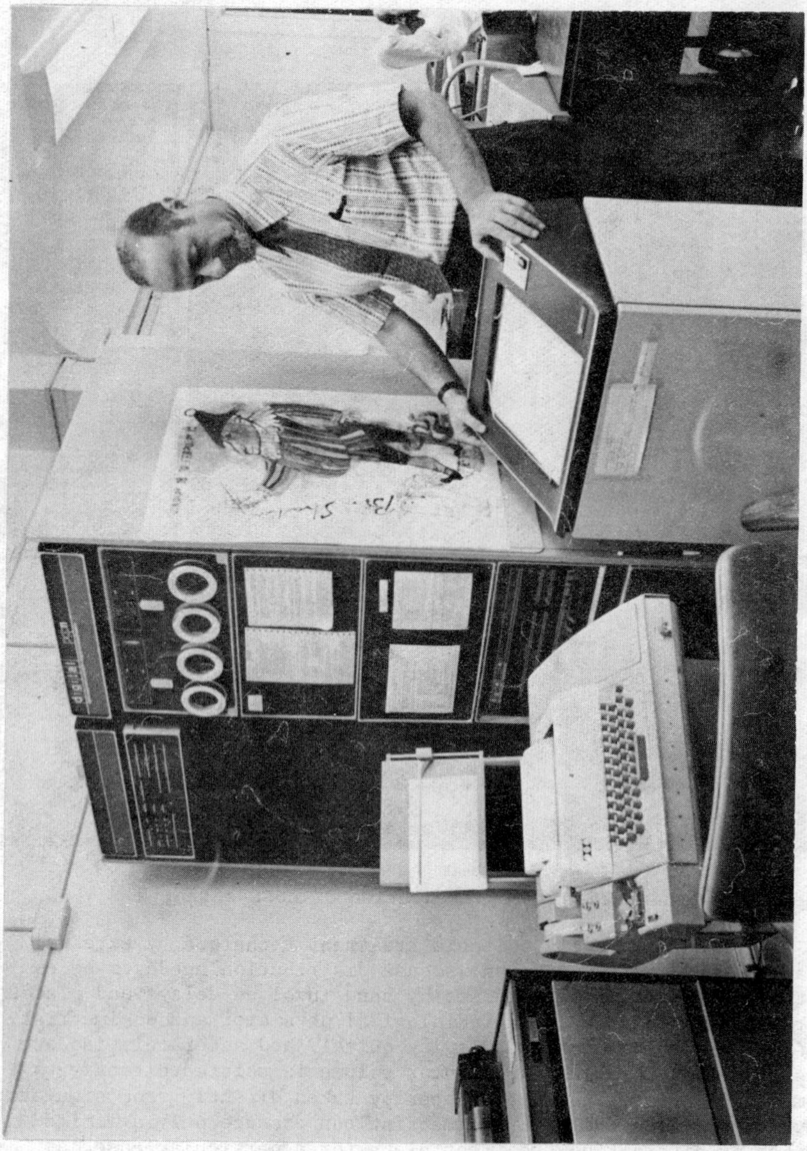

Fig. 7. PDP 11 computer system with high speed plotter printer at right

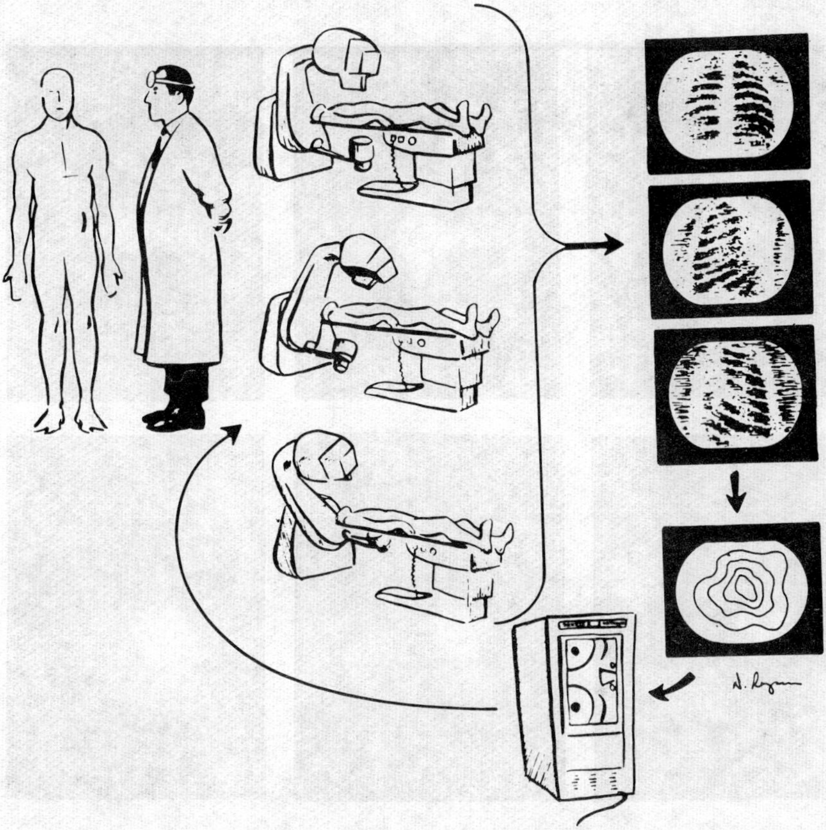

Fig. 8. Computer implemented therapy planning

Few radiotherapists keep an entire library of isodose distributions in their head, but most experienced radiotherapists have a catalog of useful isodose distributions for all of the important sites. The impact of computerized isodose computation service is to make available to the professional radiotherapist many more isodose distributions within a reasonable time of his request. At the present time too few radiotherapists think in 3-dimensions. Computer assistance will in part develop this ability. When the senior members of the department request 3-dimensional distributions more frequently and they are readily available, it will be more likely that the juniors and trainees will develop a healthy regard for this important concept.

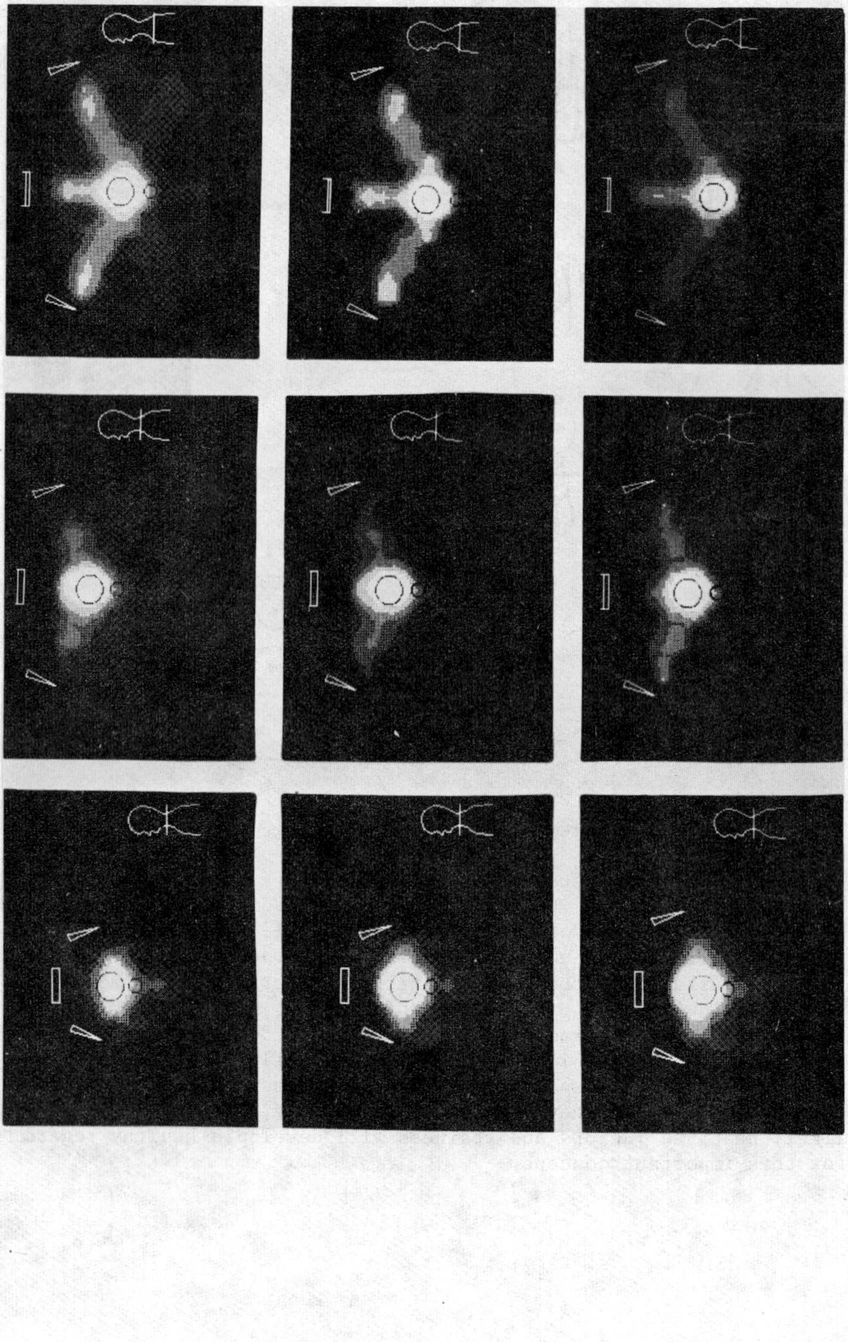

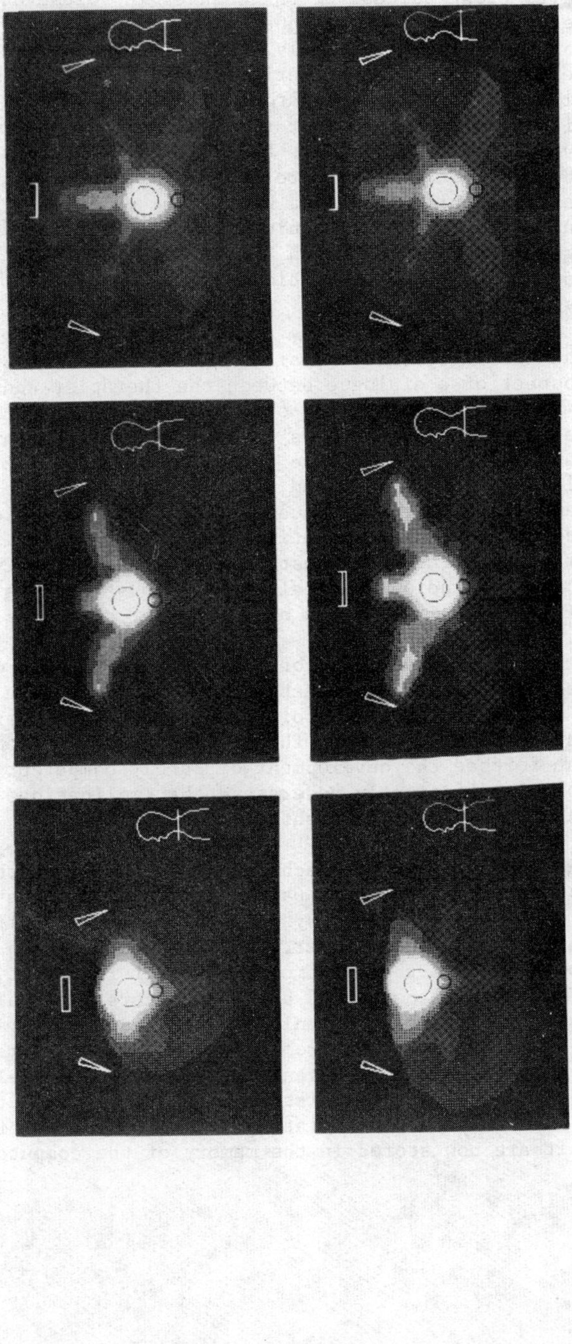

Fig. 9. Dose strength analysis for several beam patterns. The plane of analysis is indicated on the homunculus at the lower right corner of each image

A 3-dimensional display for the management of a tumor of the upper third of the esophagus is illustrated in Fig. 9. This is a complex area to treat because of the changes in volume of tissue that need be traversed from the upper part of the lesion to the lower part of the lesion. Secondly, the volume to be treated is moving posteriorly as it goes inferiorly in the body. A 3-field technique with wedges and compensators has been developed. Fifteen representative cuts from the upper to the lower part of the target volume are visualized. Optimally, the dose must encompass the esophagus, but may not deliver more than a third of this tumor dose to the spinal cord which lies just behind the esophagus. These distributions were produced in conjunction with Dr. Theodor Sterling's group at the Washington University in St. Louis and were recently shown at the 4th International Conference on Computers in Radiotherapy at Uppsala.

With the interactive mode available to us at Mount Sinai today, the prospect of a dialogue between the therapist and the computer is now feasible, from which optimum treatment techniques could emerge. Optimization offers an extension of the inventiveness, ingenuity and insight of the therapist. The utilization of various qualities of radiation and perhaps various particles in the same treatment plan to develop unusual isodose distributions is a likely consequence. Many combinations can be envisioned. Included in the optimization procedures must be fractionation equivalences, such as NSD and the radiobiological effectiveness factors for different qualities of X-irradiation and different particles.

The extension of useful radiotherapeutic techniques offers the hope of developing a wider approach and in establishing a whole new prospective of the applicability of radiotherapy. However, unless a sophisticated dialogue between the physician and the computer ensues, one can foresee the development of barely competent physicians who do not sufficiently understand the implications of treatment planning to even ask the right questions.

Once the radiotherapeutic technique is selected on the simulator, the prescription for this particular treatment can be fed directly to the computer memory system. In order to verify the accuracy of the data in the computer, it is asked to set up the simulator as though it were the treatment unit. If incorrect, the computer information is corrected and the factors are again tested. Before the patient leaves the simulator verification films are taken based on the information from the computer. A permanent record is made also of the image intensifier view of all fields to be used and of the display of the distribution of energy in the patient. All necessary factors relating to the operation of the treatment unit are now stored in the memory of the computer.

Fig. 10. Computer interaction in therapy planning, scheduling set up and monitoring, post therapy analysis and record keeping

The patient's identification, his treatment plan, prescription and dosage schedule appear on a monitor in the treatment room and on the control panel of the therapy unit (Fig. 10). A readout of the actions of the apparatus in fulfilling the requirements of each prescription is available to the therapist and the technologist at all times in the treatment room and at the control desk. Upon verification that the treatment technique is precisely that which has been prescribed, the apparatus can be activated.

The location of the radiation beam with respect to the patient is still the most critical condition to be fulfilled. It has been necessary to develop systems which can guarantee maintenance of the spatial relationship of the patient and the apparatus. One method currently employed is the mechanical immobilization of the patient, (Fig. 11) either by clamps or the preparation of individually molded casts. Alternatively, a light sensing device has been built in collaboration with the physics group at Michael Reese Hospital, Chicago, under the direction of Drs. James J. Nickson and Jacques Ovadia (Fig. 12). This light sensing device is a piece of reflectance tape which is constantly being seen by a TV camera. When the patient moves beyond a critical distance so that the reflectance from the tape does not fall within a critical zone, the apparatus is automatically turned off (Fig. 13). Ideally, with computer assistance and suitable servosensing devices, a dynamic treatment technique can be developed to automatically adjust for patient movement.

A major advantage of the integrated computer assistance system is in reproducibility with precision and accuracy of the treatment technique. Although well trained radiographers are capable of so doing, it may take as long as 15 minutes to position the patient accurately, the so-called setup time. In view of the very short treatment times, it is uneconomic to use a majority of the time to position the patient if realistic alternatives are available. With an automated treatment technique, the time required to setup a patient may be reduced to one-half or one-third that required with the present day methods. Finally, automatic recording of data, including delivered dose, would greatly decrease the routine work required of radiologists and technologists and increase the accuracy of the records being kept.

The opportunity to integrate and improve the many decisions necessary for the selection of the proper treatment of patients with cancer is a major consideration. The interaction which the oncologist has with his tumor registry in selecting the most appropriate form of treatment can significantly increase the survival rate of patients with cancer. With the computer technology available today the physician is given the possibility to define,

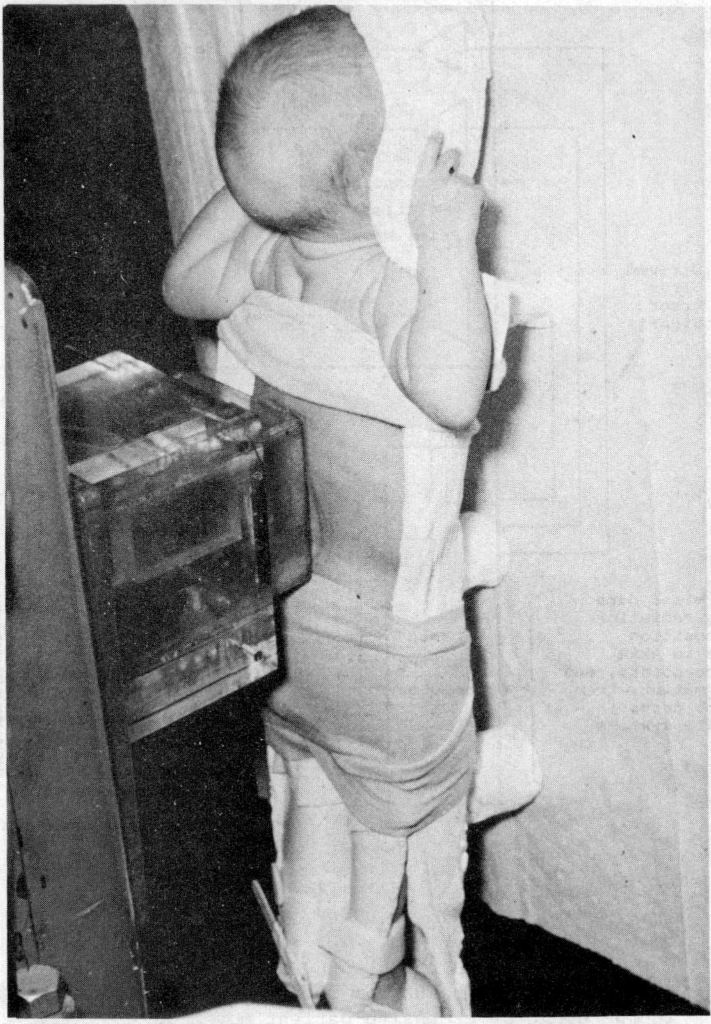

Fig. 11. Obtaining planned dose levels currently requires immobilization of the patient

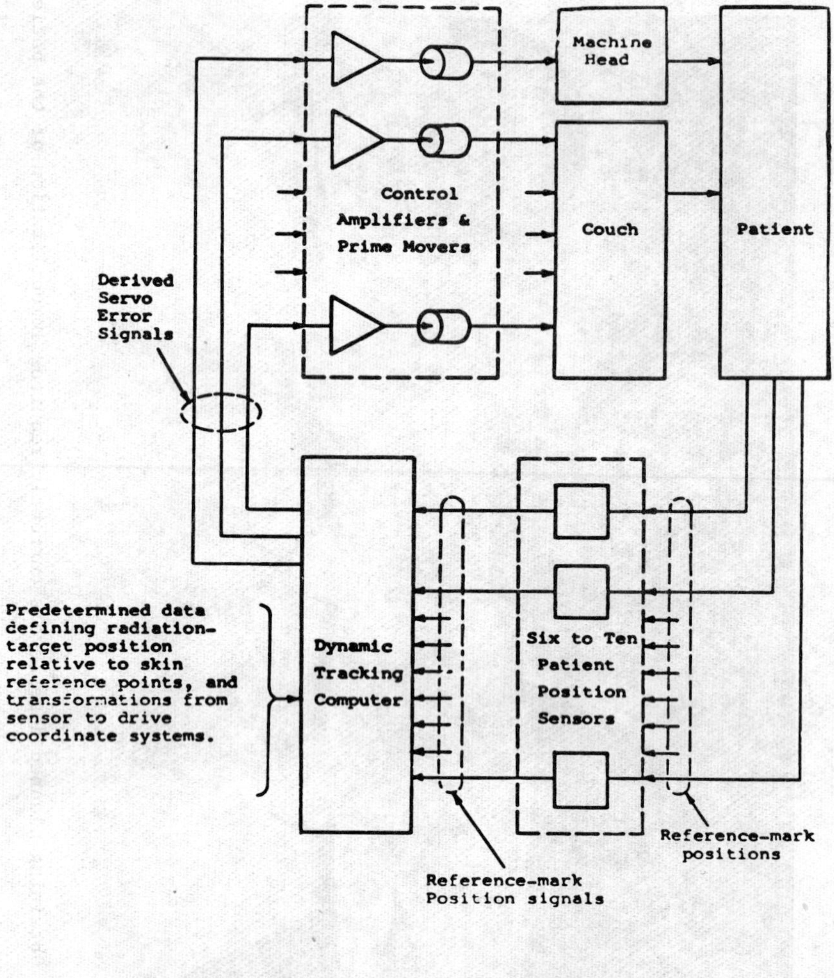

Fig. 12. Schematic of apparatus for interrupting radiation therapy in the event of excessive patient movement

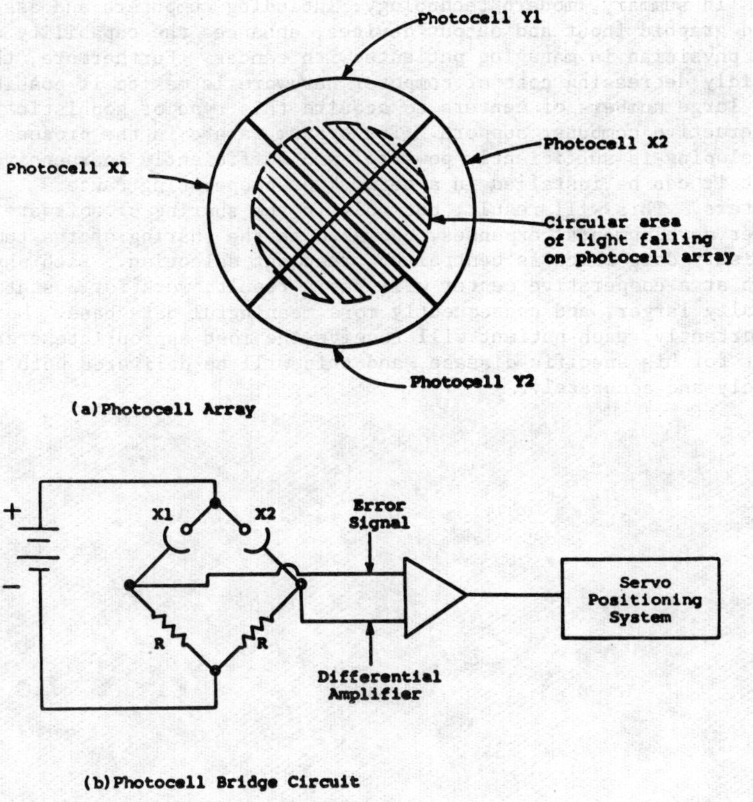

Fig. 13. Schematic of photocell positioning system

control and monitor constantly the management of the patient for whom he is responsible.

CONCLUSION

In summary, modern technology, including computers and associated graphic input and output devices, enhances the capability of the physician in managing patients with cancer. Furthermore, the rapidly decreasing cost of computer hardware is making it possible for large numbers of centers to acquire this type of sophisticated interactive computer support. The system we are in the process of developing is sufficiently powerful and sufficiently inexpensive so that it can be installed in a network of cooperating cancer centers. This will result, not only in the sharing of software and other developmental expenses, but also in the sharing of the tumor registry data which is central to treatment selection. Each physician at a cooperative center will, as a result, work for a statistically larger, and consequently more meaningful data base. More importantly, each patient will receive the most appropriate treatment for his specific disease, and this will be delivered both precisely and accurately.

OPERATIONAL ANALYSIS OF A RADIOLOGY DEPARTMENT BY COMPUTER SIMULATION*

B. LEV

School of Business Administration, Temple University

R. CALTAGIRONE

The Diagnostic Radiology Research Laboratory, Temple University, School of Medicine, Philadelphia, Penn. 19140, U.S.A.

SUMMARY

At the Department of Radiology, Temple University Hospital, a simulation model of patient flow in the Radiology Department has been developed. The model was written in GPSS/360 simulation language and implemented on an IBM 360/75 computer. The results show a good approximation to the working of the department. The simulation has been used to test various hypotheses about scheduling and waiting times.

INTRODUCTION

The operation of a diagnostic radiology department can be viewed as a general production system in which a product (patients) has to be processed in a given amount of time with a given set of resources (X-ray technicians, orderlies, and examination rooms). Such a system operates efficiently if the patients are processed with little or no waiting, and if the resources experience small amounts of idle time. In studies conducted at Temple University Hospital's Diagnostic Radiology Department it was shown that patient waiting times in excess of 1½ hours are not uncommon and that resources (X-ray technicians and examination rooms) were used less than 50% of the time [1]. To improve on these findings the operation of the radiology department was analyzed to get a better understanding of how patients interact with the system. In particular, the investigations aimed at revealing if bottlenecks occurred at any points in the system, and if so, what changes could be made to alleviate them. A further aim was to observe how changes to one part of

*Supported by Grant GM 14548-07, National Institute of General Medical Sciences, United States Public Health Service.

the system affected other parts, and to develop relationships based on these observations. This paper reports on the analysis of the Radiology Department with the aid of a computer simulation model. Results of experimentation with the model give a better understanding of system delays and their causes. The model also provides some predictive capability of system performance when controllable parameters such as the X-ray technicians and transport personnel are varied.

SYSTEM DESCRIPTION

The Department of Radiology at Temple University handles approximately 160 routine patient examinations per 8-hour day. The ratio of inpatients to outpatients is about 2:1. The department conducts over 200 different types of radiologic examinations which have been grouped into 13 major categories for purposes of model construction. Differences within a category are minor. Each category is characterizied by similar equipment needs and similar examination times and procedures. There are 14 rooms assigned to routine studies, several of which can perform many types of radiologic examinations, while others are dedicated to a single type of examination. Ten X-ray technicians are available, and each of them can perform any of the radiologic studies.

Figure 1 represents the series of service stations each patient passes through in order to complete his processing. Inpatients are transported by orderlies and arrive in the department at the control desk. Outpatients enter the department at the reception desk where initial patient data are collected. A majority (80%) is required to undress. Subsequently at the control desk room-assignment is made for both inpatients and outpatients depending on several patient characteristics as well as the study requirements. Once the assignment is complete the patient waits until the assigned room and a technician are simultaneously available. The examination is then performed, and the patient is sent back to the waiting room until his films are processed and checked for technical quality. If the films are approved the patient is released from the department, if the films are not approved the patient re-enters at the control desk with top priority in the queues.

MODEL VALIDATION

A model of the above system was written in GPSS/360 simulation language and implemented on an IBM 360/75 computer. In addition to GPSS/360 language, Fortran IV language was used to

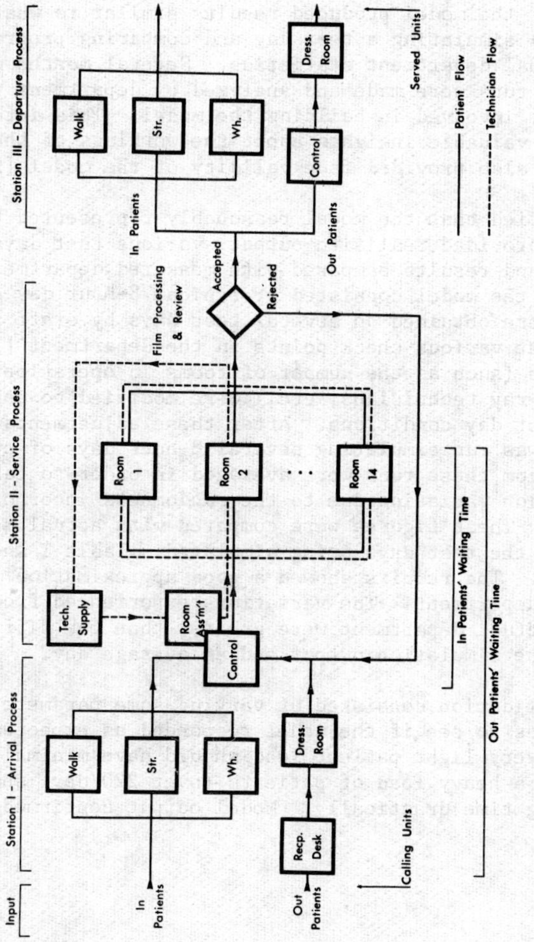

Fig. 1. Flow diagram of patient processing

write subroutines for some of the complicated decision processes concerning room-assignments. These subroutines were then accessed by the main GPSS program. Validation of the simulation model consisted of two parts; 1) analysis of initial program output to see if the model produced results similar to what was expected, and 2) simulating a test day and comparing program output with actual department statistics. Several months of trial and error runs were made and analyzed by department personnel and those involved in building the model. This interaction provided valuable insights about the workings of the department, and also provided face validity of the model [2].

Once satisfied that the model reasonably represented the department and provided realisitc output, various test days were simulated and results compared with measured department data. Input to the model consisted of typical 8-hour day statistics which were obtained on several test days by staff personnel located at various check points in the department [1]. System variables (such as the number of rooms in operation, the number of X-ray technicians, etc.) were modified to correspond with test day conditions. After these adjustments were made the model was run simulating several 8-hour days of operation. Output from these runs were averaged in order to take into consideration variation due to the randomness incorporated into the model. These figures were compared with actual measured data from the test days being simulated. Table I shows this comparison. The results showed a good approximation to the actual working department. The variations experienced from day to day in the actual department were greater than the difference found between the simulation output and an average day.

A final validation consisted of varying some parameters to extreme values to see if the model responded as expected. For example, a very light patient load should have minimal waiting time, while a heavy load of patients (over 220/day) should increase waiting time drastically. Model output confirmed the above.

EXPERIMENTATION

A future goal of this research is to improve the patient flow problem that exists in the radiology department. This can be accomplished by analyzing the system under various operating conditions so that relationships between input parameters and system performance can be established.

Experimentation began by varying the number of X-ray

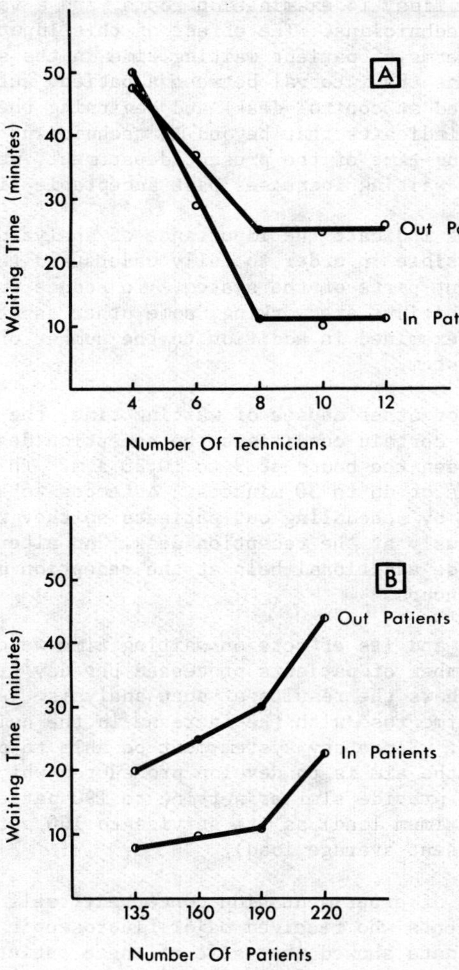

Fig. 2. A. Patient waiting time as a function of the number of X-ray technicians in the system (160 patients and 10 orderlies)

B. Patient waiting time as a function of the number of patients serviced (10 technicians and 10 orderlies) technicians in the system. All other parameters were held constant. Thus, the operating conditions of this experiment consisted of 10 orderlies, 14 examination rooms, and a variable number of X-ray technicians. The effect of this input parameter was measured in terms of patient waiting time in the system, which is defined as the interval between a patient entering the department (arrived at control desk) and beginning the examination. Figure 2A indicates that beyond 10 technicians we cannot improve waiting time of the present department, while below 8 technicians the waiting increases past acceptable limits.

These results indicate the importance of analyzing as many parameters as possible in order to fully understand the interaction of different parts of the system. To reduce waiting time when 8 to 10 technicians are working, some other aspect of the system has to be examined in addition to the number of technicians in the system.

In looking for other causes of waiting time, the model showed that under certain conditions the reception desk created a bottleneck between the hours of 9 to 10:30 a.m. This alone could cause delays of up to 30 minutes. Attempts to solve this problem were made by scheduling out-patients so they would not arrive simultaneously at the reception desk. An alternative would be to provide additional help at the reception desk between these peak hours.

Patient load and its effects on waiting time were evaluated by varying the number of patients processed per day from 135 to 220. Figure 2B shows the results of such analysis. As expected, patient waiting time rose with the increase in the number of patients serviced. Since any system must be able to perform at its maximum load the aim is to develop procedures which allow the department to provide similar service to 190 patients (which is its present maximum load) as its service to 160 patients (which is its present average load).

Another area of experimentation concerned itself with waiting times of patients who received major fluoroscopic examinations. Measured data showed that some of these patients experienced waits in excess of 2 hours. Fluoroscopic examinations usually require a series of films to be taken over a long period of time. In between films, mandatory waits are necessary. To schedule such patients requires that arrivals of some patients coincide with the mandatory wait period of others. In this way long waiting times can be eliminated and utilization of rooms improved. Table II compares measured and simulated waiting times of a major fluoroscopic examination. These data were

TABLE I - Comparison of simulated output and measured data

	135 PATIENTS		160 PATIENTS	
	RANGE OF SIMULATION	MEASURED	RANGE OF SIMULATION	MEASURED
TECHNICIAN UTILIZATION (%)	31 - 36	36	51 - 55	50
ORDERLY UTILIZATION (%)	38 - 43	42	56 - 71	54
ROOM UTILIZATION (%)	34 - 41	31	38 - 44	38
WAITING TIME (MINS.)	23 - 29	22	19 - 25	21
TOTAL TIME (MINS.)	73 - 84	74	61 - 68	69

(Conditions: 10 Technicians, 10 Orderlies, 12 Examination Rooms for 135 Patients and 14 for 160 Patients)

TABLE II. Comparison of measured waiting time and simulated waiting time for a major fluoroscopic examination

BARIUM ENEMA

WAITING TIME BEFORE STUDY (MINS.)

	MEASURED	SIMULATION
	20	24
	28	27
	30	53
	60	73
	60	107
	125	122
	189	170
MEAN	73	82

TABLE III. Results of scheduling experimentation with major fluoroscopic examination

BARIUM ENEMA

WAITING TIME BEFORE STUDY (MINS.)

SIMULATION (OLD SCHEDULE)				SIMULATION (NEW SCHEDULE)			
RUN # 1	2	3	4	RUN # 1	2	3	4
1	1	12	2	1	1	1	1
20	1	14	13	1	1	1	1
34	1	16	17	8	1	2	1
40	17	22	29	16	1	15	7
59	37	22	33	17	2	15	17
	44	28	34	18	11	28	24
		63	40	19	36	30	30
			41	20	38	43	38
MEAN NUMBER OF CASES = 7				MEAN NUMBER OF CASES = 8			
AVERAGE WAITING TIME = 25 MINS.				AVERAGE WAITING TIME = 14 MINS.			

produced with one room available for Barium Enema examinations, while in scheduling experiments two rooms were available.

A heuristic scheduling approach was employed with the aid of the simulation model in an attempt to reduce waiting time. The simulation was run with the present scheduling to produce results which could be compared with output generated by other scheduling procedures.

A comparison of the old scheduling procedure with an improved one produced a reduction in average waiting time for all Barium Enema examinations, and also a reduction in the maximum waiting time experienced by any one patient (see Table III). The latter type of improvement is important to the administration because potential complaints concern long waiting times by these patients.

CONCLUSIONS

A computer simulation model of a diagnostic radiology department has been developed which accurately represents the workings of an actual department. It is used as an inexpensive tool for evaluating changes which can improve the present department's operation. This model also serves as a basis for the development of future simulation models which are necessary due to the construction of a new facility and new philosophies concerning the radiology department. It is also used to predict performance of the department under changing conditions (such as an increase in patient load).

Despite variation due to randomness and lack of data in some areas, the model has demonstrated, with the aid of much sensitivity analysis, its ability to predict the kind of response that is expected. Program output has been modified to allow quick comparison of several runs under different operating conditions. As a result, considerable insight, knowledge, and experience has been gained about the operation of the radiology department. Simulation has reinforced some intuitive feelings about the department and refuted others. An infinite number of experiments can be performed with the aid of the simulation model. Work is now focused upon developing a realistic plan for use of the model.

REFERENCES

1. G. REVESZ, F.J. SHEA and M.C. ZISKIN, "Patient flow and utilization of resources in a diagnostic radiology department" *Radiology 104*, 21-26 (July, 1972).

2. B. LEV, R. CALTAGIRONE and F.J. SHEA, "Patient flow and utilization of resources in a diagnostic radiology department: analysis by simulation techniques" *Investigative Radiology 7*, 517 (1972).

USE OF CHEMICAL AUTOMATION AND COMPUTER TECHNIQUES IN STUDYING BIOLOGICAL FACTORS INFLUENCING BLOOD CONSTITUENTS IN HEALTHY HUMAN SUBJECTS

D.M. GOLDBERG and D.A. WINFIELD

Department of Chemical Pathology, Royal Hospital, Sheffield, England

A.J. HANDYSIDE

Department of Community Medicine, The University, Sheffield, England

SUMMARY

A study of the influence of age, body weight, social class, blood pressure and smoking habit upon the fasting serum concentrations of urea, uric acid, total protein, cholesterol, inorganic phosphate, calcium and magnesium, was conducted by investigating over 500 subjects drawn from a well-population screening clinic and laboratory staff. Chemical estimations were made by auto-analyser techniques and the results together with biometric details were transferred to punch-cards. The combined data were analysed firstly by a product moment correlation program using the ICL 1907 computer, and secondly by a multiple linear regression program with 4 independent variables (age, weight, social class and blood pressure) for each chemical constituent. Results are described.

INTRODUCTION

Well-population screening is an accepted procedure in many countries. Biochemical investigations play an important role in such screening programs [1-3]. The concentrations of many chemical constituents can be measured fairly readily in the blood serum of human subjects. Values outside certain limits may indicate an underlying disease process and call for further investigation. The limits selected for each constituent may be based upon published reference values or upon the previous experience of the investigators gained in the study of a population assumed to be normal. For the most part the criteria and the limits chosen are arbitrary; while they may have general statistical validity, they usually fail to make allowance for demographic factors which may influence the serum concentration of chemical constituents. This in turn may lead to misclassification of subjects - a number of those with underlying disease being missed, and a number of healthy subjects being exposed to unnecessary investigative follow-up.

It is conceivable that recognition and quantitation of demographic influences could improve the efficiency of biochemical screening programs. Many constituents such as uric acid [4-10] and cholesterol [11-14] vary with the age, weight, race, smoking habits, and social class of the subject. Only within recent years have widely ranging investigations been conducted to determine the levels of chemical constituents in healthy subjects and to study their relationship to age and sex [15-18]. Although much useful information has accrued, the mathematical treatment of these relationships has been unsophisticated, the demographic variables studied have been few, and their influence has not been expressed in a practically useful format.

The present study was undertaken to define these demographic factors, to quantify their influence, and to develop refined criteria as alternatives to the 'normal range' concept which could prove more accurate and useful in health screening.

MATERIALS AND METHODS

Source

The source of clinical material was a screening clinic in Baslow, Derbyshire, supplemented by healthy laboratory staff. Some aspects of this clinic have already been described [19]. An outline of its organisation is given in Fig. 1. Patients proceeded to eight sets of examination:

1) *Urine Testing*. This was carried out by commercial 'stick' tests for glucose and protein capable of interpretation by the patients with referral of doubtful and positive results to the medical staff. The information contributed to the overall 'Clinical Assessment' defined in Table 2.

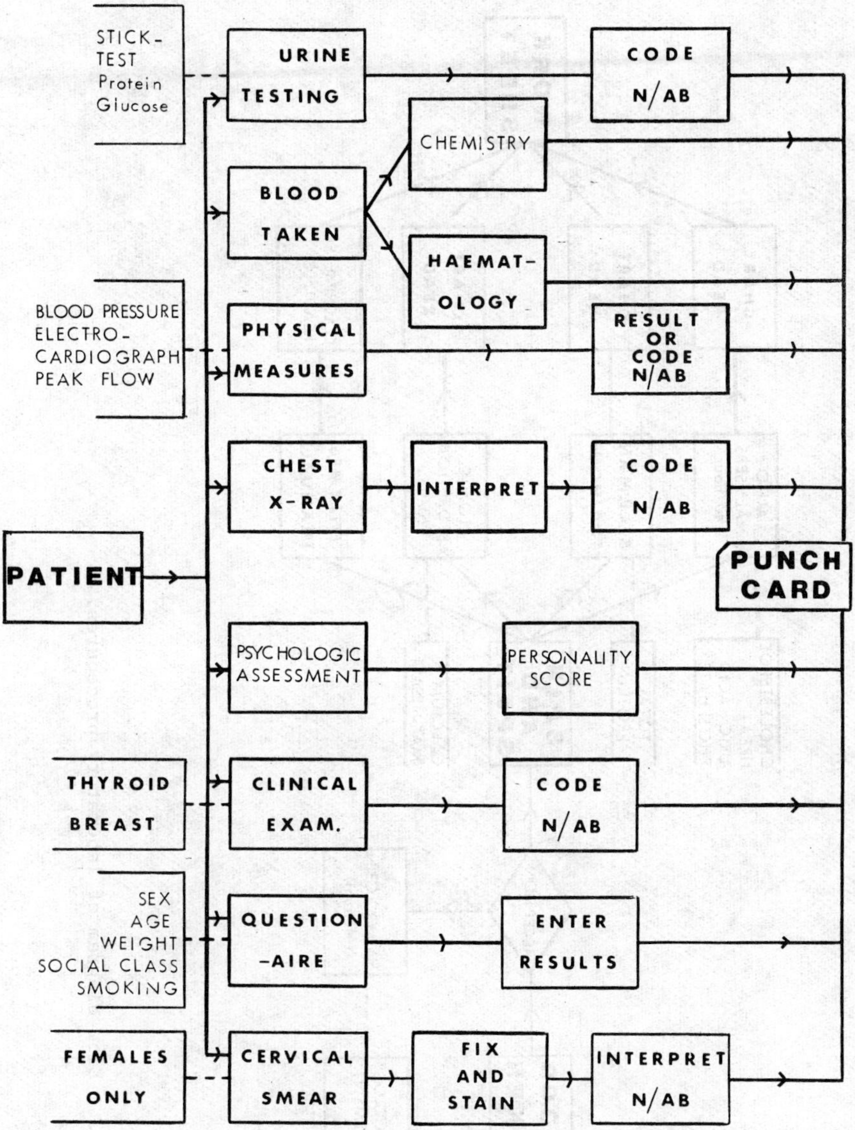

Fig. 1. Flow diagram of procedures associated with screening clinic.

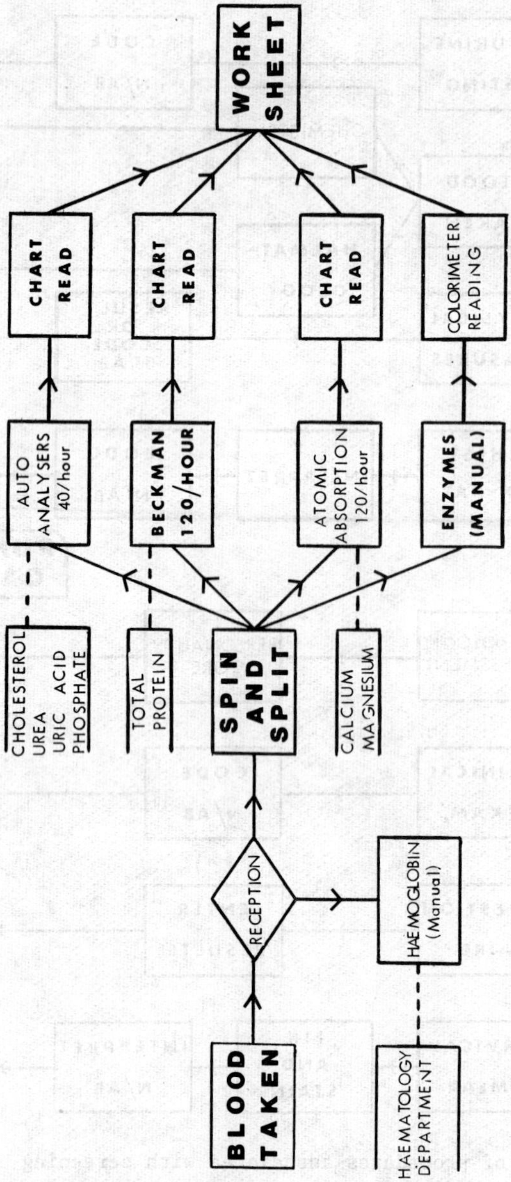

Fig. 2. Flow diagram of laboratory procedures.

2) *Venepuncture*. Blood was taken for chemical and haematological tests to be described in the next section.

3) *Physical Measurements*. Pulmonary function was measured by the Wright Peak Flow Meter, blood pressure as the diastolic reading, and a six-lead electrocardiograph (ECG) was carried out. The latter was coded NORMAL or ABNORMAL.

4) *Chest X-Ray*. These were taken by a Mobile Mass X-Ray Unit, interpreted by medical staff, and coded NORMAL or ABNORMAL.

5) *Psychologic Assessment*. This was conducted by trained staff and a score allotted [20].

6) *Clinical Examination*. In addition to asking the patient questions aimed at excluding major disease and ascertaining previous illness and surgery attendance, examinations of the thyroid gland in all subjects and of the breasts in females were specifically conducted by medical staff and the results coded as NORMAL or ABNORMAL.

7) *Questionnaire*. The patient entered sex, age, weight and height (scales provided), daily cigarette consumption, and information allowing assessment of social class. The percentage of ideal weight was derived from tables of the Metropolitan Insurance Company.

8) *Cervical Smear*. These were taken by medical staff, fixed and stained by laboratory staff, and coded NORMAL or ABNORMAL by medical staff.

Laboratory Procedure

The processes involved are outlined in Fig. 2. On reaching the laboratory, part of the blood sample was sent for estimation of whole blood haemoglobin. The remainder was allowed to clot, serum was removed by centrifugation and divided into at least four portions. One portion went for assay of cholesterol, urea, uric acid and phosphate. These estimations were done sequentially on single-channel AutoAnalyzers (Technicon Instruments Co. Ltd., Basingstoke, Hants, England) at a rate of 40 tests per hour, the samples meantime being stored at 4°C. Standard AutoAnalyzer

TABLE 1. Methods and Instrumentation Used in Biochemical Investigations

Constituent	Chemistry	Instrumentation	Rate per Hour
Urea	Diacetyl monoxime	AutoAnalyzer Mk I	40
Uric acid	Phosphotungstate + cyanide	AutoAnalyzer Mk I	40
Cholesterol	Ferric chloride	AutoAnalyzer Mk I	40
Inorg. phosphate	Am. molybdate + ANSA	AutoAnalyzer Mk I	40
Total protein	Biuret	Technicon Mk II Sampler + Beckman DB Spectrophotometer and Recorder	120
Calcium	Atomic absorption spectroscopy	EEL - AAS plus Technicon Mk II Sampler plus Beckman Recorder	120
Magnesium	Atomic absorption spectroscopy	EEL - AAS plus Technicon Mk II Sampler plus Beckman Recorder	120

chemical routines were used for these tests (Table 1). A second portion was stored for a few weeks at -20°C and estimated for total protein concentration by an automated system comprising a Technicon Mark II Sampler, a Beckman DB Spectrophotometer and a slave recorder [21]. The rate of analysis was 120/hour. A third portion after storage at -20°C was used to estimate calcium and magnesium by the EEL Atomic Absorption Spectrophotometer with output to slave recorder, and fed by a Technicon Mark II Sampler at a rate of 120/hour.

In all the above estimations results were presented as a recorder peak, the height of which was read manually and converted to concentration units by reference to standard calibration curves. All data were entered on work sheets and passed for addition to the punch-card profile of each subject.

A fourth portion was used to determine enzyme activities. The procedures used were mainly manual, and since certain of the results have already been reported [22-24] this aspect of the study will not be considered further.

Data Processing and Computing

Punch-cards were prepared, one for each subject, containing the information outlined in Table 2. Data sheets were printed and cases with abnormalities detected during the screening process were rejected on inspection by the medical staff. No account was taken at this stage of the biochemical results. Those subjects who passed this preliminary inspection were then machine-sorted by sex, by weight, and by age to produce histograms of distribution of the biochemical values by age and by weight intervals for each sex independently. Analysis was continued for males and females separately by application of a program written in Fortran IV for the ICL 1907 computer in which an x by x matrix was constructed and the value of the product moment correlation coefficient for each variable with every other variable was calculated and presented together with the mean and SD of the variables. The significance of the differences in the means between the sexes for each variable, and the significance of the correlation coefficients was calculated manually, standard tables to assess statistical significance being used [25].

The Punch-cards were next analysed by the computer using a media conversion program written in Fortran IV,

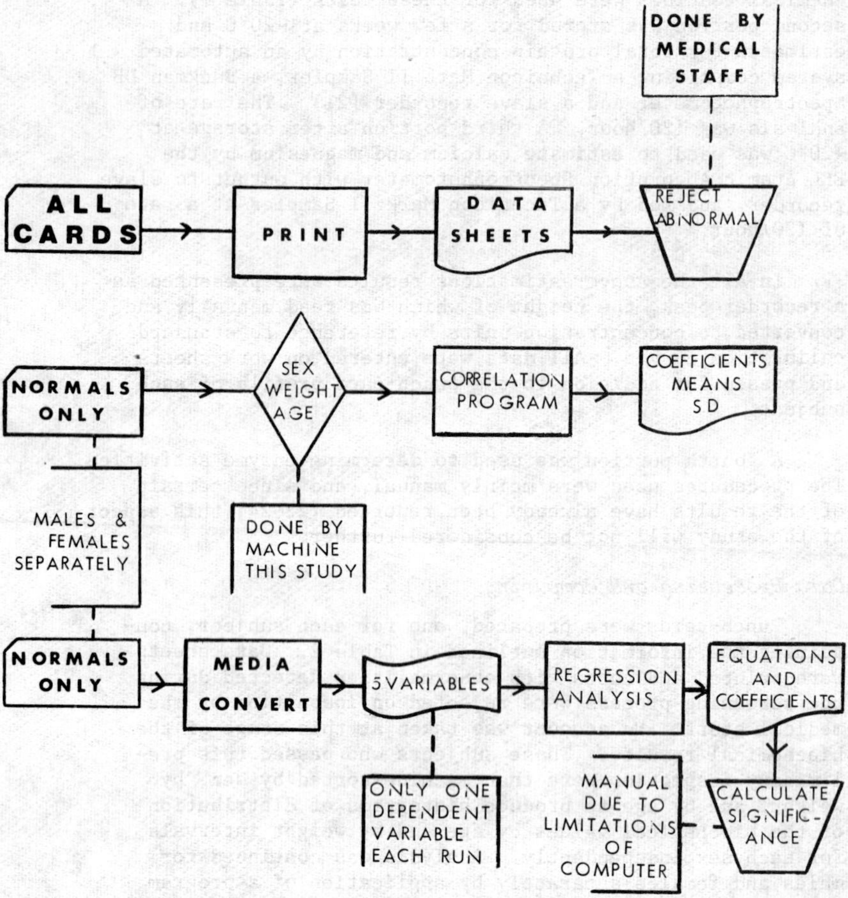

Fig. 3. Flow diagram of computing procedures.

output on paper tape giving the values for males and females separately of one dependent variable (biochemical result) and the following four independent variables: age, weight, social class and blood pressure. This information was then analysed using a modified Mercury Autocode Library program for multiple linear regression generating coefficients (m, n, o, p) and constant term for the following equation:

Biochemical Value = m Age + n Weight + o Blood Pressure + p Social Class + Constant (1)

Output also included the variance of each coefficient and its covariance with other coefficients in the same equation; raw means of all the variables; total and residual sums of squares, and degrees of freedom.

TABLE 2. Allocation of Columns on Punch Cards

Information	No. of columns	Information	No. of columns
Survey number	3	Chest X-Ray	2
Sex	1	Breast	2
Age	2	Laboratory number	3
Social class	1	Blood chemistry:	
Haemoglobin	3	a) urea	2
Diastolic blood pressure	3	b) uric acid	2
Electrocardiograph	2	c) inorg. phosphate	2
Smoking (cigarettes/day)	2	d) cholesterol	3
Psychologic assessment	2	e) total protein	3
Cervical cytology	2	f) calcium	3
Clinical assessment	2	g) magnesium	2
No. of surgery visits during past year	2	Serum enzymes:	
		a) alkaline phosphatase	2
Lung function:		b) aspartate transaminase	3
a) F. E. F.	3	c) alanine transaminase	3
b) C. P.	3	d) creatine phosphokinase	3
Weight (lbs)	3	e) 5'nucleotidase	2
Percent ideal weight	3	f) hydroxybutyrate dehydrogenase	3
Thyroid:			
a) size	1		
b) history	2		

Further tests were conducted manually because of limitations of the program:

a) The multiple regression coefficient R was calculated as $\sqrt{\frac{\text{total sum of squares} - \text{residual sum of squares}}{\text{total sum of squares}}}$ and its significance obtained from tables [25].

b) The significance of the variable associated with a coefficient was assigned 95% probability if the value for the coefficient exceeded twice the square root of its variance.

c) Confidence limits were derived at the 95% level by calculating the overall standard deviation of the equation

$$D = t'_{95} \times \sqrt{\frac{\text{residual sum of squares}}{\text{degrees of freedom}}} \qquad (2)$$

RESULTS

A total of 519 subjects comprising 248 males and 271 females on whom full biochemical results were available passed as normal and proceeded to further analysis. The mean biochemical data are presented in Table 3. Values for urea, uric acid, calcium, and magnesium were significantly higher in males. As demonstrated in Table 4, age showed a positive correlation with urea, uric acid, cholesterol, and magnesium among females, and uric acid showed a highly significant correlation with weight. Uric acid showed a highly significant correlation with total body weight also in males, but a negative correlation with age was obtained. Urea and cholesterol showed a positive correlation with age in males, but this association was less striking than among females.

Neither age nor weight showed any significant correlation with the concentration of calcium, inorganic phosphate, or total protein in either sex. Except for a highly significant correlation between diastolic blood pressure and uric acid concentration in females ($r = 0.243$; $P < 0.001$), the remaining demographic factors studied did not correlate with any of the biochemical measurements.

The equations derived from the regression analysis, where the value for the overall regression coefficient was statistically significant, are presented in Table 5 for males and Table 6 for females. The validity of these equations was established by utilising a computer program, written in Fortran IV, to derive the predicted value of the biochemical parameters for each subject based on sex, age, weight, social class, and blood pressure. Defining the demographic component by the term 'd', and using the values for C and D derived from the regression analysis, the

TABLE 3. Biochemical Values in Populations Studied (Mean ± SD)

Constituent	Males	Females	t
Urea (mg/100 ml)	38.7 ± 8.6	35.6 ± 9.6	3.48
Uric acid (mg/100 ml)	5.9 ± 1.2	4.9 ± 1.0	9.54
Cholesterol (mg/100 ml)	230 ± 43	237 ± 51	-
Magnesium (mg/100 ml)	2.1 ± 0.2	2.0 ± 0.2	5.17
Calcium (mg/100 ml)	9.7 ± 0.7	9.5 ± 0.5	3.52
Phosphate (mg/100 ml)	3.2 ± 0.5	3.2 ± 0.5	-
Total protein (g/100 ml)	7.2 ± 1.3	7.4 ± 1.3	-

TABLE 4. Product Moment Correlation Coefficients for Biochemical Constituents with Age and Weight (Significant Results Only)

Constituent	Males		Females	
	Age	Weight	Age	Weight
Urea	0.239^{b}	-	0.293^{c}	-
Uric acid	-0.182^{a}	0.341^{c}	0.301^{c}	0.394^{c}
Cholesterol	0.172^{a}	-	0.363^{c}	-
Magnesium	-	-	0.172^{b}	-
Calcium	-	-	-	-
Phosphate	-	-	-	-
Total protein	-	-	-	-

^{a} $P < 0.05$; ^{b} $P < 0.01$; ^{c} $P < 0.001$

TABLE 5. Regression Equations Relating Biochemical Value to Age (A), Social Class (SC), Diastolic Blood Pressure (BP), and Weight (W) for Males[a]

Urea	=	0.204	A	-0.439	SC	-0.015	BP	-0.008	W	+32.8	(±16.4)
	R =	0.289 (P < 0.001)									
Uric acid	=	-0.0122	A	+0.0118	SC	+0.0011	BP	+0.0131	W	+4.2	(±2.02)
	R =	0.389 (P < 0.001)									
Cholesterol	=	0.93	A	+0.314	SC	-0.240	BP	+0.025	W	+202	(±81)
	R =	0.212 (P < 0.01)									

[a] Equations given where value for multiple regression coefficient (R) was significant at $P < 0.05$

TABLE 6. Regression Equations Relating Biochemical Value to Age (A), Social Class (SC), Diastolic Blood Pressure (BP), and Weight (W) for Females[a]

Urea	= 0.226	A	-0.635	SC	+0.010	BP	+0.022	W	+24.3	($\pm$18.0)
	R = 0.305 (P < 0.001)									
Uric acid	= 0.0191	A	+0.0158	SC	+0.0043	BP	+0.0163	W	+1.16	($\pm$1.87)
	R = 0.470 (P < 0.001)									
Cholesterol	= 1.55	A	+0.398	SC	-0.237	BP	-0.009	W	+182	($\pm$93)
	R = 0.399 (P < 0.001)									
Magnesium	= 0.0227	A	+0.083	SC	-0.0013	BP	-0.0004	W	+1.91	($\pm$0.35)
	R = 0.171 (P < 0.01)									
Calcium	= 0.0487	A	-0.097	SC	-0.013	BP	-0.0226	W	+9.7	($\pm$1.1)
	R = 0.145 (P < 0.05)									

[a] Equations given where value for multiple regression coefficient (R) was significant at $P < 0.05$

TABLE 7. Relationship Between Regression Equation Constant (c), Demographic Component (d)[a] and Mean Value ($\bar{x}$). (All data as mg per 100 ml)

Constituent	Males				Females			
	C ± D[b]	$\bar{x}(\pm SD)$	$\frac{C}{\bar{x}}(\%)$	$\frac{d}{\bar{x}}(\%)$	C ± D[b]	$\bar{x}(\pm SD)$[b]	$\frac{C}{\bar{x}}(\%)$	$\frac{d}{\bar{x}}(\%)$
Urea	32.8 ± 16.4	38.7 ± 8.6	85	15	24.3 ± 18.0	35.6 ± 9.6	68	32
Uric acid	4.2 ± 2.0	5.9 ± 1.2	71	29	1.16 ± 1.87	4.9 ± 1.1	24	76
Cholesterol	202 ± 81	230 ± 43	88	12	182 ± 93	237 ± 51	77	23
Magnesium	1.95 ± 0.41	2.1 ± 0.2	93	7	1.91 ± 0.35	2.0 ± 0.2	95	5
Calcium	9.8 ± 1.2	9.7 ± 0.7	101	-	9.7 ± 1.1	9.5 ± 0.5	102	-

[a] The demographic component represents that fraction of the value for each constituent due to age, social class, diastolic blood pressure and weight calculated from the equations listed in Tables 5 and 6

[b] D represents the quotient for expressing the 95% confidence limits of the regression equation. SD is the standard deviation of the mean — the 95% confidence limits in this formulation would approximate ± 2SD

TABLE 8. Comparison of Classification of Female Subjects According to Orthodox and Demographically Corrected Criteria with Final Clinical Diagnosis

Constituent (Total number of subjects)	Number of subjects in whom value for constituent was 90 - 100% of mean + 2SD		100 - 110% of mean + 2SD	
	Number of subjects in whom		Number of subjects in whom	
	Value - d<C+D	Value - d>C+D	Value - d<C+D	Value - d>C+D
Cholesterol (46)	17	9	10	10
Disease established[a]	2	6 (3)	2 (1)	4 (3)
Uric acid (50)	18	6	14	12
Disease established[a]	1 (1)	4 (3)	3 (2)	6 (4)
Urea (70)	30	8	6	26
Disease established[a]	3 (2)	4 (4)	2 (1)	20 (17)

[a] This column gives number of subjects in whom organic disease of any kind was diagnosed within twelve months of analysis. The figure in brackets refers to number of cases in whom the disease was one known to be highly associated with raised values for constituent measured.

following relationship held for 95% of the population tested where the overall regression coefficient was statistically significant:

$$\text{Biochemical Value} = d + C \pm D \qquad (3)$$

The contribution of the demographic component (d) and of the non-demographic component (C) to each biochemical parameter was expressed as a percentage of the mean ($\bar{x}$) for that parameter (Table 7). It is obvious that demographic factors influence the value of all biochemical parameters much more profoundly among women than among men, and that among the latter, biologic variation not accountable in demographic terms represents the main source of intra-individual variation in the concentration of chemical constituents of the blood serum.

Equation(3) was re-arranged as follows:

$$\text{Biochemical Value} - d = C \pm D \qquad (4)$$

This permitted the establishment of reference values for the normal population as an alternative to the customary mean $\pm$ 2SD range. The usefulness of this proposal was tested among patients referred for out-patient investigation since there were insufficient subjects with proven illness arising from the screening clinic. Comparison was restricted to urea, uric acid, and cholesterol among females in whom organic disease was firmly excluded or a final diagnosis reached after not more than 12 months of investigation. Patients were randomly selected on the basis of having a value between 100-110% of the upper normal limit of mean + 2SD (and classified as abnormal) or between 90-100% of this limit (and classified as normal). Re-classification was based on computer-assisted analysis and calculation of the function:

Biochemical Value - d

If this exceeded C + D the classification was abnormal and, if less, the subject was classified as normal. The results of the original biochemical classifications, and of the final clinical assessment, are given in Table 8. To avoid bias and duplication no patient was included in respect of more than one biochemical result; the other biochemical constituents were not estimated, or their values were <90% or >110% of the mean + 2SD limit. Since the conditions of selection were rigorous, the number for each biochemical constituent was relatively small. It does seem, however, that correction for demographic variability made each test more accurate in predicting an underlying disease state, and that the disease in question more often than not was one accepted as having a high association with a particular biochemical abnormality (e.g. urea and uric acid in renal disease; urea and cholesterol in ischaemic heart disease, hypertension, diabetes, and vascular disease; cholesterol in hypothyroidism; uric acid in gout and related arthropathies, and blood dyscrasias).

FUTURE IMPLICATIONS

The results of the pilot study outlined in Table 8 indicate some promise in the use of demographically corrected reference values for female subjects. The data summarised in Table 7 make it appear less likely that a similar treatment for male subjects would seriously enhance the diagnostic accuracy of biochemical tests since the demographic component is very much smaller. In view of the strong racial factors known to operate for some biochemical constituents [9,10,26, 27,28,29] it cannot be assumed that the equations derived in this study would hold for other populations. A safer procedure would be for each laboratory to establish these equations for its own population. An analysis of the resources required for this study is therefore presented (Table 9) based upon the number of hours work in various professional categories for each stage. No allowance is made for capital and running costs of equipment and building, or for consumables such as chemicals, X-Ray plates, needles and syringes, ECG traces and recorder charts, etc. Although the estimate is based upon our own experience and costs the procedures at the screening clinic, these go far beyond what would be essential to ensure that a healthy population was being selected; this could be done very simply, and with little error, by excluding all those who visited their medical practitioner over a specified period prior to blood being drawn for the survey. The estimate for the actual analyses is also greatly in excess of what can be achieved at the present time with more sophisticated automated equipment, but since this is very variable, it will depend on the facilities at each laboratory.

The estimate for computing time given is that applicable to library programs available as ICL 1900 series software modified by the Computing Service of the University of Sheffield (copies on application to senior author) and providing in a single operation all of the output required for this type of study. The amount of computing time actually used in this

TABLE 9. Man-Hours Required for Total Investigations in this Study Based on 500 Subjects Equally Divided as to Sex

Procedure	Number of man-hours required	
	Medical	Technical[a]
Screening clinic		
Venepuncture	-	25
Physical measures		
A) Blood pressure	15	-
B) ECG	5	25
C) Peak flow	-	40
Chest X-Ray	15	40
Personality score	20	-
Clinical examination		
A) General	30	-
B) Goitre	30	-
C) Breast	10	-
Cervical smear	20	25
TOTAL	145	155
Laboratory procedures		
Reception	-	10
Haemoglobin estimation	-	10
Biochemical assays		
A) Cholesterol + urea + uric acid + inorg. phosphate	-	25
B) Total protein	-	5
C) Calcium + magnesium	-	10
TOTAL	-	60
Computing procedures		
Card punching	-	5
Medical inspection	10	-
Machine sorting[b]	-	20
Correlation program[c]	-	2.5
Media conversion[d]	-	2.5
Regression analysis[c]	-	2.5
TOTAL	10	32.5

[a] Includes radiographers, scientific staff, computing and secretarial staff, and non-qualified ancillary grades.

[b] This could be done in approximately five minutes by computer.

[c] These estimates are based upon currently available computing procedures each requiring about 5 minutes real-time, but not available when this study was undertaken.

[d] Not now required as above programs suitable for punch-card input; but some additional programming would be needed to select information for correlation and regression analysis if punch-cards contained patient profiles as detailed as those constructed in this study (Table 2).

study was, through inexperience, misunderstandings, and poor liaison, excessive in comparison with facilities that are nowadays widely available, and it would be utterly misleading to base the estimate given in Table 9 upon our efforts.

CONCLUSIONS

A study of the influence of age, body weight, social class, blood pressure and smoking habit upon the fasting serum concentrations of urea, uric acid, total protein, cholesterol, inorganic phosphate, calcium and magnesium, was conducted by investigating over 500 subjects drawn from a well-population screening clinic and laboratory staff. Chemical estimations were made by auto-analyser techniques and the results together with biometric details were transferred to punch-cards. The combined data were analysed firstly by a product moment correlation program using the ICL 1907 Computer, and secondly by a multiple linear regression program with 4 independent variables (age, weight, social class and blood pressure) for each chemical constituent.

In both sexes, age was a positive determinant of urea and cholesterol, this effect being more pronounced in females than in males. Weight was a powerful determinant of uric acid in both sexes; but age seemed to affect this constituent in opposite directions in the two sexes. Blood pressure correlated with uric acid in females only. No other significant biometric relationships were revealed.

The regression analysis permitted computation of the demographic component in intra-individual variation. This was more striking for females than for males, especially with respect to uric acid, urea and cholesterol. Demographically corrected reference values for these constituents provided a more accurate discriminant of disease than conventional mean + 2SD limits.

ACKNOWLEDGEMENTS

We are grateful to Drs. S.M. Evans, E. Wilkes and D. Dalrymple-Smith who organised the Baslow Screening Clinic; to Professors Arthur Jordan and John Knowelden for encouragement and the use of departmental facilities; to Messrs. K. Trout, J. Hanson and J.R. Brooke for guidance on the computing and systems analysis associated with the project;

to Professor A.M. Walker for advice on statistics; and to the medical and technical staff of the United Sheffield Hospitals who made this study possible.

REFERENCES

1. WILSON, J.M.G., "Current trends and problems in health screening" *Scand. J. Clin. Lab. Invest. 29*, Suppl. 126, 21.1 (1972).

2. SACKETT, D.L., "Evaluation of health screening programs by laboratory tests" *Scand. J. Clin. Lab. Invest. 29*, Suppl. 126, 21.2 (1972).

3. NORDEN, A., "Discrimination into healthy and sick in health screening" *Scand. J. Clin. Lab. Invest. 29*, Suppl. 126, 21.3 (1972).

4. MIKKELSEN, W.M., DODGE, H.J. and VALKENBURG, H., "The distribution of serum uric acid values in a population unselected as to gout or hyperuricemia" Tecumseh, Michigan 1959-1960 *Amer. J. Med. 29*, 242 (1965).

5. KRIZEK, V., "Serum uric acid in relation to body weight" *Ann. Rheum. Dis. 25*, 456 (1966).

6. BROOKS, G.W. and MUELLER, E., "Serum urate concentrations among university professors. Relation to drive, achievement and leadership" *J. Amer. Med. Assoc. 195*, 415 (1966).

7. MONTOYE, H.M., FAULKNER, J.A., DODGE, H.J., MIKKELSEN, WILLIS, P.W. III, and BLOCK, W.D., "Serum uric acid concentration among business executives. With observations on other coronary heart disease risk factors" *Ann. Intern. Med. 66*, 838 (1967).

8. LELLOUCH, J., SCHWARTZ, D., TRAN, M.H. and BEAUMONT, J.L., "The relationships between smoking and levels of serum urea and uric acid. Results of an epidemiological survey" *J. Chron. Dis. 22*, 9 (1969).

9. ACHESON, R.M., "Social class gradients and serum uric acid in males and females" *Brit. Med. J. 4*, 65 (1969).

10. ACHESON, R.M. and FLOREY, C. du V., "Body-weight, ABO blood-groups, and altitude of domicile as determinants

of serum-uric-acid in military recruits in four countries" *Lancet 2*, 391 (1969).

11. LEWIS, L.A., OLMSTED, F., PAGE, I.H., LAWRY, E.Y., MANN, G.V., STARE, F.J., HANIG, M., LAUFFER, M.A., GORDON, T. and MOORE, F.E., "Serum lipid levels in normal persons. Findings of a cooperative study of lipoproteins and atherosclerosis" *Circulation 16*, 227 (1957).

12. SCHILLING, F.J., CHRISTAKIS, G.J., BENNETT, N.J. and COYLE, J.F., "Studies of serum cholesterol in 4244 men and women: an epidemiological and pathogenetic interpretation" *Amer. J. Public Health 54*, 461 (1964).

13. BOYLE Jr., E., MORALES, I.B., NICHAMAN, M.Z., TALBERT, C.R. Jr., and WATKINS, R.S., "Serum beta lipoproteins and cholesterol in adult men. Relationships to smoking, age, and body weight" *Geriatrics 23*, 102 (1968).

14. BOYNS, D.R., CROSSLEY, J.N., ABRAMS, M.E., JARRETT, R.J. and KEEN, H., "Oral glucose tolerance and related factors in a normal population sample. 1. Blood sugar, plasma insulin, glyceride, and cholesterol measurements and the effects of age and sex" *Brit. Med. J. 1*, 595 (1969).

15. ROBERTS, L.B., "The normal ranges, with statistical analysis for seventeen blood constituents" *Clin. Chim. Acta 16*, 69 (1967).

16. KEATING, F.R. Jr., JONES, J.D., ELVEBACK, L.R. and RANDALL, R.V., "The relation of age and sex to distribution of values in healthy adults of serum calcium, inorganic phosphorus, magnesium, alkaline phosphatase, total proteins, albumin, and blood urea" *J. Lab. Clin. Med. 73*, 825 (1969).

17. WERNER, M., TOLLS, R.E., HULTIN, J.V. and MELLECKER, J., "Influence of sex and age on the normal range of eleven serum constituents" *Z. Klin. Chem. u. Klin. Biochem. 8*, 105 (1970).

18. REED, A.H., CANNON, D.C., WINKELMAN, J.W., BHASIN, Y.P., HENRY, R.J. and PILEGGI, V.J., "Estimation of normal ranges from a controlled sample survey. 1. Sex- and age-related influence on the SMA 12/60 screening group of tests" *Clin. Chem. 18*, 57 (1972).

19. EVANS, S.M., WILKES, E. and DALRYMPLE-SMITH, D., "Presymptomatic diagnosis. A study in a country practice" *J. Roy. Coll. Gen. Practit.* *17*, 237 (1969).

20. KERRY, R.J., ORME, J.E. and WILKES, E., "Personality testing: a new diagnostic aid" *Practitioner* *205*, 217 (1970).

21. WARD, A.M. and HIRST, A.D., "The automated ultramicroestimation of total serum protein and protein fractions, with the changes due to renal tract disease in children with spina bifida" *Amer. J. Clin. Path.* *51*, 751 (1969).

22. BELFIELD, A. and GOLDBERG, D.M., "Application of a continuous spectrophotometric assay for 5'nucleotidase activity in normal subjects and patients with liver and bone disease" *Clin. Chem.* *15*, 931 (1969).

23. WORTHY, E., WHITEHEAD, P. and GOLDBERG, D.M., "Advantages and limitations of a simplified colorimetric assay for ATP: creatine phosphotransferase activity in human serum" *Enzymol. Biol. Clin.* *11*, 193 (1970).

24. HIRST, A.D. and GOLDBERG, D.M., "Application of a new ultra-micro automated spectrophotometric determination for serum hydroxybutyrate dehydrogenase activity to the diagnosis of myocardial infarction" *Brit. Heart J.* *32*, 114 (1970).

25. *Documenta Geigy Scientific Tables* (J.R. Geigy S.A., Basle, Switzerland, 5th edition, 1956).

26. O'BRIEN, W.M., BURCH, T.A. and BUNIM, J.J., "Genetics of hyperuricaemia in Blackfeet and Pima Indians" *Ann. Rheum. Dis.* *25*, 117 (1966).

27. BRONTE-STEWART, B., KEYS, A. and BROCK, J.F., "Serum cholesterol, diet and coronary heart disease: an interracial survey in the Cape Peninsula" *Lancet* *2*, 1103 (1955).

28. MILLER, K., RUBENSTEIN, A. and ASTRAND, P.O., "Lipid values in Kalahari Bushmen" *Arch. Int. Med.* *121*, 414 (1968).

29. SIEVERS, M.L., "Serum cholesterol levels in Southwestern American Indians" *J. Chron. Dis.* *21*, 107 (1968).

THE PROSPECTS FOR MACHINE DIAGNOSIS

B. JAMES

The Doctors' House, Claremont Road, Marlow, Bucks., U.K.

SUMMARY

The current method of diagnosis in medicine is based on pattern recognition and is for the most part initiated by the patients complaint. This has serious limitations since it appears that advances in medicine presuppose the discovery of techniques for making diagnoses at a much earlier stage. The prospect of developing an implanted pill which can detect and diagnose a state of disease is discussed together with its method of operation.

In their early stages diseases are easy to cure but difficult to diagnose. In their late stages they are easy to diagnose but difficult to cure. The patient consults the doctor when he thinks that he is ill and depending on his skill the doctor can diagnose and treat his malady. This procedure is bound to fail if the patients nervous systems cannot diagnose a state of illness before it can be adequately dealt with. Routine screening for disease is a possible solution and has been a significant factor in the control of pulmonary tuberculosis. A more effective method might be to implant some instrument into the patient's body to monitor various biological parameters and raise some sort of alarm when their normal range was exceeded. This would in fact pre-empt his nervous system and hopefully bring his condition to the doctors attention at a stage when it could be effectively dealt with. This requires that the pill besides being compatible with the host should have the means to monitor biological parameters and to assess the significance of any abnormality.

In the latter case the current procedure is to regard a variation equal to three standard deviations as being a significant degree of abnormality; however this is probably unnecessarily large.

In its simplest form the pill would monitor a number of bodily parameters and record their values in some form of memory. About once a month a patient would attend a centre where his pill could be interrogated by radio and the results fed into a computer for analysis.

This would have the minor defect that the public at large could be unwilling to attend a centre once a month for however trivial a cause but the more serious objection is that a person can fall ill and die within 24 hours of some serious disease.

It is, therefore, important that the pill should have the capability of diagnosing disease as well as detect signs and symptoms, however to diagnose disease by pattern recognition requires that it should carry a very large amount of information in its memory with which to compare the incoming information and thus diagnose disease. What is required is some concept of disease in the abstract which obviates the need for specific diagnosis and merely ensures that the patient presents himself for further investigation. The human adult body consists of about 10^{16} cells (Fig. 1). When 10^{14} are abnormal due to disease death usually occurs. With many diseases such as cancer or infections the fact that the pathological process is composed of a clone suggest that the disease commences as a single event affecting a single cell. The smallest clinical condition which can be accurately diagnosed is probably a small wart which consists of about 10^6 - 10^7 cells. Therefore on our diagram we can state that the lower limit for the disease is one cell and the upper limit 10^{14} cells; diagnosis usually occurring after 10^{10} cells are affected.

The time scale lying between the 2×10^4 days which constitute a lifetime. Within the limits of 10^7 and 10^{14} some 3×10^4 separate diseases are recognised, but between 1 and 10^7 there may be a several million unrecognised diseases fortunately of no clinical significance. There are about 10^7 genes in the human genotype so there are potentially an even greater number of hereditary diseases alone.

It is probable that the vast majority of diseases are unicellular and that diseases which gain recognition as clinical entities are unusual and unrepresentative of the whole group.

All those diseases which gain clinical recognition do so by means of a rapid reproductive rate invariably requiring logarithmic growth. This gains confirmation by theoretical consideration concerning the nature of health and disease.

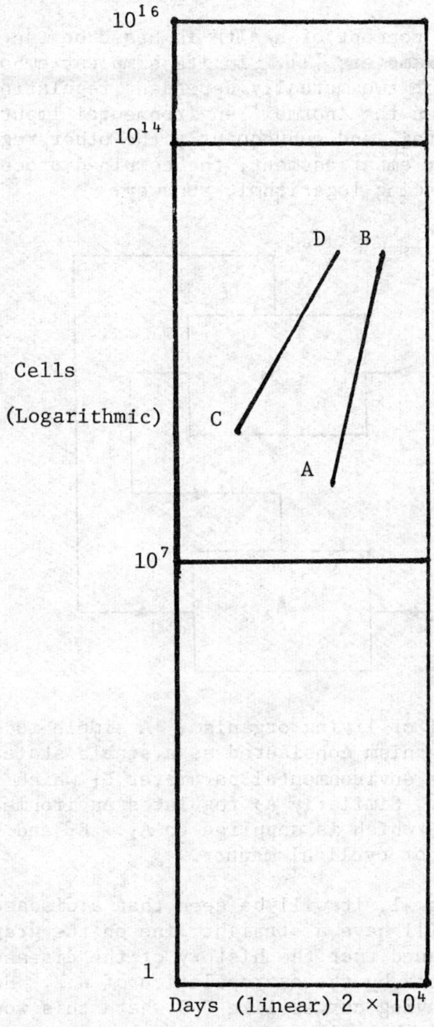

Fig. 1. Disease, death and number of cells. Diseases CD and AB are plotted on a graph of the number of cells in the body 10^{16} and the number of days in a lifetime. The earliest possible diagnosis is when 10^7 cells are affected. Death usually supervenes when about 10^{14} cells are affected.

BIOLOGICAL PARAMETERS

The most useful concept of health is based on the stability of biological parameters [1]. In its simplest embodiment this takes the form of two mutually dependant regulating mechanisms (Fig. 2). When the 'normal' environmental imput to one is exceeded it will fail and subsequently the other regulating mechanism will suffer embarrassment, the combined process being unstable and experiencing logarithmic runaway.

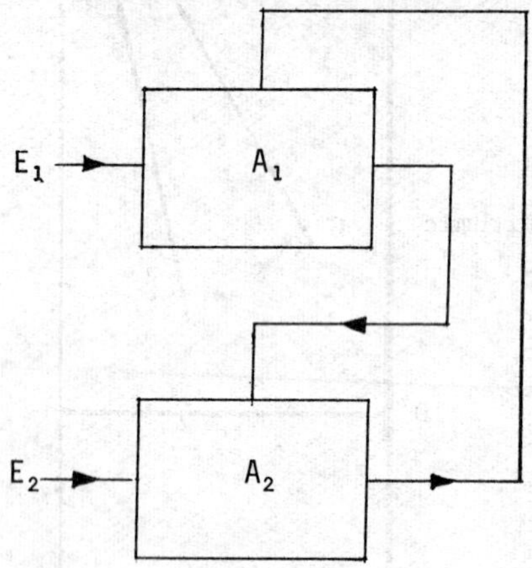

Fig. 2. Simple model of living organism. A simple model of a living organism considered as a stable state device. A_1 regulates environmental parameter E_1 which is supplied to A_2. Similarly A_2 regulates environmental parameter E_2 which is supplied to A_1. E_1 and E_2 vary in a random or cyclical manner.

Referring to Fig. 1, it will be seen that a disease having logarithmic growth will have a straight line on the graph e.g. A B. It might be argued that the history of the disease may be adequately described by the extrapolation of A B. However there are diseases having curves like C D where this would be absurd, furthermore in Malaria for example, we have a disease which has an early intrahepatic stage which is disimilar to the later stages. In the experimental treatment of certain neoplasms, cure by stimulation of the immunity mechanism is only possible when 1,000 or less cells are injected and the diseases currently most effectively treated such as smallpox and diptheria are dealt with while they are at this order of magnitude. Therefore, it seems important to attemp to diagnose diseases at a much earlier stage than is currently contemplated. Logically we can draw a flow chart (Fig. 3) of an abstract disease in which the disease is measured by counting the number of cells primarily affected (which we can call the characteristic parameter). This in turn will produce a number of secondary effects which we can call derived parameters, the whole flow chart having a tree like structure having the characteristic parameter as the trunk and the derived parameters as branches.

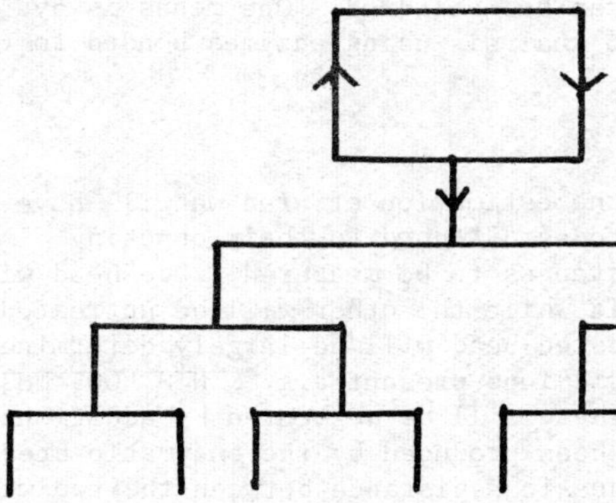

Derived parameters

Fig. 3. Flow chart of a disease. The flow chart of a disease may be considered as a characteristic parameter generated by a process of positive feedback which in turn gives use to derived parameters (signs and symptoms).

In practical terms the diagnosis of disease involves a process of pattern recognition allied with some logical deduction whereby the characteristic parameter which is usually inaccessible is deduced from the derived parameters which are not.

In practice derived parameters prefer to depart from the normal in one direction. Thus the blood pressure rises, the temperature rises and the blood urea rises. If each parameter is monitored separately it will tend to fluctuate in a random manner. If the threshold for sounding an alarm is set too low it will be set off unnecessarily. If it is set too high it will be too late. If a large number of derived parameters are weighted by coefficients then lumped together by addition or some similar operation the random signals will tend to cancel out but the diagnostic signals will tend to combine. This can best be accomplished if each parameter is set to be zero in health and the signals from each sensor are squared added and the square root of the sum is estimated. In the case of disease this is most likely to increase logarithmically with time, so the procedure will be to pass the signal through some sort of circuit which reacts only to a signal which changes logarithmically with time. This might be accomplished using a transistor to convert the signal to log signals and an RC circuit to a comparator which reacts to a linear variation greater than a certain rate. This leaves the more important consideration as to how more parameters can be monitored. One means is by differential conductimetric analysis using enzymes bonded to resin gels.

EXAMPLE

Taking as an example the estimation of urea we will have two resin beads with electrodes attached to their opposing faces to enable their resistances to be measured. One bead will have urease bonded within it while the other will be untreated. The resistance of the untreated bead will be largely determined by the amount of electrolytic ions present e.g. $K^+N^+H^+HCO_3^-$ NH_3^- etc. In the treated bead these will be augmented by additional ions H^+HCO_3 NH_3 which have been produced by the enzymatic breakdown of urea. The difference in resistance between the two will be a measure of the amount of urea present. By suitable use of ingenuity a considerable number of biochemical parameters may be monitored using this basic procedure.

Conductimetric analysis has the advantage that the conductivity is proportional to concentration squared so that the squaring of the signal before addition becomes unnecessary.

It should be pointed out that the hydrogen ion being about thirty times more mobile than any other ion is the main ion responsible for any increase in conductivity. Fortunately under most conditions the bodily pattern is remarkably constant so it is unlikely to be a disturbing factor. The detection of 10^7 cells in 10^{16} cells by metabolic abnormality supposes the ability to detect a variation of one part is 10^9 in a biological parameter. Even though differential amplification of a signal by this amount is practicable; in practice few bodily biochemical parameters can be estimated with an accuracy of 1 part in 10^2. Nevertheless if 10^{10} abnormal cells can be detected it would in most cases be a considerable advance on current diagnostic practice particularly in the case of the most inaccessible diseases. However attractive in theory the widespread application of implanted diagnostic devices does not appear to be likely to occur in the near future for the healthy population, however for patients at special risk there may be an almost immediate application.

The dialysis patient might well have an implanted urea electrode along the lines described above. Three terminals would project from his skin in a suitable position and by connecting them to a simple measuring instrument he could estimate his blood urea and therefore decide when dialysis was required. Dialysis being an expensive procedure if by this means its frequency can be reduced only marginally the indwelling urea electrode can rapidly justify its existence. In the same way a glucose electrode or ketone electrode could be valuable to an unstable diabetic. There is little limitation to the smallness of the electrodes except that when very small one might become covered by a white corpuscle. A complex array of electrodes mounted on a cannula could be inserted into the patients vein during anaesthesia or intensive care in order to monitor numerous parameters. In effect it would be equivalent to taking the clinical pathological laboratory and inserting it into the patient's vein. The technology of making small planar electrodes is well advanced, they would merely require to be coated with a suitable gel and 'doped' with the required enzyme. This principle is currently under active investigation and it is hoped that practical results will be shown in the near future.

REFERENCES

1. D.B. JAMES, "Computers and medicine" *Biokybernetik III*, 88-91 (1971).

OPTIMUM HOSPITAL LAYOUT USING TOPAZ

D.S. WHITE

Hardwicke Associates, Richmond, Virginia, U.S.A.

J.W. DICKEY

Urban and Regional Planning Program, Virginia Polytechnic Institute and State University, Blacksburg, Virginia 24061, U.S.A.

SUMMARY

One important aspect of hospital design concerns travel within the facility. Nurses, doctors, and other medical personnel often are forced to make longer trips than are really needed to serve patients. In this study, an attempt is made to determine the manner in which activities in hospitals of a given size should be arranged so as to minimize travel by health personnel. The problem is viewed in a type of quadratic assignment format, which is solved using a fairly efficient iterative technique known as TOPAZ (Technique for the Optimum Placement of Activities in Zones). Results indicate that single level layouts of hospitals are preferable to multilevel and that vertical transportation modes (e.g., elevators) should be separated, not grouped together in a core area.

INTRODUCTION TO THE TECHNIQUE

The optimal assignment of activities to locations is a combinatorial problem that is difficult to solve efficiently. For example, Dickey and Hopkins note that for a 15 activity and 15 location problem in which each location can contain one and only one activity, there exist 10^{12} feasible solutions. A computer which can evaluate 10^5 arrangements per second would take over four years to try all the possible solutions [1].

Most optimum producing procedures to date are efficient only for very small problems. For the present study, a computerized layout technique known as TOPAZ has been employed. As utilized in this study, TOPAZ not only arranges various hospital activities in three dimensional space through the iterative use of linear approximations to the quadratic assignment problem but also locates elevators and stairways to achieve "optimum" operational efficiency.

INTRODUCTION TO THE PROBLEM

Several recent computer applications have been made with the objective of reducing the total distance that medical staff in a hospital must travel during a typical day [3], thereby decreasing the cost of operation. These applications have generally relied upon two major assumptions: (1) that hospitals design can can be studied as a two dimensional space allocation problem, and (2) that "optimum" architectural designs are achieved through a balancing of rather exacting functional criteria. Yet neither of these assumptions is highly relevant to hospital design. Consequently, the layouts thus produced cannot be considered totally reliable.

With the technique proposed here, however, we can explore optimum layout solutions without reliance upon either assumption. Optimum three dimensional layouts can be determined on the basis of transit costs or, on a more complex level, through a set of independently weighted activity relationships. TOPAZ then can be employed to search automatically for an optimum solution or simply to evaluate designer-suggested solutions.

MODEL STRUCTURE

The structure of an existing or proposed hospital can be categorized in two ways: areal zones and functional activities. The zones represent distinguishable divisions of the total floor area. The activities represent distinguishable divisions of human action. The zones in this conceptualization serve to physically house the activities. The activities, in turn, serve to describe the use to which particular zones are put.

Within an existing hospital the average number of trips made by hospital employees between any pair of activities within a specified time period can be determined with relative ease. These measurements then can be used to estimate, within certain definable ranges, the expected number of trips between activity pairs in new facilities [4]. Thus, if we know certain basic operating policies for a proposed health facility, a trip frequency matrix for inter-activity travel can be established.

Significantly, the number of trips between two activities in hospitals generally is not a function of the distance between them. With the exception of trips between patient rooms, the expected travel between any two activities can be considered a constant. For example, studies by Freeman indicate that the degree of sickness of the patient and not his room location determine the number of inter-activity trips. Similar relationships exist between most other activity pairs [5].

Since the number of trips between each pair of activities can safely be assumed constant, it then is possible to develop a trip production coefficient, $p_{j\ell}$, between activity j and ℓ. This would be measured in trips per year per square feet of activity j per square feet of activity ℓ. There also would be an associated cost for travel, which would depend both on the travel time, t_{ik} (in secs/trip), between a pair of zones (i and k) where certain activities are located and the value, $d_{j\ell}$ (in dollars/second), of time spent in going between activities j and ℓ. Then, if travel is assumed to follow the rectangular distance between centroids of fixed-in-place zones, a minimum yearly travel cost allocation of activities to zones could be developed. The objective for this allocation would be:

$$\min Z = \sum_{i=1}^{m} \sum_{k=1}^{m} \sum_{j=1}^{n} \sum_{\ell=1}^{n} d_{j\ell} t_{ik} p_{j\ell} x_{ij} x_{k\ell}, \tag{1}$$

where x_{ij} is the square feet of activity j allocated to zone i (or of activity ℓ to zone k), m is the number of zones, and n is the number of activities.

Of course, there would have to be constraints. All of the area in each zone would have to be utilized (that is, if the total area of activities equals the total area of all zones). Thus:

$$\sum_{j=1}^{n} x_{ij} = a_i, \text{ (all i)} \tag{2}$$

where a_i is the area available in zone i (ft.^{2}). Then too, all activities must be allocated, which gives:

$$\sum_{i=1}^{m} x_{ij} = b_j, \text{ (all j)} \tag{3}$$

where b_j is the amount of activity j to be allocated (ft.^{2}). Also,

$$x_{ij} \geq 0, \text{ (all i, j)}. \quad (4)$$

In combining the objective in Eqn. (1) with the constraints in Eqns. (2) to (4), a quadratic assignment problem similar to those discussed by Nugent, Vollman, and Rum [6] is obtained. TOPAZ then can be employed to determine the amounts of the different activities to allocate to the various zones to minimize travel costs. The linearized, iterative solution procedure utilized in TOPAZ is discussed elsewhere [1,2,7].

THREE DIMENSIONAL DESIGN

To this point, inter-zonal travel time has been computed according to the rectangular distance between zonal centroids. However, circulation which necessitates vertical movement usually does not conform to the standard measure of three dimensional rectangular distance. If, for example, vertical movement were assumed to be provided by elevators, all trips from zone i to zone k, where i and k are on different levels, would normally go through the zone of location of elevator, where s is the elevator which provides the shortest distance between i and k. Travel time from i and k then would equal the sum of the travel time from i to s on the level of i, the time within s, and the travel time from s on the level of k to k.

Vertical circulation within the hospital is generally provided by both stairways and elevators. These vertical transit modes can be considered as activities within the facility, and the number of trips they "generate" when allocated to a specific zone will not be a function of the number of square feet assigned to the zone but of the number of trips for which the mode provides the shortest distance between other zones. A new, three dimensional, assignment problem thus needs to be developed in this case.

Let w_i equal the vertical coordinate of zone i and let all interpersonal trips be categorized into one of the following two types:

1. Trips originating and ending on the same floor (excluding those to and from vertical transit modes); and

2. Trips originating and ending on different floors.

Now, if each vertical mode on each floor is designated as an "activity", and if these v activities are assigned the first v numbers on the list of all activities, then the objective function for the three dimensional design problem can be stated as:

$$\text{Min } z = \sum_{i=1}^{m} \sum_{k=1}^{m} \sum_{j=v+1}^{n} \sum_{\ell=v+1}^{n} d_{j\ell} t_{ik} p_{j\ell} x_{ij} x_{k\ell} + \qquad (\text{for } w_i = w_k)$$

$$\sum_{i=1}^{m} \sum_{k=1}^{m} \sum_{j=v+1}^{n} \sum_{\ell=v+1}^{n} d_{j\ell} t'_{ij} p_{j\ell} x_{ij} x_{k\ell} \qquad (\text{for } w_i \neq w_k) \tag{5}$$

subject to

$$\sum_{j=1}^{n} x_{ij} = a_i \qquad (\text{all } i) \tag{6}$$

$$\sum_{i=1}^{m} x_{ij} = b_j \qquad (\text{all } j) \tag{7}$$

$$x_{ij} \geq 0. \qquad (\text{all } i, j). \tag{8}$$

In Eq. 5

$$t'_{ij} = \min_{s} \quad (t_{is} + t_{sk} + t''_s + \sum_{r=w_i}^{w_k-1} t'''_{rs}), \tag{9}$$

where:

t'_{ik} = minimum vertical and horizontal travel time between zones i and k (secs.),

t_{is} = travel time (on floor of i) from zone i to vertical mode s (secs.),

t_{sk} = travel time (on floor of k) from s to zone k (secs.),

t''_s = expected vertical transit mode s waiting time (secs.), and

t'''_{rs} = expected vertical transit mode s travel time between floors r and r+1 (secs.).

The optimization strategy using TOPAZ for the three dimensional model is similar to that described for the quadratic assignment problem in Eqns. (1) to (4).

A MULTI-LEVEL HOSPITAL ANALYSIS

Hospitals have traditionally been designed with vertical towers providing the major circulation routes. The main form determinant with this approach has been the "service core" around which units of various shapes have been vertically stacked. Adjacent to the nursing wing there has usually been a "service wing" in which ancillary departments also have been stacked. To go from one activity to another in such a scheme quite often requires use of an elevator. Such travel would usually necessitate a short waiting time at the floor level of trip origin and a mode service time between each floor of from 15 to 20 seconds. These times translate into substantial increases in the travel cost between activities separated vertically. Thus, although the design itself is physically more compact, its "service core" actual operation often results in transit costs equivalent to a much larger horizontally planned area.

When programmed to arrange a typical set of activities into a three dimensional space to minimize travel costs, TOPAZ consistently restricted development to one level rather than vertically about an elevator core. This result seemed to occur primarily because of the expected elevator waiting time on each floor of 25 seconds and the expected service time of 20 seconds between each floor.

When the same activities were initially arranged in a typical broad-based but vertical nursing "tower", TOPAZ immediately removed all activities from upper levels and again arranged the entire facility on one level in a plan quite similar in cost to the "optimum" design described previously. However, the cost of operation calculated for the initial designer-imposed, three-level solution was more than 20 percent over that for the same activities located "randomly" on one level. For a vertical design to be equivalent to a horizontal one, the expected waiting time at each floor level had to be reduced to less than ten seconds and the service time to less than five.

In another exercise, the same activities were allocated to a more restricted space than that previously discussed.

When multiple elevator shafts were provided, TOPAZ tended to spread them apart rather than group them in some central location. This decentralization of elevators resulted in only slight reductions in total transit cost, however, Yet the vertical plan was still not competitive with the horizontal plan for the prescribed activities. In fact, the cost of operation for the multi-shafted vertical design (three levels) was some 40 percent higher than the "optimal" one-level design.

CLOSING COMMENTS

The study reported here has several limitations, but three appear to be of significance:

(1) The results are highly contingent upon reliable trip production coefficients, travel time measures, and time values.

(2) Reduced travel needs for health personnel may not necessarily be passed on to the patients, whose well-being should be central to the study.

(3) Costs for construction of facilities and for purchase of land are not included.

The latter limitation is particularly important since totally horizontal hospital layouts probably would require more land and greater capital expenditures for construction.

REFERENCES

1. J.W. DICKEY and J.W. HOPKINS, "Campus building arrangement using TOPAZ" *Transportation Research 6*, 1 (March, 1972).

2. J.F. BROTCHIE, A.R. TOAKLEY and R. SHARPE, "On an urban planning model" In: *Analysis of Urban Development*, Proceedings of the Tewksbury Symposium (Melbourne University, Melbourne, July, 1970).

3. *Costs of Health Care Facilities*, Report to a Conference of the National Academy of Engineering (Washington, D.C., 1968).

4. G.L. DELON and H.E. SMALLEY, *Quantitative Methods for Evaluating Hospital Design*, Final Report, Research Grant No. HM00529 (United States Public Health Service, Washington, D.C., April, 1970).

5. T. AU, E.W. PARTI, and A.K.C. WONG, *Hospital System Design Simulation*, Final Report, Research Grant No. HS00073 (United States Public Health Service, Washington, D.C., August, 1970).

6. C.E. NUGENT, T.E. VOLLMANN, and J. RUML, "An experimental comparison of techniques for the assignment of facilities to locations" *Operations Research 16*, 1 (Jan. - Feb., 1968).

7. J.W. DICKEY, P.A. LEONE and A.R. SCHWARTE, "Use of TOPAZ for generating alternate land use schemes" *Highway Research Record*, 422 (1973).

NEURAL CONTROL OF FOOD INTAKE: A SYSTEMS APPROACH

G.M. BARNWELL

Southwest Research Institute, San Antonio, Texas 78284, U.S.A.

SUMMARY

A mathematical model of the neural control of food intake in vertebrates is developed. The neural control system detects metabolic deficits, initiates hunger motivation, and controls all subsequent steps until a satiety state is attained; it includes contributions of brain regions affecting food intake. A significant feature is the inclusion of several positive feedback loops which are controlled by negative feedback loops. The model includes most of the factors known to affect food intake. Both long- and short-term regulation of food intake and body weight are accounted for. The model can simulate food intake for a variety of natural conditions and experimentally produced alterations.

INTRODUCTION

> To eat or not to eat — that is the question. Whether 'tis nobler in the mind to suffer the admonitions and reprimands of one's will power, or to take up food against the pangs of hunger, and by eating end them.

The above distortion of a familiar quote illustrates only one aspect of the complex decision-making processes controlling food intake — that when food is abundant, the decision is whether to eat or not to eat, and when to stop. The tendency to overeat in the midst of plenty underscores the positive feedback aspects of food intake.

In this presentation, I hope to convey some idea of the extreme complexity of the food intake control subsystems and of the great value of the systems theoretic approach in attacking the problem, to discuss the role of positive feedbacks in food intake, and to present a mathematical model of the neural control of food intake.

Some of the many factors which have been implicated as contributing to control of food intake are gastric contractions, gastric distension, hunger hormones, temperature, blood glucose, caloric intake, intestinal absorption, circulating metabolites, and oropharyngeal stimuli. Several review articles [1-14] discuss evidence for the various factors as controlling agents and illustrate the complexity of the food intake system.

According to the dual-center theory of Anand and Brobeck [1] hunger sensations and food intake are initiated by activity of neurons in the lateral hypothalamic area (LH), termed the "feeding center", while the satiety mechanism is provided by activity of neurons in the ventromedial hypothalamic nucleus (VMH), termed the "satiety center". The satiety center terminates food intake by inhibition of the feeding center.

The dual-center theory was the first attempt at unification of diverse experimental observations. However, extra-hypothalamic areas were subsequently shown to be involved in food intake [10, 15, 16]. Further, aside from postulating that the single factors are integrated by the "feeding" and "satiety"centers and that glucose and other factors act upon neurons in these key hypothalamic regions, no systematic attempts to propose neural integrative mechanisms have been made. Thus, there is a need for a multiple factor neural integrative theory of the control of food intake. Such a theory can be formulated in terms of systems theory.

LEVELS OF COMPLEXITY IN COMPARTMENTAL MODELS AND BIOLOGICAL FEEDING SYSTEMS

When I first began my efforts to construct systems theoretic models of the neural control of food intake, I immediately focused on the nervous system, and in particular, on the interrelations among several neural subsystems involved in food intake control. Eventually, I realized that I was proceeding in the wrong direction and changed course. The new approach is based on parallels between the levels of complexity of compartmental models and of animal feeding systems.

The most general case is a nonlinear, time-varying coefficient compartmental model in which the coefficients are functions of variables whose levels are controlled by interacting feedback subsystems in an integrated manner, and in which environmental temperature is not an overall rate-limiting factor. Biologically, this type of model describes mammalian species. Special cases of the model apply to inframammalian species.

ROLE OF POSITIVE FEEDBACKS

Since eating is of primary importance for the survival of the individual, it seems that the neural circuitry would be designed by natural selection to insure the persistence of food-seeking and food-ingesting behaviors. Considerable evidence has accumulated in support of some type of positive feedback mechanism involving the lateral hypothalamic area (LH), medial forebrain bundle (MFB), reticular activating system (RAS), limbic system (LS), and possibly other areas.

Electrical or chemical stimulation at many different loci in the MFB, LS, or RAS has been found to evoke eating, drinking and associated behaviors [17-22]. The bulk of these studies involving lesions or electrical or chemical stimulation of extrahypothalamic regions are concerned with anatomical sites within the MFB, LS, and RAS, all of which project into or away from the LH and VMH [23]. If these various fiber systems do indeed form multiloop reciprocating circuits as Morgane [23] suggests, such positive feedback loops could increase the probability of recurrence of whatever behavior initially activated them.

Positive Feedback Loops and Metabolic Monitoring

Neural circuits containing chemosensitive neurons organized into positive feedback loops could initiate and maintain internal neural activity increases which correlate with food deprivation, i.e., such loops could comprise a biological basis for "hunger", "motivation", or "drive". Some mechanisms are suggested below.

Suppose that a localized population of neurons is more sensitive to concentration changes of some nutrient than surrounding neurons, and firing rates of these neurons are increased by decreased nutrient availability. Such a system could function as a detector or monitor for the nutrient. The efficiency of such a system could be increased by inserting it into a positive feedback neural circuit. Any change in concentration would produce signals which would be amplified by the positive feedback loops, allowing more rapid and sensitive detection.

Another possible mechanism could consist of a positive feedback neural circuit in which all the component neurons were more sensitive to decreased availability of a certain chemical than surrounding neurons.

Finally, one could even assume that all CNS neurons are identical in their sensitivity to decreased availability of some nutrient. By virtue of their connective pattern, any subset of neurons forming a positive feedback loop would be more sensitive to the nutrient availability and could, therefore, serve as a detecting or monitoring system.

Frequency Threshold Properties

A second property of a positive feedback neural circuit is that it possesses frequency threshold properties. Activity in the network will decay, persist, or increase for different conditions. The threshold for maintained activity is inherent in the structure of the network (i.e., convergence, divergence, resting membrane potentials, neuronal time constants, time delays between neurons) and the nature of the input. Thus, some input frequencies will produce activity in the network which decays with time, while other frequencies could evoke sustained activity. MacGregor [24] has presented a mathematical model, with calculated activity patterns produced by various input frequencies in a network of this type.

Theory of Food Intake Control

Now, integrating the ideas of chemical effects on neuronal membrane potentials and of frequency thresholds in neural nets, it is possible to suggest a detailed neurophysiological decision-making mechanism for food intake control. The lateral hypothalamus, septal area, limbic midbrain, and several other regions involved in initiation of food intake are links in parallel positive feedback neural circuits and are centers of convergence for a variety of internal and external sensory inputs. Further, the neurons in one or more of these neural centers are sensitive to certain nutrients or circulating metabolites. A decreased availability of a particular nutrient (or perhaps an increased concentration of some metabolite) alters the membrane potentials of the neurons in one of these centers such that the average excitability of each neuron is increased. The increased excitability increases the probability of neurons in this center firing in response or particular impulse patterns produced by food-associated stimuli. As the nutrient concentration drops still lower, the activity of one or more regions of the loop is gradually raised so that the loop becomes increasingly likely to propagate activity in response to sensory inputs signalling food. Finally, at least one positive feedback loop is activated and sustained activity of the loop initiates food-seeking and food ingestion. The taste of food activates one or more additional positive feedback loops which are already receiving facilitating inputs from the first active loops. Each bite of food reactivates these loops, so that the events leading to the ingestion tend to be repeated.

During the meal, increases in blood glucose and body temperature, and finally stomach distension begin to simultaneously decrease the excitability of positive feedback loop neurons and increase the excitability of ventromedial hypothalamic neurons. The VMH neurons inhibit LH neurons, some reticular system neurons, and possibly others in the positive feedback loops, and the increasing inhibition prevents propagation of the cyclic neural activity through the inhibited regions. A complete cut off eventually results and a state of satiety is attained.

The extreme importance of the LH is due to its strategic location at the intersection of these positive feedback loops. Thus, activation of the LH is more likely to result in propagated activity around one of the loops than activation of any other region. Similarly, inhibition of the LH by the VMH is very effective since activity of all loops is inhibited.

MATHEMATICAL MODEL

A preliminary mathematical model of the neural control of food intake in vertebrates has been developed as a first step in modeling approach. The present model deals only with glucose and does not yet attempt to incorporate protein, fat, vitamins, or other dietary factors. Several other simplifications have been made with respect to the equations.

Compartmental Model of Digestive Tract

Fig. 1 shows a compartmental model of the main portions of the digestive tract. Bile from the gall bladder and pancreatic enzymes are not included since the model excludes fat and protein. The pancreatic hormones, glucagon and insulin are included in the model, although they are not represented in Fig. 1. Each Q_i in Fig. 1 represents the amount of glucose in compartment i, and each k_{ij} is a variable rate parameter controlling the flow rate of glucose into compartment i from compartment j. Parameters a_{08}, b_{08}, c_{08}, and d_{08} are the fractions of glucose excreted or utilized by the corresponding tissues. Q_0 denotes the amount of food available.

Equations (1) through (10) describe the compartmental subsystem in terms of the components shown in Fig. 1.

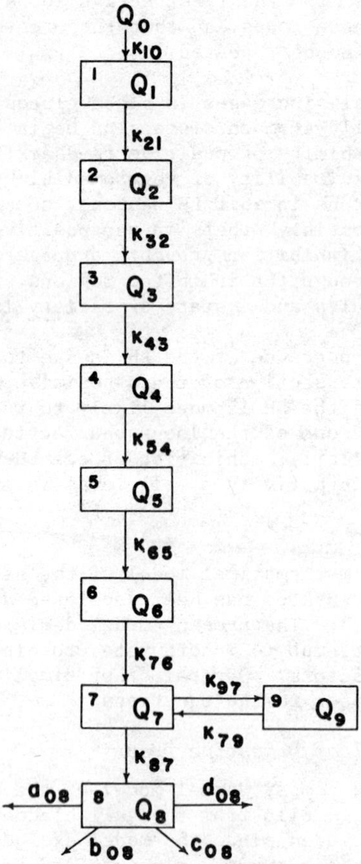

Fig. 1. Compartmental model of main portions of digestive tract. Compartments correspond to mouth (1), orophoryrgeal region (2), stomach (3), duodenum (4), lower small intestine (5), hepatic portal system (6), liver (7), blood circulation (8), and liver glycogen stores (9). Coefficients a_{08}, b_{08}, c_{08}, and d_{08} correspond respectively to execretion, CNS utilization, muscle utilization, and other tissue utilization of glucose.

$$\frac{dQ_0}{dt} = -k_{10}Q_0 \tag{1}$$

$$\frac{dQ_1}{dt} = k_{10}Q_0 - k_{21}Q_1 \tag{2}$$

$$\frac{dQ_2}{dt} = k_{21}Q_1 - k_{32}Q_2 \tag{3}$$

$$\frac{dQ_3}{dt} = k_{32}Q_2 - k_{43}Q_3 \tag{4}$$

$$\frac{dQ_4}{dt} = k_{43}Q_3 - k_{54}Q_4 \tag{5}$$

$$\frac{dQ_5}{dt} = k_{54}Q_4 - k_{65}Q_5 \tag{6}$$

$$\frac{dQ_6}{dt} = k_{65}Q_5 - k_{76}Q_6 \tag{7}$$

$$\frac{dQ_7}{dt} = k_{76}Q_6 + k_{79}Q_9 - (k_{87} + k_{97})Q_7 \tag{8}$$

$$\frac{dQ_8}{dt} = k_{87}Q_7 - (a_{08} + b_{08} + c_{08} + d_{08})Q_8 \tag{9}$$

$$\frac{dQ_9}{dt} = k_{97}Q_7 - k_{79}Q_9 \tag{10}$$

Each of the rate parameters in equations (1) through (10) may be a function of one or more variables, defined in other equations. For example, in equation (11),

$$k_{10} = m_{10}f_{LMC}, \tag{11}$$

m_{10} is a proportionality constant, and f_{LMC} is the output function of the lower motor center described in the CNS subsystem.

Thus, when $k_{10} = 0$, no food intake is occurring; food intake is initiated by outputs from the lower motor centers controlling feeding reflexes, and in this case k_{10} has a positive value.

Further equations define the other variable rate parameters in terms of controlling variables. Space limitations do not permit the inclusion of these equations. Also omitted is an eight-compartment temperature subsystem, which provides inputs to the food intake control subsystem.

Fig. 2 is a schematic diagram of the CNS subsystem for food intake control. Input lines terminating as arrows denote excitatory effects; those terminating as small circles denote inhibitory effects. The output functions represented in Fig. 2 are defined in equations, and the set of equations defining the complete model interrelates the CNS food intake control subsystem, the temperature subsystem, the blood glucose subsystem, and the digestive tract. Body weight and activity are also included in the model. The inclusion of positive feedback loops and impulse propagation time delays between neural centers is an important feature of the model.

The model agrees with experimental evidence and hypotheses for neural positive feedback loops [19, 23, 25], with Morgane's [26] suggestion concerning separate motivational and feeding circuits traversing the LH, and with Hoebel's [25] more psychologically-oriented theory of food intake control. The model incorporates many variables known to affect food intake and is compatible with a wide variety of experimental evidence.

Future goals include computer simulations based on the preliminary model, then application of the model to a particular species for behavioral predictions. Eventually, fat, protein, vitamins, and other dietary factors can be incorporated. And of course, the ultimate modeling goal is a complete adaptive system - given a set of initial conditions and food-associated stimuli, the system would decide whether to eat or not to eat and implement the decision.

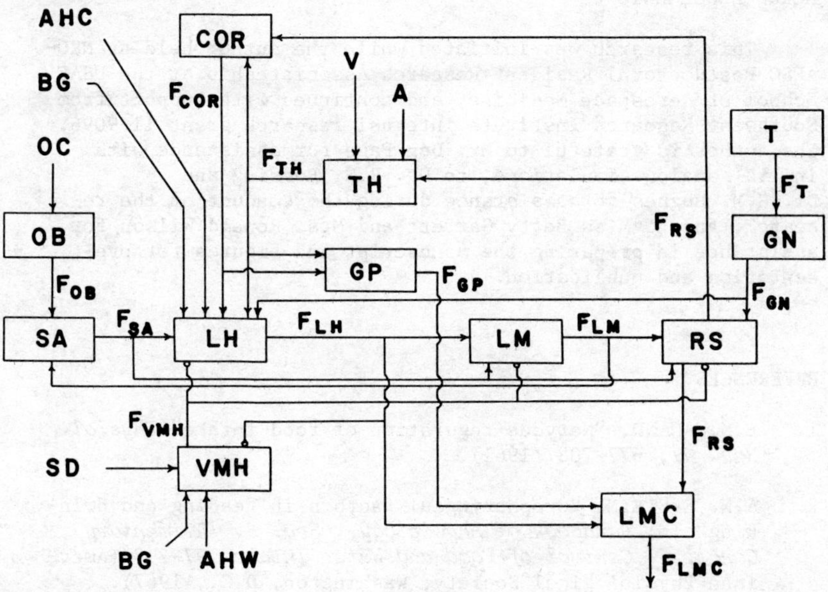

Fig. 2. CNS food intake control system. Inputs are from anterior hypothalamic temperature sensitive neurons for detecting warmer (AHW) or cooler (AHC), blood glucose level (BG), odorant concentration (OC), visual stimuli (V), auditory stimuli (A), stomach distension (SD). Neural regions shown are olfactory bulb (OB), septal area (SA), cortex (COR), lateral hypothalamic area (LH), ventromedial nucleus (VMH), thalamus (TH), globus pallidus (GP), limbic midbrain area (LM), taste receptors (T), gustatory nucleus (GN), reticular system (RS), lower motor centers (LMC).

ACKNOWLEDGEMENTS

This research was initiated while the author held an NRC-AFSC Postdoctoral Resident Research Associateship at the USAF School of Aerospace Medicine, and continued with support from Southwest Research Institute internal research grant 11-9096. The author is grateful to Mr. Don Page for assistance with initial analog simulations, to Dr. R.G. Rossing and Dr. H.M. Hughes for assistance during the conduct of the research, and to Miss Betty Garrett and Mrs. Ronald Wilson for assistance in preparing the manuscript and figures for presentation and publication.

REFERENCES

1. B.K. ANAND, "Nervous regulation of food intake" *Physiol. Rev. 41,* 677-708 (1961).

2. A.N. EPSTEIN, "Oropharyngeal factors in feeding and drinking" In: *Handbook of Physiology. Sec. 6. Alimentary Canal. I. Control of Food and Water Intake* 197-218 (American Physiological Society, Washington, D.C., 1967).

3. C.L. HAMILTON, "Food and Temperature" In: *Handbook of Physiology. Sec. 6. Alimentary Canal. I. Control of Food and Water Intake* 303-317 (American Physiological Society, Washington, D.C., 1967).

4. A.E. HARPER, "Effects of dietary protein content and amino acid pattern on food intake and preference" In: *Handbook of Physiology. Sec. 6. Alimentary Canal I. Control of Food and Water Intake* 399-410 (American Physiological Society, Washington, D.C. 1967).

5. B.G. HOEBEL, "Feeding: neural control of intake" *Ann. Rev. Physiol. 33,* 533-568 (1971).

6. H.D. JANOWITZ, "Role of the gastrointestinal tract in regulation of food intake" In: *Handbook of Physiology. Sec. 6. Alimentary Canal I. Control of Food and Water Intake,* 219-224 (American Physiological Society, Washington, D.C., 1967).

7. G.C. KENNEDY, "The hypothalamic control of food intake in rats" *Proc. roy. Soc. B 137*, 535-549 (1950).

8. J. MAYER, and D.W. THOMAS, "Regulation of food intake and obesity" *Science 156*, 328-337 (1967).

9. N.E. MILLER, "Experiments on motivation" *Science 126*, 1271-1278, (1957).

10. P.J. MORGANE and H.L. JACOBS, "Hunger and satiety" In: *World Review of Nutrition and Dietetics*, G.H. BOURNE (ed.) *10*, 100-213 (1969).

11. K.N. SHARMA, "Receptor mechanisms in the alimentary tract: their excitation and functions" In: *Handbook of Physiology. Sec. 6. Alimentary Canal I. Control of Food and Water Intake*, 225-237 (American Physiological Society, Washington, D.C., 1967).

12 A. SOULAIRAC, "Control of carbohydrate intake" In: *Handbook of Physiology. Sec. 6. Alimentary Canal I. Control of Food and Water Intake*, 387-398 (American Physiological Society, Washington, D.C. 1967).

13. P. TEITELBAUM, "Motivation and control of food intake" In: *Handbook of Physiology. Sec. 6. Alimentary Canal I. Control of Food and Water Intake*, 319-335 (American Physiological Society, Washington, D.C. 1967).

14. P. TEITELBAUM, "The encephalization of hunger" *Prog. in Physiol. Psychol. 4*, 319-350 (1971).

15. S.P. GROSSMAN, "Hypothalamic and limbic influences on food intake" *Fed. Proc. 27*, 1349-1360 (1968).

16. S.P. GROSSMAN, "A Neuropharmacological analysis of hypothalamic and extrahypothalamic mechanisms concerned with the regulation of food and water intake" *Ann. N.Y. Acad. Sci. 157*, 902-917 (1969).

17. A.E. FISHER, "The role of limbic structures in the central regulation of feeding and drinking behavior" *Ann. N.Y. Acad. Sci., 157*, 894-901 (1969).

18. B.W. ROBINSON, "Forebrain alimentary responses: some organizational principles" In: *Thirst*, M.J. WAYNER (ed.), 411-427 (The MacMillan Company, New York, 1964).

19. A.E. FISHER, "Chemical stimulation of the brain" *Scientific American 210* (6), 60-68 (June, 1964).

20. A.E. FISHER, and J.N. COURY, "Chemical tracing of neural pathways mediating the thirst drive" In: *Thirst*, M.J. WAYNER (ed.) 515-531 (The MacMillan Company, New York, 1964).

21. S.P. GROSSMAN, "Some neurochemical aspects of the central regulation of thirst" In: *Thirst*, M.J. WAYNER (ed.) 487-514 (The MacMillan Company, New York, 1964).

22. W. WYRWICKA and R.W. DOTY, "Feeding induced in cats by electrical stimulation of the brain stem" *Exp. Brain. Res. 1*, 152-160 (1966).

23. P.J. MORGANE, "The function of the limbic and rhinic forebrain - limbic midbrain systems and reticular formation in the regulation of food and water intake" *Ann. N.Y. Acad. Sci. 157*, 806-848 (1969).

24. F.J. MACGREGOR, "Intrinsic oscillations in neural networks: A linear model for the nth order loop" *Mathematical Biosciences 11*, 317-336, (1971).

25. B.G. HOEBEL, "Feeding and self-stimulation" *Ann. N.Y. Acad. Sci. 157*, 758-778 (1969).

26. P.J. MORGANE, "Distinct 'feeding' and 'hunger motivating' systems in the lateral hypothalamus of the rat" *Science 133*, 887-888 (1961).

DYNAMIC PROPERTIES OF NERVOUS NETS IN THE VISUAL SYSTEM

W.v. SEELEN

Batelle-Institut E.V., Frankfurt/M., Am Römerhof 35, Germany (FDR)

SUMMARY

Both moving and stationary images of our environment are transformed by the movement of our eyes into dynamic stimuli. It is, therefore, necessary to consider the dynamic properties of the information-processing nervous nets also in pattern recognition. The homogeneous nervous nets of the retina and the geniculate body are interpreted in this paper as combined linear space-time filters and quantitatively described on the basis of methods of Systems Theory. The quality of the description is investigated from the results of a published electrophysiological and a psychophysical experiment. In both cases a satisfactory quantitative interpretation is possible, which can also be used as the basis for the interpretation of complex optical illusions.

1. INTRODUCTION

In the optical environment of vertebrates a wide variety of time-dependent stimuli occurs. These signals frequently contain vital information for the individuals. It is, therefore, necessary for the optical system to be capable of evaluating dynamic stimuli. Since, at least in man, the environmental image on the retina is always moving, owing to the spontaneous movement of the eyes, all optical stimuli are time-dependent, i.e. not only the analysis of moving patterns or of patterns brightness-modulated in the time domain, but also the perception of stationary images are critcally influenced by the dynamic properties of the visual system.

In this paper some fundamental properties of the nervous nets in the visual system will be theoretically investigated. The basic models are nets of laterally connected neurons acting additively and substractively on one another.

2. DESCRIPTION OF NERVOUS NETS

One of the most important functions of the visual system is pattern recognition, i.e. the assignment of two-dimensional brightness distribution of the environment to specific previously acquired or inherited classes of meanings on the basis of significant characteristics. Pattern recognition is, in general, effected in two steps:

1. Extraction of significant pattern characteristics.

2. Classification of the patterns according to the extracted characteristics.

In the visual system of vertebrates the extraction of characteristics is effected in two-dimensional nerve nets in which the input signal does not only act on the associated cell, but with a specific weight factor also influences the lateral units. The modes of coupling are illustrated in fig. 1.

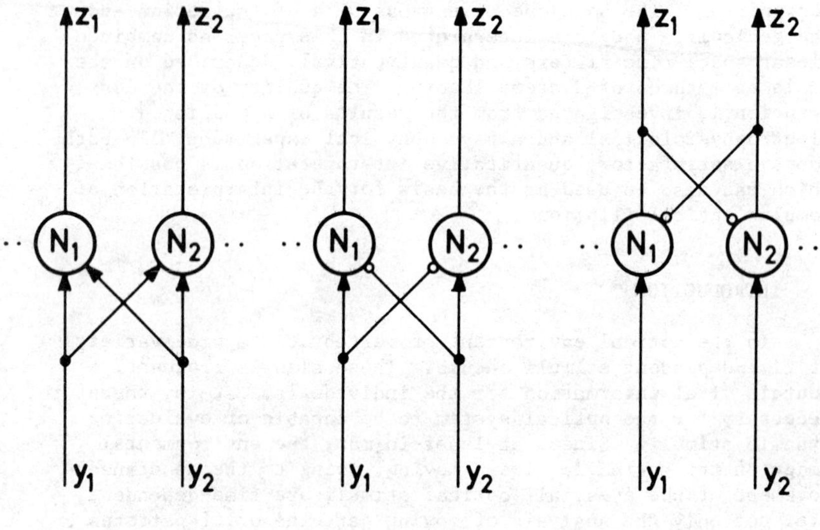

Fig. 1. Connection schemes in nerve nets.

They include forward inhibition, backward inhibition and facilitation. The positive input signals are marked by arrows, the negative signals by circles. Since nets with backward inhibition can be replaced by equivalent nets with forward inhibition, substractive couplings are described below by forward inhibition [1].

For a quantitative description of the system the following simplifying assumption can be made:

1. The transformations in the nervous nets are linear.
2. The nervous nets are homogeneous, i.e. all the neurons are connected in the same way, independent of space.
3. The patterns are much larger than the neuron spacing.

The errors involved in these assumptions are easy to estimate [2]. If H(r,s,t) denotes the coupling function dependent on space (r,s) and time (t), an input signal y(r,s,t) appears at the output of the nerve net as

$$z(r,s,t) = \int_{0}^{+}\int\int_{-\infty}^{\infty} H(r-r',s-s',t-\tau)\; y\,(r',s',\tau)\; dr\; ds\; d\tau \quad (1)$$

Eq. (1) is a convolution integral and describes a two-dimensional space filtering process. The time-dependent variation of this process is governed primarily by the time-dependent behaviour of the synaptic coupling. The characteristic of the system, the pulse reaction function g(r,s,t), is given by

$$g(r,s,t) = H(r,s,t) \quad (2)$$

Thus, the system can be described by the space and time-dependent coupling function. The receptive fields normally measured represent a section through the coupling functions at H(r,s) = 0. They only indicate the sign of the signal action and thus are not sufficient for a description of the system.

An interpretation of the nervous nets as space filters implies that the patterns of our visual environment can be regarded as superposed space-dependent periodic oscillations, which are evaluated by the nervous nets as a function of their space-frequency content. As measurements of the receptive fields show, the coupling functions have positive and negative areas. This implies that the Fourier transform F(g(r,s)) for the retina and the geniculate body are characterised by band-pass-filters.

For the transformation of dynamic stimuli not only the space-dependent coupling but also the time-dependent signal properties at the synapses have to be considered. Based on previous measurements the following assumptions can be made for an approximate description of the system:

1. The time-dependent behaviour of the coupling factors can be approximated by a low-pass filter of the first order, the time constants for facilitation (T_1) and inhibition (T_2) being different.

2. The low-pass time constants are independent of the coupling width.

The first condition is decisive for the dynamic behaviour of the system. The effect of the assumed time-dependent coupling can be illustrated by choosing the step function in the space and time domains

$$y(r,t) = \sigma(r)\,\sigma(t) \tag{3}$$

as input signal for a one-dimensional system. The response of the nerve net, calculated from Eq. (1) with the aid of the Fourier transform and the law of residues, is shown in fig. 2, if

$$H(r,t) = \frac{m_1}{T_1} \exp\left(-\frac{t}{T_1}\right) \exp\left(-\frac{r^2}{B_1^2}\right) - \frac{m_2}{T_2} \exp\left(-\frac{t}{T_2}\right) \exp\left(-\frac{r^2}{B_2^2}\right)$$

and if in

$$T_2 = nT_1 \tag{5}$$

and

$$B_2 = kB_1 \tag{6}$$

$k = n = 3$. When the signal is switched on, a distinct rise in aplitude compared with the stationary condition is induced after a period of about $T_1/2$. If in Eq. (5) $n < 1$, the amplitude rises when the signal is switched off. The on- and off-reactions measured electrophysiologically may thus be interpreted as the effect of the different low-pass time constants of facilitation and inhibition. The character of the time-dependent response is constant throughout the receptive field. In higher vertebrates, however, the on-response predominates in the central areas and the off-response in the

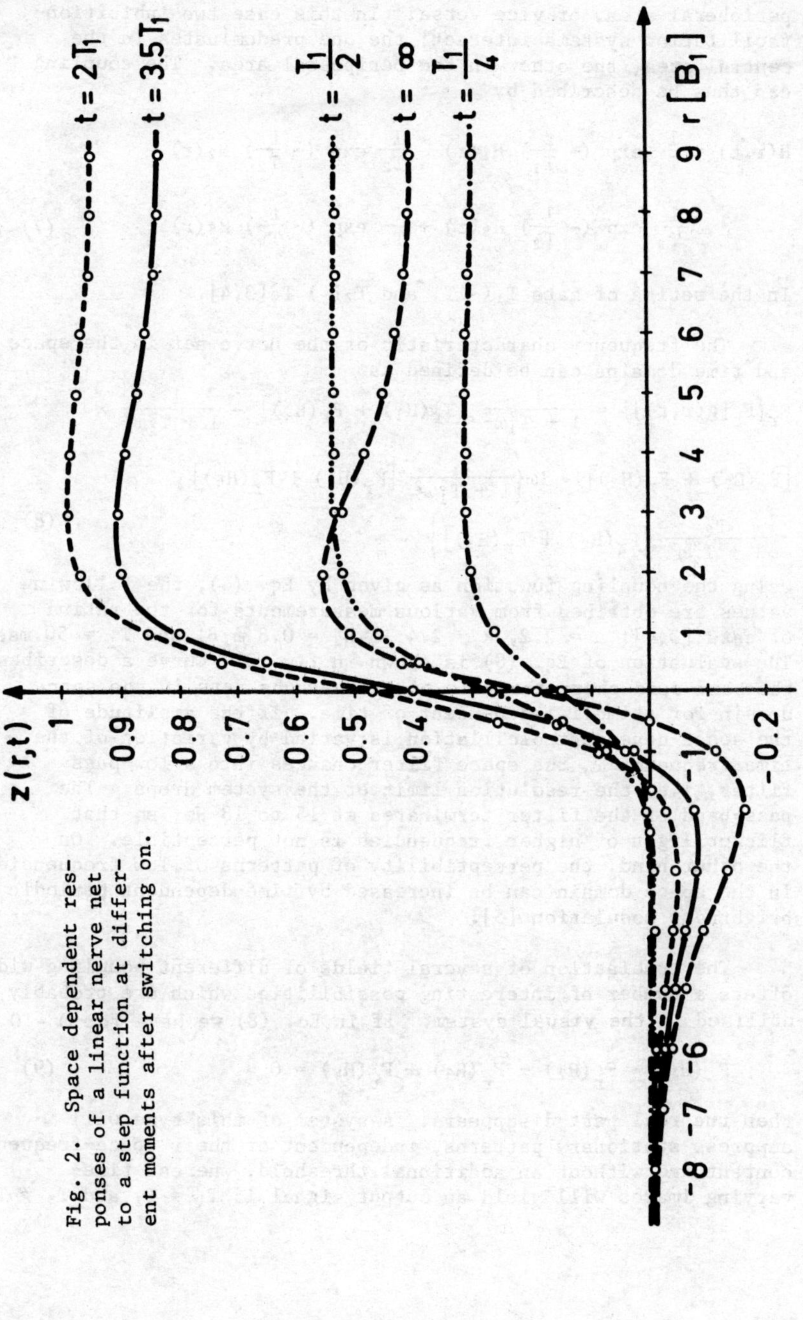

Fig. 2. Space dependent responses of a linear nerve net to a step function at different moments after switching on.

peripheral area, or vice versa. In this case two inhibition-facilitation systems interact; the one predominates in the central area, the other in the peripheral area. The coupling can thus be described by

$$H(r,t) = \frac{1}{T_1} \exp\left(-\frac{t}{T_1}\right) H_1(r) - \frac{1}{T_2} \exp\left(-\frac{t}{T_2}\right) H_2(r) -$$

$$\frac{1}{T_3} \exp\left(-\frac{1}{T_3}\right) H_3(r) + \frac{1}{T_4} \exp\left(-\frac{t}{T_4}\right) H_4(r) \qquad (7)$$

In the retina of cats $T_1(\approx)T_3$ and $T_2(\approx)\, T_4$[3,4].

The frequency characteristic of the nerve net in the space and time domains can be defined as

$$F_r\big(F_t[g(r,t)]\big) = \frac{1}{1+T_1^2\omega^2}\big[F_r(H_1) + F_r(H_4)\big] - \frac{1}{1+T_2^2\omega^2} \times$$

$$\big[F_r(H_2) + F_r(H_3)\big] - i\omega\left\{\frac{T_1}{1+T_1^2\omega^2}\big[F_r(H_1) + F_r(H_4)\big]\right.$$

$$\left. - \frac{T_2}{1+T_2^2\omega^2}\big[F_r(H_2) + F_r(H_3)\big]\right\} \qquad (8)$$

Using the coupling function as given by Eq. (4), the following values are obtained from various measurements for the retina of cats [3,4]: $n = 2.2$, $k = 2.4$, $m_2 B_2^2 = 0.8\, m_1 B_2^2$ and $T_1 = 50$ msec The evaluation of Eq. (8) is shown in fig. 3. Curve a describes the band-pass characteristic of the nervous nets in the space. domain for stimuli independent of time. If the amplitude of the space-dependent oscillation is varied by variation of the time frequency ω, the space filter changes into a low-pass filter, i.e. the resolution limit of the system drops. The pass-band of the filter terminates at 15 to 18 Hz, so that flicker light of higher frequencies is not perceptible. On the other hand, the perceptibility of patterns of low frequencies in the space domain can be increased by time-dependent periodic brightness modulation [5].

The combination of several fields of different coupling widths offers a number of interesting possibilities which are probably utilised in the visual system. If in Eq. (8) we have for $\omega = 0$

$$F_r(H_1) - F_r(H_2) - F_r(H_3) + F_r(H_4) = 0 \qquad (9)$$

then the real part disappears. A system of this type will suppress stationary patterns, independent of their space-frequency content and without an additional threshold, whereas time-varying images will yield an output signal if $T_1 \neq T_2$ and $T_3 \neq T_4$.

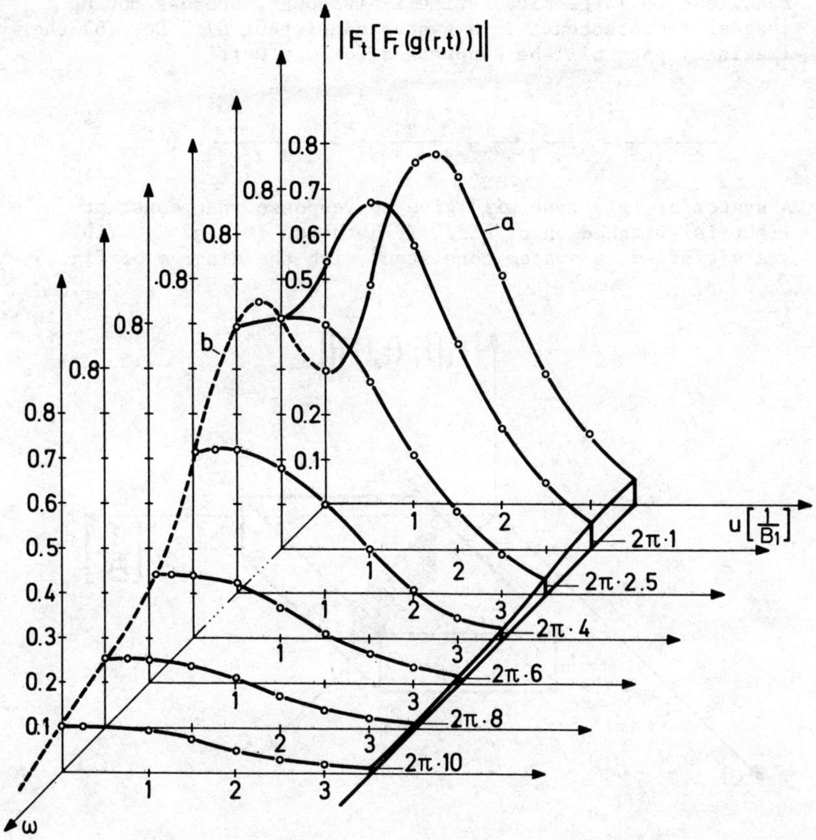

Fig. 3. Space frequency characteristic of the cat's retina for different values of the time frequency ω.

The disappearance of stabilised retinal images would thus be easy to interpret. In the retina of cats the condition of Eq. (9) is not satisfied, since the on- and off-systems have different areas of preference in the space domain. It may be assumed that the stationary image will be suppressed according to the above procedure if the coupling functions of the geniculate body and Area 17 are included in the calculation.

In the measurements on the visual cortex of cats, not only the response to stationary patterns, but also the on- and off-reactions to large-sized stimuli disappear, whereas moving images are detected. In a system consistent with Eq. (8) the imaginary part will be suppressed for u = 0 if

$$\frac{T_1}{1 + T_1^2\omega^2} - \frac{T_2}{1 + T^2\omega^2} - \frac{T_3}{1 + T_3^2\omega^2} + \frac{T_4}{1 + T_4^2\omega^2} = 0 \qquad (10)$$

A system of this type will give no response when constant light is switched on or off. If both Eq. (9) and Eq. (10) are satisfied, a system consistent with the diagram of fig. 4

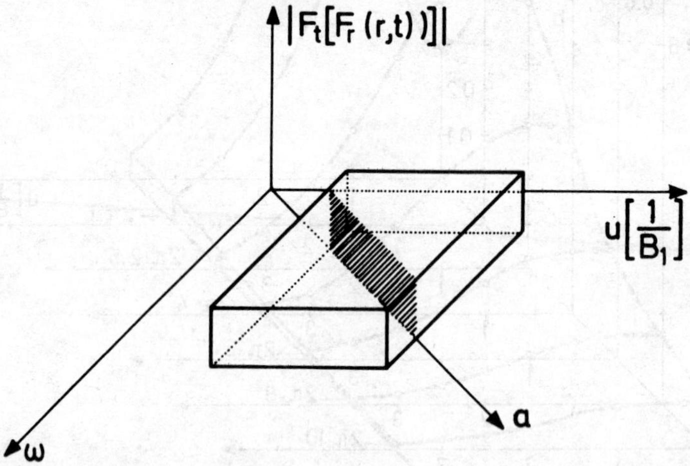

Fig. 4. Filter characteristic of a system answering mainly to moving stimuli.

is obtained, in which not only the response to stationary patterns but also the on- and off-reactions to patterns of low space frequencies are suppressed. Considering the biological conditions in the visual system, two systems as defined by Eq. (8) have to be combined. Neurons with the properties discussed have been found in Areas 18 and 19 of the visual cortex of cats.

If the time delay of the signals is ascribed to the synaptic contact, the low-pass time constant may be assumed to be independent of the coupling width. If, however, the transit time of the signals in the dendrites influences the transformation, the transit time will increase as the distances between neurons increases. Since a change of sign of the action of nervous signals requires an additional neuron, the following assumptions can be made [6].

1. The velocity of the signals in the dendrites is constant, i.e. the transit time increases with increasing cell spacing.

2. Signals propagated by inhibitory and facilitatory coupling have different transit times (T_1^*, T_2^*).

If the coupling is described by

$$F_t[H(r,t)] = m_1 \exp(-i\omega T_1^*|r|)\exp(-|r|/B_1) - m_2 \exp(-i\omega T_2^*|r|)\exp(-|r|/B_2) \tag{11}$$

the absolute value of the combined space and time frequency characteristic can be written as

$$\left|F_r[F_t(g(r,t))]\right|^2 = \left[\frac{1}{1+(\omega T_1^*+u)^2} + \frac{1}{1+(\omega T_1^*-u)^2} - \frac{1}{1+k^2(\omega n T_1^*+u)^2} - \frac{1}{1+k^2(\omega n T_1^*-u)^2}\right]^2 + \left[\frac{(\omega T_1^*+u)}{1+(\omega T_1^*+u)^2} + \frac{(\omega T_1^*-u)}{1+(\omega T_1^*-u)^2} - \frac{k(\omega n T_1^*+u)}{1+k^2(\omega n T_1^*+u)^2} - \frac{k(\omega n T_1^*-u)}{1+k^2(\omega n T_1^*-u)^2}\right]^2 \tag{12}$$

where $2\,m_1B_1 = 2\,m_2B_2 = 1$. The space frequency characteristics of the system are plotted in fig. 5 for different values of and $n = k = 2$. The basic structure of these characteristics is consistent with that of fig. 3. A remarkable feature is the broadening of the filter in the space domain at specific values of ω; this broadening is dependent on the ratio of the transit time. This effect is relevant to several optical illusions and will be discussed in Section 4. In real systems both low-pass coupling and transit times have to be considered. Thus, the dynamic properties of the linearisable part of the system can be described. The application of the basic equations to moving stimuli requires several special effects. This is discussed below.

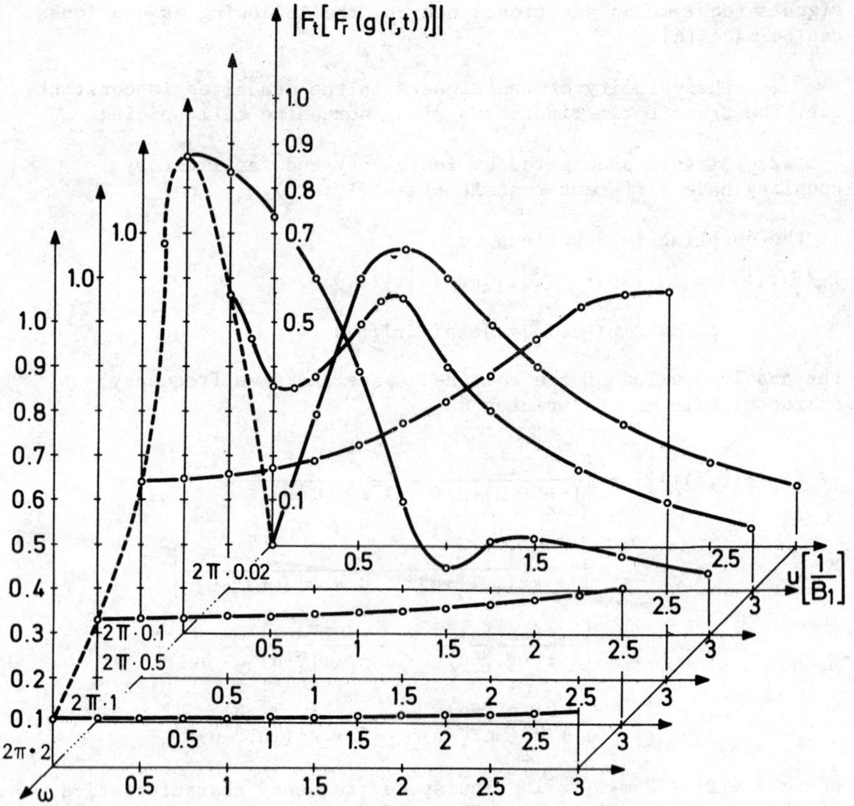

Fig. 5. Space-frequency characteristic of a system with distance dependent transit time of the dendritic signals.

3. TRANSFORMATION OF MOVING STIMULI

In the case of moving stimuli we have to consider the system, dependent transformation of the patterns, on the one hand, and the velocity of the stimuli to be measured on the other. For pattern recognition the first-mentioned problem is mainly important; it is necessary to take into account both the movement of the stimulus and the movements of the eyes. For reasons of simplicity of representation, the system is assumed below to be one-dimensional in space, and the movement is assumed to be constant. If the input signal is a Dirac pulse moving at the velocity $\bar{v}$, i.e.

$$y(r,t) = \delta(r + \bar{v}t) \tag{13}$$

the frequency characteristic results from Eq. (1) to be

$$F_r[F_t(g(r,t))] = F_r[F_t(H(r,t))]\ \delta\ (w - \bar{v}u) \tag{14}$$

In the $F_r[F_t(g(r,t))]$, u, ω - system all values of the frequency characteristic are on a straight line (Fig. 4, curve a) whose slope in the u,ω-plane depends on the velocity. In spite of radially symmetric coupling, the movement results in a phase characteristic. In fig. 6 the frequency characteristic in the space domain is plotted for various velocities, if the coupling function is described by Eq. (4) and

$$P = \frac{T_1\bar{v}}{B_2} \tag{15}$$

With increasing velocity the band-pass system becomes a low-pass filter. Eq. (3) and Eq. (14) can be used to determine the transformation of arbitrary patterns. The combined effect of attenuation and phase characteristics can be demonstrated if

$$y(r,t) = \sigma(r + \bar{v}t)\ \sigma(t). \tag{16}$$

The step response of the system for r = 0, determined from Eq. (3) and Eq. (14), is illustrated in fig. 7. As may also be seen from electrophysiological experiments, the movement of the stimulus causes stronger excitation than the on-response. It is possible to determine the velocity by measuring the amplitude at the edges of the pattern; this has not yet been thoroughly investigated when this method or the auto-correlation function of the pattern [7] is used. The motion-dependent variations of the pattern characteristics are of special importance, in particular in very simple visual systems, such as that of the frog.

4. APPLICATION OF THE DESCRIPTIVE METHODS

The descriptive equations derived from published findings are used below to interpret a recent electrophysiological and a psycho-physical experiment.

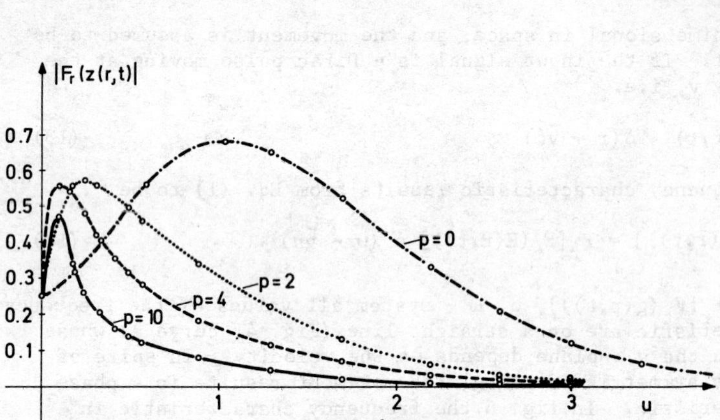

Fig. 6. Space-frequency characteristic of a system with moving stimuli ($\overline{v}$), n = 4, k = 2 and $m_1B_1 = 0,\ 8m_2B_2$.

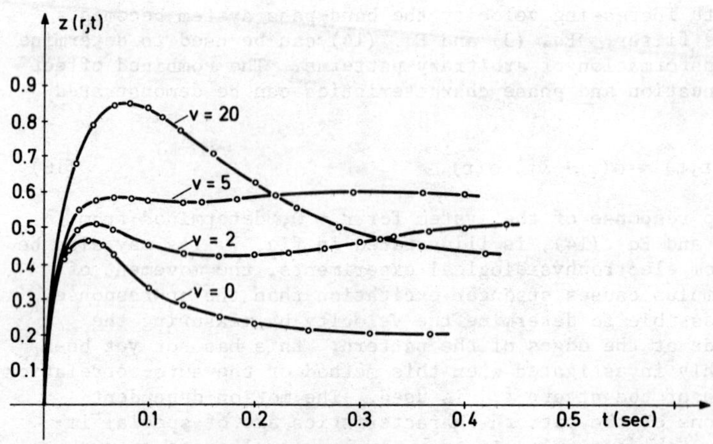

Fig. 7. Time dependent responses at r = 0 of a system with a step function at the input.

In the centre of the receptive field of an on-ganglion cell in a cat's retina small sinusoidally modulated light stimuli were applied at two points of identical sensitivity. The maximum respones of the ganglion cell and its response averaged over one period have been plotted as a function of the frequency and the time-dependent phase shift of the sinusoidal stimulus. The result shows a dependence of the response on the cosine of half the phase angle and a maximum of the reaction averaged over one period [8] at about 5 Hz. Calculations using the input stimulus

$$y(r,t) = \delta(r - r_0)\sin\left(\omega_0 t + \frac{\phi}{2}\right)\delta(r + r_0)\sin\left(\omega_0 t - \frac{\phi}{2}\right) \qquad (17)$$

on the basis of Eq. (1) yield

$$z(r,t) = \cos\frac{\phi}{2}\left[\frac{H_1(r_0)}{1 + T_1^2\omega_0^2}(\sin\omega_0 t - T_1\omega_0\cos\omega_0 t) - \frac{H_2(r_0)}{1 + T_2^2\omega_0^2}(\sin\omega_0 t - T_2\omega_0\cos\omega_0 t)\right] \qquad (18)$$

For low frequencies ω_0 we thus obtain the observed dependence of the reaction on $\cos\phi/2$, while the phase shift proportional to $T_1\omega_0$ or $T_2\omega_0$ increases with increasing frequency to lead to the deviation from the $\cos\phi/2$ -dependence observed by Büttner et al. [8].

If the response is averaged over a period where $z(r,t)_{r=0}$ is positive, we obtain the curve shown in fig. 8 for the dependence of the averaged reaction $z(r)_{r=0}$ on the stimulus frequency, where $T_1 = 20$ ms, $T_2 = 60$ ms and $[H_2(r_0)]/[H_1(r_0)] = 0.65$. The two parts of the experiments can be interpreted with good approximation as the dynamic transformations of the nervous net of the retina.

Thorson et al. recently published a psychophysical experiment which can be interpreted by the dynamic behaviour of the retinal nerve nets [9]. If two small light points are positioned such that they cannot be resolved by the observer, one of the points being first visible for a period Δt and the second point appearing subsequently for the same period Δt after a time interval $T/2$, the observer has an impression of motion. This apparent movement occurs in the direction from the first to the second point. The distance of motion exceeds the distance between the points by a multiple; at the periphery of the eye it is approximately five times larger than in the fovea. The optimum impression of motion is obtained if $T/2$ is about 60 ms.

In order to demonstrate the principle of the effect, a one-dimensional nervous net in the space domain is assumed, whose dynamic properties are determined in particular by the transit times of the signals on the dendrites. With the input signal

$$y(r,t) = \delta(r + r_0)\,\delta(t) - \delta(r - r_0)\,\delta\left(t - \frac{T}{2}\right) \qquad (19)$$

we obtain from Eq. (1)

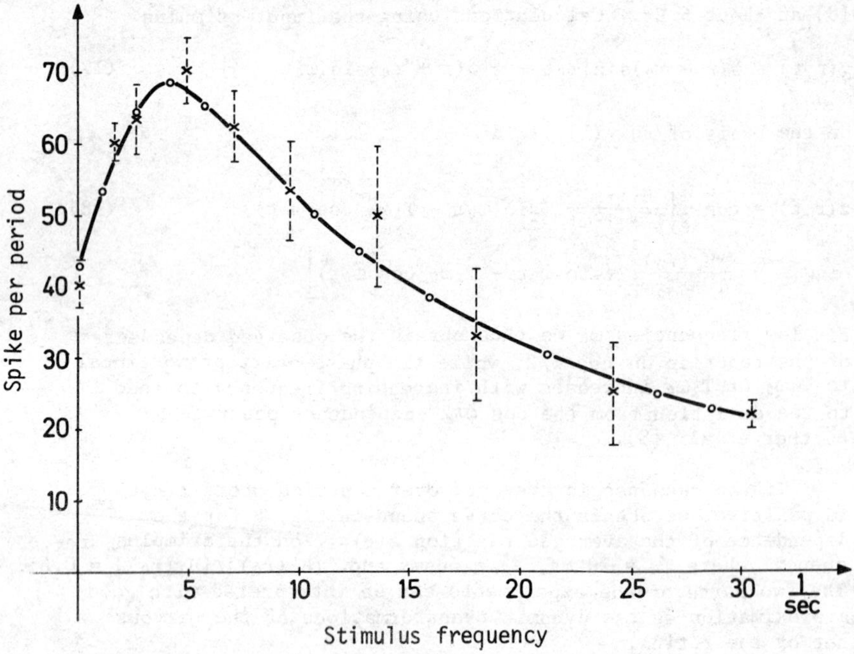

Fig. 8. Averaged response of a neuron to a stimulus consisting of two light-points. The amplitude of the stimulus was periodically changed (w_0). The measurements (dotted lines) were done by Büttner and Grüsser (1971).

$$z(r,t) = m_1H_1(r+r_0)\ \delta(t-T_1^*|r+r_0|) + m_1H_1(r-r_0)\ \delta(t-(\tfrac{T}{2} + T_1^*|r-r_0|))$$

$$- m_2H_2(r+r_0)\ \delta(t-T_2^*|r+r_0|) - m_2H_2(r-r_0)\ \delta(t-(\tfrac{T}{2} + T_2^*|r-r_0|)) \quad (20)$$

The evaluation of Eq. (20) is shown in fig. 9. The local distribution of excitation has been plotted for several points of time. If the second stimulus is applied when the excitation wave of the first stimulus reaches the place where the second stimulus is applied, this leads to summation, and the amplified excitation wave is propagated so far to the right as the coupling H(r) extends. As the coupling values at the periphery of the eye exceed those in the fovea, the region of motion at the periphery must be larger than in the centre; this is supported by experimental results. Because of the high intensity of the stimuli and the non-linear

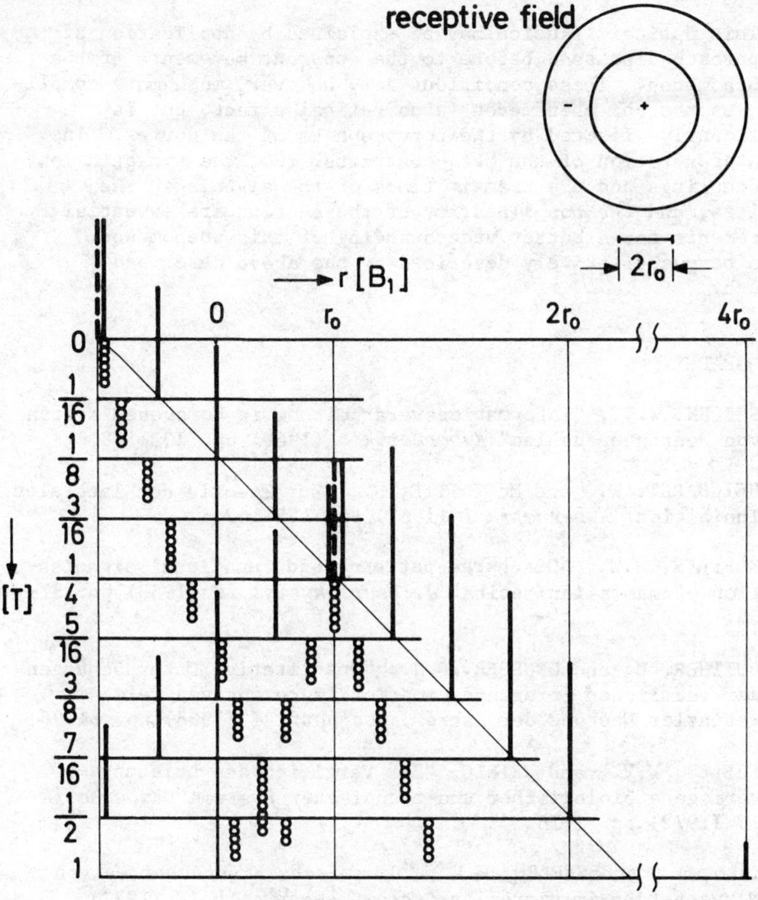

Fig. 9. Space and time dependent signals in a nerve net with time delay in the dendrites. Exitation and inhibition (dotted lines) move with different velocities.

characteristic of the neurones, the intensity of the moving point appears to be constant over a large range.

If the finite width of the stimuli, the low-pass coupling of the synapses and the presence of a superposed off-system are taken into account, the excitation wave and the inhibition wave approach each other and are smoothed. The principle of the effect, however, remains unchanged.

This optical illusion may be explained by application of the approach discussed before to the apparent movements of the phi phenomenon. These conditions are, however, much more complicated, as the phi phenomenon is no retinal effect, but is significantly affected by the nervous nets of the cortex. In the interpretation of the meta-contrasts, too, the synaptic low-pass couplings and the transit times of the signals in the dendrites, and the non-linearity of the neurons are essential requirements for a better understanding of this phenomenon. It can be quantitatively described by the above described approach.

BIBLIOGRAPHY

1. SEELEN, W.V., "Informationsverarbeitung in homogenen Netzen von Neuronenmodellen" *Kybernetik 5* (1968) pp. 133-148.

2. REICHARDT, W., and McGINITIE, S., "Zur Theorie der lateralen Inhibition" *Kybernetik 1* (1962) pp. 155-163.

3. KUFFLER, S.W., "Discharge patterns and functional organisation of mammalian retina" *J. Neurophysiol 16* (1953) pp. 37-68.

4. BÜTTNER, U. and GRÜSSER, O.J., "Quantitative Untersuchungen der räumlichen Erregungssummation im rezeptiven Feld retinaler Neurone der Katze" *Kybernetik 4* (1968) pp. 61-96.

5. SEELEN, W.V., and REINIG, "Zur Vergleich des Leistungsvermögens biologischer und technischer Systeme" *Kybernetik 10* (1972) pp. 1-16.

6. KORN, A., and SEELEN, W.V., "Dynamische Eigenschaften von Nervennetzen im visuellen System" *Kybernetik 10* (1972) pp. 64-77.

7. REICHARDT, W., and VARJU, D., "Übertragungseigenschaften im Auswertesystem für das Bewegungssehen" *Zeitschr. f. Naturforschung 14* (1959) pp. 674-689.

8. BÜTTNER, CH., BÜTTNER, U., and GRÜSSER, O.J., "Interaction of excitation and direct inhibition in the receptive field centre of retinal neurons" *Pflugers Arch. 332* (1971) pp. 1-22.

9. THORSON, M., THORSON, J., and LANGE, D., "Apparent movement due to closely spaced sequentially flashed dots in the human peripheral field of vision" *Vision Res. II* (1972) pp. 889-903.

AN ELECTRICAL MODEL FOR COMPUTER SIMULATION OF ISOTONIC CONTRACTION OF SKELETAL MUSCLES FOLLOWING MAGNETO-INDUCTIVE STIMULATION

F.K.A. ALLOTEY, K.A. ESSUMAN AND D.P. PHOTIADES*

University of Science and Technology, Kumasi, Ghana

SUMMARY

Following work on a new method of stimulating skeletal muscles of incapacitated and disabled human limbs by eddy currents induced from pulsating magnetic fields in an air core solenoid surrounding the limb, an equivalent electrical circuit model of the neuro-muscular apparatus was derived. This assumed cable and certain semiconductor (diode) properties in accordance with recent trends. In the first instance, a linear approximation is assumed and a digital computer is programmed to find a solution to the case where a response is elicited in the muscle, whenever an eddy current type of impulse is generated and induced by rapidly changing magnetic fields.

INTRODUCTION

It was recently shown [1,2,3] that it was possible to induce drowsiness and light sleep in humans by exposing the head to magneto-inductive energy from a short horizontal solenoid surrounding but not actually touching the forehead. As other workers had tentatively reported that in animals exposed to pulsed magnetic fields, muscles were stimulated indirectly, and as we had also observed this phenomenon in our human volunteers during the above mentioned electric sleep experiments, we embarked on a special study [4] to clarify the role that induced energy from rapidly changing magnetic fields played in the excitation of striated (skeletal) muscle; we also showed during this study, that such fields could be advantageously utilized to stimulate skeletal muscles of incapacitated human limbs without recourse to contact electrodes.

*Dr. D.P. Photiades, School of Medicine and Pharmacy, University of Benin, Benin City, Nigeria.

During the course of this enquiry [4], it was established that if the integrity of the motor nerve was disturbed in any way, muscle excitation became difficult or at times impossible, due to the altered chronaxie [5]. Furthermore, in order to elucidate some of these problems, we very recently undertook to derive an equivalent electrical circuit model of the skeletal neuro-muscular apparatus, following the work of earlier investigators [6,7,8,9], and to analyse it by a digital computer.

This initial communication, therefore, outlines the problem and depicts the analogous electrical circuit diagram through the various stages. It should be emphasized here that this is a preliminary study, and that considerably more work is required before the final solution.

PROCEDURE

This will be considered from the following aspects:- Production of the pulsed magnetic fields, their action on the neuro-muscular apparatus, some of the underlying problems, and the derivation of the model.

Pulsed magnetic fields are produced when a high tension source (2000-5000 volts dc) charges up a bank of condensors, which are then periodically (1/2 to 2 times a second) made to discharge through a low inductance short solenoid surrounding but not actually touching a certain part of the human body to be studied. This rapidly changing magnetic field induces eddy currents and the movement of charge carriers in the most conducting parts of the tissues.

It has been repeatedly shown during experiments [10,11] that this type of magneto-inductive energy stimulates skeletal muscles indirectly (via the motor nerve) provided that the stimulus is of a threshold value, and the neuro-muscular apparatus is unimpaired. The induced eddy currents, if adequate (threshold or liminal) initiate membrane depolarization and a nerve action potential which leads to muscle excitation and contraction.

If, on the other hand, the integrity of the motor nerve is disturbed (in cases of lower motor neurone lesions such as nerve trauma and acute anterior poliomyelitis) the normal chronaxie is lengthened, and the induced eddy currents will be subliminal and unable to initiate nerve membrane depolarization; consequently the muscle will not respond to the stimulus. However, if the intensity of the magnetically induced energy were now somehow increased sufficiently to overcome the lengthened chronaxie of the denervated muscle, it should be possible to elicit a response directly from the muscle [10]. Moreover, the chronaxie of different groups of skeletal muscles and of various types of somatic nerves differs. These were some of the problems that arose during the course of the above mentioned investigations. It was therefore decided, in the first instance, to draw up an equivalent circuit model of the skeletal neuro-muscular apparatus from data already available as a preliminary step to digital computer analysis. The circuit (Fig. 1b) was modified from earlier well known ones (Fig. 1a) [6,7,8,9]. Cable properties were assumed, since the nerve fibre has a uniform cable-like structure, with a conducting core, an external conducting path, and a surface membrane exhibiting both resistance and capacitance. Each motor nerve innervated a number of striated muscle fibres. Certain semiconductor (diode) properties were also assumed at the neuro-muscular synapse although such properties will be extended further in subsequent studies as outlined by other investigators [12].

The following points were stressed in the model:

1. The resting motor nerve has a definite threshold, below which no action occurs, and above which it fires (all or none phenomenon).

2. When a motor nerve fires, we get propagation of a wave of depolarization in a finite time interval.

3. After a motor nerve has fired, it exhibits a transient refractory period, but soon recovers its resting state.

An IBM 1620 Computer is programmed, after assuming a linear approximation, to find a solution to the case where a response is elicited in the skeletal muscle, whenever an eddy current type of impulse is induced in the corresponding nerve. The computer is still being used to program the expression derived from the ensuing pages.

It can be shown that the charge on capacitor C_0 is given by:

$$q = \frac{E_0 C_0 R_1}{(R_1 + R_0)} \left[1 - e^{\frac{-(R_1 + R_0)t}{R_0 R_1 C_0}} \right] + q_0 \, e^{\frac{-(R_1 + R_0)t}{R_0 R_1 C_0}} \qquad (1)$$

Assuming that at the instant when the external pulse is applied, steady state conditions have been reached.

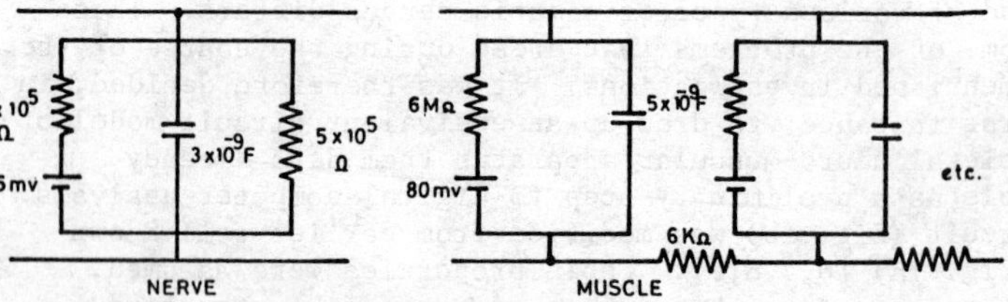

(Fig. 1a)

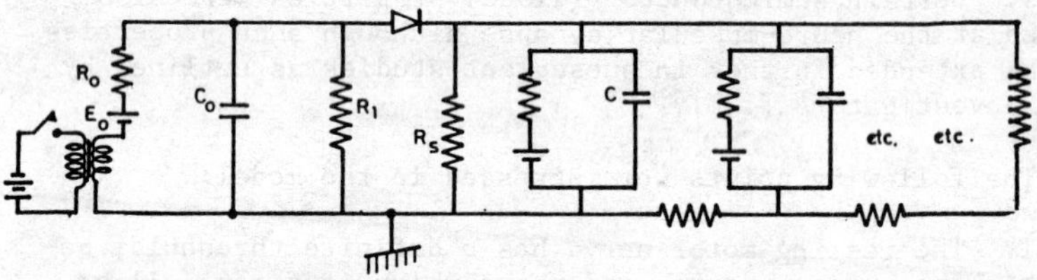

(Fig. 1b)

Fig. 1. Equivalent circuit model of the skeletal neuromuscular apparatus.

List of Symbols

C_0	=	Nerve membrane capacitance.
C	=	Muscle membrane capacitance.
R_0	=	Nerve membrane resistance.
R_1	=	Presynaptic resistance of nerve membrane (reciprocal of membrane conductance).
E_0	=	Electromotive force at rest (resting membrane potential).
q	=	Charge on nerve membrane capacitance.
q_s	=	Steady state charge on nerve membrane capacitance at rest.
Z_a	=	Generalized impedance of muscle fibres.
Z_{in}	=	Input impedance of muscle fibres.
$v(T)$	=	Output voltage response on nerve across C_0.
V_0	=	Output voltage response at end of the muscle fibre.

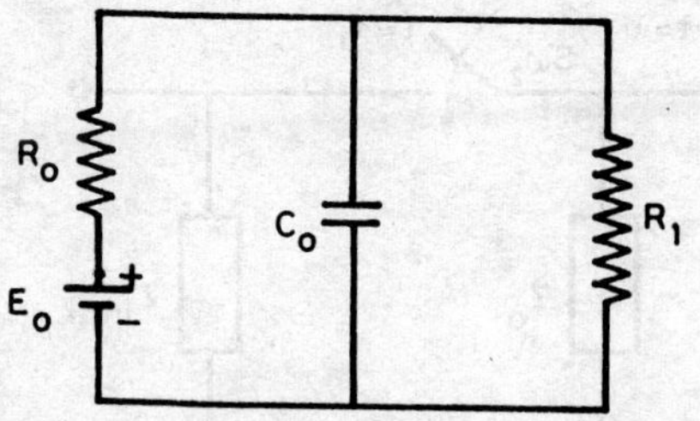

Fig. 2. Network of nerve membrane

$$q_s = \frac{E_0 C_0 R_1}{(R_1 + R_0)} \tag{2}$$

After the application of the external pulse,

$$q = \frac{-E\ C_0 R_1}{(R_1 + R_0)} \left[1 - e^{\frac{-(R_1 + R_0)t}{R_0 R_1 C_0}}\right] + q_s\ e^{\frac{-(R_1 + R_0)t}{R_0 R_1 C_0}} \tag{3}$$

$$q = \frac{-E\ C_0 R_1}{(R_1 + R_0)} \left[1 - e^{\frac{-(R_1 + R_0)t}{R_0 R_1 C_0}}\right] +$$

$$\frac{E_0 C_0 R_1}{(R_1 + R_0)}\ e^{\frac{-(R_1 + R_0)t}{R_0 R_1 C_0}} \tag{4}$$

Using the relation

$$q = C_0 v \tag{5}$$

in equation (4) and simplifying gives:

$$v = \frac{R_1}{(R_1 + R_0)} \left[-E + (E + E\ )\ e^{\frac{-(R_1 + R_0)t}{R_0 R_1 C_0}}\right] \tag{6}$$

Assume that when S_2 is closed at $t = t_1$, the first transient has not ended.

Let $T = t - t_1$

For T o, the opencircuited voltage across S_2 is given by:

$$v(T) = \frac{R_1}{(R_1 + R_0)} \left[-E + (E + E_0)\ e^{\frac{-(R_1 + R_0)(t_1 + T)}{R_0 R_1 C_0}}\right] \tag{7}$$

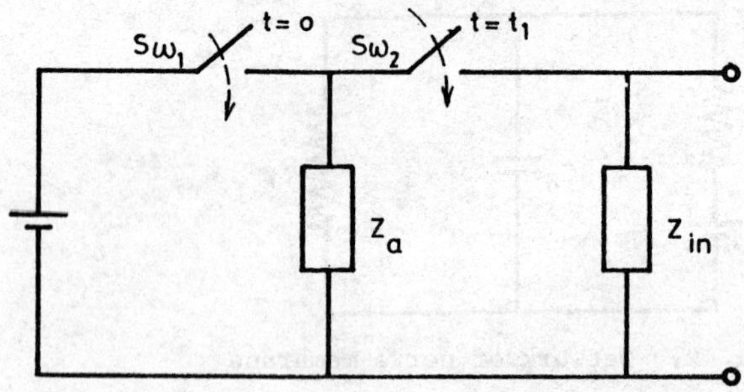

Fig. 3. Network showing the switching action of the synapse. Switch S_1 is closed at $t = 0$; switch S_2 is closed at $t = t_1$.

The neuro-muscular network may be redrawn as in Fig. 4a, where Z_{in} is the input impedance of the muscular fibre network. With switch S_2 open, the open circuited voltage across the switch is the voltage across Z_{in} and is equal to v(T). The impedance looking into the (open) terminals of switch $S_2 = Z_a + Z_{in}$. The current flowing through Z_{in} is given by:

$$\frac{v(T)}{(Z_a + Z_{in})}$$

Therefore, the voltage v_0 across Z_{in} is given by:

$$v_0 = \frac{Z_{in}\, v(T)}{(Z_a + Z_{in})} \tag{8}$$

A chain of n identical L-networks having the form of Fig. 5a may be recast as in Fig. 5b. This resolves into (n - 1) symmetrical T-networks, with residues at each end.

Residue (1) is a combination of shunt admittance and series impedance. The transfer matrix of residue (1) is given by:

$$\begin{bmatrix} 1 & -Z/2 \\ 0 & 1 \end{bmatrix} \begin{bmatrix} 1 & 0 \\ -Y & 1 \end{bmatrix} \quad \text{i.e.} \quad \begin{bmatrix} 1 + ZY/2 & -Z/2 \\ -Y & 1 \end{bmatrix}$$

The voltage and current (V_x, I_x) at any junction x on the (n - 1) symmetrical ladder network may be expressed in terms of the input voltage and current ($V_1 I_1$) as follows:

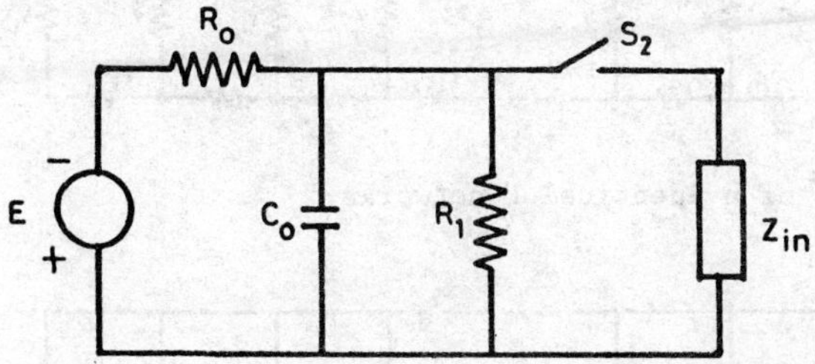

(Fig. 4a)

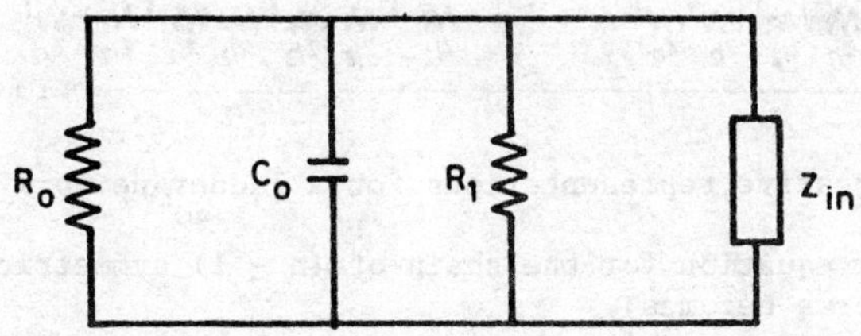

(Fig. 4b)

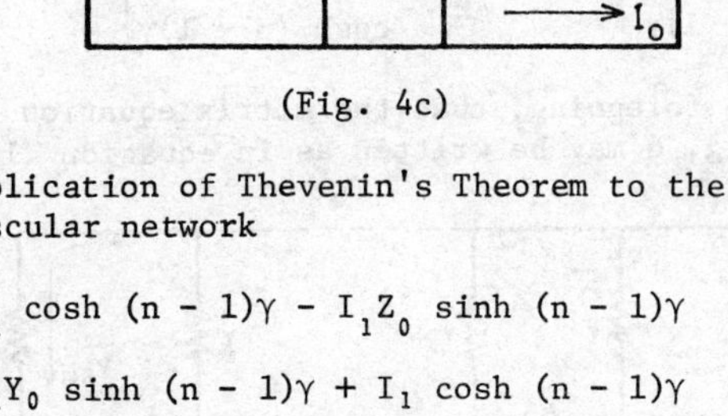

(Fig. 4c)

Fig. 4. Application of Thevenin's Theorem to the neuromuscular network

$$V_x = V_1 \cosh (n - 1)\gamma - I_1 Z_0 \sinh (n - 1)\gamma \qquad (9)$$

$$I_x = V_1 Y_0 \sinh (n - 1)\gamma + I_1 \cosh (n - 1)\gamma \qquad (10)$$

where γ = propagation coefficient per T network section
and Z_0 = characteristic impedance.

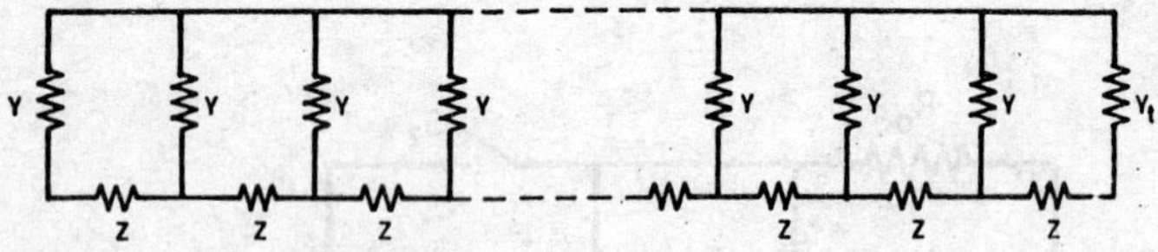

Fig. 5a. Chain of n identical L-networks.

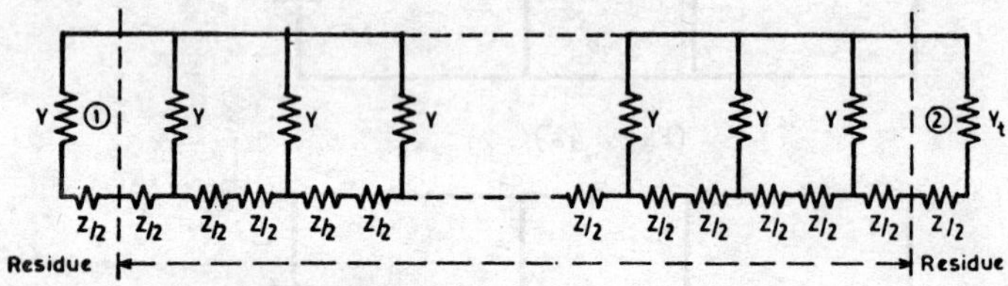

Fig. 5b. Alternative representations for a ladder network.

The matrix equation for the chain of (n - 1) symmetrical identical networks becomes:

$$\begin{bmatrix} V_{n-1} \\ I_{n-1} \end{bmatrix} = \begin{bmatrix} \cosh (n-1)\gamma & -Z_0 \sinh (n-1)\gamma \\ -Y_0 \sinh (n-1)\gamma & \cosh (n-1)\gamma \end{bmatrix} \begin{bmatrix} V_1 \\ I_1 \end{bmatrix} \tag{11}$$

Hence the transfer-matrix for the (n - 1) symmetrical identical networks is:

$$\begin{bmatrix} \cosh (n-1)\gamma & -Z_0 \sinh (n-1)\gamma \\ -Y_0 \sinh (n-1)\gamma & \cosh (n-1)\gamma \end{bmatrix}$$

It follows from the foregoing, that the matrix equation for the network shown in Fig. 6 may be written as in equation (12).

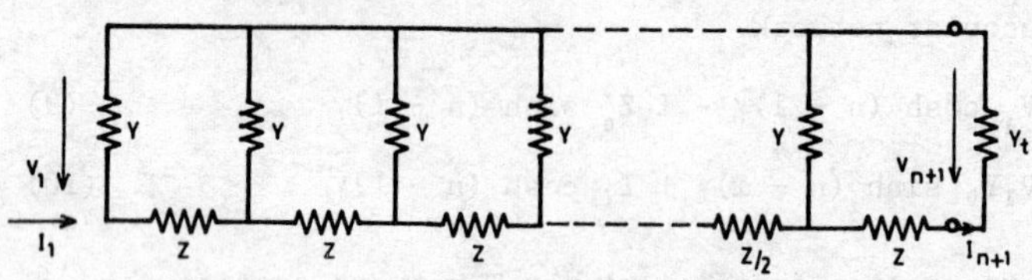

Fig. 6. A network (n - 1).

$$\begin{bmatrix} V_{n+1} \\ I_{n+1} \end{bmatrix} = \begin{bmatrix} 1 & -Z/2 \\ 0 & 1 \end{bmatrix} \begin{bmatrix} \cosh (n-1)\gamma & -Z_0 \sinh (n-1)\gamma \\ -Y_0 \sinh (n-1)\gamma & \cosh (n-1)\gamma \end{bmatrix} \times$$

$$\begin{bmatrix} 1 + (ZY/2) - Z/2 \\ -Y \quad\quad 1 \end{bmatrix} \begin{bmatrix} V_1 \\ I_1 \end{bmatrix} \tag{12}$$

or as:

$$\begin{bmatrix} V_{n+1} \\ I_{n+1} \end{bmatrix} = \begin{bmatrix} a & b \\ c & d \end{bmatrix} \begin{bmatrix} V_1 \\ I_1 \end{bmatrix} \tag{13}$$

where

$$a = (1 + ZY) \cosh (n-1) + [Z_0 + (Z^2Y_0/4) + (ZY_0/2)] \times \sinh (n-1)\gamma \tag{14}$$

$$b = -\{Z \cosh (n-1)\gamma + Z_0 + (Z^2Y_0/4) \sinh (n-1)\gamma\} \tag{15}$$

$$c = -\{Y \cosh (n-1)\gamma + Y_0\ 1 + (ZY/2) \sinh (n-1)\gamma\} \tag{16}$$

$$d = \cosh (n-1)\gamma + (Y_0Z/2) \sinh (n-1)\gamma \tag{17}$$

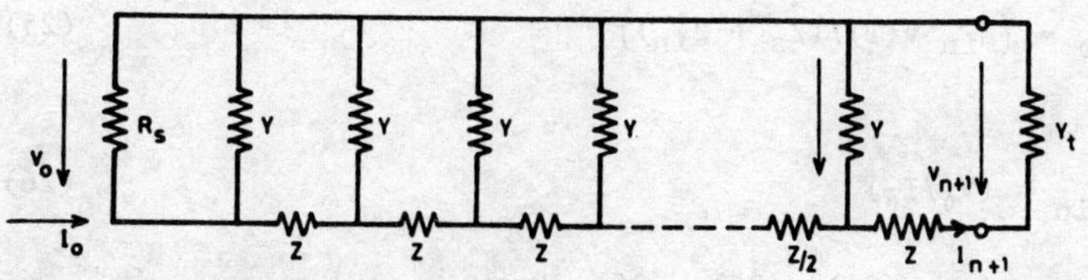

Fig. 7. An extended network

The matrix equation for Fig. 7 is given by:

$$\begin{bmatrix} V_{n+1} \\ I_{n+1} \end{bmatrix} = \begin{bmatrix} a & b \\ c & d \end{bmatrix} \begin{bmatrix} 1 & 0 \\ -1/R_s & 1 \end{bmatrix} \begin{bmatrix} V_0 \\ I_0 \end{bmatrix}$$

which gives:

$$\begin{bmatrix} V_{n+1} \\ I_{n+1} \end{bmatrix} = \begin{bmatrix} a - b/R_s & b \\ c - d/R_s & d \end{bmatrix} \begin{bmatrix} V_0 \\ I_0 \end{bmatrix} \tag{18}$$

Equation (18) may be written as:

$$\begin{bmatrix} V_{n+1} \\ I_{n+1} \end{bmatrix} = \begin{bmatrix} A & B \\ C & D \end{bmatrix} \begin{bmatrix} V_0 \\ I_0 \end{bmatrix} \tag{19}$$

where

$$A = \{1 + Z[Y + 1/R_s]\} \cosh (n - 1)\gamma + \{Z_0 + (Z^2Y_0/4)(Y + 1/R_s) + (ZY_0/2)\} \sinh (n - 1)\gamma \tag{20}$$

$$B = -\{Z \cosh (n - 1)\gamma + [Z_0 + (Z^2Y_0/4)] \sinh (n - 1)\gamma\} \tag{21}$$

$$C = -\{(Y + 1/R_s) \cosh (n - 1) + Y_0[1 + Z/2(Y + 1/R_s)] \times \sinh (n - 1)\gamma\} \tag{22}$$

$$D = \cosh (n - 1)\gamma + (Y_0Z/2) \sinh (n - 1)\gamma \tag{23}$$

It follows from equation (19) that:

$$V_{n+1} = AV_0 + BI_0 \tag{24}$$

From equation (8)

$$V_0 = \{Z_{in}\, v(T)/(Z_a + Z_{in})\} \tag{25}$$

Also

$$Z_{in} = (V_0/I_0) \tag{26}$$

Using equations (24), (25), (26) gives:

$$V_{n+1} = \{(A\, Z_{in} + B)/(Z_a + Z_{in})\} v(T) \tag{27}$$

where

$$v(T) = \frac{R_1}{(R_1 + R_0)}\left[-E + (E + E_0)\, e^{\frac{-(R_1 + R_0)(t_1 + T)}{R_0 R_1 C_0}}\right] \tag{28}$$

$$Z_a = \frac{1}{\left([(R_0 + R_1)/R_0 R_1] + SC_0\right)} \tag{29}$$

$$Z_{in} = \frac{R_s\left\{4Z_0(1+ZY_t) + [2Z + (4Z_0^2+Z^2)Y_t]\tanh(n-1)\gamma\right\}}{4Z_0\left\{(1+ZY_t)(1+YR_s) + R_sY_t\right\} + \left\{\begin{matrix}(1+YR_s)[2Z + (4Z_0^2+Z^2)Y_t] \\ + 2R_s(2+ZY_t)\end{matrix}\right\}\tanh(n-1)} \tag{30}$$

$$Z_0 = \sqrt{(Z/Y + Z^2/4)} \tag{31}$$

$$\gamma = \cosh^{-1}(1 + ZY/2) \tag{32}$$

$$Y = (1/R + SC) \tag{33}$$

Details concerning transfer-matrices, input impedance and transfer networks may be obtained from the authors of this paper.

REFERENCES

1. D.P. PHOTIADES, R.J. RIGGS, S.C. AYIVORH and JUDITH M. KILBY, *I.E.S.A. Inform. J. 10*, 37(1970).

2. D.P. PHOTIADES, R.J. RIGGS, S.C. AYIVORH and JUDITH M. KILBY, *The Nervous System and Electric Currents 2*, Eds. N.L. Wulfsohn and A. Sances Jr. (Plenum Press, N.Y., 1971) p. 75.

3. D.P. PHOTIADES, S.C. AYIVORH and JUDITH M. KILBY, *Abstracts 9th Intern. Conf. Bio-Med. Engng.* Melbourne (1971) p. 172.

4. D.P. PHOTIADES and S.C. AYIVORH, *Proceedings Human Locomotor Engng. Conf.* Univ. Sussex (1971) p. 29.

5. D.P. PHOTIADES, *Med. News Tribune 4*, 9(1972).

6. A.L. HODGKIN and W.A.H. RUSHTON, *Proc. Roy. Soc. Ser. B 133*, 444 (1946).

7. A.L. HODGKIN and A.F. HUXLEY, *J. Physiol. 117*, 500 (1952).

8. A.L. HODGKIN, *Proc. Roy. Soc. Ser. B 148*, 1(1958).

9. I. TASAKI, *Nervous Transmission* (C.C. Thomas, Springfield, 1953).

10. A.K. ABAITEY, S.C. AYIVORH and D.P. PHOTIADES, *8th Biennial Conf. West Afr. Sci. Assoc.* Accra (1972).

11. R.G. BICKFORD and B.D. FREMMING, *Digest 6th Intern. Conf. Med. Electr. Biol. Engng.* Tokyo (1965) p. 112.

12. L.W. WEI, *Digest 7th Intern. Conf. Med. Biol. Engng.* Stockholm (1967) p. 476.

A COMPUTERISED REGISTER SYSTEM FOR ASCERTAINMENT AND PREVENTION OF INHERITED DISEASE

H.M. MOORES, C. SMITH and A.E.H. EMERY

Edinburgh Regional Computing Centre, Department of Human Genetics, Edinburgh University, The Kings Buildings, Mayfield Road, Edinburgh 9, U.K.

SUMMARY

A computerised genetic register has been devised for ascertaining individuals at risk and preventing further cases of inherited disease. Clinical and computer staff have co-operated to design the system. The system enables medical staff to vet data and create a series of structured files which can subsequently be interrogated in order to assess the degree of risk to individuals. Details of file structure, access times, data chaining techniques, retrieval language and data security are presented in this paper.

INTRODUCTION

With the control of many infectious diseases and the improvement of environmental conditions, inherited disease is becoming relatively more important than in the past as a source of morbidity and mortality. For example, in a survey of child mortality in hospital it was found that some 40% of cases were due either directly or indirectly to genetic effects [1]. Because of the inherited or intrinsic nature of genetic disease, special methods are required for the ascertainment of families, assessment of risk, genetic counselling and prevention of further cases of the disease in the family. In order to integrate information from these various activities a genetic register system has been developed [2]. This paper describes the establishment of a computing system to control the data handling of this genetic register.

An approach was made by the Department of Human Genetics in the University of Edinburgh to the Regional Centre to examine the possibility of setting up a computer based register. The initial proposals for a fully comprehensive scheme were considered to be too ambitious for the resources available to both parties. By mid 1970 a simplified system had been proposed with the following specification:

1. To design and implement a file system with fast access and a good degree of security.

2. To design a data capture system which was convenient and easy to check.

3. To design and implement a suite of programs to be used for file initialisation, data retrieval and file maintenance.

Using this specification it was possible to produce a system within a year. The available resources consisted of the part time effort of staff at the Regional Centre and the Department of Human Genetics and a total of about 30 hours C.P.U. time on the Regional Centre's I.C.L. 4-75 using the Edinburgh Multi-Access System (E.M.A.S.) [3].

This economy both of financial and human resources was necessary in view of the fact that for both parties the project was one of many activities.

FILE DESIGN

From the outset it was not clear how large a filing system would be required. Clearly the size of the file would be related to the geographical area covered. In view of the Regionalisation of hospital areas it was decided to design a file system capable of holding about 25-30,000 people.

The design of the file format was dictated by the method of data capture. A pre-formatted data card has been designed to enable non-technical staff to use the system easily. The layout is arranged in such a way that a person's data falls into four categories:

1. Personal details

2. Medical details

3. Disease and family history details

4. Visit and counselling details

Once a person has been placed on the register it is unlikely that any of his personal, disease or medical details will alter, but several visits at different time may be recorded. On this basis the data file was split into two sub-files, one for the fixed data and one for the visit data. This also has the advantage of protecting at least part of the data in the event of file corruption.

With the record format defined it remained only to determine how records could be addressed directly and how to connect like records. The solution of this problem was influenced by two factors.

1. The entire system was to be run on the Regional Centre I.C.L. 4-75 under the E.M.A.S. operating system.

2. The programming language to be used was IMP [4].

The IMP language can be regarded as a subset of PL/1, but with some extra features for bit and character manipulation. Also an extremely useful direct access I/O feature was available enabling the user to transfer data easily between core and a direct access storage device.

With these available facilities a unit of information called a 'PAGE' was defined as 4096 characters. This definition coincides with the 'page size' used by the virtual addressing unit on the I.C.L. 4-75. 'PAGES' are used for both sub-files, the only difference being the number of records per 'PAGE' and hence the addressing of each record.

For the fixed data a record length of 256 characters was chosen. This enables 16 records to be held in one 'PAGE'. To address this record the user only has to know the 'PAGE' number and the record position within the 'PAGE'. It was decided to use a 16 bit address mechanism for this file, 5 bits for the record position and 11 bits for the PAGE number. This allows a maximum page address of $2^{11}-1$ or 2047 giving a total file capacity of 32,752 people. This may not appear to be an excessive number, but it should be remembered that a consultant may have several sets of files for different regions.

The addressing technique for the visit data file is the same as that used for the fixed data file. The only difference is that because the record length is shorter, 96 can be put into one 'PAGE'. This increase in the number of records requires more bits to address each one and so a 24 bit address system is used. 16 bits are used to address the PAGE and 8 bits used to define the record position. The longer addressing field allows the visit data file to be larger than the fixed data file. This may be necessary in view of the fact that a person may have as many visits, and up to nine are recorded.

For the system to have a logical method of data retrieval, some method for linking related records had to be defined. On the fixed data files a closed loop chain was defined with forward and backward pointers. The two way pointer system was to allow a person to be easily deleted from the file without too much chain reorganisation. Each record was linked into at least three of the following chains:

1. A family list
2. A disease list
3. A list of people at risk to a disease
4. A list of people affected by a disease

Access to these chains is in two ways. To enter the family chain a lookup is made on a table of family numbers. Associated with each family number is an address of a person in that particular family chain.

For the disease chains there exists a list of diseases with three addresses. The first pointer is to the first person in the disease chain, the remaining two are for the first person in the risk and affected chains respectively. All these lists are held in a separate file and are copied into local storage at run time. For the visit file data a simple chain is used. Each record containing visit data also has a pointer to that person's next visit record. The last visit in the chain is denoted by a zero value pointer. The addresses of the first and last visits in the chain are held in the fixed data files.

To complete the file design one only needs some way of defining when a record is attached to the register or not. For both files a technique of 'bit mapping' is used. With this technique a single bit is used to represent a record. The setting of this bit to '1' or '0' is used to indicate whether the record is attached or not. In the case of the fixed data records a single contiguous area is used to map the file and this is held permanently in core. For the visit data several maps are used. There is a main map which is used for the visit 'PAGES'. To supplement this each 'PAGE' has its own map which is used for the records within that 'PAGE'. With this method it is easier to find a partially empty 'PAGE' and then the actual empty records within that 'PAGE'.

PROGRAM DESIGN

A modular approach was made to the program design. It is far easier for staff not programming regularly to link together a set of modules and produce results rather than write complete programs each time. Three main modules have been written and are described below.

File Handling

This module is the kernel of the system. It handles all data transfer between the core store and the direct access store, manages the file space and the bit maps. In order to try and cut down file I/O during random access searches an intermediate work area or 'cache' arrangement has been used. When the file system is opened all the chain address tables are copied into local arrays in the program. At the same time eight pages from the fixed data and visit files are copied into a fixed working area. Associated with this work area is a table of the actual 'PAGE' numbers and an indix of when the 'PAGE' was last referenced. As new 'PAGES' are requested the last used 'PAGES' are copied back to disk and the index is updated. At the end of each run all the 'PAGES' and tables are copied back to the correct location on disk.

Text Processing

This module contains routines both for data checking and analysing data retrieval commands. The data retrieval method used is to set up a search or retrieval vector with a set of default values. On the acceptance of a retrieval command the input text is analysed and the appropriate flags are set in the search vector. Any item not referred to will retain its default value. When this vector is complete and no errors have been found, it is handed on to the retrieval process.

Retrieval and Output Control

This module contains the chain searching routines and a set of routines to output the data in an easily readable form. Included in this module is the routine to decode the data.

Results and Remarks

All the previously described components of the system have now been written and tested. A set of trial data has been made up and the system is currently being assessed for ease of use and response. The trial system is about 64 'PAGES' in total and the access times for data have been very encouraging.

The security of the data is ensured by the need for a password to log in to E.M.A.S. and a further password when a data retrieval command is given. As indicated above all data in the files is encoded and is only decoded on receipt of the correct password. For easy file maintenance several other programs have been set up. These include a program to initiate a file and define its passwords and a program to dump the direct access files onto a sequential tape file.

The computing system is now being handed over to the Department of Human Genetics for field trials leading to its full integration in the Genetic Register system. From now on the role of the Regional Centre will be that of a Consultant in implementing the system in practice.

Finally, although the system has been written in IMP and runs on an I.C.L. 4-75, the Regional Centre has developed an IMP system to run on an IBM 360 or 370. It is possible to move the entire system onto a 360 or 370 operating under O.S. and use it either in a batch mode or possibly under T.S.O. from a terminal.

REFERENCES

1. D.F. ROBERTS, J. CHAVEZ and S.D.M. COURT, "The genetic component in child mortality" *Archives of Disease in Childhood 45*, 33-38 (1970).

2. A.E.H. EMERY and C. SMITH, "Ascertainment and prevention of genetic disease" *Brit. Med. J.*, *3*, 636-637 (1970).7.

3. *Edinburgh Multi-Access System Reference Manual*. Edited by H. Whitfield,

4. *Edinburgh IMP Language Manual*. Edited by A. McKendrick.

FUTURE ROLE OF BIOSIMULATION IN A MEDICAL CURRICULUM

M.J. PEDELTY

Medical College of Virginia, Richmond, Virginia 23219, U.S.A.

G.D. FORD

Department of Physiology, M.C.V.-V.C.U., Richmond, Virginia 23219, U.S.A.

SUMMARY

It is proposed to integrate on-line uses of a digital computer into a medical curriculum at the Medical College of Virginia. Starting in about September, 1974 computer applications will gradually be introduced into the laboratories to 1) simulate complex experiments which the student would otherwise not have time or ability to perform, and 2) alleviate the burden of complex calculations (e.g., cardiac output during real experiments by providing on-line data collection and analysis). This paper will describe the engineering, software, and hardware considerations for such a system, and the types of simulation envisaged.

OBJECTIVES

The methodology described in this paper is designed:

To improve the quality of Health Science laboratory teaching methods by means of certain hardware and software enhancements to a laboratory computer facility.

To enrich the learning experience generally, and, as a secondary effect, to remove some of the awe with which computers are erroneously endowed. To display variables which are not automatically available as a transducer output, and to simulate those relationships which are difficult or impossible to measure directly in the context of a student laboratory exercise.

RATIONALE AND ASSUMPTIONS

It is assumed that the quality of laboratory education for the Health Professional can be substantially enhanced by means of 1) simulation of medical problem relationships by electronic means, 2) on-line capture of experimental data for computer reduction and display. Such a computer should be able to display the values of both the variables commonly recorded in a non-automated environment, and those variables which are the result of some computational process, and which, although they are highly significant, it would be impracticable to display without computer intervention.

It is, therefore, felt that the College should establish a very flexible facility for computer-student station interaction in a laboratory setting, so that additional applications can constantly be added, primarily by writing appropriate software to handle them. We shall use the term "on-line" to designate the communication of data to and from a student station during a laboratory exercise. Much of this data will be in analog format.

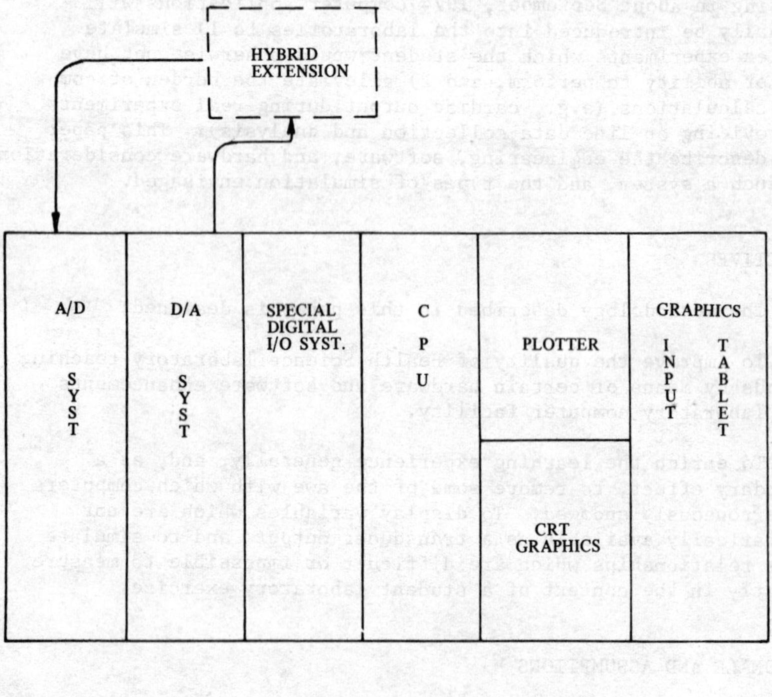

Fig. 1. Real-time computer system.

The intent of this project is to broaden and enhance the capabilities of a computer system for on-line experimentation and clinical analysis laboratory training, and to provide for equipment for on-line simulation of medical, pharmacological and physiological interactions. The computer system is thought to be quite powerful in these respects, and it requires only the addition of certain peripheral attachments, a communications system, and appropriate software to bring the capability into the teaching environment.

It is expected that a digital computer would be a more economical resource for our needs (where up to 20 users must be serviced simultaneously) than a hybrid computer would be. Since the outputs are continually updated, in a typical application of this type, the program never "stops." To service 20 users, some kind of "round robin" scheduling must occur, with hardware queuing of software service calls. The computer envisaged appears well adapted to these needs and it can handle several programs in foreground, depending on the amount of core available.* It is assumed that, in most cases of interest, the machine cycle time will allow 20-user access. This will depend on the data rates involved and the amount of computing required to display an output variable.

Facilities To Be Made Available

The third-generation computer already installed is an IBM 370 model 145, to which the real-time CPU will be connected by telephone line and data modem. Next to the computer, there will be an experiment room allowing apparatus to be coupled to the computer. There will be 32 channels of analog input and several digital i/o channels available to the experimenter, as well as analog outputs for driving an oscilloscope and/or X-Y plotter, and a means for recognizing commands generated by the experimenter in a control box, (e.g., "start data," "abort"). A teletype will also be provided. Real-time data will be collected in core memory and transferred to the disc or tape for storage and analysis. Other peripherals available will include a card reader and printer. Thus the real-time CPU can also serve as a remote terminal to the batch processor (370/145). The experiment room will be large enough to accommodate a class of student-observers.

In addition to serving the experiment room, it is intended to wire several other labs in this 15 story building so as to

---

*A Sigma 6 computer with 32K words of core will be used. Each word consists of 32 bits. The operating system is RBM.

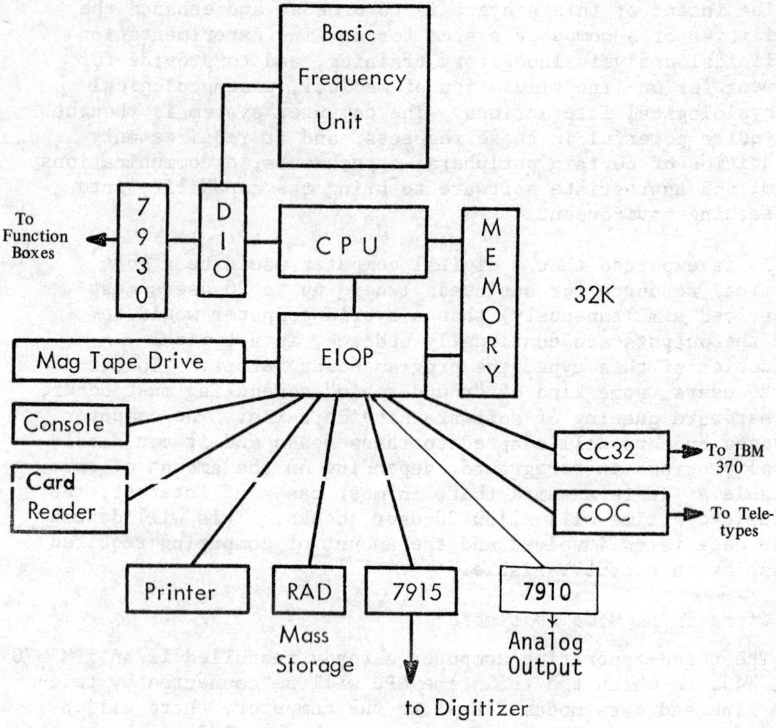

Fig. 2.

provide similar on-line capability. In this connection, the Department of Visual Education has already wired the building and other parts of the campus, including the Dental School, for closed circuit TV. It is believed that these circuits would be entirely adequate for our analog signals, provided suitable modulators or "op. amps." are obtained.

METHODOLOGY

It is proposed to augment a real-time facility by providing for student access to the computer by providing the faculty with the means to create meaningful learning experiences by means of

1. transmission of real-time experimental data to the computer (and, in some cases, transmission back of computed

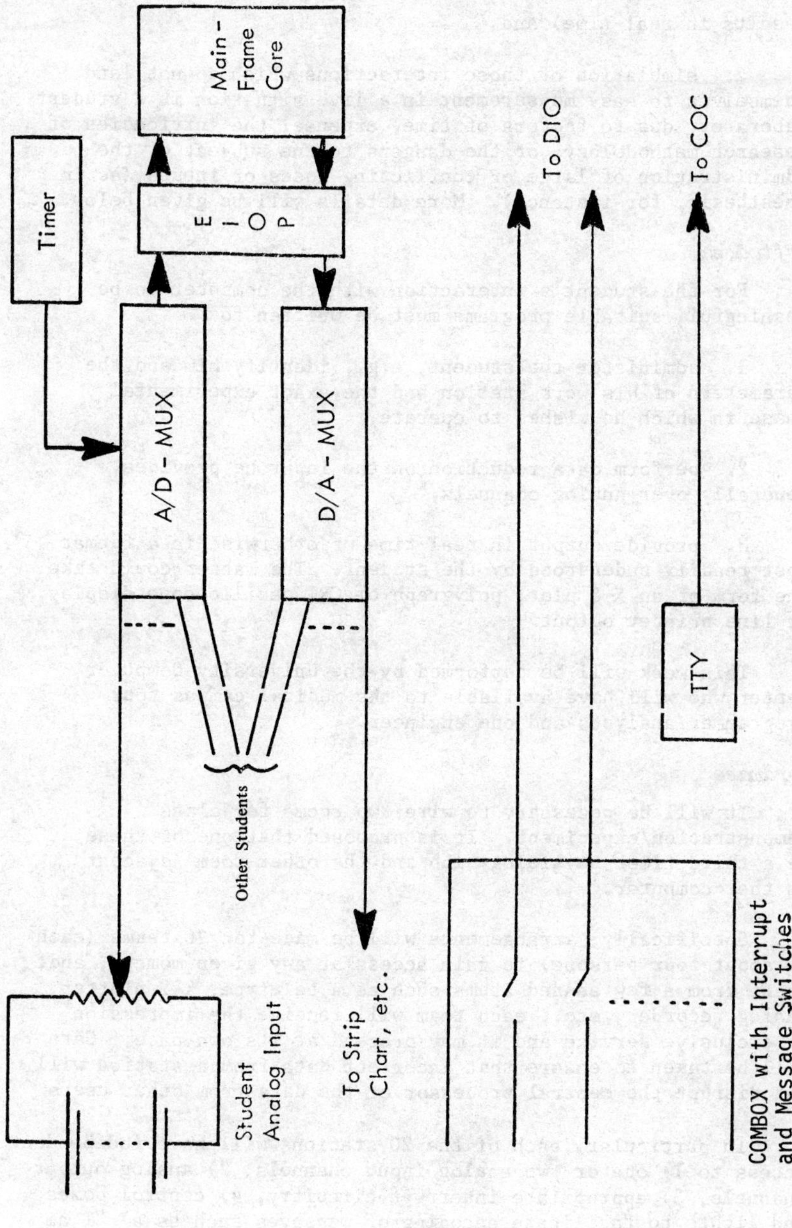
Timer
Main-Frame Core
E I O P
A/D - MUX
D/A - MUX
To DIO
To COC
TTY
Other Students
Student Analog Input
To Strip Chart, etc.
COMBOX with Interrupt and Message Switches

Fig. 3.

results in real-time) and

2. simulation of those interactions which do not lend themselves to easy measurement in a live situation in a student laboratory due to factors of time, expense, the intricacies of research methodology, or the dangers to the subject of the administration of large or conflicting doses or inputs (as in anesthesia, for instance). More details will be given below.

Software

For the student's interaction with the computer to be meaningful, suitable programs must be written to

1. administer the student, e.g., identify him and the parameters of his work station and the exact experimental phase in which he wishes to operate,

2. perform data reduction on the input he provides, generally over analog channels,

3. provide output in real-time or otherwise in a format most readily understood by the student. The latter could take the form of an X-Y plot, polygraph or CRT oscilloscope display, or line printer output.

This work will be performed by the University Computer Center who will have available to the medical campus four programmer/analysts and one engineer.

Hardware

It will be necessary to wire two rooms for class demonstration/experiment. It is proposed that one of these be a third-floor physiology lab and the other room adjacent to the computer.

Specifically, arrangements will be made for 20 teams (each of about four persons) to gain access at any given moment, and, apart from a few shared items such as a teletype, X-Y plotter, analog recorder, etc., each team will receive the impression of exclusive service and it may proceed at its own pace. Care will be taken to ensure that incorrect data from a station will not disrupt the central processor or the data from other users.

In particular, each of the 20 stations will have independent access to 1) one or two analog input channels, 2) analog output channels, 3) appropriate interrupt circuitry, 4) control boxes and lights to facilitate encoding of messages such as a) "I am injecting drug number 2 now," or b) "I need to see the resting potential now." This convention will be recognized by the computer software, provided the student has identified his station and experiment name via the teletype.

Laboratory Methodology

Students will be handed a sheet showing what it is they are expected to accomplish in the lab. In a few cases, this may be organized on a "self-study" basis whereby a student schedules an appointment with the computer. In case the experiment involves a simulation, the "sheet" will explain the relationship between a student station control panel and physiological or drug variables being simulated. This panel will generally have one or two analog variables (dial) and several thumb-wheel switches. For example, pushing a button may be the equivalent of injecting a solution, the "strength" of which has been set on the dial. The system may be set to run in real-time, (in which case one second of elapsed laboratory time equals one second of simulated time) or not, e.g., one minute equals one hour, so that a student may observe a 24-hour reaction in 24 minutes. This does not have to be linear or even continuous, e.g., if a student is to try 3 "drugs" but does not wish to wait for the effect of each to fully decay, he could call upon the computer to supply different time slices - say 6 hours apart in simulated time - but requiring

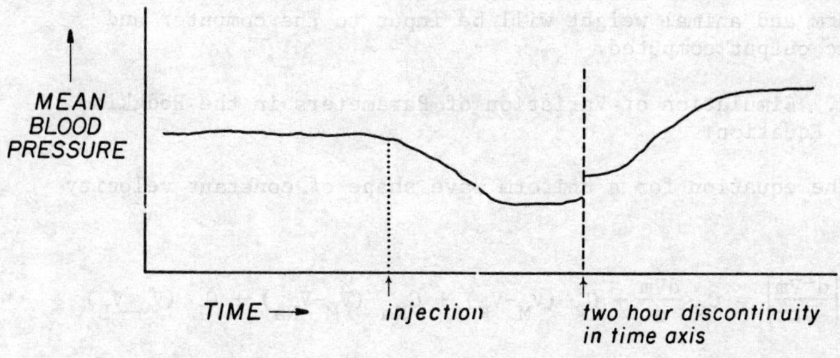

Fig. 4.

only moments of laboratory time to reach each new equilibrium. Thus, a suitable simulation could compress into one session what might otherwise require several days of observation. In another case, the "sheet" might not tell the student the drug or class, but require him to deduce this on the basis of observation. It would not matter if the computer went into "shock" or "died" in the process.

On the basis of the physical facilities available (or easily constructed), each teaching department will be asked to suggest experiments/demonstrations it would like to see performed by student-computer interaction. At last, they could be freed from recording only those variables that are easily measured, since the computer can, in theory, provide almost any kind of an output plot, e.g., mean blood pressure vs. time or vs. drug concentration.

Brief Discussion of Candidate Experiments/Demonstrations

1. Computation of Cardiac Output:

From a pressure transducer (catheter), a wave-form of two peaks and a valley [1] is recorded. These have been the input to a lengthy "hand" calculation performed by the student. This calculation is not regarded by the responsible faculty member as having any significance as a learning experience and it should be automated. This would free the student to concentrate on the significance of the variables in his experiment. The pressure waveform and animal weight will be input to the computer and cardiac output computed.

2. Simulation of Variation of Parameters in the Hodgkin-Huxley Equation:

The equation for a uniform wave shape of constant velocity is:

$$\left(\frac{a}{2RA^2}\right)\left(\frac{d^2Vm}{dt^2}\right) = C_M \frac{dVm}{dt} + G_K\ (V_M - V_K) + G_{Na}\ (V_M - V_{Na}) + G_L\ (V_M - V_L)$$

Thus the membrane potential is a function of the potassium and sodium conductances, G_K and G_{Na}, which in turn are functions of (instantaneous) membrane potential and time. By means of a digital simulation, the student will be able to input transients in G_K and G_{Na}, to control their amplitude and duration, and observe V_M, in pseudo real time.

A model by E. R. Lewis [2] (based on the work of Hodgkin, et al., Eccles and Bullock) will be used to demonstrate certain wave propagation phenomena and pacemaker activity.

At a later time, additional simulations illustrating synaptic conduction will be programmed [3].

The following three applications are designed for first year Medical and Dental students.

3. Simulation of Renal Physiology (see appendix for details).

4. Simulation of Cardiovascular Physiology (see appendix for details).

5. Simulation of Endocrine Physiology (see appendix for details).

6. Teaching of Medical Diagnosis by Simulation:

Written medical symptoms will be provided to the student who will then call for additional "tests." These will be simulated by the computer, which will provide outputs to be interpreted by the student, for example an e.k.g. waveform or a typeout from an automated clinical laboratory computer. After one or more such "tests," the student will be asked to indicate his diagnosis to the computer.

This simulation will be created in "layers" from modest beginnings. It is possible that the earliest e.c.g.'s will not be synthesized but merely stored in digital form. The effects of drugs will be added, as in the following case.

7. Simulation of I.C.U. Monitor Functions for Myocardial Infarction Training:

A simulated patient with symptoms of M.I. will be displayed via oscilloscope, with appropriate alarms. The presently used Arrhythmia Simulator is less realistic, since, for given dial settings, every wave cycle is identical. Drug effects will be programmed. An attempt will be made at a later time to incorporate some of the features of the NIH-MIRU Project, now using XDS Sigma 3 computers.

8. Effect of Drugs and Drug-Inhibitors on Blood Pressure:

A simulated animal (dog, human) will be programmed to respond to drugs of variable dosage, administered intravenously. These will be input at the student lab station by means of dials and switches. A polygraph output will show mean blood pressure vs. time.

Effects of drug habituation can also be programmed into the model.

9. Simulation of Anesthesia Administration:

In a similar demonstration the vital signs of a human patient will be provided as outputs responding to various gas or i.v. concentrations.

EVALUATION

The main criterion upon which to judge the success of the biosimulations and experiments conducted is: was each laboratory experience meaningful? For example, was it pertinent to the remainder of the course, was it realistic, did it have any permanent impact on the student?

Factors affecting the above are: selection and timing of the topic to be illustrated, in relation to the rest of the course, preparation of the student by oral, graphic or written means, technical excellence of the hardware and software used, their exact use in relation to the problem illustrated, and the actions of the student during and after the exercise.

Tests and questionnaires will be devised to measure both the subjective and objective results of each laboratory encounter, to measure both the strength of that lesson module and the characteristics of those students who derive greatest benefit from a computerized learning experience. This phase will be carried out in conjunction with the Office of Educational Resources and Research, and with Miss Hampton, Biomedical Communications Specialist, Visual Education Department.

Each simulation or on-line experiment programmed and in use will be judged according to its value to 1) the responsible faculty member, 2) his students.

A questionnaire will be made up and administered to test for reactions. Examples of questions to be asked are: "Were the objectives of this demonstration clear to you?" "How well were the stated objectives met?" "What changes would you have made?" "Do you think the availability of the computer was important **in** this exercise?" "In what ways will this experience contribute to your competency?"

Student reactions will be graded on a scale from positive to negative and correlated with school attended and age or year in program. These statistics will form the basis for improving individual teaching modules, and for the selection of classes for future computer-controlled experiences. (Student reactions to individual lecturers are already being recorded for computer input at MCV)*.

REFERENCES

1. W.F. HAMILTON, "Measurement of the cardiac output" chapter 17 of *Handbook of Physiology* Sec. 2: Circulation, I (American Physiology Society, Washington, D.C., 1962).

2. E.R. LEWIS, "Using electronic circuits to model simple neuroelectric interactions" *Proc. IEEE 56* 931-949 (June, 1968).

3. C.F. STEVENS, "Synaptic Physiology" *Proc. IEEE 56* 916-930 (June, 1968).

4. D.S. RIGGS, *Control Theory and Physiological Feedback Mechanisms* (Williams & Wilkins, Baltimore, Md., 1970).

---

*Details of simulations concerning renal, cardiovascular and endocrine physiology are available from the authors.

ON RASHEVSKY'S MODEL FOR NERVOUS STIMULATION

T. POSTELNICU

Center of Mathematical Statistics of the Romanian Academy, 21 Calea Griviței, Bucharest 12, Romania

SUMMARY

Certain biophysico-mathematical theories concerning nervous stimulation are presented. Proceeding from the "two factors theory" of N. Rashevsky, the author studies the use of a sinusoidal current whose amplitude varies exponentially in stimulation experiments. In this case, an equation of the rheobase is obtained.

INTRODUCTION

H.A. Blair considers [1] only one exciting agent or substance in the theory of excitation. But in the light of the experimental knowledge we may feel fairly certain that the exciting substance is either ionic in its nature or at least closely related to some ionic reactions. All ionic theories admit that cations are responsible for the excitation, thus accounting for the fact that excitation occurs at the cathode upon passing a current. But it is usually omitted that the current will bring to the cathode both exciting (monovalent) and inhibiting (bivalent) ions, so that a consideration of the accumulation at the cathode of only one kind of ions, or of their total sum, does not represent even approximately the actual facts. This leads to a two-factor theory of excitation, developed originally by N. Rashevsky [2].

He considers that the nerve contains two substances (or two groups of substances), the concentrations of which we denote by ε and j; the ratio ε/j determines the excitation. Whenever the ratio ε/j becomes longer than a certain constant, h, excitation occurs. Let the concentrations in the resting nerve be ε_0 and j_0. We may put h = 1 and thus excitation occurs for

$$\varepsilon \geqslant j \tag{1}$$

From the fact that a resting nerve is not spontaneously excited, it follows that $\varepsilon_0 < j_0$.

Whenever the current flows along the axon, various substances which are ionized are transported in one or another direction. To start with, four assumptions are possible. Let us consider that both exciting and inhibiting substances are transported from anode to cathode, so that ε and j decrease at the former, while at the latter they increase. We assume that the rate of change due to the current is proportional to the latter and that also any excess of ε or j over ε_0 and j_0, respectively, or any deficiency below those values tends to decrease at a rate proportional to that excess or deficiency. So we have at the cathode the Rashevsky's differential equations system:

$$\frac{d\varepsilon}{dt} = KI - k(\varepsilon - \varepsilon_0)$$

$$\frac{dj}{dt} = MI - m(j - j_0) \tag{2}$$

where K,M,k and m are constants. Formally these equations (2) are identical with Blair's equation.

Let the current I in equations (2) be of the form

$$I = I_0 e^{-\lambda t} \sin \omega t \tag{3}$$

Introducing (3) into (2) and integrating them we find

$$\varepsilon = \varepsilon_0 + Ce^{-kt} + \frac{KI_0}{\omega^2+(k-\lambda)^2}\left[(k-\lambda)\sin \omega t - \omega \cos \omega\right] e^{-\lambda t}$$

$$j = j_0 + C_1 e^{-mt} + \frac{MI_0}{\omega^2+(m-\lambda)^2}\left[(m-\lambda)\sin \omega t - \omega \cos \omega t\right] e^{-\lambda t} \tag{4}$$

Only for small t does the terms e^{-kt} and e^{-mt} play a role. Its effect is to increase the maximal value of ε and j. As t becomes large, the exponential terms become negligible, and ε and j are represented by

$$\varepsilon = \varepsilon_0 + \frac{KI_0}{\omega^2+(k-\lambda)^2}\left[(k-\lambda)\sin \omega t - \omega \cos \omega t\right] e^{-\lambda t}$$

$$j = j + \frac{KI_0}{\omega^2+(k-\lambda)^2}\left[(k-\lambda)\sin \omega t - \omega \cos \omega t\right] e^{-\lambda t} \tag{5}$$

The quantities ε and j have a series of equidistant extrema, occuring at times given by

$$\frac{d\varepsilon}{dt} = 0, \frac{dj}{dt} = 0$$

and we obtain:

$$t_\varepsilon = \frac{1}{\omega} \text{arctg} \frac{k\omega}{\lambda k-\lambda^2-\omega^2}, \ t_j = \frac{1}{\omega} \text{arctg} \frac{m\omega}{m\lambda-\lambda^2-\omega^2} \tag{6}$$

Introducing these values for t into (5) we find ε_{max} and j_{max}. Using an elementary procedure we obtain the amplitude or the maximum value of ε - j:

$$(\varepsilon-j)_{max} = \varepsilon_0 - j_0 + I_0 \sqrt{(A\omega-B\lambda)^2 + (A\lambda+B\omega)^2} \exp(-\frac{\lambda}{\omega} \text{arctg} \frac{A\omega-B\lambda}{A\omega+B\lambda}) \tag{7}$$

where

$$A = \frac{K(k-\lambda)}{\omega^2+(k-\lambda)^2} - \frac{M(m-\lambda)}{\omega^2+(m-\lambda)^2}, \ B = \frac{M\omega}{\omega^2+(m-\lambda)^2} - \frac{K\omega}{\omega^2+(k-\lambda)^2} \tag{8}$$

EXCITATION BY ALTERNATING CURRENTS

We shall now discuss the excitation by alternating currents. First, we shall consider the case in which

$$\frac{K}{k} = \frac{M}{m} \tag{9}$$

The rheobase R for cathodic excitation, (the cathodic rheobase R_c) is found by considering that for that value of the current, that is, for I = R_c, the ε- and j-curves just touch each other at one point. In fact, for I = R_c, we not only have ε = j but also $d\varepsilon/dt = dj/dt$, at a time t = t*. Thus, we obtain:

$$R_c = \frac{k}{k-m} I_0 \sqrt{(A'\omega-B'\lambda)^2 + (A'\lambda+B'\omega)^2} \exp(-\frac{\lambda}{\omega} \text{arctg} \frac{A'\omega-B'\lambda}{A'\lambda+B'\omega}) \tag{10}$$

where A',B' are obtained from (8) using (9).

Let us consider now in (3) the particular case λ = 0, when the current I in equation (2) will be of the form

$$I = I_0 \sin\omega t \tag{3'}$$

Introducing (3') into (2) and integrating them, we find

$$\varepsilon - \varepsilon_0 = \frac{I_0 K}{k^2+\omega^2} (k \sin\omega t - \omega \cos\omega t)$$

$$j - j_0 = \frac{I_0 M}{m^2+\omega^2} (m \sin\omega t - \omega \cos\omega t) \tag{11}$$

Hence

$$\varepsilon - j = I_0 \left[\left(\frac{Kk}{k^2+\omega^2} - \frac{Mm}{m^2+\omega^2}\right) \sin\omega t - \left(\frac{K\omega}{k^2+\omega^2} - \frac{M\omega}{m^2+\omega^2}\right) \cos\omega t \right] + \varepsilon_0 - j_0 \tag{12}$$

By a procedure similar to that used before, we find that the amplitude or the maximum of $\varepsilon - j$ is equal to

$$(\varepsilon - j)_{max} = I_0 \sqrt{\left(\frac{Kk}{k^2+\omega^2} - \frac{Mm}{m^2+\omega^2}\right)^2 + \left(\frac{K\omega}{k^2+\omega^2} - \frac{Mm}{m^2+\omega^2}\right)^2} + \varepsilon_0 - j_0 \tag{13}$$

After elementary rearrangements, using (9) we find

$$(\varepsilon - j)_{max} = I_0 \frac{(K-M)\omega}{\sqrt{(k^2+\omega^2)(m^2+\omega^2)}} + \varepsilon_0 - j_0 \tag{14}$$

From the Rashevsky's formula for the cathodic rheobase we have:

$$j_0 - \varepsilon_0 = \frac{R_c(K-M)}{k} \tag{15}$$

Excitation by an alternating current will just occur when the amplitude I_0 of the current is high enough to make

$$(\varepsilon - j)_{max} = 0 \tag{16}$$

Introducing (15) into (14) and the latter into (16), we find

$$\frac{I_0}{R_c} = \sqrt{\left(1 + \frac{\omega^2}{k^2}\right)\left(1 + \frac{m^2}{\omega^2}\right)} \tag{17}$$

Equation (17) gives us the ratio of the limiting amplitude of an alternating sinusoidal current to the limiting value of a constant current in terms of the frequency ω. A.V. Hill has derived [3] a similar expression from a different theory.

Considering the case when both exciting and inhibiting substances are transported from cathode to anode we find that equation (2) remains the same except for a change in the signs of I. As regards the cases when the exciting substances are transported from anode to cathode, the inhibiting ones are in the opposite direction and, conversely, these must be discarded as not agreeing with the experiments.

Other contributions to the two-factor theory have been made by A.S. Householder [4].

REFERENCES

1. H.A. BLAIR, *J. Gen. Physiol. 16*, 177 (1932).

2. N. RASHEVSKY, *Mathematical Biophysics 389* (1960).

3. A.V. HILL, *Proc. Roy. Soc. London B 119*, 305 (1936).

4. A.S. HOUSEHOLDER, *Bull. Math. Biophysics 6*, 157 (1944).

5. T. POSTELNICU, *Fiziologia 4*, 319 (1965).

COMPUTER-AIDED LOCALIZATION OF LESIONS IN THE NERVOUS SYSTEM

A.U. MEYER

Professor of Electrical Engineering, Newark College of Engineering, 323 High Street, Newark, New Jersey 07102, U.S.A.

W.K. WEISSMAN

Assistant Professor of Surgery (Neurosurgery), College of Medicine and Dentistry of New Jersey, New Jersey Medical School, 65 Bergen Street, Newark, New Jersey 07103, U.S.A.

SUMMARY

A process for the localization and demonstration of disease within the human nervous system is presented utilizing computer analysis of the physician's examination of his patient. The results of a standard clinical neurological examination serve as data input to a computer. The process is based on knowledge of the association of neural pathways with the various outcomes of clinical tests. The output is a display of factors indicative of the incidence of involvement of specific neural pathways whose total effect produces a map of probable lesion in the nervous system. The method is suitable for clinical application as well as the teaching of neuroanatomy, neurophysiology and neuropathology. The application of the process to the localization of a brainstem lesion is presented.

INTRODUCTION*

The human nervous system encompasses a variety of phenomena suitable to study and speculation and each such class poses a range of appropriate method and technique. This paper investigates certain known properties of the nervous system of man

---

*This paper discusses a new process developed by the authors for localization of lesions in the nervous system. A portion of the material of this paper was presented at the Symposium on Computer-Aided Medical Diagnosis, held on May 31, 1972 at Newark College of Engineering [13]. Presented here is a modification of a comprehensive treatment of the subject [16]. Emphasis on the medical aspects will be published in a medical journal.

affliced by disease and develops a practical method for demonstrating the location of the disease process (lesion) by means of computer analysis.

This topic, naturally, implies medical diagnosis. But we disclaim, in this paper, any attempt to describe the "making of a diagnosis", a process more complex than that which we do effect, namely, that of localizing a lesion within the nervous system.

The Encyclopaedia Britannica has treated, at length, the concept, "Diagnosis" [1]. Pertinent to this paper are these excerpted quotations: "In making a diagnosis, the physician consciously or subconsciously follows certain definite procedures in logic . . . he collects data that more clearly outline the problem . . . he compares the actual facts with the suggestions to see if there is an identity between the facts established and the suggested solutions . . . to assemble the data, to make use of the relevant and to discard the irrelevant information . . . often requires a mental ability of the highest order".

These quoted excerpts from sentences and phrases serve to indicate selected aspects of the general problem of diagnosis [2]*. Several approaches to computer-aided neurologic diagnosis have been employed, some based on data from the clinical history [3,4], others adding data from clinical signs [5,6], but these methods do not localize the neural lesion which remains the prime requisite for both generality of method and practicality.** Although we adhere to the conceptual approach to diagnosis as previously quoted, the method of localization to be described does not simulate the physician's mental technique, but employs algorithmic manipulation relating the data supplied by the examining physician to anatomical knowledge to produce a map of probable lesion.

NEURAL PATHWAYS AND NEUROLOGICAL TEST-OUTCOMES

In a clinical neurological examination, each test-outcome depends on function or malfunction of a sequence of neural generators and pathways, the knowledge of which is established

*For a discussion of the general problems of computer-aided medical diagnosis, as well as a review of pertinent literature up to 1965, see Ledley [2], pp. 418-485.

**Publication of work in the field of computer-aided neurological diagnosis is scant. Analysis of the logic of neurologists' method of diagnosis bears on the subject indirectly. See Kleinmuntz [14] and Barrons [15].

in the field of the neurosciences; anatomy [7,8,9], physiology [10], pathology [11] and neurology [12]. In other words, each test-outcome is associated with signal-flow and/or signal-flow failure through certain neural pathways. Thus, any signal-flow failure may be an indication of a lesion anywhere along the particular pathway involved.

In this paper, the physical structure of the nervous system is represented in terms of a set of elements which are chosen as volume-units.* The size of each volume-unit is selected as a compromise between desired resolution and simplicity. Each volume-unit contains portions of various neural pathways and generators. Thus, the signal-flow associated with test-outcomes can be traced in terms of a set of involved elements.

Each outcome of a neurological test may fall in any of the following categories:

(a) A specific set of elements is functioning.

(b) Malfunction is likely to be present in a specific set of elements; function in another set of elements may also be indicated.

(c) No interpretative significance — no inference can be made.

For example, as part of a clinical meurological examination, a patient is asked to close his eyes. Among the possible test-outcomes, the following three are representative of categories (a), (b) and (c) respectively:

(a) Patient closes both eyes.

(b) Patient closes right eye only.

(c) Patient does not close either eye.

The respective inferences for these test-outcomes are:

(a) A specific set of elements is *functioning* (namely the set of all volume-units containing neural pathways associated with signal flow relevant to this test-outcome).

---

*In the remainder of this paper, the terms "elements" and "volume-units" have the same definition and will be used synonymously.

(b) There exists *malfunction* in one or more of a specific set of elements, namely those containing neural pathways leading to the left eyelid. On the other hand, those volume-units containing neural pathways leading to the right eyelid are functioning.

(c) *No inference* can be made. For example, the patient may be deaf, may not understand the language, or some other unknown factor may be present.

The probability of malfunction in an element increases with the number of test-outcomes that indicate possible malfunction in a set containing this element (category (b) above). To give an illustration, suppose that a test-outcome (of category (b) occurs that implicates, say, 10 elements of possible malfunction. In the absence of other information, equal probability of malfunction exists for each of these 10 elements. Suppose now that a later test has also an outcome of category (b) associated with a different set of elements of possible malfunction except for one. The common element then contains two pathways of possible malfunction. Therefore, after occurance of the second test-outcome of category (b), the malfunction probability of the common element increases considerably, whereas that for all the other elements associated with malfunction decreases considerably. If any subsequent test-outcome of category (b) occurs which again includes the same element for possible malfunction (but none of the other elements implicated previously for possible malfunction by test-outcomes of category (b)), then the malfunction probability of that common element is even further increased, while that of the other elements is still further decreased.

The malfunction probability of each element depends not only on the number of test-outcomes implicating this element in malfunction, but also on the spatial probability distributions of all implicated pathways and on other factors. A realistic computation of malfunction probabilities for all elements, based on a large number of test-outcomes, is a rather complex task and will not be attempted here. The process described in the next section offers a practical solution to the problem of locating elements of probable malfunction as well as elements of probable function.

THE LOCALIZATION PROCESS

(a) *Malfunction Factors and Function Factors:*

Each element is identified by some suitable code; in the illustration to be presented in this paper, K elements will be considered, designated by numbers k, k = 1,2,...,K. To each element k, some factors are assigned which are indicative of malfunction or function.

The most basic of these factors is the "*malfunction factor*", M(k), which indicates the number of involvements of element k in pathways of malfunction [13]. In addition to the malfunction factor, this paper introduces other factors which advance the utility of the localizing process. Analogous to the malfunction factor, the "*function factor*", F(k), is defined to indicate the number of involvements of element k in pathways of function. Other factors will be introduced later. Initially, M(k) and F(k) are zero for all elements k = 1,2,...,K. Whenever a test-outcome indicates malfunction (or function) of certain neural pathways, then M(k) (or F(k)) will be incremented by some value or set of values for all elements k involved.

Each test-outcome is identified by some suitable code; for the purpose of illustration, let there be I test-outcomes considered, designated by numbers i, i = 1,2,...,I. Each test-outcome i falls into one of the three categories, (a), (b) or (c), described in the previous section. For each possible test-outcome i in categories (a) or (b), the set $\mathcal{M}(i)$ of elements k involved in pathways of malfunction, as well as the set $\mathcal{F}(i)$ of elements k involved in pathways of function, are stored. Moreover, incrementation factors $\Delta M(i,k)$ and $\Delta F(i,k)$ are stored (for all values of k in the set $\mathcal{M}(i)$ and all values of k in the set $\mathcal{F}(i)$ respectively) by which the malfunction factors M(k) and function factors F(k) are to be increased respectively if test-outcome i has occurred. Since I is the number of *possible* test-outcomes considered (for which data are stored in the computer), the number N of test-outcomes that do occur during a total neurological examination is less than I.

The basic data processing procedure is illustrated in the signal flow diagram shown in Fig. 1. During or after the neurological examination, the N test-outcomes that have occurred will be entered into the computer. Let i(n) be the nth of these test-outcome numbers entered. If this test-outcome i = i(n) indicates no inference (category (c)), a next test-outcome, i = i(n+1), will be entered. If test-outcome i = i(n) indicates any set $\mathcal{M}(i)$ of elements k included in pathways of malfunction,

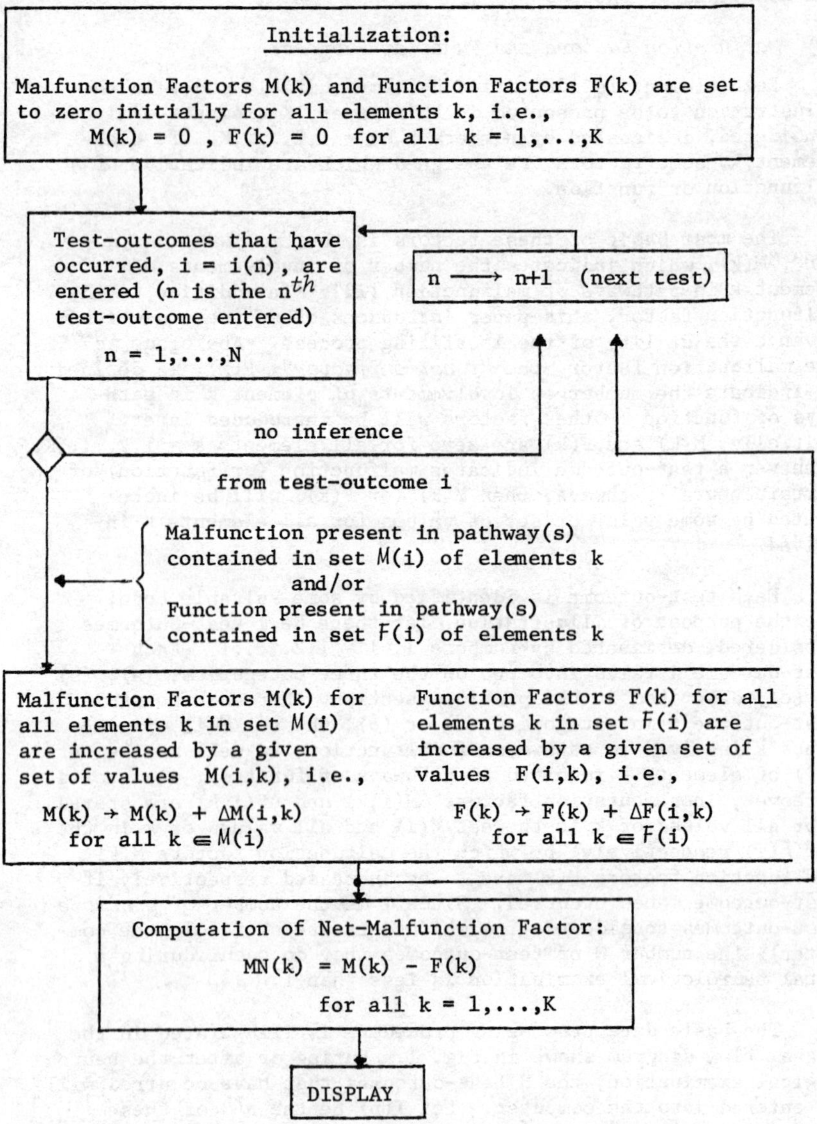

Fig. 1. Flow-diagram of the localization process.

then the malfunction factors M(k) for all elements k in the set $\mathcal{M}(i)$ will be increased by the (previously stored) incrementation factors $\Delta M(i,k)$. Likewise, for any set $\mathcal{F}(i)$ of elements k included in pathways of function, the function factors F(k) will be increased by the incrementation factors $\Delta F(i,k)$.

The incrementation factors are pre-selected. The simplest choice would be to take $\Delta M(i,k) = 1$ (and $\Delta F(i,k) = 1$) for all $k \in \mathcal{M}(i)$ (and $k \in \mathcal{F}(i)$ respectively)* and for every i for which malfunction pathways (function pathways) exist. More involved configurations of incrementation factors may be chosen depending on knowledge of relevance and relative weight of various test-outcomes.

(b) *Display of Factors:*

The simplest form of a display would consist of two separate lists of all malfunction factors and function factors for all elements k. A more informative output may be a display of the malfunction factors and function factors on a large 3-dimensional model of the particular portion of the nervous system under examination, with little lights placed at the centers of all volume-units. The intensity of each light (at volume-unit k) can be modulated as a function of the malfunction factor M(k) and/or the function factor F(k) for that volume-unit. A lesion would then be indicated by a concentration of light due to high M(k)'s in that region. A computer-generated display on a cathode-ray tube might offer even more attractive possibilities. None of these optical methods of display have yet been used by the authors.

A considerably simpler display can be given by computer printout in such a way that the values of M(k), F(k) or some suitable function of M(k) and F(k) are printed in locations corresponding to some suitable representation of the anatomy. This approach was applied by the authors to the brainstem. It was done by considering a pyramid that encloses the brainsteim (see Fig. 2) and by "slicing" this pyramid into ten sections. Each section, in turn, is subdivided into 100 volume-units. Thus, the brainstem is represented here in terms of 1000 elements (volume-units). The output display then is a printout of 10 square sections, as illustrated in Fig. 3. Here, the element numbers k are defined such that they give a logical representation of the section and its coordinates (described in caption of Fig. 3).

---

*The symbol "$\in$" means "belonging to the set", i.e., $k \in \mathcal{M}(i)$ means "all values of k belonging to the set $\mathcal{M}(i)$; $k \in \mathcal{F}(i)$ means "all values of k belonging to the set $\mathcal{F}(i)$.

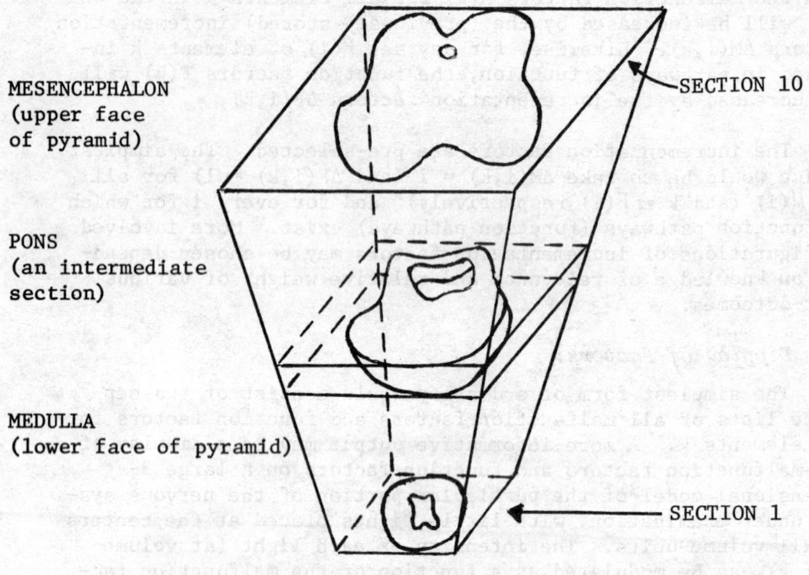

Fig. 2. Assignment of volume-units to the brainstem on the basis of physical interposition of the neural structure within a pyramid. This pyramid is then divided into ten horizontal sections, each passing through neural structures of anatomical interest. The lowest section is at the caudal terminus of the medulla oblongata, which will continue as the spinal cord. The highest section passes through the rostral mesencephalong to enter the interbrain and terminate the brainstem. Sections are numbered in ascending order. Each horizontal section is further divided by a grid into square areas, producing 100 volume-units each (see Fig. 3).

SECTION 1:

L= \ N=	0	1	2	3	4	5	6	7	8	9
10					1					
11				1	2	1				
12				1	2	1				
13					1	1				
14										
15										
16										
17										
18										
19										

SECTION 2:

L = \ N=	0	1	2	3	4	5	6	7	8	9
20					1					
21				1	2	2	1			
22				2	4	3	2	1		
23					1	2	1	1		
24						1	1	1		
25										
26										
27										
28										
29										

SECTION 10:

..... L =

L = \ N=	0	1	2	3	4	5	6	7	8	9
100										
101										
102										
103										
104										
105										
106										
107										
108										
109										

Fig. 3. Printout display of malfunction factors, M(k), on locations representing elements (volume-units) k = 10L + N. For example, for k = 235 (i.e., L = 23, N = 5), it is M(k) = M(235) = 2; for k = 224 (i.e., L = 22, N = 4), it is M(k) = M(224) = 4. In this display system, there are K = 1000 elements (volume-units), k = 100,101,..., 1099. Zero-values of M(k) are not displayed.

As mentioned before, the quantities displayed on each element (location) k may be the malfunction factor M(k), the function factor F(k), or some relation of both (or either) M(k) and/or F(k). Useful information on both malfunction and function in the nervous system will be provided by the *net-malfunction factor*, defined by

$$MN(k) = M(k) - F(k)$$

$$\text{for all } k = 1,2,\ldots,K.$$

This new factor has the feature that, if any element k is involved not only in a pathway or pathways of malfunction but also in a pathway or pathways of function, then M(k) will be diminished by F(k). The display of positive factors will indicate locations of probable malfunction, whereas the display of negative factors will indicate locations of probable function. Thus, one display provides an indication of locations of both probable malfunction and probable function.

In the interest of clarity, no factor of zero value is displayed when the printout is given in the form shown in Fig. 3. This holds for all of the factors defined in this paper.

In addition to its clinical use, the process has a natural application in the teaching of neurosciences. For example, it is possible to obtain on a computer console an instant printout or plot, in some suitable didactic form, of the neural pathways associated with the response to a neurological test, e.g., to demonstrate normal pathways of specific sensory modalities and their normal efferent course.

EXAMPLE: APPLICATION OF THE PROCESS TO THE CLINICAL EXAMINATION OF THE BRAINSTEM

(a) *Data Input to the Computer:*

Figure 4 shows a portion of the printout which lists the tests and their outcomes obtained during the performance of a clinical neurological examination of a given patient. The total number of tests performed and the order in which the test-outcomes are entered into the computer is arbitrary. In the example presented here, 28 neurological tests were administered to a patient in a standard but incomplete sequence.

The format of entering the data to the computer is subject to great flexibility. One approach would be to supply the

```
OBSERVE PUPILLARY SIZE * UNEQUAL; LEFT CONSTRICTED, RIGHT LARGER
SHINE LIGHT IN RIGHT PUPIL * RIGHT CONTRACTS MARKEDLY, LEFT MINIMALLY
OBSERVE PUPILS * RIGHT REDILATES
SHINE LIGHT IN LEFT PUPIL * RIGHT CONTRACTS MARKEDLY, LEFT MINIMALLY
OBSERVE PUPILS * LEFT REMAINS MIOTIC
ASK PATIENT TO LOOK UP TO RIGHT, THEN UP TO LEFT * MOVEMENTS NORMAL
ASK PATIENT TO LOOK DOWN TO RIGHT, THEN DOWN TO LEFT * MOVEMENTS NORMAL
ASK PATIENT TO FOLLOW MOVING FINGER HORIZONTALLY * NYSTAGMUS PRESENT
ASK PATIENT TO FOLLOW RISING FINGER * RIGHT LID ELEVATES, LEFT DROOPS
TOUCH PATIENT,S FOREHEAD TO ESTIMATE MOISTURE * RIGHT MOIST, LEFT DRY
ASK PATIENT TO DEMONSTRATE CHEWING ABILITY * JAW MOTION NORMAL
PIN-PRICK APPLIED TO RIGHT FACE * PATIENT COMPLAINS OF SHARP PAIN
PIN-PRICK APPLIED TO LEFT FACE * NO PAIN EXPERIENCED
TOUCH RIGHT CORNEAL EDGE WITH COTTON WHISP * BOTH EYELIDS BLINK
TOUCH LEFT CORNEAL EDGE WITH COTTON WHISP * NEITHER EYELID CONTRACTS
ASK PATIENT TO SQUEEZE EYELIDS SHUT AND EXAGGERATE SMILE * FACE SHOWS SYMMETRICAL GRIMACE
PLACE SWEET, SOUR OR SALT SOLUTION ON EACH ANTERIOR HALF-TONGUE * RIGHT SAVORS,LEFT IMPAIRED
PLACE SWEET,SOUR OR SALT SOLUTION ON EACH POSTERIOR-THIRD TONGUE* RIGHT SAVORS,LEFT DOES NOT
```

Fig. 4. Partial printout of tests and their outcomes obtained during the performance of a clinical neurological examination of a given patient. An asterisk separates the test-description from the test-outcome, which is entered by the physician. The physician may choose the tests to be performed as well as their sequence.

physician a catalog of all tests and their possible outcomes considered in the computer program. The actual test-outcomes can be entered into the computer by means of some suitable code; for example, by numbers supplied by the catalog. The catalog lists the tests in an order convenient to the physician. A reasonable format would be a list of tests in the sequence of a typical standard clinical neurological examination; however, the physician is free to modify the sequence or to omit any test.

Instead of having an external catalog, a statement of each test to be performed together with a list of its possible outcomes may be provided to the physician on a computer terminal. As soon as he enters on the terminal the actual test-outcome, or a statement of his choice to omit the test, the description of the next test and a list of its possible outcomes will appear on the terminal. The sequence of tests appearing on the terminal may, again, follow that of a typical clinical neurological examination, or may be predetermined by the physician according to his preference.

A possible extension of the present work would be to incorporate into the computer program a decision process which provides the physician with suggestions regarding the order of forthcoming tests to be performed, as a function of the previous test-outcomes. Such an extension would be subject to considerable investigation.

(b) *Computer Output:*

The computer output is given in terms of sets of 10 plots in the form of Fig. 3, one set each for malfunction factors, function factors, and net-malfunction factors. Each plot is used in conjunction with a transparent overlay which contains a schematic representation of the anatomy of the particular section of interest. Figure 5 shows the overlay, Section 4, taken through the medulla near the mid-olivary level. Reference to an anatomic atlas of this section (not illustrated) allows identification of the neural structures [7,8,9].

This overlay is to be used with the computer printout plots for this section of the various factors. Figure 6 shows the printout of malfunction factors for Section 4, derived from the test-outcomes for the same patient as previously indicated (Fig. 4). The malfunction factors have a scatter pattern whose significance would be appreciated by the application of overlay of Section 4.

The concentration of malfunction factors over the right of the plot of Fig. 6 (representing the left of the brainstem of

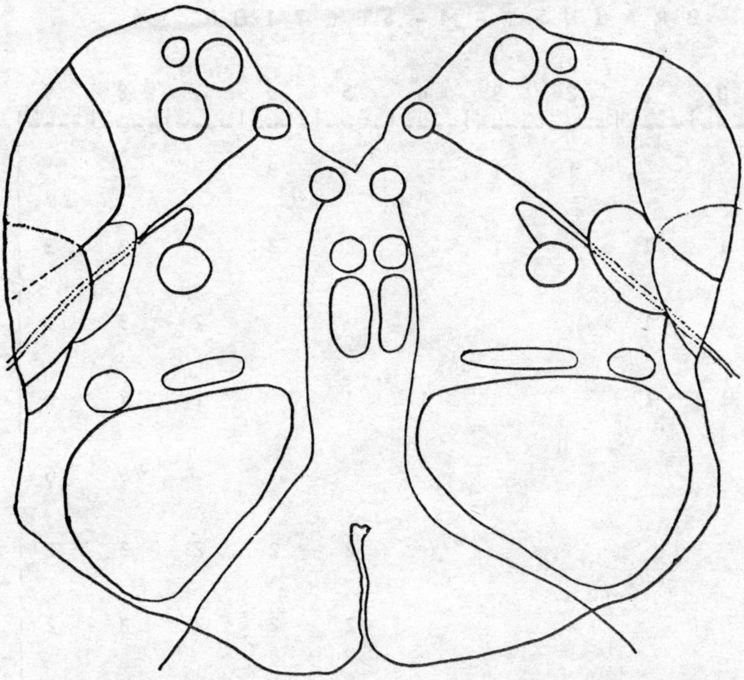

Fig. 5. A drawing representing a transverse section of medulla through the near mid-olivary level, identified as Section 4. This drawing serves as a transparent overlay to be applied upon a printout of various factors. Coincidence of the marked corners to indicies on the printout facilitates proper alignment. Reference to an anatomical atlas of this section allows identification of the outlined neural structures.

MALFUNCTION FACTORS:

B R A I N S T E M - S E C T I O N 4

	0	1	2	3	4	5	6	7	8	9
40			1	1			3	3		
41	1	1		1			3	3	3	3
42	1	1						2	3	3
43	1	1			1	1		2	7	5
44									6	6
45						2	2	2	3	2
46						2	2	2	2	2
47							2	2	2	
48										
49										

Fig. 6. Printout of the malfunction factors whose elements (volume-units) lie in Section 4 (see Fig. 5). The format follows that illustrated in Fig. 3. This output is derived from the test-outcomes of the same patient as previously indicated. The malfunction factors have a scatter pattern whose significance would be appreciated by overlay application. See Fig. 9 for overlay application to a different set of factors.

FUNCTION FACTORS:

BRAINSTEM-SECTION 4

	0	1	2	3	4	5	6	7	8	9
40			2	2						
41	2	2	1	2				1		
42	2	2	2							
43	4	6	2		2	2				
44	6	4			2	2				
45		3	2	2						
46		2	2	2						
47		2	2	2						
48										
49										

Fig. 7. Printout of function factors whose elements (volume-units) lie in Section 4. The format, for all factors described, follows that illustrated in Fig. 3, and the output is derived from the test-outcomes for the same patient as previously indicated. The scatter pattern of the function factors is dominantly on the left side of the plot, readily distinguishable from the plot of malfunction factors (see Fig. 6). However, some function factors are coincident with malfunction factors; for their interpretation see text and Figs. 8 and 9.

the patient) indicates that the lesion has a left lateralization. The higher numbered malfunction factors are related to anatomical structures of greater implication in the lesion. The total pattern of malfunction factors in this section is indicative of a lesion located in the left dorso-lateral medulla of the patient. A study of all sections would reveal the extent of the lesion in three dimensions providing additional information of diagnostic value.

For the same patient and the same brainstem section, the printout of function factors is shown in Fig. 7. The scatter pattern demonstrates the concentration of number on the left of the plot; these too were derived from the test-outcomes as accomplished for the malfunction factors (Fig. 4). The normalcy of these test-outcomes, hence the normalcy of their associated neural pathways, becomes more certain as the numerical value of the factor increases. For this patient, the probability of structural normalcy of the right half of the brainstem at this level is high.

The printout of the net-malfunction factors for the same patient and same brainstem section is shown in Fig. 8. This derived factor, representing the signed factoral difference, malfunction minus function, occurring within a common volume-unit, demonstrates simultaneously, the plot of probable malfunction (positive values) and the plot of probable function (negative values). As the number of test-outcomes increases, more information would be supplied, in a typical case, by a likely filling of all empty volume-units with negative numbers, except for those of zero value.

By applying the overlay of Section 4 to the printout of the net-malfunction factors (Fig. 9), the physical significance of the process is demonstrable; the positive numbers define the region of probable malfunction, while the negative numbers indicate the region of probable function. The numeral "1", for any factor, has the least indicative value and could be disregarded without loss of information relevant to the localization of a lesion. Figure 9 demonstrates the probable lesion to be localized to the left half of the brainstem (right of plot), at this level, and concentrated in its dorsal quadrant. The lesion is consistent with occlusion of an artery supplying the left dorsolateral brainstem, giving rise to Wallenberg's syndrome. The high probability of function of the right half of this patient's brainstem is also indicated.

NET-MALFUNCTION FACTORS:

BRAINSTEM-SECTION 4

	0	1	2	3	4	5	6	7	8	9
40			-1	-1			3	3		
41	-1	-1	-1	-1			3	2	3	3
42	-1	-1	-2					2	3	3
43	-3	-5	-2		-1	-1		2	7	5
44	-6	-4			-2	-2			6	6
45		-3	-2	-2		2	2	2	3	2
46		-2	-2	-2		2	2	2	2	2
47		-2	-2	-2			2	2	2	
48										
49										

Fig. 8. The printout of net-malfunction factors, MN(k) = M(k) − F(k), whose elements (volume-units) lie in Section 4. If the difference is zero, no symbol appears, otherwise, the signed value is printed; positive values indicate probable malfunction, negative values indicate probable function. See Fig. 9 for interpretation.

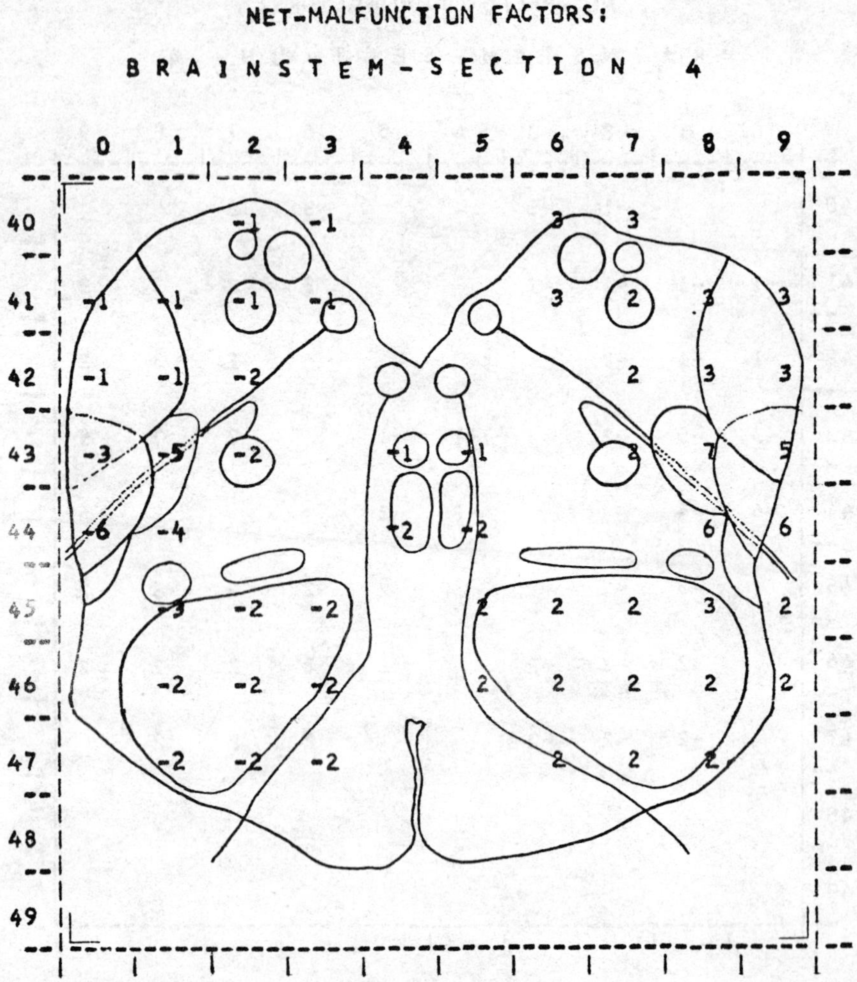

Fig. 9. Application of the overlay of Section 4 (Fig. 5) to the printout of net-malfunction factors (Fig. 8). This relates the factors to the anatomical structures whose function has been tested (Fig. 4). For this patient, the region of probable malfunction (positive numbers) is predominantly in the left dorsolateral quadrant of the mid-medulla, while the region of probable function is on the right (left of plot). The location of the lesion is consistent with an occlusion of an artery supplying the left dorsolateral brainstem.

REFERENCES

1. R.H. MAJOR, "Diagnosis" *Encyclopaedia Britannica* (William Benton, Pub., Chicago, 1971).

2. R.S. LEDLEY, *Use of Computers in Biology and Medicine* (McGraw Hill, New York, 1965) pp. 418-495.

3. F. FREEMON, "Computer diagnosis of headache" *Headache 8*, 49-56 (July 1968).

4. E.F. VASTOLA, Chapter on automated screening in general neurology, to be published in *Computers in Biomedical Research 4* (1973).

5. N.J. MOISEEVA and V.V. USOV, "Problems in classifying and systematizing data for a neurological examination and the computerized diagnosis" *Problems in Psychiatry and Neuropathology 13*, 504-513 (1968) Institute of Experimental Medicine, AMN, USSR.

6. D.A. MARKOV, A.SH. BLOCKH, A.L. LEONOVICH, G.I. MIRKIN and V.A. ORLOV, "The use of computers for the diagnosis of disseminated sclerosis" *S.S. Korsokov Journal of Neuropathology and Psychiatry 69*, 1624-1628 (1969).

7. E.C. CROSBY, T. HUMPHREY and E.W. LAUER, *Correlative Anatomy of the Nervous System* (Macmillan, New York, 1962).

8. R.C. TRUEX and M.B. CARPENTER, *Human Neuroanatomy*, 6th ed. (Williams and Wilkins, Baltimore, Md., 1969).

9. H.A. RILEY, *Atlas of the Basal Ganglia, Brain Stem and Spinal Cord*, rev. ed. (Hafner Publishing Co., New York, 1960).

10. T.C. RUCH et al., *Neurophysiology* (W.A. Saunders Co., Philadelphia, 1965).

11. J.G. GREENFIELD et al., *Neuropathology* (Edward Arnold Pub., London, 1959).

12. H.H. MERRITT, *A Textbook of Neurology* 4th ed. (Lea and Febiger, Philadelphia, 1967).

13. A.U. MEYER and W.K. WEISSMAN, "Computer analysis of the clinical neurological examination" *Computers in Biology and Medicine* (to be published).

14. B. KLEINMUNTZ, "The processing of clinical information by man and machine" In: *Formal Representation of Human Judgement* B. Kleinmuntz (ed.) (Wiley, New York, 1968) Ch. 6. pp. 149-186.

15. H.S. BARRONS and K. BENNETT, "The diagnostic (problem solving) skill of the neurologist" *Archives of Neurology 26*, 273-277 (March 1972).

16. A.U. MEYER and W.K. WEISSMAN, "Localization of lesions in the human nervous system by computer analysis" *IEEE-Transactions on Biomedical Engineering*, Vol. BME-20, No. 3, (May 1973) pp. 194-200.

A MATHEMATICAL MODEL OF THE MONOSYNAPTIC ARC REFLEX FOR REPETITIVE ELECTRICAL STIMULATION

M. CRIVELLINI*, M. DECANDIA**, L. DIVIETI* and M. MAINI***

Istituto di Elettrotecnica ed Elettronica del Politecnico di Milano, Italy.

***Istituto di Fisiologia Umana dell' Università di Milano, Italy.*

****Centro Ricerca di Automatica, ENEL, Milano, Italy.*

SUMMARY

In this paper results of some tests are analyzed in order to describe habituation in a mono-synaptic arc reflex. This phenomenon consists of decreasing efferent responses to repetitive afferent electrical stimulation. The acquisition and analysis of data are implemented on a hybrid computer. A mathematical model of the monosynaptic junction is proposed for the study of habituation and the results are compared with experimental data.

INTRODUCTION

The aim of this work is to analyze the depression of the monosynaptic reflex discharge following electrical stimulation of Group I afferent fibres at different rates.

Many authors have faced this problem [1,2] from a static point of view and have presented the frequency-firing index relationships. In what follows the firing index is the ratio between responses and stimuli. As the frequency of stimulation increases, low frequency depression increases in magnitude and the firing index tends to zero. It is shown in this paper that the firing index tends to zero, since the stimuli increase while the responses remain almost constant. Low frequency depression is a complex phenomenon and in this paper its dynamical behaviour is examined. The diagram of Fig. 1 shows the monosynaptic reflex arc and its connections. There is a synapse between the afferent neuron and the motorneuron, and there are other nerve pathways to the nervous system. Between the afferent fibre and the motorneuron there are many nerve chains. These chains differ one from the other in length and complexity, the monosynaptic chain being the shortest. The motorneuron shows a recurrent collateral ending on a Renshaw cell, which in turn sends its inhibitory axon to the motorneuron.

Some nerve pathways coming from the higher centers impinge upon the motorneuron. The whole system is represented by the block-diagram of Fig. 2.

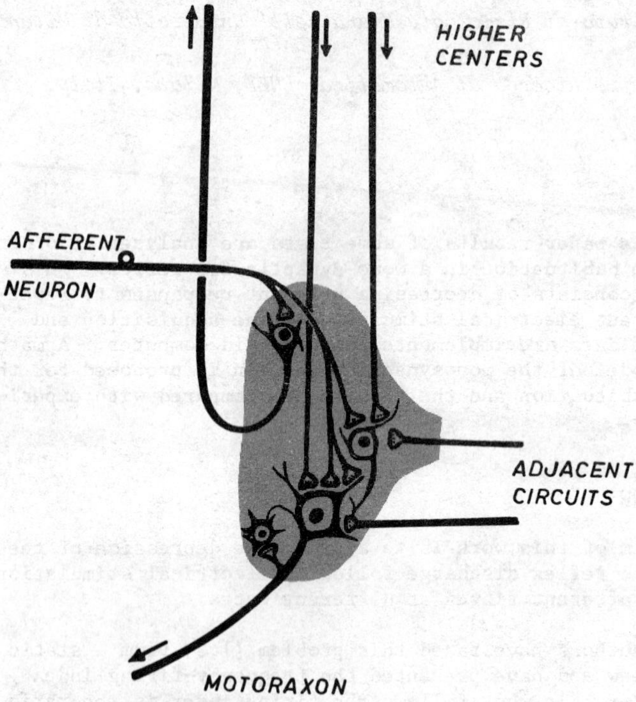

Fig. 1. Monosynaptic reflex arc and its connections

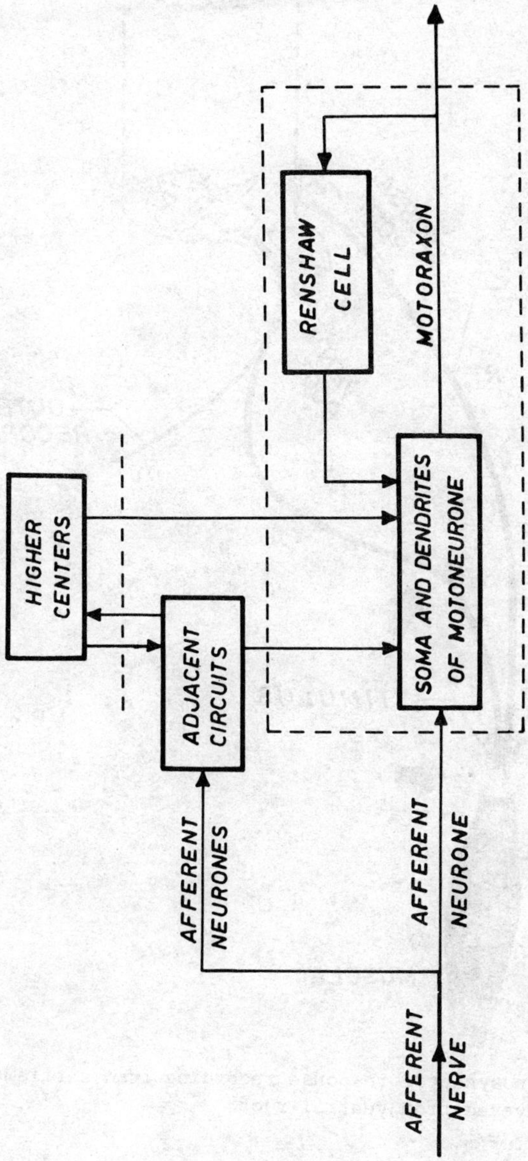

Fig. 2. Block diagram of the monosynaptic reflex arc and its connections

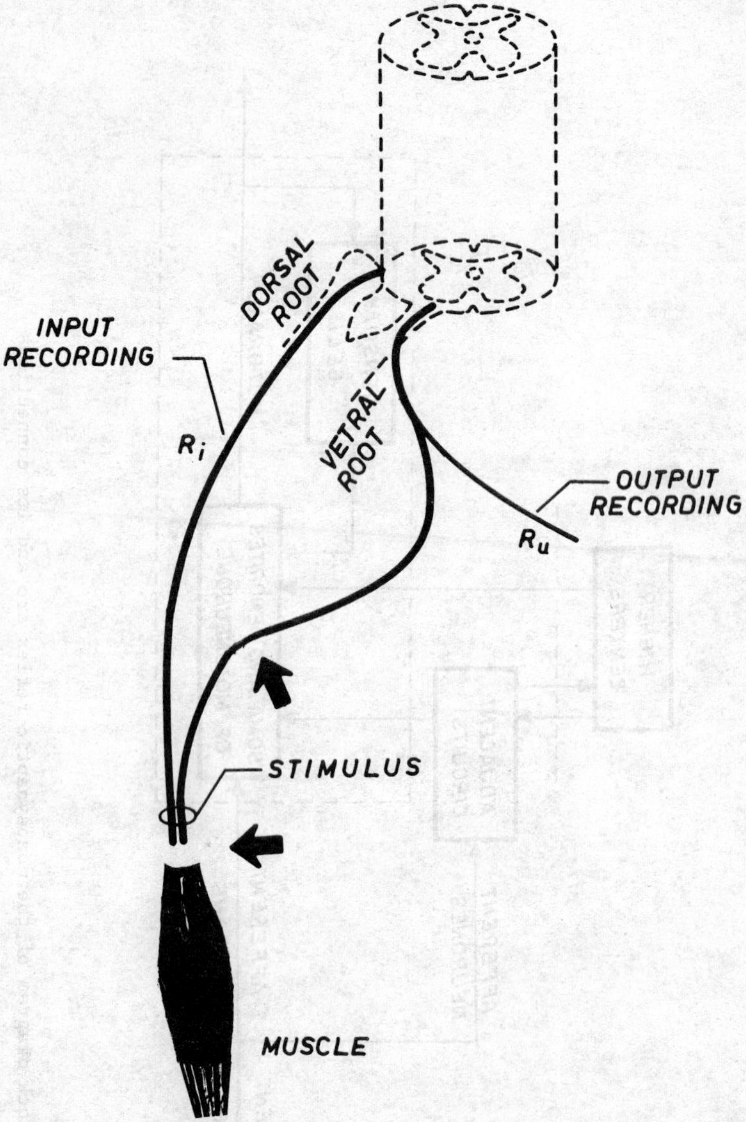

Fig. 3. Monosynaptic response recording from a filament severed from ventral root

METHOD

The experiments were carried out in anemically decerebrated cats four hours after ether anaesthesia was discontinued.

Electrical stimuli were applied at Group I strength to the gastrocnemius-soleus nerve cut peripherally. The afferent input was monitored from the S_1 dorsal root and the all-or-none monosynaptic responses were recorded from a filament severed from the S_1 ventral root cut distally (see Fig. 3).

Blood pressure, temperature and artificial ventilation were controlled and kept constant at physiological values. The surgical preparation enabled us to avoid either influences from higher centers or effects of anaesthesia on the monosynaptic circuit under study; however, effects of the adjacent circuits were present. The block diagram of Fig. 4 shows the whole system. The electrical stimuli to the peripheral nerve were applied at different frequencies starting from a frequency for which the firing index was 1.

Different trials were performed every three minutes, starting after a one minute resting period, the two minute stimulation having constant frequency.

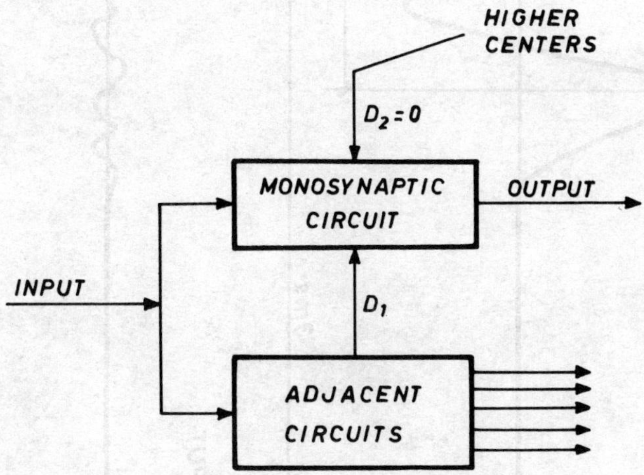

Fig. 4. Block diagram of the whole system $D_2 = 0$ for decerebrated and spinalized cats

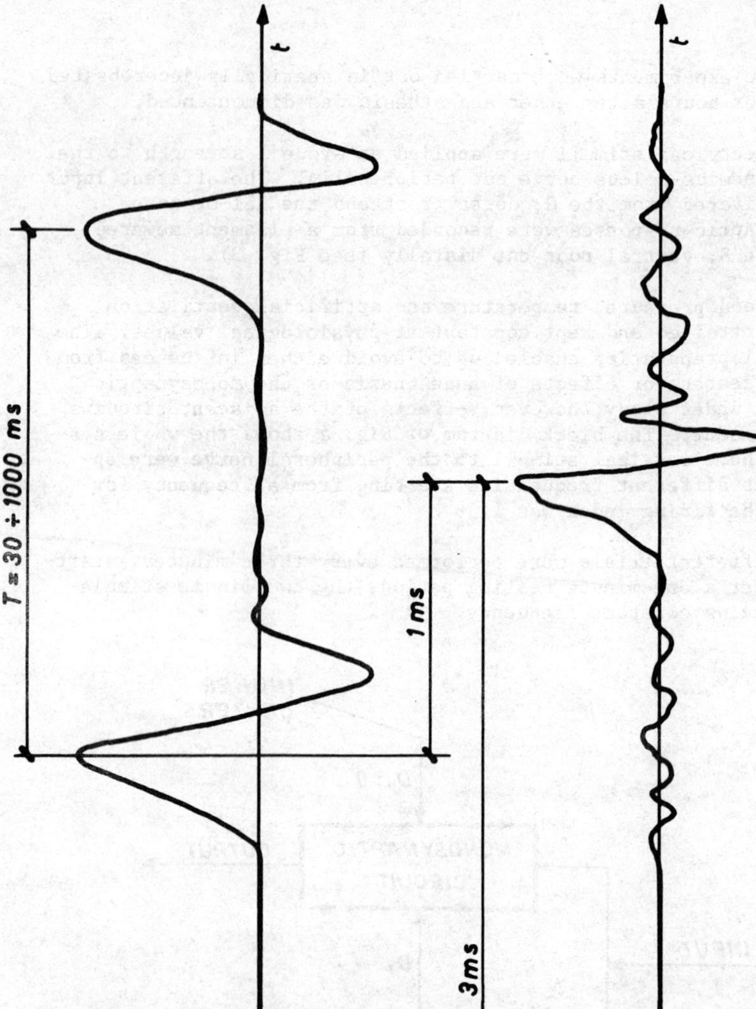

Fig. 5. Input and output pulses as recorded before conditionement

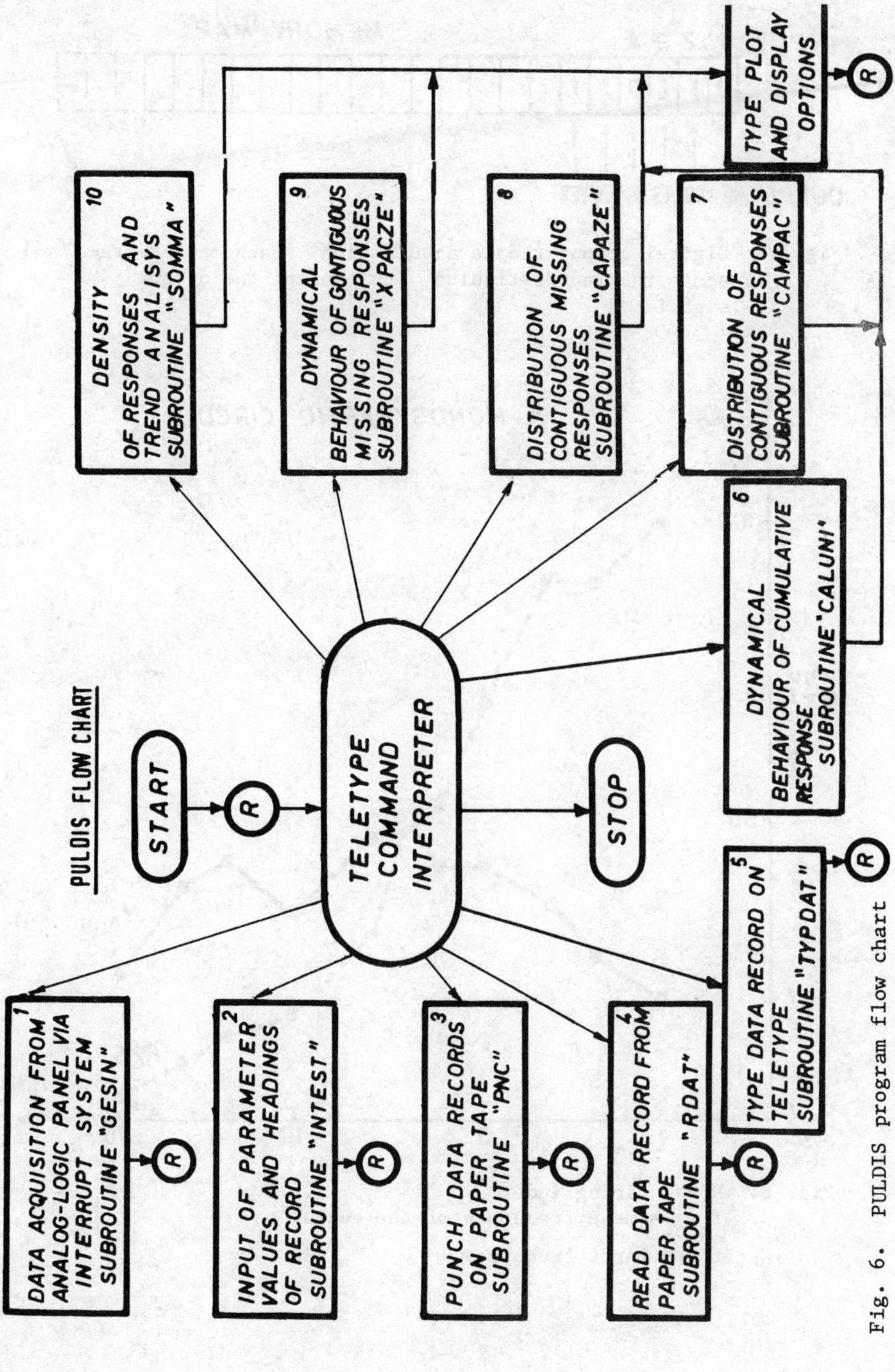

Fig. 6. PULDIS program flow chart

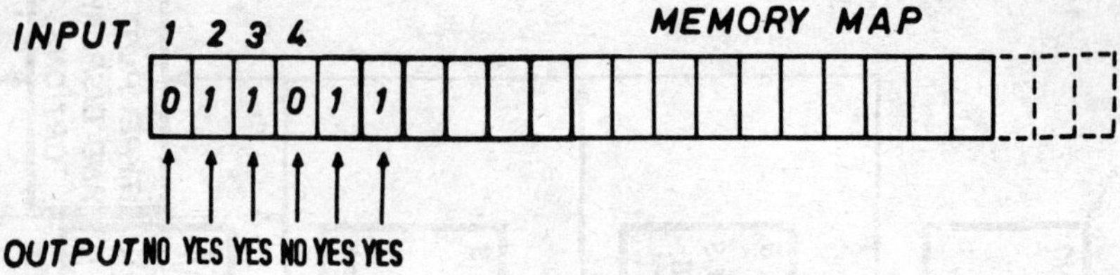

Fig. 7. Digital computer data acquisition. Each cell represents the input stimulus, its content the output signal

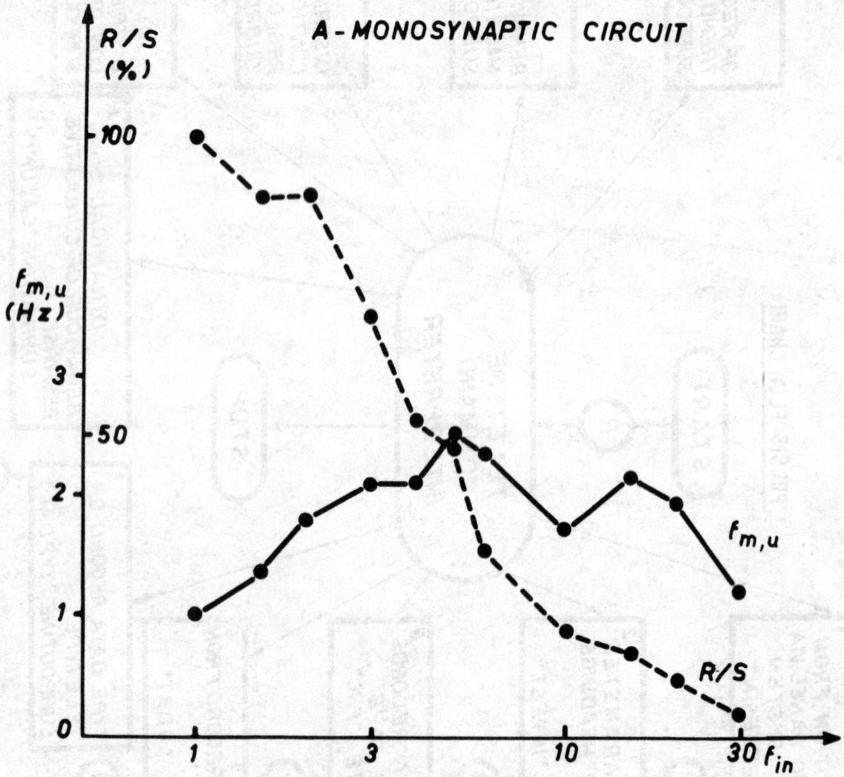

Fig. 8. R/S = firing index
$f_{m,u}$ = mean frequency of the output
f_{in} = input frequency

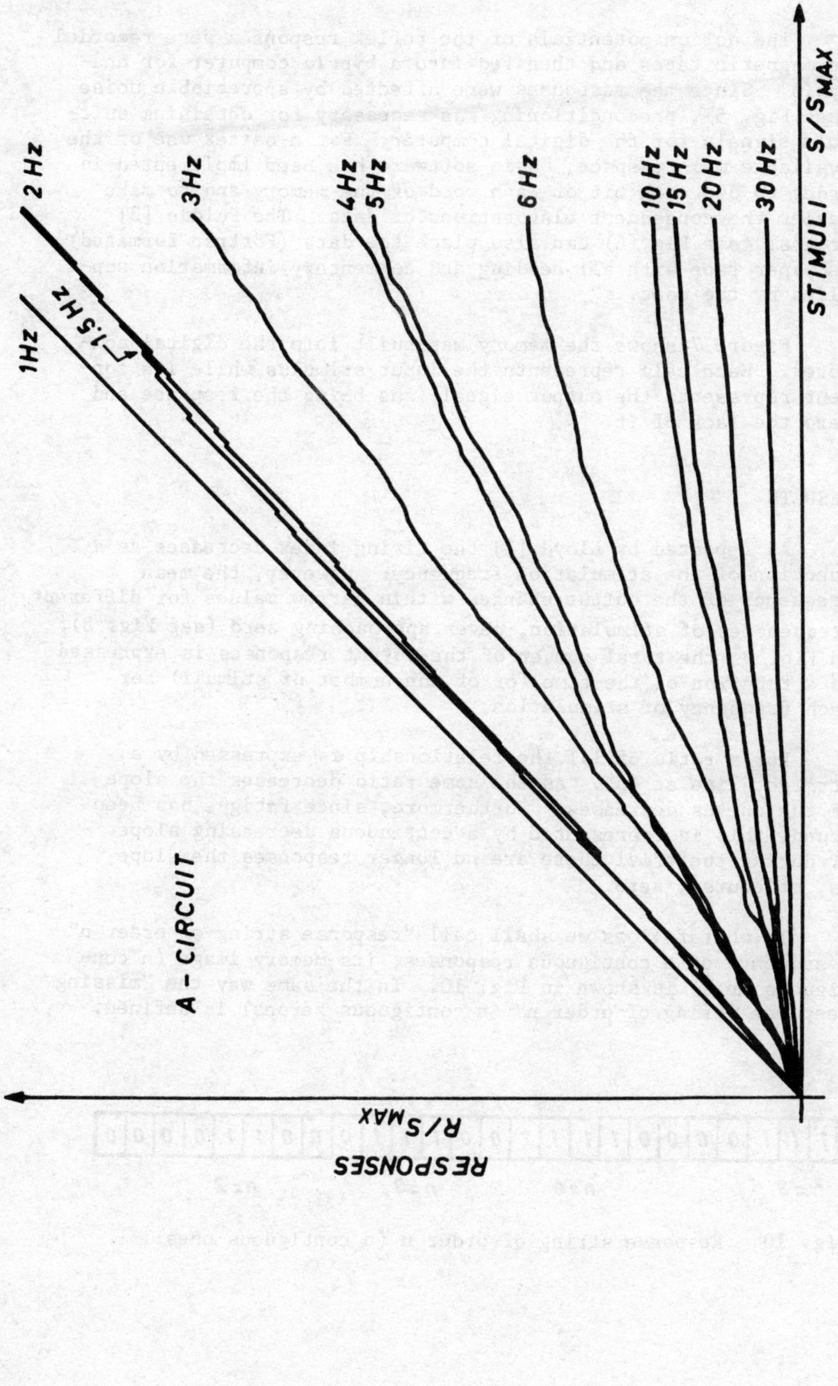

Fig. 9. The total number of responses versus the total number of stimuli at different frequencies

The action potentials of the reflex responses were recorded on magnetic tapes and then fed into a hybrid computer for analysis. Since the responses were affected by appreciable noise (see Fig. 5), preconditioning was necessary for obtaining suitable signals for the digital computer. For a better use of the available memory space, basic software has been implemented in order to use each bit of each word of the memory and to make easier the consequent elaborations of data. The Puldis [3] program (see Fig. 6) can also place the data (Fortran formated) on paper tape with all heading and commentary information supplied by the user.

Figure 7 shows the memory map built into the digital computer. Each cell represents the input stimulus while its content represents the output signal, one being the response and zero the lack of it.

RESULTS

As reported by Lloyd [1] the firing index decreases as a function of the stimulation frequency. However, the mean frequency of the output changes within narrow values for different frequencies of stimulation, never approaching zero (see Fig. 8). In Fig. 9, the total number of the output responses is expressed as a function of the time (or of the number of stimuli) for each frequency of stimulation.

For a ratio of 1:1 the relationship is expressed by a straight line at 45°. As the same ratio decreases the slope of the curves decreases. Furthermore, since fatigue has been found, this is represented by a continuous decreasing slope. If during the trial there are no longer responses the slope is, of course, zero.

In what follows we shall call "response string of order n" a sequence of n contiguous responses; its memory image (n contiguous ones) is shown in Fig. 10. In the same way the "missing response string of order n" (n contiguous zeroes) is defined.

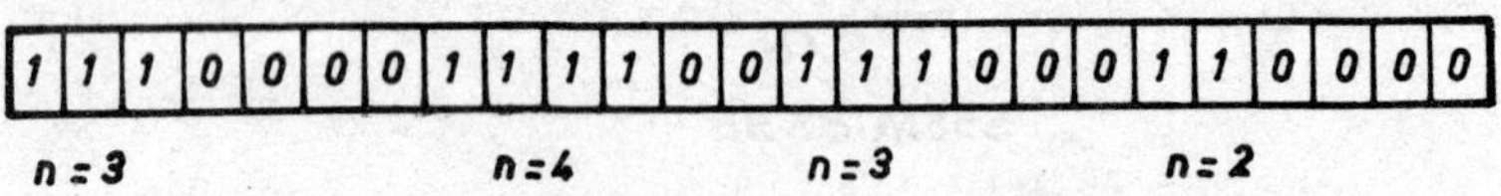

Fig. 10. Response string of order n (n contiguous ones).

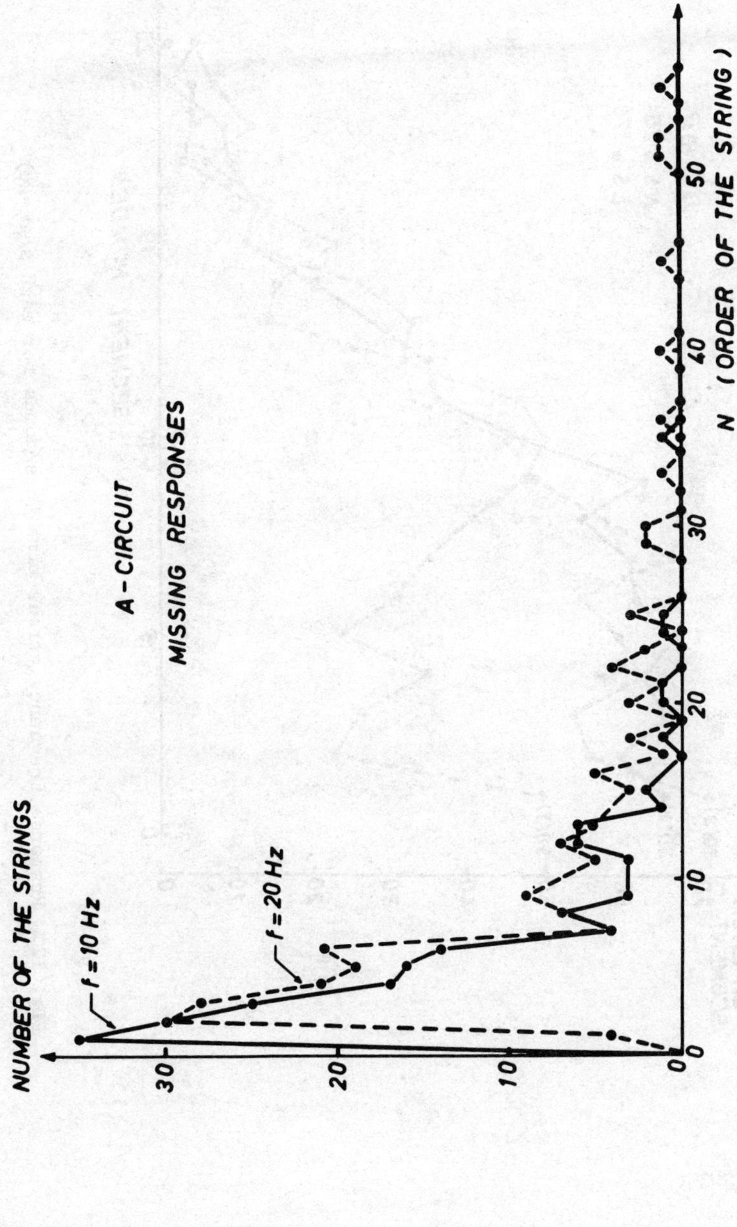

Fig. 11. Distribution of contiguous missing responses

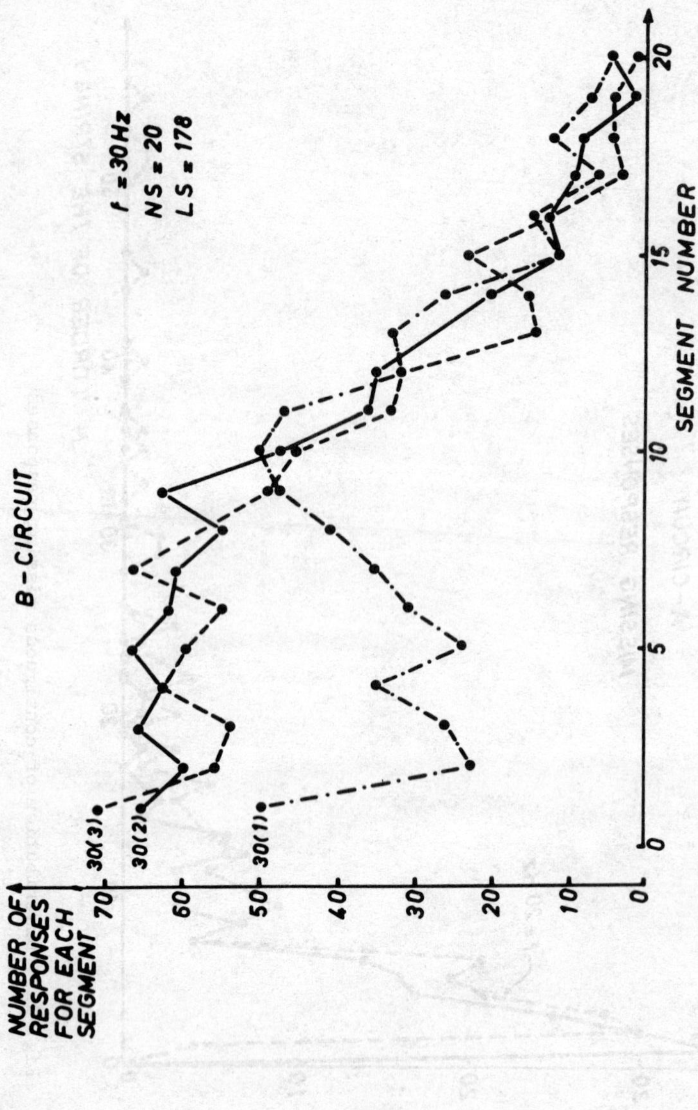

Fig. 12. Response frequency versus time (6 seconds for each segment)

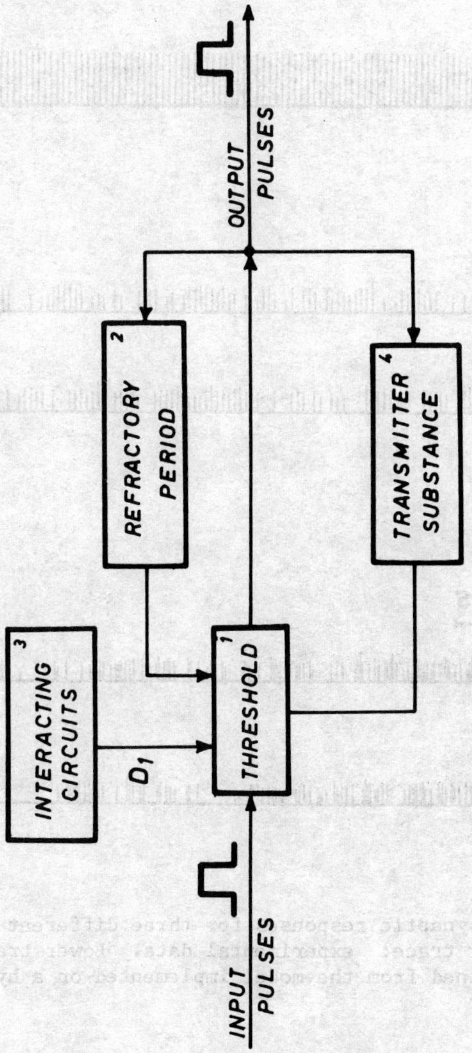

Fig. 13. Block diagram of the model

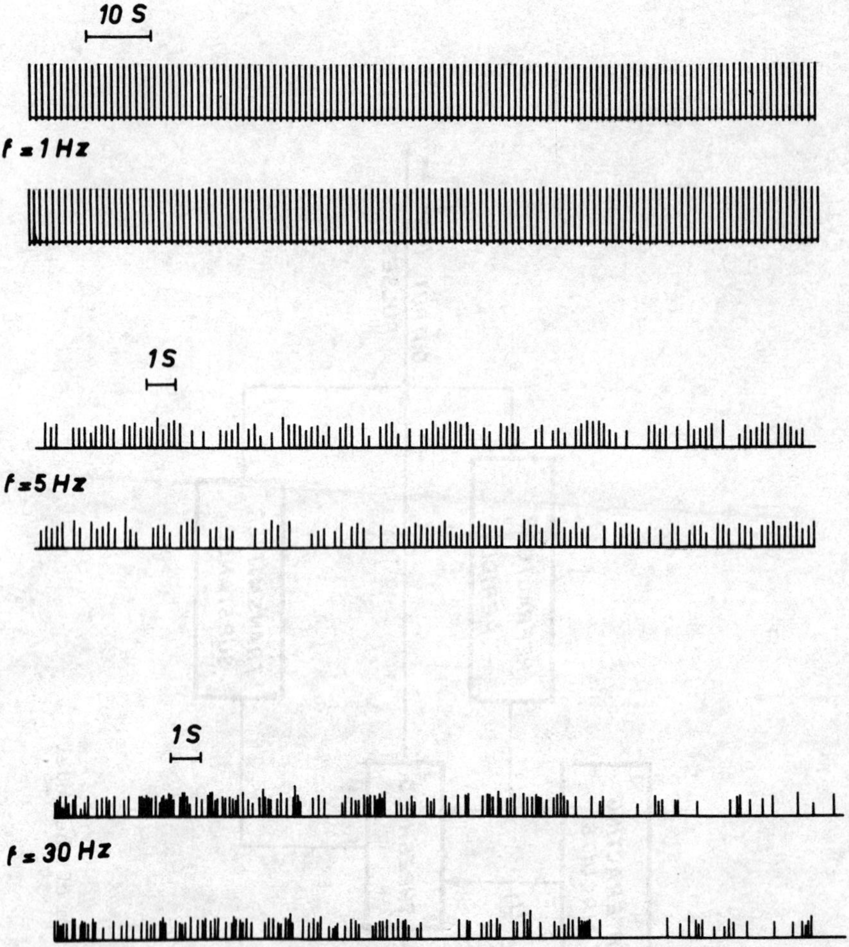

Fig. 14. Monosynaptic responses for three different frequencies. Upper trace: experimental data. Lower trace: data obtained from the model implemented on a hybrid computer

In Fig. 11 are plotted the results of the Capaze subroutine processing [4] for two different frequencies. It is clear that with increasing frequency the probability of high order strings of missing responses also increases.

For each trial the record has been split in NS segments. As plotted in Fig. 12 the number of the responses for each segment has been computed. This graph can also be viewed as the behaviour of response frequency versus time, where the response frequency is computed as the ratio of the number of responses and time corresponding to a segment. As already mentioned, the shape of the graph suggests a fatigue of the synapse.

MATHEMATICAL MODEL

All the data obtained from anatomy, physiology and experimental results have been integrated in a mathematical model. The aim of this model is to explain the depression of the monosynaptic reflex discharge following electrical stimulation of Group I afferent fibres. The input of the model, implemented on the hybrid computer, is given by a sequence of pulses which simulate the afferent nerve signals; the output signals may be considered as response spikes on the motoraxon (see Fig. 13). The model has been implemented following four considerations:

a) The Renshaw cell has been simulated as a negative feedback from the efferent axon to the synapse. Its effect is to inhibit conduction for a given period (refractory period). Experimental results show that at the output there are no pulses closer than 50 ms.

b) The conduction of the synapse has been simulated by means of a threshold circuit giving output pulses. This hypothesis is valid because, for the purpose of the model, the only thing we take into account of the pulse is its presence and not its shape.

c) The exhaustion of the available chemical transmitter has been simulated by a first order circuit where an energy balance is accomplished taking into account the energy produced and the energy spent for generating response spikes.

d) The interactions of conducting adjacent circuits with the synapse have been simulated by noise affecting the threshold. Data of the noise have been adopted according to Katz [5].

As an example, in Fig. 14 the experimental data and the data obtained from the model at different frequencies are reported.

This research is now in its infancy and the parameters of the model are not completely identified.

REFERENCES

1. D. LLOYD, "Monosynaptic reflex response of individual motorneurons as a function of frequency" *J. Gen. Physiol. 60*, No. 3 (1957).

2. B.G. WICHELGREN, "Habituation of spinal motorneurons" *J. Neurophysiol. 30*, 1404-1423 (1967).

3. P. GUBELLINI and M. MAINI, "Puldis: a program for the acquisition and analysis of sequences of spikes" (in Italian) *R.I.G 3/9-2, Centro di Ricerca Automatica* (ENEL, Milano, 1972).

4. M. CRIVELLINI, M. DECANDIA, L. DIVIETI and M. MAINI, "Automatic analysis of biological signals in repetitive electrical stimulation" *Kongress Medizin-Technik* (Stuttgart, 1972).

5. B. KATZ, *Nerve, Muscle, and Synapse* (McGraw-Hill, New York, 1966).

INTERFERENCE PHENOMENA IN THE HIPPOCAMPAL CORTEX*

A.C. SANDERSON**, T.W. CALVERT***, and KENG-CHIANG YANG

Biotechnology Program and Electrical Engineering Department, Carnegie-Mellon University, Pittsburgh, Pennsylvania 15213, U.S.A.

SUMMARY

In this paper we describe a model of the hippocampal cortex consisting of a primary layer of pyramidal cells and a layer of basket cells which mediate recurrent and lateral inhibition. By considering a spatially uniform input, we simplify this model to a single excitatory neuron and a single recurrent inhibitory neuron. The mean rate gain characteristics of this simple configuration are derived using the methods of renewal theory and emphasizing the role of regularity or coherence in the input spike train in determining the gain of the network. Experimental results have been reported in the literature which associate the specific frequency of the theta rhythm in the hippocampus with particular modes of activity. The primary inputs to the hippocampus are from the entorhinal area and from the septum. Our results suggest that the frequency and coherence of septal pacemaker activity could effectively modulate the gain of the hippocampal network to incoming spike train coded information.

---

*This work was supported in part by Research Grant No. NS 08167 from the National Institute of Neurological Diseases and Stroke. Mr. Sanderson was supported by an NSF traineeship.

**Presently with Applied Physics Department, Delft University of Technology, Delf, The Netherlands.

***Presently with Department of Kinesiology, Simon Fraser University, Burnaby, B.C., Canada.

INTRODUCTION

Recent discussion of the neural correlates of optical holography [1,2,3] has stimulated interest in interference phenomena in the brain. The fundamental requirement for the distributed 'holographic' storage of information is that there should exist some substrate where the information pattern to be stored interferes with a reference pattern and modifies the properties of the substrate. While it is only possible to speculate what neural structures may be involved, it is known that the hippocampus plays an important role in short-term and immediate memory [4,5,6]. In this paper we will examine a particular class of interactions which can take place between coherent and incoherent neural signals in sheets of neural tissue with properties similar to the hippocampus.

THE PHYSIOLOGY OF THE HIPPOCAMPUS

The hippocampus is a sheet of neural tissue situated bilaterally on the internal surfaces of the temporal lobes of the cerebrum. As shown in Fig. 1, the hippocampus has roughly

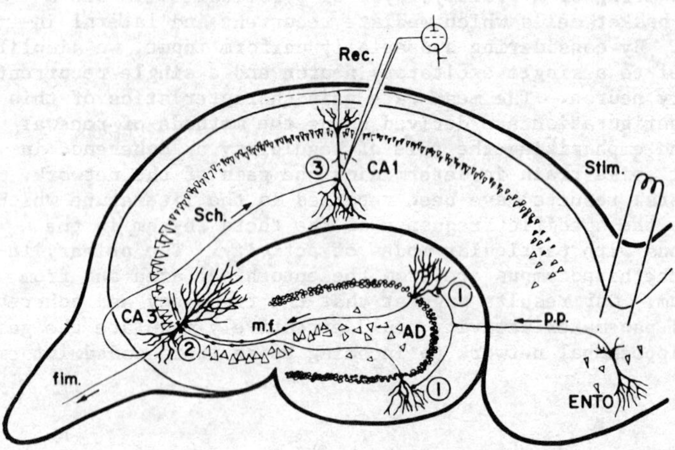

Fig. 1. Diagram of the hippocampal formation with the different cell types activated from the entorhinal area. The encircled numbers give the successive synaptic stations activated. AD — dentate area; ENTO — entorhinal area; fim. — fimbria; m.f. — mossy fibers; p.p. — perforant path; Sch. — Schaffer collateral. (From Andersen and Lømo [7]).

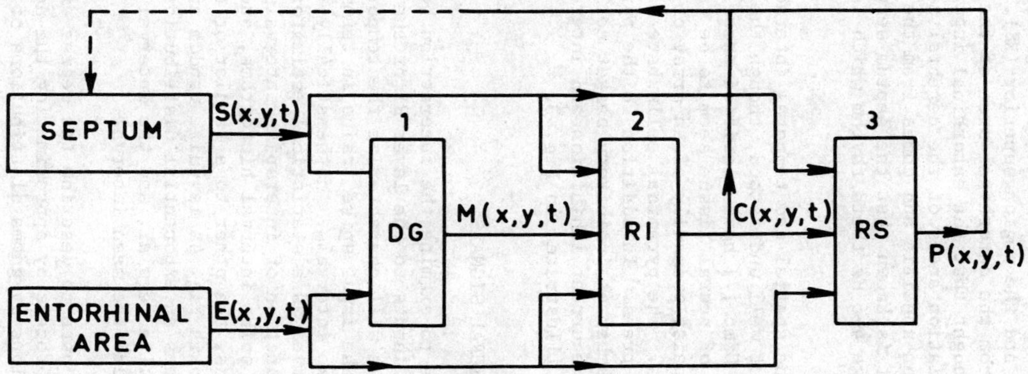

Fig. 2. Schematic diagram illustrating the input, output, and internal interconnections of the hippocampus. The primary inputs are from the septum and from the entorhinal area. The three primary layers of neural tissue are the dentate gyrus (DG), the region inferior (RI), and the region superior (RS).

the shape of a comma with the head of the comma capped by another sheet of neural tissue — the dentate gyrus. The input, output, and internal interconnections of the hippocampus are quite complex, as is shown in Fig. 2. Basically, there are three layers of tissue in series, the dentate gyrus (DG), the region inferior (RI), and the region superior (RS). The principal afferents are from the entorhinal area of the cortex and the septum. It is thought that the entorhinal inputs come from the sensory and association areas of the cerebral cortex, while the septal input is non-specific and comes from the reticular activating system. It is known that the septum serves as the pacemaker for the large 4-6 Hz theta rhythm which is observed in the hippocampus.

The details of the spatial and temporal interactions in the hippocampus are not well understood, though the investigations of Andersen and Lømo [7] have clarified these mechanisms somewhat. The layers of neural tissue seem to be rather simply interconnected and consist primarily of an array of closely packed pyramidal cells. The pyramidal cells have large apical and basilar dendritic trees. In addition to the pyramidal cells, there are a smaller number of inhibitory basket cells. These basket cells provide recurrent inhibition and interconnect the array laterally as is illustrated in Fig. 3.

RANDOM AND COHERENT NEURAL SIGNALS

It is our purpose to examine the interaction between the septal and entorhinal inputs to the layer RI of the hippocampus. In order to do this, we will characterize the temporal pattern of spike activity in the input spike trains in terms of the distribution of interspike intervals. Mathematically, the spike interval histogram serves as a statistical estimator of the probability density function of interspike intervals. Fig. 4 shows examples of two spike interval histograms, one corresponding to a random process, the other to a regular or coherent process. The spike train in Fig. 4a is quite random and the interval histogram approaches an exponential distribution. The spike train in Fig. 4b is quite regular, and the interval histogram is sharply peaked around the mean interval.

It is convenient here to describe the degree of randomness or regularity of the process by approximating the actual probability density functions by gamma distributions of the form:

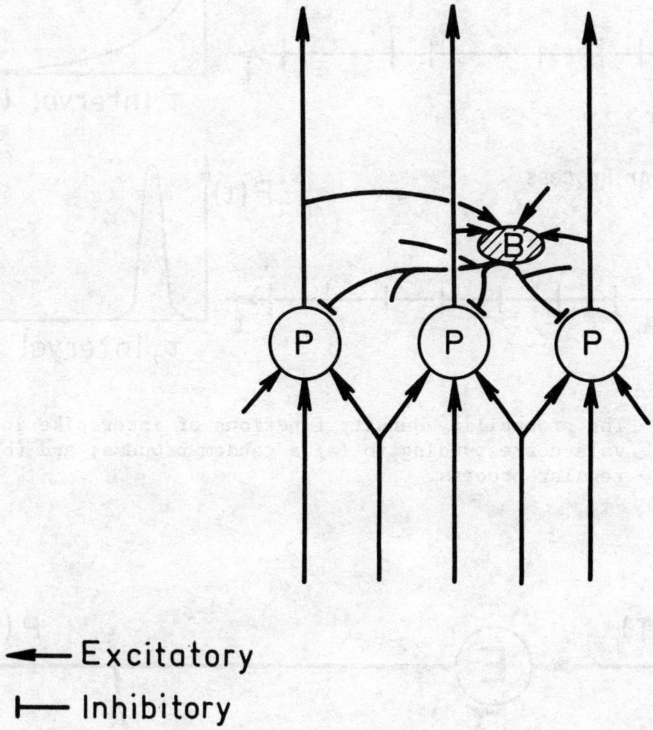

Fig. 3. Schematic diagram illustrating the interconnections of the principal cells in each layer of the hippocampus. The pyramidal cells, P, receive the primary inputs. The basket cells, B, provide recurrent inhibition and interconnect the array of pyramidal cells laterally.

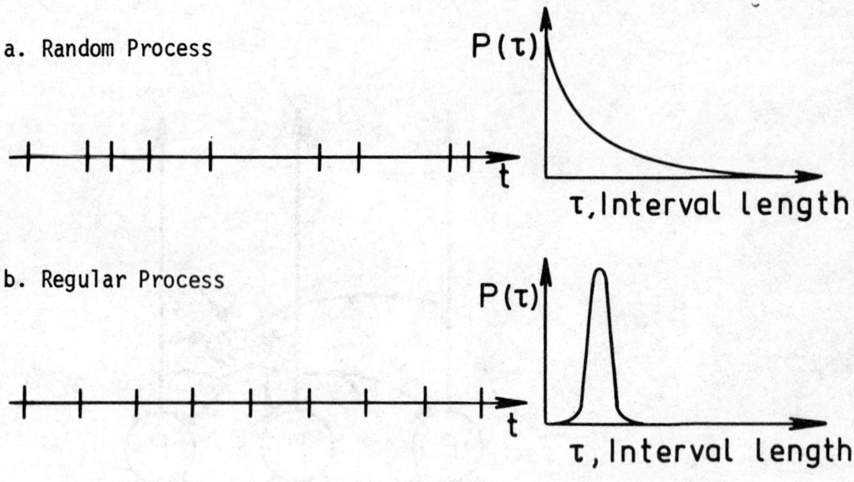

Fig. 4. The probability density functions of interspike intervals corresponding to (a) a random process, and (b) a regular process.

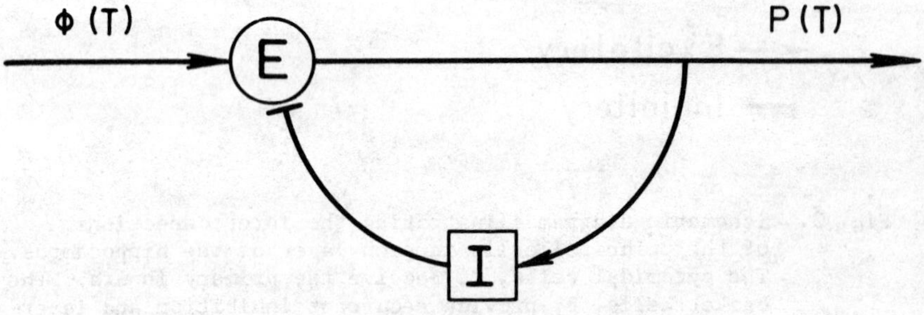

Fig. 5. A simplified recurrent inhibition network consisting of one excitatory cell and one inhibitory cell. The input process has probability density function $\phi(\tau)$ and the output process has probability density function $p(\tau)$.

$$g(\tau;n,\mu) = \begin{cases} \dfrac{\mu^n \tau^{n-1} e^{-\mu\tau}}{\Gamma(n)}, & \tau \geq 0, \mu > 0, n < 0 \\ 0, & \tau < 0, \end{cases} \tag{1}$$

where

$$\Gamma(n) = \text{gamma function}$$

$$= \int_0^\infty r^{n-1} e^{-r} dr, \tag{2}$$

and τ is a random variable referring to the length of the interval. The mean interval for this distribution is

$$\bar{\tau} = n/\mu. \tag{3}$$

The parameter n designates the order of the gamma distribution. For n = 1, the distribution is exponential corresponding to a completely random, or Poisson, process. As $n \to \infty$, the process becomes increasingly regular, approaching a normal distribution in the limit.

We have previously described the role of the interspike interval distribution in determining the output from a simple deletion model, the interaction of excitatory and inhibitory inputs to a single neuron, and from a simple network with lateral inhibition [8,9]. In the case of the hippocampus, we are interested specifically in the interaction of two excitatory inputs with a recurrent inhibition network such as that illustrated in Fig. 3. If we assume that the inputs to the network are spatially uniform then it is possible to consider the network as a single excitatory cell and a single inhibitory cell as shown in Fig. 5. This simplified model will have the following characteristic parameters:

$\phi(\tau)$ = probability density function of combined entorhinal and septal spike train inputs.

m_ϕ = mean firing rate of input

$p(\tau)$ = probability density function of pyramidal cell output

m_p = mean firing rate of output

E = pyramidal cell with excitatory and inhibitory inputs and excitatory outputs. Every excitatory input spike causes an output spike unless it is deleted by a preceding inhibitory spike. The inhibitory effectiveness decays with time with time constant 1/a.

I = basket cell inhibitory interneuron with excitatory input and inhibitory output which after a pure delay, T, produces one inhibitory output spike for every excitatory input.

THE MEAN RATE GAIN FUNCTION

In order to characterize the recurrent inhibition network, we define the mean rate gain function

$$T_0 = m_p/m_\phi, \tag{4}$$

the ratio of the output mean rate to the input mean rate. In order to calculate the mean rate gain function of the network we use the methods of renewal theory [10], treating the problem as a modified type I counter [11]. If we define $\psi_1(\tau)$ as the probability density function of the delay time considered as a random variable, $\psi_2(\tau)$ as the probability density function for the duration of the inhibition (the length of time which the counter is locked), and g(t) as the product density of the input process, then the product density of the output process is:

$$h(t) = K(t) + \int_0^t g(u)K(t-u)\,du, \tag{5}$$

where

$$k(t) = \phi(\tau)\Big[\int_t^\infty \psi_1(u)\,du + \int_0^t \psi_{12}(u)\,du\Big], \tag{6}$$

and

$$\psi_{12}(\tau) = \int_0^\tau \psi_1(v)\psi_2(\tau-v)\,dv. \tag{7}$$

The mean rate of the output process is

$$m_p = \lim_{t\to\infty} h(t), \tag{8}$$

with the assumption that the output is not strictly periodic.

In order to examine specifically the role of coherence in determining the mean rate gain function of the recurrent inhibition network, we consider inputs in the form of the gamma distribution:

$$\phi(\tau) = \frac{\mu^n \tau^{n-1} e^{-\mu\tau}}{\Gamma(n)} . \qquad (9)$$

If we define

$$c(t) = \int_t^{\infty} \psi_1(u)du + \int_0^t \psi_{12}(u)du, \qquad (10)$$

then the mean rate gain function for a given order of deletions is

$$T_0 = \frac{\mu^n(-1)^{n-1}}{\Gamma(n)}\left[\frac{d^{(n-1)}}{ds^{(n-1)}} C(s+\mu)\right]_{s=0}, \qquad (11)$$

where C(s) is the Laplace-Stieltjes transform of c(t). If we evaluate equation (11) for the specific case of a discrete delay time, T:

$$\psi_1(\tau) = \delta(\tau-T), \qquad (12)$$

and for an exponentially decaying inhibitory effectiveness:

$$\psi_2(\tau) = ae^{-a\tau}, \qquad (13)$$

then we obtain

$$T_0 = 1 - \frac{\alpha^{n-1}e^{-\alpha}}{(n-1)!(1+\beta)} \sum_{j=0}^{n-1} \left[\frac{j!}{\alpha^j (1+\beta)^j}\right], \qquad (14)$$

where n is an integer,

$$\alpha = \mu T, \qquad (15)$$

the relative inhibition delay, and

$$\beta = a/\mu, \tag{16}$$

the relative inhibition duration.

Equation (14) is an expression for the mean rate gain function for a given order of deletions, that is, for deletion of the first, second, or n^{th} spike event following t = 0. If we assume that the deletion of incoming events is a mutually exclusive process, that is, that each inhibitory event can delete one and only one excitatory event, then we can write the general mean rate gain function in the following form:

$$T_0 = \prod_{\ell=1}^{\infty} \left[1 - \frac{n(\alpha\ell/n)^{\ell n-1}}{(\ell n-1)!(1+\beta)} e^{-(\alpha\ell/n)} \sum_{j=0}^{\ell n-1} \left(\frac{j!}{(\alpha\ell/n)^j (1+\beta)^j} \right) \right]. \tag{17}$$

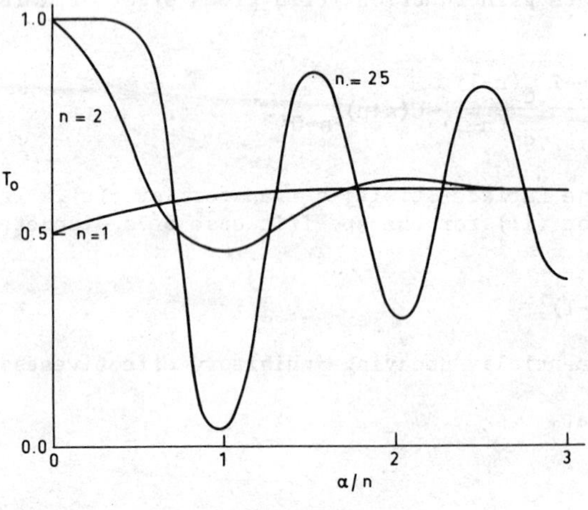

Fig. 6. The mean rate gain function, T_0, for the recurrent inhibition network, plotted versus α/n, the relative inhibition delay adjusted to the actual mean rate, for three different input gamma distributions, n = 1, n = 2, n = 25. This graph illustrates the basic dependence of the transfer properties of the network on the regularity or coherence of the input process.

In Fig. 6, the mean rate gain function for the recurrent inhibition network is plotted versus α/n, the relative inhibition delay adjusted to the actual mean rate, for three different input gamma distributions, n = 1, n = 2, n = 25. This result illustrates the basic dependence of the transfer properties of the network on the regularity or coherence of the input process. For the Poisson process, n = 1, the response is almost constant as the mean rate is increased relative to the delay time. For the regular process, n = 25, the mean rate gain function shows a marked periodic variation. The recurrent inhibition network acts as a frequency selective filter for the regular process, while it has nearly constant gain for the random process.

HIPPOCAMPAL FUNCTION

The result summarized in Fig. 6 shows clearly that if the combined entorhinal and septal input to the recurrent network is random, then the gain of the network is relatively independent of the network time constants. However, if the septal input becomes regular due to pacemaker activity, then the gain of the network becomes crucially dependent on the relation between the frequency of the regular input, the coherence of the regular input, and the network time constants. If n = 25, for example, the gain of the network can change by a factor of 10 for a 50% change in the frequency of the regular input. Black [12] has shown that animals can control the frequency of their theta rhythm very precisely in the range 4-8 Hz. This experimental result suggests that there is potentially a very fine vernier control of the sensitivity of the hippocampus to different entorhinal inputs and that this sensitivity is closely related to the frequency of ongoing rhythmicity in the structure.

While the hippocampus is probably not the site of short-term memory storage, it is almost certainly involved in the attention mechanism which allows the selective storage of sensory inputs. We have shown in this paper that the frequency of the theta rhythm could be used to selectively modulate the gain of the hippocampus to different sensory information.

REFERENCES

1. K.H. PRIBRAM, *Languages of the Brain* (Englewood Cliffs, N.J. Prentice-Hall, 1971).

2. P.R. WESTLAKE, "The possibility of neural holographic processes within the brain" *Kybernetik 7*, 129-153 (1970).

3. J.P. CAVANAGH, *Holographic Processes Realizable in the Neural Realm: Prediction of Short Term Memory Performance* (Ph.D. Thesis, Carnegie-Mellon University, Pittsburgh, Pennsylvania, U.S.A., 1972).

4. B.A. CURTIS, S. JACOBSON and E.M. MARCUS, *An Introduction to the Neurosciences* Philadelphia: W.B. Saunders, 1972).

5. R.J. DOUGLAS, "The hippocampus and behaviour" *Psychol. Bull. 67*, 416-422 (1967).

6. J. OLDS, "The behavior of hippocampal neurons during conditioning experiments", In: *The Neural Control of Behavior*, ed. R.E. WHALEN et al. (New York: Academic Press, 1970).

7. P. ANDERSEN and T. LØMO, "Mode of control of hippocampal pyramidal cell discharges", In: *The Neural Control of Behavior*, ed. R.E. WHALEN et al. (New York: Academic Press, 1970).

8. A.C. SANDERSON, *Stochastic Models of Information Processing in the Nervous System* (Ph.D. Thesis, Carnegie-Mellon University, Pittsburgh, Pennsylvania, U.S.A., 1972).

9. A.C. SANDERSON, W.M. LOZAK and T.W. CALVERT, "Distribution coding in the visual pathway" (submitted for publication).

10. D.R. COX, *Renewal Theory* (London: Methuen, 1962).

11. S.K. SRINIVASAN and G. RAJAMANNAR, "Counter models and dependent renewal point processes related to neuronal firing" *Math. Biosci. 7*, 27-39 (1970).

12. A.H. BLACK, "The direct control of neural processes by reward and punishment" *American Scientist 59*, 236-245 (1971).

L'ETHIQUE COMME INSTANCE RÉGULATRICE SUPÉRIEURE DE LA VIE MENTALE

P.R. BIZE

Professeur au Conservatoire National des Arts et Métiers, Paris, France

SUMMARY

This paper discusses the relation between two biostatic systems: the neurology of a neurostatic system and the mental "life" of a psychostatic system. The author then considers the four principal levels in mental "life". The role of ethics as a supreme regulatory force is examined.

Le but de cette communication est un essai d'interprétation de la morale en termes de régulations, de circuits, de niveaux opératoires, et, de ce fait, dans une optique cybernétique.

Au même titre qu'il existe des régulations mécaniques, électro-chimiques, électro-physiques, etc., la biologie nous montre l'existence de bio-stats, la neurologie de neuro-stats, la vie mentale présente bien à considérer des psycho-stats. Le système nerveux, en effet, comme l'avait bien pressenti Hughling-Jackson, est constitué de toute une série d'étages, hiérarchiquement organisés, se subsumant les uns les autres, par le jeu de processus inhibiteurs ou facilitateurs.

Effectivement, la trajectoire situation-initiale ⟶ situation-finale que présente toute action n'est adaptée que si elle est assujettie à un processus de régulation. Il faut que ce que l'on peut appeler la "grande machine", c.a.d. la trajectoire cause-objectif, soit régulée par une "petite machine", c.a.d. un système approprié de contrôle. Dans sa forme canonique la plus simple, ce dispositif de régulation présente à considérer un tripole constitué d'un détecteur (la quantité présentée dans la grande machine), un comparateur (la quantité optimum à atteindre) et un correcteur (la quantité à laisser passer dans la grande machine).

Pour que l'action soit efficace, il convient qu'elle satisfasse un certain nombre de critères se définissant par les diverses réponses à apporter à un certain nombre de questions:

1) quel est l'objectif à atteindre.

2) quelle est la procédure, la stratégie, à faire intervenir

3) quels sont les paramètres qui doivent être retenus: l'économique, le pratique, le scientifique, l'esthétique, l'humain, l'effet psychologique, voire le philophique. On retrouve là les diverses "valeurs" si bien indiquées par Spranger.

Certes l'action peut être guidée par un seul ou quelques uns de ces paramètres, ceux notamment qui traitent surtout des grandeurs, c.a.d. des aspects exclusivement quantitatifs du problème en jeu, tandis que sont négligés les aspects qualitatifs; l'inverse est d'ailleurs également possible: on ne s'occupe que du qualitatif tandis que le quantitatif est mis entre parenthèses. Or l'action n'est véritablement efficace, aussi bien à court terme qu'à long terme, que si quantitatif et qualitatif font également partie de l'équation.

C'est, en effet, lorsque la qualité est négligée et que le facteur humain avec toute sa "malice" est omis, que l'action entreprise parait devoir être satisfaisante à court terme, mais à long terme expose à un "rebound", un effet en boomerang qui va à l'encontre des effets bénéfiques escomptés, sous la forme notamment de tous ces effects négatifs que suscite cette malice de l'animal: agressivité, revendication, refus de l'effort, primauté de l'hédonisme, déviations perverses, etc.

Ainsi se trouve posé sur des bases, non plus spéculatives, mais fort positives, le problème même du bénéfique et du maléfique, tant pour soi, que pour autrui et, on le sait de plus en plus, pour l'environnement, voir pour la planète. L'éthique apparait ainsi comme la fonction indispensable et ultime de régulation de nos actions, comme cette finalité suprême sans laquelle l'action risque de devnir nocive...un jour ou l'autre.

LES DIFFÉRENTS NIVEAUX DE LA VIE MENTALE

Concernant l'homme, en effet, on se trouve en présence d'un agencement général en quatre niveaux principaux de régulation ou de "petites machines" qui confèrent cohérence et objectifs à la vie mentale: à savoir:

1) *un plan quasi-mécanique* d'opérations se déclanchant et se succédant sur un mode stéréotypé, avec un minimum d'intervention du psychisme; telles sont les conduites dites instinctives avec leurs tropismes, leurs tactismes et leurs programmes d'obtention en partie génétiquement fixé.

2) *un plan émotivo-puslif* où émergent et sont ressentis des états émotionnels et sentimentiels de type bi-polaire, procédant de la congruence ou de la non-congruence des stimuli reçus avec notre système d'affects, donnant ainsi lieu à des régulations de compatibilité ou de non-compatibilité entre les évenements et notre agencement de modèles affectifs, relevant de programmes acquis par voie de conditionnement, de type instrumental principalement, c.a.d. en fonction des expériences favorables ou défavorables subies.

3) *un plan d'élaboration cognitive* permettant à la pensée de résoudre les divers problèmes qui se posent à elle et ainsi d'acquérir des connaissances, ceci selon deux modes principaux:

a) celui de l'élaboration élémentaire qui fait appel à des processus syncrétiques et utilise les inférences analogiques qui suscitent des comportements d'essais et d'erreurs, d'où surgissent des modèles empiriques de stratégie régulant nos actes au mieux de nos désidérata.

b) celui de la pensée discursive ou réfléchie, de type analytico-synthétique, où se succédent analyse, raisonnements inductifs et déductifs, synthèse; ceci en faisant appel à des régulations, issues des principes directeurs de la connaissance, se traduisant par la genèse de modèles logiques.

4) *un plan d'optimisation* en rapport avec les interactions possibles, fastes ou néfastes, qui sont la conséquence de nos actions sur l'environnement; ceci selon plusieurs modes:

a) celui de l'optimisation utilitaire, où la décision est précédée de pondérations sur des échelles de valeur en vue d'établir la formule appropriée de valeurs au but considéré, c.a.d. des modèles moraux, les quels sont essentiellement fonction du système de valeurs hic et nunc et résultent de ce fait à la fois de processus conditionnants passifs de type pavlovien et aussi de type actif, par la voie d'essais et d'erreurs, et donc de "calculs" opportunistes.

b) celui de l'optimisation exhaustive ou éthique proprement dite, où s'effectue le bilan réfléchi de toutes les valeurs possibles, dans une optique d'objectivité et de dépassement de soi, de consequence de nos actes à la fois à court-terme et à long-terme, et ainsi de responsabilité personnelle et d'intégration coamique, c.a.d. de sacralisation générale de nos actes. Ce qui nécessite déconditionnement, décomplexation, travail sur soi, approfondissement, mise en résonance cosmique, dépassement de la dualité et recherche de l'unité. Ce n'est plus tellement à des modèles qu'il est fait appel ici, encore moins à des principes, mais à l'éveil de certaines sphères du psychisme par le biais d'états de sur-conscience.

On conçoit que ce chemin soit bien long, parsemé d'embuches dont les plus importantes sont l'orgueil, le narcissisme et l'auto-suggestion.

LES ÉLÉMENTS DU DÉBAT

Tandis que la vie extra-consciente n'est que choix spontané, c.a.d. option en fonction des préférences d'ordre biologique ou affective, la vie consciente est choix délibéré, autrement dit débat entre instances opposées, entre pulsions antagonistes, entre solutions multiples; non seulement débat du pôle préférentiel, mais encore sur la distance de l'écart par rapport au centre du vecteur considéré.

On conùoit que le "connais-toi/toi-même" de par nos propres efforts, mais surtout grâce à la connaissance psychologique scientifique et aux techniques psycho-analytiques, soit indispensable; sinon on ne connait de soi que ce que la censure nous permet seulement de connaitre, autrement dit seulement ce que nous pouvons aimer de nous!

Tout se passe en notre psyché comme si nous nous trouvions dans un système de sortes de roses des vents, constituées de vecteurs multiples, souvent de type bipolaire, ce qui autorise toutes ces oscillations qui permettent l'adaptation: le système des inacceptions, celui des valeurs, celui des conduites, celui des attitudes. Le pôle choisi, le vecteur choisi, la position choisie sont chacun le résultat d'un débat.

Au niveau subconscient, la psycho-analyse nous a bien montrée quelles étaient les instances qui intervenaient: le ça, le surmoi, l'idéal du moi, sous la forme d'un tripole centré par le moi et entouré par l'environnement, la réalité; soit un débat entre des pulsions, des anti-pusions, des aspirations, avec un compromis à établir entre elles d'une part et entre le moi et la réalité d'autre part.

Le but de la conscience est de faire émerger tous les élements du débat et de leur donner solution.

Reste le problème de l'évolution de l'homme et celui de la voie qu'il pourrait suivre pour accéder au niveau d'optimisation exhaustive, niveau qu'il conviendrait que quelques uns, tout au moins, atteignent; nos dirigeants notamment. Peut-être le symbole du Sceau de Salomon nous donne une clef; il est, en effet, constitué de deux tripoles enchevetrés; un tripole à sommet supérieur où pourraient se situer les trois instances freudiennes qui régissent la vie automatique et commandent même notre conscience, et un tripole à sommet inférieur qui représente le chemin inverse que nous devrions suivre pour nous constituer un trans-ça (au lieu du ça), un sur-soi (au lieu du sur-moi), un idéal du soi (au lieud de l'idéal du moi), avec au centre un soi au lieu du moi, et autour l'environnement cosmique (au lieu de celui de notre entourage immédiat).

Il semble que les temps soient venus de nous préoccuper de cette évolution, car nous sommes devenus des causes et causes singulièrement efficientes, voire dangereusement efficientes.

CONCLUSION

Au même titre qu'il existe des régulations mécaniques, électro-chimiques, électro-thermiques, etc., la biologie nous montre l'existence de bio-stats, la neurologie de neuro-stats et la vie mentale de psycho-stats. Le système nerveux et la vie mentale présentent à considérer toute un série d'étages, hiérarchiquement organisés, se subsumant les uns les autres par le jeu de processus inhibiteurs ou facilitateurs, c'est-à-dire des niveaux successifs de régulation.

S'agissant de la vie mentale, on se trouve en présence de quatre niveaux principaux de régulation: celui sous-psychique de la vie instinctive, celui psychoide des processus émotivo-pulsifs, celui des processus cognitifs et celui de l'optimisation en fonction des conséquences fastes ou néfastes de nos actes.

L'éthique apparait comme la rpgulation suprême; tant qu'elle n'est pas developpée par une sorte de travail sur soi, elle est remplacée par la morale, avec ses variations hic et nunc. Elle implique donc qu'aux régulations issues de programmes génétiques ou acquis par conditionnement passif ou actif, fasse suite des régulations contractées en pleine conscience dans une optique d'intégration cosmique.

INFORMATION-THEORETIC ANALYSIS OF NEURAL COMMUNICATION

R.E. RINK

University of Alberta, Edmonton 7, Alberta, Canada

SUMMARY

There have been a number of attempts to apply Shannon's measure of information and the associated mathematical theory to communication processes in the nervous system. Although these attempts were made in hope of thereby gaining deeper understanding of the possibilities and limitations of such processes, the results have been rather inconsistent and inconclusive. Indeed, many neurophysiologists and cyberneticians are presently of the opinion that the probabilistic measure of information and ideas of channel capacity are quite irrelevant and useless to the analysis of biological communication. General questions of the applicability of information-theoretic methods are considered in this paper and some features discussed.

INTRODUCTION

Shannon's mathematical theory of communication [1], first published in 1948, provided a conceptual and quantitative basis for the analysis and evaluation of systems used to transmit messages from a source to a receiver. The theory presupposes the existence of source and receiver, each "knowing" the same set of potential messages. The messages $x_i \in X$ may or may not have semantic meaning or survival value; the only specifications required by the theory are their relative probabilities $p(x_i)$ of being selected for any one transmission.

The fundamental measure of *information* is defined as the negative logarithm of the message probability,

$$I_i = - \log p(x_i),$$

commonly expressed in binary units or "bits" when the logarithm is taken to the base 2. Apart from the mathematical niceties which result from this definition, it has intuitive appeal in that the amount of information conveyed with a message is related, through the use of probabilities, to the unpredictability or "surprise value" of the message, and, further, in that the information is additive for compound messages.

Following from this definition is that of average information content, or *information entropy*, of the source message set,

$$H(X) = -\sum_i p(x_i) \log_2 p(x_i) \text{ bits.}$$

The theory then focusses on the processes of encoding messages from X onto sequences of the symbols which are physically transmitted over the channel between source and receiver, and on the subsequent decoding from received sequences to received messages $y_j \in Y$. The channel may be variable or "noisy", so errors are possible, and the average information received in a single transmission is

$$I(X/Y) = \sum_{i,j} p(x_i,y_j) \log_2 \frac{p(x_i/y_j)}{p(x_i)} = H(X) - H(X/Y) \text{ bits,}$$

where $p(x_i/y_j)$ is the conditional probability that x_i was sent when y_j is received, and H(X/Y) is the conditional entropy of X (or average residual uncertainty about X) when a message in Y is received.

The information capacity C of the channel is then defined as the supremum of

$$\lim_{T\to\infty} \frac{I(X_T/Y_T)}{T} \text{ bits/sec,}$$

over all possible ways of encoding compound messages onto channel sequences of temporal duration T. The importance of this definition stems from Shannon's Fundamental Theorem, which states that there exist ($T\to\infty$) codes which approach the average information rate C bits/sec. and yield vanishing probability of message error.

There have been a number of attempts made to apply the theory to the process of neural communication, generally to estimate the information capacities of sensory nerves or of individual nerve cells. Jacobson [2,3], using data from psychophysical measurements of sensory acuity, estimated capacities per cell of 0.3 and 5 bits/sec for auditory and optic nerve, respectively. These rates are somewhat lower than those computed by Stein [4] for single cells under assumptions of a neural-impulse-frequency code and of certain stochastic models for the neuronal variability. Jacobson's channel capacity of 8,000 bits/sec for the auditory nerve is, however, consistent with the results [5] of a theoretical treatment of that nerve as a distributed channel, again assuming a frequency code and a Poisson model for neuronal variability, but taking into account the effect of parallel redundancy within the nerve bundle.

There is, however, a large discrepancy between these estimates of sensory capacity and the maximum information-processing rates achieved by human subjects during sustained perception-response activity. The latter have been reported by Quastler [6] to be only about 25 bits/sec.

This sort of discrepancy, plus certain objections to the probabilistic measure of information, has led many neurophysiologists and cyberneticists to doubt the usefulness of the Shannon theory to the analysis of biological communication. Indeed, in a recent symposium on information processing in the nervous system, the Shannon theory was scarcely mentioned, and then only in a comment [7] which deemed it inappropriate.

I shall attempt to show that when information theory is applied carefully, taking into account certain constraints which apply in real-life communication, it can lead to consistent and useful results. The suitability of the probabilistic measure itself will not be defended; adequate discussion of that question has been given by Shannon and Weaver [1] and by Cherry [8].

CONSTRAINTS PRESENT IN SENSORY COMMUNICATION

There remains the paradox: Why are the information capacities of the sensory channels so enormously greater than the throughput capacity of the animal?

The answer has been suggested by Cherry [8], Keidel [9], Stein [4], and others. The principle function of the senses is not to transmit a steady stream of data on a long sequence of standard symbols, as in telegraphy, for example. It is, rather, to be ready to signal the occurrence of a single, life-threatening event whose sensible features may lie anywhere within a wide range of stimulus type and intensity. In other words, the channel must be *adaptable* as to symbol type rather than specific, and it must perform reliably with little time delay, when called upon.

The range of stimuli which can be signalled by a sensory channel is reflected in the sensor arrangement. In vision, for example, the spatial distribution of retinal cells provides a structure for classifying external objects as to position. Thus the optic nerve channel must transmit signals which are patterns on a two-dimensional spatial mosaic. It must have, therefore, enough capacity over its crossection to reliably and simultaneously transmit a sufficient number of independent pattern elements, or degrees of freedom, to support the required fineness of spatial resolution. Jacobson [3] has estimated the number 240,000 acuity squares per mosaic.

In the auditory system, likewise, the distribution of hair cells and nerve endings along the cochlea provide a structure for classifying acoustic stimuli as to frequency content. Signals on the auditory nerve are, therefore, patterns with one spatial dimension, and the nerve must transmit reliably a sufficient number of independent pattern elements (degrees of freedom) to support the required frequency resolution. This number is much smaller than for vision, it has been estimated [10] to be either 4 or 6, depending on how the relevant pattern elements are defined.

Similar comments can be made for the other senses. Because of such crossectional patterning of nerve signals, a number N of degrees of freedom can be specified for each sensory nerve. These might also be viewed as N independent channels in parallel, but serving the cause of flexibility rather than that of redundancy.

The second constraint on the neural channel is called the *real time constraint* because the animal must, at some definite times as it is receiving sensory information, make decisions based on the information which has been received prior to those times. It cannot afford the luxury of waiting forever to achieve that perfect reliability of information at maximum capacity which is promised by Shannon's theorem. Indeed, even when waiting is possible, the memory requirement for the decoding of very long signals is a forbidding one. Thus there is specified a maximum allowable real time interval T for the encoding, transmission, and decoding of a particular message on a particular sensory channel.

Even though Shannon's theorem is not applicable with T constrained to be finite, the notion of channel capacity is still relevant. The probability of message error can be tightly upper-bounded through use of the *channel reliability function* E(R), according to [11]

$$P \leq A \cdot 2^{-TE(R)}$$

where R is the data rate in bits/sec ($0 \leq R \leq C$), E(R) is a monotone decreasing function which is maximum at R = 0 and reaches zero at R = C, and A is a slowly-varying (algebraic) function of T and R. Thus for a given value of T, the reliability of the channel is greatest for low data rates and least for rates approaching the channel capacity.

It has recently been shown [12] that when the channel is being used to provide feedback information about N state variables (degrees of freedom) for the control of a linear system, if CT>>1 there exists an optimum data rate which is the solution of the equation $2R = N \cdot E(R)$. This rate represents the optimum compromise between high rates, which are conducive to message errors and hence loss of control, and low rates, which lead to poor control through lack of enough information. For any specified N and channel reliability function E(R), the equation has a unique solution between R=0 and R=C. Typically, for N=1 the optimum rate may be about 0.3C, increasing with N and approaching C in the limit as N becomes very large.

The precise form of the function E(R) is not known for nerve channels, but those reliability functions which have been derived for other channels all have shapes roughly similar to one another. One may, perhaps, extrapolate to the present case. If this is done, and if N is taken to be 6 for the auditory nerve, the optimum rate turns out to be [12] about 0.5C = 4000 bits/sec. For the optic nerve, on the other hand, taking N = 240,000 gives the optimum rate $R_{opt} \simeq C = 4.3 \times 10^6$ bits/sec, using Jacobson's figure [3] for the channel capacity.

RESULTS AND CONCLUSIONS

To summarize, sensory nerves are characterized, as information channels, by N-fold spatial diversity and limited block encoding time T. These features are essential for the survival of the animal, and it can now be demonstrated that, in consequence, the very large channel capacities that have been found are also essential.

The error probability for one message is of the exponential order

$$P \sim 2^{-T \cdot E(R_0)} = 2^{-\frac{2R_0}{N} T}$$

where R_0 is the optimum data rate. The encoding time T can be estimated from consideration of the time-span of intersymbol constraints.

For the auditory nerve, one measure of this time-span is the time constant of the compound action potential for stepwise changes in stimulus intensity. From the results of Keidel and Spreng [9], this is about 3.24 milliseconds. This value is also roughly the reciprocal of the maximum discharge rate for the primary neurons, and is approaching the refractory period and synaptic integration time which characterize the underlying physiological mechanisms responsible for temporal encoding at the periphery. Therefore, taking $T = 3.24 \times 10^{-3}$ sec, $R_0 = C/2 = 4 \times 10^3$ bits/sec, and $N = 6$ for the auditory nerve,

$$\log_2 P \sim - \frac{2(4\times10^3)(3.24\times10^{-3})}{6}$$

$$= -4.32$$

so the probability of message error is of the order of 1/20.

For the optic nerve, on the other hand, the photochemical effects in the retina provide mechanisms for longer block encoding times. Jacobson [3] used an average fusion time of 0.054 seconds as the time-span of the intersymbol constraints. Using that figure and taking $N = 240{,}000$ and $R_0 = C = 4.3 \times 10^6$ bits/sec, the error probability for elementary visual messages is of the order

$$\log_2 P \sim \frac{2(4.3\times10^6)(5.4\times10^{-2})}{2.4 \times 10^5}$$

$$= -1.93$$

so $P \sim 1/4$.

Thus we have estimated bounds of 1/20 and 1/4 on the achievable error probabilities for elementary messages on the auditory and optic nerves, respectively. The point to be made with these admittedly crude estimates is that these error probabilities are *not* negligibly small, as might have been expected from the huge channel capacities of the respective nerves. It may be, in fact, that the channel performance is adequate for long-term survival only because single-message errors are rarely fatal, there being time to correct initial response errors in the majority of cases.

REFERENCES

1. C.E. SHANNON and W. WEAVER, *The Mathematical Theory of Communication* (University of Illinois Press, Urbana. Reprinted 1962).

2. H. JACOBSON, "Information and the human ear" *J. Acoust. Soc. Am. 23* no. 4, 463-471 (1951).

3. H. JACOBSON, "The informational capacity of the human eye" *Science 113*, 292-293 (1951).

4. R.B. STEIN, "The information capacity of nerve cells using a frequency code" *Biophys. J. 7*, 797-826 (1967).

5. R.E. RINK, "Information theory of neural noise in hearing" *Math. Biosciences 16*, 129-142 (1973).

6. H. QUASTLER, "Studies of human channel capacity", In: *Information Theory, 3rd London Symposium*, ed. C. CHERRY (Academic Press, New York, 1956).

7. K.N. LEIBOVIC, final session on "Information theory", In: *Information Processing in the Nervous System*, ed. K.N. LEIBOVIC (Springer-Verlag, New York, 1969).

8. C. CHERRY, *On Human Communication* second edition (M.I.T. Press, Cambridge, Mass. 1966).

9. W.D. KEIDEL, "Tuning between central auditory pathways and the ear" *IEEE Transactions on Military Electronics MIL-7* nos. 2 & 3, 131-143 (1963).

10. R.E. RINK, "Degrees of freedom of cochlear patterns" *J. Acoust. Soc. Am. 48*, 1379-1382 (1970).

11. R.G. GALLAGER, Chapter 5, *Information Theory and Reliable Communication* (John Wiley and Sons, Inc., New York, 1968).

12. R.E. RINK, "Optimal utilization of fixed-capacity channels in feeback control" *Automatica 9*, 251-255 (1973).

CONTROL OF THRESHOLD SYSTEMS AND NERVOUS SYSTEMS

T. ISHIHARA and H. TAKAHASHI

Department of Mathematical Sciences, University of Osaka Prefecture, Sakai, Osaka, Japan

SUMMARY

When inputs (control) are fed into a threshold system, three types of behavior are found. In this paper we study these three types of system behavior by means of some examples. We also refer to the relation between these threshold systems and nervous systems in the brain.

INTRODUCTION

Various electro-physiological experiments containing EEG evoked potentials, etc., related to the complex neuro-physiological phenomena in the brain, have been carried out and considerable information has been accumulated. Of course, most of these data have been analyzed; they often explain in a satisfactory manner the mechanism of the complex phenomena [1].

It seems, however, that only a qualitative description of the mechanism is usually given, and there are few mathematical models which give a quantitative clarification of the problem. [1,2,3]. In this paper we study the control of threshold systems and investigate the basic quantitative behaviour of the nervous system under influence of various cyclic inputs.

CONTROL OF THRESHOLD SYSTEMS

We consider a network consisting of n linear threshold elements interconnected by means of positive or negative coupling coefficients.

Denoting by i_h, u_h, and o_h the state of the h-th input, internal and output elements respectively, the evolution of a system in time can be described by the following set of equations:

$$u_h((m+1)\tau) = 1[\sum_{r=0}^{\alpha(h)} \sum_{k=1}^{n} a_{hk}^{r} u_k(m\tau - r\tau) +$$

$$\sum_{r=1}^{\alpha(h)} \sum_{p=1}^{n_i} b_{hp}^{r} i_p^{r}(m\tau - r\tau) - \theta_h]$$

$$(h=1,2,\ldots,n) \qquad (1)$$

$$O_h((m+1)\tau) = 1[\sum_{r=0}^{\beta(h)} \sum_{k=1}^{n} c_{hk}^{r} u_k(m\tau - r\tau) +$$

$$\sum_{r=0}^{\beta(h)} \sum_{q=1}^{n_0} d_{hq}^{r} i_q^{r}(m\tau - r\tau) - \theta_h]$$

$$(h=1,2,\ldots,n_0)$$

where n, n_i, n_0, denote respectively the number of the internal, input and output elements. The function $1(x)$ is the Heaviside unit step-function defined as:

$$1(x) \begin{cases} = 1 \ , & x \geqq 0 \\ = 0 \ , & x < 0; \end{cases}$$

θ_h denotes the threshold of the h-th element. In this model the time variable is quantized and considered as a multiplé $t = m\tau$ of a small constant time τ.

The system without input (control) is described by the following equations

$$u_h((m+1)\tau) = 1[\sum_{r=0}^{\alpha(h)} \sum_{k=1} a_{hk} u_h(m\tau - r\tau) - \theta_h] \qquad (2)$$

$$(h=1,2,\ldots,n)$$

and in the case all $\alpha(h) = 0$, the equations

$$u_h((m+1)\tau) = 1[\sum_{k=1}^{m} a_{hk} u_k(m\tau) - \theta_h] \qquad (h=1,2,\ldots,n) \quad (2a)$$

For the sake of simplicity we study mainly about (2a). One can classify 2^n possible states of this system in transition sequences as follows:

$$S^i(1) \rightarrow S^i(2) \rightarrow \ldots \rightarrow S^i(k) \longrightarrow S^i(k+1) \ldots \longrightarrow S^i(k+R_i) \qquad (i=1,\ldots,m)$$

and $$S(k) = S(k+R_i),$$

where

$$\tilde{U}_i^R i = \{S^i(k),\ S^i(k+1),\ldots,S^i(k+R_i-1)\}$$

gives a resonance (periodic transition) of period R_iT and the other states $S^i(1),\ldots,S^i(k-1)$ are called triggers to $\tilde{U}_i^R i$. The resonances $\tilde{U}_1^R 1,\ldots,\tilde{U}_m^R m$ are called proper (*reverberations*) resonances of the system.

Let us ask the following question: If we force some input sequences into the system, will the system change the initial proper resonance to another proper resonance, or remain in the same resonance or produce a new resonance?

There are three possible types of input sequences: (i) finite sequences; (ii) infinite cyclic sequences; (iii) infinite acyclic sequences.

It is evident that under the first kind of input sequences the system drops into one of the proper resonances determined by the state at the moment when the control is not operating.

We only take here the second kind of input sequences, since the third kind of input sequences contain non-countable types of variations and are less interesting.

Since the problem is complicated, we first show by means of the following examples that various types of system behaviour occur which follow input sequences and ways of interactions containing their synchronizations.

We further confine our considerations to the resonances in the closed chain C_n of n elements, that is, $C_n = \{u_1,\ldots,u_n\}$, $u_1(t) = u_n(t-1)$, $u_2(t) = u_1(t-1),\ldots,\ u_i(t) = u_{i-1}(t-1),\ldots,$ $u_n(t) = u_{n-1}(t-1)$.

Remark: Every state in a proper resonance of this system has same number of non-vanishing components. The number of the proper resonances whose states have k non-vanishing components is ${}_nC_k/n$ if the greatest common measure of n and k is 1. In this case the period of those resonances is n. If n and k have a common divisor d, there exist some resonances with a period n/d.

Example 1. Consider C_n with p inputs $i_1,\ldots,i_p$ connecting to $u_{j1},\ldots, u_{jp}$ respectively. We assume that i_k (k=1,...,p) are excitatory inputs such that $u_{jk}(t)=1$ if $i_k(t-1)=1$.

If p=1 and the periodic input sequence $\tilde{I}_i^k=1\overbrace{00\ldots0}^{k-1}1\overbrace{0\ldots0}^{k-1}1\ldots$ with period k is injected into the zero state $u_i(0)=0$ (i=1,...,n), then all the resonances in which the state transition finally appears by means of $\tilde{I}_1^k$(k=1,...,n-1) are the proper resonances. If k and n are relatively prime, the resonance elicited by $\tilde{I}_1^k$ contains only one state each of whose components is 1. Generally, we can see that the following property holds: If n and k have the greatest common measure d, then the elicited proper resonance consists of states which have n/d non-vanishing components.

We can see that if the p inputs sequences $\tilde{I}_1,\ldots,\tilde{I}_p$ are injected into C_n through p channels (elements), then the elicited resonance is $\tilde{U}_{j_1}+\tilde{U}_{j_2}+\ldots+\tilde{U}_{jp}$, where $\tilde{U}_{jk}$ represent the resonance elicited by $\tilde{I}_k$(k=1,...,p), and $\tilde{U}_1+\tilde{U}_2$ is that whose state vectors are obtained by the element-wise Boolean summation of state vectors $S_1(t)$ and $S_2(t)$ belonging to $\tilde{U}_1$ and $\tilde{U}_2$, respectively.

As an example we show a table of a state transition of C_6 with inputs i_1 and i_2.

$$
\begin{pmatrix} u_1 \\ u_2 \\ u_3 \\ u_4 \\ u_5 \\ u_6 \end{pmatrix}
\begin{array}{ccccccccccccc}
0 & \boxed{1} & 0 & 0 & 0 & 0 & \textcircled{1} & \boxed{1} & 0 & \textcircled{1} & 0 & 0 & \textcircled{1} \\
0 & \textcircled{1} & \boxed{1} & 0 & 1 & 0 & 0 & \textcircled{1} & \boxed{1} & 0 & \textcircled{1} & 0 & 0 \\
0 & 0 & \textcircled{1} & \boxed{1} & 0 & 1 & 0 & 0 & \textcircled{1} & \boxed{1} & 0 & \textcircled{1} & 0 \\
0 & 0 & 0 & \textcircled{1} & \boxed{1} & 0 & 1 & 0 & 0 & \textcircled{1} & \boxed{1} & 0 & \textcircled{1} \\
0 & 0 & 0 & 0 & \textcircled{1} & \boxed{1} & 0 & 1 & 0 & 0 & \textcircled{1} & \boxed{1} & 0 \\
0 & 0 & 0 & 0 & 0 & \textcircled{1} & \boxed{1} & 0 & \textcircled{1} & 0 & 0 & \textcircled{1} & \boxed{1}
\end{array}
$$

$$
\begin{pmatrix} i_1 \\ i_2 \end{pmatrix}
\begin{array}{ccccccccccccc}
1 & 0 & 0 & 0 & 0 & 0 & 1 & 0 & 0 & 0 & 0 & 0 & 1 \\
1 & 0 & 0 & 1 & 0 & 0 & 1 & 0 & 0 & 1 & 0 & 0 & 1
\end{array}
$$

where $\boxed{1}$ and $\textcircled{1}$ are generated by i_1 and i_2 respectively.

Similarly, we also obtain the resonance $\tilde{U}_0+\tilde{U}_i$ in the case $\tilde{U}_0=\{S_0(0),\ldots,S_0(R_0-1)\}$ is the initially given proper resonance and input sequence $\tilde{I}_i$ is added. $\tilde{U}_i=\{S_i(t),\ldots, S_i(t+R_i-1)\}$ represents the resonance elicited from the zero state by the injection of the input $\tilde{I}_i$ at t=0.

Example 2. Next we consider the case in which the system receives inhibitory inputs $i_1^-,\ldots, i_q^-$ (such that $u_{kj}^-(t)=0$ if $i_j^-(t-1)=1$) and also excitatory inputs $i_1^+,\ldots, i_p^+$ where the elements u_{kj}^- accept i_j^-, and u_{kj}^+ accept i_j^+ $(1<p+q\leqq \bar{n})$. Let $\tilde{I}_1^+,\ldots, \tilde{I}_p^+, \tilde{I}_1^-,\ldots, \tilde{I}_q^-$ be the cyclic inputs to the elements $u_1^+,\ldots, u_p^+, u_1^-,\ldots, u_q^-$. We denote by $\tilde{N}_j$ the resonance elicited by $\tilde{I}_j^-$ injected into the element u_j^- assuming as if i_j^- were an excitatory element.

When the input sequences $\tilde{I}_1^+,\ldots, \tilde{I}_p^+, \tilde{I}_1^-,\ldots, \tilde{I}_q^-$ are injected to the state in the resonance $\tilde{U}_0$, the resonance obtained is $\{\tilde{U}_0+\sum_{k=1}^{p}\tilde{U}_k\} - \{\sum_{j=1}^{q}\tilde{N}_j\}$, where $-$ is a binary operation such that 1-1=0, 1-0=1, 0-0=0 and 0-1=0.

Example 3. In the nervous system, if a neuron once fires, it does not fire until the refractory time is over.So we consider the effect of the refractory time.

In the system C_3, cyclic input sequence 10 is excitatorily given from i_1, to u_1 at the zero state. The state transition without refractory time is

$$\begin{pmatrix} u_1 \\ u_2 \\ u_3 \end{pmatrix} \begin{array}{ccccccc} 0 & 1 & 0 & 1 & 1 & 1 & 1 \\ 0 & 0 & 1 & 0 & 1 & 1 & 1 \\ 0 & 0 & 0 & 1 & 0 & 1 & 1 \end{array}$$
$$\begin{pmatrix} i_1 \end{pmatrix} \begin{array}{ccccccc} 1 & 0 & 1 & 0 & 1 & 0 & 1 \end{array}$$

In the case when each element u_i of C_3 has the refractory time 2τ, that is, $u_i\ (t+1) = 0$ and $u_i\ (t+2) = 0$ if $u_i\ (t) = 1$, the state transition is

$$\begin{pmatrix} u_1 \\ u_2 \\ u_3 \end{pmatrix} \begin{array}{cccccccccc} 0 & 1 & 0 & 0 & 1 & 0 & 0 & 1 & 0 & 0 \\ 0 & 0 & 1 & 0 & 0 & 1 & 0 & 0 & 1 & 0 \\ 0 & 0 & 0 & 1 & 0 & 0 & 1 & 0 & 0 & 1 \end{array}$$
$$\begin{pmatrix} i_1 \end{pmatrix} \begin{array}{cccccccccc} 1 & 0 & 1 & 0 & 1 & 0 & 1 & 0 & 1 & 0 \end{array}$$

The refractory time 2τ causes the 2τ elongation of the original period of u_i

If u_1, u_2 and u_3 have τ, 2τ and 3τ refractory times respectively, then the state transition is

$$\begin{pmatrix} u_1 \\ u_2 \\ u_3 \end{pmatrix} \begin{array}{ccccc} 0 & 1 & 0 & 1 & 0 \\ 0 & 0 & 1 & 0 & 0 \\ 0 & 0 & 0 & 1 & 0 \end{array}$$
$$\begin{pmatrix} i_1 \end{pmatrix} \begin{array}{ccccc} 1 & 0 & 1 & 0 & 1 \end{array}$$

In this case the refractory times $\{\tau, 2\tau, 3\tau\}$ cause the elongation of the original period by $\{\tau, 3\tau, 3\tau\}$ of $\{u_1, u_2, u_3\}$.

Example 4. Periodic input sequences can sometimes produce other resonances in a system than proper resonances. As an example consider the system $U=\{u_i, a_{ij}, \Theta_i;\ 1 \leqq i,j \leqq 3\}$ with inputs i_1 and i_2 which are connected to u_1 and u_2 by means of coupling coefficients b_{11} and b_{22}, respectively.

$$\left(a_{ij}\right) = \begin{pmatrix} 0.8 & 0 & 0 \\ 0 & -0.1 & 0.9 \\ 0.6 & -0.3 & 0 \end{pmatrix},\ \Theta_i = 0.5(i=1\sim 3),\ b_{11} = b_{22} = 1.$$

The proper state transition is

$$\begin{pmatrix} u_1 \\ u_2 \\ u_3 \end{pmatrix} \begin{matrix} 1 & 1 & 1 & 1 \\ 1 & 1 & 0 & 0 \\ 1 & 0 & 0 & 1 \end{matrix} \quad \text{and} \quad \begin{matrix} 0 & 0 & 0 & & 0 \\ 1 \rightarrow & 1 \rightarrow & 0 & & 0 \\ 1 & 0 & 0 & & 1 \end{matrix}$$

If the periodic input sequences $\begin{pmatrix} i_1 \\ i_2 \end{pmatrix} = \begin{matrix} 1 & 0 & 0 \\ 0 & 1 & 0 \end{matrix}$ are injected into the zero state, then the state transition in this system is

$$\begin{matrix} \begin{pmatrix} u_1 \\ u_2 \\ u_3 \end{pmatrix} & \begin{matrix} 0 & 1 & 1 & 1 & 1 & 1 \\ 0 & 0 & 1 & 1 & 0 & 1 \\ 0 & 0 & 1 & 0 & 0 & 1 \end{matrix} \\ \begin{pmatrix} i_1 \\ i_2 \end{pmatrix} & \begin{matrix} 1 & 0 & 0 & 1 & 0 & 0 \\ 0 & 1 & 0 & 0 & 1 & 0 \end{matrix} \end{matrix}$$

Thus the generated resonance differs from any of the proper ones.

Moreover, some input sequences can make the state transition which never occurs autonomously. We demonstrate this extreme case by an example.

Consider the system $U = \{u_1, u_2\}$ with input i_1 and i_2 described by the next equations

$$u_1(t+1) = 1[u_1(t)+i_1(t)-i_2(t)-0.5]$$

$$u_2(t+1) = 1[0.6u_1(t)-2u_2(t)+i_1(t)-0.5]$$

By injecting input sequences

$$\begin{pmatrix} i_1 \\ i_2 \end{pmatrix} \begin{matrix} 1 & 1 & 0 & 0 \\ 0 & 0 & 1 & 0 \end{matrix}$$

we can obtain the state transition

$$\begin{matrix} \begin{pmatrix} u_1 \\ u_2 \end{pmatrix} & \begin{matrix} 0 & 1 & 1 & 0 \\ 0 & 1 & 0 & 1 \end{matrix} \\ \begin{pmatrix} i_1 \\ i_2 \end{pmatrix} & \begin{matrix} 1 & 1 & 0 & 0 \\ 0 & 0 & 1 & 0 \end{matrix} \end{matrix}$$

In this state transition $u_1(t+1) = 1$ for $\begin{bmatrix} u_1(t) \\ u_2(t) \end{bmatrix} = \begin{bmatrix} 1 \\ 1 \end{bmatrix}$ and $\begin{bmatrix} 0 \\ 0 \end{bmatrix}$ and $u_1(t+1) = 0$ for $\begin{bmatrix} u_1(t) \\ u_2(t) \end{bmatrix} = \begin{bmatrix} 1 \\ 0 \end{bmatrix}$ and $\begin{bmatrix} 0 \\ 1 \end{bmatrix}$. This behaviour of u_1 cannot occur without input.

We can regard the system behaviour in these examples as those mainly depending on the inputs.

Example 5. We next show the system behaviour mainly depending on the structure of the system as an opposite example to Example 4.

Consider the first system given in example 4. Set $b_{11} = 0.6$, $b_{22} = 0.2$, and other values to be equal to the values in Example 4. Then the state transition under the same input sequence is

u_1	0	1	1	1	1	1	1	1	1	1	1	1	1	1
u_2	0	0	0	1	1	0	0	1	1	0	0	1	1	0
u_3	0	0	1	1	0	0	1	1	0	0	1	1	0	0
i_1	1	0	0	1	0	0	1	0	0	1	0	0	1	0
i_2	0	1	0	0	1	0	0	1	0	0	1	0	0	1

In this example input sequences only cause the proper resonance and have no other influence on the behaviour of the system.

CONTROL OF THRESHOLD SYSTEMS AND NERVOUS SYSTEMS

So far we have investigated the periodic behaviour of the threshold systems under control. Here we consider the periodic behaviour in the nervous systems. There exist many neuro-physiological phenomena that we believe are caused by the reso-nances. The direct detection of reverberations (resonances) is made, e.g. between the thalamus and the neocortex and be-tween the nucleus interpositus and the nucleus reticularis tegmenti pontis [7]. Theoretical investigations of information processing in the nervous systems based on the resonances have been discussed [4-6].

We may think that in the nervous system there are three

types of relations, as shown in the preceding examples, between input sequences and proper resonances.

1) In the primary sensory cortex, e.g., visual cortex area 17, auditory cortex area 41 and 42, input information must be found. We can naturally imagine that in these areas the system under the particular specific input sequences takes on a characteristic behaviour. Hence we may consider that the process shows that the information depends on the input like in Example 4.

2) As regards information processing in the memory fields of the brain, we can reasonably consider that the input sequences in this area act as triggers, and the resulting behaviour shows the distinctive memory which is characteristic of the structure of the system. Therefore, we can consider this process like the one in example 5.

3) In the association area there must be some comparison of two distinct information sets compatible in the same domain. Hence we can imagine the process to be like the one shown in example 1 or 2.

REFERENCES

1. E.R. CAIANIELLO, "An outline of thought processes and thinking machines" *J. Theoret. Biol. 1*, 204 (1961).

2. E.R. CAIANIELLO, A. DE LUCA and L.M. RICCIARDI, "Reverberations and control of neural networks" *Kybernetik 4*, 10 (1967).

3. L.M. RICCIARDI, "Formalized neurons and neural networks" *1st European Biophysics Congress, Vienna* (1971).

4. T. ISHIHARA, "Local reverberations in the nervous system and conditioned reflex" *Math. Biosci. 12*, 23 (1971).

5. T. ISHIHARA, "Local reverberations in the nervous system and memory" *Math. Biosci. 12*, 225 (1971).

6. T. ISHIHARA and H. TAKAHASHI, "Some mathematical models of information processing in the nervous system" *4th International Biophysics Congress, Moscow* (1972).

7. N. TSUKAHARA, T. BANDO, S.T. KITAI and T. KIYOHARA, "Cerebello-pontine reverberating circuit" *Brain Research 33*, 233 (1971).

8. H.T. CHANG, "Dendritic potential of cortical neurons as produced by direct electrical stimulation of the cerebral cortex" *J. Neurophysiol. 14*, 1 (1951).

A CYBERNETIC-HOLOGRAPHIC MODEL FOR THE CEREBRAL CORTEX ACTIVITY

C. BĂLĂCEANU, E. NICOLAU AND G. DONA

Polytechnic, Bucharest, Rumania

SUMMARY

Although information processing, storage and retrieval have been of importance to both biological and engineering sciences, it has not been readily appreciated that we do not have a perfect model for cerebral cortex activity. Contemporary concepts pertinent to Cybernetics (as defined by Wiener) and Communication Theory (in Shannon's approach) were primarily developed for the physical and technical sciences, and secondarily applied to human sciences and to man's body. It seems to us that holography now is in the same position. The aim of this paper is to present a model of information processing, storage and retrieval in the cerebral cortex, which is based directly on cybernetics and holography, as well as on the anatomy and physiology of the nervous system.

The cerebral cortex can be considered as a system, the inputs of which are all afferent ways of the nervous system, and the outputs of which are represented by the effectory ways. The cerebral cortex is occupying a special position in the general plan of the system. It is the site of the most sophisticated information processing because of the complexity of its structure.

From a structural standpoint, the cerebral cortex is a stochastic network, consisting of information-treating microsystems (the neurons) and of transmitting microsystems (the neuronal axons and the synapses). The neuronal density in the human cerebral cortex is of about 50 neurons per 0.001 m^3, bringing the total number up to 10^{10}. These neurons could be divided in two classes: Pyramidal and the rest. The fundamental operational element of the cerebral cortex is represented by the pyramidal neurons.

PYRAMIDAL NEURONS

Every pyramidal neuron is to be considered as a system of information processing of two input groups (at the apical tree branches and at the level of the basal dendrites) and also of an output formed by the pyramidal axon.

To every pyramidal neuron are attached one or more resonance circuits [29] (in the Lorente de No's sense). These functioning as a hysteresis mechanism (Rashewsky) are conferring a memory on the pyramidal neuron; this is evidently only a limited one.

The experimental data justify also the existence of some memory elements of long duration (on a biochemical basis), attached to the pyramidal neurons. There can be modifications at the level of RNA molecules [18] or of the synapses [23].

We shall now consider the pyramidal neuron as system with two types of inputs, an output and with memory elements.

Like every system the neuron is also characterized by his states. We consider the pyramidal neuron to display four possible states: The indifferent or rest state (Er); the activity or excitation state (Ec); the inhibition state (Ein); the disinhibition or rebuilding state (Ed). The last occurs after the cessation of the inhibitory signal. The inhibition does not disappear instantly, but is progressively exhausted during the Ed state, having a duration D (constant for every pyramidal neuron).

THE CORTEX

From a morphological standpoint, the cerebral cortex is forming an undulated and curved layer, with a relatively constant thickness. From a theoretical standpoint it can be considered as transformed in a developed plane, like a screen in a bidimensional Euclidian plan. The transformation does not alter topologically the cortex organisation.

We shall consider the cerebral cortex like a screen on which X, Y Cartesian coordinates system can be defined.

The T (x,y) status of the cortical screen can be defined as the set of all pyramidal neurons composing it. We will have to particularly consider the excitation states Ec. In this way the state of the screen T will be defined by the distribution of the excitation states in the points of the (x,y).

We also define the cerebral cortex as a system the inputs of which are coming from all receptors of the organism. This means that the T states (x,y,t) depend on the information received from these receptors.

These data determine the distribution of the excited points of the plan (x,y) every moment (t). This distribution is certainly not accidental, but it is based on a correspondence between every input message and a certain special distribution of the excited points in the plan (x,y). We have, in other words, a coding operation. The function defined by the set of input messages, the values of which lie in the set of possible distributions of the excited points in the plan (x,y), denotes the spatial type code in which afferent messages are transcribed on the set of the pyramidal neuronal states of the cerebral cortex.

In this way messages received from the external and internal media (considered as information sources of the cortical system) are transformed in distributions of excited pyramidal neurons, realizing some bidimensional shapes on the T screen (x,y,t). These shapes represent, like a map, the semantic content of the afferent messages.

By more subtle experiments neurophysiology allows one to explain this principle. In this way a theory was elaborated, called by us the "chartographic principle" of the cerebral cortex function. It lies at the base of the Penfield and Rasmussen homunculus [32] of the parietal cortex of the tonotopic representation of the auditory cortex [41] and of the retinal projection on the calcarine cortex [17].

If we also take into consideration the resonance circuits, we have to assume that different T states (x,y,t) are remembered for a short time at their level; If we also take into consideration the long memory elements, we have to assume that these states are remembered a very long time (sometimes during the entire existence period of the cortical system). In this case we can draw an analogy between the screen (x,y) and a photographic plate. The resonating circuits and the long memory elements attached to the pyramidal cells function like photo-sensible granules of the photographic plates emulsions.

To a first approximation we can consider the coding function to operate like a lens projecting images (spatial shapes) on the screen (x,y), which are stored in the short and long term memory elements. It follows that maps transcribing the semantic content of the afferent messages are photographed, stored and retrieved. However, experimental data on the cerebral cortex memory do not agree with this model.

The researches and theories of Bianchi, Rylander, Tubb, Halstead and especially of Lashley [21] and Pavlov do not agree with the chartographic principle [15,31,36]. According to them, every element of the semantic content of the afferent messages is distributed over the entire cerebral cortex. That is why partial destruction of the cortical screen does not lead to a selective disappearance of the stored information, but to a general lowering of the precision of this information. This lowering is a function of the destroyed surface, independently of the position of the destroyed area in the (x,y) plan.

Taking into consideration these data, some authors [8,19, 33,39] advanced the hypothesis that the maps "transcription" is done in accordance with a principle of the optical holography type of D. Gabor [12,13,14].

CORTICAL SCREEN

We saw that a coding function transforms afferent messages as distributions of excited points on the cortical screen. This function is operating at a sub-cortical level (most probably at a thalamic level). The axons of the respective neurons represent the specific afferent cortical ways that penetrate the cortical layers. We can define a $\hat{T}$ state (x,y,t) of the cortical screen, taking into consideration only the states of the specific afferent fibres considered as points distributed in the plan (x,y). This $\hat{T}$ state (x,y,t) corresponds to maps postulated in the chartographic model discussed already and found by electroneurophysiological researches.

Between the $\hat{T}$ state of the screen defined as the set of the states of afferent specific fibres and the T state of the cortical screen defined as the set of pyramidal neurons there is a considerable difference. This difference is due to the fact that between the specific afferent fibres and the pyramidal neurons a "position-wave" there is interposed a translator. Due to this translator a new coding function occurs which establishes a correspondence between the position of every excited axon and an oscillating process triggered at the level of the pyramidal neuron.

Every axon ax_j is divided into a great number of terminal branches b_{ji}, which are connected to a corresponding number of pyramidal neurons N_i ($i = 1,2,\ldots.L$). This principle agrees with histological researches [11,29,37]. It was shown that b_{ji} ramifications exist at the basal dendrites of the neuron N_i. It was also shown that the lengths of the b_{ji} ramifications are different. It follows that the signal of the ax_j axon reaches at different moments every N_i neuron. This gap is a constant of the assembly, since its basis is ensured by the anatomical structure that is invariant in time.

The neurons N_i are interconnected, a fact amply demonstrated by histological researches [11,29]. The interneuronal connectors are greatly of an inhibitory type, as our researches of electronic microscopy have proved.

The inhibitory character is given by the morphologic criterion, i.e. by the form of the presynaptic vesicles, as the researches [30] of Ochizuno have proved.

We can consider that every neuron N_i sends m inhibitory connexions to neurons $N_i - q$ ($q = 1,2,\ldots m$). The most simple case is $m = 1$.

If we assume that the inhibitory signal always dominates the excitatory signal (or signals) and that the number of neurons N_i is finite, such a structure is behaving like a network with cyclic inhibition of the type of that studied by Kling [20].

Such a system is characterized by the fact that, if the axon ax_j is in an excitatory state and if there is at least one neuron N_i in an inhibitory state, every N_i neuron leaves the resting state E_r and enters into a periodical succession of states.

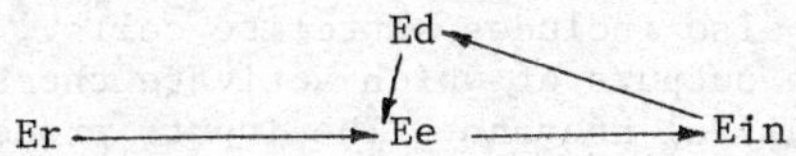

(1)

The frequency ω of this process depends on the number L of the neurons N_i the number m of the inhibitory connexions, and on the sum of the durations D_i of the disinhibition states. It also depends on the number n of the neurons N_i which are at every moment in an excitatory state in the entire system. That is:

$$\omega = F\ (\ L,m,n,\ \Sigma\ D_i\ ) \qquad (2)$$

in which F is a function.

The number n of the excited neurons at every moment t is rapidly rising during the functioning of the system and is established at a N_{max} value defined by the relation.

$$N_{max} \hat{=} \frac{1}{m+1} \qquad (3)$$

in which (m) represents the greatest integer, smaller or equal to m. As all parameters are constant, it follows that the system is characterized (in the case the axon ax_j is excited) by a periodic process with its own frequency (ω), propagating like a wave in the group of the neuron N_i.

In this case the status T (x,y,t) of the cortical screen defined on the states of the pyramidal neurons resembles a periodical process T (x,y,ω,t). It follows that the afferent messages determine at the cortex level processes of the type of some waves propagated in the T (x,y) plan, with a frequency ω and with an amplitude a_s.

The states of the pyramidal neurons do not only depend on the inputs on the level of basal dendrites. Every pyramidal neuron dispose also of an apical bunch of dendrites at the level of the molecular stratum of the cerebral cortex.

These apical dendrites receive input signals from the horizontal fibres of the molecular stratum, distributed in different directions, maintained parallel with the (x-y) plan. The signals of the fibre "influence" over 70% of the cerebral cortex cells [38].

Our researches showed that the horizontal fibres belong to an assembly which also includes sattelite cells. They form a subsystem, the outputs of which activate the apical dendrites of the pyramidal neurons. The inputs proceded either from some subcortical structures (for example the ascendant activatory system of Magoun [22] or the thalamic recruiting system [24] of Morrison and Dempsey) or from some pyramidal cells with recurrent axons (Martinotti cells).

We can assume that this subsystem, under the impact of its inputs, presents an internal oscillation with a frequency $\hat{\omega}$. This oscillation can be determined by his own arrangement of the Kling [20] networks with cyclic inhibition type or by a periodical input signal. In every respect this internal oscillation produces a periodical evolution of outputs. This makes "the influence" of the horizontal fibres system of the molecular stratum on the apical arborisations of the pyramidal cells periodical with a frequency ω. We can also assume that a certain mean $\hat{\omega}$ is not accidental, but depends on the activity of the entire cortex, either by the Martinotti cells or in a more complex cortico-subcortical way. This dependence may lead to the relation

$$\omega = \hat{\omega} \quad \text{or} \quad \omega \approx \hat{\omega} \tag{4}$$

It follows that pyramidal cells are simultaneously under the influence of two periodical processes. The first is generated by the axons forming specific afferent fibres and acting on the basal dendrites; the other is determined by the subsystem of horizontal fibres of the molecular stratum, acting on the apical dendrites. Both processes have, in accordance with the relation (4), an equal frequency. Due to the different positions of the pyramidal cells in relation to the horizontal fibres at the level of every pyramidal neuron, a phase difference $\Delta\zeta$ is obtained between the two periodical processes; $\Delta\zeta$ is different for every pyramidal neuron. Since these differences are conditioned by the positions of the neurons in the plan (x,y), they are invariant in time.

It follows that the T status (x,y,t) of the cortical screen, defined as pyramidal cells, results in combinations of periodical processes:

$$T\,(x,y,t) = a_s\,(x,y,\omega,t) \;*\; a_r\,(x,y,\hat{\omega},t) \tag{5}$$

in which $\omega = \hat{\omega}$ and the phase differences are constant at every point of the plan (x,y).

THE HOLOGRAPHIC BASE

What is stored on the memory elements is the combination between a_r (the periodical process determined by the horizontal fibres) and a_s (the periodical process determined by the specific afferent fibres). The combination of the two processes is like the interference of two wave fronts. From a mathematical point of view it is a convolution product defined by the relation:

$$T = a_s + a_r = (a_s^* + a_n)\ (a_s + a_2) = a_s a_r + a_s^* a_r + I_s + I_r \quad (6)$$

in which a is the complex conjugated of a, and I is the intensity of the periodical process (I = aa*).

The result of this interference is stored by the memory elements, considered by us to be attached to the pyramidal neurons. The "deformity" of the substratum implicated in the memory is, like in the photographic process, a quadratic function of the amplitude of the periodic process acting on it and thence as a f(a^2) ar f (a.a*) form function.

In this way we can define a set of the cortical screen T_e (x,y) as one of memory elements attached to the pyramidal neurons, depending on the relation (6). This set is invariant in time and has the physical significance of a photograph.

The action of a periodical process (a wave front) a 'r" on this "photograph", which could be the a_r wave or a part of it leads to a combination between T_e and a_r, which from a physical point of view has the significance of diffraction according to the relation:

$$a_e' \cdot T_e = a_s\ (a_2\ (+)\ a'_2\ ) = a_s \quad (7)$$

In which (+) represents a crossed correlation. It follows that the wave front a_s represents the engrammed message. The process belongs to the type described in optical holography [10,39]. In accordance with this principle the memory of the cerebral cortex has the properties attributed to it by different investigators; due to the "position-wave" translator the apparent contradiction between the chartographic model (of the cortical neurophysiology) and the holographic model may be resolved.

The holographic principle permits the engramming of a much more of information on the surface unit [7,12,13,14].

It is also sufficient that the "reference wave" a_r be oriented in different ways so that two hologrphic constructions could be engrammed. This phenomenon was experimentally verified [25,42]. The proper anatomical conditions exist, since the horizontal fibres are oriented in different directions.

Also, if it is assumed that the reference way a_r is subjected to some regular periodical transformations (in the sense of a scanning), it is possible to obtain time variable holographic constructions and reconstructions, like in holographic cinematography or television (Leithes; Upatriks).

As we can see, the holographic model fits all experimental data, and is in no contradiction (by the conditions implied) to morphological principles of organization of the cerebral cortex. Also, it represents in relation to the chartographic classical model a series of advantages regarding the amount of information, which could be treated and remembered by surface units.

REFERENCES

1. C. BALACEAUNU and E. NICOLAU, *Les fondements cybernetiques de l'activité nerveuse.* (Expansion Scientifique, Paris, 1971).

2. C. BALACEANU and E. NICOLAU, "Contributii la studiul transmiterii informatiei prin sinapsa". *Neurologia, Psihiatria, Neurochirurgia 8*, Nr. 6, 531 - 540 (1963).

3. C. BALACEANU, G. DONA and E. NICOLAU, "Les mecanismes holographiques du cortex cérébral" *Commun. Congrès Medecine Cybérnetique* Naples (1972).

4. C. BALACEANU, G. DONA and E. NICOLAU, "Bazele morfologice ale mecanismelor holografice corticale" *Com. USSM - Neurologie, Bucuresti* (1972).

5. C. BALACEANU, G. DONA, I. COTUTIU and TEODORESCU, "Structura microscop electronica a scoartei cerebrale" (Nota I) *Com. Cercul de Anat-Patol. Inst. Neurologie, Acad. RSR - Bucuresti* (1971).

6. R. BADESCU, C. BALACEANU and E. NICOLAU, "On transmission of information by synapsis" *Int. J. Bio-Med. Comput. 1*, 211-220 (1970).

7. P. BARLAI, "Informationsverarbeitung durch Halogramme" *Kybernetic 9*, 2, p.78-83 (1971).

8. T.W. BARRET, "Prolegomena to on aesthetic" *Math. Biosci 3*, 3/4 (1968).

9. S.N. BRAINES, A.V. NAPALKOV and V.B. SVECINSKII, Neurokibernetica gosizdmedlit, Moscova (1962).

10. A. BORSELINO and T. POGGIO, "Holographic Aspects of temporal Memory and Optomotor Resphases" *Kybernetik 10*, No. 1, 58-60 (1972).

11. S. CAJAL and Y. RAMON, *Histologie du système nerveux de l'homme et des vertébreux* (Doin.Paris, 1909-11).

12. D. GABOR, "A new microscopic principle" *Nature* (London) *161*,777(1948).

13. D. GABOR, "Holographic model of temporal recall". *Nature* (London) *217*, 584(1968).

14. D. GABOR, "Associative holographic memories". *IBM. J. Res. Develop. 13*, 2(1968).

15. W.C. HALSTEAD, *Brain and Intelligence*, (Chicago, 1947).

16. D.O. HEBB,"Man's frontal lobes". *Arch. Neurol. Psychiat. Chicago 54*,10-24(1945).

17. D.H. HUBEL and T.N. WISEL, "Receptive fields of single neurones in the cats striate cortex" *J. Physiol.* London *148*, 574-591 (1959).

18. F. HYDEN, "A molecular basis of neuron-glia interaction" In: *Macromolecular Specifity and Biological Memory* O.F. Schid. (MIT Press, Cambridge, 1962).

19. B. JULESZ and K.S. PENNINGTON, "Equidistributed information mapping. An Analogy to hologramms and memory" *J. Opt. Soc. Amer. 55*, 604(1965).

20. U. KLING, "Simulation neuronaler Impulsrythmen", *Kybernetik 9*, No. 4, 123-139 (1971).

21. K.S. LASHLEY, *Brain, Mechanisms and Intelligence* (Dover, New York, 1963).

22. W.H. MAGOUN, *The Waking Brain* (Springfield. Illinois, 1963).

23. K. MOLGAARD, M.C. DIAMOND, E.L. BENNET and M.R. ROSENZWEIG, "Quantitative Synaptic changes with differential experience in rat Brain". *Int. Neurosci, 2*, No. 2, 113-128 (1971).

24. R.S. MORRISON and E.W. DEMPSEY, "A study of thalamocortical relations" *Am. J. Physiol.* 281-292 (1942).

25. E. MÜHLENFELD, "Paralelle Verarbeitung zur Erklärung Beliebiger Bildmuster" *NTZ 23*, 597-603 (1970).

26. E. NICOLAU and C. BALACEANU, *Cibernetica* (Ed. stiintifica, Bucuresti 1961).

27. Idem., *Elemente de Neurocibernetica*, (Ed. ştiinţifica, Bucuresti, 1967).

28. Idem., "Contributii la studiul retelelor instruibile" *Automatica si Electronica 7*, No. 3, 100-106 (1963).

29. R. LORENTE DE, "La corteza cerebral del raton" *Trab. Lab. Invest. biol. Univ. Madrid 20*, 28-32(1922).

30. K. OCHIZUNO, "Characteristics of excitatory and inhibitory synapses in the central nervous system of the cat" *Nature 207*, 642-643(1965).

31. I.P. PAVLOV, *Prelegeri despre activitatea hemisferelor cerebrale* (Ed. Academiei RPR, 1952).

32. W. PENFIELD and T. RASMUSSEN, *The Cerebral Cortex of Man* (Mac Millan Co., N.Y., 1950).

33. K.H. PRIBRAM, "The neurophysiology of remembering" *Scientific American 220*, No. 1, 73-88(1969).

34. FR. ROSENBLATT, *Principles of Neurodynamics* (Spartan Books, Washington, 1962).

35. M.R. ROSENZWEIG, ED.L. BENNET and M.C. DIAMOND, "Brain changes in response to experience scientific" *Scient. Amer. 226*, No. 2, 22-29 (1972).

36. G. RYLANDER, "Mental changes after operation on the frontal Lobes" *Acta Psychiatr. Neurol. Supp. 20* (1943).

37. S.A. SARKISSOV and G.N. POLLIAKOW.

38. D.A. SHOLL, *The Organization of the Cerebral Cortex* (Methuen, Co, London, 1956).

39. P.R. WESTLAKE, "The possibilities of neural holographic processes within the brain". *Kybernetik VII*, No. 4, 129-153 (1970).

40. O. WIENER, "Stehende Lichtwellen und die Schwingungsrichtung polarisierten Lichtes" *Ann. de Physik 40*, 203 (1890).

41. C.N. WOOLSLEY and E.M. WALZL, "Topical projection of nerve fibers from local regions of the cochlea to the cerebral cortex of the cat." *John Hopkins Hospit.-Bull. 71*, 315-344 (1942).

42. F.T.S. YU, "Information channel capacity of a photographic film" *I.E.E.E. Trans. Information Theory 16*, 477-480 (1970).

SECTION III: ENGINEERING CYBERNETICS (AUTOMATION)

ENGINEERING CYBERNETICS AND AUTOMATED INSPECTION

M.D. FREEDMAN and J.M. IDELSOHN

Control and Data-Handling Systems Department, Information Sciences Laboratory, Bendix Research Laboratories, Southfield, Michigan 48076, U.S.A.

SUMMARY

An automated inspection technique using optical pattern recognition is described. In the application of this technique, an electro-optical scanner views a mechanical part and provides an input to a feature extraction and image classification system. The output of the classification system is then used to reject parts having defective shape or surface characteristics, thereby automating the quality control function of a production assembly line. Three examples of the application of this automated inspection technique are: a master-brake-cylinder inspection system, a jet engine turbine blade inspection system, and a power brake diaphragm alignment inspection system. All of these systems offer improved performance when compared to conventional inspection procedures. The latter application also provides an interesting example of a man-machine interaction. If the assembly machine operator does not properly align the parts to be assembled, the machine prevents the task from being completed, thereby forcing the operator to reposition the parts correctly. Thus, the operator learns to properly align the parts, and his performance is improved as a result of his interaction with the inspection system.

INTRODUCTION

The subject of optical pattern recognition, whereby visual patterns are classified into categories, has received a great deal of attention in the past decade in an effort to build a machine capable of seeing [1-4]. Ideally, such a machine would process visual patterns in much the same manner that humans do to extract information about the environment [5]. For example, by processing the information contained in aerial photographs, we are able to produce maps. By examining our surroundings, we avoid bumping into obstacles, are aided in our ability to perform complex mechanical assembly tasks, and can extract information from a printed page. How great an accomplishment it would be if we could build a machine with all of these characteristics! Fortunately, some progress has been made and machines have been built which individually possess these properties in some limited fashion. For example, robots have been built which are capable of negotiating simple obstacle courses without bumping into the obstacles [6]. Machines, called optical character readers, are capable of "reading" printed matter and converting it into machine-usable form [7]. Bendix has built photogrammetry equipment, which automatically produces mapping materials from aerial photographs [8], as well as inspection systems for automating the quality control function of a manufacturing assembly line [9]. The latter type of system optically examines a manufactured part to determine whether it is in any way defective.

This paper describes an automated inspection technique which uses an optical scanner to view a part. The scanner provides information to a preprocessor and classifier which process the scanner output to determine whether certain characteristics of the part are within prespecified tolerances. Defective parts can then be rejected automatically.

Examples of several types of inspection systems which have been built and incorporate the techniques described in this paper include: a master-brake-cylinder inspection system, a jet engine turbine blade inspection system, and a power brake diaphragm alignment inspection system. Significant performance improvements over conventional inspection procedures have been observed with these systems since boredom, which is the primary cause of poor inspector performance, does not affect the machine.

PRINCIPLES OF OPERATION

The block diagram of an automated inspection system is illustrated in Fig. 1. It consists of an *electro-optical converter*, a *preprocessor*, and a *classifier*. The *mechanical handling equipment*, which moves the part being inspected past the read station, and the *optics*, which focus the part onto the electro-optical converter, are not shown.

The *electro-optical converter* scans the part and converts the image it receives into electrical signals for further processing. Scanning can be mechanical or electronic.

The *preprocessor* examines the output of the scanner and performs all quantization and feature extraction operations.

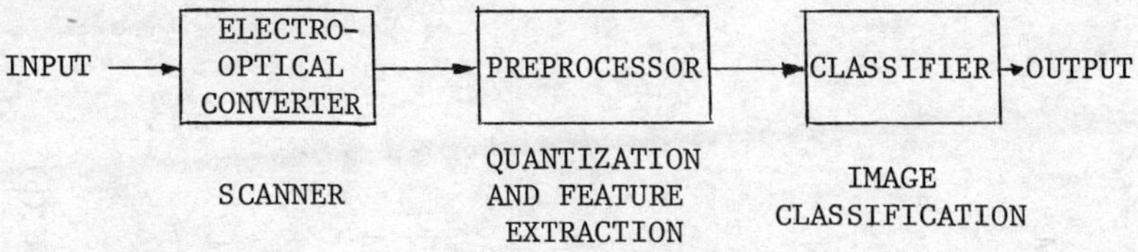

Fig. 1. Block diagram of automated inspection system

Since some inspection systems do not employ feature extraction hardware, the preprocessor may simply consist of a quantizer.

The *classifier* processes the output of the preprocessor to determine whether there are any defects in the part being examined. The output of the classifier is generally a GO/NO GO decision which causes the part to be accepted or rejected. It is often in the form of a logic command which is then sent to the mechanical handling equipment causing automatic acceptance or rejection of the part.

In the next sections, we examine in detail how each of these sub-systems operate and how they contribute to the overall functioning of the inspection system.

ELECTRO-OPTICAL CONVERSION

The conversion of an optical image into electrical signals can be accomplished in many ways. Either mechanical scanning or electronic scanning can be used. Scanning can be *active* in which case a moving spot of light from a laser is focused onto the part and its reflection is sensed by fixed photodetectors. Or it can be *passive*, in which case the entire field of view is illuminated uniformly but the sensor detects only the reflection from one small spot at a time. Two types of scan patterns are used: the *raster scan*, which is usually generated electronically, scans the entire field of view one line at a time in a manner used by commercial television cameras, and the *helical scan*, which is generated mechanically, is used to inspect the interior surface of a bored hole in one long continuous sweep.

The Raster Scan

The raster scanner examines each point of an image in a line-by-line manner using a vidicon tube. The latter is a low-cost television pickup tube which is easily adapted for use in inspection systems. The output generated by a vidicon scanner is shown in Fig. 2(b) for several scan lines located as shown in Fig. 2(a).

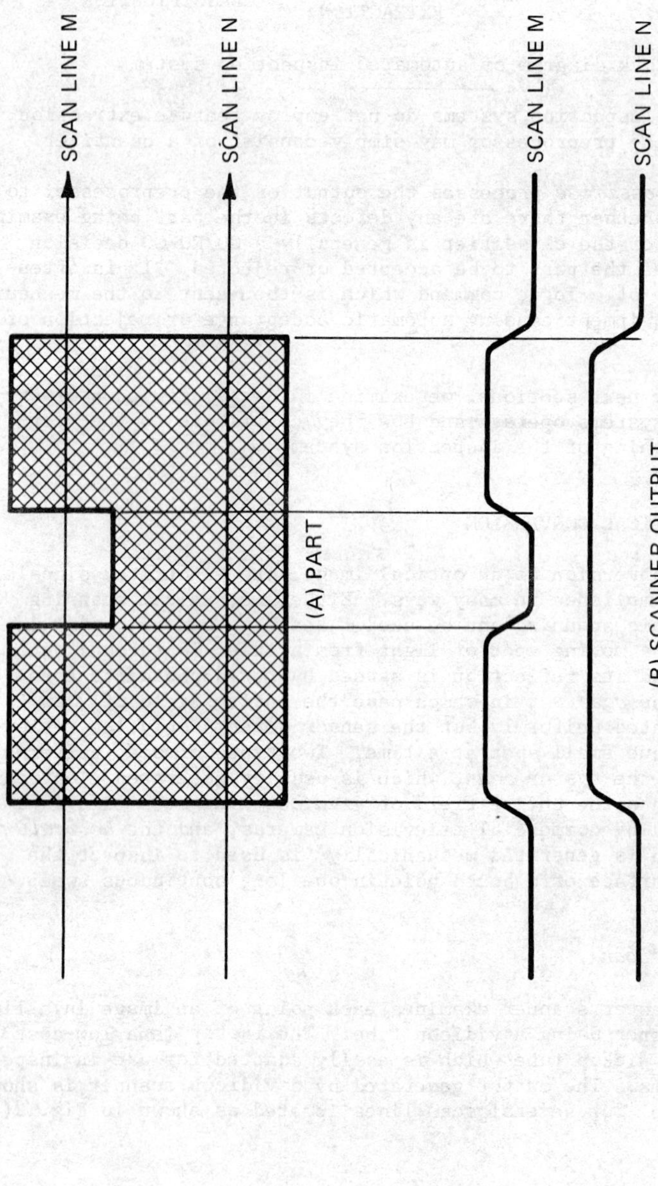

Fig. 2. Operation of vidicon raster scanner showing part being scanned (a), and output (b)

The example used in the figure is a small back-lighted object which produces a high contrast black and white image. The relevant features of the part are its outline and the location of any holes which may be present.

The Helical Scan

If the inspection system is to examine the inside surface of a bored hole, the helical scanner, shown in Fig. 3, is used.

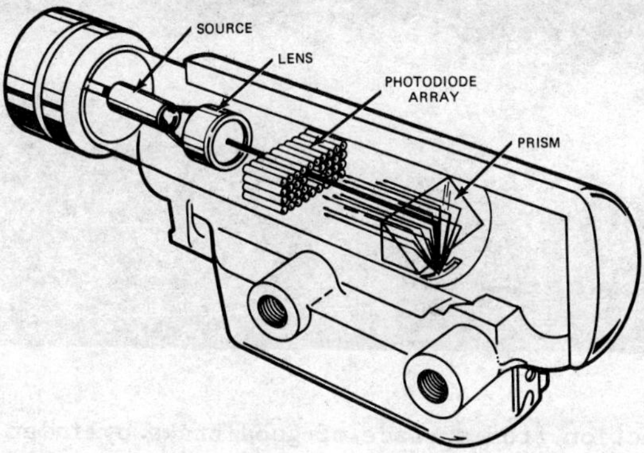

Fig. 3. Operation of helical scanner

A laser beam is focused onto the inside surface of the hole by a prism or mirror attached to the end of a probe. The probe is then rotated and slowly moved out of the hole. This results in a helical path being traced on the surface of the hole by the laser beam. The reflected light from the surface being examined is returned through the probe via the same prism or mirror and observed by an array of photosensitive devices. The relative outputs of these photodetectors are then examined to determine whether the part is defective. Figure 4 illustrates the instantaneous reflection obtained from a part of a surface which is not defective.

THE PREPROCESSOR

The preprocessor has the task of converting the scanner output signal into a form that is usable by the classifier. This task may consist of two distinct steps: *quantization* and *feature extraction*. The quantizer converts the analog signals produced by the scanner into digital signals representing light and dark areas, whereas the feature-extraction logic, if used, reduces the data to a set of features which the classifier uses to determine the quality of the part being examined.

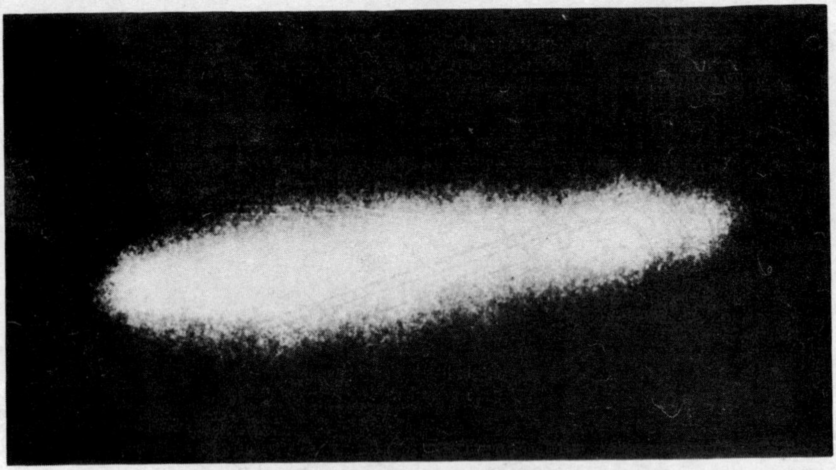

Fig. 4. Reflection from surface of good brake cylinder bore.

The Quantizer

In the simplest case, the quantizer merely consists of a circuit whose output is a logical ONE or ZERO depending upon

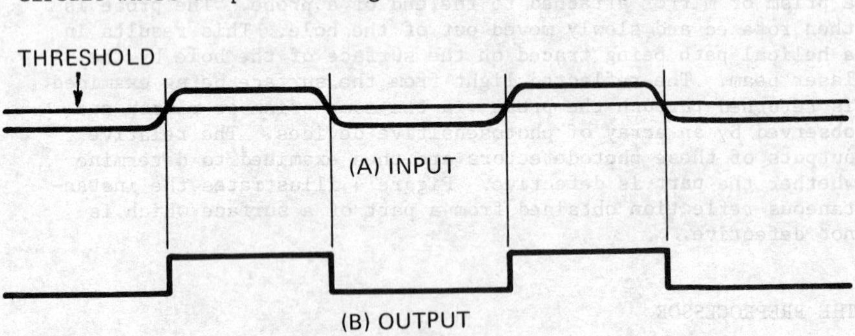

Fig. 5. Operation of simple quantizer

whether the input is below or above a preset threshold level. This is illustrated in Fig. 5. Since the scanner signals are rarely as well-defined and noise-free as in the example, more sophisticated quantizers are often used. For example the threshold can be varied to compensate for input signal changes which result from a changing background level. Or the quantizer can be designed to change state whenever the input changes by a certain preset amount, thereby causing the device to respond only to changes in scene intensity. The output of the quantizer can be fed directly to the classifier, or feature-extraction logic can be incorporated into the preprocessor as described next.

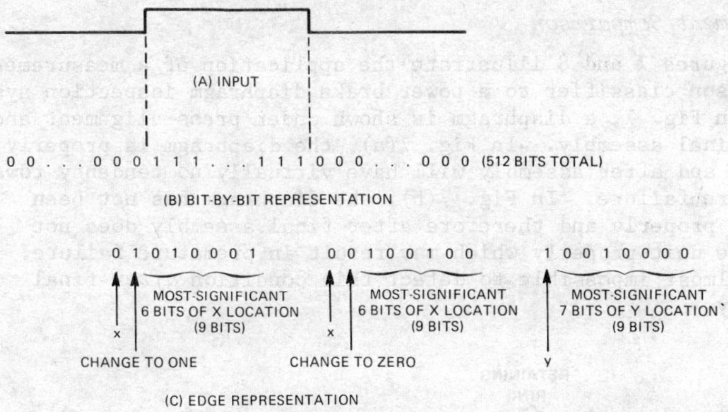

Fig. 6. Operation of edge detection feature extractor comparing bit-by-bit representation (b) and edge representation (c)

Feature Extraction

One common type of feature extraction technique used in inspection systems makes use of contrast or edge detection. In this case, rather than transmitting a ONE or ZERO for every picture element to the classifier, only the locations of the changes are sent. An example of this type of feature extraction is shown in Fig. 6 for a single scan line. In the example, only 24 bits are needed to represent a complete line using feature extraction instead of the 512 bits needed to represent the same information on a bit-by-bit basis. If a line is devoid of significant detail, no bits are used so that a great deal of data reduction is possible even with a simple edge detection feature extraction scheme.

CLASSIFICATION

Several classification schemes may be used depending on the complexity of the inspection task. These range from simple comparisons using linear measurements to spatial correlations of complete two-dimensional patterns. In each case, a decision must be reached as to whether the part meets a set of required specifications or is a reject, in which case it may automatically be sorted into a reject pile.

Measurement Comparison

Figures 7 and 8 illustrate the application of a measurement comparison classifier to a power brake diaphragm inspection system. In Fig. 7, a diaphragm is shown under press alignment and after final assembly. In Fig. 7(a), the diaphragm is properly aligned and after assembly will have virtually no tendency toward premature failure. In Fig. 7(b), the diaphragm has not been aligned properly and therefore after final assembly does not seal the unit properly which may result in premature failure. It is almost impossible to detect this condition *after* final assembly.

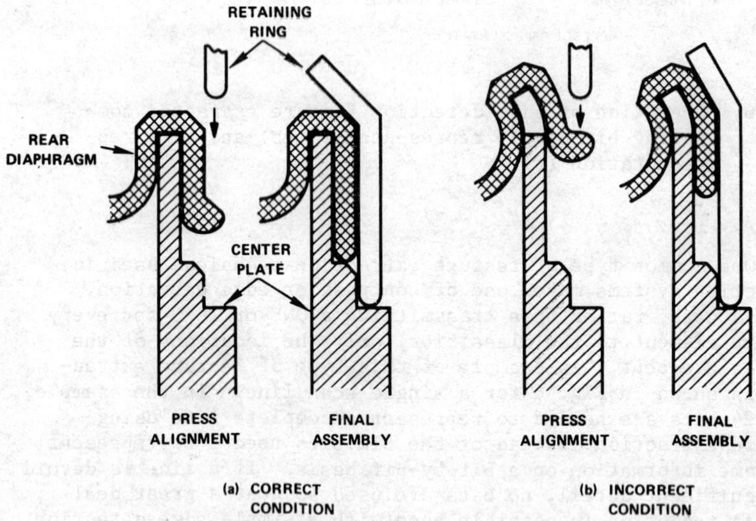

Fig. 7. Inspection conditions for power brake diaphragm alignment inspection system

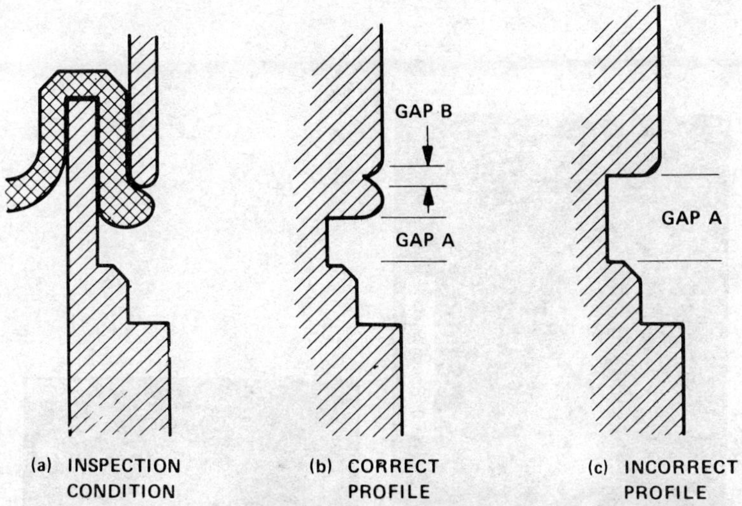

Fig. 8. Operation of measurement comparison classifier in power brake diaphragm alignment inspection system

Figure 8 illustrates how the automated inspection system operates. After press alignment by the operator, the system partially assembles the unit but stops with the retaining ring in the position shown in Fig. 8(a). The part is then back-lighted, its edge is focused onto a vidicon scanner, and the complete unit is rotated through 360 degrees. If gaps A and B (Fig. 8(b)) remain within preset tolerances, the assembly of the unit is completed. If however, the gaps deviate from the allowed limits (Fig. 8(c)), the machine is stopped and the operator informed that he should reassemble the unit. Since the system maintains a log of operator performance, a careless operator quickly improves his performance. Thus, we have an example of improved performance through man-machine interaction.

Flaw Detection

In the master-brake-cylinder inspection system and the turbine blade inspection system, the parts are examined for two-dimensional flaws such as cracks. In the former system, a helical laser scanner is used to scan the inside of the brake-cylinder bore. Figure 9 illustrates the instantaneous reflection from the surface of the bore for three conditions: (a) a good surface, (b) a rough surface, and (c) a cracked surface. For processing, the reflection is focused onto a set of

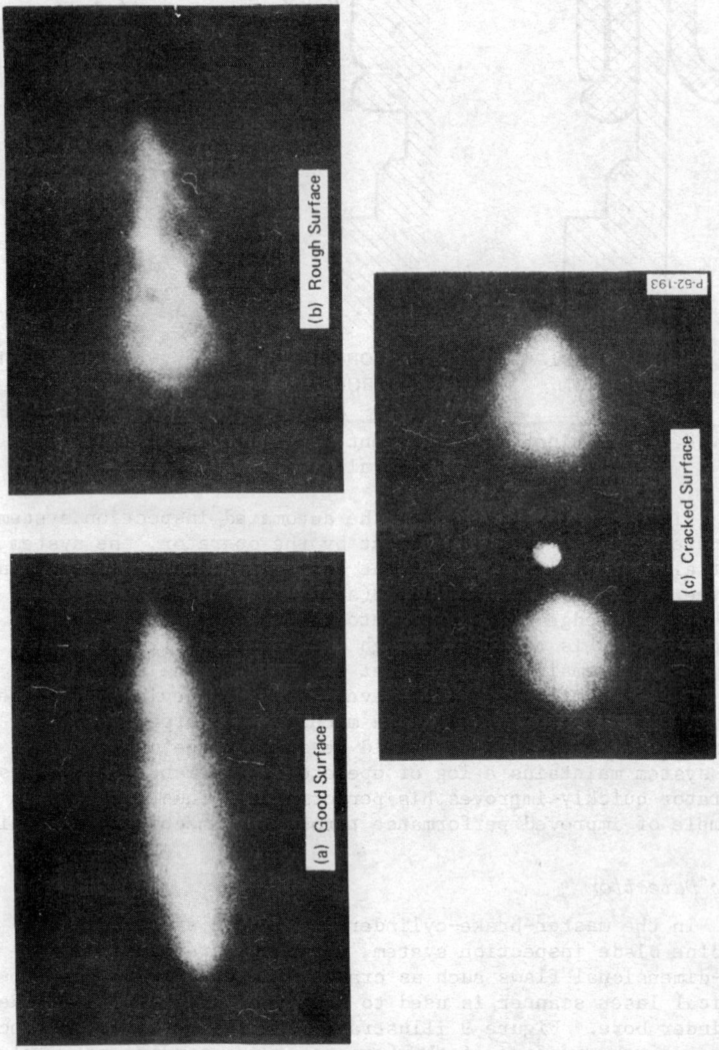

Fig. 9. Reflections from surface of brake cylinder bore during inspection illustrating flaw detection classification

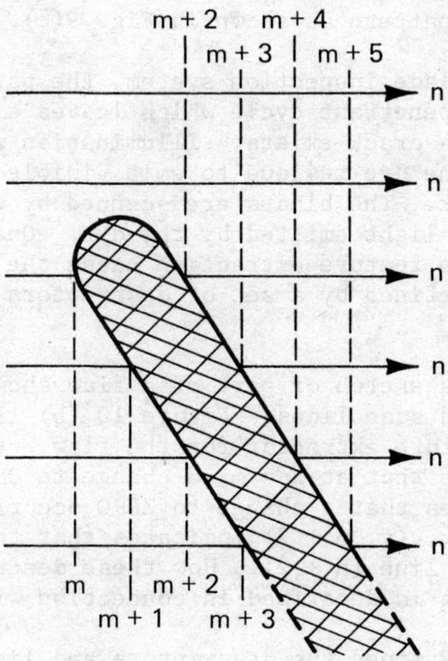

(a) Sketch of part of a flaw.

⋮ ⋮ ⋮

(x, 1, m) (x, o, m + 2) (y, n + 2)

(x, 1, m + 1) (x, o, m + 3) (y, n + 3)

(x, 1, m + 2) (x, o, m + 4) (y, n + 4)

(x, 1, m + 3) (x, o, m + 5) (y, n + 5)

⋮ ⋮ ⋮

(b) Descriptors defining flaw.

Fig. 10. Edge detection feature extraction and flaw detection classification as used in turbine blade inspection system.

photodetectors and quantized. These quantized signals are then correlated with stored patterns to classify any flaws that exist. Classification of a rough surface is a difficult task since, as shown, the output from a rough surface does not differ much from the output produced by a good surface. However, a cracked surface is readily identifiable since its reflection produces a distinctly different pattern as shown in Fig. 9(c).

In the turbine blade inspection system, the parts are processed through a dye penetrant cycle which leaves a fluorescent dye residue wherever a crack exists. Illumination with ultraviolet light causes the dye residue to emit visible light in the vicinity of each crack. The blades are scanned by vidicon cameras to detect the light emitted by the dye. Quantization and contrast detection feature extraction cause the location of each crack to be defined by a set of descriptors as illustrated in Fig. 10.

Figure 10(a) is a sketch of part of a flaw showing all pertinent coordinates and scan lines. Figure 10 (b) illustrates the output of the feature extractor for the flaw. (x, 1, m), for example, indicates that at x = m, a change to ONE occurred. (x, 0, m + 2) indicates that a change to ZERO occurred at x = m + 2, and finally, (y, n + 2) indicates that the preceding x data came from scan line (n + 2). How these descriptors are encoded for processing is described in connection with Fig. 6.

The classifier examines the descriptors and links together all descriptors which come from a particular flaw. Descriptors are therefore separated into groups which determine the size, shape, and location of each flaw. Noise can be eliminated since it tends to be random and does not fall into well-defined patterns as does flaw data.

Once the location, shape, and size of a flaw has been determined, it is compared to a set of stored patterns for classification. The part is then sorted into a reject category if it contains undesirable flaws as determined by the classifier.

CONCLUSION

In this paper, we have presented the principles of operation of automated inspection systems. We have included, as examples, three applications which illustrate the practicality of building an automated "quality control inspector" for assembly line use.

REFERENCES

1. G. NAGY, "State of the art in pattern recognition" *Proc. IEEE 56,5*, 836-862 (1968).

2. L.N. KANAL, ed., *Pattern Recognition* (Thompson Book Company, Washington, D.C., 1968).

3. S. WATANABE, ed., *Methodologies of Pattern Recognition* (Academic Press, New York, 1969).

4. A. ROSENFELD, *Picture Processing by Computer* (Academic Press, New York, 1969).

5. T.C. RUCH, "Vision" *Neurophysiology*, 2nd edition, T.C. RUCH et al., (eds.) (W.B. Saunders Company, Philadelphia) pp. 415-440 (1965).

6. N.J. NILSSON, "A mobile automaton: an application of artificial intelligence techniques" *Proceedings of the International Joint Conference on Artificial Intelligence*, D.E. WALKER and L.M. NORTON (eds.) (Washington D.C.) pp. 509-520 (1969).

7. A.W. HOLT, "Comparative religion in character recognition machines" *IEEE Computer Groups News, 2,6*, 3-11 (1968).

8. *Bendix Technical Journal*, Image Data Processing Issue *5,1* (1972).

9. R.M. CENTNER and E.D. HIETANEN, "Automated inspection using pattern recognition and numerical control" *Bendix Technical Journal 4,1*, 34-38 (1971).

PROPERTIES OF A MODEL OF SYSTEMS COMPOSED OF CONCURRENTLY OPERATING PROCESSES*

K.P. GOSTELOW

*Stichting Academisch Rekencentrum Amsterdam, Amsterdam Buitenveldert, Netherlands***

G. ESTRIN

Dept. of Computer Science, University of California, Los Angeles, Los Angeles, Calif., U.S.A.

SUMMARY

Many systems are constructed from a group of concurrently operating subsystems which interact and exchange information at various points in their operating cycles. In order to study and to model such systems, it is most useful to retain this notion of concurrent operation and cooperation among subsystems, and to prove theorems concerning such systems. This paper presents the *bigraph* model for representing such systems, and shows how it can be used to represent general system flow-of-control and resource allocation structures. Some theorems are then given concerning properties of systems, such as modularity, control storage requirements, and resource allocation and deadlock.

INTRODUCTION

Many systems are constructed from a group of concurrently operating subsystems which interact and exchange information at various points in their operating cycles. In order to study and to model such systems, it is most useful to retain this notion of concurrent operation and cooperation among subsystems and to prove theorems concerning such systems. The purpose of this paper is to present some recent results on the study of a model which exploits the notion of a system composed of concurrently operating subsystems.

---

*This research was supported in part by the U.S. Atomic Energy Commission, Contract No. AT(11-1) Gen 10, Project 14.

**Formerly with the UCLA Computer Science Department.

BIOGRAPH MODEL

Various models have been devised to display numerous aspects of concurrently operating systems. We refer the reader to the literature [1-7].

Our purpose is to study flow-of-control as a system cycles, and how subsystems interact and exchange information. Thus, the model we use is *uninterpreted*, in that no significance is ascribed to the actions or internal operations of a system.

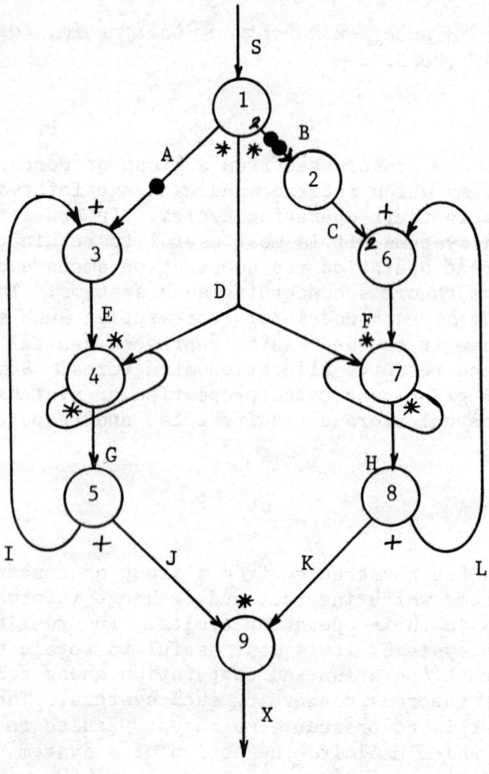

Fig. 1. Sub-bigraph model

As an example of our bigraph [6-8] model, we show a modeled system in Fig. 1. *B = (V,A,L,Q) is a sub-bigraph* where:

1) V is a finite set of vertices wherein activity relevant to the system takes place.

2) A is a set of many-to-many arcs (precedence conditions) with the restriction that, as indicated, S (X) is the distinguished entry (exit) arc into (away from) the unique entry (exit) vertex.

3) $L = (L^-, L^+)$: $V \to \{+,*\}$ are the input, output logic mappings.

4) $Q = (Q^-, Q^+)$: $V \times A \to \{1,2,\ldots\}$ are the input, output token value specifications (Q^-, Q^+ values are written only when they are different than 1. In Fig. 1 $Q^-(1,B) = 2$ and $Q^-(6,C) = 2$).

A bigraph marks its state by the placement of tokens on arcs and vertices. State transitions are defined by a "token machine" H [9] which accepts a bigraph and moves tokens according to the current state and the definitions of the symbols in a bigraph, i.e. V,A,L, and Q. We indicate a history of operation of a bigraph by a *computation sequence* [2] y, an ordered string of vertex symbols such that (for $v \in V$) "$\bar{v}$" indicates initiation of a vertex, and "v" its termination. Such a description is complete since all transitions of state are distinguishable by the rule *no two vertices may initiate or terminate at the same instant*. We now follow a processing of Fig. 1 by H: initially H places one token on S and randomly searches for vertices to process. Only vertex 1 may be initiated (no other vertex has inbranching arcs with tokens in greater number than the Q^- value; here, $Q^-(1,S) = 1$) and thus the computation sequence would be $y = \langle\bar{1}\rangle$ at this point in processing. No further processing is possible until vertex 1 terminates ($y = \langle\bar{1}1\rangle$) and places one token on each of arcs A and D, and two on arc B. Then either of vertices 2 or 3 (in fact, 2 could be initiated twice in succession since there are two tokens on arc B and $Q^-(2,B) = 1$) may be initiated. Let us say vertex 2 initiates first (recall that no two vertices may be initiated or terminated at exactly the same instant). The computation sequence then becomes $y = \langle\bar{1}1\bar{2}\bar{3}\rangle$ if 3 initiates before 2 terminates. If 3 now terminates ($y = \langle\bar{1}1\bar{2}\bar{3}3\rangle$) vertex 4 is eligible for initiation. Assume 4 initiates by removing one token from each of arcs D and E ($y = \langle\bar{1}1\bar{2}\bar{3}3\bar{4}\rangle$) and processing of 4 continues until such time that vertex 2 has initiated again (there was still a token on B) and terminated twice ($y = \langle\bar{1}1\bar{2}\bar{3}3\bar{4}\bar{2}22\rangle$). Until 4 terminates (and places a token on arc D), vertex 7 cannot initiate. At this point, given the previous actions and value of y,

$$y = \langle\bar{1}1\bar{2}\bar{3}3\bar{4}\bar{2}224\bar{6}\rangle.$$

Observing the structure of the bigraph, we see that vertices 4 and 7 in fact form two groups of vertices which are mutually exclusive in execution. Thus we can model the mutual exclusion condition by the use of multi-headed arcs. We shall not proceed further with this example to state that execution may continue until each of arcs J and K have one token present (vertices 5 and 8 are decision vertices: only one arc from such a vertex can receive tokens for each termination). At this point vertex 9 initiates, then terminates, and places a token on arc X. Computation can continue no further and the token machine halts processing. The reader should note that many different computation sequences are possible for this bigraph, but one example of a computation sequence which is *not* possible is $y = <\bar{1}1\bar{2}\bar{3}3\bar{4}\bar{7}..>$.

PROPER TERMINATION

The purpose of this section is to define a property of sub-bigraphs called *proper termination* [8] (PT). PT is best shown by example, as in Fig. 2, which is a simple modification of Fig. 1 (arc D has been extended to vertex 9). We say that a sub=bigraph is PT if:

1) only a finite number of tokens are required by H and

2) at any point in operation of the system, there is always a sequence of transitions by which the condition of "exactly one token on arc X" can be achieved as the terminal condition of operation.

We note that the sub-bigraph of Fig. 2 is PT since only a finite number of tokens are ever required. Given that the tokens are distributed in some fashion (starting originally with one token on arc S), we can always progress to vertices 5 and 8 and select, respectively, arcs J and K as the decision results. Then the tokens on arcs D,J, and K are removed by vertex 9 and the final transition places one token on arc X. No other tokens remain on the graph.

The motivation for this particular definition is quite broad. Briefly, we can see that a sub-bigraph behaving in this fashion is well-behaved because only a finite number of tokens (storage space) is required. Fig. 3 shows a sub-bigraph where finiteness of operation is not preserved. Also it is convenient to have simple initiation (one token on arc S) and termination (one token on arc X) conditions. Termination is "clean" in that reuse of the procedure implies that no tokens remain from any previous operation. Fig. 4 is an example of a sub-bigraph which is not PT because condition 2) of the definition of PT cannot be satisfied.

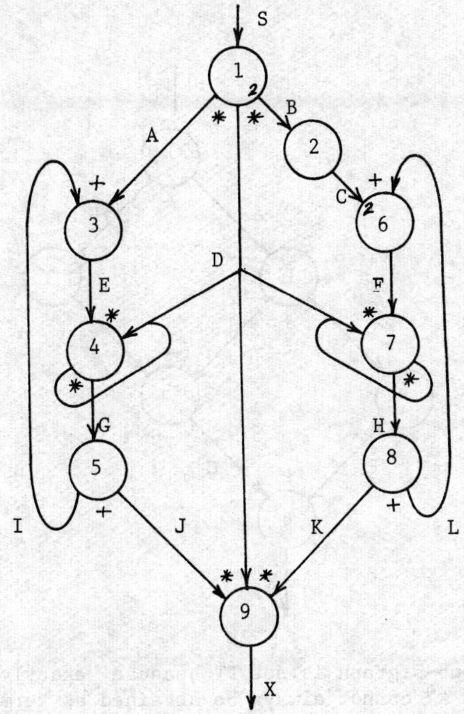

Fig. 2. A PT sub-bigraph

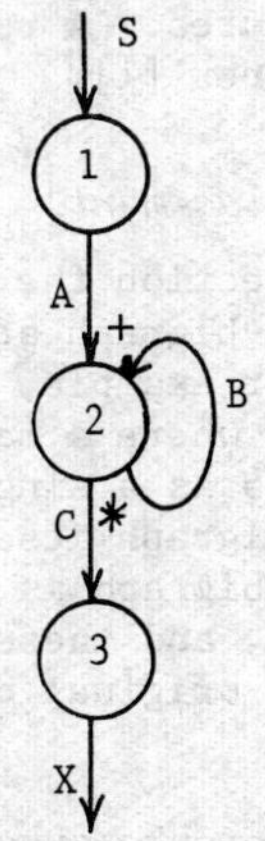

Fig. 3. An infinite number of tokens is required to operate this system

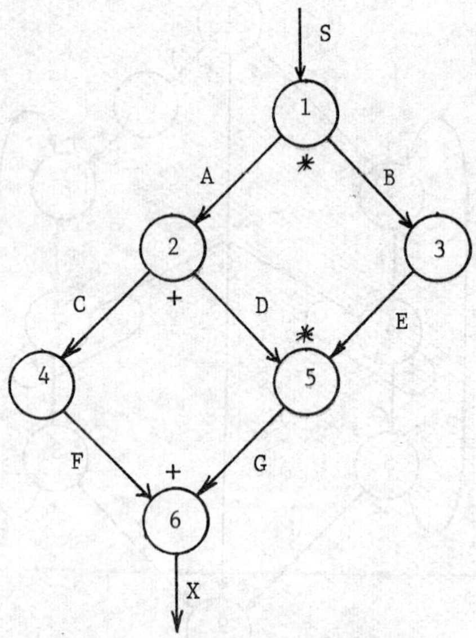

Fig. 4. This sub-bigraph is not PT because "exactly one token on arc X" cannot always be attained at termination

Systems which are PT are well-behaved in several ways, and have many convenient features. A rapid algorithm for deciding PT is given in another paper [1].

Modularity (Subsystem Replacement)

We discuss in this section the problem of replacing parts of a bigraph by other sub-bigraph structures and the resulting bigraph's properties. For example, programs are often constructed from procedures, where a main program calls a subprocedure K, which appears as a single vertex in the main program, but is actually a bigraph itself. We generalize to the following problem: if a bigraph is constructed such that various substructures are PT, and these are replaced by other PT substructures, and if the original bigraph was PT, will the resulting bigraph be PT?

We define here a *removable substructure* K of a bigraph C to be: that collection of vertices and arcs of C such that when delineated by an enclosing line, then 1) no arcs in K are cut by the enclosing line and 2) those arcs cut by the line

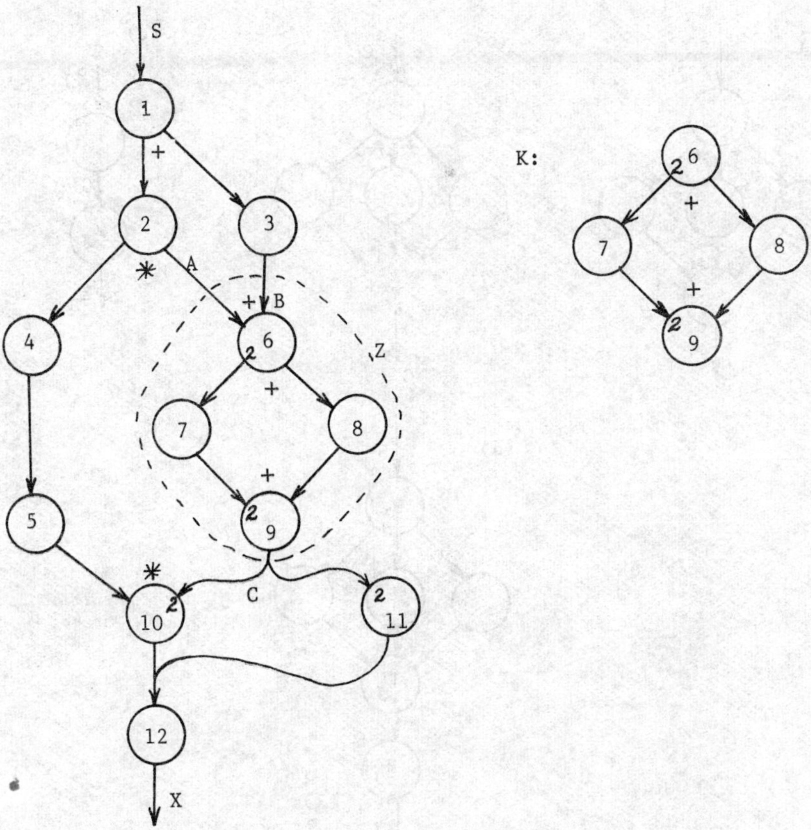

Fig. 5. A removable substructure delineated by enclosing line Z

(which are in bigraph C) either inbranch to the unique entry vertex in K; or outbranch from the unique exit vertex in K; and these arcs have Q values of 1 at the entry and exit vertices of K.

An example of a removable substructure is shown in Fig. 5. The enclosing line is marked as Z and cuts arcs A,B, and C (which are thus not part of K). These arcs have Q values of 1 at the entry (vertex 6) and exit (vertex 9) vertices of K. We also say that a *removable substructure* K of a bigraph C *is PT* if 1) we introduce arc S_k as the unique entry arc to the entry vertex of the removable substructure, and similarly

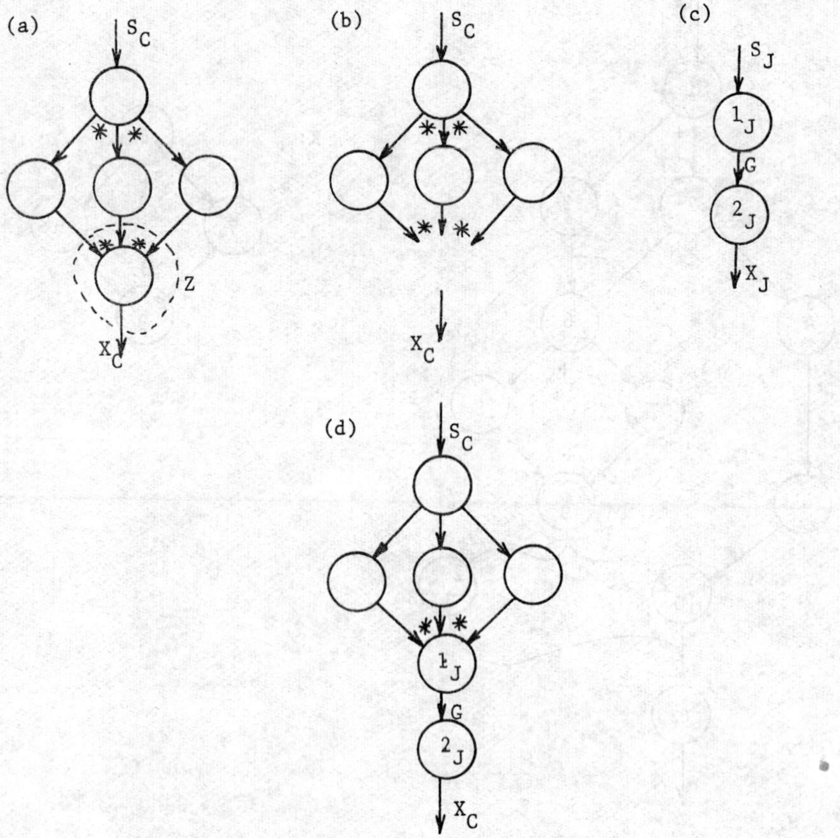

Fig. 6. Replacement of removable substructure K by J: (a) K is defined by Z. (b) K is removed. (c) Sub-bigraph J. (d) J replaces K.

introduce arc X_k to the exit vertex, then 2) the resulting sub-bigraph is PT; for example, the removable substructure K in Fig. 5 is certainly PT.

Replacement is effected by removing the substructure K from C such that those arcs (and associated logic and Q values) cut by the delineating line remain "hanging", and are subsequently attached to the entry and exit vertices of the replacing sub-bigraph J, as in Fig. 6.

Theorem: Let C be a bigraph, K a removable substructure of C, and J a sub-bigraph. Let F be the bigraph resulting from the replacement of K by J in C. If C,K, and J are each PT, then F is PT.

Observing Fig. 6, we see that it fulfills the conditions and conclusion of the theorem.

Control Storage Requirements

A system must be able to provide counters to record the (arbitrarily high) number of tokens present at any time on each arc and vertex. Thus, it would be convenient to place bounds on the sizes of these counters, since in most cases a counter with values 0 and 1 is sufficient to characterize the count status.

The class of bigraphs with which we concern ourselves is that of *simple bigraphs*: all Q values are 1 and each arc has at most one vertex at its head and one vertex at its tail (Fig. 7). Now let us take any path from S to X in the bigraph (for example, p = S,A,C,F,X in Fig. 7). At any point in the processing of that bigraph by H, we may count the number of distinct tokens occupying places (arcs and vertices) along that path.

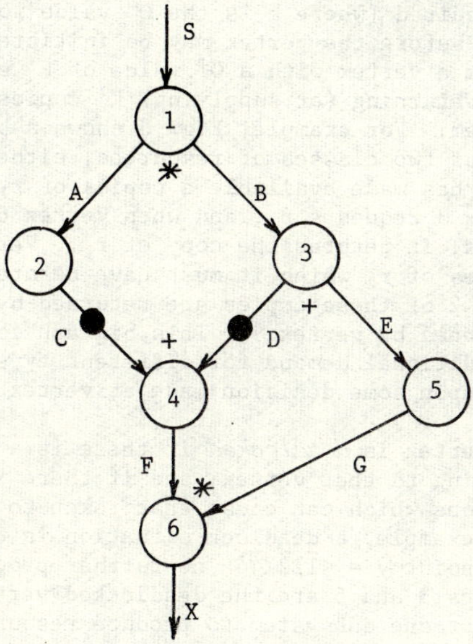

Fig. 7. A simple graph whose token count along a path may increase

We say that "n^y" is the number of distinct tokens along the selected path at that point in execution given by y, where y is the computation sequence up to that point. (Thus $y = \langle \bar{1}1\bar{2}\bar{3}32 \rangle$ defines the point shown in Fig. 7 and $n^y = 1$). Now we note the following property: if we extend the computation sequence $y = \langle \bar{1}1\bar{2}\bar{3}32 \rangle$ to $yy' = \langle \bar{1}1\bar{2}\bar{3}32\bar{4} \rangle$, then we compute $n^{yy'} = 2$ and realize that in general we can say no better than $n^{yy'} \geq n^y$.

The following theorem has been proven [8]:

Theorem: Let C be a simple bigraph which is PT. Then no path p = S,...,X will have more than one distinct token at any point in the execution of C by H. Corollary: If C is a simple and PT bigraph, then no arc or vertex of C can acquire more than one token at any time. Thus, we need only supply 1-bit counters for each arc and vertex.

Resource Allocation and Deadlock

The bigraph model can be used to model resources and allocation systems by assigning one arc as the pool of copies of one class of resource. The number of copies of that resource is represented by the number of tokens on that arc. Since tokens are indistinguishable every copy is indistinguishable. Such an arc inbranching to a vertex implies that k copies of that resource are required (where k is the Q^- value for that arc and vertex pair) before the vertex may be initiated. An arc outbranching from a vertex with a Q^+ value of k' signifies that this vertex is returning (or supplying) k' copies of that resource to the system. For example, Fig. 8 shows a bigraph with a need for one of two classes of resources, either r_1 or r_2, where the system has made available a copies of r_1, and b copies of r_2. Vertex 3 requests r_1, and when vertex 6 has completed its actions, it returns the copy of r_1. Vertex 4 is requesting 3 copies of r_2 which it must have before it can begin operation, and 2 of these copies are returned by vertex F. The last is returned by vertex 9. This bigraph is a representation of a conditional demand for different types of resources depending upon some decision made at vertex 2.

We say that a vertex is *deadlocked* if there is a token on some arc inbranching to that vertex, and if there is no sequence of transitions which can cause that token to move from that arc. For example, a deadlock situation is shown in Fig. 9 where at the point $y = \langle \bar{1}1\bar{2}2\bar{4}4 \rangle$ no further progress can be made. Vertices 3 and 5 are the deadlocked vertices. Also, it is common for one subsystem to produce resources, and another to absorb them. The production and consumption thus forms one whole system. However, a situation to be avoided

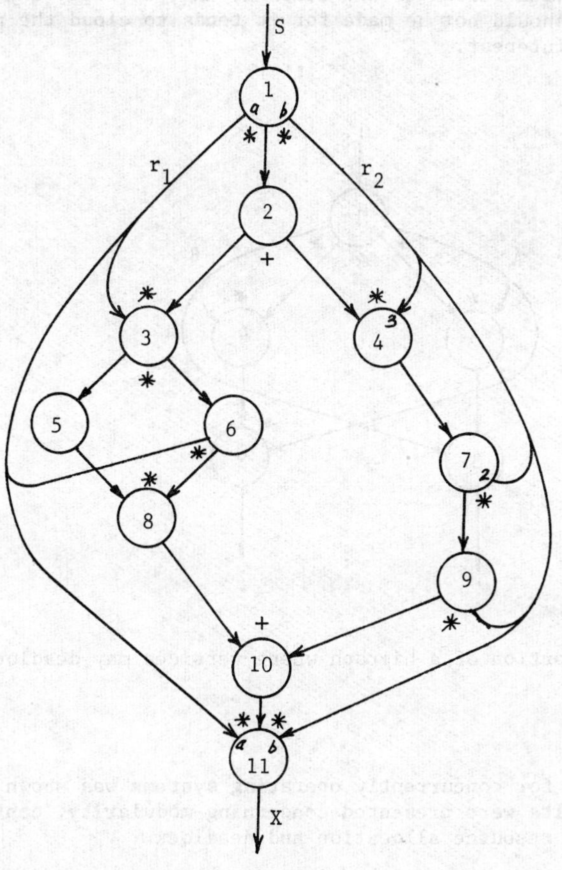

Fig. 8. A bigraph demonstrating conditional resource allocation demands

is the potential for the producer system to produce an unbounded collection of resources, thus overflowing any real system's capacity. This behavior has been described previously in terms of an infinity of tokens being required of the token machine. Holt [10] has called a system which avoids both of these situations *self-regulating*. We state the following theorem [8]:

Theorem: A PT bigraph is self-regulating.

Finally, the reader should notice that we have blurred the distinction between resources and control, and, in fact, any such distinction should not be made for it tends to cloud the real problems of interest.

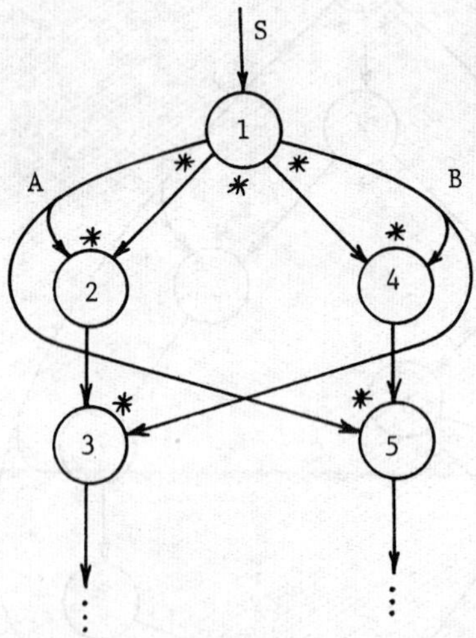

Fig. 9. A portion of a bigraph where vertices may deadlock

CONCLUSIONS

A model for concurrently operating systems was shown, and several results were presented concerning modularity, control storage, and resource allocation and deadlock.

REFERENCES

1. K. GOSTELOW, V. CERF, G. ESTRIN and S. VOLANSKY, "Proper termination of flow-of-control in programs involving concurrent processes" *Proceedings of the ACM National Conference* (1972).

2. R.M. KARP and R.E. MILLER, "Parallel program schemata" *J. Com. System Sciences 3, no. 4*, 147-195 (May 1969).

3. D.R. SLUTZ, *The Flow-Graph Schemata Model of Parallel Computation* (Ph.D Dissertation, MAC-TR-53, MIT, Sept. 1968).

4. J. RODRIGUEZ, *A Graph Model for Parallel Computation* (Sc.D. Dissertation, Dept. of Electrical Engineering, MIT, 1967).

5. T. BREDT, "A survey of models for parallel computing" *Stanford Electronics Laboratory, Digital Systems Laboratory TR-8 Stanford University* (August 1970).

6. V. CERF, *Memory Allocation, Multiprocessors, and a Graph Model of Computation* (Ph.D. Dissertation, Computer Science Dept., University of California, Los Angeles, 1972).

7. S. VOLANSKY, *Graph Model Analysis and Implementation of Computational Sequences* (Ph.D. Dissertation, University of California, Los Angeles, 1970) (UCLA-10P14-93).

8. K.P. GOSTELOW, *Flow of Control, Resource Allocation and the Proper Termination of Programs* (Ph.D. Dissertation, and Computer Science Technical Report No. UCLA-ENG-7179, University of California, Los Angeles, December 1971) (UCLA-10P14-106).

9. A. HOLT, *Final Report for the Information System Theory Project* prepared for Rome Air Development Center, Contract No. AF30 (602)-4211 (Applied Data Research, Inc. Princeton, N.J., U.S.A., 1968).

10. R. HOLT, "On deadlock in computer systems" *University of Toronto, Technical Report CSRG-6* (April 1971) (or, as a Ph.D. Dissertation from Cornell University).

CYBERNETIC IDEAS AT WORK: TEXTILE TECHNOLOGY

M. KONOPASEK

Department of Textile Technology, University of Manchester Institute of Science and Technology, Manchester, U.K.

SUMMARY

An intersection of two scientific disciplines, Textile Technology and Cybernetics, is examined with special attention to (a) the control problems of assembling the fibres, yarns etc. into higher level textile structures and (b) specific aspects of the production control, process monitoring and textile design; dyeing and garment manufacture are also considered. Basic concepts of visual topology are introduced as a convenient and computable means of the ordering of fibres and yarns into textile structures. It is shown that the role of informational and organisational aspects of textile technology justifies constitution of the cybernetic viewpoint in textile technology, or Textile Cybernetics, by analogy to the already established Textile Chemistry and Textile Physics.

INTRODUCTION

The title of my contribution might be considered in at least three different ways: The real impact of cybernetics on material and ideological innovation in textiles during the last decade or so; ideas originated independently of cybernetics though interpretable as cybernetic; the possible and desirable influence of cybernetics on further development of textile technology. Aiming to assist in the establishment of working relations between the two disciplines under consideration I shall point out what seem to be the most interesting in all the above directions.

A cybernetician hardly comes across textile technology other than as a consumer of textile goods and as an admirer of Babbage's analytical engine with the punched cards inspired by the pattern cards of a Jacquard weaving loom. Babbage's contemporary Ada Augusta, Countess of Lovelace, wrote [1]: "The distinctive characteristic of the Analytical Engine... is the introduction into it of the principle which Jacquard devised for regulating, by means of punch cards, the most complicated patterns in the fabrication of brocaded stuffs... We may say most aptly, that the Analytical Engine weaves algebraical patterns just as the Jacquard loom weaves flowers and leaves".

Let us try to invert the story as if concerning a hypothetical textile machine "Kybertex" with an integrated control and working processor depicted aptly as follows: "Kybertex orders fibres and yarns into fancy textile fabrics and garments just as the digital computer transforms and transmits signals to perform mathematical operations". Babagge's Analytical Engine became prehistory; on the other hand Jacquard's patterning devices are still in use and the above inverted story is worthy of science fiction. However, things are changing rapidly and textile technology is about to claim the old debt.

Textile problems do not belong to top priority topics of contemporary science and technology, unlike pollution, nutrition, nuclear energy, cosmic flights etc. Textile technology has, however, its own dynamics (for instance, the rate of speed increase in most of the production processes during the past 60 - 70 years is about as impressive as that of aircrafts), and at the same time it retains a comparatively stable position within the framework of the physiological, social, economic and cultural pattern of the life of humanity.

As defined 50 years ago in the Royal Charter of the Textile Institute, "Textile Technology is the knowledge of the art of producing threads and fabrics of every description in combination with the knowledge of these natural sciences which relate to the physical, chemical or other fundamental properties of any of the substances used or to any of the processes employed in such production".

The declared openness of textile technology towards any useful scientific and technological achievements from elsewhere brought into existence special scientific disciplines: Textile Chemistry (in the 2nd half of the last century) and Textile Physics (in the 1st half of this century). Cybernetics naturally, is going to follow this development, as we shall see by examination of the intersection of the scope of interest of cybernetics and textile technology.

TEXTILE TECHNOLOGY

The basic concepts we need to operate with are defined as follows [2]:

Textile - now applied to any manufacture from fibres, filaments or yarns, natural or man-made, obtained by interlacing;

Fibre - a unit of matter characterised by flexibility, fineness and high ratio of length to thickness;

Filament - fibre of indefinite length;

Yarn - an assembly of substantial length and relatively small cross-section of fibres and/or filaments with or without twist.

By analogy, we can define

Fabric - an assembly of substantial area and relatively small thickness of fibres and/or filaments and/or yarns.

It follows from the above definitions, that fibres and their assembling have about the same conceptual meaning in textile technology (scientific discipline) as the concepts of mass-energy and their transformation or information and its communication have in physics or cybernetics respectively.

Textile fibres belong to a very large and various class of thread-like material objects, natural and man-made, organic and inorganic, living and inanimate. Fibres, fibrils and the like appear to be a very common way of arranging matter for constitutive reasons (repetitive adding of the links to a chain), purposive reasons (getting a highly space-concentrated and space-oriented medium for carrying the physical or informational impulses), or both.

The subclass of textile fibres itself encompasses items with an upper limit of thickness of about 100 μ and lower limit of length-to-thickness ratio of about 1000 and a wide variety of structural features and properties [3,4]. Their common feature, which is perhaps the most general and also the most relevant to our topic is their capacity to be assembled in a mechanical way into structures satisfying certain mechanical requirements. Though assisted sometimes by adhesive, aerodynamic, electrostatic, chemical, plastification and other treatments, the ways of getting textile structures are essentially mechanical and so are the required properties of intermediate and end-use textile products.

The mechanical properties of textiles are subdivided by Backer [5] into bulk properties (i.e. deformation and disintegration resistance), surface properties (i.e. contact behaviour and abrasion resistance) and transfer properties (i.e. penetration resistance including heat transfer). As regards these requirements (not to mention aesthetic and other criteria), the standard achieved by textile technology is so high that any wide-range replacement of textile fibres and textile structures by articles made straightforwardly in different ways (e.g. chemical) is unlikely to occur at least in the near future. (The replacement of some textile goods by foams, special papers, plastic foils, etc., bears a character of border adjustment and is well compensated by the introduction of textiles in new, mainly engineering, fields - for instance textile fibre reinforced composite materials).

This point of view may seem to be conservative and, in fact, it is within the discretion of applied cybernetics to rule it out. What I mean is to employ microcontrolling (perhaps biological) devices to let the micro- as well as macro-structure grow directly in such a way as to meet or, possibly to overcome all the requirements satisfied nowadays only through complicated textile processing. A hypothetical pattern of the control mechanism required can be developed in a similar way to that described by Herman [6], but practical difficulties will prevent a materialisation of the idea before more has been done in the development of artificial biocybernetic systems.

In the meantime textile engineering, concerned with building textile structures, will continue its operation in the same way lying somewhere between mechanical engineering and chemical engineering - being closer to the first with respect to the nature of manipulating the elementary units (essentially mechanical) and being closer to the second with respect to the amount of tiny elementary units involved. There are usually millions of them (Fig. 1) and their uneveness, capriciousness and complicated causal relations make the task of an investigator more like that of a biologist.

The whole history of textile technology may be seen as consecutive improving of the tool and machine assistance to the process of ordering the fibres in the required manner. This development resulted in an enormous variety of processes and machinery and in a huge amount of descriptive knowledge*

*The Thesaurus of Textile Terms [8] set up by Backer and Valko for a computer-based information retrieval system contains 8000 key-words and 72000 relationships!

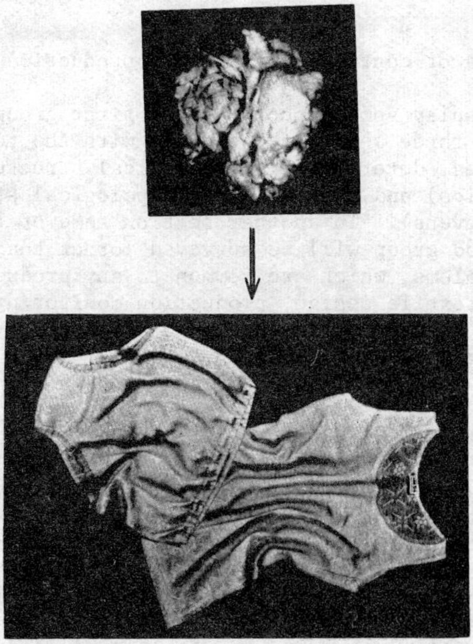

Fig. 1. Fighting entropy - textile way (about 15 million cotton fibres assembled into 2.5 km of yarn ordered into 400 thousand stitches covering the area of about 0.4 m^2; the fabric pattern repeat = 2048 bit; 6 pieces of fabric, except lace trimming, assembled into children's underwear).

---

impeding generalisations and preventing sometimes more efficient communication with the outside world and even within the textile business.

Summing up, we can consider the nature and purpose of textile processing as ordering the fibres, yarns or fabrics into the fibrous assemblies, i.e. yarns, multifold yarns, fabrics and end-use products possessing the required physical, aesthetic, economical and other properties.

Two main groups of textile technological problems may be defined as relevant for the application of the cybernetic viewpoint:

a) Problems of control of the immediate processes of ordering the lower level structural elements into their assemblies;

b) Problems of control of the whole production process.

We shall display some aspects of the first group of problems in the next three sections concerned with the topology of textile structures, deterministic topological structures (woven and knitted fabrics) and probabilistic topological structures (yarns and non-wovens). In another section some of the problems of the second group will be surveyed (other than managerial control problems, which are common to any production activity), namely textile design, production monitoring and computer assistance in the routine and creative activity of a textile technologist.

TOPOLOGY OF TEXTILE STRUCTURES

The ordering of lower elements, e.g. fibres or yarns, into higher level textile assemblies is, in fact, equivalent to imposing certain positional relations on them and may be interpreted in terms of the Topology of line-structures. Textile structures are only briefly mentioned by Lietzman [9] as topological phenomena and to our knowledge no attempt has been made in textile science to apply topological concepts. To quantify the order in textile structures and the process of ordering in a unique and computer-representable way, we find topological interpretation obvious and indispensable.

The so-called theory of knots as presented e.g. by Reidemeister [10], approaches quite closely to our textile problems, though it does not reflect the real ones. The knot is defined as a closed curve twisted and interlaced in space. Planar projection of the knot forms a graph (or directed graph when the direction of the movement along the knot is given). The number of crossing points or vertices V, the number of edges E, and the number of faces F (including that encircling the graph) are interrelated by Euler's formula for polyhedra

$$V - E + F = 2 \qquad (1)$$

All the knots obtained by deformation, overlaying or twisting of the original one are called isotopic or belonging to the same class. The order of a knot is defined as the minimum number of crossings within a given class. At present only knots up to 9th order have been fully investigated and no general method for the determination of the order of an arbitrary knot is yet known.

The vertices-edges (VE), vertices-faces (VF) and faces-edges (FE) incidence matrices may be defined on the graph as illustrated in Fig. 2. The signs in the VE and FE matrices provide information about cross functions (see below) and edge orientation. We have found, that the following relation takes place

$$\text{abs (VE)} = (\text{VF} \times \text{abs (FE)}) \text{ modulo } 2 \qquad (2)$$

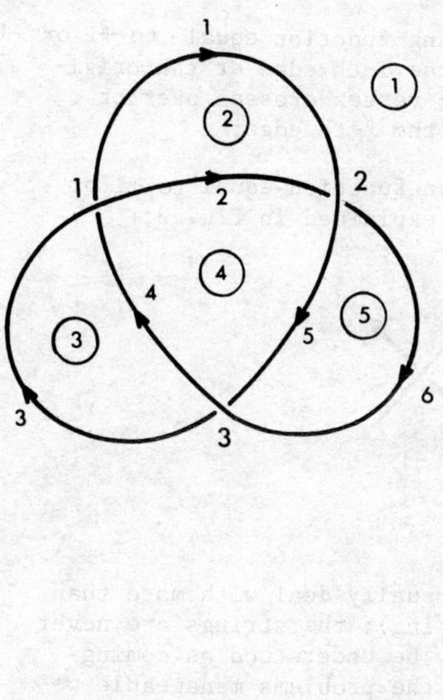

$$VE = \begin{bmatrix} 1 & 1 & 1 & -1 & 0 & 0 \\ 1 & -1 & 0 & 0 & 1 & -1 \\ 0 & 0 & -1 & 1 & -1 & 1 \end{bmatrix}$$

$$VF = \begin{bmatrix} 1 & 1 & 1 & 1 & 0 \\ 1 & 1 & 0 & 1 & 1 \\ 1 & 0 & 1 & 1 & 1 \end{bmatrix}$$

$$FE = \begin{bmatrix} -1 & 0 & -1 & 0 & 0 & -1 \\ 1 & -1 & 0 & 0 & 0 & 0 \\ 0 & 0 & 1 & -1 & 0 & 0 \\ 0 & 1 & 0 & 1 & 1 & 0 \\ 0 & 0 & 0 & 0 & -1 & 1 \end{bmatrix}$$

$$K = \begin{bmatrix} 1 & 4 & 5 & 2 & 6 & -1 & 1 \\ 2 & 3 & 6 & 1 & 5 & 1 & 1 \\ 3 & 5 & 2 & 4 & 1 & -1 & 1 \\ 4 & 6 & 1 & 3 & 2 & 1 & 1 \\ 5 & 1 & 3 & 6 & 4 & 1 & 1 \\ 6 & 2 & 4 & 5 & 3 & -1 & 1 \end{bmatrix}$$

Fig. 2. Trefoil knot and its incidence matrices and K matrix

A different way of computer-representation of knots has been found more convenient for an investigation of knots and simulation of topological operations, namely, matrix $K_{n,7}$ with one row assigned to each edge where the seven elements are defined as follows:

$k_{i,1} = i$ - pointer to itself;

$k_{j,2} = k_{i,1}$ - pointer to the previous edge;

$k_{i,3} = k_{j,1}$ - pointer to the next edge;

$k_{i,4} = k_{\ell,1}$ - pointer to the crossing edge originating at the same vertex as the i-th edge;

$k_{i,5} = k_{m,1}$ - pointer to the crossing edge originating at the vertex where i-th edge terminates;

$k_{i,6} =-k_{\ell,6}$ - crossing function equal to +1 or -1 when the i-th edge at the originating vertex crosses over or under the ℓ-th edge;

$k_{i,7} = k_{\ell,7}$ - torsion function equal to +1 or -1 as explained in Fig. 3;

Fig. 3. Torsion function

In real textile structures we usually deal with more than one fibre or yarn (or generally, string); the strings are never closed although one or both ends may be understood as coming from and going to infinity. To get the problems manageable we introduce a frame to separate a finite part of the structure. The frame is 0-knot in the topological sense or, simply, a closed line without crossing-points but with terminal points for cut-off edges called frame vertices. The relation (1) remains valid providing the graph is connected. The matrix K may also be used for investigation and manipulation of the framed structures. The elementary framed structure may be combined by removing segments of the frame and joining the free string ends. The joining of elementary or lower level topological units exhibiting orthogonal symmetry of frame vertices is of special practical importance (see an example in Fig. 4). In

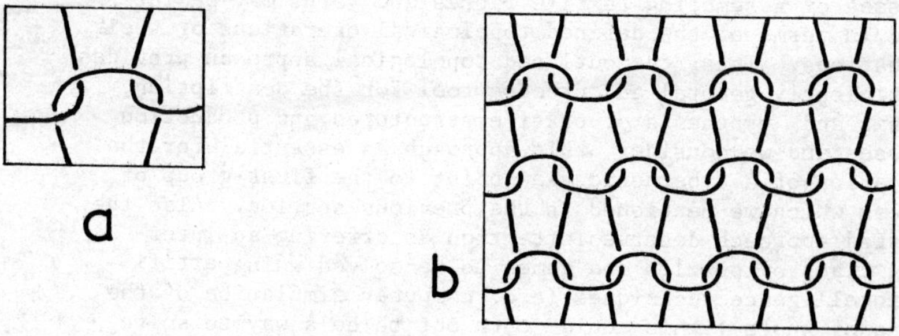

Fig. 4. Plain weft knitted fabric: elementary unit and 3 × 4 matrix

the case of repeating identical elementary structures (called repeats) there are the following relations between the number of vertices, edges and faces of one repeat and m × n matrix of repeats:

$$V_{mat} = m\,n\,V_{rep} + 2T; \quad E_{mat} = m\,n\,E_{rep} + 3T$$

$$F_{mat} = mn\,F_{rep} + T + 2\,(1 - mn)$$

where $T = an(1 - m) + bm\,(1 - n)$

a and b - number of frame vertices on the horizontal and vertical boundary respectively.

Three kinds of topological operations on a finite number of strings inside the frame may be distinguished: close-end operations, twisting or frame-vertices interchanges and open-end operations (Fig. 5). All the known and all the possible

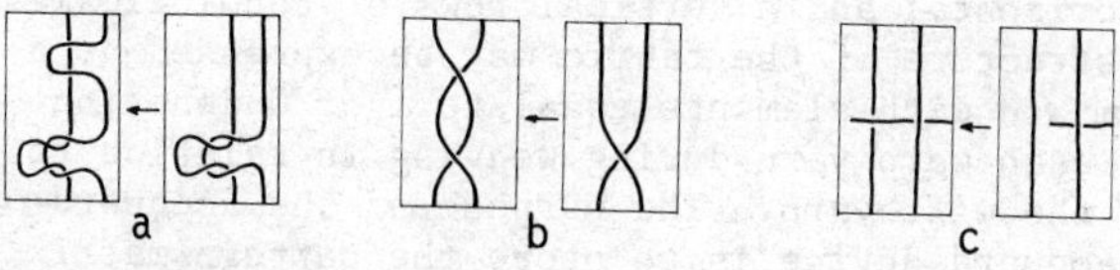

Fig. 5. Elementary topological operations in textile technology: (a) close-end operation; (b) twisting; (c) open-end operation.

processes of assembling textile fibres and yarns may be interpreted in terms of the defined topological operations or their combinations. Thus, the outlined topological approach provides a sufficiently general and precise tool for the description, analysis and synthesis of textile structures and production processes and we consider this approach as essential for the application of a cybernetic view-point to the first group of problems which we mentioned in the previous section. Also the suggested approach deserves attention as offering an interesting class of puzzles and games to be solved using artificial intelligence techniques (e.g. computer simulation of the undoing of knots); this could turn out to be a way to solve some yet unsolved problems of the theory of knots and generally of the topology of line-structures.

ORDERING THE YARNS INTO FABRICS

We shall consider here only the two most important subclasses of textile fabrics with deterministic topological structures - woven fabrics and knitted fabrics. Woven fabrics are built up in a series of open-end operations which are technically realised by pulling or throwing the weft yarn through a passage between the layers of warp yarns. By changing the location of each warp yarn from one layer to the other the required combination of the topological elements of two kinds (Fig. 6) is formed. Suppose the repeating part of the fabric

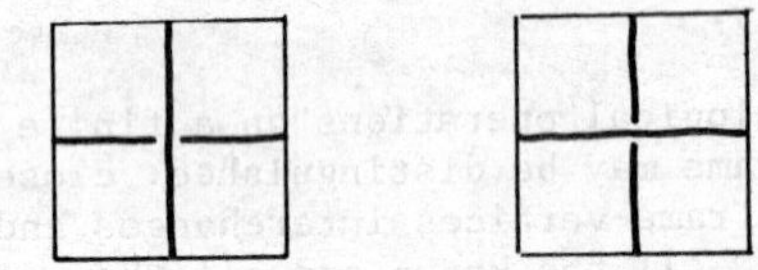

Fig. 6. Basic topological elements of a woven fabric

consists of m horizontal and n vertical rows of topological elements. The structure of the fabric may be expressed as a pattern matrix m × n with elements equal to 1 or 0 denoting the location of each warp yarn during weaving in relation to each portion of the weft yarn. The purpose of the Jacquard cards and the Jacquard device is to store the pattern matrix and to edit (in a mechanical way) the information in terms of the location of each warp yarn in each cycle of insertion of the weft yarn.

Several attempts have been made to replace Jacquard cards by other media and to use electrical signals at certain parts of the information pathway. The most advanced system was that demonstrated in the United States in 1968, comprising an IBM 360 computer and an IBM 2250 display terminal, which enabled weaving without delay of any design which had been created on the screen using the light pen. Commercial implementation of less sophisticated systems for special purposes (woven carpets, labels) is on the way and further development is to be expected.

As compared with weaving, an electronic pattern control for weft knitting machines has been in commercial use for well over 5 years and is spreading rapidly. The overall boom in knitting production during the last decades is partly responsible for that; from the topological point of view, knitting processes belong to the class of close-end operations offering bigger variety and higher efficiency in technical realisation than the others, providing there exist fine mechanisms and working parts to manipulate the yarn. On the other hand, the speed and arrangements of the weft knitting process exclude direct application of the Jacquard device in its original form and makes it difficult to use any solely mechanical pattern device in the case of large pattern areas.

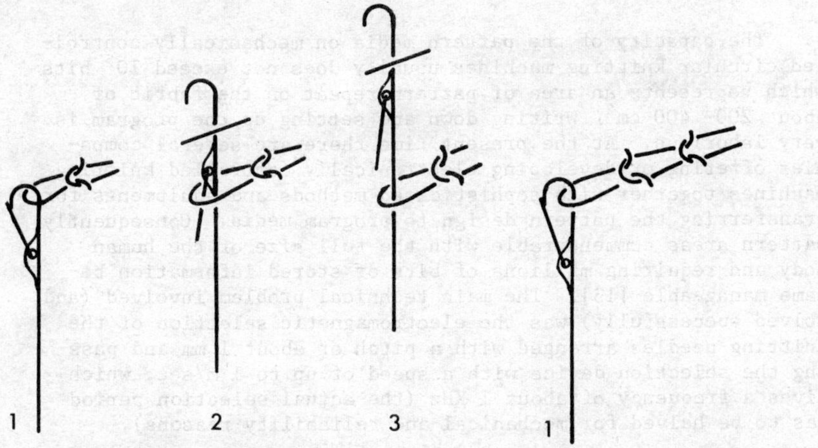

Fig. 7. Knitting cycle

The knitting cycle as performed by lifting and lowering the latch needle is shown in Fig. 7. The full cycle is needed to get every elementary topological unit or stitch as shown in Fig. 4. There are two possible pattern modifications: tuck stitch and held stitch (Fig. 8) realised by missing the third

Fig. 8. Modified weft knitted stitches: a - tuck stitch; b - held stitch.

and both the second and third stage of the knitting cycle respectively. The knitting needles are moved up and down by means of passing cams and there are various pattern devices for programming and performing any one of the three mentioned alternative actions. The needle positions as well as the other functions of the knitting machine may be expressed in terms of switching theory and Boolean algebra as shown by Offermann and Pilz [11], alternatively using ternary logic as suggested by Oberst [12].

The capacity of the pattern media on mechanically controlled circular knitting machines usually does not exceed 10^5 bits which represents an area of pattern repeat on the fabric of about 200- 400 cm^2. Writing down and setting up the program is very laborious. At the present time there are several companies offering or developing electronically controlled knitting machines together with sophisticated methods and equipments for transferring the pattern design to program media. Consequently pattern areas commensurable with the full size of the human body and requiring millions of bits of stored information became manageable [13]. The main technical problem involved (and solved successfully) was the electromagnetic selection of the knitting needles arranged with a pitch of about 1 mm and passing the selection device with a speed of up to 1 m/sec, which gives a frequency of about 1 KHz (the actual selection period has to be halved for mechanical and reliability reasons).

In general, highly sophisticated, fairly reliable and moderately expensive mechanical control devices on the modern knitting machines make the application of up-to-date digital techniques both urgent and difficult. There are some other positive examples besides the previously mentioned circular machines. The most urgent of the yet unsolved problems is electronic pattern control of the warp knitting machine (an

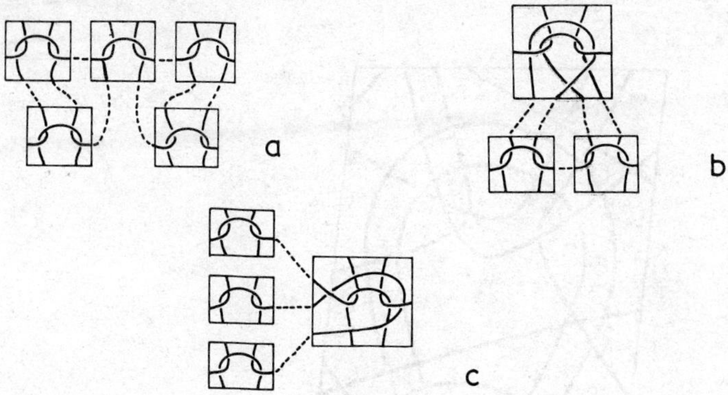

Fig. 9. Branching the weft knitted stitches; a - 2 to 3; b - 2 to 1; c - 3 to 1.

example of the topology of a simple warp knitted fabric is in Fig. 9). The problem is to select the position of up to 40 guidebars (rods about 2 m long, with a mass of about 2 kg) each of which can be moved into 20 different positions within the interval of about 50 mm with a frequency of 10 - 20 Hz. Pattern chains consisting of hundreds or thousands of expensive links, hard to manage and reset, still do the work.

The most promising direction of application for modern digital control techniques is undoubtedly fully fashioned knitting. The idea is to let the knitted fabric grow stitch by stitch in such a way as to cover more or less evenly a planar area with any contour required (without cutting it out of a sheet and getting cutting wastage) or, moreover, a surface of the given three-dimensional body (for instance human!) saving the sewing operations as well [14]. Fig. 10 shows some examples of the possible topology of the branching stitches in plain weft knitted fabric, which combined with ordinary elementary units (Fig. 4a) give a fully fashioned fabric of any required shape. This technique has been used to a limited extent in both hand and machine knitting for ages but only the recent progress in digital control technique encourages us to think about automatic knitting of the whole garment including sleeves, collar, pockets, buttonholes, etc., - all in textured and coloured pattern. A very advanced system of this kind was suggested several years ago by MacQueen [15] but it failed in commercial application. Less sophisticated systems are being produced and many others are in the stage of development. This way is perhaps the closest to the hypothetical machine "Kybertex" mentioned in the Introduction, and computer simulation of the topology of such fabrics seems to be a realistic task,

Fig. 10. Elementary unit of warp knitted fabric ('sharkskin').

though the realisation of the system in metals, plastics and fibres will probably mean complete departure from many of principles of contemporary knitting machinery.

ASSEMBLING THE FIBRES INTO YARNS AND NONWOVENS

The last section dealt with textile structures with topological relations of lower level elements which were fully determined by the actions of the working parts of the production machines*. Such structures are usually topologically and/or physically stable due to internal reactions and/or friction forces. They are manufactured by deterministic topological

*The determinism is limited to the topology while physical properties of real woven and knitted fabrics suffer from irregularities - partly inherited directly from irregular yarns and partly arising from random deviations during the physical realisation of a formation process. The latter are due to disturbances in the dynamic system, yarn-machine-fabric, which are caused by irregularities in yarn properties (the major source) as well as in machine performance. These aspects as related to the weaving process were investigated by Nosek [16].

processors (e.g. weaving looms, knitting machines etc.). These are, in fact, sequential or nonsequential automata with a more or less complicated internal logical and mechanical structure which links program information, yarn properties, actions of working parts and product properties, and with multi-level feedback control - partly built-in and partly realised by the operating staff.

A different approach has to be used to order big numbers of randomly located single fibres into spun yarns or nonwoven fabrics. The single fibres never come under individual deterministic control during the processes involved and consequently the level of their order can be defined in terms of distribution of density and orientation of fibres rather than in terms of determined topology. Therefore, the topological tools introduced in one of the previous sections have only limited use in these cases and their generalisation for probabilistic and three-dimensional lattice-like structures should be considered in future.

The coherence of the spun yarns or nonwoven fabrics is usually based on jamming due to inter-fibre friction imposed by twisting the yarns and by stitching or by other topological processing of the nonwovens or alternatively is achieved by applying adhesives. The final fixing or binding procedure is however preceded by the multistep process of getting a uniform fibre assembly with required fibre orientation and linear density for yarns or planar density for nonwovens. Let us consider the yarns first.

In a typical case at the beginning of the process we have a lap (i.e. a layer of loose fibres) made of cotton fibres (linear density .16 mg/m, mean length 25 mm) originally pressed in bales. The linear density of the lap is about 4kg/m and at the end of the spinning process a yarn is expected with a linear density of .02 g/m, which means an overall drafting ratio of 2.10^5. The process lies in the multistage repetitive combing (common meaning) of the fibres and slendering of the intermediate products, accompanied by separation, straightening and parallelisation of fibres and removing foreign matter as well as very short fibres.

The main concern of the textile technologist is to get the yarn linear density reasonably close to the required value and the irregularity of linear density and other properties below a reasonable level. Machinery defects of up to 10 different kinds at each 5-10 operations may disturb the process and cause excessive deviations in addition to those which arise from drift and fibre irregularities. Until recently the only means of keeping the process within tolerances were simple regulators of the lap linear density and off-line quality control with consequent adjustment of the drafting ratio by changing the gears on the machines. During the last decade an increasing number of automatic regulators of the speed of input or output rollers at the drafting machines have been successfully installed. There was also considerable activity in the theoretical field leading eventually to attempts to formulate the characteristics of carding machines [17] and drafting machines [18] in terms of automatic control theory.

The properties of the yarn along its axis may be interpreted as a realisation of a stationary random process. Progress has been made in the development of equipment for measuring the process characteristics and their interpretation. Particularly spectral analysis of experimental yarn-length/ yarn-linear-density curves offers a good clue for identification of the sources of excessive irregularities at earlier or later stages of the spinning process [19].

The increasing speed of machines, progressive shortening of the spinning process and overall automation of a spinning mill require more efficient control techniques. Another innovation excludes an insertion of the twist to the yarn by using a topological twisting operation (see Fig. 3b) which necessarily involves the rotation of the whole stock of yarn on the bobbin and also some other limitations. In so called open-end spinning the single fibres are ordered and twisted to the end of the created yarn in a manner covered by our definition of an open-end topological operation (an analysis of a linear dynamic system as representing the random process of fibre manipulation was given by Ripka [20]). In another new technology, self-twisted yarns, the twisting is replaced by close-end topological operation.

The original reason for the complicated process of spun yarn manufacture was the limited length and random of orientation of the raw natural fibres (except silk). On the contrary, normal arrangement of man-made fibres is parallel to the product axis. Textile technology has learnt to make maximum use of this fact during the past 2 decades. Several methods of texturing the multifilament yarns was developed to simulate the often required hairy character of spun yarns; and also there are methods of cutting man-made fibres when necessary without destroying their order.

The special class of non-woven fabrics also came into existence about 20 years ago as an innovation, aiming to rule out many of the fibre and yarn ordering processes. The nature and the problems of the first stage of manufacturing of nonwovens i.e. the formation of a fibre web, are similar to those of manufacturing yarns. Then the technology differs according to the nature of the cohesion agent applied; in one case it is stitching or some other deterministic topological operation, which belongs to the class investigated in the previous section; in the other case the order (or disorder) of the fibres in the web is fixed by creating adhesive bonds. The production speed is much higher than that of woven or knitted fabrics, sometimes by orders of magnitude, and this also involves new problems of process design and control. This and other aspects brought about the most interesting application of modern methods of design of experiments in textiles as given by Tikhomirov [21].

The last practical and theoretical achievements concerning yarn and non-woven manufacture as described above and also the understanding of their structure as exposed by Hearle [40] are impressive indeed. One has a feeling that a combination of process and structure viewpoints on one hand and a combination of the textile technologists' and control engineers' approach on the other hand should provide a higher level of theoretical coverage of control processes of assembling the fibres (including proper treatment of nonlinearities, discrete simulation of behaviour of single fibres etc.) and inspire the development of new processes.

TEXTILE DESIGN AND PRODUCTION CONTROL

Most of what has been said or written about the meaning of management cybernetics, for instance by Crawford [22], applies generally to any industry, including the textile industry and hence it is not necessary to recall it*. Here and there in flowcharts of management systems appear little boxes inscribed "Production Control", "R & D" "Quality Control", etc., implicating activities, which:

a) are not and cannot be disclosed in general texts in detail;
b) represent a good deal of complicated informational processing by themselves,

---

*Some conclusions about the level of appreciation of the topic in the textile industry may be drawn from Ref.[23] surveying advanced computer applications in the textile field, mainly in managerial control.

c) are being performed mainly by technologists in a manner depending to a large extent on specific features of the production under consideration.

Our survey would be incomplete without at least mentioning the specific role of textile technologists in acting as receivers, transformers, amplifiers and transmitters of the information at one point or another in such flowcharts. The most crucial activity of this kind is the design in a broad sense, viz. creating information about what is to be produced and how - in line with market requirements, within the limitations of manufacturing capability and at an acceptable cost. Let us have a set S of possible textile structures including raw materials and desired end-products and also a set of elementary production processes P, both sets with elements possessing a large range of technical, economic and other properties. The elementary technological process may be expressed as $p_{i,j,k}$ operation over s_i and s_j and the design means a choice of sequence of $n \geq 2$ elements of S (from s_1 to s_n) and n-1 elements of P satisfying given constraints and, possibly, optimising the production process with respect to a certain criterion.

Various aspects of computer assistance in the informational processing at the design stage of textile manufacture are considered in [24]. An easily realisable and prevailing trial-error method in textile design is its strongest and weakest point at the same time. Strongest because it prevents disastrous decisions and weakest because it often produces decisions far from optimum and with undesirable delay. The situation, however, steadily improves along with predictability of process-running and structure-properties as a result of accumulation of empirical knowledge and exact theories. A partial answer is the development of a computer-based system for calculation of geometry and mechanical properties of textile structures [25], coping with large non-linear visco-elasto-frictional deformations of the whole hierarchy of fibres, yarns, fabrics and end-use products.

Generally, design is perhaps the most skillful, knowledge demanding and time consuming activity of a textile technologist and it fully deserves to be analysed, controlled and computer assisted. Unlike design in other engineering fields with huge amounts of established numerical calculation and technical drawing, the main emphasis in Computer aided textile design will have to be on improving the accessibility of the whole body of knowledge and previous experience. Some experiments have been done with a flexible question-answering system which, operated via teletype or display terminal, is intended to serve a textile technologist in his day-to-day work [26]; we hope to supplement it with additional information, resolution power and learning ability to get some sort of artificial intelligence system.

The computerisation of the textile design in a narrower sense (i.e. creation of an artistic design and its conversion into machine instructions) does not produce any major problems. In fact, several comparatively simple systems of computer recognition and conversion of artistic ideas are already in use serving electronically controlled knitting machines [27]. Further development of these systems may be foreseen in two directions:

a) an integration to higher level design systems, assisting the textile designer not only in pattern handling and transformation but also in matching artistic ideas, manufacturing constraints and mechanical requirements as discussed in the previous paragraphs*;

b) radical changes in the working technique of an artist-designer, an establishment of a qualitatively new level of man-computer-production machine interaction and proceeding to stage two (the computer decides on alternative courses of action within imposed limits) similar to those defined by Mallary [28] concerning six levels of cybernetic art. This development will be accompanied by innovation of technology by art (complementary to innovation of art by technology mentioned by Mallary), by increasing the role of clothing fashion and pattern in the cultural environment and by stress on individual taste contrary to the ideas of some science fiction authors who dress their 3rd millenium heroes in uniform amorphous overalls.

The role of a textile technologist in the production process consists of keeping the differences between design and outcome at a tolerable level by embracing the existing (and rather scarce) or by substituting the non-existing automatic feedback connections. Typical conditions in a textile mill with equipment dispersed into hundreds of independent units acting partly in parallel and partly in series, each with several significant parameters to be measured, make the automation of data collection urgent, but also rather difficult and expensive.

However, the critical level of the benefit/expenses ratio in terms of economic values and human attitudes was reached a couple of years ago and by now hundreds of more or less sophisticated process-monitoring systems are being or have been

*Recent report by Dooner et al. [41], outlines development of a flexible Metasystem for Computer-Aided Knitted Fabric Design enabling the user to create an individual system by activating some of the variety of input and output facilities and design handling capabilities including retrieval and processing of the management information - as required in particular environment.

installed world-wide, many of them operated by mini-computers or integrated into higher level computer control systems [29, 30]. Machine efficiency, down-times and stoppages (classified with respect to causes) and additional characteristics of machine performance and product quality are monitored and analysed continuously or periodically. The immediate gain in human and machine efficiency makes the installations pay for themselves within 2-4 years. Furthermore, their use for identification of the true characteristics of the production process as a controlled system should influence positive development of textile technology as a whole.

DYEING, FINISHING, GARMENT MANUFACTURE

Two important branches of textile business have not been considered yet. The first one, dyeing and finishing, is by nature of the processes closely related to chemical engineering. Textile chemistry is traditionally more advanced in the understanding of the causal relationships and in the description and prediction of relevant phenomena than mechanical technology of textiles and, naturally, is keeping ahead in computer aided design and computerized production control.

Computer colour matching i.e. the prediction of the dyeing recipe to match spectrophotometric characteristics of a sample and other requirements, uses stored information about yield curves and other properties of dyestuffs, It has been used now for many years and represents a nice piece of automation of highly skilled and time consuming intellectual activity [31]. This development is followed by full-scale computer control of dyeing process, i.e. filling the dye becks, running the circulation pumps, adding chemicals, heating or cooling, controlling the rate of flow, the pH, etc. including feedback control via linked spectrophotometer, as described, for instance, by Squire [32].

The last lot of problems to be considered briefly is concerned with assembling the garments, which, unless knitted as fully fashioned, consist of a certain number of pieces of fabric cut out of the sheet and joined together by sewing operations. The extraordinary economic importance of the garment assembling arises from a) high labour consumption in apparel manufacture and b) the decisive role of apparel manufacture in the valuation of all the labour spent at earlier production stages. At the same time a scientific approach to the garment design and an automation of the production process is extremely difficult. The first industrial application of a numerical control of cutting and sewing processes have been known only for a couple of years. It has been made possible only after an extensive (and still continuing) development of machine manipulation of pieces of fabrics and certainly will develop further alongside other innovations like laser cutting and ultrasonic, adhesive and thermoplastic joining etc. On the theoretical side the topological approach introduced in one of the previous sections may be applied to seams consisting of one, two or more threads joining a number of pieces of cloth. A generalised topological approach might encompass positional relationships of all the pieces of cloth assembled in a garment.

The most difficult and the most beneficial classes of problems to be solved by applying various subdisciplines of cybernetics are those arising in the design of garments: Firstly, approximation of the three-dimensional body, which is to be covered, by polyhedra having faces representing single pieces of fabric and secondly, packing the pieces of fabric on the planar sheet in such a way so as to give minimum wastage in cutting. These problems have been solved empirically for ages and they constitute nowadays a great deal of the tailor's skill. There are already some computerised elements of the general problem in commercial use, for instance pattern grading (i.e. developing patterns for different sizes from the basic one). There are also some theoretical tools available as presented by Toth [33] or Rvatchev [34]. One of the first computed pattern layout was reported by Art [35] and is shown on Fig. 11. Some more information about the state of art may be drawn from [36].

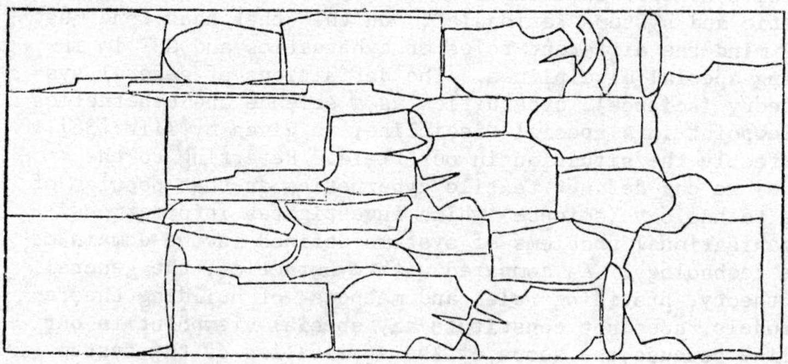

Fig. 11. Computed pattern layout for a lady's suit in two sizes.

The problems of optimum pattern layout or more general problems of optimal covering of the body plus pattern layout satisfying certain requirements are probably far from complete solution. However, partial solutions employing, possibly, a heuristic approach and suiting various practical needs seem to be within the scope of our theoretical and computing power.

CONCLUDING REMARKS

A brief excursion into the main provinces of textile technology showed numerous fields, where cybernetic ideas are or might be used directly or indirectly. There are three groups of problems deserving special attention: Digital control for assembling the yarns into woven and knitted fabrics and other deterministic topological structures; control of the processes of assembling the fibres into yarns, non-wovens and other probabilistic topological structures; assembling the garments from fabrics and general covering problems.

These problems themselves (if not to mention others including those common to any engineering discipline) fully justify the keen interest of a textile technologist in cybernetics and, I dare say, some attention of cyberneticians to what is going on in textiles. The proposed marriage is unequal as regard both age and background. It seems to me that newly developed and cultivated contacts between cybernetics and general systems theory (GST) could help to smooth the match.

Indeed, as stated by Bahr [37], "the most broadly based integrative concept existing at this time is one embracing both cybernetic and systems rationale". On the other hand, one must bear in mind the different roles of cybernetics and GST in influencing special disciplines. The definitions of general systems theory (science), cybernetics as a science and cybernetics as a viewpoint in a special discipline, as given by Klir [38], fit perfectly the situation in our field. Referring to the last one, we can define textile cybernetics as that portion of textile technology (science) which investigates informational and organisational problems of systems defined in the domain of textile technology. As compared with cybernetics, the general system theory, providing rules and methods of building theoretical models, does not constitute any special viewpoint in our discipline because the scope of the application of the system viewpoint coincides with the whole scope of the discipline itself. However, general systems theory, if mastered for instance to the level and in the way given by Klir [39], including all the necessary modern mathematical and computing techniques, will help textile technologists to operate within the realm of cybernetics as a science and to benefit from the interdisciplinary co-operation.

This is only one aspect of desirable innovation of the software of a textile technologist. The textile scientists and technologists - as serious users of cybernetic ideas, concepts and developments - of cybernetics and its subdisciplines. In this context an appropriate spreading of general and special knowledge in cybernetics through whole process of lower and higher education, both general and textile, seems to be particularly important.

REFERENCES

1. In *Charles Babbage and his Calculating Engines*, ed. by P. and E. MORRISON (Dover Publications, Inc., New York, 1961) 251-252.

2. *Textile Terms and Definitions*, 6th edition (The Textile Institute, Manchester, 1970).

3. J.W.S. HEARLE, and R.H. PETERS, (Ed.), *Fibre Structure* (The Textile Institute and Butterworths, Manchester and London, 1963).

4. W.E. MORTON, and J.W.S. HEARLE, *Physical Properties of Textile Fibres* (The Textile Institute and Butterworths, Manchester and London, 1962).

5. S. BACKER, "An engineering approach to textile structures" in *Ref. 40*, 2.

6. G.T. HERMAN, "The computing ability of a developmental model for filamentous organisms" in *Ref. 7*, 873.

7. J. ROSE (Ed.), *Progress of Cybernetics* (Gordon and Breach, London, 1970).

8. S. BACKER, and E.I. VALKO, *Thesaurus of Textile Terms Covering Fibrous Materials and Processes*, 2nd edition (M.I.T. Press, Cambridge, Mass., 1969).

9. W. LIETZMANN, *Anschauliche Topologie*, R. Oldenbourg, Munich (1955), English translation: *Visual Topology* (Chatto & Windus, London, 1965).

10. K. REIDEMEISTER, "Knothentheorie", in *Ergebnisse der Mathematik and Ihrer Grenzgebiete 1* (Julius Springer, Berlin, 1932).

11. P. OFFERMANN and S. PILZ,"Die Algebra der Logik als Hilfsmittel zur Analyse der Technik von Wirkerei- und Strickereimaschinen" *Faserforsch. u. Textiltechn. 16*, 26 (1965); continued *ibid.*, *16*, 89 (1965) and *17*, 512 (1966).

12. E. OBERST, "Beschreibung der Stenervorgange bei Wink - und Strickmaschinen mit einer ternaren Schaltalgebra" *Faserforsch. u. Textiltechn. 18*, 201 (1967) and also "Anwendungsmoglichkeiten mathematisch-logischer methoden in der strickereittechnik" *Deutsche Textiltechnik 20*, 98 (1970).

13. J.B. LANCASHIRE, *Jacquard Design and Knitting* (National Knitted Outerwear Association, New York, 1969) 41-49.

14. M. KONOPASEK, F. MACHACEK, and L. KLIMENT, "Contribution to spatial shaping of knitted fabrics" *Textile Science and Research X* (VUP, Brno, 1969).

15. "Tricoteuse "MacQueen" à commande électronique", *Moniteur de la Maille 943*, 70 (1961).

16. S. NOSEK, "Rheological dynamics of weft beat-up" and "Resonance weavibility and vibration beat-up" *J. Text. Inst.* (In press).

17. I. KH. BUTUROVICH, "Analysis of the equalizing action of the flat card from the frequency characteristics" *Tech. Tekst. Industr. U.S.S.R. 1*, 38 (1968).

18. I. DAVIES, "Some theoretical limitations of sliver autolevelling systems" *J. Text. Inst. 59*, 10 (1968).

19. J.E. BOOTH, "Principles of textile testing", 3rd Ed. (Heywood, London, 1968) 456-531.

20. J. RIPKA, "Cyclic fibre amalgamation in the spinning rotor of the BD 200 open-end spinning machine" *Textile Science and Research XI* (VUP, Brno, 1970).

21. V.B. TIKHOMIROV, "Matematicheskie metody planirovanija eksperimenta pri izuchenii netkannykh materialov" *Legkaja industrija* (Moscow, 1968).

22. A. CRAWFORD, "Management cybernetics" in J. ROSE (Ed.), *Survey of Cybernetics* (Iliffe Books, London, 1969).

23. *Computer Technology for Textiles* (W.R.C. Publishing Comp., Atlanta, Georgia, 1970).

24. J.W.S. HEARLE, M. KONOPASEK, and A. NEWTON, "Computer aided textile design", in P.W. HARRISON (Ed.), *News Ways to Produce Textiles* (The Textile Institute, Manchester, 1972).

25. J.W.S. HEARLE, M. KONOPASEK, and A. NEWTON, "On some general features of a computer based system for calculation of the mechanics of textile structures" *Textile Res. J.* (In press).

26. M. KONÓPASEK, and J.W.S. HEARLE, "On-line manipulating the property lists and property structures in CAD of textiles", in *Proceedings of International Conference on Computer-aided Design* (University of Southampton, 1972).

27. "New developments in pattern preparation procedures for double jersey fabrics" *Symposium proceedings, Hosiery and Allied Trades Research Association* (Nottingham, 1972).

28. R. MALLARY, *Computer Sculpture: Six Levels of Cybernetics* (in Ref. 7, 93).

29. W.N. ROZELLE, "Will mills buy monitoring?". in *Ref. 23*, 147.

30. H. LOCHER, and K. DOUGLAS, "Computerised control in the textile industry", in P.W. HARRISON (Ed.) *New Ways to Produce Textiles* (The Textile Institute, Manchester, 1972).

31. R.C. ALLISON, "Instrumental colour matching" in *Ref 23*, 123.

32. D.H. SQUIRE, "On-line computer control and automation in the dyehouse" *J. Soc. Dyers & Colourists 87*, 426 (1971).

33. L.F. TOTH, *Lagerungen in der Ebene, auf der Kugel und im Raum* (Springer, Berlin, 1953).

34. V.L. RVACHEV, *Geometricheskie prilozhenija algebry logiki* (Technika, Kiev, 1967).

35. R.C. ART Jr., "An approach to the pattern layout problem in the garment industry" *J. Apparel Res. Foundation 2*, No. 2, (1967).

36. "A fit subject for cooperative research, computerised marker making" (editorial), *J. Apparel Res. Foundation 4*, No. 1. 1 (1970).

37. F.R. BAHR, "Man-machine symbiosis, fusing systems theory and cybernetics to define the total information requirements of modern organisational activity" *Kybernetes 1*, 169 (1972).

38. G.J. KLIR, "Cybernetics and general systems theory" in *Ref. 7*, 155.

39. G.J. KLIR, *An Approach to General Systems Theory* (Van Nostrand - Reinhold, New York, 1970).

40. J.W.S. HEARLE, P. GROSBERG and S. BACKER, *Structural Mechanics of Fibres, Yarns and Fabrics, 1*, (Wiley-Interscience, New York, 1969).

41. N.P. DOONER, J.R. LOURIE and P. VELDERMAN, "A metasystem for computer-aided knitted fabric design and manufacture", Proceedings of Hosiery Trade Journal International Symposium on Electronics in Knitting, Leicester, 1973.

LEARNING IDENTIFICATION OF DYNAMIC PLANTS

W.R. WOUTERS*

Department of Electrical Engineering, University of Texas, Austin, Texas 78712, U.S.A.

SUMMARY

The problem of identification or, more appropriately the problem of finding the characteristics of controlled objects (plant characteristics) and of control actions, is one of the basic problems of automatic control systems. The identification of linear systems is discussed in noise-free and noisy environments. Particular attention will be paid to a generalized algorithm that performs very well under very general assumptions concerning measurement and plant noise.

INTRODUCTION

One of the basic problems in automatic control is the problem of identification, i.e. the characterization of a system.

The following two problems must be distinguished in an identification process:

1) The problem of determining the structure and the parameters.

2) The problem of determining the parameters for a given or an assumed structure.

If the first problem has to deal with a "black" non-transparent box, then the second is related to a "grey", semi-transparent one. Any information about the possible plant structure, or a sufficient general permissible structure, can

---

*Formerly at KUL-Louvain University, Belgium.

considerably accelerate the process of identification. Therefore, as it is usually done in practice, main attention will be paid to the solution of the second problem, mostly called "parameter estimation".

If there is an uncertainty in our *a priori* knowledge of a process, we may try to gather information by observing the behavior of the system and its responses to artificial test signals.

Most of the early identification procedures are of a non-sequential nature, i.e. they often require large amounts of data to be accumulated over relative long periods of time. This stored information is then processed in order to extract the features of the system.

In the context of learning and adaptive systems, the possibility of identifying processes during their normal operation is important. Also, as a result of the availability of today's high-speed digital computers, sequential identification procedures (these are procedures that make use of information as it becomes available) have been developed. Furthermore, it was no longer necessary to store all the measurements. Indeed, information is extracted at every instant, such that the new estimate shows up as a function, parameterized by the extracted information, of the previous estimate and the new observation.

In what follows, some of these procedures, also referred to as algorithms for on-line parameter estimation, will be discussed. We will limit our attention to time-invariant processes, i.e. the estimation of constant parameters. In the next section a formal introduction and problem statement is given. Next, attention is paid to the identification of linear processes. It is certainly not our intention to give a complete survey of all possible on-line estimation schemes, but we believe that the algorithms presented here are worthy of some discussion.

A very complete survey on identification, in general, with an extensive bibliography can be found in a recent paper by K.J. Åström and P. Eykhoff [1].

GENERAL PROBLEM STATEMENT

As stated in the introduction, we shall deal in this paper with the problem of parameter identification. First, we will give some definitions relevant to this problem.

Let $Z^N \triangleq \{\zeta(1),\ldots,\zeta(N)\}$ be a sequence of N observations over a system with parameters $\Theta_0 \varepsilon M$, where M is a separable metric space with distance function d. Based on the observations $\zeta(1)$, $\zeta(2),\ldots$ our objective is to estimate the true parameter Θ_0.

Definition 1: An estimate of Θ_0 based on the observation sequence Z^N is a measurable function of Z^N, and is denoted by

$$\hat{\Theta}(N) \triangleq \hat{\Theta}(N, Z^N) \tag{II.1}$$

Definition 2: An on-line estimate of Θ_0 based on the observation sequence Z^{N+1} is a measurable function F of $\zeta(N+1),\Theta(N)$ and $P(N)$, where $\zeta(N+1)$ is the (N+1)th observation, $\hat{\Theta}(N)$ is the Nth estimate of Θ_0 and $P(N)$ is a matrix parameterizing the function F, and containing extracted information from the observation sequence Z^N. The on-line estimate is denoted by:

$$\hat{\Theta}(N+1) \triangleq F(\zeta(N+1),\hat{\Theta}(N)\,|\,P(N)) \tag{II.2}$$

$$P(N+1) = G(\zeta(N+1),P(N)) \tag{II.3}$$

Definition 3: A sequence of estimates $\{\hat{\Theta}(i)\}_{i=1}^{\infty}$ is said to be consistent in probability, if for any $\delta,\varepsilon > 0$ and arbitrary small, there exists an $N(\varepsilon,\delta)<\infty$ such that for $k > N(\varepsilon,\delta)$

$$\text{Prob}\ \{d(\hat{\Theta}(k),\Theta_0) > \delta\} < \varepsilon \tag{II.4}$$

Formally, we write $\hat{\Theta}(k) \overset{P}{\to} \Theta_0$

We can formulate our problem now as follows: Construct a filter $F(\cdot)$ which is excited by the observation sequence $\{\zeta(k)\}$, and that yields a sequence of consistent estimates $\{\hat{\Theta}(k)\}$.

Mostly a filter of the following form is used:

$$\hat{\Theta}(k+1) = \hat{\Theta}(k) + \varepsilon(k)\Gamma(k) \tag{II.5}$$

where

$$\Gamma(k) = \Gamma(P(k),\zeta(k+1)) \tag{II.6}$$

The precise definition of $\varepsilon(k)$ and $\Gamma(k)$ is strongly problem-depending, i.e. it depends on what we know or assume about our system.

Another important notion is that of identifiability of the parameters [2]. It is not our intention to discuss this here, but we will assume in the following that the conditions for identifiability are fulfilled. Note that [2]:

Definition 4: The parameter Θ_0 is said to be identifiable if there exists a sequence of estimates $\{\hat{\Theta}(i)\}_{i=1}^{\infty}$ which is consistent in probability, i.e., $\hat{\Theta}(i) \overset{P}{\to} \Theta_0$.

IDENTIFICATION OF LINEAR SYSTEMS

a) Introduction

In this section we shall be concerned with the on-line parameter estimation problem for linear systems. We will restrict our attention to single-input, single-output constant discrete-time systems of the n-th order, governed by a difference equation of the form:

$$x(k) = \sum_{i=1}^{n} a_i x(k-i) + \sum_{j=1}^{m} b_j (u(k-j)+w(k-j)) \qquad \text{(III.1)}$$

$$y(k) = x(k) + n(k) \qquad \text{where } m \leq n. \qquad \text{(III.2)}$$

The sequence $\{u(k)\}$ represents the perfectly measurable control input. However, there is plant noise which can be represented by an extra additive input sequence $\{w(k)\}$, and a noise corrupting the output measurements $\{n(k)\}$.

Assumptions about these sequences will be given below, where we will consider first the case where $w(k) = n(k) = 0$ for all k. In this case we can use a method which has been called the gradient algorithm. When the noise is not zero, we must use different algorithms, depending on the noise characteristics.

b) Noise-Free Situation

First we will discuss a very simple algorithm, the gradient algorithm. This algorithm, together with its most important properties, has been derived in Mendel [3,4], Nagumo and Noda [5] and Wouters [6].

Let us define a measurement-vector

$$\mathbf{z}^T(k) \triangleq \{z_1(k),\ldots,z_{n+m}(k)\}$$
$$\triangleq \{y(k-1),\ldots,y(k-n),u(k-1),\ldots,u(k-m)\} \qquad \text{(III.3)}$$

the unknown parameter is

$$\mathbf{\Theta}_0^T \triangleq \{\Theta_{01},\ldots,\Theta_{0\,n+m}\}$$
$$\triangleq \{a_1,\ldots,a_n,b_1,\ldots,b_m\} \qquad \text{(III.4)}$$

Since the measurement noise is assumed to be zero, we have $y(k) = x(k)$ for all k, so we may write

$$y(k) = \sum_{i=1}^{n+m} \Theta_{0i}\, z_i(k) = \mathbf{\Theta}_0^T \mathbf{z}(k) \qquad \text{(III.5)}$$

Having an estimate $\hat{\Theta}(k)$, we can define an error

$$e(k) = y(k) - \hat{\Theta}^T(k)\ z(k) = \tilde{\Theta}^T(k)z(k) \qquad \text{(III.6)}$$

where

$$\tilde{\Theta}(k) = \Theta_0 - \hat{\Theta}(k) \qquad \text{(III.7)}$$

So, clearly e(k) is zero for all k if $\tilde{\Theta}$ is zero, and this is what we want. Defining now a cost function

$$V(e(k)|\hat{\Theta}) \triangleq \tfrac{1}{2}e^2(k) \qquad \text{(III.8)}$$

we minimize this function with respect to $\hat{\Theta}(k)$, using the gradient descent procedure

$$\Theta(k+1) = \Theta(k) - R(k)\ \mathbf{grad}_{\hat{\Theta}}\{V(e(k))\} \qquad \text{(III.9)}$$

where R(k) is a (n+m) (n+m) positive definite symmetric gain matrix, with elements to be specified.

From (III.6) and (III.8) it follows that

$$\mathbf{grad}_{\hat{\Theta}}\{V(e(k)|\hat{\Theta}) = -e(k)z(k) \qquad \text{(III.10)}$$

If we choose for R(k) to be a scalar $\rho(k)$, one can show that

$$\rho(k) = (z^T(k)z(k))^{-1} \qquad \text{(III.11)}$$

is the best choice for $\rho(k)$[3].

When we choose for R(k) to be a positive definite symmetric matrix, the best choice can be shown to be

$$R(k) = \frac{P(k)}{z^T(k)P(k)z(k)} \qquad \text{(III.12)}$$

where P(k) is a positive definite symmetric matrix. Algorithm (III.9) with R(k) as in (III.11) and (III.12) has the "error correcting" property, this means that

$$y(k) = \hat{\Theta}^T(k+1)z(k) \qquad \text{(III.13)}$$

Convergence of this algorithm can be proved very easily, see e.g. *reference* 6. However, we can ask whether we can't find an optimal R(k), optimal in this sense that $\tilde{\Theta}^T(k+1)\tilde{\Theta}(k+1)$ would be minimized at every instant of time. Let us define therefore

$$Q(k+1) \triangleq \tilde{\Theta}(k+1)\tilde{\Theta}^T(k+1) \qquad \text{(III.14)}$$

One can show that algorithm (III.9) with

$$R(k) = \frac{Q(k)}{z^T(k)Q(k)z(k)} \qquad \text{(III.15)}$$

minimizes $Tr\{Q(k+1)\}$. When we apply this algorithm, we find also easily an iterative form for $Q(k)$

$$Q(k+1) = \left(I - \frac{Q(k)}{z^T(k)Q(k)z(k)}\right)Q(k) \qquad \text{(III.16)}$$

If we can define now an initial value $Q(1)$ to start the iteration scheme, we have in the combination of (III.9,10,15) and (III.16) the optimal gradient estimator.

Actually $Q(1)$ is the outer product of the error in the parameters with itself, so $Q(1) = (\Theta_0-\hat{\Theta}(1))(\Theta_0-\hat{\Theta}(1))^T$. However, since we don't know Θ_0, we cannot define $Q(1)$ exactly. When we take $\hat{\Theta}(1) = \mathbf{0}$, we may take an estimate

$$Q(1) = q(1) \cdot I \qquad \text{(III.17)}$$

so that $y^2(1) = z^T(1)\Theta_0\Theta_0^T z(1) = z^T(1)Q(1)z(1)$

$$= q(1)z^T(1)z(1)$$

thus $\quad q(1) = y^2(1)/z^T(1)z(1) \qquad \text{(III.18)}$

c) Plant Noise

Let us assume for a moment that our measurement noise is zero, but that we have some plant noise $\{w(k)\}$, thus our system is described now by

$$x(k) = \sum_{i=1}^{n} a_i x(k-i) + \sum_{j=1}^{m} b_j u(k-j) + \sum_{j=1}^{m} b_j w(k-j) \qquad \text{(III.19)}$$

$$y(k) = x(k)$$

Further we shall assume that the noise sequence $\{w(k)\}$ is generated by filtering a white sequence $\{r(k)\}$, independent of $\{x(k)\}$ and $\{u(k)\}$, with bounded variance σ_r^2, through a (m-1)th order filter

$$w(k) = -\frac{1}{b_1}(b_2 w(k-1) + \ldots + b_m w(k-m-1)) + \frac{1}{b_1} r(k) \qquad \text{(III.20)}$$

We see that in this case we also can write our system equation as

$$y(k) = \Theta_0^T z(k) + r(k-1) \qquad \text{(III.21)}$$

where Θ_0 and $z(k)$ are as defined in (III.3,4) and $\{r(k-1)\}$ is a white sequence.

Several approaches to the parameter estimation are now possible.

(i) *Stochastic approximation* [7.8]

Defining a cost function

$$J(\hat{\Theta}) \triangleq E\{V(e(k)|\hat{\Theta})\} \qquad \text{(III.22)}$$

where $e(k)$ and $V(e(k)|\hat{\Theta})$ are as defined in (III.6,8), we can see that the value Θ_0 minimizes $J(\hat{\Theta})$ with respect to $\hat{\Theta}$. Indeed, we have

$$J(\hat{\Theta}) = E\{\tfrac{1}{2}(\tilde{\Theta}^T z(k))^2\} + \tfrac{1}{2}\sigma_r^2 \qquad \text{(III.23)}$$

and this clearly has a minimum for $\tilde{\Theta} = 0$, thus $\hat{\Theta} = \Theta_0$. Furthermore we have the property that

$$\mathbf{grad}_{\hat{\Theta}} J(\hat{\Theta}) = E\{\mathbf{grad}_{\hat{\Theta}} V(e(k)|\hat{\Theta})\} \qquad \text{(III.24)}$$

and thus we are in the possibility of applying the well-known Robbins-Monro stochastic approximation scheme.

$$\hat{\Theta}(k+1) = \hat{\Theta}(k) - \rho(k)\mathbf{grad}_{\hat{\Theta}} V(e(k)|\hat{\Theta}) \qquad \text{(III.25)}$$

with

$$\rho(k) > 0, \sum_{k=1}^{\infty} \rho(k) = \infty, \quad \sum_{k=1}^{\infty} \rho^2(k) < \infty$$

for which convergence $\hat{\Theta}(k) \xrightarrow{P} \Theta_0$ can be proved [8].

(ii) *Iterative least squares* [1,9]

Suppose we have measurements $z(k)$ over N instants of time, we can define the cost function

$$J_N(\hat{\Theta}) \triangleq \sum_{k=1}^{N} (y(k) - \hat{\Theta}^T z(k))^2 = (Y_N - Z_N\hat{\Theta})^T (Y_N - Z_N\hat{\Theta}) \qquad \text{(III.26)}$$

where $\mathbf{Y}_N^T \triangleq \{y(1),\ldots,y(N)\}$

(III.27)

and $Z_N^T \triangleq \{\mathbf{z}(1),\ldots,\mathbf{z}(N)\}$

In order to minimize this cost function, we set $\mathbf{grad}_{\hat{\Theta}} J_N(\hat{\boldsymbol{\theta}}) = \mathbf{0}$, which yields

$$Z_N \mathbf{Y}_N - Z_N^T Z_N \hat{\boldsymbol{\theta}} = \mathbf{0} \tag{III.28}$$

When we solve this equation with respect to $\hat{\Theta}$ we find the least squares estimate based upon N observations

$$\hat{\boldsymbol{\theta}}(N+1) = (Z_N Z_N)^{-1} Z_N \mathbf{Y}_N \tag{III.29}$$

In order to have an on-line least square estimator, we will propose now an iterative scheme. Define

$$P^{-1}(N+1) = Z_N^T Z_N = Z_{N-1}^{\ T} Z_{N-1} + \mathbf{z}(N)\mathbf{z}^T(N) = P^{-1}(N) + \mathbf{z}(N)\mathbf{z}^T(N) \tag{III.30}$$

There exists a matrix inversion lemma [9], that for an inverse given as in (III.30) states:

$$P(N+1) = P(N) - \mathbf{z}(N)(\mathbf{z}^T(N)P(N)\mathbf{z}(N) + 1)^{-1}\mathbf{z}^T(N)P(N) \tag{III.31}$$

So (III.29,30 and 31) combined give us

$$\hat{\boldsymbol{\theta}}(N+1) = \hat{\boldsymbol{\theta}}(N) + \frac{P(N)}{\mathbf{z}^T(N)P(N)\mathbf{z}(N)+1}\, e(N)\mathbf{z}(N) \tag{III.32}$$

where $e(N) = y(N) - \hat{\Theta}^T(N)\mathbf{z}(N)$.

In order to start our iterative scheme (III.32,31), we have to find initial values $\hat{\boldsymbol{\theta}}(1)$ and $P(1)$. Now is $P(1) = (\mathbf{z}(1)\mathbf{z}^T(1))^{-1}$, and this does not exist, since $\mathbf{z}(1)\mathbf{z}^T(1)$ is singular. So we can make an approximation

$$\hat{P}(1) = \mathrm{diag}\{z_1^{-2}(1),\ldots,z_{n+m}^{-2}(1)\} \tag{III.33}$$

also we will usually take $\hat{\boldsymbol{\theta}}(1) = \mathbf{0}$

(iii) *Kalman filtering* [10,11]

Considering the unknown parameter vector Θ_0 as the state of a linear system, we can apply Kalman Filter theory to derive an optimal estimator $\hat{\Theta}(k)$.

Since Θ_0 was assumed to be constant, the system equations given by

$$\Theta_0(k+1) = I\Theta_0(k)$$

$$y(k+1) = \mathbf{z}^T(k)\Theta_0(k) + r(k-1) \tag{III.34}$$

where $\mathbf{z}(k)$ is considered as the state observation matrix.

The filter equations are heavily simplified, since here $\hat{\Theta}(k+1|k) = \hat{\Theta}(k|k)$ and $P^*(k+1|k) = P^*(k|k)$. Denoting $\hat{\Theta}(k|k)$ by $\hat{\Theta}(k)$ and $P^*(k|k)$ by $P^*(k)$ we find

$$\hat{\Theta}(k+1) = \hat{\Theta}(k) + \mu(k)[y(k) - \hat{\Theta}^T(k)\mathbf{z}(k)] \tag{III.35.a}$$

$$\mu(k) = [\mathbf{z}^T(k)P^*(k)\mathbf{z}(k) + \sigma_r^2]^{-1}P^*(k)\mathbf{z}(k) \tag{III.35.b}$$

$$P^*(k+1) = (I-P^*(k)\mathbf{z}(k)(\mathbf{z}^T(k)P^*(k)\mathbf{z}(k) + \sigma_r^2)^{-1}\mathbf{z}^T(k))P^*(k) \tag{III.35.c}$$

Remark that $P^*(k)$ is defined herein as

$$P^*(k) \triangleq E\{\tilde{\Theta}(k)\tilde{\Theta}^T(k)\} \tag{III.36}$$

The only problem that remains now is the estimation of $P^*(1)$, in order to start our recursive scheme. An appropriate choice when $\hat{\Theta}(1) = \mathbf{0}$, is

$$\hat{P}^*(1) = y^2(1)(\mathbf{z}^T(1)\mathbf{z}(1))^{-1}\, I \tag{III.37}$$

(iv) *Some remarks*

By definition, the estimate obtained using the Kalman Filter is the optimal one (minimum variance in the error of the estimate). It is clear that (III.35) reduces to the optimal gradient estimator (III.9,10,15,16) when $\sigma_r^2 = 0$.

We can also see that the Kalman Filter estimator resembles strongly the iterative least squares estimator. For the latter we can see that

$$\mathbf{Y}(k) = Z_k\Theta_0 + \mathbf{R}(k) \tag{III.38}$$

where

$\mathbf{R}^T(k) \triangleq \{r(0),\ldots,r(k-1)\}$

$\tilde{\Theta}(k+1) = \Theta_0 - \hat{\Theta}(k+1) = \Theta_0 - [Z_k^T Z_k]^{-1} Z_k^T (Z_k \Theta_0 + \mathbf{R}(k))$

$$\tilde{\Theta}(k+1) = -[Z_k^T Z_k]^{-1} Z_k^T \mathbf{R}(k) \qquad \text{(III.39)}$$

$$E\{\tilde{\boldsymbol{\Theta}}(k+1)\tilde{\Theta}^T(k+1)\} = E\{([Z_k^T Z_k]^{-1} Z_k^T \mathbf{R}(k))([Z_k^T Z_k]^{-1} Z_k^T \mathbf{R}(k))^T\} = \qquad \text{(III.40)}$$

$[Z_k^T Z_k]^{-1} Z_k^T \; E\{\mathbf{R}(k)\mathbf{R}^T(k)\} Z_k [Z_k^T Z_k]^{-1}$

Now, if r(k) is a sample function from a stationary white sequence (as we assumed), with variance σ_r^2, we find

$E\{\tilde{\boldsymbol{\Theta}}(k+1)\tilde{\Theta}^T(k+1)\} = \sigma_r^2 [Z_k^T Z_k]^{-1}$

$$E\{\tilde{\Theta}(k+1)\tilde{\boldsymbol{\Theta}}^T(k+1)\} = \sigma_r^2 P(k+1) \qquad \text{(III.41)}$$

For the Kalman Filter (minimum variance estimator) we have by inversion of (III.35.c)

$$P^{*-1}(k+1) = P^{*-1}(k) + \mathbf{z}(k)\frac{1}{\sigma_r^2}\mathbf{z}^T(k) =$$

$$P^{*-1}(1) + \frac{1}{\sigma_r^2}\sum_{i=2}^{k} \mathbf{z}(i)\mathbf{z}^T(i) \qquad \text{(III.42)}$$

and for the least squares estimator we have (III.30)

$$P^{-1}(k+1) = P^{-1}(1) + \sum_{i=2}^{k} z(i)z^T(i) \qquad \text{(III.43)}$$

We can see that for k large the influence of $P^*(1)$ and $P(1)$ will disappear, so

$$P^{*-1}(k) \approx \frac{1}{\sigma_r^2} P^{-1}(k) \quad \text{for k large}$$

or

$$P(k) \approx \frac{1}{\sigma_r^2} P^*(k) \quad \text{for k large} \qquad \text{(III.44)}$$

Comparing (III.41) with (III.44), we can see that both the least squares estimator and the Kalman Filter estimator are minimum variance estimators of the parameter Θ_0.

d) Known Measurement Noise and Plant Noise

Here our system can be described by the equations (III.1,2), where the following is assumed concerning the sequences $\{u(k)\}$, $\{w(k)\}$ and $\{n(k)\}$.

*) $\{u(k)\}$ is the measurable input sequence

*) $\{w(k)\}$ and $\{n(k)\}$ are zero mean stochastic white sequences, mutually uncorrelated, uncorrelated with $\{u(k)\}$, and independent of the state of the system.

Here also, several solutions are possible.

(i) *A stochastic approximation* algorithm can be applied when the variances of the sequences $\{n(k)\}$ and $\{w(k)\}$ are known. Let us define a $(n+m)x(n+m)$ matrix S

$$S \triangleq \text{diag}\,\{\sigma_w^2,\dots,\sigma_w^2,\sigma_n^2,\dots,\sigma_n^2\} \qquad \text{(III.45)}$$

where

$$\sigma_w^2 = E\{w^2(k)\} \qquad \sigma_n^2 = E\{n^2(k)\}$$

then the following algorithm

$$\hat{\Theta}(k+1) = [I + \rho(k)S]\hat{\Theta}(k) + \rho(k)(y(k) - \hat{\Theta}^T(k)\mathbf{z}(k))\mathbf{z}(k) \qquad \text{(III.46)}$$

where $\mathbf{z}^T(k) \triangleq \{y(k-1),\dots,y(k-n),u(k-1),\dots,u(k-m)\}$

$$\rho(k) > 0 \qquad \sum_{k=1}^{\infty} \rho(k) = \infty \qquad \sum_{k=1}^{\infty} \rho^2(k) < \infty$$

will yield consistent estimates. A convergence proof can be found in Saridis and Stein [12].

The presence of S in the algorithm is necessary in order to remove the bias in the estimates. Indeed, when the variances of the noise processes are not known exactly, (III.46) will yield biased estimates. Also the least squares estimates will be biased, and this bias can be removed only if the variances of the noises are known exactly.

(ii) *The extended Kalman Filter*

The relationship between the recursive least squares and Kalman Filter theory was obtained by introducing the parameters of the identification problem as state variables. We thus found that there are in principle no differences between parameter estimation and state estimation. A parameter estimation problem can be regarded as a state estimation problem by introducing the unknown parameters as auxiliary state variables.

A system description in state space notation will be used. Let our single-input single-output process be given by

$$\mathbf{y}(k+1) = \Phi\mathbf{y}(k) + \boldsymbol{\beta}u(k) + \mathbf{w}(k) \tag{III.47.a}$$

$$\Phi \triangleq \left|\begin{matrix}\mathbf{0} & I \\ & \mathbf{a}^T\end{matrix}\right| \quad c^T \triangleq [0,\ldots,0,1]$$

with measurements

$$z(k) = \mathbf{c}^T\mathbf{y}(k) + n(k) \tag{III.47.b}$$

The noise is assumed to be Gaussian with the following characteristics

$$E\{\mathbf{w}(i)\mathbf{w}^T(j)\} = Q\delta_{ij} \qquad E\{n(i)n(j)\} = \sigma_n^2\delta_{ij}$$

$$E\{n(i)\mathbf{w}(j)\} = \mathbf{0} \qquad \text{for all } i,j$$

and is uncorrelated with the state $\mathbf{y}$ of the system.

The extended system becomes:

$$\mathbf{x}(k+1) = \mathbf{f}(\mathbf{x}(k)) + \mathbf{w}^*(k)$$

$$z(k) = \mathbf{c}^{*T}\mathbf{x}(k) + n(k)$$

with $\mathbf{x}^T(k) = [\mathbf{a}^T, \boldsymbol{\beta}^T, \mathbf{y}^T(k)]$

$$\mathbf{f}(\mathbf{x}(k)) \triangleq \begin{bmatrix} x_1(k) \\ x_2(k) \\ \cdot \\ \cdot \\ \cdot \\ x_{2n}(k) \\ x_{2n+2}(k) + x_{n+1}(k)u(k) \\ x_{2n+3}(k) + x_{n+2}(k)u(k) \\ \cdot \\ \cdot \\ \cdot \\ x_{3n}(k) + x_{2n-1}(k)u(k) \\ \sum_{i=1}^{n} x_i(k)x_{2n+i}(k) + x_{2n}(k)u(k) \end{bmatrix}$$

$$\mathbf{w}^{*T}(k) \triangleq [0,\ldots,0,\ \mathbf{w}^T(k)]$$

$$\mathbf{c}^{*T} \triangleq [0,\ldots,0,\ldots,0,1] \tag{III.48}$$

As can be seen, this system is non-linear of the second degree.

It can be shown* that the following relationships define a sub-optimal linear estimator for the state of the extended system.

I. *EXTRAPOLATION*

$$\hat{\mathbf{x}}(k+1|k) = \mathbf{f}(\hat{x}(k|k)) + \mathbf{g}(P(k|k)) \tag{III.49.a}$$

$$P(k+1|k) = F(\hat{\mathbf{x}}(k|k))P(k|k)F^T(\hat{\mathbf{x}}(k|k)) + Q^* + G(P(k|k)) \tag{III.49.b}$$

where $Q^* = E\{W^*(k)W^{*T}(k)\}$

$\mathbf{g}(P(k|k))$ is a linear vector valued function of the elements of $P(k|k)$

$F(\hat{\mathbf{x}}(k|k))$ is the matrix of the first derivatives of $f(\mathbf{x}(k|k))$ with respect to $\mathbf{x}(k|k)$ in the point $\hat{\mathbf{x}}(k|k)$

$G(P(k|k))$ is a non-linear matrix valued function of the elements of $P(k|k)$

As for the normal Kalman Filter, $\hat{\mathbf{x}}(k+1|k)$ denotes an unbiased estimate of the state at time (k+1) and based upon measurements up to time k, and $P(k+1|k)$ denotes the error covariance matrix of this estimate.

II. *UPDATE*

$$\hat{\mathbf{x}}(k+1|k+1) = \hat{\mathbf{x}}(k+1|k) + \mathbf{K}^*(k+1)(z(k+1) - \mathbf{c}^{*T}\hat{\mathbf{x}}(k+1|k)) \tag{III.50.a}$$

$$\mathbf{K}^*(k+1) = P(k+1|k)\mathbf{c}^*(\mathbf{c}^{*T}P(k+1|k)\mathbf{c}^* + \sigma_n^2)^{-1} \tag{III.50.b}$$

$$P(k+1|k+1) = [I - \mathbf{K}^*(k+1)\mathbf{c}^{*T}]P(k+1|k) \tag{III.50.c}$$

Note that these are the normal update equations for the Kalman Filter. This is because our extended non-linear system remains linear in the observations.

---

*Details available from author.

e) Unknown Measurement and Plant Noise

When the noise variances are not known, the previous methods will yield biased, thus inconsistent, estimates. Special identification schemes such as the extended matrix method, and other related schemes, try to estimate both the noise and plant characteristics (for references see e.g. Åström and Eykhoff [1]). Although some of these algorithms seem to have a fair performance, they are rather complicated, and no formal proof exists for convergence.

The method we propose is based on the fact that in the stationary case the cross-correlation function between the output and the input of a linear system is uniquely determined by the auto-correlation function of the input and the parameters of the system. This means that any other signal, not correlated with input and output of the process, does not affect the value of the cross-correlation function. This result is very well known, and perhaps its most popular application is the determination of the impulse response of a plant by correlating a (pseudo) white input sequence with the observed output.

In some recent papers [13,14] the author proposed an algorithm that yields on-line consistent estimates of the parameters of a time-invariant linear discrete system of known order (structure), using an ergodic input sequence and measurements of the output.

The estimator has the following form

$$\hat{\theta}(k+1) = \hat{\theta}(k) + \frac{P(k)\mathbf{v}(k+1)}{\mathbf{s}^T(k+1)P(k)\mathbf{v}(k+1)+1}\,(y(k+1) - \mathbf{s}^T(k+1)\hat{\theta}(k)) \quad \text{(III.51.a)}$$

$$P(k+1) = \left(I - \frac{P(k)\mathbf{v}(k+1)\mathbf{s}^T(k+1)}{\mathbf{v}^T(k+1)P(k)\mathbf{s}(k+1)+1}\right) P(k) \quad \text{(III.51.b)}$$

where $y(k+1)$ is the noise corrupted measurement of the output, and the $(n+m,1)$ columnvectors $\mathbf{v}(k)$ and $\mathbf{s}(k)$ are defined as follows

$$\mathbf{v}^T(k) \triangleq [u(k-1), \ldots, u(k-n-m)]$$

$$\mathbf{s}^T(k) \triangleq [y(k-1), \ldots, y(k-n), u(k-1), \ldots, u(k-m)] \quad \text{(III.52)}$$

The initial values for this scheme may be taken to be $\hat{\theta}(1) = 0$ and $P(1) = I$ where I is the $(n+m) \times (n+m)$ unit matrix.

Note that eqs. (III.51) define an easy to implement on-line algorithm. Convergence to the true parameter values is assured under very general conditions, and there is no need for a priori knowledge of the stochastic environment. Note also that the algorithm, in essence realizes nothing but identification by deconvolution.

CONCLUSION

In the previous section, applicable on-line identification techniques have been discussed. The author performed several computer simulations with each of the mentioned algorithms, and, in all but one case, no convergence problems arose, even with very poor signal to noise ratios. Convergence difficulties arose while using the extended Kalman Filter. The usability of this algorithm is questionable therefore.

As indicated in the introduction, it is not our purpose to give a complete picture, although we think that the most important algorithms have been discussed. Our discussion was limited to parameter estimation for linear systems; however, many of the concepts discussed herein are also useful in understanding the behavior of identification algorithms, when the identified system is non-linear. This is because a non-linear process is mainly approximated by a model that is linear in the parameters. Although the linearity constraint is quite restrictive, there are many important applications.

ACKNOWLEDGEMENTS

The author wishes to thank Prof. Ir. H.P. Debruyn, who made possible the research described in this paper, and is much obliged to his colleagues for the many useful hints and discussions.

A special thank also to the Education Office of the Belgian government, which partially supported this research programme.

REFERENCES

1. K.J. ÅSTRÖM and P. EYKHOFF, "System identification - a survey" *Automatica 7*, 123-169 (1971).

2. E. TSE and J. ANTON, "On the identifiability of paramters" *Proc. of the 1971 IEEE Control and Decision Conf.*, (Miami Beach, Florida, December 1971) pp. 498-502.

3. J.M. MENDEL, "Gradient identification for linear systems", In: *Adaptive, Learning, and Pattern Recognition Systems - Theory and Applications*, edited by J.M. MENDEL and K.S. FU (Academic Press, N.Y. and London, 1970).

4. J.M. MENDEL, "Property of the equation-error approach to parameter identification" *IEEE Vol. AC-15, No. 6*, pp. 676-678 (December 1970).

5. J. NAGUMO and A. NODA, "A learning method for system identification" *IEEE Vol. AC-12, No. 3*, pp. 282-287 (June 1967).

6. W.R. WOUTERS, "Learning identification for a state space model" *see ref.* 2, pp. 503-507.

7. Ya.Z. TSYPKIN, *Adaptation and Learning in Automatic Systems* (Academic Press, New York and London, 1971).

8. R.L. KASHYAP, C.C. BLAYDON and K.S. FU, "Stochastic approximation", *see ref.* 3.

9. P.C. YOUNG, "The use of linear regression and related procedures for the identification of dynamic processes" *Proc. of the IEEE Symp. on Adaptive Processes* (December 1968).

10. A. GELB, et al., "Short course on Kalman Filter theory and application" (edited by The Analytic Science Corp., Reading, Mass., 1971).

11. J. WIESLANDER and B. WITTENMARK, "An approach to adaptive control using real time identification" *Automatica 7, No. 2*, 211-218 (March 1971).

12. G.N. SARIDIS and G. STEIN, "Stochastic approximation algorithms for linear discrete-time system identification" *IEEE Vol. AC-13*, pp. 515-523 (October 1968).

13. W.R. WOUTERS, "On-line identification in an unknown stochastic environment" *IEEE Vol. SMC-2, No. 4* (November 1972).

14. W.R. WOUTERS, "On-line parameter estimation in an unknown stochastic environment" (presented at *The Systems Symposium, Purdue University*, Lafayette, Ind., October 1972).

FUNCTIONAL OPTIMIZATION FOR QUANTUM DYNAMICAL SYSTEMS DEFINED BY SCHROEDINGER'S EQUATION BASED ON MODERN CONTROL THEORY

R. MUTABŽIJA

Institute "Rudjer Bošković", Zagreb, Yugoslavia

SUMMARY

Functional optimization is introduced for quantum-dynamic systems, starting from known performances. The Pontryagin maximum principle is applied for this purpose in cases where the dynamics of the controlled system is defined by the Schroedinger equation. The optimal control functions are determined by the variational calculus methods, starting from known integral probabilistic performances. Some approximations in time dependent perturbational theory are used to approximate the time-dependent Schroedinger equation by a finite set of differential equations in probability amplitudes. The perturbational functions appearing in this set as part of the Hamiltonian of the system allow a control of the solutions for the probability amplitudes. This procedure is equivalent to the control functions introduction in quantum mechanical interactions, effecting the optimal performance on the basis of the Pontryagin principle. This represents an extension of the functional optimization for the classical dynamic systems.

INTRODUCTION

General dynamic systems, organized by external control or self-organized, appear as natural and artificial objects all around us. The aim of nature and that of artificial design is to optimize functions of such objects. The optimization is performed for the classical dynamic systems by the known control theory methods. The aim of this paper is to apply the standard method of functional optimization in modern control theory to the quantum-dynamic systems. It is well known that in published papers and books on the subject matter, in general, one can find analytical treatments of the quantum-dynamic systems concerned with the investigation and determination of properties for given physical and mathematical structures. An analytical approach is applied to quantum systems with time-independent Hamiltonian, as well as to the less investigated time-dependent Hamiltonians, and corresponding Schroedinger equations.

The synthetic approach to the problem of optimal performance for the quantum-dynamic systems by powerful means of modern control theory, has not been introduced till now, as far as the author knows. This paper is an attempt to introduce logically and formally this synthetic approach. In addition to its theoretical meaning, the developed approach introduces optimal design, starting from the given probabilistic performances at the level of quantum engineering; one could also use it for artificial design. The developed approach is probably used by nature for the organization and control of natural physical, chemical and biological phenomena [1.2.3].

QUANTUM SYSTEM DYNAMICAL BEHAVIOUR DESCRIBED BY THE SCHROEDINGER EQUATION REDUCED TO A SET OF COUPLED DIFFERENTIAL EQUATIONS

To describe the time development of a quantum system, one postulates the existence of a Hamiltonian H for the system, and requires that the state vector for the system $|\Psi(t)>$ changes in accordance with the Schroedinger equation

$$i\hbar \frac{\partial|\Psi(t)>}{\partial t} = H|\Psi(t)> , \qquad (1)$$

In the case of a conservative system, $H = H_0$ is explicitly independent of time. In that case it is possible to integrate eq. (1) and obtain

$$|\Psi(t)> = U(t,t_0)|\Psi(t_0)> , \qquad (2a)$$

where

$$U(t,t_0) = \exp\left[-\frac{iH_0(t-t_0)}{h}\right] \qquad (2b)$$

and $|\Psi(t_0)>$ is the state of the system at time t_0.

Obviously, conservative quantum system analysis, although relatively simple, is not interesting from the standpoint of the modern control theory. The dynamic behaviour of a quantum system under the influence of the time variable external forces or fields represents a non-conservative quantum system, analogous to the non-conservative classical system. The Hamiltonian

$H = H_0 + H_c$ is in this case an explicitly time-dependent function. Such a system behaviour can be controlled, by properly choosing the time variable external fields or forces, within the ramifications of the classical systems.

This procedure can be applied to quantum-dynamic systems, taking into account some specific properties.

The control function may be derived, starting from the given time-dependent atomic transition probabilities. Such a problem formulation is actually a control theory problem, different from standard quantum theoretical task of finding the transition probability functions for given quantum systems and known excitation fields.

According to the time-dependent perturbation theory, the time development for quantum-dynamic system is given by the solutions of the Schroedinger equation

$$i\hbar \frac{\partial|\Psi(t)>}{\partial t} = (H_0 + H_c)|\Psi(t)> \quad , \tag{3}$$

where H_c introduces a correction to H_0, or control in our interpretation. We can first consider the uncontrolled (unperturbed) problem corresponding to H_0, relating to the Schroedinger equation

$$i\hbar \frac{\partial|\phi(t)>}{\partial t} = H_0|\phi(t)> \tag{4}$$

Since H_0 is assumed to be independent of time, we may write the solution as

$$|\phi(t)> = \exp(-\frac{i}{\hbar} H_0 t)|\phi(0)> \tag{5}$$

In the energy representation of the uncontrolled system, the complete set of orthonormal state vectors, which are eigenvectors of H_0, will be designated by $|n>$ where

$$H_0|n> = E_n|n> \qquad <n|m> = \delta_{mn} \tag{6}$$

The E_n are the eigenvalues of H_0, and we may expand the arbitrary initial state ket $|\phi(0)>$ in terms of this complete set $\{|n>\}$ by

$$|\phi(0)> = \sum_n C_n(0)|n> \tag{7}$$

Since by (6)

$$\exp(-\frac{i}{h} H_0 t)|n> = \exp(-\frac{i}{\hbar} E_n t)|n> \tag{8}$$

it follows from the above and (7), that the most general solution of the uncontrolled Schroedinger equation is given by

$$|\phi(t)\rangle = \sum_n C_n(0)\exp(-\frac{i}{\hbar} E_n t)|n\rangle \tag{9}$$

According to the general theory

$$|C_n(0)|^2 = |\langle n|\phi(t)\rangle|^2 , \tag{10}$$

is the probability that one will find the system in state $|n\rangle|$ and $C_n(0)$ is called the probability amplitude. If $|\phi(t)\rangle|$ is normalized to unity

$$\langle\phi(t)|\phi(t)\rangle = 1 \tag{11}$$

it follows that

$$\sum_n C_n(0)|^2 = 1 , \tag{12}$$

since the probability of finding the system in same state is certain.

If we observe, according to our point of view, the controlled Schroedinger equation, we may expand the solution $|\Psi(t)\rangle$ in terms of the complete set of uncontrolled solutions, and we have

$$|\Psi(t)\rangle = \sum_n C_n(t)\exp(-\frac{i}{\hbar} E_n t)|n\rangle , \tag{13}$$

where the probability amplitude $C_n(t)$ must depend on time.

This time-dependence is introduced by the time-dependent control functions, which can modify the solutions according to our specifications. The remaining important problem is to find the $C_n(t)$ in terms of the control function entering the time-dependent Hamiltonian $H_c(t)$; this would supply a powerful tool in synthetic quantum system problems, leading to straightforward quantum engineering. Before proceeding in this direction, it is necessary to note the following two items:

a) Under the action of an outside control function, say H_c, the state of the H_0 system will undergo changes. The control H_c causes transitions among the states of the uncontrolled system; as a result, the probability amplitudes $C_n(t)$ will change with time.

b) Although the expansion (13) is valid for arbitrary H_c

unless it is small compared with H_0 the convergence of the series becomes an important problem.

Let us now find the probability amplitudes $C_n(t)$. Substituting (13) in (3) and using (6) we have

$$i\hbar \sum_n \frac{\partial C_n(t)}{\partial t} \exp(-\frac{i}{\hbar} E_n t)|n\rangle = \sum_s H_c|s\rangle \exp(-\frac{i}{\hbar} E_s t) C_s(t) \qquad (14)$$

Multiplying both sides from left by $\langle n|$, and using the orthogonality relation, we find that the expansion coefficients must satisfy the set of coupled equations,

$$i\hbar \frac{\partial C_n(t)}{\partial t} = \sum_s \langle n|H_c|s\rangle e^{i\omega_{ns} t} C_s(t) \qquad (15)$$

where $\hbar\omega_{ns} = E_n - E_s$. Equation (15) is exact and represents a set of coupled equations for the probability amplitudes $C_n(t)$. It is equivalent to the original Schroedinger equation (3).

In order to solve this equation the coefficients $C_s(t)$ in (15) may be expanded in a series

$$C_s(t) = C_s^{(0)}(t) + C_s^{(1)}(t) + C_s^{(2)}(t) + \ldots \qquad (16)$$

where $C_s^{(1)}(t)$ is of order of the coupling constant, $C_s^{(2)}$ is of order of squared coupling constant, and so on. Since the matrix element $\langle s|H_c|n\rangle$ in (15) is of order of coupling constant, if we substitute (16) into both sides of (15), we obtain set of approximate equations

$$i\hbar \frac{dC_n^{(0)}(t)}{dt} = 0 \qquad (17)$$

$$i\hbar \frac{dC_n^{(1)}(t)}{dt} = \sum_s \langle n|H_c|s\rangle e^{i\omega_{ns} t} C_s^{(0)}(t)$$

$$i\hbar \frac{dC_n^{(2)}(t)}{dt} = \sum_s \langle n|H_c|s\rangle e^{i\omega_{ns} t} C_s^{(1)}(t)$$

and so on. Each of these equations may be solved successively.

The expansion of the solution for the controlled Schroedinger equation in terms of the complete set of uncontrolled solutions, results in equivalent set of the coupled equations for the time-dependent probability amplitudes $C_n(t)$, given by (15) or (17). The time-variable coefficients in coupled equations depend, upon the transition frequencies of the system and the control function entering the Hamiltonian $H_c(t)$. It is known from the differential equations theory and control theory, that the dynamic systems given by (15) or (17) can be controlled, according to same specifications or prescriptions, by properly choosing the control functions and leading to some sort of the controlled Hamiltonian $H_c(t)$ in (15) and (17). Similar systems are well-known in classical general dynamics, and their variable changes can be optimized with respect to some criteria, using extremal principles of the calculus of variations. The controlled quantum system time development, represented by the set of the coupled equations in probability amplitudes (15) or (17), can be considered in an analogous way, as similar classical dynamic system. Because of the quantum nature, such a system is represented in terms of the probability amplitudes instead of classical state variables.

FUNCTIONAL OPTIMIZATION BY THE PONTRYAGIN MAXIMUM PRINCIPLE FOR THE QUANTUM DYNAMICAL SYSTEM DEFINED AS A SET OF COUPLED DIFFERENTIAL EQUATIONS

The first part of this paper showed, how a quantum-dynamic system can be formally reduced to the analytical representation commonly used in analysis of classical-dynamic systems. Here we shall continue the functional optimization of the quantum system development in accordance with the known control theory.

The probability amplitude vector $\vec{C}(t)$, governed by the control matrix $H_{c_{ns}}$ corresponding to the Hamiltonian H_c incorporating system control function, can be written as

$$\frac{dC_i}{dt} = f_i(\vec{C}, H_{c_{ns}}, \omega_{ns}t) \qquad i = 1,2,3,\ldots,N \qquad (18)$$

where $\omega_{ns}t$ represents the oscillation at the transition frequencies, appearing in eqs. (15) and (17).

At each moment in real physical systems, the components of the control matrix $H_{c_{ns}}$ in eq. (18) are limited to some definite magnitude by

$$a_{ns} \geq H_{c_{ns}} \geq -b_{ns} \qquad \begin{matrix} n,s = 1,2,3,\ldots,N \\ a_{ns},\ b_{ns} \geq 0 \end{matrix} \tag{19}$$

In addition to the transition frequencies ω_{ns}, on the right side of eq. (18) could be included external disturbances or noises; this complicates but does not impair the developed approach.

According to the quantum theory, the average expected value of an observable $<\bar{K}>$ corresponding to an operator K, when the system is in the state Ψ is in Dirac's notation given by

$$<\bar{K}> = <\Psi_i|K|\Psi_j> \tag{20}$$

where the integral is taken over the configuration space. In the case, that the wave function ψ can be separated into spatial and temporal part, or depends on time as in eq. (13), the result of the integration according to eq. (20) is a functional of the probability amplitudes

$$F(t) = F[C_1(t), C_2(t), C_3(t), \ldots C_n(t)] \tag{21}$$

assuming $\frac{dC_n(t)}{dt} << \frac{i}{\hbar} E_n$.

This function represents the measure of the average expected value of an observable measurement in the controlled quantum-dynamic system, defined by the set of coupled equations in probability amplitudes (15).

The evaluation of the functional (21) will be performed as a terminal control problem, reduced to the generalized mode of optimal control. A terminal control system is one which controls the variables of the system, in this particular case the probability amplitudes $C_i(t)$, to specified values at some fixed, terminal time in the future. The concept of the terminal control for probability amplitudes is based on the fact, that if the initial probability amplitudes are given, for the system described by a set of coupled differential equations in probability amplitudes (18), the future response of the system can be predicted. The desired terminal state is attained by continuous control and prediction of the terminal conditions. The quantum system (18) is controlled to the desired final value by the properly choosen control matrix $H_{c_{ns}}$. The general description of the terminal control, for the average expected value of an observable measurement, may be stated as the determination of the control matrix $H_{c_{ns}}$ such that in a given time interval T, the functional of the final probability amplitudes vector $F[\vec{C}(T)]$, is maximized. In other words, this optimum control problem requires the determination of an admissible control matrix $H_{c_{ns}}$ to make the function $F[\vec{C}(T)]$ a maximum.

Let us now introduce an additional new probability amplitude, identical with the function (21),

$$C_{N+1}(t) = F[C_1(t), C_2(t), \ldots, C_n(t), \ldots C_N(t)], \tag{22}$$

being proportional to the average expected value of the considered observable measurement eq. (20) for the controlled quantum-dynamic system eq. (18). The initial value of the N+1 probability amplitude is given by

$$C_{N+1}(0) = F[C_1(0), C_2(0), \ldots, C_n(0), \ldots, C_N(0)] \tag{23}$$

Taking the first derivative of the probability amplitude introduced by the eq. (22) with respect to t yields

$$\frac{dC_{n+1}(t)}{dt} = \frac{\partial F(\vec{C})}{\partial C_1}\frac{dC_1}{dt} + \frac{\partial F(\vec{C})}{\partial C_2}\frac{dC_2}{dt} + \ldots + \frac{\partial F(\vec{C})}{\partial C_N}\frac{dC_N}{dt} \tag{24}$$

In view of eq. (18), the rate of change of the new introduced probability amplitude representing the average expected value of the observable measurement is

$$\frac{dC_{N+1}(t)}{dt} = \sum_{i=0}^{N} \frac{F(\vec{C})}{\partial C_i} f_i(\vec{C}, H_{c_{ns}}, \omega_{ns} t) \tag{25}$$

The rates of change of other probability amplitudes, are given by eq. (18).

The terminal control of the quantum-dynamic system is now reduced to the problem of the optimization with respect to the new probability amplitude C_{N+1} at the final moment of time. We introduced, starting from eq. (20) and (21), by eq. (22) the probability amplitude C_{N+1} as proportional to the average expected value of the considered observable. The optimization with respect to the amplitude C_{N+1}, because of that, corresponds to the optimization of the particular observable measurement by the transition stimulating field entering the control matrix.

To determine the optimal transition control matrix $H_{c_{ns}}$

in (18) and (25) it is necessary to maximize the functional

$$C_{N+1}(T) = F[C_1(T), C_2(T), \ldots, C_n(T), \ldots, C_N(T)] \quad (26)$$

It is differentiable, and describes the result of the controlled observable measurement, at the end of the measurement period given by T.

The differential equations describing the augmented system after the introduction of the new variable are

$$\frac{dC_i(t)}{dt} = f_i(\vec{C}, H_{c_{ns}}, \omega_{ns}\, t) \qquad (i = 1,2,\ldots,N)$$

$$\frac{dC_{N+1}(t)}{dt} = \sum_{i=0}^{N} \frac{\partial F(\vec{C})}{\partial C_i} f_i(\vec{C}, H_{c_{ns}}, \omega_{ns}\, t) \quad (27)$$

Initial conditions

$$\vec{C}(t_0) = \vec{C}_0,\; C_{N+1}(t_0) = F_0 \quad (28)$$

define the probability amplitudes, and the average expected value of an observable measurement, at the beginning of the controlled measurement process.

The Maximum Principle of Pontryagin provides an elegant method of obtaining the optimal solution for the integral average expected value of an observable detection, as formulated in this paper.

In terms of the components of the probability amplitude vector for the augmented dynamic system (27), the Pontryagin function P may be expressed as

$$P = \sum_i A_i C_i(T) + A_{N+1} C_{N+1}(T) \qquad i = 1,2,3 \ldots N \quad (29)$$

For the augmented quantum-dynamic system given by (27), and the optimization with respect to the average expected value of an observable detection given by its variable N+1, the Pontryagin function can be reduced to

$$P = C_{N+1}(T) \quad (30)$$

supposing A_i equal to zero in (29) and A_{N+1} equal to unity.

The maximum (or minimum) principle states that, if the transition control matrix $H_{c_{ns}}$ is optimal, i.e. if it maximizes (or minimizes) the Pontryagin function (29), the corresponding criterion function defined as

$$B(\vec{C},\vec{A},H_{c_{ns}},\omega_{ns}t) = (\vec{A},\vec{f}) = \sum_i A_i f_i \qquad i = 1,2,\ldots N+1 \quad (31)$$

is to be minimized (or maximized) with respect to the control matrix $H_{c_{ns}}$, over the control interval. The vector $\vec{A}$ is an auxiliary variable in classical physical systems, ordinarily forming the product $\vec{A}\vec{f}$ with the dimension of energy.

In the discussed quantum-dynamic system, the integral average expected value of an observable measurement

$$P = C_{N+1}(T) = \int_0^T \sum_i \frac{\partial F(\vec{C})}{\partial C_i} f_i(\vec{C},H_{c_{ns}},\omega_{ns}t)\,dt \qquad (32)$$

$i = 1,2,\ldots N$

is maximized, if the corresponding criterion function written as

$$B = A_{N+1} \sum_i \frac{\partial F(\vec{C})}{\partial C_i} f_i(\vec{C},H_{c_{ns}},\omega_{ns}t) \qquad (33)$$

is minimized with respect to the components of the control matrix $H_{c_{ns}}$ equating to zero the derivatives

$$\frac{\partial B}{\partial H_{c_{ns}}} = 0 \qquad (34)$$

The components of the probability amplitude vector $\vec{C}$ and the components of the auxiliary vector $\vec{A}$ are evaluated from the canonical equations

$$\dot{C}_i = \frac{\partial B}{\partial A_i} \qquad (35a)$$

$$i = 1,2,\ldots,N$$

$$\dot{A}_i = -\frac{\partial B}{\partial C_i} \qquad (35b)$$

From the formulae (32), (33), (34), (35a) and (35b) it is evident that the control matrix is defined by the properties of the function $F(\vec{C})$ that includes the effect of the operator corresponding to a particular observable measurement and the dynamic properties of the quantum system given by the set of coupled differential equations in probability amplitudes. In fact, the movement of the probability amplitudes vector is controlled in such a way that the integral of the average expected value of an observable measurement is maximized.

CONCLUSION

The aim of the present paper is to introduce functional optimization for dynamic systems, including quantum physical elements, starting from the defined performances. The *Pontryagin Maximum Principle* is applied for this purpose, in the cases where the dynamics of the controlled system are defined by the Schroedinger equation. The optimal control functions for quantum-dynamic systems are determined by variational calculus methods, starting from the prescribed integral probabilistic performances and probabilistic quantum system response to control functions, defined by the time-dependent Schroedinger equation. This equation is approximated by a finite set of differential equations in probability amplitudes defining the dynamics of the probability amplitudes change.

The time development of the quantum system, given by the state vector transformation is determined by the dynamics of the differential equations in probability amplitudes. The perturbational functions, appearing in this set as part of the Hamiltonian of the system, determine the solutions for the probability amplitudes. This process is equivalent to the introduction of control functions in quantum-mechanical interactions, effecting the optimal performance on the basis of the *Pontryagin Maximum Principle*. The functional optimization for controlled classical-dynamic systems, given by a set of differential equations in classical variables, is extended by the functional optimization for controlled quantum-dynamic systems, given by a set of differential equations in probability amplitudes.

REFERENCES

1. L. BRILLOUIN, *Science and Information Theory* (Academic Press Inc., New York 1956).

2. V.M. FAIN and Ya.I. KHANIN, *Quantum Electronics* (Pergamon Press, London 1969).

3. D. BELL and A.W. GRIFFIN, *Modern Control Theory* (McGraw Hill, London 1969).

MEASUREMENT AND CYBERNETICS

L. FINKELSTEIN

Instrument Systems Centre, Department of Systems and Automation, The City University, St. John Street, London EC 1, England

SUMMARY

This paper discusses one principal aspect of the problem, namely the relation of the basic concepts of measurement to that of information as it is understood in cybernetics. It is shown that the concepts of measurement and information are closely related.

INTRODUCTION AND SCOPE OF PAPER

This paper outlines certain principal points from an oral presentation on the above subject presented at the Congress.

Cybernetics, being concerned with information should, of course, consider fundamental problems of measurement. However, the philosophy of measurement is not treated in the literature of cybernetics and is not known to many cyberneticians. The presentation attempted to review the basic concepts of measurement, and to draw them to the attention of an audience working in the field of cybernetics. However, the limitations of length imposed on the written papers, prevent the review from being reproduced here.

The survey was based on material from a lecture course by the author, not available in published form. Some references on the subject are listed at the end and will constitute a good introduction to the problems, as well as providing extensive bibliographies.

This paper will thus confine itself to discussing one principal aspect of the presentation: The relation of the basic concepts of measurement to the concept of information as it is understood in cybernetics. However, some familiarity with the philosophy of measurement is presupposed.

DEFINITION OF MEASUREMENT

Measurement [1,2,3] can be defined as the assignment of numbers to conceptual entities in such a way as to describe them.

The basis of measurement is a concept which defines a class of entities, by means of a rule which determines by an examination of attributes whether or not an entity belongs to a given class. Thus measurement of force, for example, is based on a definition of force as that which changes, or tends to change, the motion of a body.

Consider now Q, a set of extra-mathematical entities defined as above. Let N be a set of numbers, defined as a set of symbols with a structure or set of relations defined on it. Measurement is a mapping procedure M which assigns to every $q_i \in Q$ one, and only one, element $n_i \in N$, such that relations on Q are formally similar to relations on N.

The majority of writers on the philosophy of measurement consider measurement as the descriptive assignment of real numbers only. In consequence they are concerned with the analysis of the necessary and sufficient conditions for the establishment of a correspondence between a class of extra-mathematical entities and the empirical relations on them, and the set of real numbers and a structure defined on it. The writers require that a measure should be a quantitative description of an entity, involving relations of "greater than" and "less than" with respect to other entities of the same kind, as well as a notion of "distance" between entities.

However, it is suggested here that this is too restrictive. The basic function of measurement is to provide a precise and concise description of an entity in mathematical form. Any mapping which assigns the same element of a set of symbols to all entities of the same kind which are indistinguishable from each other, and never assigns the same element of the symbol set to distinguishable entities, constitutes measurement.

Given such a procedure of assignment of symbols to entities to describe them, facts and conventions about the entity can be expressed in the formal language of mathematics.

INFORMATION

Cybernetics is concerned with information in many kinds of systems. In a galvanometer the angular deflection of the movement carries information about the current being measured; in a speech communication system an electric waveform carries information about words spoken into the receiver; in language a word carries information about a concept; in an animal organism nerve impulse frequency carries information about stimuli to a sensor.

Each of these cases is an illustration of a general concept of information. Let S be a set of entities (e.g. symbols or states of a physical variable) termed signals, let Q be some set of messages and let C be a mapping of Q to S which may be termed a code. Then given an element $s \in S$ together with the code C, we know the corresponding elements of Q. We can say that S and C carry information about Q.

In general, the mapping C may be many to many. In human language, the same word may correspond to a number of concepts and the same concept may be expressed by a number of words. In an on-off thermostat there are generally only two output states of the thermometer element, one corresponding to all the temperatures below the desired value and the other to those above; an example of many to one mapping.

The precision of the label provided by a signal $s_i \in S$ depends on the sizes of Q_i the subset of Q which is mapped into s_i relative to the size of Q. The smaller Q_i relative to Q the more precise the information.

In information carrying systems it is commonly required that C should be a one to one mapping, as for example in the case of the relation between galvanometer current and deflection.

It is often required that the mapping C should be structure preserving so that relations between signals s_i, $s_j \in S$ represent the relation between the corresponding messages q_i, $q_j \in Q$. However, this is not an essential feature of an information system.

4. COMPARISON BETWEEN INFORMATION AND MEASUREMENT

It will be seen that the concepts of measurement and information as defined here are closely related.

A measure is a particular form of information about an entity, a number n together with the mapping M carrying information about the measurand q.

Information is a more general concept, since, as illustrated, there are other ways of carrying information than in the form of numbers, even when number is as generally defined as in the present paper.

Measures have also the property that relations between measures represent relations between corresponding measurands (even if only the relation of identity and difference). This is not necessarily true of other forms of information carrying signal.

REFERENCES

1. L. FINKELSTEIN, "Principles of measurement" *Trans. Soc. Instr. Technol.*, 181-189 (September, 1963). (Read at a meeting of the Society of Instrument Technology, 26th March 1963).

2. B. ELLIS, *Basic Concepts of Measurement* (Cambridge University Press, Cambridge, 1968).

3. J. PFANZAGL, *Theory of Measurement* (Physica-Verlag, Würzburg-Vienna, 1968).

ENGINEERING AND MEDICAL APPLICATIONS OF STATISTICAL DATA REDUCTION TECHNIQUES

F. CSÁKI AND B. SZÜCS

Department of Automation, Technical University, Budapest, Hungary,

and

E. MONOS

Experimental Research Department, Semmelweiss Medical University, Budapest, Hungary.

SUMMARY

Two applications of statistical identification methods of control systems are described: One is taken from the engineering field, the other from the physiological field. Proposals of length of the observation period and that of stationarity test of stochastic signals are presented. An appendix contains the theoretical bases used in the presented applications.

INTRODUCTION

In science and engineering one of the fundamental problems is the identification of processes and systems. The analysis of systems used to be performed, for sake of simplicity, by assuming inputs of predetermined regular course. The inputs of physical and physiological systems, however, show in reality random variations, and may only be described in a statistical manner. For these so-called stochastic processes the analysis of systems may be realized, though with certain limitations [1].

Statistical techniques for practical calculation of signal-structures and dynamic relationships of variables in engineering and biological systems are becoming of increasing importance now that low-cost computing facilities are available. Comparing the computed statistical characteristics obtained from repeated measuring series, practical problems of observation period and stationarity are discussed.

OBSERVATION PERIOD AND STATIONARITY

In theoretical statistical investigations the stationarity of the processes is generally assumed. But, in practice, the statistical characteristics of signals of technical and biological systems can undergo essential alterations.

The changes of statistical characteristics (correlation functions, spectra, means and mean square values, etc.) determined for real processes by computation are due not only to the instationarity of the process or signal under examination but also to the shortness of the observation period (OP).

For stationary signals a simple approximate connection can be given to determine the necessary observation period [2]. On the basis of the desired maximal error $\varepsilon(\%)$ the averaging time constant T (Sec) can be determined in dependence of the low boundary frequency f_{min} (Hz) of the signal to be investigated. The necessary observation period T_0 (Sec) should be at least double of T:

$$T_0 \geq 2T \geq \frac{2}{0.01\ \varepsilon f_{min}}$$

If an averaging time constant, which ensures the desired accuracy of the computation, is applied, the instationarity of the signal, during an essentially longer OP than is necessary, can be quantitatively described by the value of the observed changes in the computed statistical characteristics.

In the case of simpler systems optional statistical characteristics can be chosen for the stationarity test. For example, changes of the variance curves of vertical vibration accelerations measured in a bus running on concrete road are shown in Fig. 1. In this case the signals excited by the stochastic road-profile undergo similar alterations statistically.

In the study of complex processes it is more useful to examine simultaneously the formation of some statistical characteristics. Besides, the changes of a given statistical characteristic, dervied from different, simultaneously observed signals of the system under test, can demonstrate various tendencies, as is shown in Fig. 2. The variance of pulsatile pressures measured in the ascending aorta, iliac artery and right atrium and that of pulsatile flow obtained in the iliac artery of a dog (see Table I) exhibit different kinds of changes. The periods marked by shaded areas may be regarded as stationary.

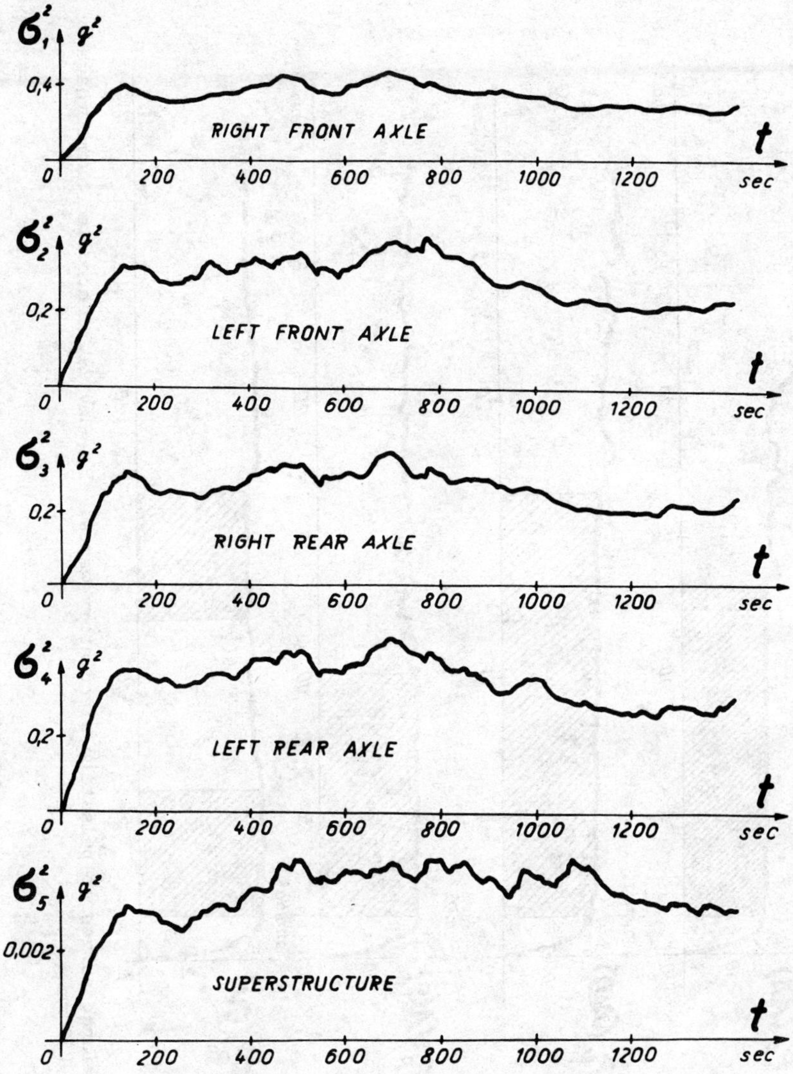

Fig. 1. Variance changes in vertical accelerations measured in a running bus. Averaging time constant T = 80 sec.

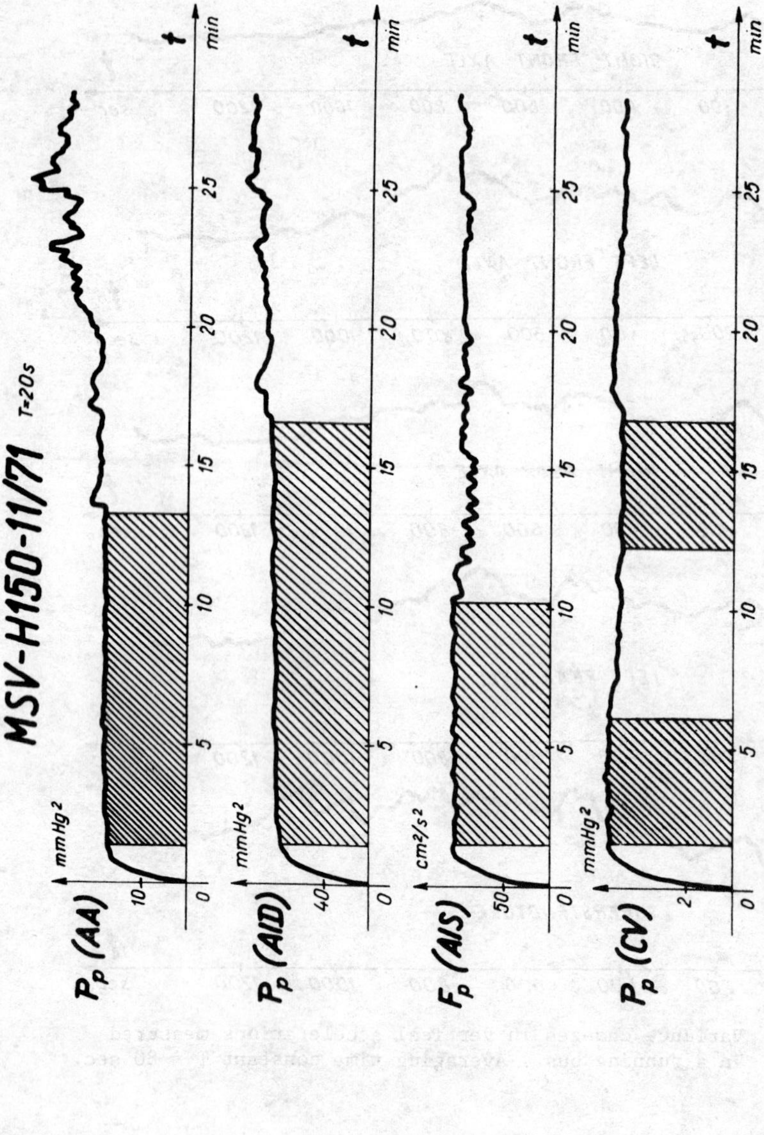

Fig. 2. Variance curves of pulsatile circulatory waves. Dog No. 11, controlled haemorrhage at 150 mmHg.

TABLE I. Variance Values Obtained on Dog. No. 11

Measured pulsatile signal	Variance of component	Arterial mean pressure level, mmHg							
		Normo-tension	Bleeding					Reinfusion	
		155	150	130	110	90	70	120	150
Pressure in ascending aorta, $P_p(AA)$	periodic (mmHg)	16.8	11.6	14.6	17.4	7.6	28.3	35.5	65
	stochastic	27.8	12.5	15.7	19	23	23.7	26.2	45
Pressure in right iliac artery, $P_p(AID)$	periodic (mmHg)	49.3	33.6	50	55	21.3	99	131	161
	stochastic	112	70	57	69	123	69	99	113
Flow in left iliac artery, $F_p(AIS)$	periodic (cm /s)	64	46	59	46.5	not measured			
	stochastic	139	74	84	114				
Pressure in right atrium $P_p(CV)$	periodic (mmHg)	3.33	3.59	3.69	4.28	4.31	7.68	4.8	3.4
	stochastic	3.11	2.93	1.39	2.76	6.88	3.95	2.0	4.3

STATISTICAL NATURE OF PULSATILE CIRCULATORY WAVES

Stochastic influences of the internal and external environment belong to the important but not often studied problems of physiology. Stochastic components contained in different circulatory variables may be characteristic of the stress effect suffered by the cardiovascular system (CVS), or they may even show the ability of the system to eliminate disturbances. As it was shown earlier, statistical methods of control engineering might be properly applied for studying dynamics of the CVS [3,4].

In the course of present study the signal-structure of pulsatile blood pressure and flow waves has been analysed in graded hypotension by steps of 20 mm Hg. The experiments were performed on anaesthetised dogs. The schematic diagram of experimental set-up is presented in Fig. 3. The blood pressure was measured in the ascending aorta, right iliac artery and right atrium with Statham inductive transducers. For measuring the velocity of the blood flow in the left iliac artery a Ward ultrasonic flow meter was used. The analogue electrical signals were recorded by a Hottinger instrument tape-recorder. At each mean pressure level stabilized by a buffer reservoir system, an observation period of 30 min duration was applied after the transient elicited by the bleeding off. Based upon general properties of the measured signals in the frequency domain, every single pulsatile component was automatically separated during playback from the magnetic tape. The structure analysis of signals was performed by autocorrelation functions (ACF), computed by a SAIP real-time correlator with twentyfold time compression.

As an example, a typical ACF determined from the pulsatile pressure component measured in right iliac artery is shown in Fig. 4. For large shifting times τ the ACF varies periodically with the frequency of pulse and of respiration and the variance of periodic components can be read. The sum of variances of periodic and of stochastic components can be found at $\tau = 0$. The variance of stochastic signal components as compared to the total variance of pulsatile waves, is demonstrated in Fig. 5 for different arterial mean pressure levels. Table I contains the same variance values expressed in real dimension.

It can be established that the pulsatile changes in blood pressure and flow, known as the most regular periodic processes in the organism, contain very significant stochastic components showing considerable variety in dependence of mean arterial pressure. The stochastic component is the smallest in the physiological range (about 110-130 mm Hg) of the baroceptor

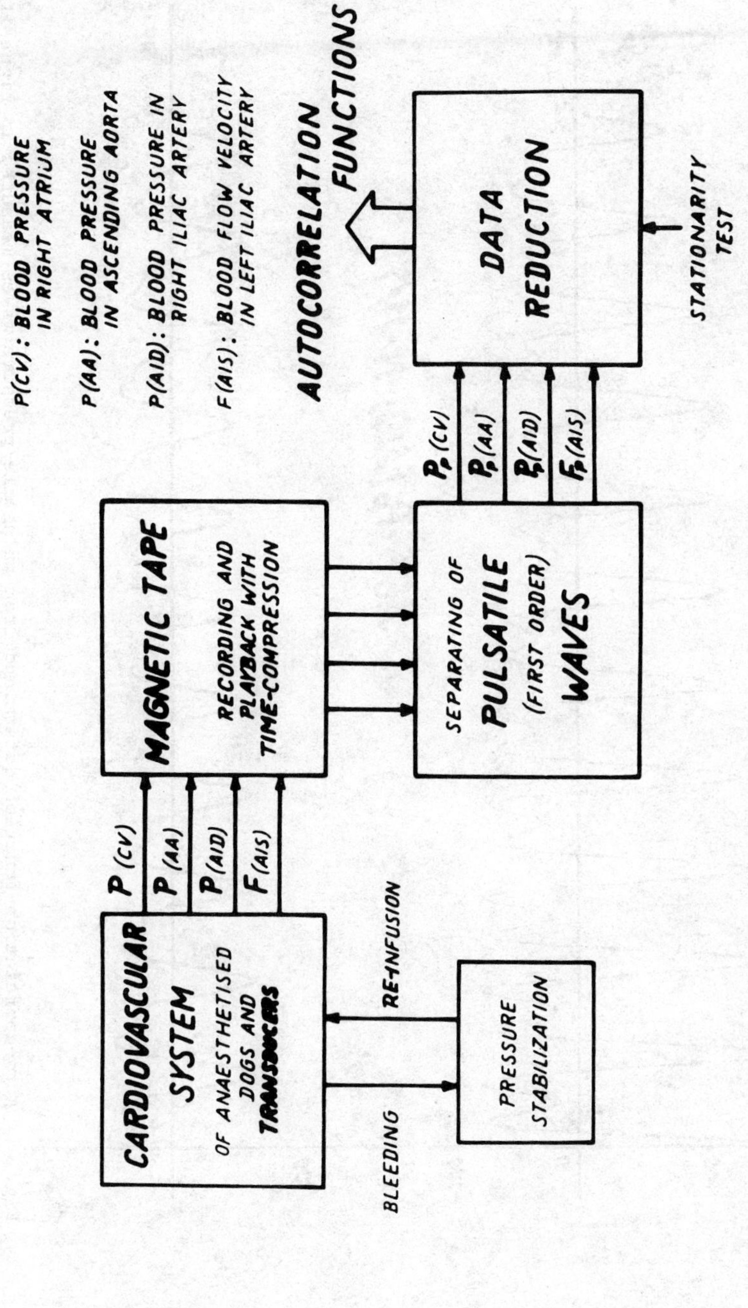

Fig. 3. Schematic diagram of measurement and computation of the circulatory variables

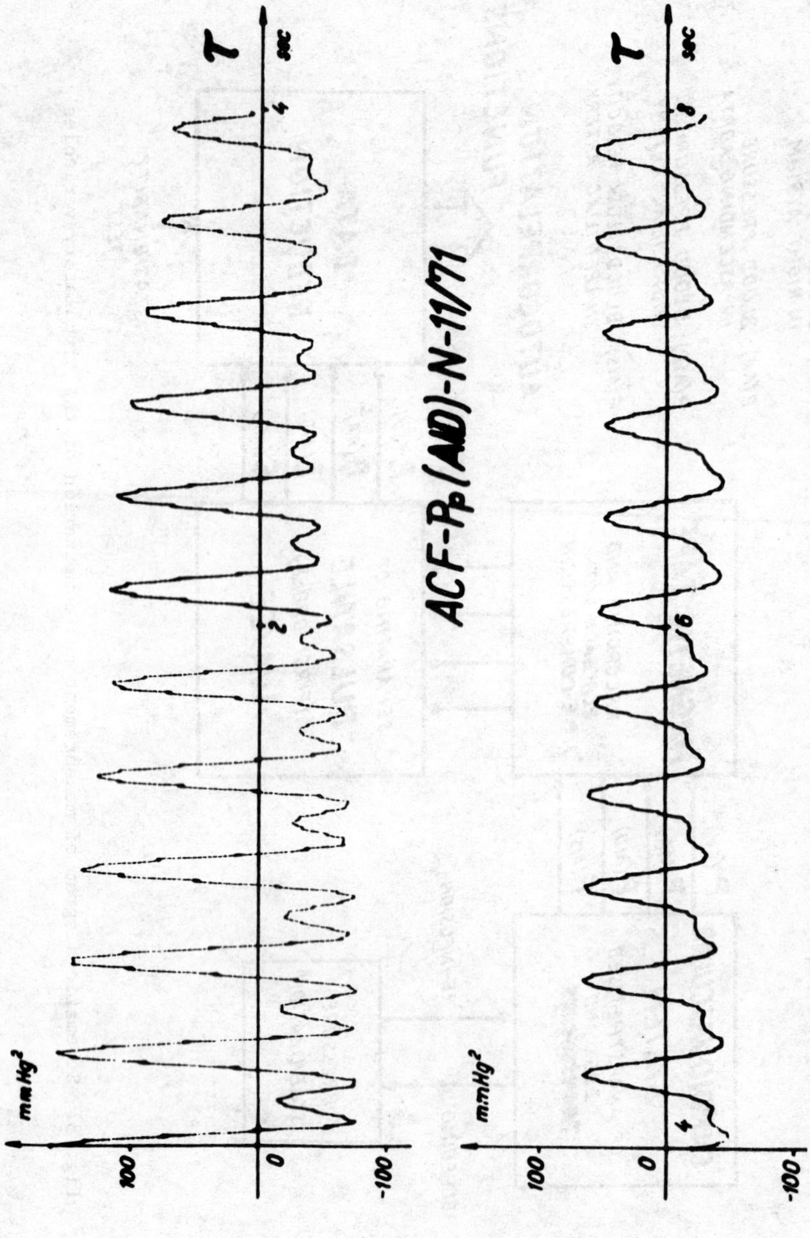

Fig. 4. Auto-correlation function determined from pulsatile pressure waves measured in right iliac artery. Dog No. 11, normotension

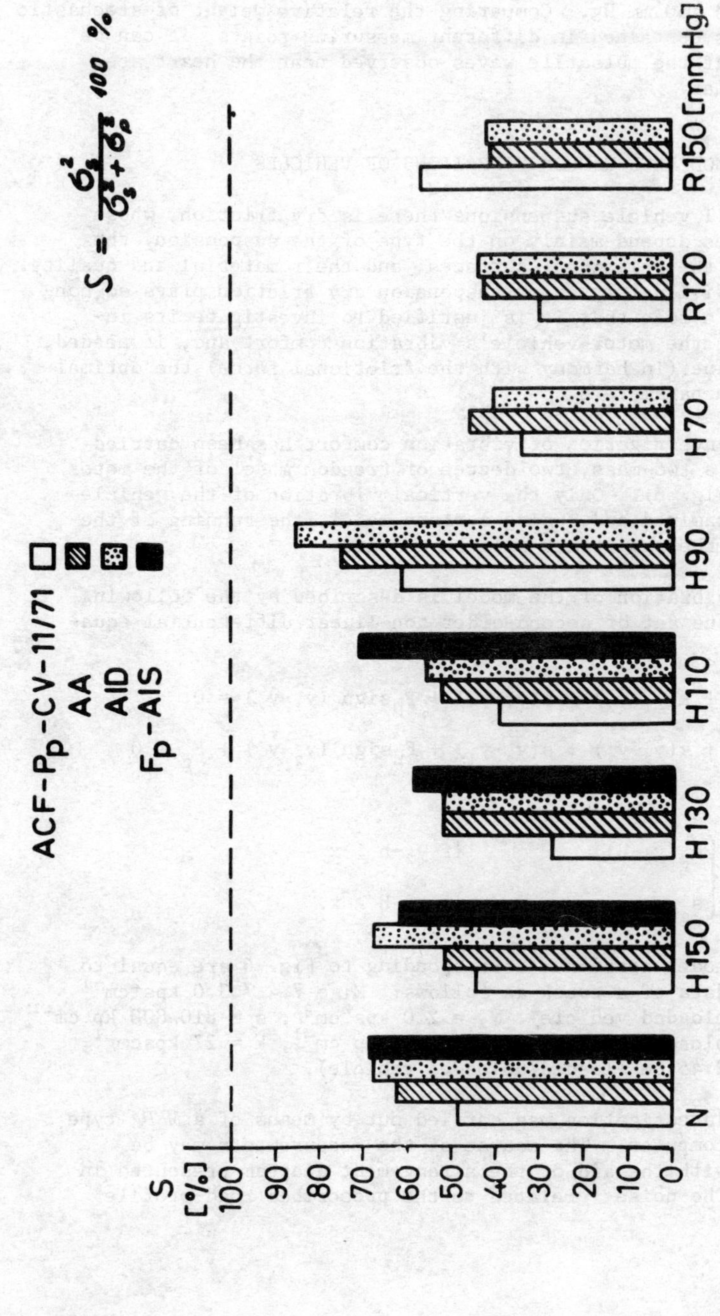

Fig. 5. Relative variance of stochastic signal components manifested in pulsatile circulatory waves. Dog No. 11

control operating mainly in the mean arterial pressure range from 90 to 150 mm Hg. Comparing the relative weight of stochastic components contained in different measuring points, it can be stated that the pulsatile waves observed near the heart are more regular.

COMPUTER-MODELLED RANDOM VIBRATIONS OF VEHICLES

In all vehicle suspensions there is dry friction, whose effect does depend mainly on the type of the suspension, the number of the frictional surfaces, and their material and quality. In the individual types of suspension dry friction plays so considerable a role that it is justified to investigate its influence on the motor-vehicle's vibration comfort and, if needed, to determine (in harmony with the frictional force) the optimal suspension parameters.

The investigation of vibration comfort has been carried out using a two-mass, two degree of freedom model of the motor vehicle (Fig. 6). Only the vertical vibration of the vehicle will be examined and, using a plane model, the running of the wheels on the same track will be assumed.

The vibration of the model is described by the following simultaneous set of second-order non-linear differential equations:

$$M_1\ddot{y}_1 + k(\dot{y}_1-\dot{y}_2) + s(y_1-y_2) + F_\mu \text{sign}\,(\dot{y}_1-\dot{y}_2) = 0$$

$$M_2\ddot{y}_2 + k(\dot{y}_2-\dot{y}_1) + s(y_2-y_1) + F_\mu \text{sign}\,(\dot{y}_2-\dot{y}_1) + F_g = 0$$

where

$$F_g = \begin{cases} s_g(y_2-h), & \text{if } y_2-h \leqq x \\ s_g x, & \text{if } y_2-h > x. \end{cases}$$

The model constants corresponding to Fig. 6 are equal to the real data of a truck as follows: $M_1 = 7.4\ /\ 3.0$ kps^{2}cm^{-1} (loaded/unloaded vehicle), $M_2 = 2.0$ kps^{2}cm^{-1}, $s = 810/800$ kp cm^{-1} (loaded/unloaded vehicle), $s_g = 2000$ kp cm^{-1}, $k = 27$ kpscm^{-1}, $x = 4.65/2.45$ cm (loaded/unloaded vehicle).

The investigation was carried out by means of a *MEDA* type analogue computer. The course of the measurements may be followed with the aid of the arrangement diagram presented in Fig. 7. The noise — related to the prescribed road-profile

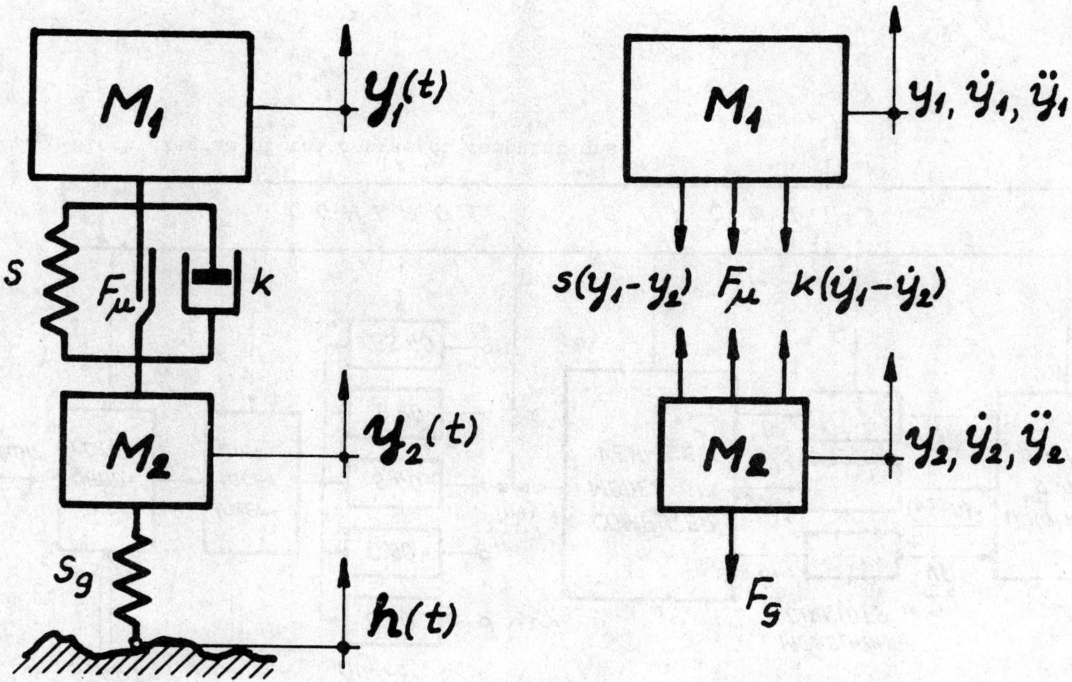

Fig. 6. Vibration model of a motor vehicle suspension with two degrees of freedom

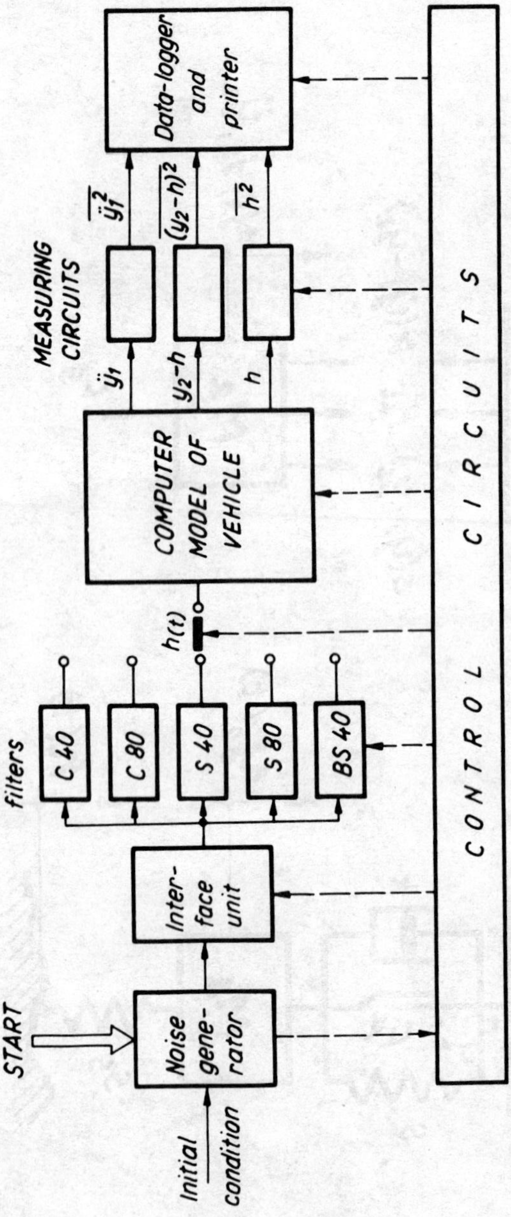

Fig. 7. Block diagram of the course of computations

filters by an interface unit of automatic mean-value compensation. The model may be excited by a road-profie analogue signal h(t) selected from among 5 possibilities corresponding to Table II.

TABLE II. Data of Road-Profiles

Road-type and running speed	$S_h(j\omega)$ Power-density spectrum, $(cm^2 s)$	σ_h Standard deviation of the profile, (cm)
Concrete 40 km/h	$\frac{0.91}{1+0.36\omega^2}$	0.87
Concrete, 80 km/h	$\frac{0.455}{1+0.09\omega^2}$	0.87
Stony, 40 km/h	$\frac{1.30}{1+0.04\omega^2}$	1.81
Stony, 80 km/h	$\frac{0.653}{1+0.01\omega^2}$	1.81
Bad stony, 40 km/h	$\frac{1.95}{1+0.032\omega^2} + \frac{0.00854(1+0.002\omega^2)}{1-0.0039\omega^2+4.10^{-6}\omega^4}$	2.52

After selecting the road-type and setting the vehicle parameters on the model, the noise generator was started and the measurement was carried out automatically by means of control circuits attached to the computer. The sequence is as follows: When starting the noise generator, the road-profile filters are set in "compute" position, then after a period of 10 s the already stationary signal h(t) is connected to the input of the model and at the same time the measurement devices are also started. The duration of the measurement section is $T_0 = 40$ s, which represents at a speed of 80 km/h a distance traveled of about 880 m. At the end of this period the control circuit brings the computer into "hold" position and the results are read out. By pressing the initial condition button of the noise generator the whole system is brought into the starting-state, and after setting another parameter combination the subsequent measurement is carried out in the same way as described above. Direct control of the measuring process by means of only two press-buttons considerably reduces the possibility of mistakes.

In the course of the studies, the evaluation has been carried out with the following widely used vibration-comfort indicators:

1) $\sigma^2_{\ddot{y}_1}$, the variance of the vertical vibration accelerations of the sprung mass (superstructure),

2) $\sigma^2_{(y_2-h)}$, the variance of the displacement of the unsprung mass relative to the ground,

3) $S_{\ddot{y}_1}(j\omega)$, the power-density spectrum of the acceleration of the sprung mass.

Though the detailed discussion from the vehicle technology point of view is beyond the scope of this paper, the description of some results [5] may be of interest.

The comfort of an unloaded vehicle — independently of the road quality — will be considerably worsened due to the frictional force (Fig. 8). For a loaded motor vehicle dry friction improves the comfort up to a certain extent. For a loaded vehicle running on a stony road of good or bad quality the optimum frictional force is about 900 kp and a 20% decrease of the acceleration variance can be reached (Fig. 8). With an increase of the frictional force beyond the optimum value comfort will decrease. At a given frictional force ($F\mu \sim 2000$ kp) the acceleration variance will again be around the level corresponding to the $F\mu = 0$. It appears that the given frictional force would not have any effect on comfort.

By comparing the acceleration-power density spectra computed for $F\mu = 0$ and for $F\mu = 2000$ kp (Fig. 9) of the loaded motor vehicle running on a bad stony road, it will, however, be clear, that due to dry friction vibration comfort will be worsened. At the frictional force of $F\mu = 2000$ kp a second resonance peak will be formed in the power density spectrum at about 3.8 Hz, and these vibrations will be less bearable by the human organism. In consequence of the high frictional force vibrations of the unsprung mass can be significantly transferred to the superstructure without considerable damping.

Finally, it is to be noted that the applied hybrid-like computing method has proved very economical in comparison with digital computer simulation and with a great number of equivalent highway instrumental investigations, because financial expenditure is about a sixth of those of others.

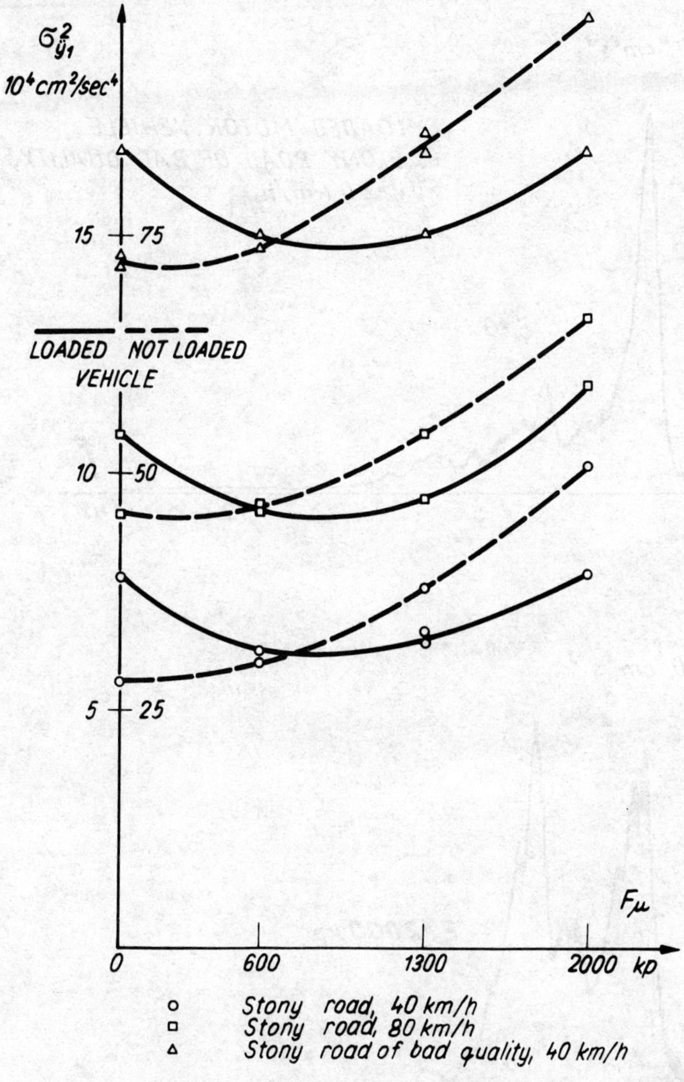

Fig. 8. Acceleration variance curves of a motor vehicle's superstructure, running on stony roads

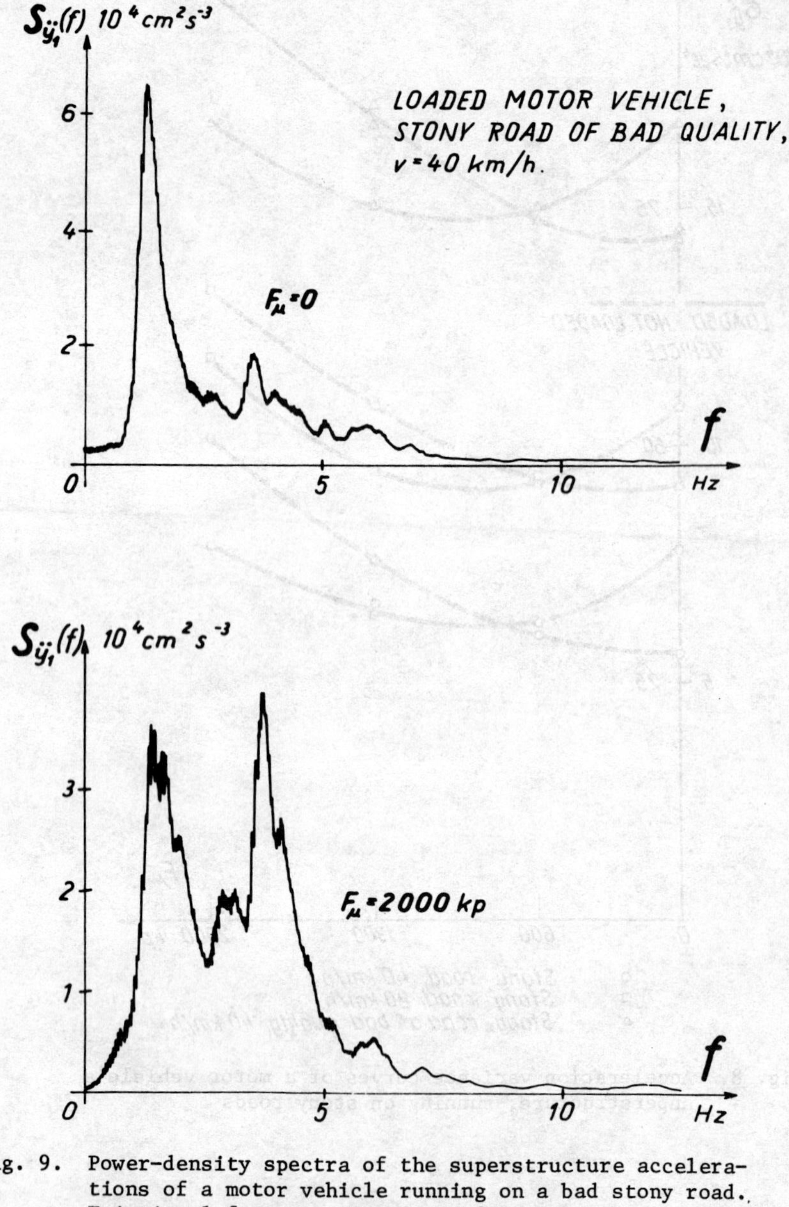

Fig. 9. Power-density spectra of the superstructure accelerations of a motor vehicle running on a bad stony road. Frictional forces: Fμ = 0 and 2000 kp.

APPENDIX

For a stationary process x(t), by the aid of time average, the definition of the autocorrelation function (ACF) is:

$$\phi_{xx}(\tau) = \lim_{T\to\infty} \frac{1}{2T} \int_{-T}^{T} x(t)x(t+\tau)dt = \overline{x(t)x(t+\tau)}$$

If the stochastic signal has zero mean value $\overline{x(t)} = 0$, then the ACF at zero time displacement ($\tau=0$) is equal to the variance of x(t):

$$\phi_{xx}(0) = \overline{x^2(t)} = \sigma_x^2.$$

If x(t) includes a periodic component

$$x(t) = a(t) + b\cos(\omega t+\Theta)$$

then

$$\phi_{xx}(\tau) = \phi_{aa}(\tau) + \frac{b^2}{2}\cos\omega\tau,$$

and the ACF varies periodically also for large values of τ.

According to the so-called *WIENER-HINTSIN* relations,

$$\phi_{xx}(\tau) = \frac{1}{2\pi} \int_{-\infty}^{+\infty} S_{xx}(j\omega)\exp(j\omega\tau)d\omega$$

and the variance of x(t) may be obtained from its power-density spectrum $S_{xx}(j\omega)$ after substituting $\tau = 0$:

$$\sigma_x^2 = \frac{1}{2\pi} \int_{-\infty}^{+\infty} S_{xx}(j\omega)d\omega.$$

Based upon the relationship between the power-density spectra of input signal x(t) and output signal y(t) of a linear system with transfer function W(s),

$$S_{yy}(j\omega) = |W(j\omega)|^2 S_{xx}(j\omega),$$

the transfer function of road-profile filters can be determined.

REFERENCES

1. F. CSÁKI, "Application of statistical techniques in science and technology" *Proc. JUREMA, Zagreb*, 51-64 (1971).

2. B. SZÜCS and F. CSÁKI, "On evaluation of statistical characteristics of stochastic signals" *Preprints of the V. IMEKO Congress, D-TH-25* (1970).

3. B. SZÜCS and E. MONOS, "Circulatory system analysis by a stochastic method using an analogue correlator" *Int. J. Bio-Medical Computing, 1*, 87-102 (1970).

4. B. SZÜCS, E. MONOS and F. CSÁKI, "On a method for identification of the cardiovascular system" *Preprints of 2nd Prague IFAC Symposium, 1970, 2.11.5*, (1970).

5. L. ILOSVAI and B. SZÜCS, "Random vehicle vibrations as effected by dry friction in wheel suspensions", *Vehicle System Dynamics, 1*, 197-209 (1972).

ON THE LEARNING BEHAVIOR OF FUZZY AUTOMATA

G.A. WONG and D.W.C. SHEN

Moore School of Electrical Engineering, University of Pennsylvania, Philadelphia, Pa. 19104, U.S.A.

SUMMARY

The learning behavior of a fuzzy automaton operating in a random environment is reflected by its variable structure via a reinforcement scheme. Linear and nonlinear reinforcement algorithms are employed to vary directly the membership function of the state. Convergence properties of these reinforcement schemes are studied. Conditions for the fuzzy automata to achieve optimal behavior are also derived. The application of a fuzzy automaton for solving parameter optimization problems is discussed and simulation results verify the theoretical predictions.

INTRODUCTION

A fuzzy automaton owes its origin to the fuzzy set theory introduced by Zadeh [1]. The mathematical formulation of a fuzzy automaton was given by Wee and Fu [2]. When a fuzzy automaton is used as a model of learning systems, the elements of the fuzzy state transition matrix are varied via a linear reinforcement scheme [2,3]. In this manner, the fuzzy automaton exhibits a variable structure. In this paper, we modify the membership function of the state directly. The advantages are computational economy and analytical convenience. For the situation of a 2-state fuzzy automaton operating in a random environment that yields either penalty or reward, its learning efficiency in terms of optimality is examined in detail. Certain classes of linear and nonlinear reinforcement schemes for changing the automaton structure are considered. Finally, the fuzzy automaton is used to solve the parameter optimization problems on line. The objective is to find the parameter value that maximizes the expected value of a noisy multimodal performance function. Simulation studies are carried out to verify the theoretical analysis.

FINITE FUZZY AUTOMATA

A finite fuzzy automaton can be described by a quintuple [2] [X, S, Y, f, g] where

X: a set of inputs $(x_1, x_2, \ldots, x_q)$

S: a set of states $(s_1, s_2, \ldots, s_n)$

Y: a set of outputs $(y_1, y_2, \ldots, y_r)$

f: membership function that maps (X,S,S) into closed interval (0,1)

g: membership function that maps (S,Y) into closed interval (0,1)

The above is a formulation of the Moore type of fuzzy automata. Usually the membership functions f and g are represented by transition matrices $Q_t(x_\ell)$ and G_t, respectively. When the input at time t is x_ℓ, the elements of the fuzzy state transition matrix $Q_t(x_\ell)$ is given by $f_{ij}{}^{\ell}(t)$ where

$$f_{ij}^{\ell}(t) = f[x(t) = x_\ell,\ s(t) = s_i,\ s(t+1) = s_j] \tag{1}$$

Similarly, the element of the output fuzzy matrix G_t at time t is given by

$$g_{ij}(t) = g[s(t) = s_i,\ y(t) = y_j] \tag{2}$$

It should be noted that f and g are membership functions of fuzzy sets in the spaces (X,S,S) and (S,Y), respectively. To be strictly correct, subscripts denoting the particular fuzzy sets should be attached to f and g in eqs. (1) and (2) but they are omitted for notational simplicity.

BEHAVIOR OF THE LEARNING FUZZY AUTOMATON IN A RANDOM ENVIRONMENT

In the application of fuzzy automata as models of learning systems [2], the elements of the fuzzy transition matrix $Q_t(x_\ell)$ are changed according to a linear reinforcement scheme. Here we modify the membership function of the state.

At time t, suppose that the fuzzy automaton is in state s_i with grade of membership $f_i(t)$,

$$f_i(t) = f[s(t) = s_i]$$

the elements of the fuzzy state transition matrix are given by $f_{ij}^{\ell}(t)$. If the input to the automaton is x_{ℓ}, then the grade of membership of next state is given by [1]

$$f_k(t+1) = \mathrm{Max}_i \min[f_i(t),\ f_{ik}^{\ell}(t)] \tag{3}$$

Similarly, the grade of membership of the output at t + 1 is

$$g[y(t+1) = y_m] = \mathrm{Max}_k \min[g_{km}(t+1),\ f_k(t+1)] \tag{4}$$

Therefore, the modification of $f_{ij}^{\ell}(t)$ or $f_i(t)$ affects the input-output characteristic of the fuzzy automaton. The modification of the state membership function is preferred since there are only n states whereas the modification of f_{ij}^{ℓ} involves $n \times n$ elements. In addition, the former is more convenient to deal with analytically. It is interesting to note that in the learning section of the learning system in reference 2, a composite fuzzy automaton is needed for the convergence of the learning algorithm. If the state membership function is modified rather than f_{ij}^{ℓ}, convergence is easily obtained and the composite fuzzy automaton is unnecessary.

The fuzzy automaton is assumed to have two states and the states are mapped one-to-one to its outputs. At time t, if $f_k(t) \geq f_j(t)$, y_k is the output of the automaton as well as the input to the random environment. A penalty $x(t) = 1$ occurs at the output of the environment with probability p_k, and reward $x(t) = 0$ with probability $1-p_k$. This output of the environment is then incorporated into a reinforcement scheme to change the structure of automaton by modifying its state membership function. The performance of the automaton in the random environment is the asymtotic average penalty, denoted by M^*. If $M^* \triangleq \lim_{t\to\infty} E[x(t)] = \mathrm{Min}(p_1, p_2)$, then the automaton is optimal. Finally, certain linear and nonlinear reinforcement schemes used in stochastic automata [5,6,7] are considered below:

A) Linear reward and punishment reinforcement scheme

Assume the state is s_i

$$\begin{aligned} f_i(t+1) &= af_i(t) + (1-a)\ [1-x(t)] \\ f_j(t+1) &= af_j + (1-a)\ x(t), \text{ for } j \neq i \end{aligned} \tag{5}$$

where $0 < a < 1$

For steady-state situation, the asymtotic expected value of the state membership function satisfies the Martingale equations.

That is,

$$\Delta f_i = E[f_i(t+1)/F(t)] - f_i(t) = 0 \qquad i = 1, 2 \tag{6}$$

where F(t) stands for the vector $[f_1(t), f_2(t)]$

$$\begin{aligned} E[f_1(t+1)/F(t)] &= af_1(t)\ P[s(t) = s_1,\ x(t) = 1] \\ &+ [af_1(t) + (1-a)]\ P[s(t) = s_1,\ x(t) = 0] \\ &+ [af_1(t) + (1-a)]\ P[s(t) = s_2,\ x(t) = 1] \\ &+ af_1(t)\ P[s(t) = s_2,\ x(t) = 0] \end{aligned} \tag{7}$$

but

$$\begin{aligned} P[s(t) = s_1,\ x(t) = 1] &= P[x(t) = 1/s(t) = s_1]\ P[s(t) = s_1] \\ &= p_1\ P[f_1(t) \gtrsim f_2(t)] \end{aligned} \tag{8}$$

From eq. (5) it is noted that

$$f_1(t) + f_2(t) = 1 \tag{9}$$

Substituting eq.(9) into eq.(8) we obtain

$$P[x(t) = 1,\ s(t) = s_1] = p_1\ P[f_1 \gtrsim \tfrac{1}{2}] \tag{10}$$

The other probability terms in eq.(9) can be obtained in similar manner and Δf_1 becomes

$$\Delta f_1 = (1-a)\ \{-\ f_1 + p_2 + (1-p_1-p_2)\ P[f_1(t) \gtrsim \tfrac{1}{2}]\} \tag{11}$$

Similarly,

$$\Delta f_2 = (1-a)\ \{-\ f_2 + p_1 + (1-p_1-p_2)\ P[f_2(t) \gtrsim \tfrac{1}{2}]\} \tag{12}$$

Discounting the case in which the solutions to the Martingale equations ($f_1{}^*$ and $f_2{}^*$) are equal, $f_1{}^*$ is either greater than ½ or less than ½. Therefore two possible solutions for $f_1{}^*$ could exist. Once $f_1{}^*$ is calculated, $f_2{}^*$ can be found directly from the normality condition of eq. (9).

Solution 1) $f_1{}^* > \frac{1}{2}$

from $\Delta f_1 = 0$, $f_1{}^* = 1-p_1 > \frac{1}{2}$, which means that the restriction on p_1 is that $p_1 < \frac{1}{2}$.

Therefore,

$(f_1{}^*, f_2{}^*) = (1-p_1, p_1)$

The overall performance of the automaton is calculated by

$$M^* = \lim_{t\to\infty} E[x(t+1)]$$

$$= \lim_{t\to\infty} \sum_{i=1}^{2} P[x(t+1) = 1/s(t) = s_i]\, P[f_i^* > ½]$$

$$= p_1$$

Solution 2) $f_1^* < ½$

similarly,

$(f_1^*, f_2^*) = (p_2, 1-p_2)$ and $p_2 < ½$

$M^* = p_2$

For a given environmental condition $p_i < p_j$, in order for the fuzzy automaton to achieve optimal behavior, the restrictions on p_i and p_j are $p_i < ½$ and $p_j > ½$. In the stochastic automata case, optimality is unreachable except for the situation that either p_i or p_j is zero.

B) Linear Reward and Inaction Algorithm

When automaton is in state s_i

$$f_i(t+1) = af_i(t) + (1-a) \qquad \text{for } x(t) = 0$$
$$f_j(t+1) = af_j(t) \qquad \text{for } x(t) = 0,\ j \neq i$$
$$f_i(t+1) = f_i(t) \qquad \text{for } x(t) = 1$$

Applying the Martingale equation, we get

$$\Delta f_1 = (1-a)\ \{(p_2-1)\ f_1(t) + [(p_1-p_2)\ f_1(t) +$$
$$+ (1-a)\ (1-p_1)]\ P[f_1(t) \geq ½]\}$$

There are two sets of solutions to the Martingale solutions:

Solution 1) $f_1^* > ½$

$(f_1^*, f_2^*) = (1-a, a)$ and $a < ½$

$M^* = p_1$

Solution 2) $f_1{}^* < \frac{1}{2}$

$$(f_1{}^*, f_2{}^*) = (0, 1)$$

$$M^* = p_2$$

From the above solutions, it may be seen that if $a > \frac{1}{2}$ and $p_2 < p_1$ then optimal behavior is possible. However, if $p_1 < p_2$, and $a < \frac{1}{2}$, M^* may not be p_1 and hence optimality is not guaranteed.

C) Beta Model (Nonlinear Reinforcement)

for $s(t) = s_i$,

$$f_i(t+1) = af_i(t)/[1 - (1-a)\ f_i(t)] \quad \text{for } x(t) = 1$$

$$f_k(t+1) = f_k(t)/[1 - (1-a)\ f_i(t)] \quad \text{for } x(t) = 1 \text{ and } k \neq i$$

$$f_i(t+1) = f_i(t)/[a + (1-a)\ f_i(t)] \quad \text{for } x(t) = 0$$

$$f_k(t+1) = af_k/[a + (1-a)\ f_k(t)] \quad \text{for } x(t) = 0 \text{ and } k \neq i$$

There are four admissible solutions to the Martingale equations. We omit the detail steps for economy of space. For nonlinear reinforcement schemes, the solutions must be stable [5,7], in the sense that

$$\left.\frac{d\Delta f_i}{df_i}\right|_{f_1{}^*, f_2{}^*} < 0 \qquad i = 1,2$$

We list the solutions and the stability conditions:

Solution 1) $f_1{}^* > \frac{1}{2}$

$$(f_1{}^*, f_2{}^*) = (1, 0)$$

stability condition: $p_1 < \dfrac{a}{a+1}$

$$M^* = p_1$$

Solution 2) $f_1{}^* > \frac{1}{2}$

$$(f_1{}^*, f_2{}^*) = \frac{1-(1+a)p_1}{1-a}, \frac{(1+a)p_1-a}{1-a}, \quad p_1 < \tfrac{1}{2}$$

stability condition: $\dfrac{a}{(1+a)^2} < p_1\ (1-p_1)$

$$M^* = p_1$$

Solution 3) $f_1^* < \frac{1}{2}$

$(f_1^*, f_2^*) = (0, 1)$

stability condition: $p_2 < \frac{a}{a+1}$

$M^* = p_2$

Solution 4) $f_1^* < \frac{1}{2}$

$(f_1^*, f_2^*) = \frac{(1+a)p_2-a}{1-a}, \frac{1-(1+a)p_2}{1-a}, p_2 < \frac{1}{2}$

stability condition: $\frac{a}{(1+a)^2} < p_2(1-p_2)$

$M^* = p_2$

The above results indicate that optimality is attainable but with restrictions on a, p_1, and p_2. If $p_1 < p_2$, and $p_2 > \frac{1}{2}$ then $M^* = p_1$, but the restrictions imposed on solutions 1 and 2 must be obeyed.

D) Instantaneous Nonlinear Reinforcement

for $s(t) = s_i$ and 2-state case,

$$f_i(t+1) = f_i^2(t) \qquad \text{if } x(t) = 1$$

$$f_j(t+1) = f_j(t) + f_i(t) - f_i^2(t) \qquad \text{if } x(t) = 1 \text{ and } j \neq i$$

$$f_i(t+1) = 1 - f_j^2(t) \qquad \text{if } x(t) = 0$$

$$f_j(t+1) = f_j^2(t) \qquad \text{if } x(t) = 0 \text{ and } j \neq i$$

Similarly, we obtain the following results:

Solution 1) $(f_1^*, f_2^*) = (1, 0)$

stability condition: $p_1 < \frac{1}{2}$

$M^* = p_1$

Solution 2) $(f_1^*, f_2^*) = (0, 1)$

stability condition: $p_2 < \frac{1}{2}$

$M^* = p_2$

Clearly, if $p_i < p_j$ and $p_j > \frac{1}{2}$, $p_i < \frac{1}{2}$, the desired optimal performance $M^* = p_i$ is obtained.

APPLICATION OF FUZZY AUTOMATA TO PARAMETER OPTIMIZATION PROBLEMS

The problem of parameter optimization is concerned with finding a parameter (α_{opt}) that would maximize (or minimize) the performance function $I(\alpha)$ of a given system. The performance function, $I(\alpha)$, is multimodal and since it may be of stochastic origin, it is commonly expressed as $I(\alpha) = E[Z(\alpha,v)]$, where v is a random variable. In general, the explicit functional relationship between $Z(\alpha, v)$ and α is not known but observations of $Z(\alpha, v)$ are available to the system designer. Stochastic automata have been applied to the solution of parameter optimization problems [6]. The advantage of using fuzzy automata is due to its structural simplicity. The first step is to discretize the parameter α into n possible values, $\alpha = (\alpha_1, \alpha_2, \ldots, \alpha_n)$. If α is multidimensional, more discrete level would have to be dealt with, but the added dimensions of α does not pose new problems. The block diagram of the learning model is given in Fig. 1. Each state s_k corresponds to a α_k. When the automaton is in state s_k at time t, α_k is sent out as an input to the multimodal, unknwon system, from which a particular value of $Z(\alpha_k,v)$ is observed. The most recent observation of $Z(\alpha_k, v)$ is used to update the estimate of $I(\alpha_k)$ by

$$\bar{I}(\alpha_k) = \left(\frac{L_k - 1}{L_k}\right) \bar{I}^*(\alpha_k) + \frac{1}{L_k} Z(\alpha_k, v)$$

where L_k is the number of times α_k has been selected up to the present time and $\bar{I}^*(\alpha_k)$ is the stored previous estimate of $I(\alpha_k)$. The updated value $\bar{I}^*(\alpha_k)$ is then compared with the maximum value of the stored estimates, $\bar{I}^*(\alpha_j)$, $j \neq k$. Penalty and reward in terms of 1, 0, respectively, are then used to change the membership functions of the states according to a selected reinforcement scheme. The new output of the fuzzy automaton is chosen corresponding to the state with the maximum grade of membership function. If more than one state has the maximum membership value, then a random strategy is used for the selection of a suitable output. The convergence of this optimization procedure can be shown as follows: For large t, $\bar{I}(\alpha_j) \to I(\alpha_j)$ for $j = 1, 2, \ldots, n$, then a reward is always sent out so that

$$f_j(t+1) \to \begin{cases} 1 & \text{for } I(\alpha_j) \text{ is the extremum} \\ 0 & \text{for } I(\alpha_j) \text{ not the extremum} \end{cases}$$

Therefore α_{opt} is the output of the fuzzy automaton with probability 1. As a numerical example, we consider the objective

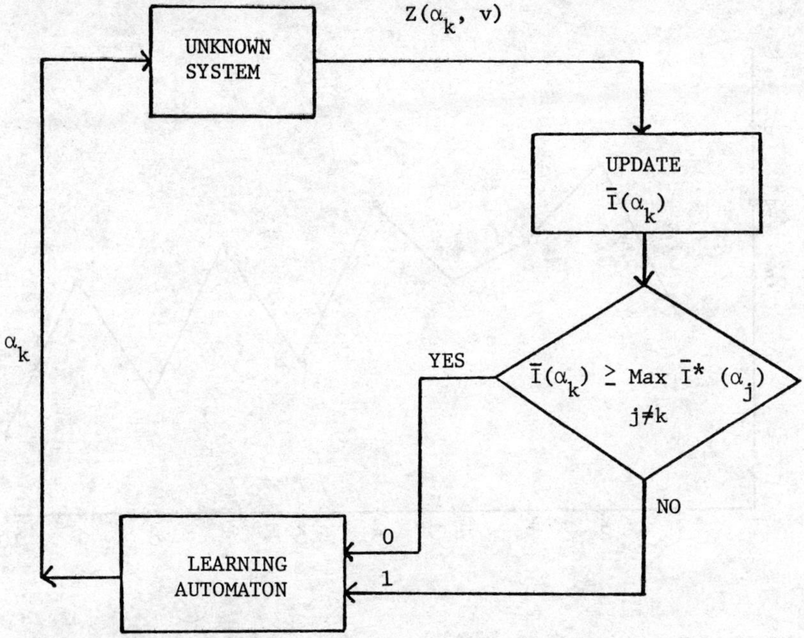

Fig. 1. Block diagram for parameter optimization

function $I(\alpha)$ of the form $I(\alpha) = Z(\alpha, v) = Z(\alpha) + v$ where v is a normal random variable with zero mean and standard deviation σ, and $Z(\alpha)$ as the noiseless objective function. α is discretized into 10 levels and $Z(\alpha)$ is shown in Fig. 2. Simulation of the learning model is carried out for 50 runs with $\sigma = 1, 2$. The average values of some of the membership functions $\sigma = 1$ and $\sigma = 2$ are shown in Figs. 3 and 4, respectively. Initially, all membership functions are set equal to 1/10 and the one noise observation $Z(\alpha_k, v)$ is stored. Figures 3 and 4 demonstrate that the average value of f_2, which corresponds to the choice α_{opt}, tends to go to 1 and the f_j's ($j \neq 2$) tend to decrease to 0.

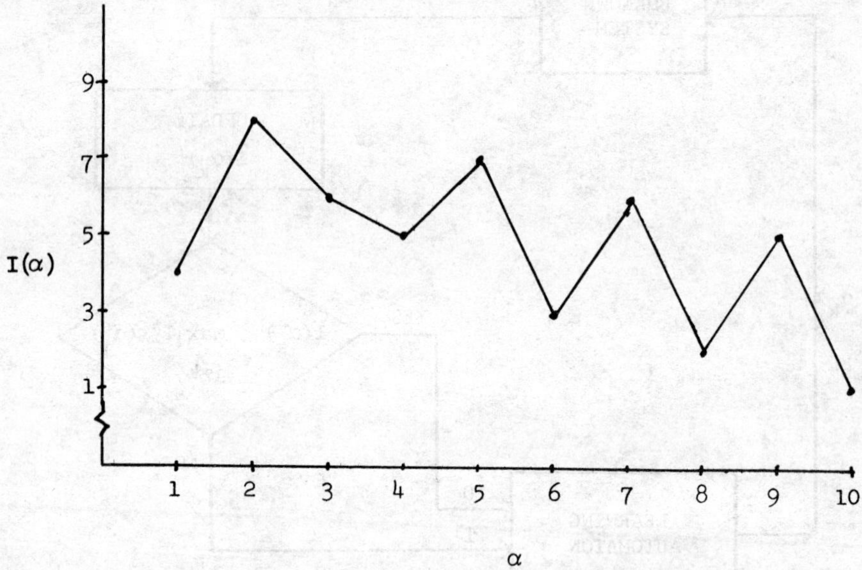

Fig. 2. Objective function

CONCLUSION

The performance of a variable-structure 2-state fuzzy automaton operating in a penalty-and-reward type of stationary random environment has been considered. Optimality, a measure of the efficiency of learning of the automaton, is shown to be attainable under certain restrictions. The restrictions are placed on the statistical parameters of the environment and sometimes on the coefficient in the reinforcement algorithms.

The fuzzy automaton is shown to be capable of seeking the best parameter value in the optimization of a noisy multimodal performance function. In the learning process, the structure of the automaton is self-organised in the following manner: the membership function of the state that moves the performance function toward its optimum value will approach 1, while those of the states that do not will approach 0. Hence, the parameter corresponding to the state with a grade of membership equal to one will be selected. Simulation studies yield reasonable results.

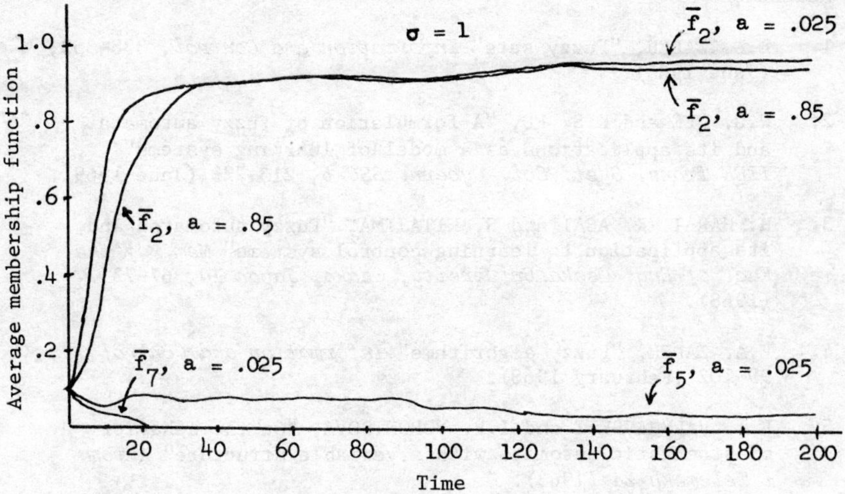

Fig. 3. Average membership function vs. time

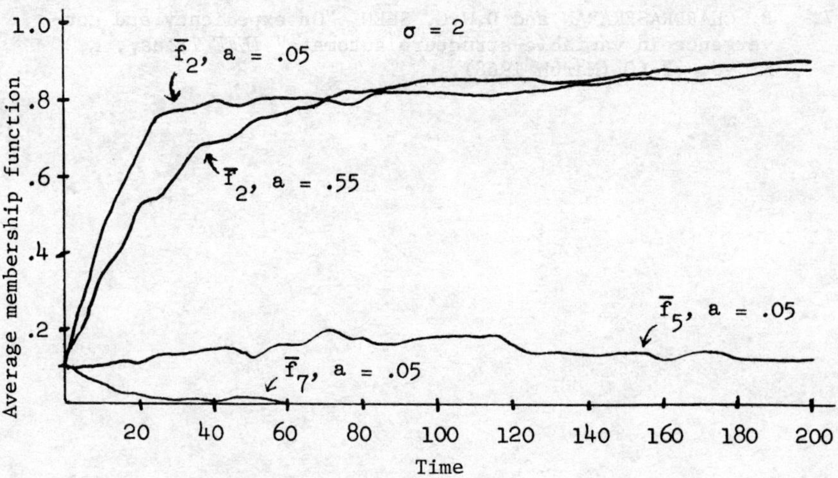

Fig. 4. Average membership function vs. time

REFERENCES

1. L.A. ZADEH, "Fuzzy sets" *Information and Control*, 338-353, (June 1965).

2. W.G. WEE and K.S. FU, "A formulation of fuzzy automata and its applications as a model of learning systems" *IEEE Trans. Syst. Sci. Cybern. SSC-5*, 215-223 (June 1969).

3. H. HARAI, K. ASAI and S. KITAJIMA, "Fuzzy automaton and its application to learning control systems" *Mem. of the Fac. of Eng. Osaka University, Osaka, Japan 10*, 67-73 (1968).

4. L.A. ZADEH, "Fuzzy algorithms" *Information and Control 12*, 99-102 (February 1968).

5. V.I. VARSHAVSKII and I.P. VORONTSOVA, "On the behavior of stochastic automata with a variable structure" *Autom. i Telemekh 24* (1963).

6. I.J. SHAPIRO and K.S. NARENDRA, "Use of stochastic automata for parameter self-optimization with multimodal performance criteria" *IEEE SSC-5*, 352-360 (October 1969).

7. B. CHARDRASEKARAN and D.W.C. SHEN, "On expediency and convergence in variable-structure automata" *IEEE Trans., SSC-4*, 52-60 (March 1968).

THEORY OF MOBILE AUTOMATA

G.E. LASKER

School of Computer Science, University of Windsor, Windsor, Ontario, Canada

SUMMARY

The article introduces a new theoretical framework for studying finite-state sequential systems which have the capability to move within the boundaries of a two-dimensional cellular space from one position to another. A mobile automaton is defined in terms of automata algebra as a mobile sequential machine, which can successively enter and occupy a finite, non-empty set of distinct cellular positions. The move to be made by the automaton at any specific time is determined through the move function μ (or positional function π) by a configuration of systems' dispositional variables at that time. An example is presented which illustrates the structural and functional properties of an automaton whose moves are restricted to a specified part of its operation environment. In a final section of this article a system is described, which can be guided (under sequential application of specific inputs) through a predetermined trajectory according to an "a priory" defined timetable.

This paper introduces new types of sequential discrete systems which have the capability to move within the boundaries of a specified environment from one physical position to another. These systems, subsequently called *mobile automata*, are formally defined as finite-state sequential machines which can successively move in specified directions and which can successively enter a finite, non-empty set of distinct physical positions in an arbitrarily defined environment [1-5].

The environment in which a mobile automaton is assumed to operate will be called an operational space or operational environment of the automaton and will be denoted by Ω. In general, this environment can be defined in numerous ways. In this article, the Ω-environment will be defined as a two-dimensional cellular space, i.e. a space which is partitioned into a finite, non-empty set C of adjacent cells $c_{00}, c_{01}, \ldots, c_{09}$; $c_{10}, c_{11}, \ldots, c_{19}$; ...; $c_{90}, c_{91}, \ldots, c_{99}$ (see Fig. 1). Each of these cells is assumed to represent a position which the automaton under certain conditions can enter and occupy for a definite period of time. Each position is assumed to contain a specific information which the automaton may treat as a "positional" input.

00	01	02	03	04	05	06	07	08	09
10	11	12	13	14	15	16	17	18	19
20	21	22	23	24	25	26	27	28	29
30	31	32	33	34	35	36	37	38	39
40	41	42	43	44	45	46	47	48	49
50	51	52	53	54	55	56	57	58	59
60	61	62	63	64	65	66	67	68	69
70	71	72	73	74	75	76	77	78	79
80	81	82	83	84	85	86	87	88	89
90	91	92	93	94	95	96	97	98	99

Fig. 1. Generalized operation space Ω for automaton A

Formally, the mobile automaton A can be defined as follows:

$$A = (X, Q, Y, M, \delta, \lambda, \mu) \qquad (1)$$

where

X = a finite non-empty set of inputs $x_1, x_2, \ldots, x_n$

Q = a finite non-empty set of internal states $q_1, q_2, \ldots, q_m$

Y = a finite non-empty set of outputs $y_1, y_2, \ldots, y_z$

M = a finite non-empty set of permissible moves $m_0, m_1, m_2, \ldots, m_r$

δ = a state-transition function, mapping $X \times Q \rightarrow Q$

λ = an output function, mapping $X \times Q \rightarrow Y$

μ = a move function, mapping $X \times Q \rightarrow M$

It is assumed that A can successively take on a set Q of internal states $q_1, q_2, \ldots, q_m$. The state, that A takes on at a specified time t is defined recursively by the formula

$$\begin{cases} q(0) = q_i & \text{for } q(0), g(t), g(t+1) \in Q \\ q(t+1) = \delta[x(t), q(t)] & x(t) \in X \end{cases} \tag{2}$$

where

$q(0) = q_i$ = the initial internal state of A

$x(t)$ = the present input

$q(t)$ = the present internal state

$q(t+1)$ = the next internal state of A

Provided that q(0) is specified, the formula (2) basically indicated that the present input x(t) and the present internal state q(t) determines the next-state q(t+1).

The output, which the automaton A generates at a specific time t is defined through the function λ as follows

$$y(t) = \lambda[x(t), q(t)] \tag{3}$$

where $y(t) \in Y$, $x(t) \in X$ and $q(t) \in Q$. The formula (3) indicates that the output y(t) occurs as soon as the input x(t) is applied to $A|q(t)$. The symbol $A|q(t)$ is used as an abbreviation of the phrase "the automaton A in the state q(t)".

It is assumed that within a defined operation space Ω the automaton A can successively make a series of distinct moves $m_0, m_1, m_2, \ldots, m_r$. Each of these moves is *a priori* specified by the direction in which the automaton A should travel and by the distance which the automaton should traverse from a specific position within a predetermined period of time. Each move can be also specified by the spatial transition of A from one position to another or by the route that the automaton should take in order to reach a specific position in Ω-space.

A move m(t) to be made by the automaton A at a specific time t is defined through the move function μ according to the following formula

$$m(t) = \mu[x(t), q(t)] \tag{4}$$

where $m(t) \in M$, $x(t) \in X$, $q(t) \in Q$.

Each move $m(t) \in M$ can be specified by a transition of the automaton from the position $c(t)$ to a new position $c(t+1)$, (provided that $c(t), c(t+1) \in C | C = \{c_k;\ k = 1, 2, \ldots, u\}$). In this respect the set C of cellular positions $c_1, c_2, \ldots, c_u$ may be incorporated into the definition of A as a set of dispositional variables and the move function μ can be replaced by an operationally equivalent positional function π, defined recursively as follows:

$$\begin{cases} c(0) = c_{jk} & \text{for } c(0), c(t), c(t+1) \in C \\ q(0) = q_i & q(0), q(t) \in Q \\ c(t+1) = \pi[x(t), q(t), c(t)] & x(t) \in X \end{cases} \tag{5}$$

where

$c(0) = c_{jk}$ = the initial position of A

$q(0) = q_i$ = the initial state of A

$c(t)$ = the present position of A

$c(t+1)$ = the next position to be entered by A

AN EXAMPLE

To illustrate the functional properties of the above described mobile automata let us consider an automaton A defined as follows:

$$A = (X, Q, Y, M, \delta, \lambda, \mu)$$

where

$X = \{x_1, x_2\}$

$Q = \{q_1, q_2, q_3\}$

$Y = \{0, 1\}$

$M = \{m_1, m_2, m_3, m_4\} = \{N, E, S, W\}$

TABLE I. Tabular Representation of δ, λ and μ-functions

δ, λ, μ:

Q \ X	x_1	x_2
q_1	q_2, 1, m_1 = N	q_1, 0, m_2 = E
q_2	q_3, 1, m_3 = S	q_2, 1, m_1 = N
q_3	q_1, 0, m_4 = W	q_3, 0, m_1 = N

The automaton A is assumed to operate within the boundaries of Ω-space, illustrated by Fig. 1. It is assumed that A can make four distinct moves m_1, m_2, m_3 and m_4. Each move is defined as a single step (a transition) to an adjacent cellular position in one of four designated directions (North, East, South and West). Thus m_1 means: move one square north, m_2 means: move one square east, m_3 means: move one square south and m_4 means: move on square west.

It is assumed that A is initially in the state $q(0) = q_1$ occupying the cellular position $c(0) = c_{33}$. Under sequential application of admissible input x_1 or x_2 the automaton A can successively move in directions specified by Table I. It is assumed that each move is completed within a unit period of time.

To illustrate the actual trajectory of A under application of specific inputs, let us consider a situation in which the input $x_1 \in X$ is initially applied to $A|q_1$. Since we know that the initial internal state $q(0) = q_1$ and the initial position $c(0) = c_{33}$, we can compute the initial move m(0) of A through the function μ as follows:

$m(0) = \mu[x(0), q(0)] = \mu[x_1, q_1] = m_1 = N$. This means that under application of x_1 the automaton A will move from the initial position $c(0) = c_{33}$ one square north to a new position $c(1) = c_{23}$. Upon arrival to this position at time $t = 1$, the automaton will assume a new internal state $q(1) = q_2$ and it will produce an output $y(1) = 1$. If at this time an input x_1 is applied again, the automaton A will make a new move m(1), specified by the configuration of x(1) and q(1). Since $x(1) = x_1$ and $q(1) = q_2$ the move $m(1) = \mu[x(1), q(1)] = \mu[x_1, q_2] = m_3 = S$, which means that A will move from the present position $c(1) = c_{23}$ one square south to the subsequent position $c(2) = c_{33}$ (in this case - to the initially occupied position). Upon arrival to this position at time $t = 2$, the automaton will assume the state $q(2) = q_3$ and it will produce the output $y(2) = 1$. If at this stage an input x_2 is applied to $A|q_3$, then the automaton will make a further move $m(2)$. Since $x(2) = x_2$ and $q(2) = q_3$ the move $m(2) = \mu[x(2), q(2)] = \mu[x_2, q_3] = m_1 = N$ which means that under the input x_2 the automaton A will move from the presently occupied position $c(2) = c_{33}$ one square north to a subsequent position $c(3) = c_{23}$. Upon arrival to this position at time $t = 3$, the automaton will maintain its previous internal state q_3 and it will generate an output $y(3) = 0$. As it follows from Table I, the internal state $q(3) = \delta[x(2), q(2)] = \delta[x_2, q_3] = q_3$ and the output $y(3) = \lambda[x(2), q(2)] = \lambda[x_2, q_3] = 0$. Under further application of specific inputs the subsequent moves of A can be calculated with the aid of Table I in the same way as outlined above.

The trajectories to be assumed by A under application of various input sequences can be traced from the flow-diagram, presented in Fig. 2. This diagram has been constructed on the basis of data provided by Table I.

In general, the presented trajectorial diagram provides us with an information about the behavior of A under various operation conditions. From the diagram it follows that if the input x_2 is initially applied to $A|q_1$, the automaton moves instantly one square east, maintaining its initial internal state q_1 and producing an output 0. Under repeated application of x_2 to $A|q_1$, the automaton will successively move in the eastern direction, maintaining its q_1-state and producing 0 - output.

If the input x_1 is repeatedly applied to A, then the automaton will make the following moves:

$m_1, m_3, m_4, m_1, m_3, m_4, \ldots, m_1, m_3, m_4, \ldots$ or equivalently N, S, W, N, S, W,..., N, S, W,...

From the diagram it also follows that the east-bound automaton $A|q_1$ cannot move directly from the East to the South. Such transition can be realized only indirectly by moving first one step north. This is achieved by applying the input sequence (x_1, x_1) to the east-bound automaton $A|q_1$. Similarly, a north-bound automaton $A|q_2$ cannot move directly to the East. The North-East transition of $A|q_2$ can be realized only through two intermediary moves m_3 and m_4 (or S and W) i.e. by moving first one step South and then one step West. This can be achieved by applying the input sequence (x_1, x_1, x_2).

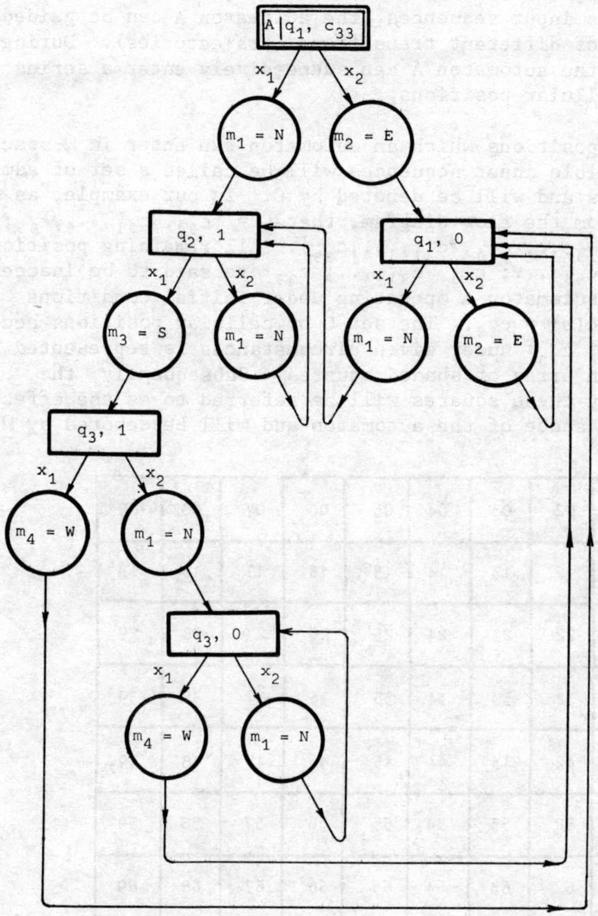

Fig. 2. Flow-diagram of positional transitions for $A|q_1, c_{33}$.

From the diagram it is also apparent, that once the machine is put on an East-bound course it can be kept on it by repeated application of the input x_2. Similarly, the North-bound machine can be kept on its course by repeated application of the input x_2. However, as it follows from the diagram, the South-bound or the West-bound automaton cannot be continually kept on its course, since there is no input which would preserve the continuity of the moves m_3 and m_4.

In general, the flow-diagram indicates, that under application of various input sequences, the automaton A can be guided through a set of different transitions (trajectories). During this guidance the automaton A can successively enter a series of specific cellular positions.

A set of positions which an automaton can enter in Ω-space under all possible input sequences will be called a set of admissible positions and will be denoted by $\hat{C}$. In our example, as it is apparent from the flow diagram, that $\hat{C} = \{c_{00}, c_{01}, \ldots, {}_{09};$ $c_{10}, c_{11}, \ldots, c_{19}; \ldots; c_{30}, c_{31}, \ldots, c_{39}\}$. All remaining positions $c_{40}, c_{41}, \ldots, c_{49}; \ldots; c_{90}, c_{91}, \ldots, c_{99}$ are said to be inaccessible for the automaton A operating under initial conditions $q(0) = q_1$ and $c(0) = c_{33}$. The set $\hat{C}$ of cellular positions accessible to $A|(q_1, c_{33})$ under given circumstances is represented in Fig. 3 by an array of shaded squares. Subsequently, the area covered by these squares will be referred to as the effective operation space of the automaton and will be denoted by Ω^*.

00	01	02	03	04	05	06	07	08	09
10	11	12	13	14	15	16	17	18	19
20	21	22	23	24	25	26	27	28	29
30	31	32	33	34	35	36	37	38	39
40	41	42	43	44	45	46	47	48	49
50	51	52	53	54	55	56	57	58	59
60	61	62	63	64	65	66	67	68	69
70	71	72	73	74	75	76	77	78	79
80	81	82	83	84	85	86	87	88	89
90	91	92	93	94	95	96	97	98	99

Fig. 3. An effective operation space Ω^* for $A|q_1, c_{33}$.

DESIGN OF MOBILE AUTOMATA

In what follows it will be illustrated how it is possible to design a model A* of the mobile automaton (X,Q,M,δ,μ) which under sequential application of specific inputs can be guided in cellular space Ω on a trajectory specified by Table II and illustrated in Fig. 4.

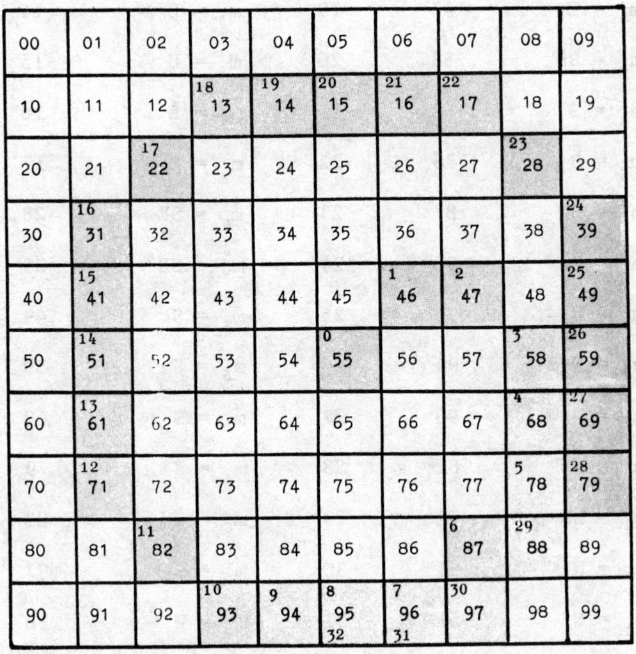

Fig. 4. Prescribed trajectory for A*

A given task assumes that under sequential application of arbitrarily determined inputs the automaton A* can successively realize a set M of moves m_0, m_1, m_2, ..., m_8 defined as follows:

TABLE II. Prescribed Trajectory for $A^*|[q_1, 55]$

Time t	Move m (t)	Entered Position	Time t	Move m (t)	Entered Position
0	m_0 = O	55	17	m_2 = NE	22
1	m_2 = NE	46	18	m_2 = NE	13
2	m_1 = E	47	19	m_3 = E	14
3	m_4 = SE	58	20	m_3 = E	15
4	m_5 = S	68	21	m_3 = E	16
5	m_5 = S	78	22	m_3 = E	17
6	m_6 = SW	87	23	m_4 = SE	28
7	m_6 = SW	96	24	m_4 = SE	39
8	m_7 = W	95	25	m_5 = S	49
9	m_7 = W	94	26	m_5 = S	59
10	m_7 = W	93	27	m_5 = S	69
11	m_8 = NW	82	28	m_5 = S	79
12	m_8 = NW	71	29	m_6 = SW	88
13	m_1 = N	61	30	m_6 = SW	97
14	m_1 = N	51	31	m_7 = W	96
15	m_1 = N	41			
16	m_1 = N	31			

$m_0 = 0$ = zero move, (means: maintain the present position)
$m_1 = N$ = move one square north
$m_2 = NE$ = move one squre north-east
$m_3 = E$ = move one square east
$m_4 = SE$ = move one square south-east
$m_5 = S$ = move one square south
$m_6 = SW$ = move one square south-west
$m_7 = W$ = move one square west
$m_8 = NW$ = move one square north-west

Under sequential application of steering inputs the automaton should enter a series of predetermined cellular positions according to the schedule specified by Table II. To safeguard the prescribed trajectory of A* in Ω-space it is necessary to completely define the characteristics X,Q,δ and μ. As a matter of convenience these characteristics can be defined as follows:

$X = \{x_1, x_2\}$

$Q = \{q_1, q_2, q_3, q_4, q_5, q_6, q_7, q_8\}$ when $q(0) = q_1$

TABLE III. Tabular Representation of δ and μ Function for A*.

δ, μ: Q \ X	x_1	x_2
q_1	q_1, N	q_2, NE
q_2	q_2, NE	q_3, E
q_3	q_3, E	q_4, SE
q_4	q_4, SE	q_5, S
q_5	q_5, S	q_6, SW
q_6	q_6, SW	q_7, W
q_7	q_7, W	q_8, NW
q_8	q_8, NW	q_1, N

It is assumed that the automaton A* is initially in the state $q(0) = q_1$ and occupies the position $c(0) = 55$. If the input x_2 is applied to $A^*|q_1$, the automaton A* will instantly move north-east from the position $c(0) = 55$ to the position $c(1) = 46$ and it will assume there a new internal state $q(1) = q_2$.

Subsequently, the automaton should move one square east to enter the position c(2) = 47. As it follows from Table III, the automaton $A^*|q_2$ can move east to reach the position c(2) = 47 from the position 46 only if the input x_2 is applied; since $\mu[x(1), q(1)] = \mu[x_2, q_2] = m_1 = E$. Under application of x_2 the automaton $A|q_2$ will also assume a new internal state q_3. Thus at time t = 2 the automaton $A^*|q_3$ occupies position 47. In the next period of time the automaton A* should move south-east to enter the position c(3) = 58. This position can be reached by $A^*|q_3$ only under the input x_2 which also transforms the state $q(2) = q_3$ into a state $q(3) = q_4$. At time t = 3 the automaton $A^*|q_4$ occupies the position 58. From the Table III it is thus possible to successively determine the sequence of inputs which should be applied to the automaton A* in order to guide this machine on a prescribed route (trajectory). The individual positional transitions to be realized by A* under application of steering inputs x_1 and x_2 are schematically described by the flow-diagram displayed in Fig. 5. From this diagram it follows that the automaton $A^*|[q_1, 55]$ (which is initially in state q_1 and occupies position 55) can be guided on a prescribed trajectory through the inputs x_1 and x_2 applied in the following order:

$$x_2, x_2, x_2, x_2, x_1, x_2, x_1, x_2, x_1, x_1, x_2, x_1, x_2, x_1,$$
$$x_1, x_1, x_2, x_1, x_2, x_1, x_1, x_1, x_2, x_1, x_2, x_1, x_1, x_1$$
$$x_2, x_1, x_2.$$

The above described model A* illustrates only one of several possible variants which can be designed to follow the trajectory, specified by Table II. In general, a large variety of functionally equivalent models can be designed which would have the capability to accomplish the same task.

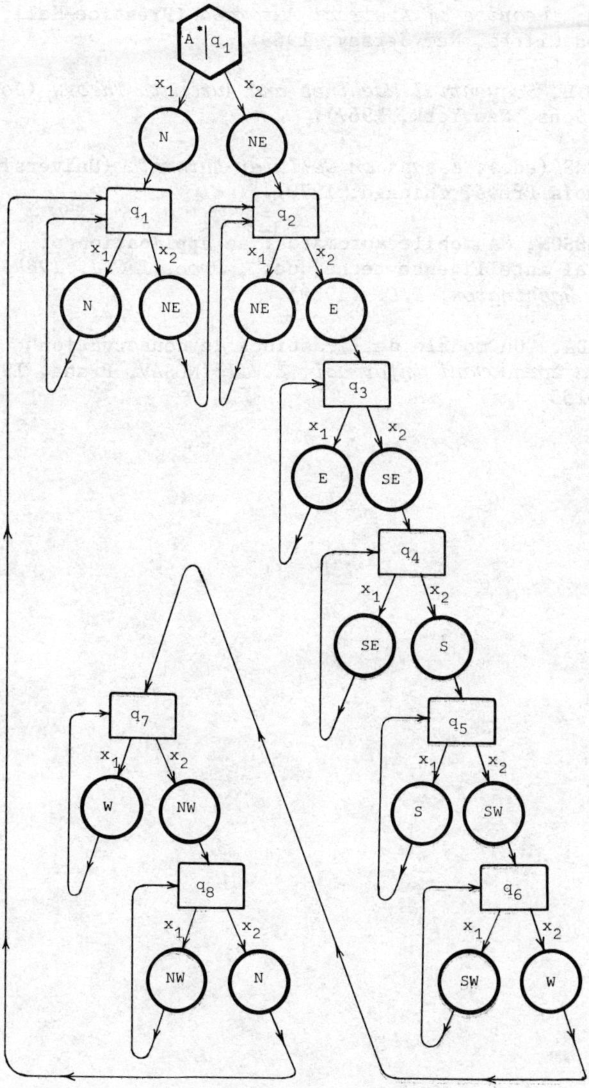

Fig. 5. Flow-diagram of positional transitions for $A^*|[q_1, c_{55}]$

REFERENCES

1. M. ARBIB, *Theories of Abstract Automata* (Prentice-Hall, Englewood Cliffs, New Jersey, 1969).

2. T.L. BOOTH, *Sequential Machines and Automata Theory* (John Wiley & Sons, New York, 1967).

3. A.W. BURKS (ed.), *Essays on Cellular Automata* (University of Illinois Press, Chicago, 1970).

4. N.J. NILSSON, "A mobile automaton: an application of artificial intelligence techniques", *Proc. IJCAJ, 1969, May 7-9, Washington, D.C.* (1969).

5. A. SVOBODA, "Un modèle de l'instinct de conservation" *Stroje na zpracování informací, č.VII* (NČSAV, Praha, 1960) pp. 147-155.

THRESHOLD AUTOMATA

G.E. LASKER

School of Computer Science, University of Windsor, Windsor, Ontario, Canada

SUMMARY

The paper introduces several new types of input-output threshold systems which can operate in descrete steps. These systems, called threshold automata, are described in terms of automata algebra as modified sequential machines whose input, state-transition and output functions are defined as threshold functions. It is assumed, that each of these machines has the capability to take on a series of distinct internal states. Each internal state determines (through a specific configuration of threshold operators) a unique input-output relationship to be realized. This relationship can be defined in the form of K-ary valued switching function. As a consequence, a single machine, which assumes in discrete steps a number of different internal states, can successively realize a variety of distinct switching functions.

INTRODUCTION

This article introduces new types of finite-state threshold systems which shall be referred to as threshold automata [1-13]. Formally, these systems are described in terms of automata algebra as sequential machines whose input, state-transition and output functions are defined as threshold functions. It is assumed that each of these machines has the capability to take on a series of distinct internal states such that each state is associated with a configuration of specific threshold characteristics on the basis of which it is determined:

1) which input will be accepted (or rejected) by the machine;
2) which state transition will be realized under the effect of the accepted input; and

3) which output will be produced by the machine under the accepted input.

Each internal state of the machine specifies a distinct configuration of threshold characteristics through which a unique input-output relationship can be realized. Formally, this relationship can be represented by a k-ary valued switching function (for $k = 1,2,\ldots\ldots,n$). As a consequence, a single machine which assumes a series of discrete internal states can successively realize a number of various switching functions.

SYSTEM MODEL

Definition 1. A generalized threshold automaton M is a completely specified finite-state sequential discrete system defined as follows:

$$M = (X,Q,Y,W,T,\alpha,\beta,\gamma) \quad (1)$$

where

X = a finite, non-empty set of input variables $x_1,x_2,\ldots,x_n$.
Q = a finite, non-empty set of internal states $q_1,q_2,\ldots,q_m$.
Y = a finite, non-empty set of outputs $y_1,y_2,\ldots y_z$.
W = a finite, non-empty set of input weights $w_1,w_2,\ldots,w_s$.
T = a finite, non-empty set of thresholds $T_1,T_2,\ldots,T_u$.
α = an input function $W \times X \times Q \times T \to X$
β = a state-transition function $W \times X \times Q \times T \to Q$
γ = an output function $W \times X \times Q \times T \to Y$

It is assumed that M can successively take on a finite, non-empty set Q of distinct internal states $q_1,q_2,\ldots,q_m$ such that each internal state $q_i \in Q$ is associated with a configuration τ_i of threshold characteristics (A_i,B_i,C_i) where

A_i represents a set of input thresholds
B_i represents a set of state-transition thresholds
C_i represents a set of output thresholds

In general it is assumed that $\tau_i \in \mathcal{T} | \mathcal{T} = \{\tau_1,\tau_2,\ldots,\tau_m\}$ where $\mathcal{T}$ is defined as a set of threshold configurations $\tau_1,\tau_2,\ldots,\tau_m$, specified by the set Q of internal states $q_1,q_2,\ldots,q_m$. Thus for each $q_i \in Q$ there exists a triplet $\tau_i = (A_i,B_i,C_i) | A_i \subseteq T;\ B_i \subseteq T;\ C_i \subseteq T$.

Let us consider that the system M is at time t in the state $q(t) \in Q$ (symbolically denoted as $M|q(t)$) and that $q(t)$

at time t specifies a configuration $\tau(t) \in T$ of threshold characteristics A(t), B(t) and C(t) as follows:

$A(t) = \{A_k(t)\}$ where $A_k(t) \in T$ for $k = 1,2,\ldots,$
$B(t) = \{B_0(t), B_1(t),\ldots,B_n(t)\}$ where $B_0(t) < B_1(t) <\ldots< B_n(t)$
$C(t) = \{C_0(t), C_1(t),\ldots,C_z(t)\}$ where $C_0(t) < C_1(t) <\ldots< C_z(t)$

Let us further consider that at time t a combination $x(t) \in X$ of binary-valued inputs $x_1(t), x_2(t),\ldots,x_r(t)$ is applied to $M|q(t)$ and that each elementary input $x_i(t) \in x(t)$ applied to $M|q(t)$ is associated at time t with a specific input weight $w_i(t) \in w(t) | w(t) = \{w_1(t), w_2(t),\ldots,w_r(t)\}$ where $w(t) \subsetneq W$ and $w_i(t) \geq 0$. In general, the input weight can be defined by one of the following functions:

$$\text{(i)}\quad g : X \to W \implies w_i(t) = g[x_i(t)]$$
$$\text{(ii)}\quad h : Q \to W \implies w_i(t) = h[q(t)]$$

The mapping (i) indicates that the weight $w_i(t) \varepsilon W$ is a function of a specific input $x_i(t) \in X$; the mapping (ii) indicates that the input weight $w_i(t)$ is a function of a specific internal state q(t) assumed by M at time t. Unless specified otherwise, the input weight $w_i(t)$ of M will be defined by relation (i).

In order to define an operational value of each input applied to $M|q(t)$ at time t, a new auxiliary function is introduced. This function, subsequently denoted as value function ϕ is represented by mapping as follows:

$$\phi : W \times X \to V \tag{2}$$

where W and X are defined by (1); and $V = \{v_i | v_i \geq 0 \text{ for } i = 1,2,\ldots,n\}$

Let $x(t) = (x_1(t), x_2(t),\ldots,x_r(t)) : x_i(t) \in \{0,1\}$ for $i = 1,2,\ldots,r$ and $w(t) = (w_1(t), w_2(t),\ldots,w_r(t)) : w_i(t) \in N | N = \{0,1,2,3,\ldots,Z\}$* then the value $v_i(t)$ of each elementary input $x_i(t) \in x(t)$ is defined as follows:

---

*The symbol N denotes a set of non-negative integers including zero. It is assumed that $W \subseteq N$.

$$v_i(t) = v[x_i(t)] = \phi[w_i(t),\ x_i(t)] = w_i(t),\ x_i(t)$$
$$= g[x_i(t)]\cdot x_i(t) \qquad (3)$$

where $v_i(t) \in V | V = \{v_1(t),\ v_2(t),\ldots,v_r(t)\}$; $w_i(t) \in W$ and

$$x_i(t) \in X.$$

The value $v(t)$ of the total input pattern $x(t)$ applied to $M|q(t)$ is defined by the sum of values of all elementary inputs contained in $x(t)$. Thus

$$v(t) = v[x(t)] = \phi[w(t),\ x(t)] = v[(x_1(t),\ x_2(t),\ldots,x_r(t)]=$$

$$= \sum_{i=1}^{r} w_i(t) = \sum_{i=1}^{r} w_i(t)x_i(t) = \sum_{i=1}^{r} g[x_i(t)]x_i(t) \qquad (4)$$

As follows from Eq. (4) the value $v(t)$ of the input pattern $x(t)$ has been defined as a linear arithmetic function. In certain situations however, the operational value of $x(t)$ may be a non-linear combination of values of individual inputs. As a consequence, the actual value of $x(t)$ may be smaller or larger than the sum of values of individual inputs. In such a case, the value function ϕ must be modified accordingly.

Under the condition that $q(t) \in Q$ at time t completely specifies a configuration $\tau(t)$ of threshold characteristics $A(t)$, $B(t)$ and $C(t)$ and on the assumption that the value of each input pattern $x(t)$ can be numerically calculated from the weights of elementary inputs, the functions α, β and τ can be defined as follows:

Input Function α:

The α -function determines for each combination $x(t) \subseteq X$ of inputs $x_1(t),\ x_2(t),\ldots,x_r(t)$ whether or not the system $M|q(t)$ will accept $x(t)$ at time t. Formally

$$\alpha_{A(t)}[x(t)] = \begin{cases} 1 \text{ if } v(t) = \sum_{i=1}^{r} w_i(t)x_i(t) \geq T_k(t) \\ 0 \text{ if } v(t) = \sum_{i=1}^{r} w_i(t)x_i(t) < T_k(t) \end{cases} \qquad (5)$$

The input pattern $x(t)$ is said to be accepted by $M|q(t)$ at time t if and only if the value of input function α is 1; otherwise $x(t)$ is said to be rejected by $M|q(t)$ at time t. The value of the function $\alpha_{A(t)}[x(t)]$ is 1 if and only if the operational value $v(t)$ of input pattern $x(t)$ is greater than or equal to the input threshold $A(t) = T_k(t)$; otherwise $\alpha_{A(t)}[x(t)] = 0$. Since $v(t) = \sum_{i=1}^{r} w_i(t)x_i(t)$, we can also say that $x(t)$ is accepted by $M|q(t)$ if and only if the value of the sum $\sum_{i=1}^{r} w_i(t)w_i(t)$ of weighted elementary inputs exceeds or equals a specific threshold $T_k(t)$; if the value of the sum $\sum_{i=1}^{r} w_i(t)x_i(t)$ is smaller than $T_k(t)$, the input pattern $x(t)$ is not accepted by $M|q(t)$

State Transition Function β

The state transition function β defines the next internal state $q(t+1)$ of M on the basis of $x(t)$, $q(t)$ and $B(t)$ according to the following recursive formula

$$\begin{cases} q(0) = q_i \\ q(t+1) = \beta_{B(t)}[x(t),q(t)] = \begin{cases} q_1(t+1) \text{ if } B_1(t) > v(t) \geq B_0(t) \\ q_2(t+1) \text{ if } B_2(t) > v(t) \geq B_1(t) \\ \vdots \\ q_z(t+1) \text{ if } B_z(t) > v(t) \geq B_{z-1}(t) \end{cases} \end{cases} \tag{6}$$

where

$q(0)$ = the initial internal state of M.
$x(t)$ = an admissible present input pattern.
$v(t)$ = an operational value of the present input pattern $x(t)$.
$q(t)$ = a present internal state of M.
$B(t)$ = a present state-transition threshold characteristic.
$q_k(t+1)$ = the next internal state of M, i.e. the state that

will be assumed by M at time t+1 if $B_k(t) > v(t) > B_{k-1}(t)$ for $B_k(t)$, $B_{k-1}(t) \in B(t)$ and $k \in \{1,2,...,z\}$

In general it is assumed that the input x(t) which was accepted by $M|q(t)$ at time t may transform the present internal state q(t) into one of the subsequently available internal states $q_1(t+1), q_2(t+1),...,q_z(t+1)$ defined on a set $Q(t+1) \subseteq Q$, where $Q(t+1) = \{q_k(t+1) : k = 1,2,...,z\}$. Which internal state will be reached by M at time t+1 under input x(t) depends: (i) on the value of the present internal state q(t), (ii) on the value of the presently accepted input pattern x(t) and (iii) on the configuration B(t) of state-transition thresholds $B_0(t), B_1(t), B_2(t),...,B_z(t)$, associated with the state q(t).

The input pattern x(t) is said to transform a specific present state q(t) into a subsequent state $q_k(t+1)$ if and only if the value v(t) of x(t) is within the interval $[B_k(t), B_{k-1}(t)]$, i.e. if $B_k(t) > \sum_{i=1}^{r} w_i(t)x_i(t) \geq B_{k-1}(t)$ for k = 1,2,...,z, provided that $q(t) \in Q$ and $q_k(t+1) \in Q(t+1)$, where Q(t+1) is defined as a finite set of internal states $q_1(t+1)$, $q_2(t+1),..., q_z(t+1)$ directly accessible from the state q(t) under input x(t).

The Output Function γ

The γ-function determines the output y(t) of $M|q(t)$ on the basis of x(t), g(t) and C(t) according to the following formula

$$y(t) = \gamma_{C(t)}[x(t), q(t)] = \begin{cases} y_1(t) \text{ if } C_1(t) > v(t) \geq C_0(t) \\ y_2(t) \text{ if } C_2(t) > v(t) \geq C_1(t) \\ \cdot \\ \cdot \\ \cdot \\ y_n(t) \text{ if } C_n(t) > v(t) \geq C_{n-1}(t) \end{cases} \quad (7)$$

The formula (7) indicates that the output y(t) has the value $y_j(t)$ if and only if the value v(t) of x(t) falls within the specified interval $[C_j(t) : C_{j-1}(t)]$, i.e. if

$$C_j(t) > \sum_{i=1}^{r} w_i(t)x_i(t) > C_{j-1}(t) \text{ for any } j = 1,2,...,n.$$

In general it is assumed that threshold automaton M may produce various types of outputs. Which type of output will be produced by $M|q(t)$ under the effect of $x(t)$ depends exclusively on the nature of the output threshold characteristic $C(t)$ specified by the state $q(t)$. To illustrate this, let us consider a situation in which the characteristic $C(t) = T_j(t)$, where $T_j(t) \in T$ represents a single threshold value defined on N. In that case the output $y(t)$ of $M|q(t)$ is defined through the threshold output function γ as follows:

$$y(t) = \gamma_{C(t)}[x(t), q(t)] = \begin{cases} 1 \text{ if } v(t) \geq T_j(t) \\ 0 \text{ if } v(t) < T_j(t) \end{cases} \quad (8)$$

Since $C(t)$ is represented by a single threshold value $T_j(t)$, the function γ defines the output $y(t)$ as a binary variable which can take on the value 0 or 1. The formula (8) basically indicates that for each admissible combination $x(t)$ of binary-valued input variables $x_1(t), x_2(t), \ldots, x_r(t)$ the output $y(t) = 1$ if and only if the value $v(t)$ of $x(t)$ exceeds or equals the value of the threshold $T_j(t)$, i.e. if $\sum_{i=1}^{r} w_i(t)x_i(t) \geq T_j(t)$. If, however, the value $v(t) < T_j(t)$, then the output $y(t) = 0$.

In the context of the above considered situation, the threshold automaton M yields a binary-valued output $y(t)$ for each combination $x(t)$ of binary-valued inputs $x_1(t), x_2(t), \ldots, x_r(t)$ and consequently the output $y(t)$ can be viewed and treated as a switching function of the input variables $x_1(t), x_2(t), \ldots, x_r(t)$.

An Example:

Let us consider a threshold automaton D illustrated in Fig. 1. This automaton can be viewed as an output-driven threshold device which has two types of inputs and two types of outputs. One type of input called "regular input" represents a combination $x^1(t)$ of binary-valued inputs $x_1^1(t), x_2^1(t), \ldots, x_n^1(t)$. It is assumed that this input has the following properties:

(i) the input pattern $x^1(t)$ is always accepted by $D|q(t)$;
(ii) each $x_j^1(t) \in x^1(t)$ is associated with a corresponding input weight $w_j^1(t) \in w^1(t)$ specified by the state $q(t)$;
(iii) $x^1(t)$ has no direct effect on the internal state $q(t)$ of D;
(iv) $x^1(t)$ determines (through the composite γ-function) the values of outputs $y^1(t)$ and $y^2(t)$ of D.

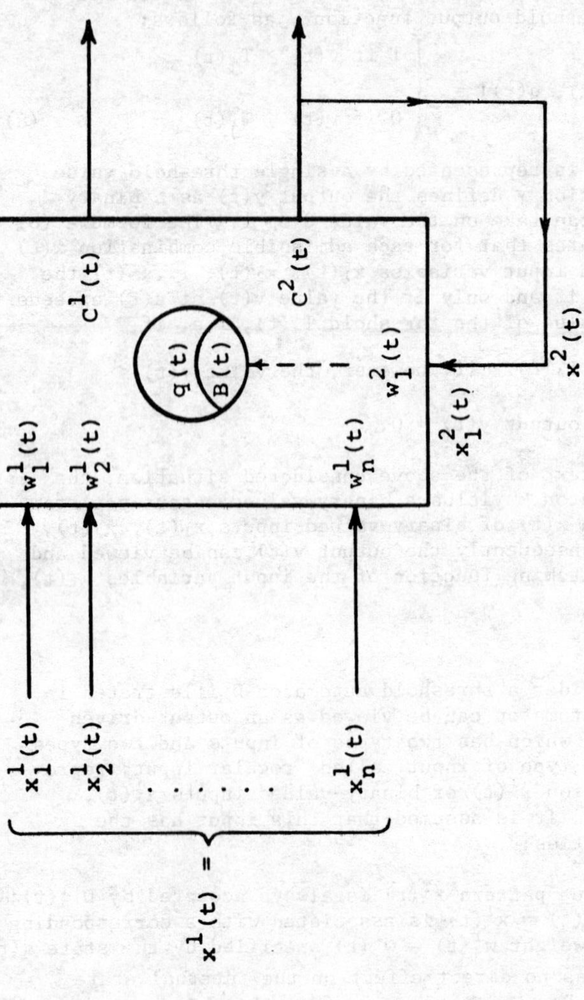

Fig. 1. The diagrammatic representation of a threshold automaton D.

The second type of input, denoted $x^2(t)$ and called "steering" input, represents a k-ary valued variable $x_i^2(t)$, which is generated by the automaton D as an output $y^2(t)$. This input is assumed to have the following properties:

(i) each $x^2(t) \in X$ is accepted by $D|q(t)$;
(ii) each $x^2(t) \in X$ is produced by $D|q(t)$ as $y^2(t)$;
(iii) each $x^2(t)$ is produced by $D|q(t)$ under the effect of $x^1(t)$;
(iv) each $x_j^2(t) \in x^2(t)$ is associated with an input weight $w_j^2(t) \in W$ specified by the stated $q(t)$;
(v) each $x^2(t)$ has an exclusive capability to transform one internal state of D into another.

Provided that $Q = \{q_1, q_2, \ldots, q_m\} | q(t) \Longrightarrow \tau(t) = \{B(t),\ C(t)\}$ where $B(t) = \{B_j(t):\ j = 0,1,\ldots,m\}$; $B_j(t) \in T$ and $B_0(t) < \ldots < B_m(t)$, $C(t) = \{C^1(t), C^2(t) | C^1(t) = T^1(t)$ and $C^2(t) = [T_j{}^2(t):\ j = 0,1,\ldots,n\}$ where

$T^1(t),\ T^2{}_j(t) \in T$ and $T^2{}_{j+1}(t) > T^2{}_j(t)$ for $j \in J | J = \{0,1,\ldots,n\}$

then

$$\beta_{B(t)}[x^2(t), q(t)] = \begin{cases} q^1(t+1) \text{ if } B_1(t) > v^2(t) \geq B_0(t) \\ q^2(t+1) \text{ if } B_2(t) > v^2(t) \geq B_1(t) \\ \vdots \\ q^m(t+1) \text{ if } B_n(t) > v^2(t) \geq B_{n-1}(t) \end{cases} \quad (9)$$

under the condition that $q(0) = q_i \in Q$. The operational value $v^2(t)$ of $x^2(t)$ is defined as a product $w_i^2(t) \cdot x_i^2(t)$ for each $w_i^2(t) \in W$ and $x_i^2(t) \in X$.

$$\gamma_{C(t)}[x^1(t), q(t)] = \begin{cases} \to y^1(t) = \begin{cases} 1 \text{ if } v^1(t) \geq T^1(t) \\ 0 \text{ if } v^1(t) < T^1(t) \end{cases} \\ \to y^2(t) = \begin{cases} z_1 \text{ if } T_1^2(t) > v^1(t) \geq T_0^2(t) \\ z_2 \text{ if } T_2^2(t) > v^1(t) > T_1^2(t) \\ \vdots \\ z_n \text{ if } T_n^2(t) > v^1(t) \geq T_{n-1}^2(t) \end{cases} \end{cases} \quad (10)$$

where $z_j \varepsilon\ Z | Z = \{z_1, z_2, \ldots, z_n\}$ represent the value of a k-ary valued output $y^2(t)$ if and only if $T_j{}^2(t) > v^1(t) \geq T_{j-1}^2(t)$ for $j \in J$. The operational value $v^1(t)$ of $x^1(t)$ is defined as a sum $\sum_{i=1}^{n} v_i^1 = \sum_{i=1}^{n} w_i^1(t)x_i^1(t)$.

The configuration w(t) of input weights $w_1^1(t)$, $w_2^1(t)$,..., $w_n^1(t)$; $w_1^2(t)$ associated at time t with the regular and steering inputs is determined by the state q(t) through the function h. Thus

$$w(t) = h[q(t)] \tag{11}$$

where $q(t) \in Q$ and $w(t) \in W$.

From the above example it follows, that the output-driven threshold automata can be defined which may have a built-in capability to adjust their internal states (and responses) to the anticipated inflow of inputs. Such automata could maintain the realization of a required logic functions at a predetermined level over a specified period of time and could be ultimately used as framework models for designing various types of self-adaptive threshold logic elements, analog to digital converters and various portions of a specialized computing hardware.

REFERENCES

1. M. ARBIB, *Theories of Abstract Automata* (Prentice-Hall, Englewood Cliffs, New Jersey, 1969).

2. T.L. BOOTH, *Sequential Machines and Automata Theory* (John Wiley & Sons, New York, 1967).

3. F.O. HADLOCK and C.L. COATES, "Realization of sequential machines with threshold elements" *IEEE Trans. on Computers C-18*, 428-439 (May 1969).

4. J. HARTMANIS and R.E. STEARNS, *Algebraic Structure Theory of Sequential Machines* (Prentice-Hall, Englewood Cliffs, N.J., 1966).

5. F.C. HENNIE, *Finite-State Models for Logical Machines* (John Wiley & Sons, New York, 1968).

6. G.E. LASKER, "CONSITRON - A threshold element control device for automatic control systems" *Proc. 6th Int. Congress on Cybernetics, Namur,* Section 3, 667-675, (7-11 September, 1970).

7. G.E. LASKER, "TRANSITRON - A new multifunctional threshold cell" *Cybernetica No. 3*, (Namur, 1972), 235-249.

8. W.S. McCULLOCH and W. PITTS, "A logical calculus of the ideas immanent in nervous activity" *Bull. Mat. Biophysics*, *5*, 115-133 (1943).

9. W.S. MEISEL, "Variable - threshold threshold elements" *IEEE Trans. on Computers, C-17*(7), 656-667 (July 1968).

10. W.S. MEISEL, "Nets of variable-threshold threshold elements" *IEEE Trans. on Computers, C-17*(7), 667-676 (July 1968).

11. M. MINSKY, *Computation - Finite and Infinite and Infinite Machines* (Prentice-Hall, Englewood Cliffs, New Jersey, 1967).

12. M. MINSKY and S. PAPERT, *Perceptron* (M.I.T. Press, Cambridge, Mass., 1969).

13. G.W. MOW and K.S. FU, "An approach for the realization of multithreshold threshold elements" *IEEE Trans. on Computers, C-17*(1), 36-46 (January 1968).

WALSH FUNCTIONS AND THEIR APPLICATION FOR COMMUNICATION CONTROL AND SIGNAL PROCESSING

K.G. BEAUCHAMP

Computing Centre, Cranfield Institute of Technology, Cranfield, Bedford, U.K.

SUMMARY

A common basis for the theory of communication and control engineering is found in the use of sine/cosine functions in continuous systems. The last decade has seen the development of a new system of orthogonal functions, paralleling the role of the sine/cosine functions, but particularly suited to discontinuous systems, such as solid-state binary logic. These are known as Walsh functions. This paper considers the basic properties and generation of these functions and their transforms in comparison with those of the sine/cosine functions. A number of application are discussed and conclusions drawn concerning the usefulness of these functions to application areas in digital technology.

INTRODUCTION

This paper discusses a fairly new concept in function representation providing a basis for application to two-state devices in much the same way as the sine/cosine functions have been applied to continuously-variable devices.

The most important of these representations is undoubtedly the set of orthogonal functions proposed by J.L. Walsh [1] in 1923. Other orthogonal function sets such as the Haar functions [2], and a complex Walsh function [3], have been described for specific uses but lack generality of application using digital logic found with the original Walsh function.

The Walsh functions form an ordered set of rectangular waveforms taking only two amplitude values, +1 and -1 defined over a limited time interval, T, known as the time base. Two arguments are required for complete definition, a time period, t normalised to the time base as t/T, and an ordering number, n related to frequency in a way which is described later. The function is written:-

$$\mathrm{WAL}(n,t) \tag{1}$$

For most purposes a set of such functions is ordered in ascending value of the number of zero crossings found within the time base. Figure 1 shows the first 32 of these with the ordering arranged in this way.

The function series can be obtained by means of a difference equation [4], as products of Rademacher functions [5], or by the use of a Hademard matrix [6]. The last two methods are more informative concerning the structure of the series and are considered below.

A subset of the Walsh functions known as the Rademacher functions are obtained from an appropriate set of sinusoidal functions through amplification followed by hard limiting Fig. 2. A complete set of Walsh functions may be obtained from these by taking selected function products.

Thus, if we represent the Rademacher functions as R(i,t) where i represents the order by number of zero crossings shown in Fig. 2 then a given Walsh function is obtained from:

$$\mathrm{WAL}(n,t) = \prod_{i=1}^{m} b_i \, R(i,t) \tag{2}$$

Here, n, the order number, is expressed in binary form as a Gray code and b_i gives the relevant bit positions. Hence to find WAL(9,t) we first express 9 in binary code as 1001 and then rearrange this in Gray code as 1101.
The second bit position gives $b_i = 0$ so that we can write directly from (2):

$$\mathrm{WAL}(9,t) = R(4,t).\,R(3,t)\,R(1,t)$$

A simple hardware realisation of a Walsh function generator using Rademacher products is shown in Fig. 3. Here the +1 and -1 levels are exchanged for binary 1 and 0 levels which permits the process of multiplication by +1 and -1 to be replaced by an exclusive-OR operation. A set of Rademacher functions is produced by a binary division counter having $\log_2 N$ stages. Appropriate functions are selected from this

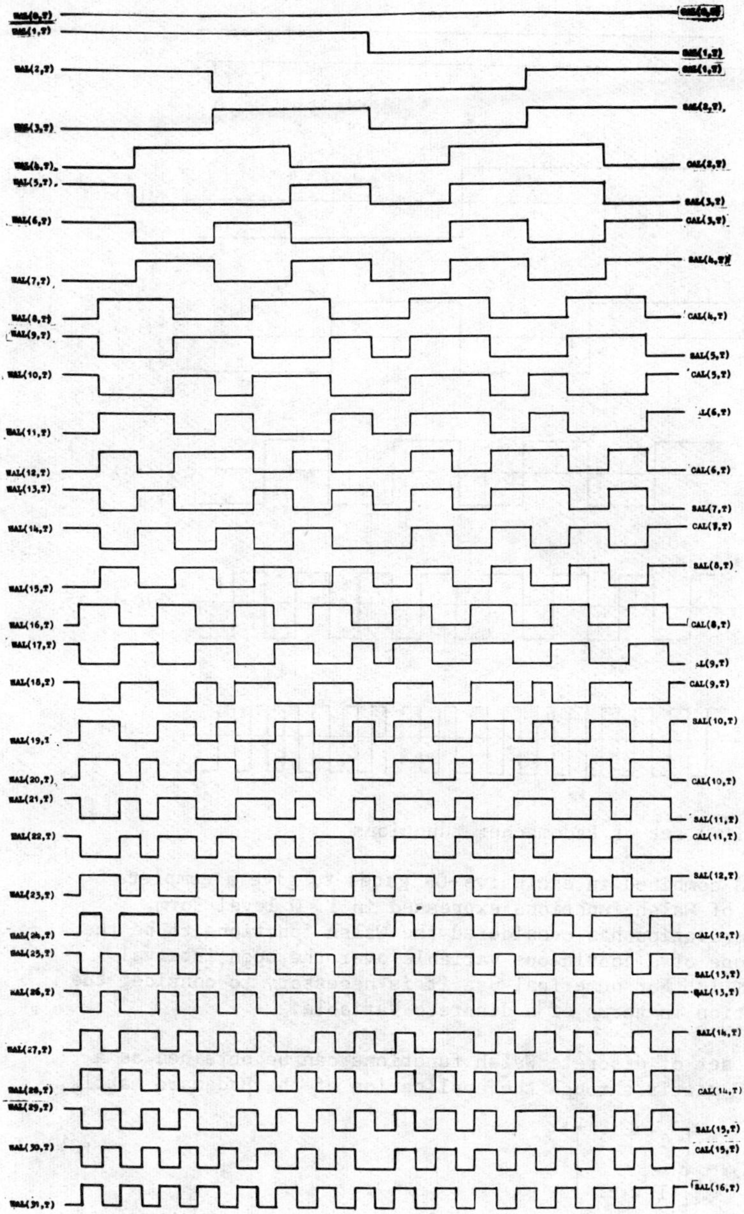

Fig. 1. The first 32 Walsh functions arranged in sequency order.

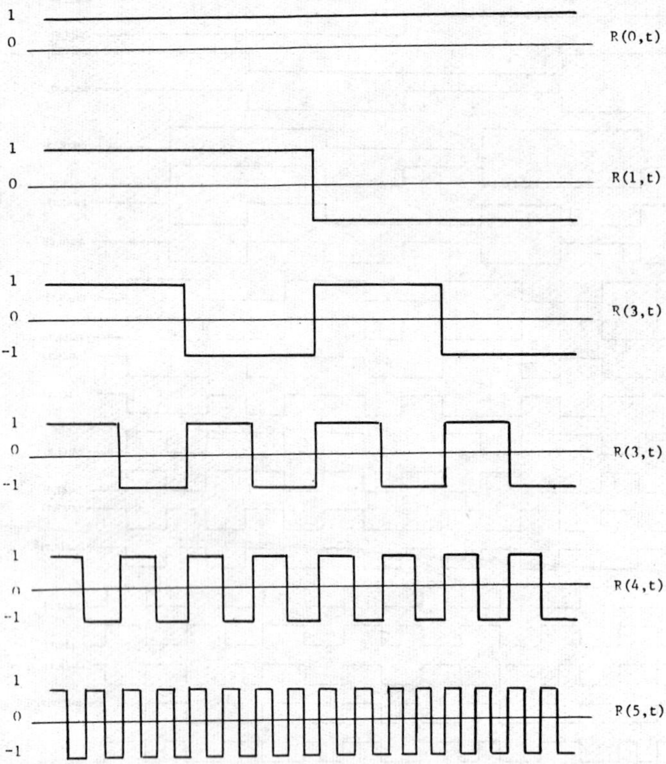

Fig. 2. A set of Rademacher functions

set and combined in exclusive-OR gates to give a complete series of Walsh functions expressed in 1, 0 level form. This derivation has considered the Walsh functions to be the functions of a continuous variable over the open interval $0 < t < 1$. For numerical use it is necessary to consider the derivation in terms of a discrete variable.

A set of discrete Walsh functions can be obtained as a $2^n \times 2^n$ matrix through the application of the Hadamard matrix,

$$H_2 = \begin{bmatrix} 1 & 1 \\ 1 & -1 \end{bmatrix} \tag{3}$$

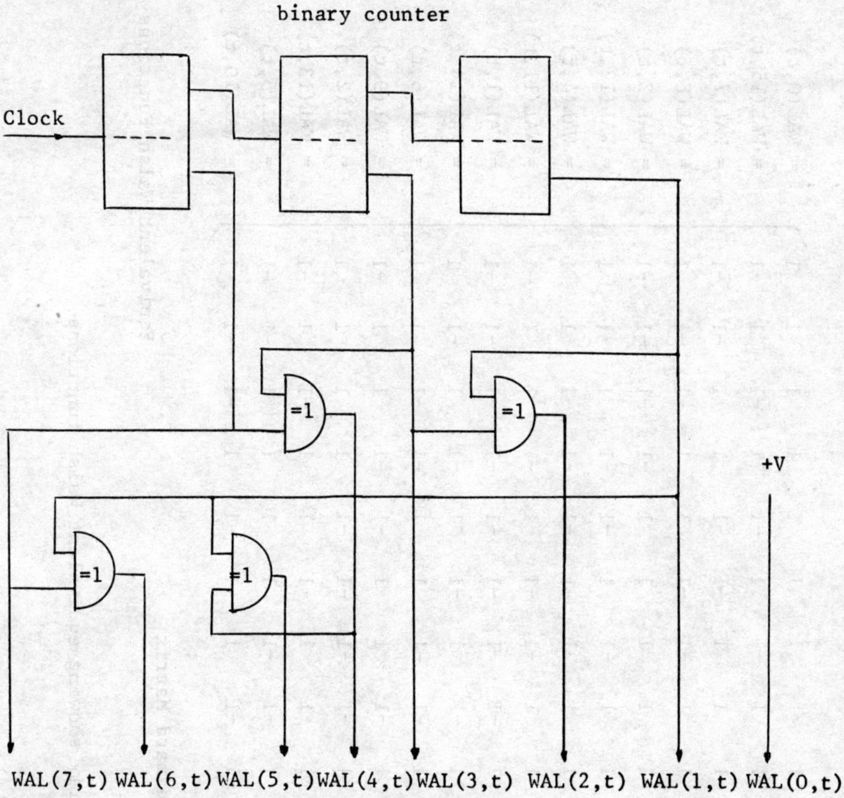

Fig. 3. A hardware Walsh function generator.

from the recursive relation:-

$$H_N = H_{N/2} \otimes H_2 \tag{4}$$

where $\otimes$ denotes the direct or Kronecker product and

$$N = 2^n, \quad n = 2,3.........$$

Figure 4 shows this carried out for a 16 order Hadamard matrix. This produces an identical set of functions to those shown in Fig. 1, but arranged in a different order. The relationship between the ordering of the rows of a Hadamard matrix and a set of Walsh functions is given elsewhere [7].

$$
\begin{bmatrix}
1 & 1 & 1 & 1 & 1 & 1 & 1 & 1 & 1 & 1 & 1 & 1 & 1 & 1 & 1 & 1 \\
1 & -1 & 1 & -1 & 1 & -1 & 1 & -1 & 1 & -1 & 1 & -1 & 1 & -1 & 1 & -1 \\
1 & 1 & -1 & -1 & 1 & 1 & -1 & -1 & 1 & 1 & -1 & -1 & 1 & 1 & -1 & -1 \\
1 & -1 & -1 & 1 & 1 & -1 & -1 & 1 & 1 & -1 & -1 & 1 & 1 & -1 & -1 & 1 \\
1 & 1 & 1 & 1 & -1 & -1 & -1 & -1 & 1 & 1 & 1 & 1 & -1 & -1 & -1 & -1 \\
1 & -1 & 1 & -1 & -1 & 1 & -1 & 1 & 1 & -1 & 1 & -1 & -1 & 1 & -1 & 1 \\
1 & 1 & -1 & -1 & -1 & -1 & 1 & 1 & 1 & 1 & -1 & -1 & -1 & -1 & 1 & 1 \\
1 & -1 & -1 & 1 & -1 & 1 & 1 & -1 & 1 & -1 & -1 & 1 & -1 & 1 & 1 & -1 \\
1 & 1 & 1 & 1 & 1 & 1 & 1 & 1 & -1 & -1 & -1 & -1 & -1 & -1 & -1 & -1 \\
1 & -1 & 1 & -1 & 1 & -1 & 1 & -1 & -1 & 1 & -1 & 1 & -1 & 1 & -1 & 1 \\
1 & 1 & -1 & -1 & 1 & 1 & -1 & -1 & -1 & -1 & 1 & 1 & -1 & -1 & 1 & 1 \\
1 & -1 & -1 & 1 & 1 & -1 & -1 & 1 & -1 & 1 & 1 & -1 & -1 & 1 & 1 & -1 \\
1 & 1 & 1 & 1 & -1 & -1 & -1 & -1 & -1 & -1 & -1 & -1 & 1 & 1 & 1 & 1 \\
1 & -1 & 1 & -1 & -1 & 1 & -1 & 1 & -1 & 1 & -1 & 1 & 1 & -1 & 1 & -1 \\
1 & 1 & -1 & -1 & -1 & -1 & 1 & 1 & -1 & -1 & 1 & 1 & 1 & 1 & -1 & -1 \\
1 & -1 & -1 & 1 & -1 & 1 & 1 & -1 & -1 & 1 & 1 & -1 & 1 & -1 & -1 & 1
\end{bmatrix}
\begin{matrix}
= \mathrm{WAL}(0,t) \\
= \mathrm{WAL}(15,t) \\
= \mathrm{WAL}(7,t) \\
= \mathrm{WAL}(8,t) \\
= \mathrm{WAL}(3,t) \\
= \mathrm{WAL}(12,t) \\
= \mathrm{WAL}(4,t) \\
= \mathrm{WAL}(11,t) \\
= \mathrm{WAL}(1,t) \\
= \mathrm{WAL}(14,t) \\
= \mathrm{WAL}(6,t) \\
= \mathrm{WAL}(9,t) \\
= \mathrm{WAL}(2,t) \\
= \mathrm{WAL}(13,t) \\
= \mathrm{WAL}(5,t) \\
= \mathrm{WAL}(10,t)
\end{matrix}
$$

Hadamard Matrix — Equivalent Walsh Functions

Fig. 4. A 16 order Hademard matrix showing equivalent Walsh functions.

The ordering shown in Fig. 1 is known as Sequency order. Sequency is a term proposed by Harmuth [4], to describe a periodic repetition rate which is independent of waveform. It is defined as:- 'one half of the average number of zero crossings per unit time interval'. From this we see that frequency can be regarded as a special measure of sequency applicable to sinusoidal waveforms only.

A further notation has also been introduced by Harmuth to classify the Walsh functions in terms of even and odd waveform symmetry, viz:

$$\begin{aligned} &WAL(2k,t) = CAL(k,t) \\ &WAL(2k-1,t) = SAL(k,t) \qquad (5) \\ &\quad k = 1, 2 \ldots\ldots\ldots\ldots (^{N}/_{2} - 1) \end{aligned}$$

defining two further Walsh series having close similarities with cosine and sine series.

Using the Walsh function series any complex waveform can be represented by superposition of a number of elements of the series having appropriate amplitudes in an exactly analogous manner to Fourier synthesis. It will be found that fewer Walsh functions are required to represent a discontinuous waveform, compared with synthesis using sine/cosine functions, and that the converse holds true for smoothly-varying waveforms. This brings out an important difference between the two sets of functions, indicating their respective roles in signal analysis and other applications.

THE WALSH TRANSFORM

Decomposition of a time series function x(t) into a Walsh series is similar to Fourier series representation thus:

$$x(t) = a_0 + a_1\, WAL(1,t) + a_2\, WAL(2,t) + \ldots\ldots \qquad (6)$$

where the sequency coefficients are given by:-

$$a_k = \int_0^1 WAL(k,t)\, x(t)\, dt \qquad (7)$$

A finite discrete Walsh transform pair can be described for a time series x_i comprised of N samples:

$$X_k = \frac{1}{N} \sum_{i=0}^{N-1} x_i \ \mathrm{WAL}(k,i) \qquad (8)$$

$$k = 0,1,2.......N-1$$

$$x_i = \sum_{k=0}^{N-1} X_k \ \mathrm{WAL}(k,i) \qquad (9)$$

$$i = 0,1,2........N-1$$

Similar transforms, $X_c(k)$ and $X_s(k)$ can be obtained using Harmuth's CAL and SAL functions.

The transform and is inverse are obtained by matrix multiplication using the digital computer. Since the matrices are symmetrical for the Walsh transform (unlike the Fourier transform) then both transform and inverse transform are identical, except for a scaling factor, 1/N.

If we compare equation (8) with the corresponding discrete Fourier transform:-

$$X_f = \frac{1}{N} \sum_{i=0}^{N-1} x_i \exp(-j2\pi if/N) \qquad (10)$$

$$f = 0,1,2.......N-1$$

we note that whilst WAL(k,i) is real and limited to values ±1, exp(-j2if/N) is complex and can assume N different values. As a direct consequence of this the Walsh transform proves considerably easier and faster to calculate using digital methods. A fast Walsh transform algorithm (F.W.T.) exists having comparable computational features to the fast Fourier transform [8] (F.F.T.). If the transform is evaluated directly using equation (8) then N^2 addition/subtractions are required. Using the F.W.T. only $2N\log_2 N$ mathematical operations are required to transform N values, where N is expressed as a power of 2 . Further the Walsh transform requires only real additions and subtractions, compared with the complex multiplications needed for the Fourier transform.

The properties of the Walsh function and the Walsh transform are summarised and compared with the sine/cosine functions in Table 1.

TABLE I. Equivalents Between Walsh and Fourier Discrete Series of Length, N.

WALSH		FOURIER	
time index	i	time index	i
sequency index	k	frequency index	n
	$i,k,n = 0,1,2 \ldots\ldots N-1$		
cal function	$cal(k,i) = \omega al(2k,i)$	cos function	$\cos \frac{2\pi ni}{N}$
sal function	$sal(k,i) = \omega al(2k-1,i)$	sin function	$\sin \frac{2\pi ni}{N}$
Walsh function	$\omega al(k,i)$	Complex function	$\exp j \cdot \frac{2\pi ni}{N}$ $= \cos \frac{2\pi ni}{N} + j \sin \frac{2\pi ni}{N}$

TABLE I. Cont.

WALSH		FOURIER	
time series	$x_i = a_0 \ \omega al(0,i) + a_1 \ \omega al(1,t)$ $+ \ldots\ldots\ldots + a_N \ \omega al(N,i)$	time series	$x_i = A_0 + A_1 \exp\left[\frac{2\pi i}{N}\right]$ $+ A_2 \exp\left[\frac{4\pi i}{N}\right] + \ldots\ldots + A_N \exp(\pi i)$
sequency coefficients	$a_0, a_1 \ldots\ldots\ldots a_N$	complex frequency coefficients	$A_0, A_1 \ldots\ldots\ldots A_N$
Walsh series	$a_i = a_0 \ \omega al(0,1) +$ $\sum_{m=1}^{N/2} \sum_{p=1}^{N/2-1} a_m sal(m,i) + b_p cal(p,i)$	Fourier series	$a_i = \frac{a_0}{2} + \sum_{m=1}^{N} \left[a_m \cos\left[\frac{2\pi ni}{N}\right] + b_m \sin\left[\frac{2\pi ni}{N}\right]\right]$
Walsh transform	$X_k = \frac{1}{N} \sum_{i=0}^{N-1} x_i \omega al(k,i)$	Fourier transform	$X_n = \frac{1}{N} \sum_{i=0}^{N-1} x_i \exp\left[-j\frac{2\pi ni}{N}\right]$
Walsh inverse transform	$x_i = \sum_{i=o}^{N-1} X_k \ \omega al(k,i)$	Fourier inverse transform	$x_i = \sum_{i=0}^{N-1} X_n \exp\left[j\frac{2\pi ni}{N}\right]$

TABLE I. Cont.

WALSH		FOURIER	
Walsh CAL transform	$X_c(p) = \frac{1}{N} \sum_{i=0}^{N-1} x_i \; cal(p,i)$	Fourier cosine transform	$X_c(p) = \frac{1}{N} \sum_{i=xi}^{N-1} \cos\left[\frac{2\pi ni}{N}\right]$
	$p = 1, \; 2 \; \ldots\ldots\ldots \frac{N}{2} - 1$		
Walsh SAL transform	$X_s(q) = \frac{1}{N} \sum_{i=0}^{N-1} x_i \; sal \; (q,i)$	Fourier sine transform	$X_s(p) = \frac{1}{N} \sum_{i=0}^{N-1} x_i \sin\left[\frac{2\pi ni}{N}\right]$
Orthogonal property	$\sum_{i=0}^{N-1} \omega al(k,i) \; \omega al(\ell,i)$ $= N \quad k = \ell$ $= 0 \quad k \neq \ell$	Orthogonal property	$\sum_{i=0}^{N-1} \exp\left[j \frac{2\pi ni}{N}\right] \exp\left[j \frac{2\pi mi}{N}\right]$ $= N \quad n = m$ $= 0 \quad n \neq m$
Symmetrical property	$\omega al(k,i) = \omega al(i,k)$	Symmetrical property	Not applicable

TABLE I. Cont.

	WALSH		FOURIER
Shift theorem	not applicable	Shift theorem	$\cos(n \mp m)\, i = \cos ni.\ \cos mi \pm \sin ni.\ \sin mi$ $\sin(n \pm m)\, i = \sin ni.\ \cos mi \pm \cos ni.\ \sin mi$
Multiplication theorem	$wal(k,i)wal(p,i) = wal[(k \oplus p), i]$ $cal(k,i)cal(p,i) = cal[(k \oplus p), i]$ $sal(k,i)cal(p,i) = sal[(p \oplus (k+1))+1, i]$ $cal(k,i)sal(p,i) = sal[(k \oplus (p-1))+1, i]$ $sal(k,i)sal(p,i) = cal[(k \oplus 1) \oplus (p-1), i)]$ $\oplus$ = modulo-2 addition	Multiplication theorem	$2 \cos ni.\cos mi = \cos(n-m)i + \cos(n+m)i$ $2 \sin ni.\cos mi = \sin(n-m)i + \cos(n+m)i$ $2 \cos ni.\sin mi = -\sin(n-m)i + \sin(n+m)i$ $2 \sin ni.\sin mi = \cos(n-m)i - \cos(n+m)i$
Dyadic convolution $\circledast$	$x_i \circledast y_i = \frac{1}{N} \sum_{i=0}^{N-1} x_i\ y(\tau \oplus i)$	Convolution $*$ τ=convolution delay	$x_i * y_i = \frac{1}{N} \sum_{i=0}^{N-1} x_i\ y(i+\tau)$
Convolution Product relation	$x_i \circledast y_i \leftrightarrow X_k \cdot Y_k$	Convolution relations $\leftrightarrow$ = Transform	$x_i * y_i \leftrightarrow X_n \cdot Y_n$
Dyadic autocorrelation	$D_{(\tau)} = \frac{1}{N} \sum_{i=0}^{N-1} x_i\ y(i \ominus \tau)$	Autocorrelation	$R_{(\tau)} = \frac{1}{N} \sum_{i=0}^{N-1} x_i\ y(i-\tau)$

TABLE I. Cont.

WALSH		FOURIER	
Dyadic Spectrum	$P(o) = X_c^{\,2}\ (o)$ $P(p) = X_c^{\,2}\ (p) + X_s^{\,2}(p)$ $P\,\frac{N}{2} = X_s^{\,2}\ \frac{N}{2}$ $p = 1, 2 \ldots\ldots \frac{N}{2} - 1$	Fourier Spectrum	$G_{(n)} = \frac{1}{N} \mid X_n \mid^2$
Dyadic Wiener-Khintchine Theory	$D(\tau) \leftrightarrow P_{(p)}$	Wiener-Khintchine theory	$R(\tau) \leftrightarrow G(n)$
Parseval's theorem	$\frac{1}{N} \sum_{i=0}^{N-1} \left[x_i\right]^2 = \sum_{k=0}^{N-1} \left[X_k\right]^2$	Parseval's theorem	$\frac{1}{N} \sum^{N-1} \left[x_i\right]^2 = \sum_{n=0}^{N-1} \left[X_n\right]^2$

Important differences, not already considered, concern the effect of circular time shift on the series to be transformed and the special behaviour of transform products.

The discrete Fourier transform is invarient to the phase of the input signal so that the same spectral decomposition can be obtained independently of the phase or circular time shift of the input signal.

This is not the case with the Walsh transform [4].

The effect is one of variation in shape and location of the dominant spectral characteristics of the signal. It is of less importance where the sum of the square of pairs of transformed coefficients of the same sequency are taken, as with power spectrum derivation, but will account for minor variations between spectra unless the time histories are obtained at the same time or adjusted for zero phase shift.

An addition relationship is found for Walsh functions, namely:

$$WAL(k,t)WAL(p,t) = WAL(k \oplus p,t) \qquad (14)$$

where $\oplus$ represents Modulo-2 addition.

This corresponds to the set of relationships

$$2\cos kt \cos pt = \cos(k-p)t + \cos(k+p)t$$

.........etc

with the important difference that a Shift Theorem for Walsh functions does not exist so that whilst the product of two Fourier transforms can be transformed to obtain a convolution of the two original time series, a similar result is not obtained with the Walsh transform.

The absence of a Walsh shift theorem successfully prevents fast correlation via the F.W.T. or applications of digital filtering through use of a defined impulse response function in the time domain.

Despite this major difficulty the Walsh function finds many important applications in processing and communication. Some of these will now be described.

Spectral Analysis

A sequency spectrum is obtained from the sum of the squares of the CAL and SAL function coefficients of the same sequency for each spectral coefficient in a manner similar to that used in Fourier analysis. Reference to Fig. 1 and equation (5) will show that N/2 + 1 spectral points will be obtained with the first and the last consisting of the square of the CAL and SAL function only viz:

$$P_{(0)} = X_c^{\,2}\,(0)$$

$$P_{(k)} = X_c^{\,2}(k) + X^2(k) \qquad (15)$$

$$P(\tfrac{N}{2}) = X_s^{\,2}\left[\frac{N}{2}\right]$$

$$k = 1, 2\ldots\ldots \frac{N}{2} - 1$$

We can regard the Walsh spectrum so obtained as having a minimum analysis bandwidth analogous to 'two degrees of freedom' obtained in the Fourier case. A wider bandwidth is obtained by summing the squares of a number of CAL and SAL coefficients for consecutive sequencies and normalising by the number of pairs taken. Some examples of Walsh spectral analysis are shown compared with the equivalent Fourier spectrum in Fig. 5. The first shows the analysis of a short-term transient signal and the second the spectrum of a pulse-coded modulation signal which is limited to two binary levels. In the latter case the precision of the Walsh analysis applied to a binary signal is apparent. The signal is decomposed into a limited number of Walsh functions whereas in the Fourier case a theoretically unlimited series of harmonic coefficients is produced.

Digital Filtering

The general principle of software Walsh digital filtering may be understood by reference to Fig. 6. The N-point signal to be filtered is transformed into the sequency domain, weighting modifications made to this and the results transformed again to give the filtered signal. The modification can take several forms. The simplest of these is known as sequency-limited filtering. In the case of low-pass filtering all the sequency coefficients above a certain value are set to zero before retransformation takes place. This is an extremely efficient process and can result in a perfect 'brick-wall' filter.

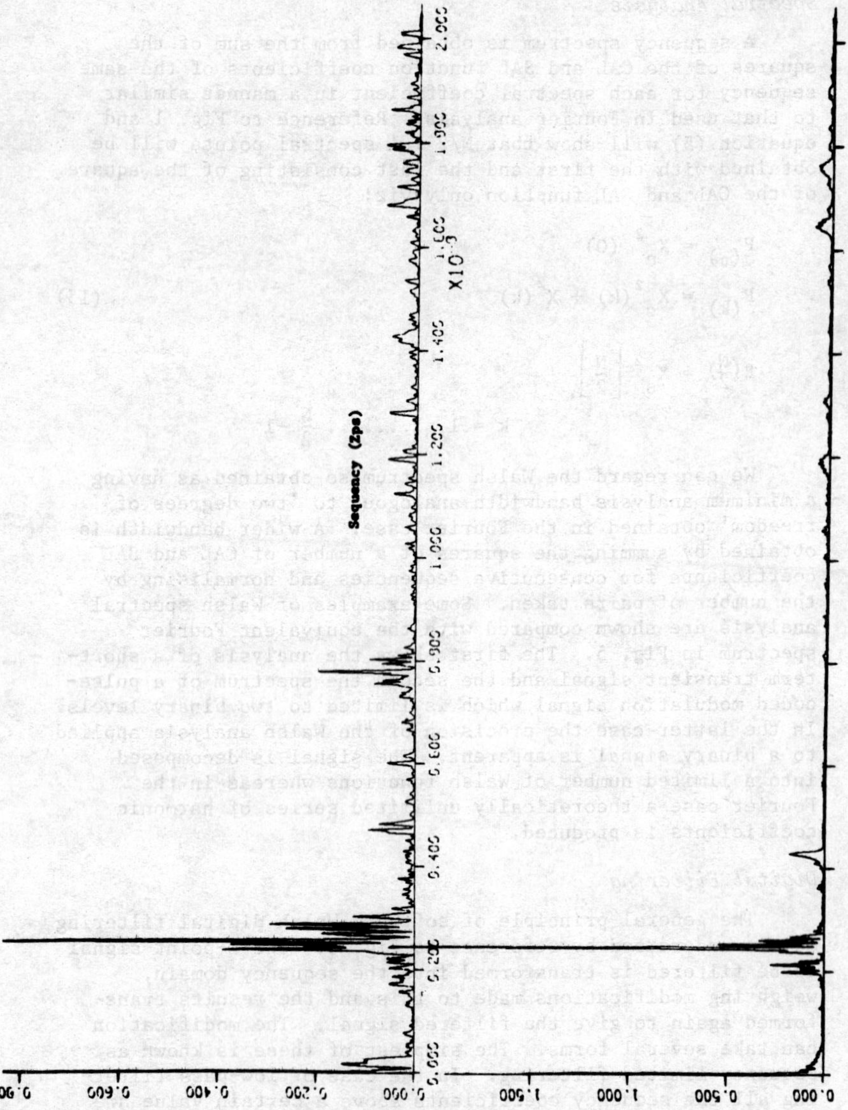

Fig. 5a. Comparison between a Sequency and Frequency Power Spectrum for a shock transient.

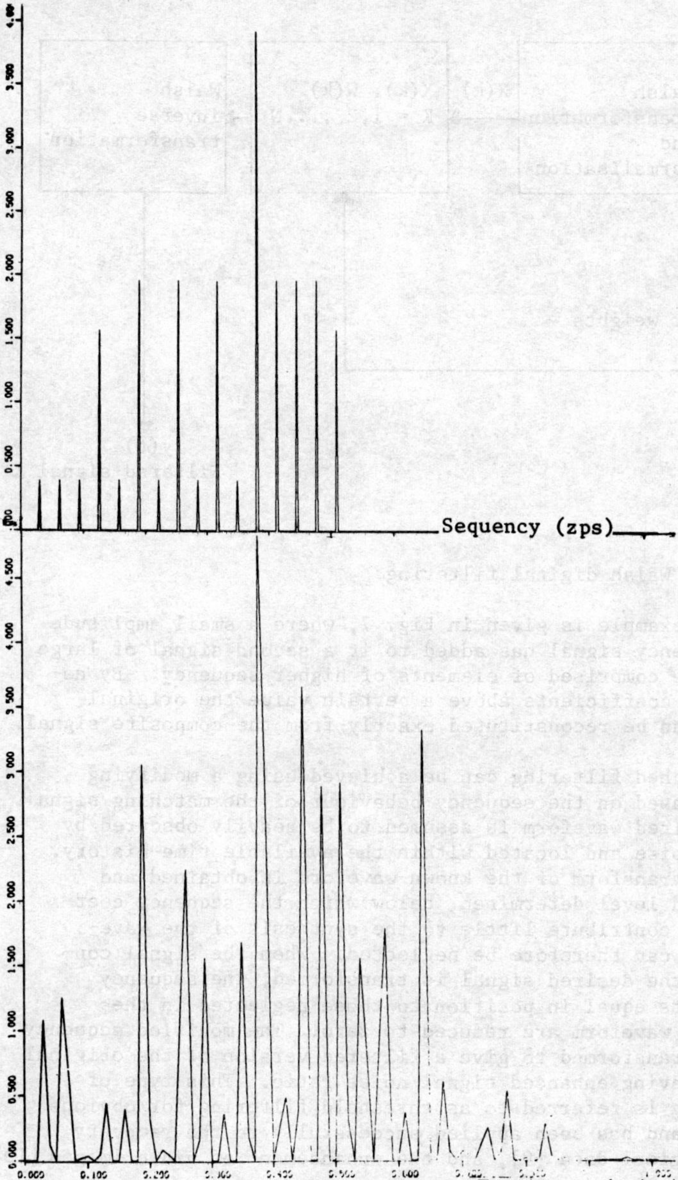

Fig. 5b. Examples of Walsh spectral analysis
Comparison between the sequency and frequency spectrum of a PCM signal coded in NRZ-M code.

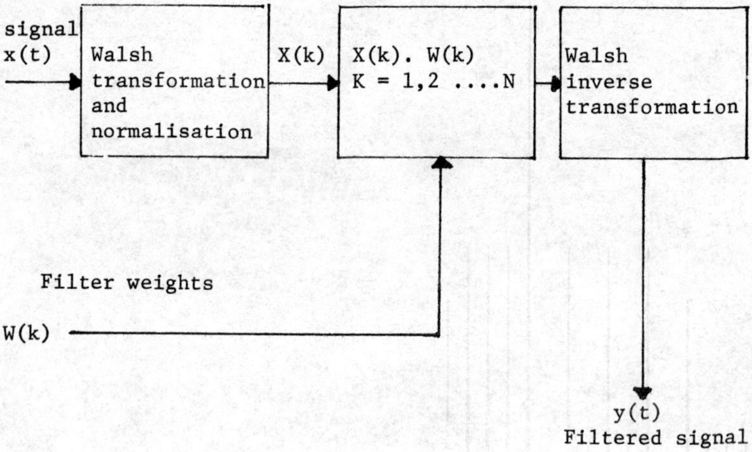

Fig. 6. Walsh digital filtering.

An example is given in Fig. 7, where a small amplitude low sequency signal has added to it a second signal of large amplitude comprised of elements of higher sequency. By neglecting coefficients above a certain value the original signal can be reconstituted exactly from the composite signal.

Matched filtering can be achieved using a modifying series based on the sequency behaviour of the matching signal. The required waveform is assumed to be heavily obscured by random noise and located within the available time-history. A Walsh transform of the known waveform is obtained and threshold level determined, below which the sequency coefficients contribute little to the synthesis of the waveform and can therefore be neglected. When the signal containing the desired signal is transformed, the sequency components equal in position to those neglected in the matching waveform are reduced to zero. The modified sequency set is transformed to give a filtered version of the original signal having enhanced signal/noise ratio. This type of filtering is referred to as threshold filtering for obvious reasons and has been applied successfully to the recovery of geological data [9], and the enhancement of video images [10].

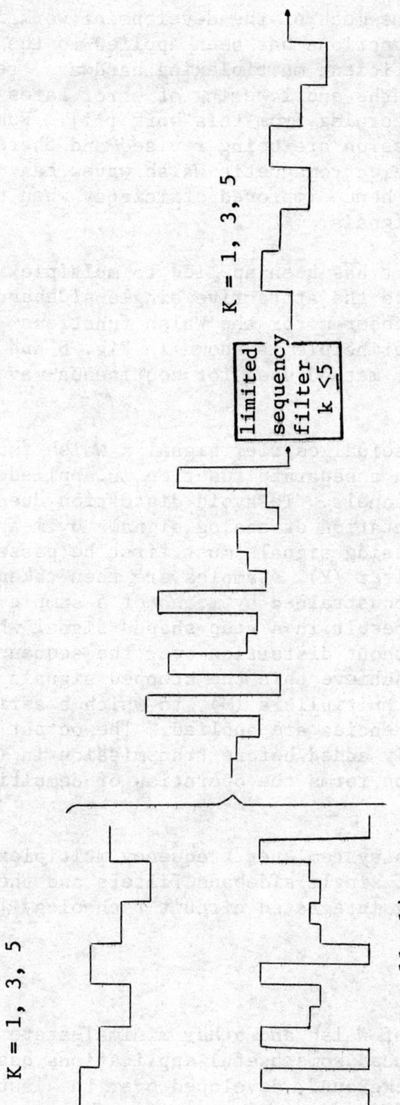

Fig. 7. Example of sequency limited filtering.

Applications in Communications

At the present time much of the development work in the application of Walsh functions has been applied to the field of communications. Efficient multiplexing hardware, reduction of transmission bandwidths and lowering of error rates are some of the benefits accruing from this work [11]. Fundamental ideas of radio transmission are being revised and there are also indications that electromagnetic Walsh waves can offer better directivity and hence improved efficiency when compared with continuous-wave signals.

Considerable effort has been applied to multiplexing systems. This is due to the attractive single-sideband features of the addition theorem for the Walsh functions (equation (14)). The principle is shown in Fig. 8 and is similar to the familiar method used for continuous-wave telemetry.

Instead of a sinusoidal carrier signal a Walsh function series is used in which a separate function is applied to each of the transmission channels. To avoid distortion due to the limitations in representation of analog signals by means of Walsh functions, the analog signals must first be passed through an aliasing filter (F). Samples are then taken at uniform intervals and constrained by means of a sample-and-hold amplifier (H) to result in a step-shaped signal which can then be transmitted without distortion over the sequency multiplex system. To achieve this the stepped signals are applied to a series of Multipliers (M), to which a series of contiguous carrier sequencies are applied. The output of the multipliers are linearly added before transmission in (S). A similar multiplication forms the operation of demultiplexing at the receiving end.

Advantages of this system over frequency multiplexing are the absence of a set of single-sideband filters and the ease of implementation using integrated circuit technology [12].

CONCLUSION

The exploutation of Walsh and other minimal-state functions has already produced some useful applications based on a sound theoretical background, developed over the last decade.

The analysis and processing methods developed using these functions are particularly suitable for solid-state technology and in view of the effort currently being expended in research

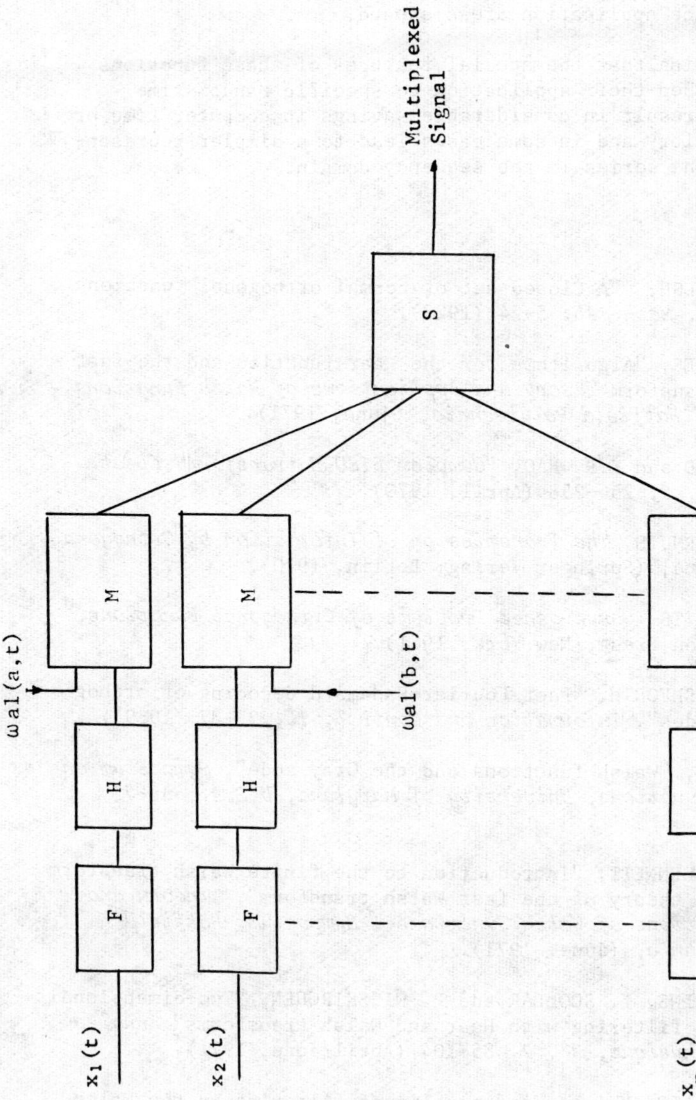

Fig. 8. Multiplexing using Walsh function carriers.

Fig. 8. Multiplexing using Walsh function carriers.

laboratories and University departments on a global basis it is obvious that the technology will benefit to an increasing extent as the application areas expand.

Providing that the special features of these functions are noted then their application to specific random time series can result in considerable savings in computer time or logic circuitry and in some cases lead to a simpler representation of the series in the sequency domain.

REFERENCES

1. J.L. WALSH, "A Closed set of normal orthogonal functions", *Amer. J. Math. 45*, 5-24 (1923).

2. H. KREMER, "Algorithms for the Haar function and the fast Haar transform *Theory and Applications of Walsh Functions - Symposium, Hatfield Polytechnic,* (june, 1971).

3. N. AHMED and K.R. RAO, *"Complex BIFORE transform" Elect. Letters, 6,* 256-258 (April, 1970).

4. H.F. HARMUTH, *The Transmission of Information by Orthogonal Functions*, (Springer Verlag, Berlin, 1970).

5. G. ALEXITS, *Convergence Problems of Orthogonal Functions,* (Pergamon Press, New York, 1961).

6. C.K. RUSHFORTH, "Fast Fourier-Hadamard decoding of orthogonal Codes", *Information and Control, 15,* 33-37 (1969).

7. C. YUEN, "Walsh functions and the Gray code", *Symposium on Walsh Functions, University of Maryland, U.S.A.,* 68-73 (1971).

8. B.L.N. KENNETT, "Introduction to the finite Walsh transform and the theory of the fast Walsh transform". *Theory and Applications of Walsh Functions - Symposium, Hatfield Polytechnic,* (June, 1971).

9. D. GUBBINS, I. SCOLLAR and P. WISSKIRCHEN, "Two-dimensional digital filtering with Haar and Walsh transforms" *Annales de Geophysique, 27,* 2, 85-104 (April/June, 1971).

10. W.K. PRATT, "Linear and non-linear filtering in the Walsh domain", *Symposium on Walsh Functions, University of Maryland, U.S.A.,* 38-42 (1971).

11. See: Applications of Walsh Functions - *A Symposium, Naval Research Laboratory, University of Maryland,* AD727000 (1971), and AD744650 (1972).

12. H. HUBNER, "Analog and digital multiplexing by means of Walsh functions", *Symposium on Walsh Functions, University of Maryland, U.S.A.,* 180-191, (1971).

SECTION IV

TOWARDS EFFECTIVE MANAGEMENT CONTROL SYSTEMS: A SYSTEMS ANALYSIS FOR SOCIO-ECONOMIC ENTERPRISES

E.A. LOWE
Division of Economic Studies, University of Sheffield, Western Bank, Sheffield S10 2TN, England

J.M. McINNES
Manchester Business School, Booth Street West, Manchester, M15 6PB, England

SUMMARY

This paper is a development of the authors' previous contribution towards a definition of the management control problem by means of systems analysis and, in terms of a macro-type model of the enterprise, describes the general characteristics of the internal systems analysis necessary for an effective management control system. The anlaysis requires extension by: an elaboration of the elements of each sub-system and the linkages between them; the linkage between the elements of these sub-systems and the substantial environment; inclusion of the behavioural aspects of the analysis; and inclusion of the implications for the structure of the organisation of the enterprise. The authors are aware of the shortcomings of this highly condensed conference paper but trust that readers will find it useful as an introduction to their work.

INTRODUCTION

A contribution towards the definition of the management control problem by means of systems analysis has already been made by the authors [1]. This paper is an extension of that work. In our previous paper emphasis was placed upon an analysis at a low level of resolution of the relationship between an organisation and its environment, from a management control viewpoint; an attempt was made to define the boundaries between a human enterprise and its environment and between the 'substantial' and 'general' parts of the environment to the enterprise. Stress was further laid upon the need for the use of an orderly analysis in terms of 'resolution levels' in defining and elaborating a model for a management control system.

It is important to emphasise that this analysis is not presently intended to advocate an approach in which systems analysis and control theory are used directly to set the level of enterprise control variables according to, for instance, a detailed computer programme; although there is an implication that this is a desirable end towards which progress should be (and is being) made [2]. In terms of management science models we are still at the stage where a better general understanding of the management control problem of the enterprise, *as a whole*, is required. A contrast may be made here between such a 'macro type' control model and the many 'micro-level' control models, for detailed aspects of control, which abound in the management science literature.

In this paper our work is extended to suggest an outline for a model which describes the general characteristics of the internal systems analysis necessary for an effective management control system.

A SYSTEMS ANALYSIS FOR AN ENTERPRISE'S INTERNAL STRUCTURE

In Fig. 1 we attempt a systems analysis of an economic, human enterprise which defines the principal parts of the internal control structure. Self evidently, and therefore the point need not be laboured, this representation is not, in any sense, an attempt to describe the internal authority and role structures or the working relationships within enterprises. Rather it attempts to define the control problem in its most general and fundamental management terms.

The enterprise is characterised here as an input-conversion-output processor. Inputs, as stimuli to the human enterprise system, are conceived in the widest of terms as 'human needs for which the enterprise is intended to provide satisfactions' and conversely the outputs, as responses to the stimuli of the inputs, are conceived in similarly wide terms as 'satisfactions of those same needs'. There are, we suggest, good reasons for such a wide conception for both inputs and outputs: firstly, in order to understand and predict, and therefore control, the behaviour of an enterprise it is necessary to include in the analysis all human values which affect the behavioural relationships as between people within the enterprise, and hence its outputs; secondly, we are seeking a long-run theory of management control and for these purposes all other consequences, as well as the most evident and immediate ones, of behaviour must be taken into account, insofar as they influence enterprise outputs significantly.

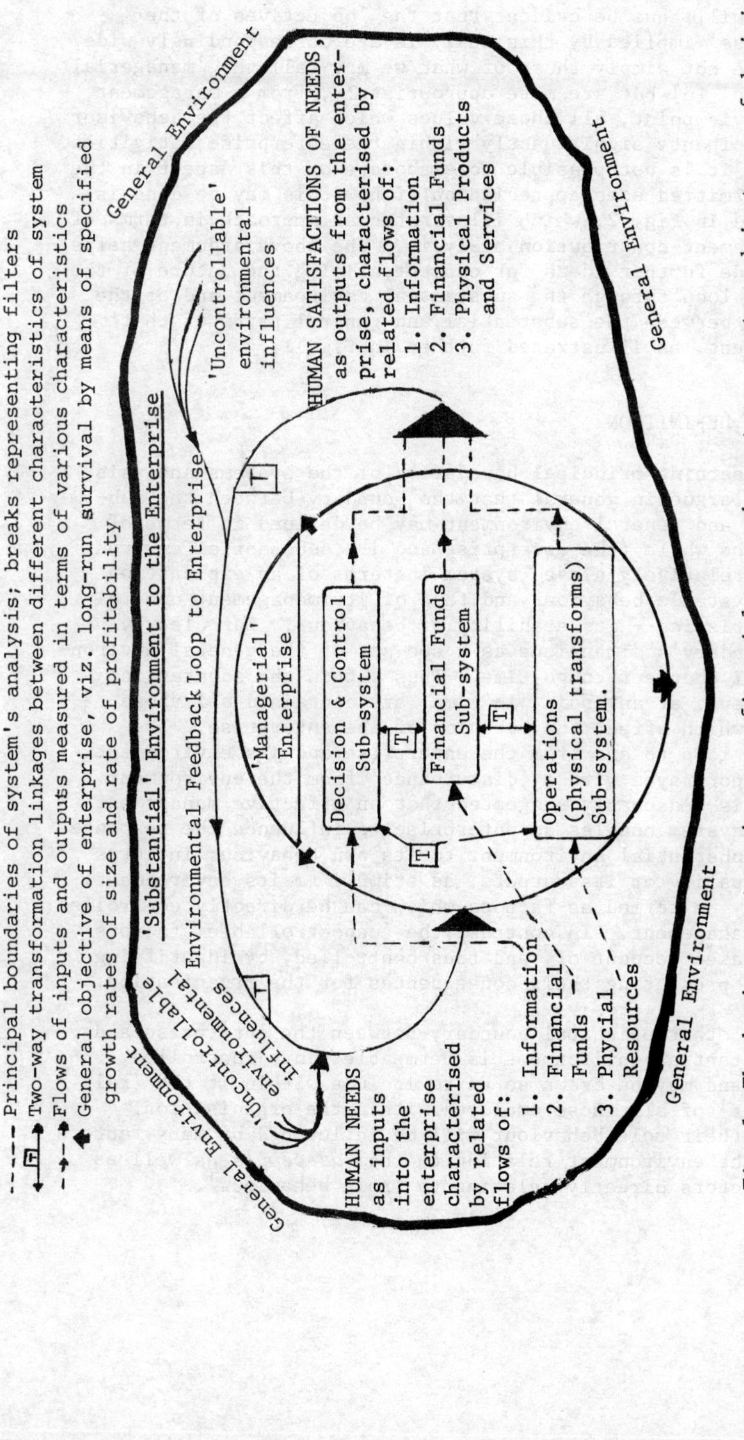

Fig. 1. The business enterprise as a financial-economic system — portrayed in terms of decision and control, funds flows and operations.

It will thus be evident that the 'objectives of the enterprise' implied by this analysis are correspondingly wide. They are not simply those of what we may call the 'managerial coalition' [3] but are more appropriately, from a management control viewpoint, all those values which affect the behaviour of participants significantly within the enterprise activities. Although it is not possible to elaborate on this aspect in the space permitted some appreciation of how this may be done is suggested in Fig. 2, which illustrates an approach in terms of an inducement-contribution analysis. The above argument helps to provide further ideas for conceptualising the nature of the feedback loop through the substantial environment and of the boundary between the substantial and general parts of that environment, as illustrated further in Fig. 1.

BOUNDARY DEFINITION

Concerning principal boundaries of the systems analysis, we would argue in general that the boundary between the substantial and general environment may be defined in terms of making the whole (the enterprise and its substantial environment) a relatively closed system in terms of an explanation of the system's behaviour and thus of its management control characteristics - its stability of behaviour. But clearly that boundary's dimensions as a sub-set of the general environment will change through time. Thus within the substantial environment, at any point in time, are contained all those factors which affect the behavior of the enterprise. The feedback loop to and from the enterprise and its environment is thus portrayed with a 'disturbance' from the environment. Thus it is reasonably suggested that an effective management control system enables an enterprise to influence the response of the substantial environment to its own behaviour in terms of the quality of its outputs, as stimuli to its environment. These may be termed as factors which can be directly controlled by the management. In contrast the 'uncontrollable' factors can be taken account of, and thus controlled, by identifying them and predicting their consequences for the organisation.

The other principal boundary-between the enterprise and its substantial environment is permeable, in a controlled manner, and may be drawn so as to include within it the 'role behaviour' of all those employed within the organisation. Clearly their role behaviour will be influenced by many factors within the environment relating to them *as people* as well as those factors directly relating to 'role behaviour'.

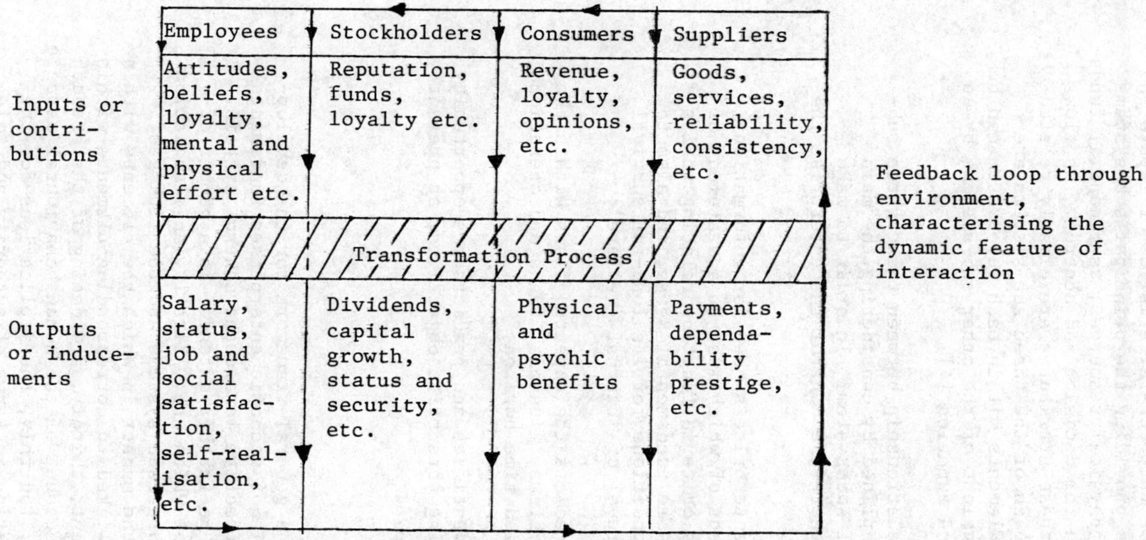

Notes: 1) The participants, inputs and outputs in the above model are only examples; each situation will be unique.

2) The employees' contributions to the firm include both task performance in respect to the operations sub-system, and the use of decision-making initiative in respect to the decision and control sub-system.

Fig. 2. The firm as a conversion process*

*We are much indebted to our colleague, A.M. Tinker, for the development of the idea for this Figure.

THE ENTERPRISE SUB-SYSTEMS

Within the enterprise three characteristics of inputs and outputs are identified as providing the principal sub-systems for control, namely: as physical resources, as financial funds flows, and as information for decision and control. As flows relating to human needs these attributes are closely related to one another and thus each of the three sub-systems are linked to one another. Elements within each sub-system can be transformed into an equivalent of the other sub-systems by an appropriate transformation function [4].

The nature of the relationship between these three sub-systems may be further outlined by considering the main elements of the principal sub-system. In order to make effective decisions and therefore control the enterprise the latter must include:

(1) a model of the enterprise's need for information; the main component of which must be a statement of the enterprise's criteria function relating to its objectives, in some fundamental sense, and also to the necessary conditions for its long-run survival at some stated level of internal 'welfare';

(2) a model which predicts the expected flows within the other two sub-systems, financial funds and operations, for some specified time horizon;

(3) a model which identifies and predicts the opportunity costs of achieving enterprise objectives, as presently formulated.

CONCLUSIONS

This paper outlines a general framework for the development of a systems analysis of economic enterprises fundamental to the construction of effective management control systems. The analysis requires to be further extended in a number of ways the most important of which are: firstly, an elaboration of the elements of the three sub-systems and the linkages between them; secondly, the manner in which the elements within each sub-system must be linked to corresponding elements within the substantial environment; thirdly, a widening of the breadth of the analysis to take account of the human behavioural aspects of this systems analysis; fourthly, the implications for the structure of the organisation in terms of authority and role relationships.

REFERENCES

1. E.A. LOWE and J.M. McINNES, "Control in socio-economic organizations: a rationale for the design of management control systems (Section 1)" *The Journal of Management Studies, 8* No. 2, 213-227 (May 1971).

2. C.P. BONINI, *Stimulation of Information and Decision Systems in the Firm* (Prentice-Hall, New York, 1963) and Y. IJIRI, *Management Goals and Accounting for Control* (North-Holland, Amsterdam, 1965).

3. R.M. CYERT and J.G. MARCH, *A Behavioural Theory of the Firm* (Prentice-Hall, New York, 1963).

4. See for instance, A. CHARNES and W.W. COOPER, "Some network characterizations for mathematical programming and accounting approaches to planning and control" *The Accounting Review* (January, 1967) pp. 24-52.

THE MANAGEMENT AND DATA PROCESSING SYSTEMS

V. PESCARU

Scientific Director of the Centre of Economic Computation and Economic Cybernetics, Bucharest, Romania

SUMMARY

Aspects regarding the contribution made by information systems, based on the electronic computer and data teleprocessing equipments in the management activity of enterprises or governmental organizations, are discussed in relation to scientific researches and at actual management activity.

In this paper requirements and conditions are presented for designing and implementing Management Information Systems, as well as the possibilities of operation and automation of decisions by means of these systems. The psychological organization and technical aspects of collaboration among analysts and designers of information systems and the managers of economic enterprises are also discussed.

THE ROLE OF MANAGEMENT IN DEFINING THE CONCEPT OF DATA PROCESSING SYSTEMS

To define the objectives of the concept and achievement of data processing systems, one sets out from the necessity of subordinating these objectives to those of management; at the same time, data processing systems (informatic systems)* are considered indispensable instruments for management.

---

*We mean by informatic system the totality of methods, techniques models, programs, specific technical means used for the collecting, registering, transmission, processing, questioning and keeping of data (including the object of these operations - data) used for presenting as quickly as possible an optimal structure of the necessary information (synthetic, selected, analytic, etc.) at various levels of information and/or decision taking points.

Since the main objective of management is the continuous increase of the efficiency of work in the respective unit, the objectives of the information systems - in their capacity as instruments of management - must also be subordinated to this main goal. Consequently, the indicators of the increase of the efficiency of work in the economic unit represent the main criterion for estimating the utility of economic-mathematical methods and of electronic computers in designing and organizing informatic systems.

Experience gained so far both in Romania and elsewhere, clearly demonstrates the efficiency of the use of methods of economic cybernetics, of operation research and of electronic computers in the qualitative growth of economic activity and of social life, in general, and in the improvement of management activity in particular [4,7,10].

The mere existence of such technical methods and means, in spite of the potential at our disposal in raising the efficiency of economic-social activity, cannot be a sure guarantee for their turning into an effective and efficient instrument of management . This desideratum may be only achieved if their real possibilities of utilization are known and used, and only if the necessary conditions for implementation are ensured; in this connection the level of professional knowledge, the high degree of organization and professional discipline are playing an extremely important role [1,3]. Hence a *first conclusion,* extremely important both for the concept and design of informatic systems and for their construction and utilization, namely in that *an extremely important role in the achievement of these systems is incumbent on management.* Management must fully play its role of taking decisions and of control over their fulfilment also in the activity of concept, design and construction of informatic systems. Without denying the important role of analysts and designers of informatic systems, of programmers and specialists in the working out and application of economic cybernetic models and of operation researchers, the fact should be stressed that leadership must not delegate to these specialists ("technicians") the task of taking decisions linked with the definition of the theme and objectives for the design of new informatic system and the establishment of the necessary and possible resources. However, the "technicians" (either in or outside the system) have the important task to help the leadership in taking decisions in these activities, to be its good advisers, to prepare the information necessary for the substantiation and taking of decisions, to elaborate and experiment with the most efficient program and model systems, and solutions.

A project theme for an informatic system can be adequately formulated only by "the user of the instrument", the only one capable of defining the utility of this instrument. Hence, the *second* important *conclusion* is that *the clarity of the objectives for* the informatic system and the very quality and performances of the system *greatly depend on the clarity and exacteness of the objectives of management at various levels of the respective system* [3,19,33,37]. Obviously, in order to actively participate in the concept and achievement of informatic systems and to use most efficiently such a complex instrument based on the application of economic-mathematical methods and on the use of electronic computers, *it is necessary for their users to know as much as possible about the possibilities of these systems.* This requirement may be considered as a *third conclusion* concerning the tasks incumbent on the leadership at various levels in the achievement of modern informatic systems.

The role of management at various levels in determining the concept and achievement of informatic systems can be described as follows:

WHY ONE MUST START WITH THE DEFINITION OF THE THEME AND OBJECTIVES

> "Finally, the correctness and efficiency of management depend on the clarity of the objectives pursued by society, of the tasks raised in various branches of activity".
>
> NICOLAE CEAUSESCU

Before passing on to the emphasis of the objectives of the informatic systems, we consider it useful to underline why it is necessary to set out objectives in the designing and construction of economic informatic system [3,19,25,30,31,32,33]. The importance of the definition of objectives and their direct influence on the results of various actions of the leadership renders this problem one for lively discussion within the scientific needs in management. "In any book about the science of management which does not begin with the objective, a big mistake is made, because the organizing principle of any structure is finality, the aim or the objective. Therefore, very many reasonings on management collapse because of the vagueness of the objective "what do we want?" This is the first question which is put*". Only after having specified the objectives that are facing the informatic systems and what tasks they must answer, we can pass on to the next stages - of determining the necessary resources (*with, what, with whom* can we achieve the objectives?) and of establishing the methods of transforming the resources (*How* shall we transform the resources?) for attaining the objectives. To find an adequate answer to this last question, we must also apply techniques of optimization for transforming the process and the use of resources.

We want to emphasize the importance of the concept of the new informatic system (the stage of study and analysis of the system) is mapping out and establishing the best ways for the achievement of such a system. The concept stage has the task of defining the theme, the objectives and the necessary and possible resources for the attainment of the objectives; only afterwards, one can pass on to the other stages of designing and use of informatic systems. Consequently, there is a necessary sequence of these stages within which, in any condition, for any system, maximum priority should be granted in due time to the stage of establishing the objectives (see Fig. 1).

Figure 1 presents in a synthetic way the stages which have to be covered by the managerial body of the unit in defining and achieving the objectives of a project of informatic system, as well as the illustration of the weight of the contribution of the managerial body at various levels of the respective unit or organization in these stages [37].

THE OBJECTIVES PURSUED IN THE ELABORATION OF INFORMATIC SYSTEMS

An Effective and Efficient Instrument of Management

As it has already been stressed, the main objective of the elaboration, design and production of informatic systems is that they must be an effective and efficient instrument for management at all levels of the respective system. Consequently, the informatic system must be put in the service of the user, in the service of the leadership and not the user in the service of the informatic system.

---

*MIRCEA MALITA, "Art or Science of Management?" *Forum 2* (Bucharest, 1971).

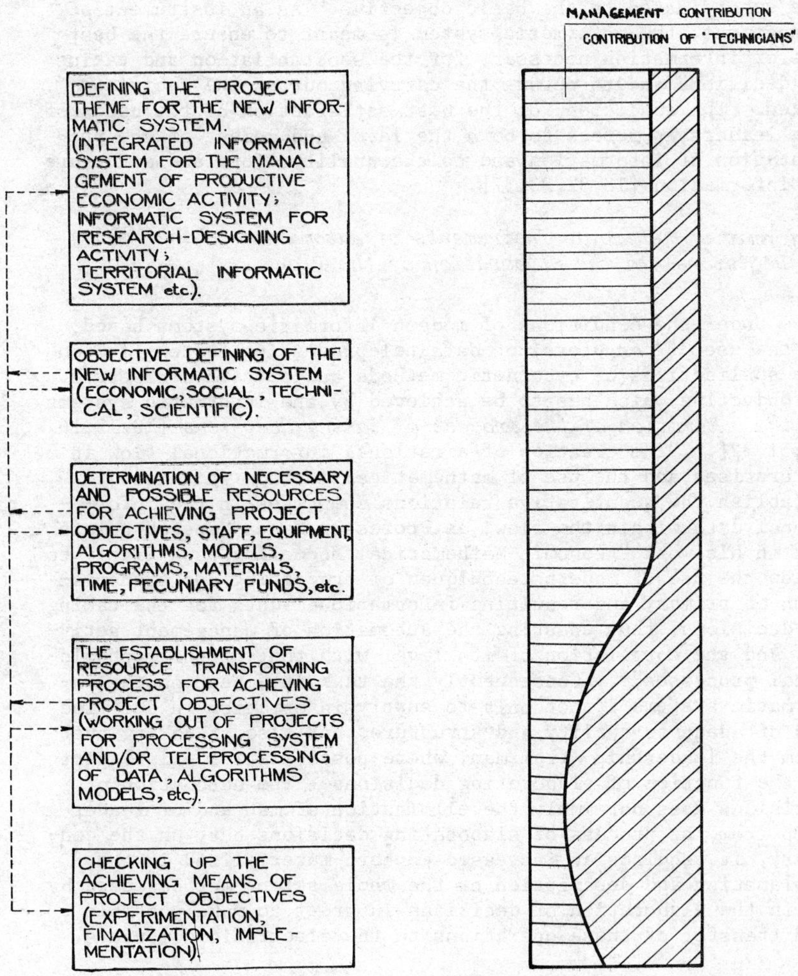

Fig. 1. Stages of defining and achieving the objectives of an informatic system project.

Setting out from the recognition of the basic objective of the elaboration, design and production of informatic systems as an *instrument for management*, one can easily establish the other objectives to be achieved by these systems, objectives which are subordinated to the basic objective. As an instrument of management, the informatic system is meant to ensure the best use of information necessary for the substantiation and taking of decisions and to pursue the carrying out of the decisions taken. The condition for the best satisfaction of the needs of the leadership refers to both the level and moment of the presentation of information and to the quality, form and structure of information [18,32,33,37[.

Informatic Systems as Instruments of Automation of the Taking of Decisions and the Elaboration of the Plans

Under the conditions of modern informatic systems based on the use of computers, of data teleprocessing systems and on the applications of cybernetic methods and operation research, an objective which has to be achieved by the informatic systems is *the automation of the process of taking decisions* [10,15,16, 26,31,32[. "The creation of a rational informational flow in enterprises and the use of mathematical methods which should establish the quantitative relations comprises in the informational data within the flow, as Professor Manea Manescu points out in his work "Economic-Mathematical Moddeling" are likely to allow the use of modern techniques of processing and transmission of primary and resulting informational data for the taking of decisions, thus ensuring the automation of management activity and the correlation of its level with that of the technological processes"*. Consequently the task incumbent on the informatic systems if not only to supply information in due time and of adequate quality and structure, but also of taking over from the leadership (from man, where possibilities exist) part of the function of elaborating decisions. The automation of decisions does not imply the elimination of man and of leadership from the process of elaborating decisions but, on the contrary, it requires an increased concern materialized in the explanation and description of the whole set of methods used by it in the elaboration of decisions in order to make possible the transfer of these operations to the electronic computers.

---

*MANEA MANESCU, *Economic-Mathematical Modelling. Contributions to the Development of the Theoretical Problems of Socialist Economy 2* (Editura Politica, Bucharest, 1971).

Of course, the passing on to the automation of the process of taking decisions is possible only in the conditions in which this process is or may be known exactly and algorithmized. The exact description of the process of taking decisions can be elaborated only by the persons who concretely and analytically know this process, i.e. by the leadership whose role is to make these decisions.

In the socialist state based on a planned economy, in which the state plan represents the main form of the decision, the application of cybernetic methods and of informatics is an indispensable instrument in the elaboration and optimization of this plan. The close link between the activity of management, of taking of decisions and planning activity leads to the necessity for a common approach to the problem of the automation of decisions and the automation of the activity for the elaboration of the activity for the elaboration of the plans and of production programmes [2,3,7,13].

The Informatic System, an Instrument of Keeping Records, of Control and Precision

It is well known that without a full exercise of the function of control over the implementation of the plans and decisions taken, the efficiency of management activity is considerably decreased [1,2,3,8,10,13].

The control of the fulfilment of production plans and programs and of the implementation of the decisions taken by the leadership at various levels is continuously generating a considerable volume of information which has to be effectively collected, transmitted, processed and analysed with a view to ensuring the taking of new decisions in due time, and for bringing the plan up to date and, if necessary, for mobilizing new resources. As it has already been pointed out, such requirements can only be adequately satisfied in conditions of existence of efficient informatic systems based on the use of cybernetic methods, of modern electronic computers and of management scientific methods [1,2,4,5,7,11,15]. The inseparable pair represented by decision and control, the plan and the pursuing of its fulfilment also point to the objectives which have to be pursued in the concept of informatic systems. When we accept as the objective of these systems automation of decisions and of activity for the elaboration of plans, we must also accept the condition for the informatic systems to represent also the main instrument for the pursuing and control of the implementation of the decisions and plan targets.

The informatic system must also be an efficient instrument for keeping records (operative technical, book-keeping, statistical, technological, etc.) and for the control over the unfolding of technological, economic and social processes, over the use of human, material and financial resources, over the relations within the respective system and over the relations with the exterior [10,26,29]. Besides these requirements, the informatic system must ensure an adequate level of exactness of information and most faithfully mirror phenomena, processes and relations characterized by it.

The Informatic System, an Instrument for Diagnosis, Simulation and Prognosis

The release of the leader, in particular, and of "the office staff", in general, from routine technical operations for processing of information on the progress of processes and phenomena in the past leads to the establishment of optimal relations between the period of time assigned to the analysis "of the past" and that assigned to the preparation of the future. Without denying the importance of the analysis of the development of economic and social phenomena and dynamic processes, of the experience gained in the past, the fact, however, should be stressed that between the time assigned to the analysis of the past and that assigned to the study of the future development of the process and of the relevant system, there should be a clear emphasis in favour of the latter.

Through its concept and construction, an informatic system must meet the requirements of provisional management, the latter being another objective of these systems. Based on the application of the methods of economic cybernetics and of operations research in the concrete economic-social activity, the task is incumbent on the informatic systems of assisting in the prognosis and simulation methods in mapping out the evolution trajectory of the system serving it, of suggesting the future trend and of being able to supply information on possible negative phenomena before the latter can become an obstacle or to cause undesired perturbations in the development of the relevant system [6,10,30,37,40]. The roles of diagnostician, simulator and of prognosis can be rightly attributed to the informatic system for management.

The objectives of the concept and construction of the above-mentioned informatic systems are characterized by a close cohesion and a high degree of mutual interaction. In this way, the weakening of the interest in achieving one of the objectives may hinder the results in attaining other connected objectives. The notion of *package of objectives* emphasizes the cohesion and interaction required by an increased efficiency of achieving these objectives. The cohesion and interaction characteristic of these objectives and conditions do not exclude but, on the contrary, imply the possibility of differentiating the intensity with which each of those may act. This differentiation is given by the concrete conditions in which the respective informatic system is going to be achieved.

This package of objectives has a high degree of generality for economic informatic systems. It has a wide sphere of action in case of complex informatic systems, characteristic of economic enterprises, of industrial centrals and groups, of production units in agriculture, in constructions and in other fields of economic-productive activity.

REFERENCES

1. *The Tenth Congress of the Romanian Communist Party* (Editura politica, Bucharest, 1969).

2. N. CEAUSESCU, *Romania on the Road to Building the Many-sidely Developed Socialist Society 1-4* (Editura politica, Bucharest, 1968-1970).

3. N. CEAUSESCU, *Speech at the Opening of the Colloquium on Problems of Management Science of Society*, 6 March, 1972 (Scinteia, Bucharest, 26 April 1972).

4. *Decision of the Executive Committee of the Central Committee of the Romanian Communist Party on the Improvement of the Social-Economic Information System; the Introduction of Management System with Data Automatic Processing Means and the Endowment of the National Economy with Computation Technique in the 1971-1980 Period* (Scinteia, Bucharest, 1971).

5. *Decision of the Council of Ministers of the Socialist Republic of Romania, No. 1719 of December 31, 1971, Regarding the Approval of the Program for the Rationalization of the Record Keeping System in the Socialist Units for the 1971-1973 Period* (Bucharest, 1971).

6. M. MANESCU, "The role of cybernetics in forecasting the social-economic development" *Studii si Cercetari de Calcul Economic si Cibernetica Economica* No. 1 (Bucharest, 1971).

7. M. MANESCU, *The Many sided Developed Socialist Society, a New Stage of the Social Economic Revolution* (Lupta de clasa No. 1. Bucharest, 1972).

8. M. MANESCU, "The economic progress of the socialist Romania" in *Contributii la Dezbaterea Problemelor Teoretice ale Economiei Socialiste Vol. 2* (Editura Politica, Bucharest, 1971).

9. M. MANESCU, "Preoccupations regarding the technique of elaborating cybernetic models in economy" *Studii si Cercetari de Calcul Economic si Cibernetica Economica* No. 2 (Bucharest, 1967).

10. M. MANESCU, "Economic-mathematical modelling" in *Contributii la Dezbaterea Problemelor Teoretice ale Economiei Socialiste Vol. 2* (Editura politica, Bucharest, 1971).

11. M. MANESCU, "Scientific preoccupations in the field of economic computation and economic cybernetics technique" *Studii si Cercetari de Calcul Economic si Cibernetica Economica* No. 1 (Bucharest, 1966).

12. M. MANESCU, "Preoccupations and directions of the applications of mathematics in organizing production and work" *Ibid.* No. 5-6 (Bucharest, 1966).

13. M. MANESCU, "Directions and trends in economic cybernetics" *Ibid.* No. 1 (Bucharest, 1968).

14. S. BIRLEA, "The training of personnel - an essential condition for achieving the national system of informatics and management" *Ibid.* No. 2 (Bucharest, 1971).

15. S. BIRLEA, "The national informatics and management system - an important instrument in improving the management and organization of economic and social life" in *Contributii la Dezbaterea Problemelor Teoretice ale Economiei Socialiste Vol. 2* (Editura politica, Bucharest, 1971).

16. S. BIRLEA, and M. PETRESCU, "Computer and informatic systems networks in economic and social management" *Studii si Cercetari de Calcul Economic si Cibernetica Economica* No. 6 (Bucharest, 1971).

17. S. BIRLEA, T. HOMOS, and S. COSTOIU, "Considerations on cybernetic modelling in the engineering industry" *Buletinul Institutului Politehnic Bucharest* No. 8 (1969).

18. V. BITA, "Automatic control and correction - a premise for the efficient utilization of electronic computer in data processing" *Studii si Cercetari de Calcul Economic si Cibernetica Economica 4* (Bucharest, 1971).

19. GH. BOLDUR, *Information and Decision in Social-Economic Management Process* (Editura politica, Studii, Bucharest, 1971).

20. GH. BOLDUR, *Informational and Decision Processes in Economy* (Editura Stiintifica, Bucharest, 1969).

21. G. BAUVIN, *L'Information de Gestion* (Editions Hommes et Techniques, Paris, 1968).

22. J. BROMIRSKI, "On the training of specialists in computation technique in the Polish people's Republic" *Studii si Cercetari de Calcul Economic si Cibernetica economica* No. 2 (Bucharest, 1971).

23. C. COJOCARU, "The attributes of management of economic organizations" *Stiinta Conducerii Societatii* (Studii Editura politica, Bucharest, 1971).

24. N. COSTAKE, "The integrated management of production" *Viata Economica* No. 32 (414), Bucharest (1971).

25. A. DELVILLE, *L'Information dans l'Enterprise* (Dunod, Paris, 1969).

26. M. DRAGANESCU, "Society as a system" in *Stiinta Conducerii Societatii* (Studii, Editura politica, Bucharest, 1971).

27. M. DRAGANESCU, "The building of a unitary informatic system" in *Contributii la Dezbaterea Problemelor Teoretice ale Economiei Socialiste Vol. 2* (Editura politica, Bucharest, 1971).

28. C.M. DRAGAN, *The Organization of the Economic Information System of the Enterprise* (IDT, Bucharest, 1970).

29. N.P. FEDORENKO, *Integrirovannie Sistemi ob Rabotki Dannih* (Izdatelstvo "Nauka", Moscow, 1970).

30. M. MALITA, "Art or science of management?" *Forum* No. 2 (Bucharest, 1971).

31. A. MODIN, "The development of automated systems for the management of industry" in *Probleme ale Perfectionarii, Organizarii si Conducerii Economiei si Vietii Sociale* No. 2 (IDT, Bucharest, 1972).

32. J. ORLICKY, *Le Système Informatique de l'Entreprise* (Editions Hommes et Techniques, Paris, 1971).

33. V. PESCARU, "Tasks of the designing and organization of informatics and management systems" in *Contributii la Dezbaterea Problemelor Teoretice ale Economiei Socialiste 2* (Editura politica, Bucharest, 1971).

34. V. PESCARU, "The national informatics and management system and the training of specialists" *Viata Economica* No. 14 (396) Bucharest, (1971).

35. V. PESCARU, "Data processing systems" in *Organizarea Sistemului Informational Economic Documentare Selectiva* No. 8 (IDT, Bucharest, 1971).

36. V. PESCARU, "The objectives of the concept and achievement of economic informatic systems" *Economic Computation and Economic Cybernetics Studies and Research* No. 3 Bucharest (1972).

37. V. PESCARU, R. HOMESCU, and C. APOSTOL, *Analysis and Designing of Economic Informatic Systems* (Academia de studii Economice, Bucharest, 1971-72).

38. V. PESCARU, "On the automation of the statistic information system" (Use of permanent data records) *Revista de Statistica* No. 7 Bucharest (1969).

39. I. STANCIOIU, and I. GUNEA, "Improvement of the information system in the scientific management of the enterprise" in *Stiinta Conducerii Societatii* (Studii, Editura politica, Bucharest, 1971).

40. *Economic and Social Prognosis. Reference material about Prognosis Methods and Techniques* (Consiliul economic, Bucharest, 1971).

DESIGN OF MANAGEMENT SYSTEMS BY MEANS OF CYBERNETIC MODELING

J.L. ELOHIM

Systems Engineering, E.S.I.M.E. Postgraduate Courses, Instituto Politecnico Nacional, Mexico D.F., Mexico

SUMMARY

The design of management procedures has been heuristic since the beginning. The increase in size and complexity of real management organisations were the cause for searching for a new approach in order to understand what they were all about and how to organize great and complex management structures. The cybernetic viewpoint of a management system has opened a new way for studying its behaviour; it offers the alternative of studying more closely management problems. Cybernetic modeling as a methodology for a scientific design of management systems offers some valuable advantages. Four cases are briefly described.

WHY CYBERNETICS TODAY?

Our era is characterized by the great number of important technological and scientific advances which are contributing little by little to a better comprehension of the complex world in which we live (Fig. 1).

There are three fields in our complex world which are distinctly identified because of their singular homogeneity:

1. The first one is concerned with the development of living creatures.

2. The second field is derived from an increasing deepness of knowledge of physical, chemical and biological laws which are ruling the behaviour of nature.

Numerous "automatic" machines resulting from the comprehension of natural laws are under development. It is claimed that they will improve the conditions for a better living, although, unfortunately, we hear very often of

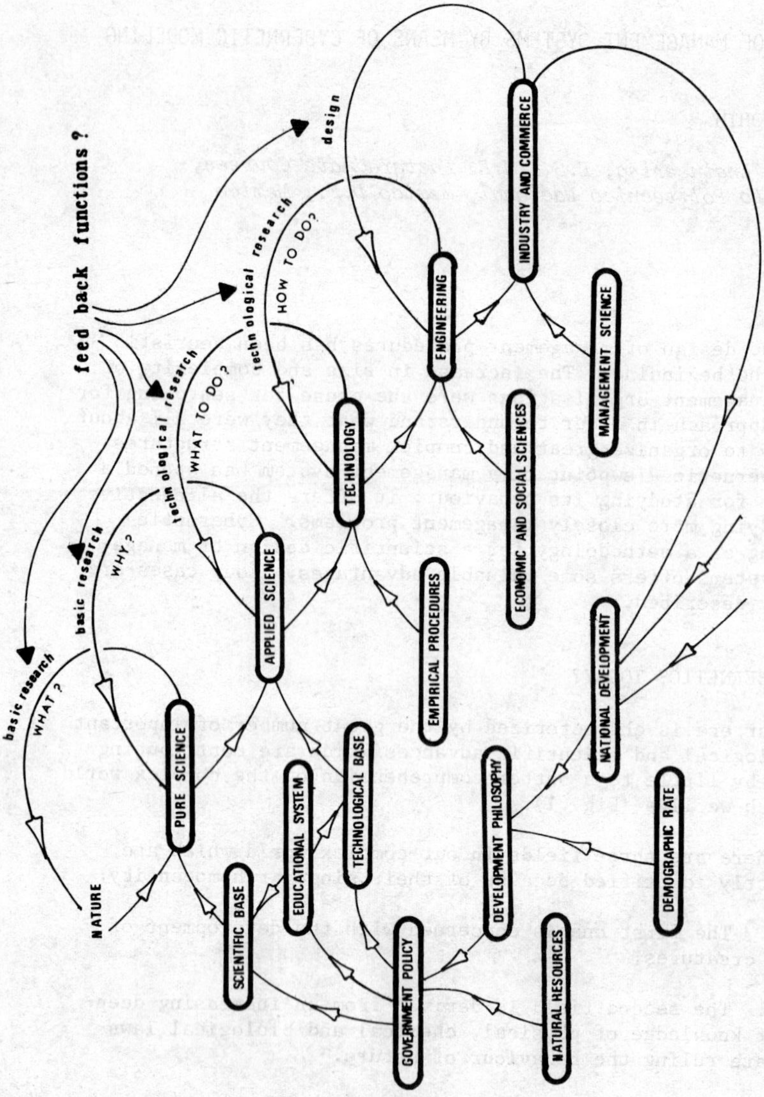

Fig. 1. The progress of science and technology

new automatic devices for the destruction of people and their culture.

3. The third one is the result of the interaction of man with other men in trying "to organize" themselves in order to comprehend the actual environment and to find a way for the individual and collective development of human beings.

The three fields have been during the last few years the object of study for those utilizing the cybernetic approach when trying to comprehend the behaviour of complex phenomena. Although the three fields are rather different from the traditional scientific point of view, they have in common a couple of very important similarities.

First of all, the behaviour of any particular system of the three fields is highly dynamic. Secondly, each of those systems is sufficiently complex in structure and behaviour so that the interchange of information with its environment produces the development of organs specialized in the realization of various partial processes, including the governing of the whole system.

When talking of biology, it is known that the degree of independence of living individual from the environment is related to that of the development and functional complexity. The physiological autonomy is the result of a great number of regulatory mechanisms, which are operated by organs doing a highly specialized kind of work.

The cells of living things are able to live only in some conditions which are defined with great accuracy (water, oxygen, mineral compounds, organic compounds, ...). These elements are combined under the influence of extracellular conditions (temperature, pressure, ...) in order to constitute the means of life (blood, plasma, amniotic fluid, chlorophyll, ...)

Through a schematic division it is possible to identify the interaction between the means of life and the set of cells. The means of life make possible the organized action of the cells integrated in highly specialized organs. The organs have the responsibility for maintaining the characteristics of the means of life between certain limits. The main objective of cybernetics in the field of biology is to prove the hypothesis formulated in order to explain the function of regulatory mechanisms.

Biological processes eventually lose part of their autonomy. This is due to structural and/or functional disequilibrium; this phenomenon is usually called disease. A second objective of cybernetics could be to provide scientific bases to those who are trying to reinstate the equilibrium, i.e. to render the biological system sufficiently autonomous again. When treating human beings, it may be better to try to reinstate the integral equilibrium of the function of the ill body, instead of treating partially only the most critical consequences of the disequilibrium (Fig. 2).

It seems that a third objective is out of question. A long time must still pass before a serious "design" of new biological means of "life" is produced. Different combinations of conditioning elements, perhaps others than those we actually know, will integrate new means of life, namely, those required for the world of the future.

The cybernetic approach in the study of natural phenomena and also of certain technological processes leads to the identification of some very useful analogies. The knowledge of the dynamics of natural and technological processes increases the chances for a successful design of regulatory mechanisms, which are to be inserted in certain devices. Along this way we arrive to the process of construction of "automatic" machines. The objective of any automatic machine has to be defined with accuracy in order to make its construction easier. The information required to correct the path followed by the behaviour process, so to reach the fixed objective, is also well defined.

The automatic machines have acquired a certain independence from the environment, although it is still not clear how to measure their degree of autonomy.

The engineer designs, builds and maintains dynamic controllable systems. He is, without realizing it, a cybernetician, who uses the accumulated experiences in order to create what could be called conditioning elements and means of life for the technological processes. This is the only way to ascertain the operation of automatic devices. The cybernetician heps the engineer to find out the best alternative solutions to the problems of integrating the governing and control processes. He assumes to have the knowledge of the general laws of the government process (Fig. 2).

Since the appearance of the human species on this earth man has "organized" and "directed" the action of human creatures in order to reach certain objectives. However, it very often happens that men do not realize that there are a number of

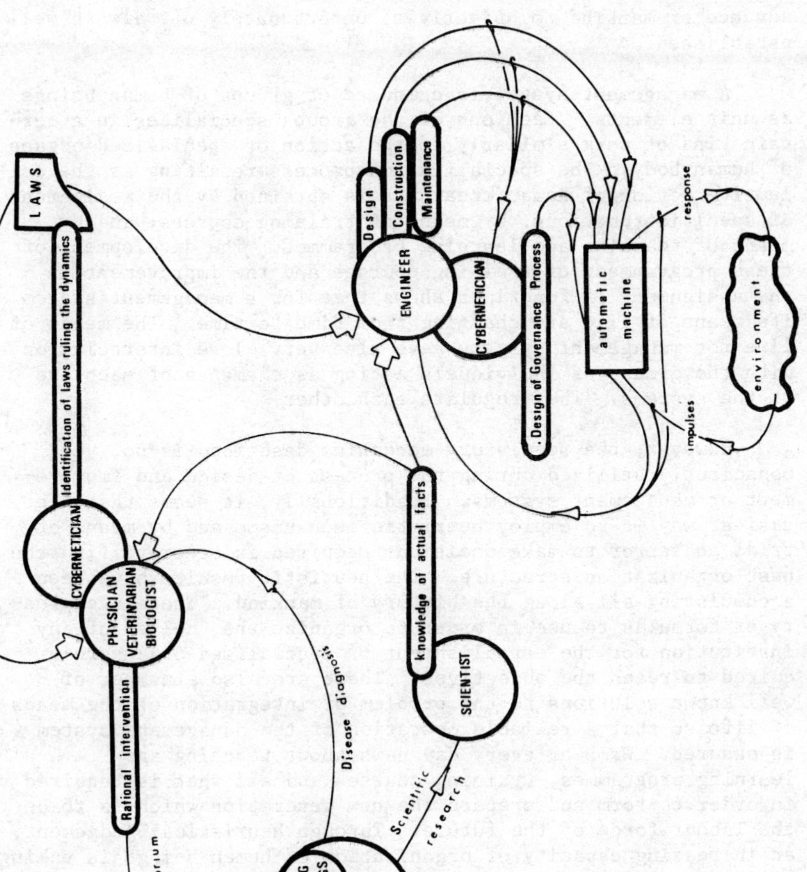

Fig. 2. Biology and engineering are closely interrelated with cybernetics

regulatory mechanisms which delay or sometimes accelerate the advance of mankind to objectives, unfortunately not always well established.

A management system is composed of groups of human beings as unit elements. Each one of the groups specializes in a certain kind of work similarly to the action of specialized organs of human body. The specialization process resulting as the collective action of human creatures is obtained by the assignment of specific functions, by means of training courses, and by means of teaching and learning programmes. The development of these programmes, of training courses and the improvement in the assignment of functions shows that for a management system its means of life are changing from time to time. The means of life for management systems have also very close interrelation with the groups of individuals acting as elements of each one of the systems. They regulate each other.

However, the regulatory mechanism described is not yet consciously utilized during the process of design and improvement of management systems. Traditionally, it seems that the easiest way is to employ heuristic mechanisms and by means of trial and error to make decisions required in order to find the best organization structure. The heuristic results have been accumulating all along the history of mankind. There are plenty of formulas to use in order to organize the "cells" of any institution for the establishment of specialized organs required to reach the objectives. There are also a number of well known solutions to the problem of integration of the means of life so that a reliable operation of the management system is assured. We hear every day news about teaching and learning programmes, training courses and all what is required in order to form and prepare the new generation which is to be the labour force of the future. Through heuristical judgement, an increasing capacity of organization of human beings is taking place all around the world. Complex management problems are solved by a number of rules of thumb for improving the efficiency of the systems. However, many people are trying to look for a scientific methodology for solving management problems.

Cybernetics is capable of dealing with the identification of the general laws of the function of management systems. The cybernetician, when working with management systems should be able to simulate and to prove whether the fixed objectives of the system are efficiently obtained by means of the organization designed for the institution concerned. He should be able to improve or even to build up again the structure of a management system.

Cybernetics is the instrument required for the development of a scientific methodology dealing with the governance of institutions and of society; in order to reach with the greatest efficiency the objectives that they (the institutions, the society) have imposed on themselves.

THE GENERAL CYBERNETIC MODEL OF A MANAGEMENT SYSTEM

Cybernetics helps to analyze the general and essential aspects: (1) of the regulation of the processes taking place in living organisms; (2) of the governing of automatic machines built by man; (3) of the governing of activities undertaken by groups of human beings in order to reach a certain objective. The general laws of making decisions in order to lead "something" to a certain objective, although being under the pressure exerted by the environment, is the subject of cybernetics when dealing with management systems. The direction of a management system is to order the structure and the functioning of the system, so that they are in accordance with the general laws governing its behaviour.

It is proposed to build the general cybernetic model of management systems in order to provide a scientific methodological frame of reference to those who analyze, design, modify or improve specific systems. This cybernetic model is based on the attitude of human behaviour when tackling problems emerging from the development of society, either as a whole or partially when it is concerned with the operation of a single institution. Management of enterprises, social and educational institutions, local and national governments, political parties, ... are extensions of individual human action when solving problems.

It is first decided WHAT are the activities to execute. This task is done in accordance with a plan, say as a result of deciding WHEN and WHERE are the activities to be executed. From a different angle the activities are executed also in accordance to rules and instructions which are the result of making a decision about HOW the action is to be done. The first function require control action so that it is assured that the activities are executed according to the plans, the rules and the instructions. The whole set of four functions is under a unique Direction, and a general Co-ordination of those aspects not included in either Plans, Rules or Instructions (Fig. 3).

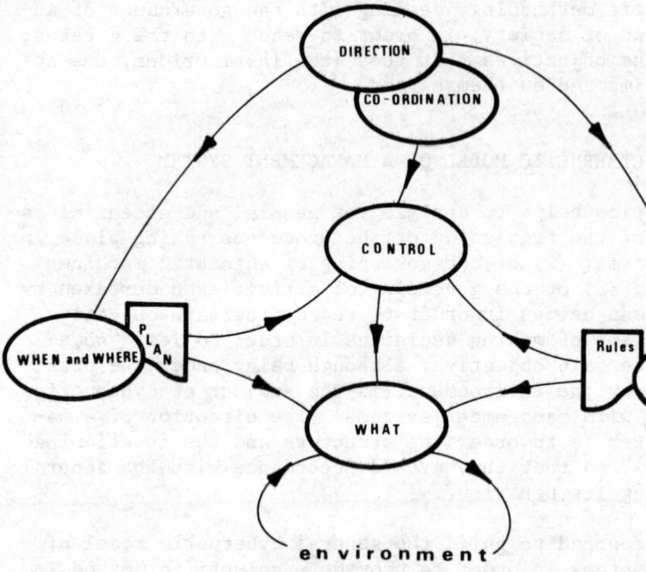

Fig. 3. Basis for the definition of the general cybernetic model of a management system

The specifications for the definition and integration of a cybernetic model of management system are as follows:

1. In order to produce adequate responses to the stimulus of its environment a management system requires to be composed of six elements specialized in the execution of the following functions:

I. Execution of basic activities; II. Control of the execution of basic activities; III. Planning; IV. Standardization; V. Co-ordination; VI. Direction.

NOTE. The graphic representation used to describe the six basic functions is based in the general concepts presented in the Appendix.

2. The EXECUTION of basic activities (Fig. 4) is the function concerned with the main objective of the management system. It is done as a reaction of the system to the stimulus originated in the environment. The response is the action of the system towards the environment. The execution of basic activities is done under the frame imposed by reference

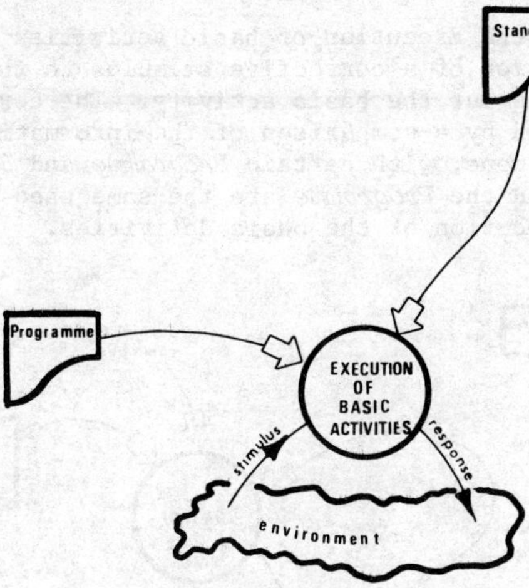

Fig. 4. The EXECUTION function.

information, which rules the execution. The reference frame is composed of prospective information (*Programme*) and of retrospective information (*Standards*)

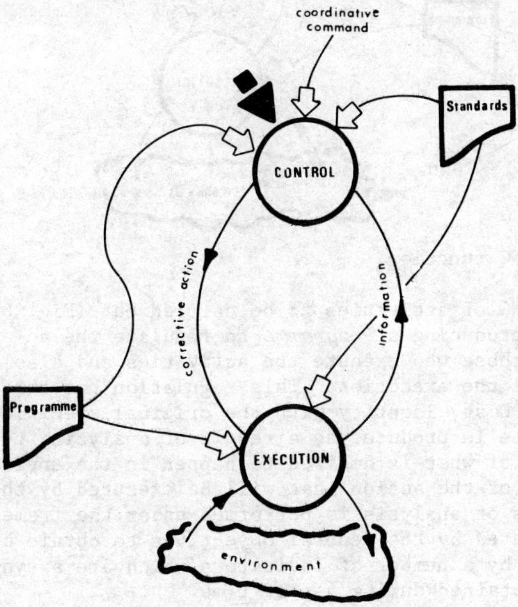

Fig. 5. The CONTROL function.

3. The CONTROL of the Execution of basic activities (Fig. 5) is the application of a corrective stimulus to the organ in charge of carrying out the basic activity. The corrective stimulus is produced by a comparison of the information related to the activity done, with certain *Programme* and *Standards*. The *Standards* and the *Programme* are the same used as a reference during the execution of the basic activities.

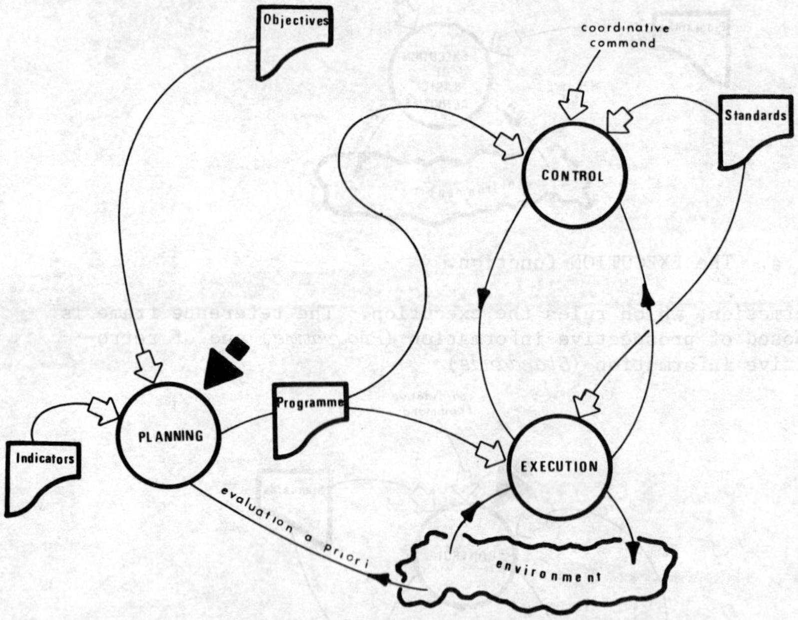

Fig. 6. The PLANNING function.

4. The PLANNING of activities to be carried out (Fig. 6) has the purpose of producing a *Programme* to regulate the actions performed by those who execute the activities and also of those who control the execution. This regulation has three main aspects: Time, Cost, Identity with the original specifications. The programme is produced as a result of analyzing the evaluation *a priori* of what is desired to happen in the environment as a result of the action that will be executed by the system. The process of analysis is performed under the frame of reference integrated by the General Objectives to obtain by the system and also by a number of Indicators which are a synthesis of results obtained during a past time.

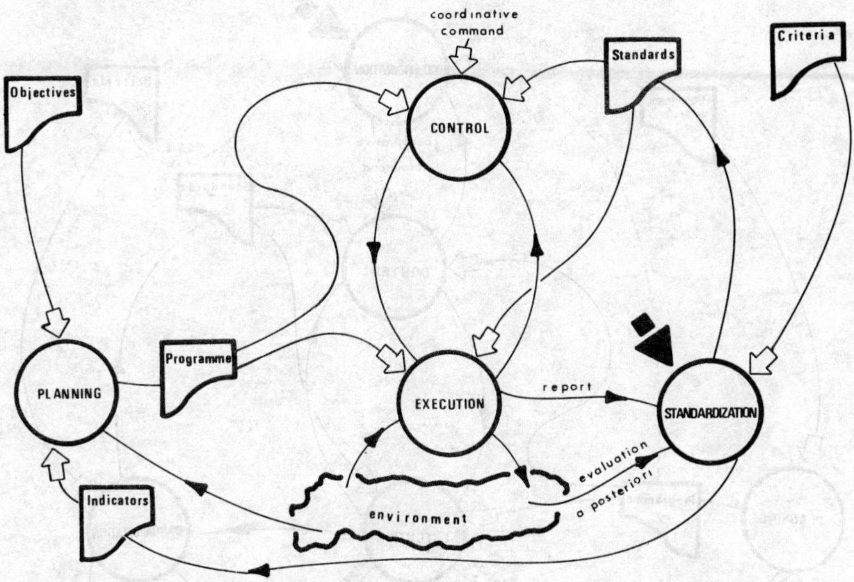

Fig. 7. The STANDARDIZATION function.

5. The STANDARDIZATION is the function required for the revision and adjustment of Standards and also for the production of new ones (Fig. 7), which are to be used for the regulation of actions performed by those who execute the basic activities and also of those who control the carrying out of these actions. This regulation has two fundamental aspects: *Quality* and *Functionality*.

The Standards are produced as a result of analyzing the evaluation *a posteriori* of what really did happen in the environment as a result of the action exerted by the system. Also used in the analysis is the interpretation of the information provided by the organ that has executed the basic activity. The process of analysis is performed in the frame of reference integrated by the General Criteria to evaluate the results. The function of Standardization produces also the Indicators to be used as a reference by the Planning function.

6. The CO-ORDINATION is the function required for making decisions in all those cases that for any particular reason, the stimulus of environment is unable of being regulated (Fig. 8). This means that the system under normal circumstances is unable to produce a response; it is due to the fact that the kind of action to produce has not been registered either in the Programme or in the Standards or in both. The

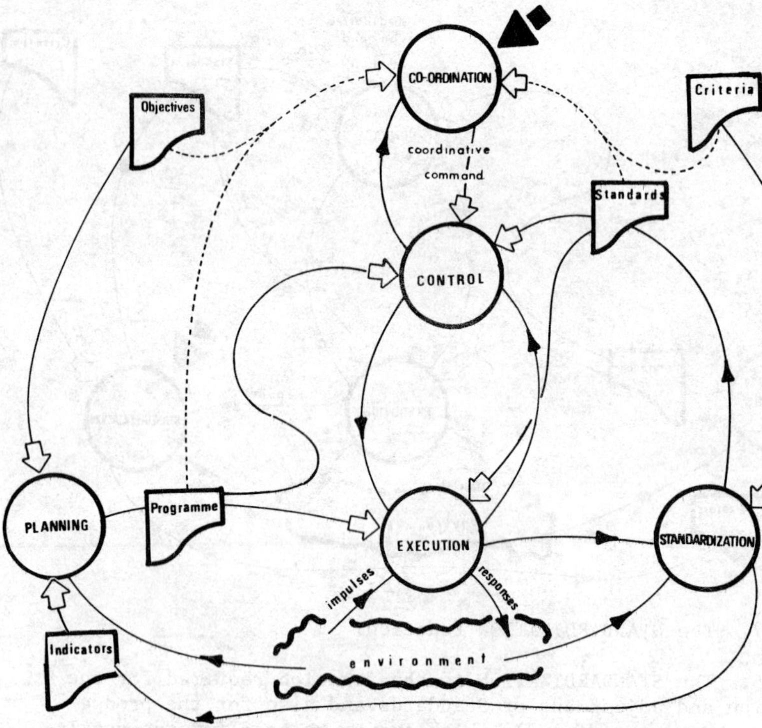

Fig. 8. The CO-ORDINATION function.

decision is made as a response to a stimulus (information sent by the organ in charge of the Control Function, after being reported by the organ in charge of the execution of the basic activities. The co-ordinate decision is produced after verifying that the case has not been contemplated under the Scheme of either the Programme or the Standards. The co-ordinate decision is basically the interpretation of the objectives of the System by the organs in charge of the governance of the system.

7. The DIRECTION has the purpose of producting (Fig. 9) the Objectives for the Planning function: the Criteria for the Standardization function and also the specific instructions for the Co-ordination function. The three results are produced by means of the analysis of the information concerned with the results of the execution of the basic activities. This information must be reliable, so the required data is obtained from the following different sources:

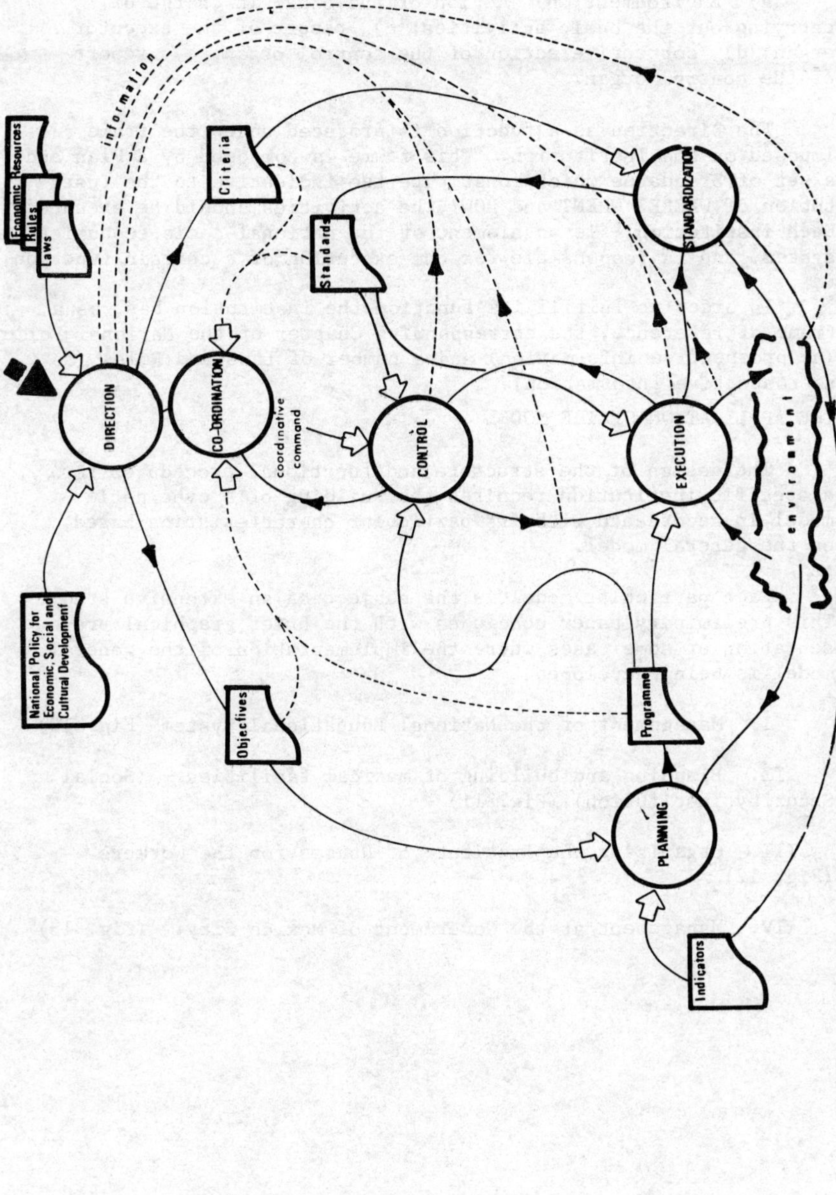

Fig. 9. The DIRECTION function.

a) Environment; b) Action of the organ in charge of carrying out the basic activities; c) report of the executor organ; d) corrective action of the control organ; e) report of the control organ.

The Direction as a function is produced under the frame imposed on the institution. This frame is composed by a Plan and a set of Standards which constitute the indicative to the institution of WHERE? WHEN? and HOW? the activities should be executed. Each institution - is an element of the national socio-economical system, and is responsible for the execution of a certain function.

In order to fulfill its function the institution has, as a frame of reference, the corresponding Chapter of the National Policy (as prospective information) and a number of Laws and Rules (as retrospective information).

THE APPLICATION OF THE MODEL

The design of the structure and functional procedures for a specific institution requires the building of a cybernetic model in accordance with its particular characteristics based on the general model.

Each particular model is the subject of an extensive study. This preliminary paper concludes with the brief graphical presentation of some cases where the implementation of the general model is being developed.

I. Management of the National Educational System (Fig. 10)

II. Planning and building of medical facilities - (Social Security Institution) (Fig. 11)

III. Organizing the Institute of Houses for the Workers. (Fig. 12)

IV. Management at the Government of Mexico City. (Fig. 13)

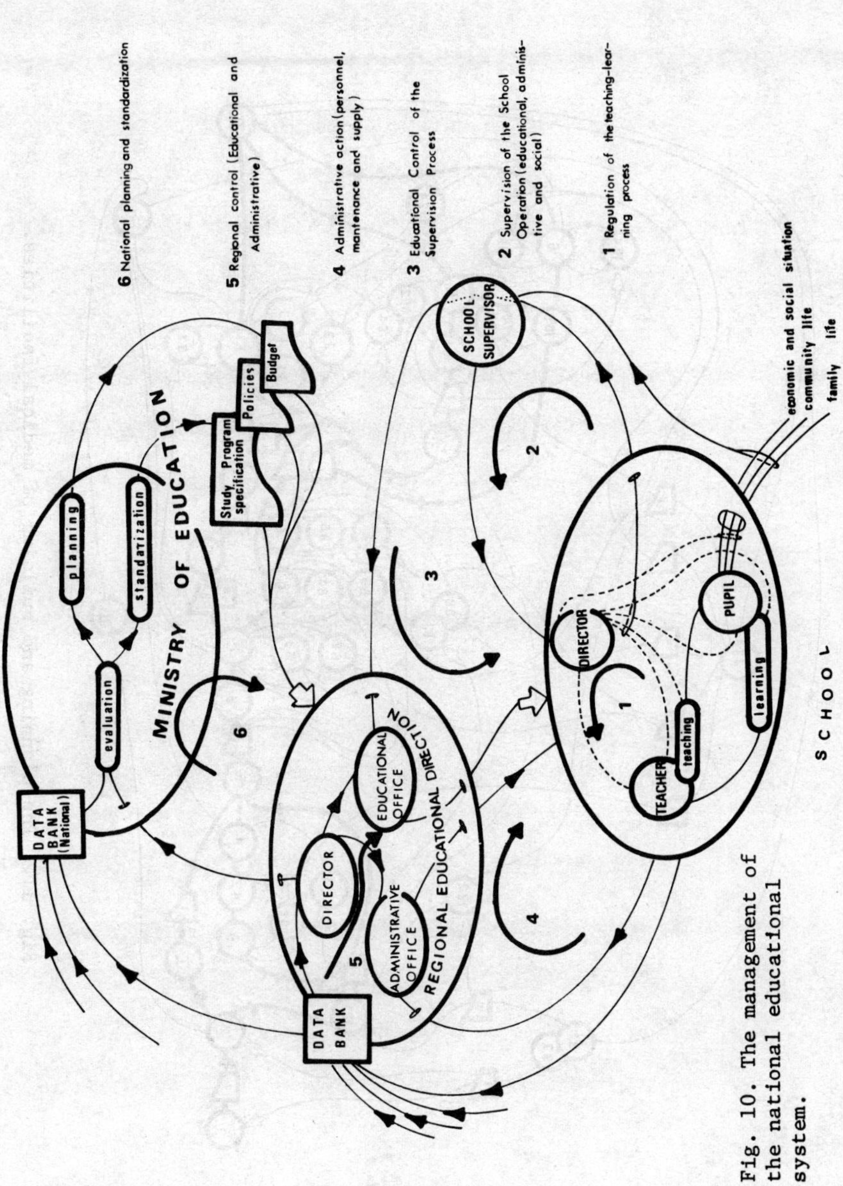

Fig. 10. The management of the national educational system.

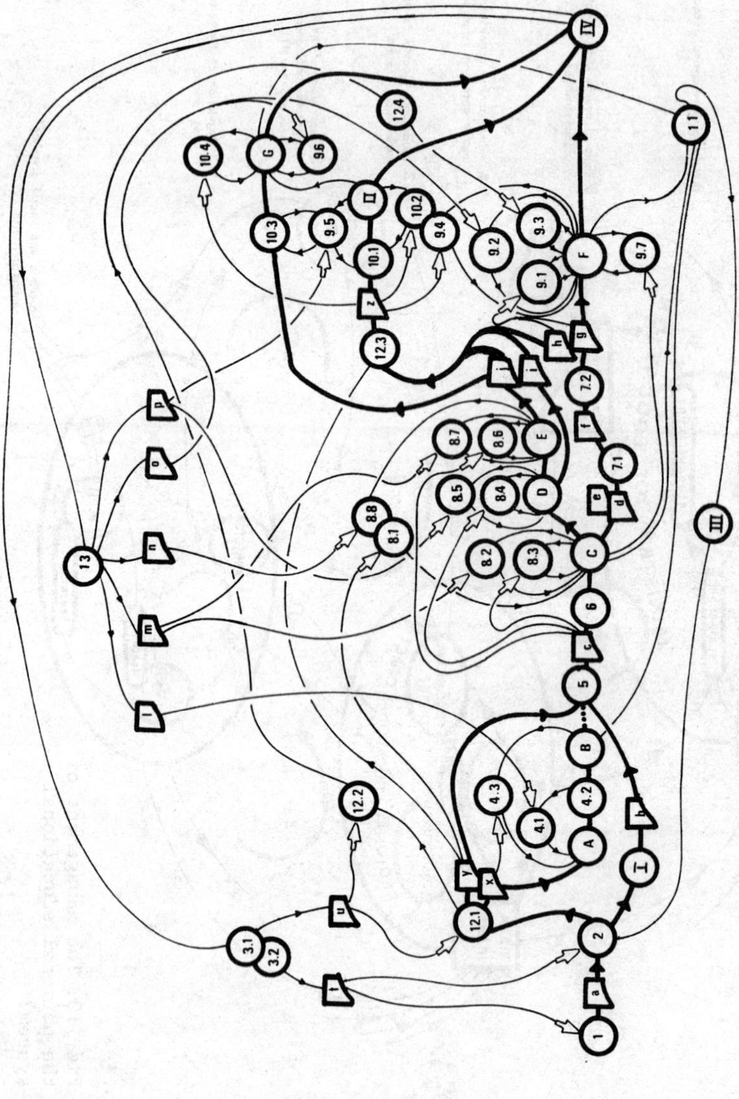

Fig. 11. The planning and building of medical facilities.

Fig. 12. Organizing the Institute of Houses for the workers.

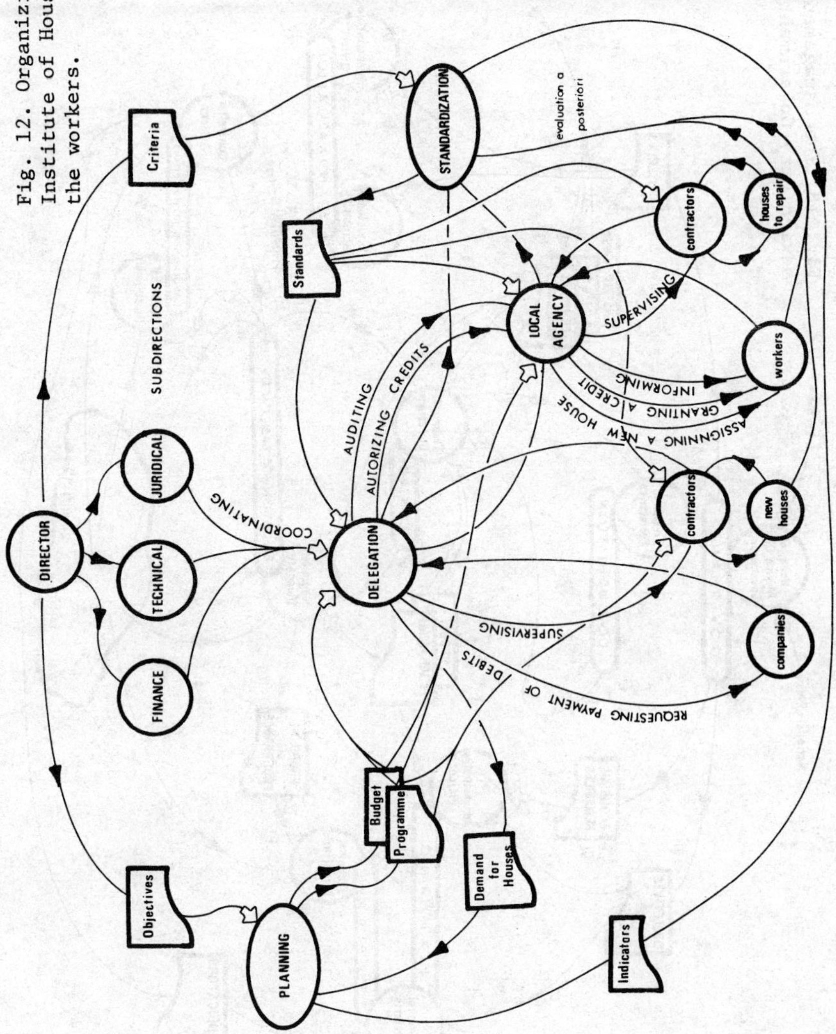

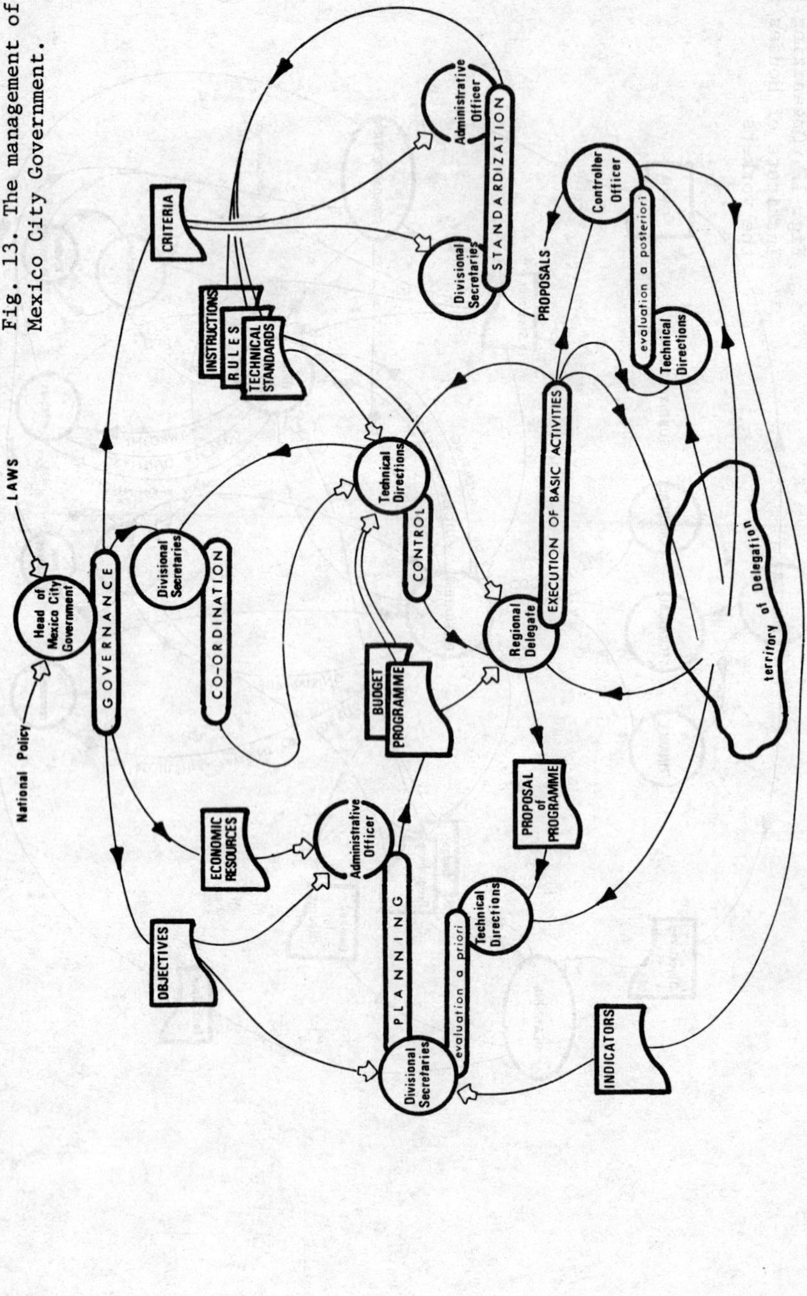

Fig. 13. The management of Mexico City Government.

APPENDIX

REPRESENTATION OF AN ACTION TO BE PERFORMED

An impulse i is transformed by T in a response r. The action of T is executed in accordance to a certain law L (Fig. 14).

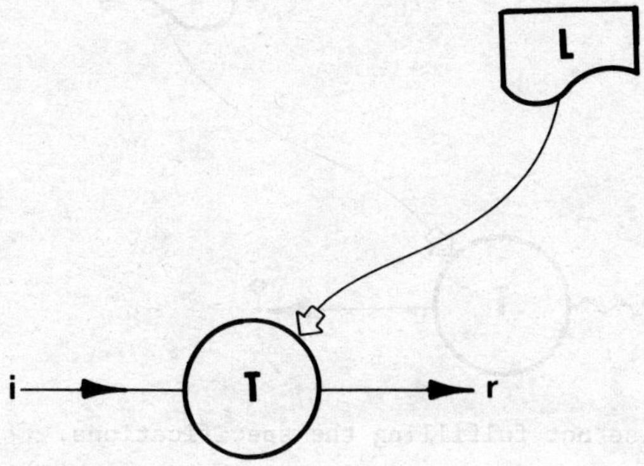

Fig. 14. The transformation process.

The transformation of i to r is quite often the desirable one. Sometimes the misinterpretation of L (Fig. 15) leads to wrong responses. it could happen also that the specification

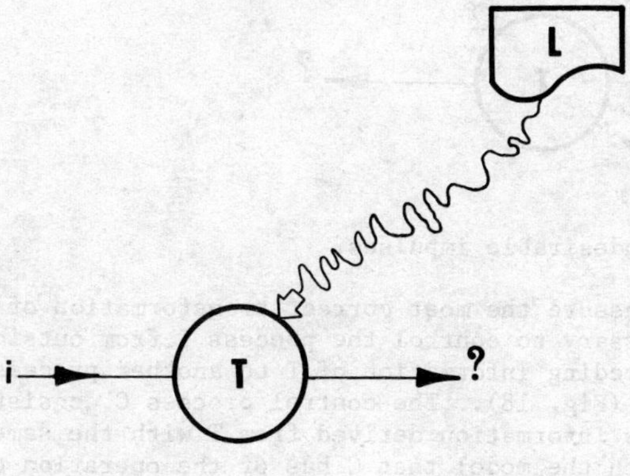

Fig. 15. A misinterpretation of transformation law.

for i is not fulfilled so the response is not the expected one (Fig. 16). In other instances the reason behind a wrong response is the insufficient autonomy of the process T, since n noisy impulses may influence the transformation T (Fig. 17).

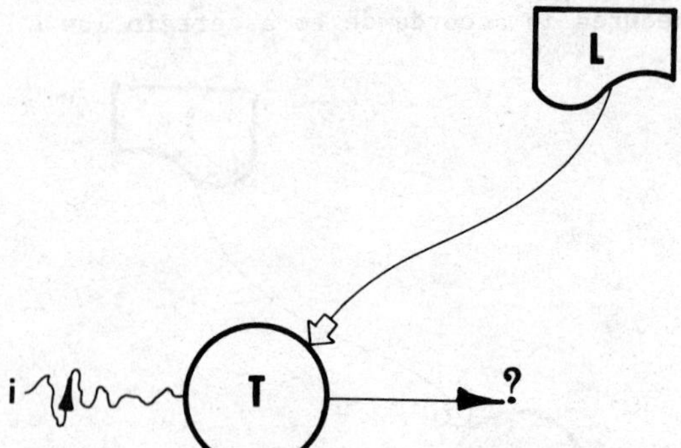

Fig. 16. An impulse not fulfilling the specifications.

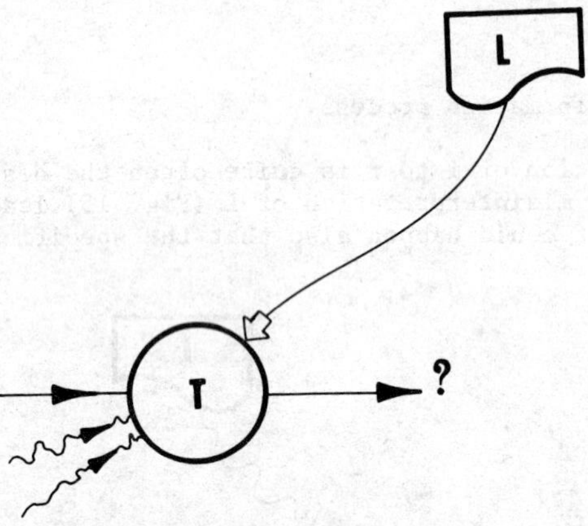

Fig. 17. Noisy undesirable impulses.

In order to assure the most correct transformation of i into r it is necessary to control the process T from outside. This is done by feeding information of T to another process named C (control) (Fig. 18). The control process C consists of confronting the information derived from T with the same law L and also with the model that C has of the operation of T (Fig. 19).

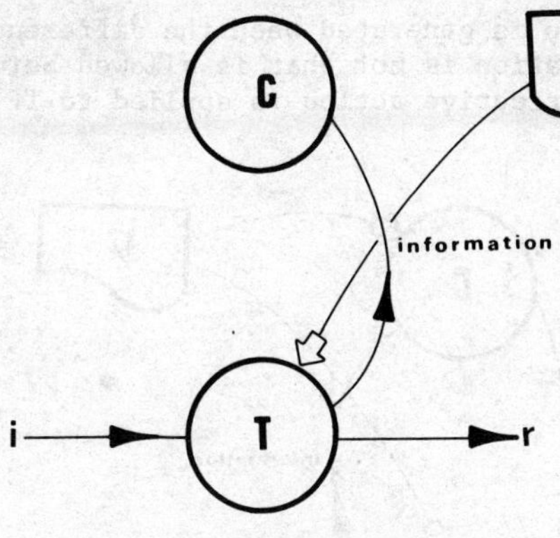

Fig. 18. Feeding the control process.

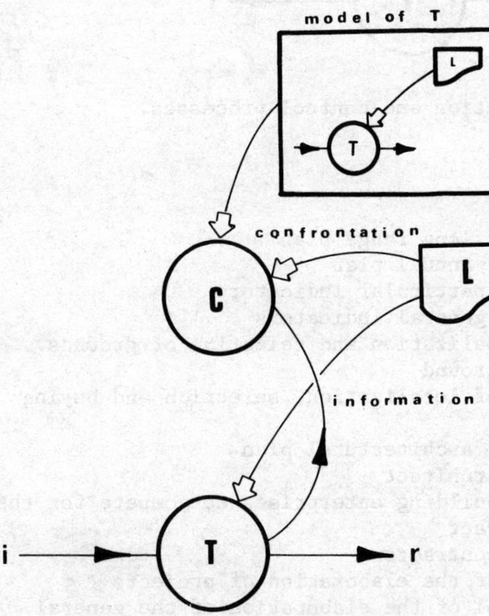

Fig. 19. Confrontation as a basis of control process.

A corrective action is generated when the difference derived from the confrontation is not what is allowed between certain levels. The corrective action is applied to T. (Fig. 20).

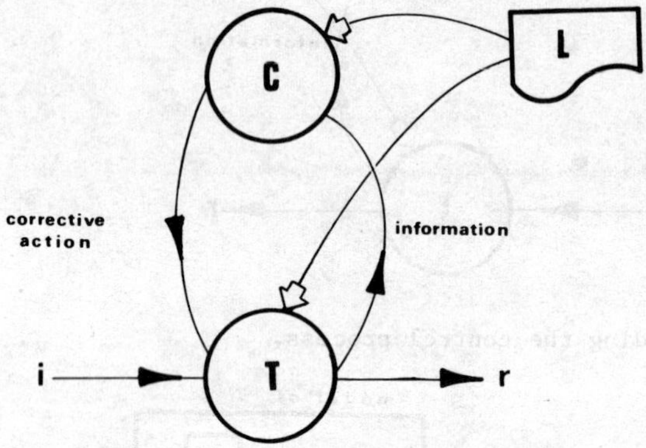

Fig. 20 The transformation and control processes.

SYMBOLS USED IN FIG. 11

1. Formulation of long range plan
2. Formulation of annual plan
3.1 Adjustment of particular indicators
3.2 Adjustment of general indicators
4.1 Control of localization and selection of grounds.
4.2 Selection of ground
4.3 Time control of localization, selection and buying of grounds.
5. Formulation of architectural plan
6. Selection of architect
7.1 Selection of building enterprises to compete for the building contract
7.2 Selection of contractor
8.1 Time control of the elaboration of projects
8.2 Quality control of the elaboration of the general project
8.3 Identity control of the elaboration of the general project
8.4 Identity control of the elaboration of the project of location of equipment and furniture
8.5 Control of selection of equipment and furniture
8.6 Identity control of the elaboration of the projects of special systems

8.7	Quality control of the elaboration of the projects of special systems
8.8	Documentation control of projects
9.1	Identity control of construction works
9.2	Quality control of construction works
9.3	Cost control for actions out of the original contract (Construction works)
9.4	Time control of construction work
9.5	Identity control of acquisition of equipment and furniture
9.6	Quality control of the installment of special systems
9.7	Architects' participation in identity control
10.1	Formulation of orders for acquisition of equipment furniture
10.2	Time control of acquisitions
10.3	Selection of equipment for special sub-systems
10.4	Time control for the installment of special sub-systems
11.	Registration of expenses
12.1	Formulation of the annual programme
12.2	Market research of material prices and labour force salaries
12.3	Formulation of the construction and supply programme
12.4	Formulation of particular budgets for works not included in the original contract
I	Formulation of particular specifications
II	Acquisition of equipment and furniture
III	Financial control of the development of the annual programme
IV	Evaluation of the operation of the medical (administrative) unit
A	Localization of ground
B	Acquisition of ground
C	Elaboration of general project
D	Elaboration of project for location of equipment and furniture
E	Elaboration of particular projects of special subsystems
F	Construction works
G	Installment of equipment of special subsystems

a	Long range plan
b	Particular specification of a certain medical (administrative) unit
c	Architectural plan
d	Drawings
e	List of partial works
f	Proposals presented for probable contractors
g	Budget of the contract
h	Drawings
i	List of equipment and furniture
j	Project of special subsystems
l	Norms for selection of ground
m	Norms of quality of projects
n	Norms of documentation per project
o	Norms of quality of the construction works
p	General catalogue of equipment and furniture
x	General programme for the acquisition of grounds
y	General programme of buildings to construct
z	Construction and supply programme

MODELS OF ORGANIZATIONAL CONTROL SYSTEMS

C.G.D. MAARSCHALK

Pedagogical Centers (Amsterdam) and Hogere Economische School (Rotterdam), The Netherlands

SUMMARY

The control of an organization (management) and the control of a machine in the widest sense (process control) are governed by the same cybernetic principles; however management is much more complicated. The paper applies the principle of "aspect system" to "management". The conclusion is that all of management can be described in terms of control models, all of which have some kind of cybernetic character. The control systems can only be partly automated.

THE SCOPE OF THE PROBLEM

Organizational control obviously pertains to management. However, the many definitions which exist of management indicate that management has many sides, which result in different pictures of the concept appealing to the many users of the word. To be sure, management covers a totality, including both foreseen and unforeseen happenings. Management is always used in relation to people and hardly understood when referring to a device which controls a machine. On the other hand, the controlling functions which can be found in such a device also belong to the managerial instruments and are used there in exactly the same way. However, there also is a difference: the essential quality of management, compared to any machine-like control, is its possibility of innovation, which is a faculty of human thinking. The term "constituting management" indicates such an innovation.

The total control system of an organization consists of a number of control systems of a different nature. One part operates like the mechanical type of control; a somewhat rigid but highly exact character. Another part can turn every section into complete innovation, with a highly flexible operation and, non-exact with a wide range of choices. Other parts are

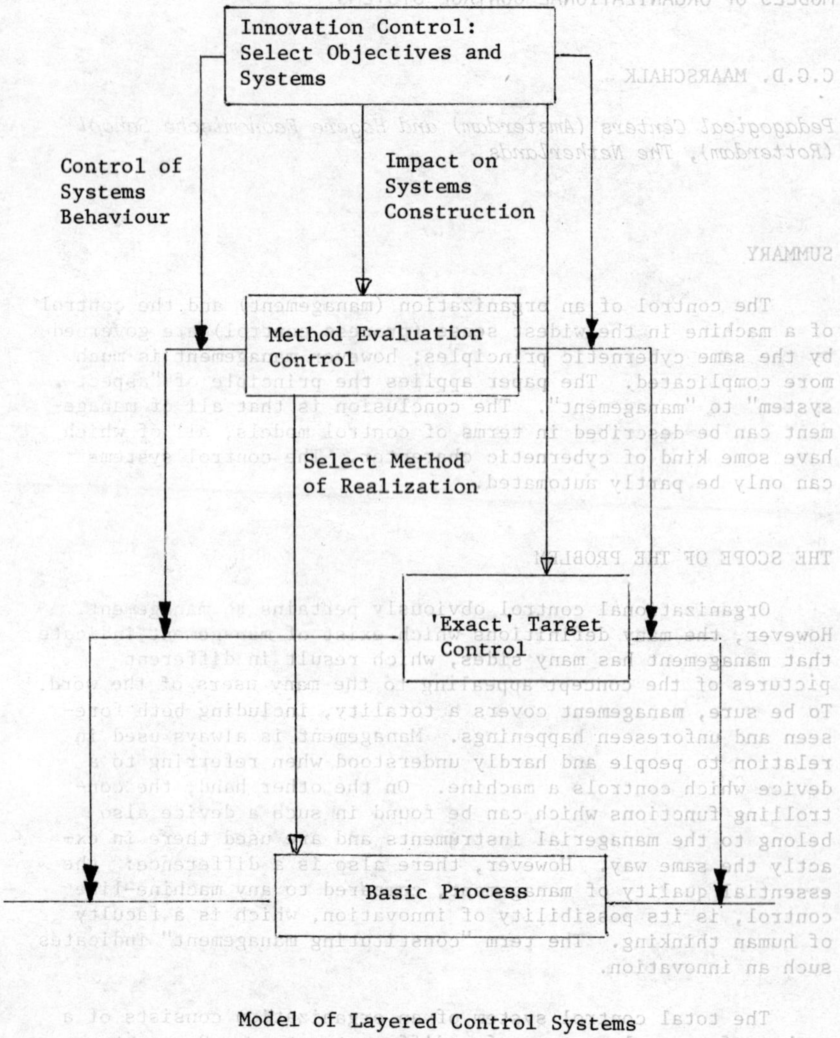

Fig. 1. Model of layered control systems

situated somewhere between these extremes. The types mentioned roughly correspond with management levels, but various factors, like nature of process, historical development and character of manager may cause considerably different pictures. The principle of such layered control system is illustrated in Fig. 1.

Nevertheless, there is always a mixture of said extremes in any organizational control system. Yet, these control systems of varying nature have to operate together; in reality the different component control systems often operate on their own accord and are even set up independently of other control systems. Naturally this causes unfavourable effects on integrated management and organizational outputs.

But there is more. For a number of years, computers have been introduced in the most obvious sections, mainly automating data flows and calculating (exact) decisions. To expand their usage it is necessary (1) to develop systems which cover also part of the management function and (2) to understand the integration of various types of sectional control systems.

The concept of such an overall system management information system was launched some years ago, but the development of its construction hardly has started. We are of the opinion that such development requires additional analytical instruments. The approach we advocate: (a) applies the principle of aspect systems [1] and (b) is process-oriented, instead of hierarchy-oriented. We found that an organizational control system is partly dependent on what is being controlled, but also carries possibilities of free choice, perhaps a wider range than often is realized. One can look separately at the efficiency of a control system and at the quality of its decisions.

Since we apply the concept of systems we shall now consider their characteristics.

THE SYSTEMS LANGUAGE

We define a system as a set of elements and their relationships; it functions as a unity or is being considered as such. Our definition of organization then is a system, in which the elements consist of people, physical and financial means, data and information or combinations, having one or more objectives.

We adopt the distinction that Control information is used in the sense of pragmatic information: Data which have a meaning to a person in relation to usually preset objectives.

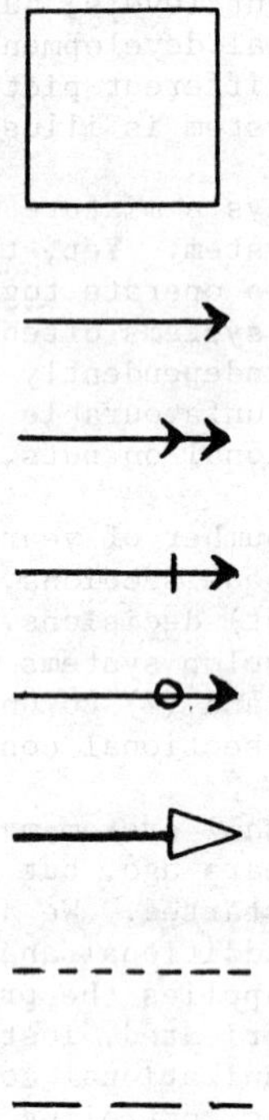

Fig. 2. Notation for charting of systems

In order to simplify the complex system of an organization we have to divide it into parts. As parts we choose the empirical aspects [1], such as the physical bread-and-butter process (e.g. manufacturing and selling), the financial process and the control or management system. The latter can be divided into two aspect systems: One whose elements are the control information and another whose elements consist of the controling people, the managers (see Fig. 4). In this paper we are concentrating our attention at the control information system, also called management information system.

The formal description of a system can be done either by charting or in symbolic notation. Both have advantages and disadvantages. We choose here the charting method, because we believe that it communicates faster the problems involved and reaches a wider circle of readers; besides, a universal symbolic systems language, capable to express these problems and solution techniques does not exist, as yet [2]. Our charting notation is given in Fig. 2.

Looking at systems, one has to distinguish between (a) the structure or construction of a system (the putting together of elements and relations) and (b) the behaviour of a system. All process aspect systems maintain input-output flows with the environment; also there is a flow of data to and from the control system (Fig. 4). Looking at flows means the study of the behaviour of a system. The way how the control information system and the hierarchy reflecting the process to be controlled, is a matter of construction.

The process aspect systems and the control (management) information system are homologous and isomorphic systems according to our approach. They have different functions but a similar structure with one-one similarity. The models of systems reviewed in this paper are shown at macro level, meaning a minimum number of elements.

MODEL OF ORGANIZATIONAL FEEDBACK CONTROL SYSTEM

The model shown in Fig. 3 is a type, well known in business organizations. The main line of this system shows how a flow of data is processed by transformation elements. As soon as such element has passed on the transformation variables to the next element, its role is finished. The preservation elements have a permanent role; their character is to preserve data. This model accentuates the "control cycle", which appears to be the transformation flow. It only deals with behaviour, not with construction. The operation of this model requires three decisions: (a) Setting performance standards (which decision should precede any operation); (b) A decision as to whether to continue, in spite of a (slight) deviation; (c) or to change directions for the future (a decision how to change).

This model, which occurs in several varieties, has a number of deficiencies. All decision elements and the total control procedure involving frequencies and timing of the various elements are absent.

THE CONCEPT OF DIRECT AND INDIRECT CONTROL IN ORGANIZATIONS

Before advancing to the next model we have to explore the fact that organizations usually operate with a double type of control.

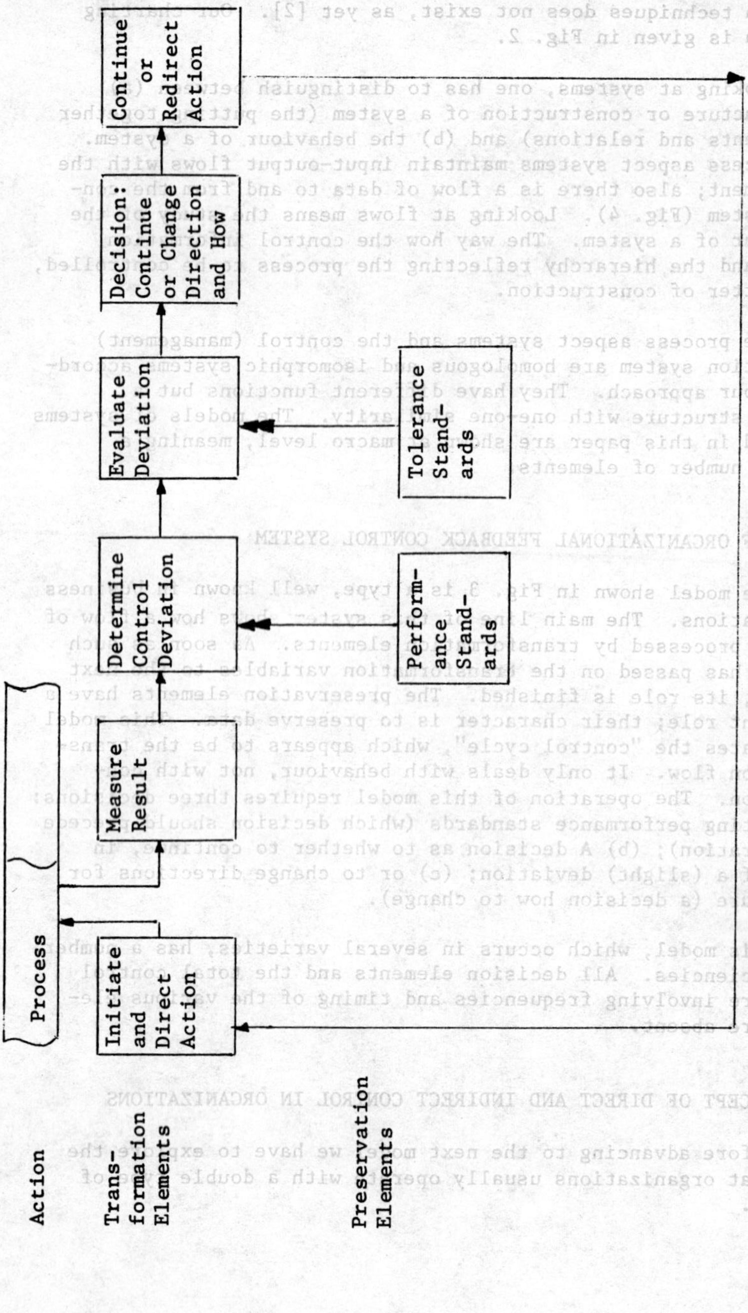

Fig. 3. Model of organizational feedback control system

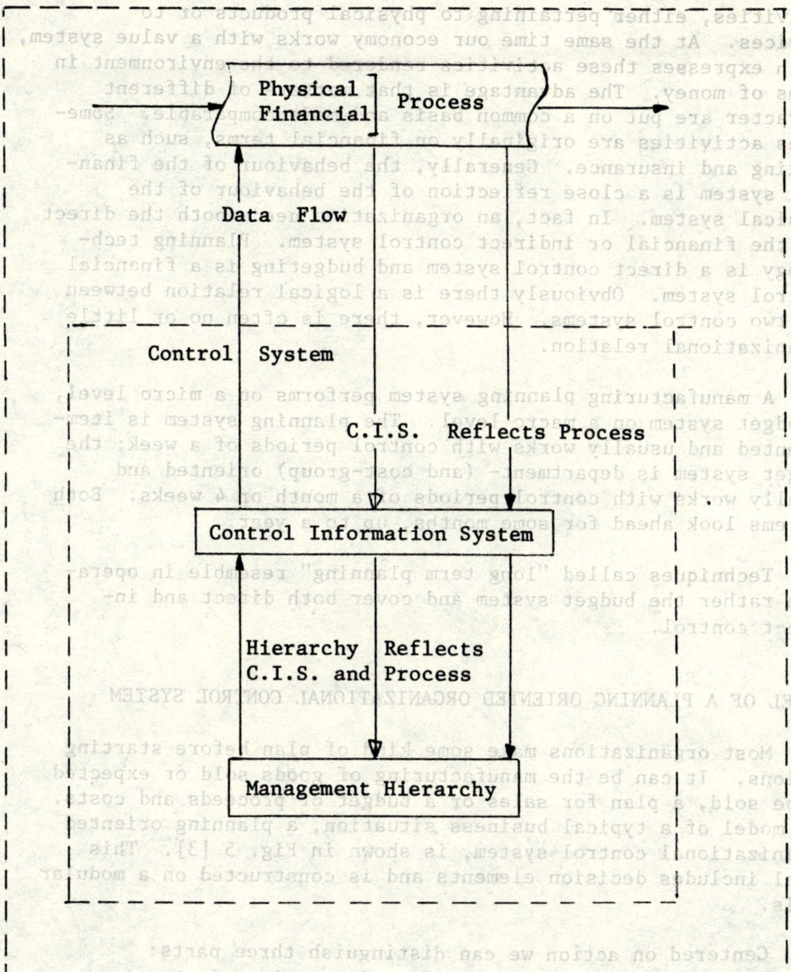

Fig. 4. Model of main organizational aspect systems

The basis for existence of an organization are its physical activities, either pertaining to physical products or to services. At the same time our economy works with a value system, which expresses these activities rendered to the environment in terms of money. The advantage is that matters of different character are put on a common basis and made comparable. Sometimes activities are originally on financial terms, such as banking and insurance. Generally, the behaviour of the financial system is a close reflection of the behaviour of the physical system. In fact, an organization needs both the direct and the financial or indirect control system. Planning technology is a direct control system and budgeting is a financial control system. Obviously there is a logical relation between the two control systems. However, there is often no or little organizational relation.

A manufacturing planning system performs on a micro level, a budget system on a macro level. The planning system is item-oriented and usually works with control periods of a week; the budget system is department- (and cost-group) oriented and usually works with control periods of a month or 4 weeks. Both systems look ahead for some months, up to a year.

Techniques called "long term planning" resemble in operation rather the budget system and cover both direct and indirect control.

MODEL OF A PLANNING ORIENTED ORGANIZATIONAL CONTROL SYSTEM

Most organizations make some kind of plan before starting actions. It can be the manufacturing of goods sold or expected to be sold, a plan for sales or a budget of proceeds and costs. The model of a typical business situation, a planning oriented organizational control system, is shown in Fig. 5 [3]. This model includes decision elements and is constructed on a modular basis.

Centered on action we can distinguish three parts:
The anterior phase; The initiation and creation of planning (the real action phase); and the late (posterior) phase covering all evaluation and possible redress [4]. The latter consists of an evaluation of the action itself and an evaluation of the contents of the anterior phase, which includes a possible decision pertaining to the next phase of action. It is interesting to compare this model with the planning and budget systems, mentioned in the preceding paragraph.

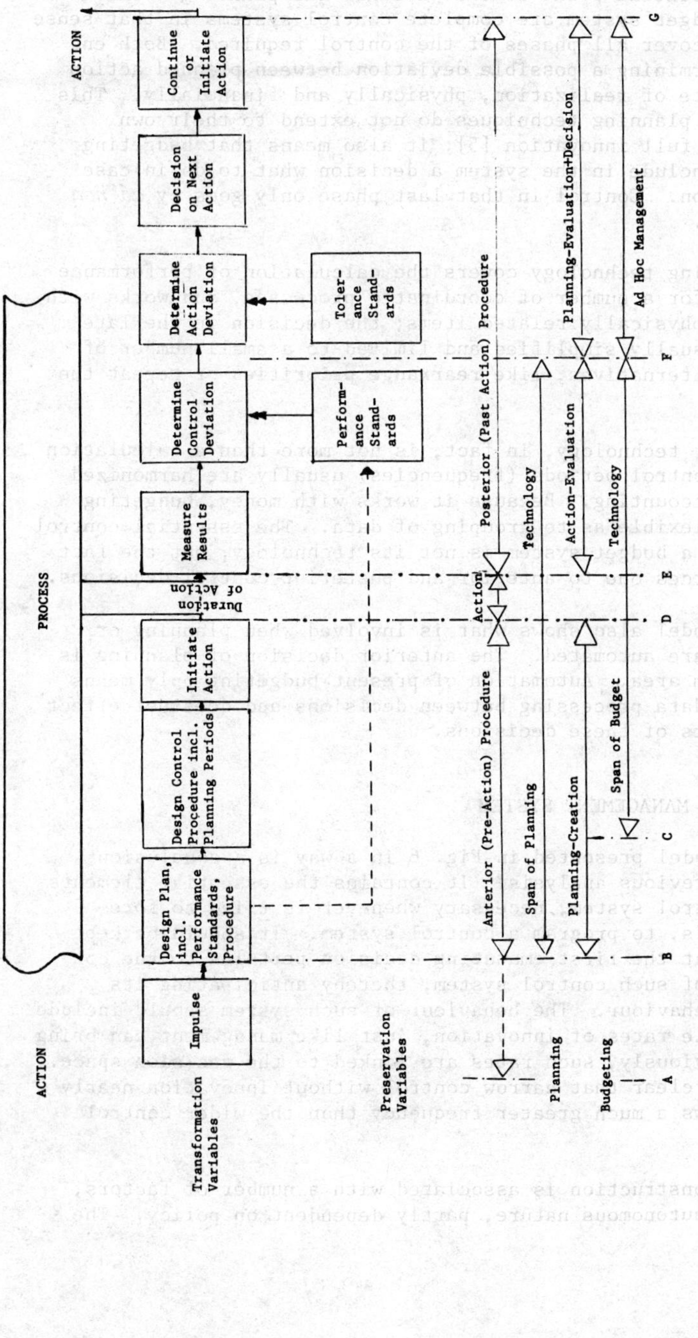

Fig. 5. Model of planning oriented organizational control system.

An essential point is that neither the planning techniques nor the budget system are complete control systems in that sense that they cover all phases of the control required. Both end after determining a possible deviation between planned action and its rate of realization, physically and financially. This means that planning techniques do not extend to their own partial or full innovation [5]; it also means that budgeting does not include in the system a decision what to do in case of deviation. Control in that last phase only goes by *ad hoc* management.

Planning technology covers the calculation of performance standards for a number of coordinated processes, and works with groups of physically related items; the decision in the late phase is usually simplified and limited to a small number of kinds of alternatives, like rearrange priorities or repeat the planning.

Budget technology, in fact, is not more than a calculation system. Control periods (frequencies) usually are harmonized with the accounting. Because it works with money, budgeting is fully flexible as to grouping of data. The essential control feature of a budget system is not its technology, but the fact that it forces one to anterior and posterior control decisions.

The model also shows what is involved when planning or budgeting are automated. The anterior decision of planning is the problem area. Automation of present budgeting only means automatic data processing between decisions and does not effect the contents of these decisions.

MODEL OF A MANAGEMENT SYSTEM

The model presented in Fig. 6 in a way is a conclusion from the previous analysis. It contains the essential elements of the control system, necessary whenever is tried to foresee, that is, to program a control system. It should be kept in mind that the first emanating decision pertains to the construction of such control system, thereby anticipating its possible behaviour. The behaviour of such system should include all possible rates of innovation, just like management can bring about. Obviously, such rates are linked to the decision space. It is also clear that narrow control without innovation nearly always shows a much greater frequency than the wider control level.

The construction is associated with a number of factors, partly of autonomous nature, partly dependent on policy. The

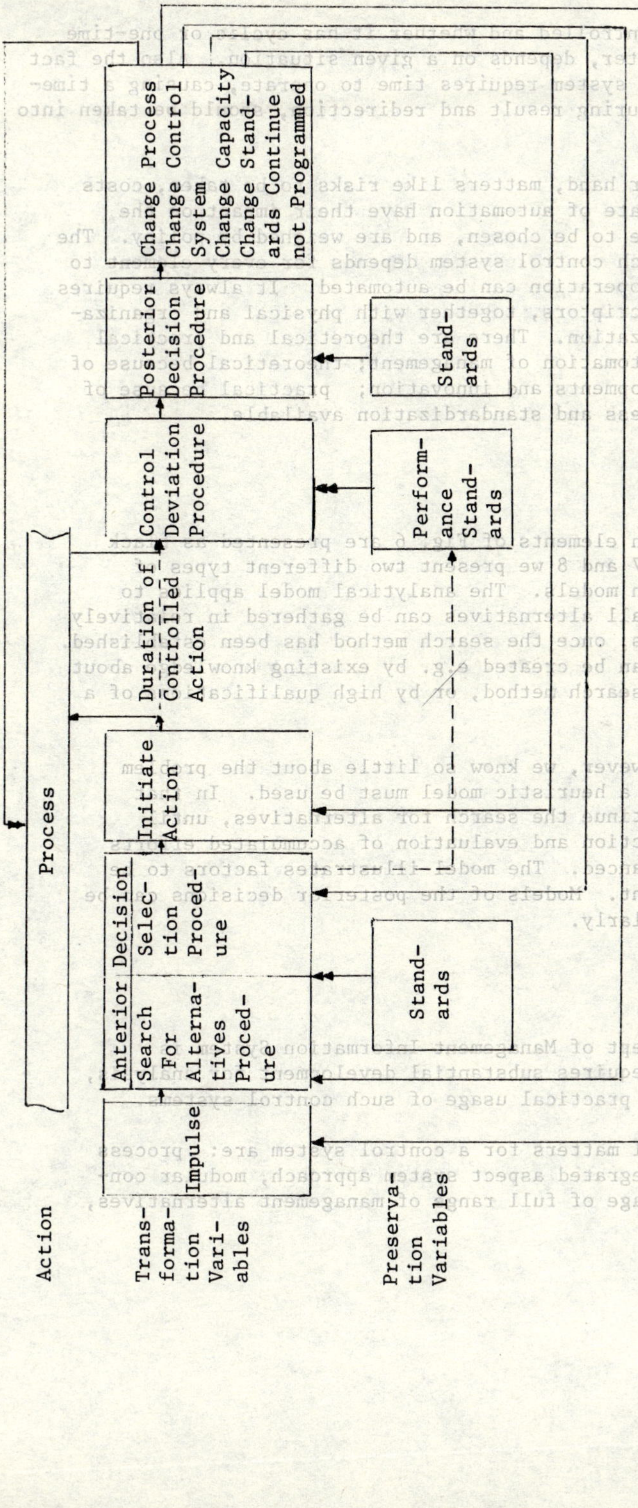

Fig. 6. Model of programmed organizational control system

process to be controlled and whether it has cyclic or one-time (project) character, depends on a given situation. Also the fact that the control system requires time to operate, causing a time-lag between measuring result and redirection, should be taken into account.

On the other hand, matters like risks to be taken, costs of control and rate of automation have their impact on the control procedure to be chosen, and are weighed by policy. The automation of such control system depends for every element to what extent its operation can be automated. It always requires exactness of descriptors, together with physical and organizational standardization. There are theoretical and practical limits to the automation of management; theoretical because of unforeseen developments and innovation; practical because of limits of exactness and standardization available.

DECISION MODELS

The decision elements of Fig. 6 are presented as black boxes. In Fig. 7 and 8 we present two different types of anterior decision models. The analytical model applies to situations that all alternatives can be gathered in relatively few search rounds, once the search method has been established. Such situation can be created e.g. by existing knowledge about the problem and search method, or by high qualifications of a manager.

Usually, however, we know so little about the problem encountered that a heuristic model must be used. In that situation we continue the search for alternatives, until relative satisfaction and evaluation of accumulated efforts are somewhat balanced. The model illustrates factors to be taken into account. Models of the posterior decisions can be constructed similarly.

FINAL STATEMENTS

a. The concept of Management Information System is essential, but requires substantial development for analysis, construction and practical usage of such control systems.

b. Essential matters for a control system are: process orientation, integrated aspect system approach, modular construction, coverage of full range of management alternatives,

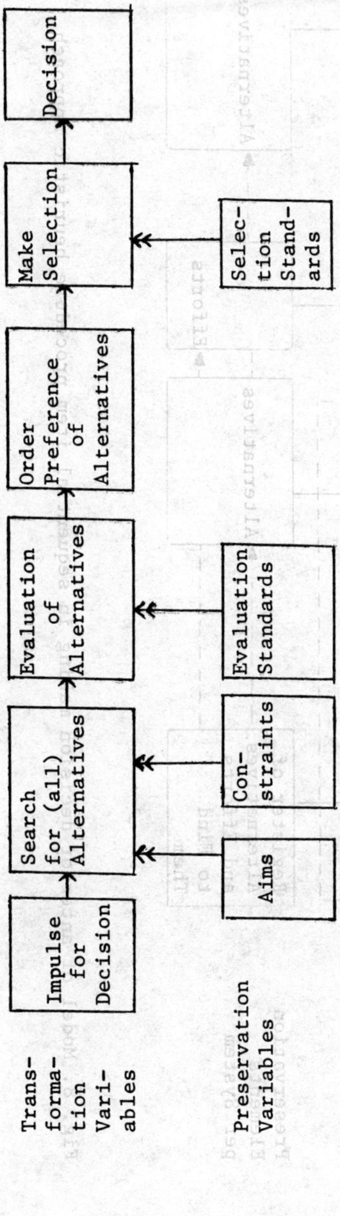

Fig. 7. Model of anterior decision making in batch procedure analytical approach

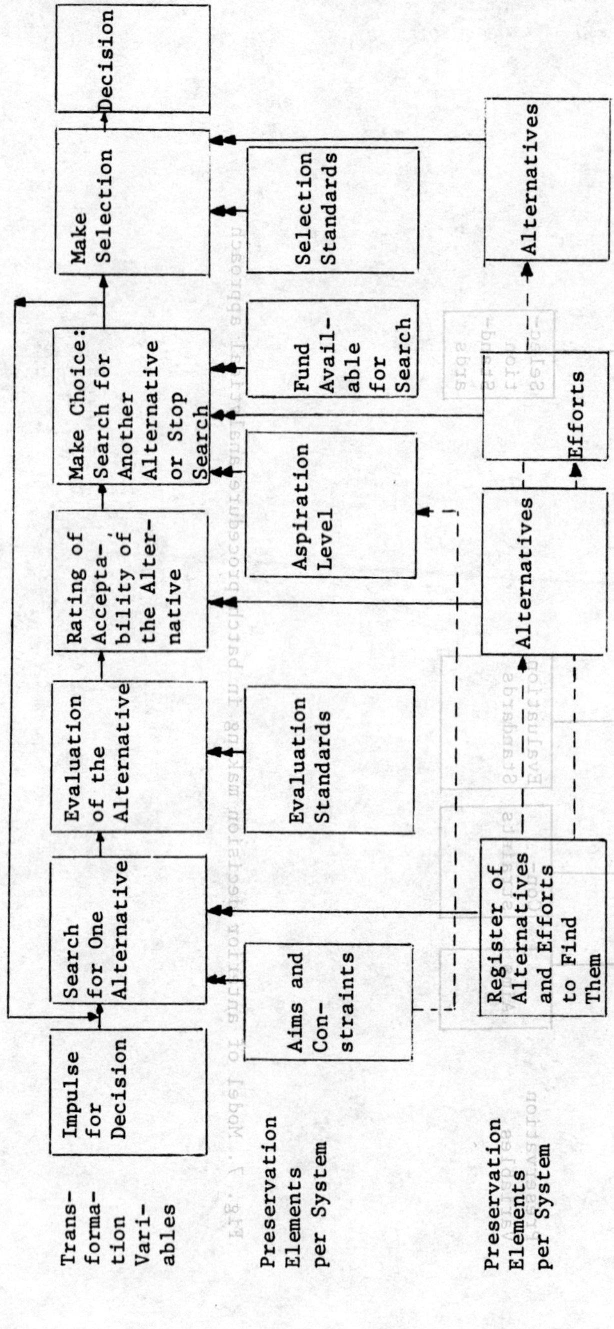

Fig. 8. Model of anterior decision making in sequential item procedure heuristic approach.

including innovation, highest possible rate of clearness and exactness.

c. The automation of data-flows between decisions has to be expanded, so far as feasible, towards automation of the full management control process.

d. Organizational structures, like hierarchy, have to be designed dependent on process-oriented control information systems.

e. Direct (physical) and indirect (financial) control must be better integrated in a management information system.

f. Control of process and control of people (managers) should be separated.

g. Successful development and implementation of M.I.S. requires that it becomes a specialized management function, which is represented in top management.

h. Size of organization, rate of complexity of processes and interests at stake determine mainly the urgency of having an effective and efficient control system, as described.

i. A symbolic language to deal with these kinds of problems has to be developed.

j. We suggest the name Systematics to indicate the field described in this paper, and perhaps Business Systematics for typical business applications.

REFERENCES

1. C.G.D. MAARSCHALK, "The use of aspect systems in a general model for organizational structure and organizational control" *Ann. Sys. Res.* (Publication of the Netherlands Society for Systems Research, The Netherlands, 1971), p. 27-41.

2. A language, based on the Set Theory has been published by A.C.J. de LEEUW, "On measurement, methodology and systems" *Ann. Sys. Res*, *1*, 17-26 (1971).

3. The author is indebted to his publisher, Stanfert Kroese, Leiden, to permit publication in this paper of some charts from his manuscript of a future publication.

4. Compare also M.R. MANTZ, "Systems theory and evolution" *Ann. Sys. Res., 1*, 42-63 (1971).

5. Compare the distinction between Planning and Control, made by A. BOSMAN, *Systemen, Planning, Newerken* (Leiden, 1969) p. 40 ff, p. 208 ff.

A PROCESS-SYSTEM THEORY TO GUIDE MANAGEMENT POLICY AT ANY LEVEL

M.R. MANTZ

Chief Scientific Advisor, Honeywell Bull, Amsterdam, Netherlands

SUMMARY

The challenge of today is to know how all the different aspects which are covered more or less by existing management theories and scientific disciplines fit together into one system and how they interact. The proposed way of thinking is based on a generalized elementary model of a process and system rules. It is found that the model offers a systematic approach to the multi-aspect problem indicating when and where a certain discipline becomes relevant. The dynamics of development and evolution can be derived from the model in a simple and consistent manner.

INTRODUCTION

The modern business enterprise strives for many objectives, carries many different products and has to meet a number of ever increasing and rapidly changing, technical, economic and social requirements. However, the means to fulfill those requirements are available. Automation is one of those means and so are the many scientific organization theories which have been set up.

The problem arises which of those theories will prevail or which are already outdated; which theory presents a one-sided view and, therefore, cannot always be relevant; which offers a true prospect or will prove to be false.

Amidst this confusing amount of possibilities and problems a systematic theory of the structure of processes, in general, is needed, supplied with rules for the structure of the interaction between production and management. Such a theory should provide an answer to many questions and give information on the changes that are taking place.

Organization Theories

It is well-known how an organization based on authority has to be structured (line organization) and how and when expert knowledge has to be called for (staff organization). It is also known how critical decision points have to be found, how cybernetic principles can be adopted for system's control and how the technique of automatic data processing can be applied for an information system.

However, much less is known about the interaction between these methods. Moreover, it does not suffice to know whether a theory is attractive, it must also be relevant to reality.

An organization changes because it grows and because of the application of technical, economic and social knowledge. Society as a whole is also constantly changing and the industrial production and management organization will have to be adjusted continuously and ever more rapidly to this development. An organization theory will have to allow for all possible changes. For this reason the design of a generally applicable theory of management organization is such an ambitious task that it would always remain a pipe dream unless the reality of practise itself would present the clue for such a theory. The solution is to be found in automation and the role it has become to play in management.

Automation and Organization

Before an object is automated it has to be analysed in detail. The object is always a process, i.e. a continuous series of interrelated operations for the accomplishment of a result. Of course research into the process will not be restricted to analysis of the process, but it will also be investigated how and where improvements can be made. A process can be improved technically (new machines), by economic rationalization (homogenization, standardization, expansion), or by adjusting to the needs of the market or changing social demands.

It may also be found necessary to accelerate a process. Above all, much attention has to be paid to the management and control of a process, and for this purpose the planning and programming of a process in *advance* is of great importance. It should be possible to recognize errors at once and to apply corrections immediately.

The integral control will not be limited to the process itself, but will extend to those fields which influence the process, e.g. the supply of raw materials, the selling of the products. The processes involved here should be included in the control and management structure. The resulting complex of processes produces the structural model of a business enterprise that is represented in elementary form in Fig. 1.

It is necessary to make a clear distinction between production processes and management processes. The former yield the product, usually by transforming raw materials into consumer goods, but the product may also be some kind of service. The management process (sometimes called control process)* implies the processing of data in such a way that the resulting information is useful for the continuation of the production process. Here lies the origin of the new science, Informatics, that studies how the computer can contribute to a better construction and functioning of management processes. Informatics is in fact based on a process theory in the same way as Cybernetics; the latter examines how cybernetic principles can improve the control of processes

It is remarkable that all improvements of management processes contribute to a better functioning of production processes. Furthermore it should be noticed that the optimum and continuous functioning of the production process is of the utmost importance within a business enterprise and that the management process serves to promote it.

Although it is through the influence of automation that organization, originally the creation of effective and efficient *relations*, now implies the creation of effective *processes*. This tendency has been noticed for some time, as this change of meaning is a logical consequence of the delegation principle. By planning everything in advance and by giving clear assignments, the management can achieve that all activities are carried out according to their wish and without their constant attention. For some time already routine operations no longer depend on ad hoc instructions given by persons with delegated authority or with expert knowledge, but were programmed in advance. A well-known example is the conveyor belt and the assembly line.

Process Organization in Relation to Traditional Organizations

It would be a mistake to suppose that the introduction of new ideas on organization would make the traditional organizational relations obsolete. It is better to see them as inadequate.

*The model to be presented here makes a difference between management and control.

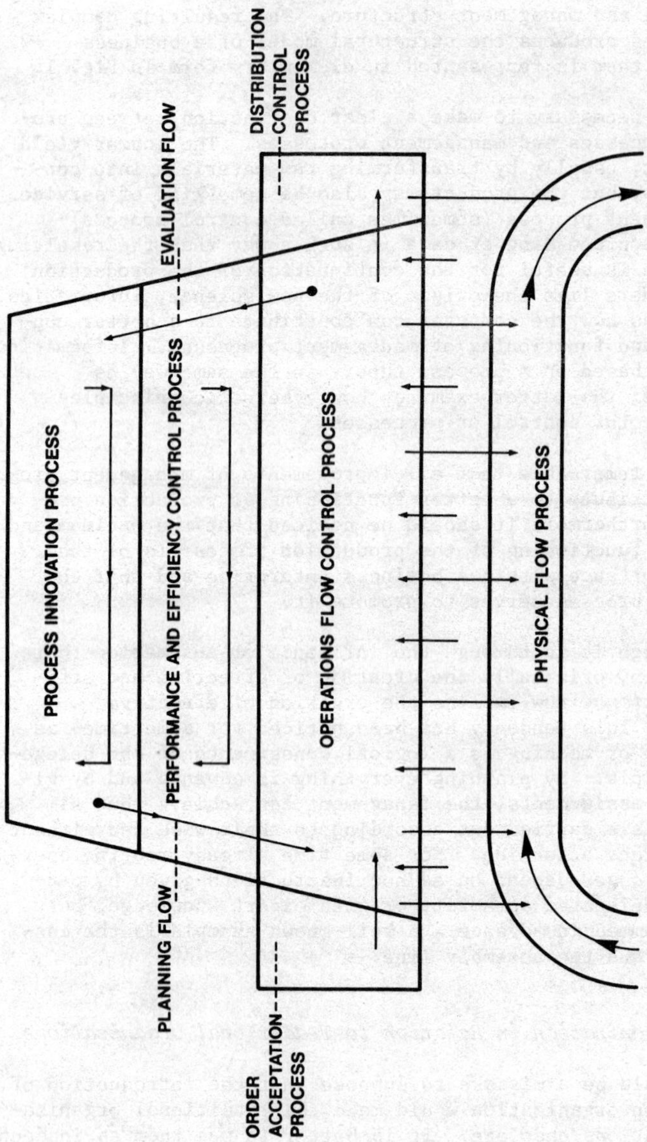

Fig. 1. Elementary model of the process structure of a company

In a primitive situation in which all that is accomplished depends on human labour, an organization based on authority (line organization) is the only possible one. As soon as expert knowledge is available the organization will become a line and staff organization. When the situation has developed in such a way that the production processes involved can be programmed in advance, the line and staff organization will gradually become a process organization. This development resembles the realization of a process that is programmed for the computer. At the beginning the initiative is taken by the authority, next the experts take care of the actual construction and realization, and at the end the operations are carried out and controlled by a program which in itself is a detailed model of the process. In case of stagnation the procedure occurs in the opposite order.

Let us consider a computer program for the daily order processing. If everything runs smoothly the order processing is carried out by an automated process that is only controlled by an operator. When the processing stagnates through an unknown cause, the operator turns to an expert for help, e.g. a programmer or someone from the maintenance department. If this person fails to find the cause of the stagnation or needs too much time to put things back in order again, the authority placed above him, e.g. the head of the department, will step in and he decides what has to be done. In other words, when a process is constructed, the authority turns to the expert who will realize the project for him; when a process stagnates, the person directly in charge (e.g. the operator) will turn to the expert and, if necessary, the latter turns to the authority who will take measures until the process is functioning well again.

Summarizing one might say that as long as the work to be done is not clearly defined, the organization in which it has to be carried out will mostly be based on authority, and that as the operations become better defined, the organizational form will gradually become a process organization.

Someone who wants to orientate himself in a business enterprise needs this knowledge absolutely. The nature of a situation must be ascertained before a policy decision can be made.

FROM MANAGEMENT TO MIS (MANAGEMENT INFORMATION SYSTEM)

Summarizing we can conclude that the steady efforts to improve management control, to apply economic rationalization by promoting homogenuity, continuity and expansion and to benefit from automation, all together show a trend to be properly oriented in line with the business and economic needs.

The conditions that favour this are that processes are predictable, not very special or exceptional, and not changing rapidly.

Improving a business organization requires, therefore, the separation of process-parts which can be rationalized and delegated to a machine (or low qualified workers) and the parts which are so unpredictable and changing that only the human mind can deal with them properly. If we speak about management tools to improve management we mean the process modules that can be delegated to others and to machines. Improving management by M.I.S. as a tool of management means that we should study the processes that can be controlled by M.I.S. and that the processes are such which can to a great extent be standardized.

How a situation can be assessed in terms of processes is illustrated by Fig. 1, the elementary model of an enterprise as, with all kinds of variations, used by automation experts, and by Fig. 2 (the model of an elementary computer operation). Although the models are shown in quite different detail (Fig. 1 gives an overall picture, Fig. 2 gives a more detailed view), the two of them are remarkably alike. The explanation for this lies in the fact that both models represent processes and that the basic construction of a process model is not sensitive to the dimensions considered.

The study of processes is receiving more and more attention. However, the description of processes is still incomplete, unmotivated, and unsystematic. A general process theory would be most useful and with this paper I hope to convince the reader that a simple and elementary model can yield an enormous gain of insight.

The introduction of automation in the enterprise has shown that automation of *existing* procedures offers only limited benefit. To profit really from the power of the computer one has to go back to the first principles of organization. Likewise,

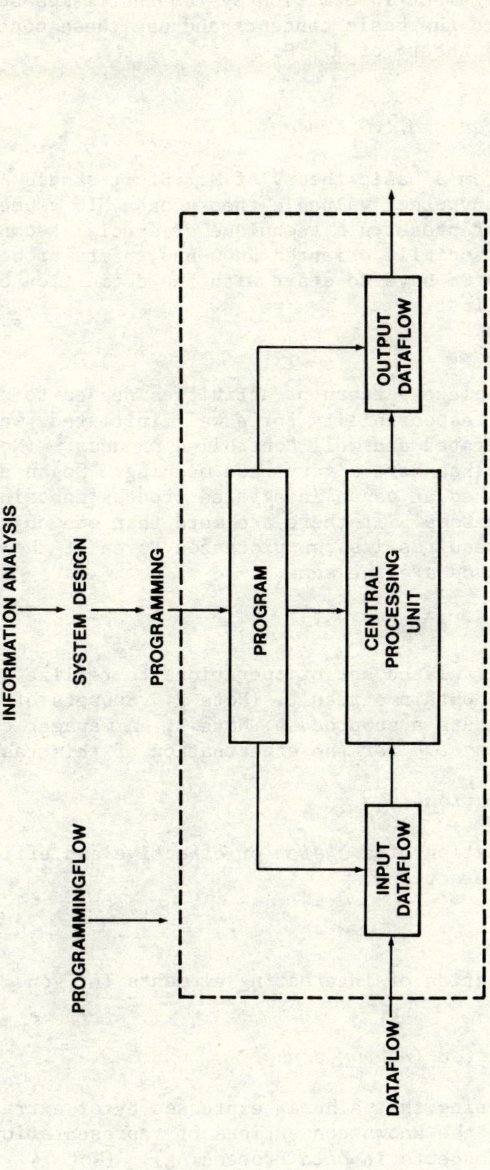

Fig. 2. Elementary model of a computer operation

a theory of Management Information System that makes sense should go back to the basic concepts and use these concepts to build up a basic theory of M.I.S.

Basic Concepts for a M.I.S. Theory

Starting from a basic theory of M.I.S. it should be possible to place any other valuable theory on a MIS aspect, which is one-sided or represents a technique or special technically, economically or socially oriented know-how in its proper context. Therefore we have to start with the definition of our basic concepts first.

a. Management

The complete pattern of activities needed to effectuate the total responsibility for a well initiated, well designed, well operated and well controlled *process*. (Note 1: The term process has here a very wide meaning. So an enterprise can be looked at as an integrated process containing numerous subprocesses. If there are more than one objective, each objective requires its own processes, even if the means and people involved are the same.)

b. Process

An interrelated set of operations to realize an objective resp. to obtain a result. (Note 2. Subsets of operations can constitute a subprocess; Note 3. A manager can create or use an *organization* for the effectuation of this task.)

c. Organization

The creation of a *system* of effective and efficient relations or interactions.

d. System

A collection of interacting elements (L. von Bertalanffy).

e. Information (narrow sense)

The meaning that a human expresses by or extracts from data by means of the known conventions of representation used. (IFIP Guide to concepts in Data Processing). (Note 4. In management environment information is used to come to a decision. A decision can initiate an action, e.g. to start, stop or to correct a process or operation, in short to control an operation. As also data processors can be initiated by a signal, which is interpreted as a command to start, stop or correct an operation we can widen the concept of information to:

f. Information (broad sense)

The significance expresses by or extracted from *data* by means of the known conventions of representations used. (IFIP Modified)

g. Data

A representation of facts or ideas in a formalized manner capable of being communicated or manipulated by some *process*. (IFIP)

Having defined some basic conepts, we can now look at the interrelations by developing a basic process-system model.

Elementary System Models

Level 1: G.S.T. model

The simplest model comes from the General Systems Theory (L. van Bertalanffy)

Input and output are defined by functions in a mathematical language. The relation between input and output is not described in the sense of how the process operates (it is a black box), but the result of the transformation is described by the relation between input and output. So the model is not intended to study the "how" question but to compute "what" actually happens. If we want to study both the how and what aspects, we shall have to make the black box less black and specify what is happening within by indicating and describing the planning, implementation and evaluation activities.

Level 2: Process Module

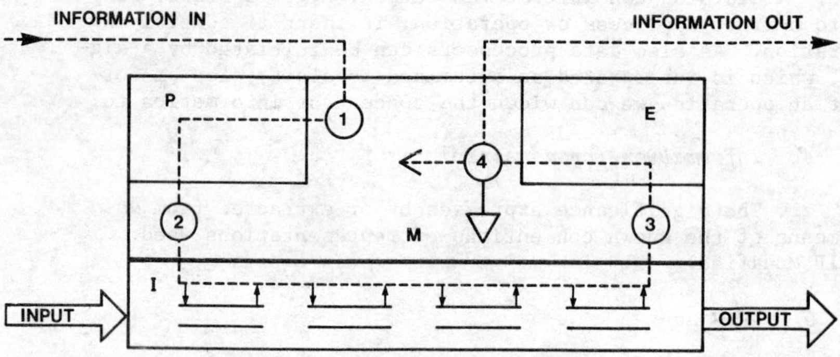

Fig. 3.

P = planning, i.e. making a *model* of the implementation process to guide implementation

I = implementation, i.e. *monitoring* the transformation process step by step.

E = evaluation of results obtained, (1) to get experience and store in the memory a picture of the situation (data base), (2) to correct planning if necessary, (3) to inform the planning function of a higher level located outside the process module.

M = management function to coordinate the whole process by

① decision to create a plan or model

② decision to implement

③ decision to deliver OUTPUT

④ decision to store data, to correct planning or to inform higher management.

Specific Management Functions

Based on this level of detail (aggregation) we can specify the management functions more in detail. A manager receives data from his environment and supplies data to the environment. By doing this he interacts with a management information system (M.I.S.). Besides the external M.I.S. the manager uses also an internal M.I.S. Each subprocess P,I and E need input data and supplies output data. By knowing the relation between output and input data, a manager can control each subprocess by comparing obtained results with expected results. In *each* interface between two successive subprocesses the manager can take resp. a decision to *initiate*, a decision to *implement*, a decision to *deliver* the result of the transformation process (physical flow) or a decision to *correct* the procedure and/or to inform *higher* management.

Level 3: Process-system Module

To come from level 1 module to level 2 module we have introduced the subprocesses P, I and E and the management function M.

Let us consider P, I and E once again as black-boxes that can be specified further, and let us suppose that the P, I, E and M specification formula can again be applied because it operated independent of the dimensions or the kind of process analyzed.

Looking at the level 3 process-system model more closely, we note that the lower part named I module is identical with the level 2 process model. The upper part, named P-E-M module can be considered as a model for a higher level planning and control process, coordinated by a higher level of management.

Moreover, we discover a relation between M and resp. M_p, M_i and M_e, which we recognize as a hierarchical structure of management authority. At this level we can summarize the management functions as follows: A manager can control a process by planning, monitoring, evaluation, and comparing the inputs and outputs of each subprocess, delegated to a sub-manager.

To elaborate the system developed as far as we can go in three directions:

I. By applying a 4th level of differentiation, which makes the model complicated.

II. By extending the physical flow from where it comes from and towards it goes.

III. By extending the information - or better called data-flow by putting another P.E.M. module on top of the level 3 process-system model.

If we follow the last possibility we obtain a three level planning and control system together with a physical flow which is exactly the company model of Fig. 1.

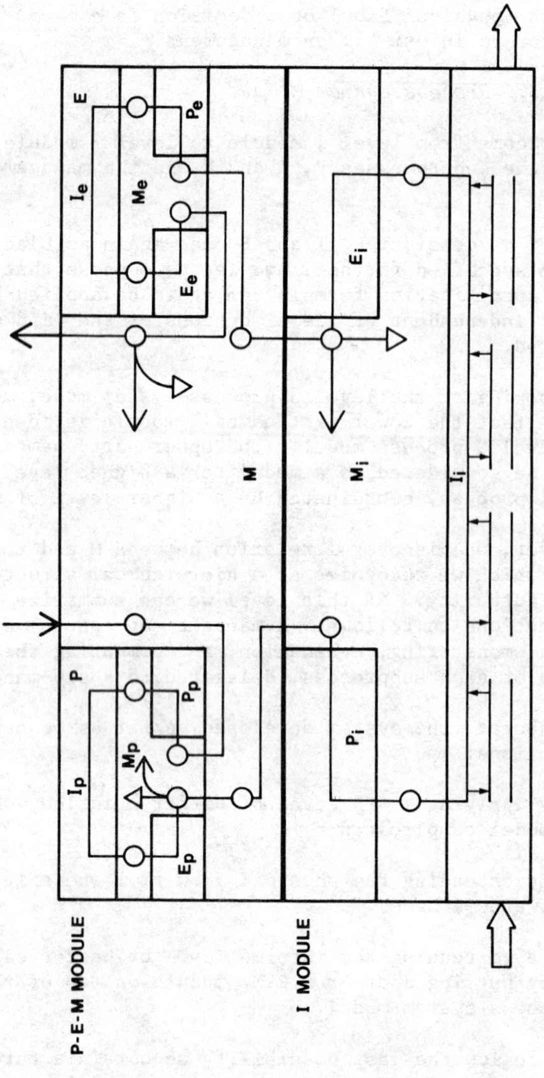

Fig. 4. Elementary process-system model

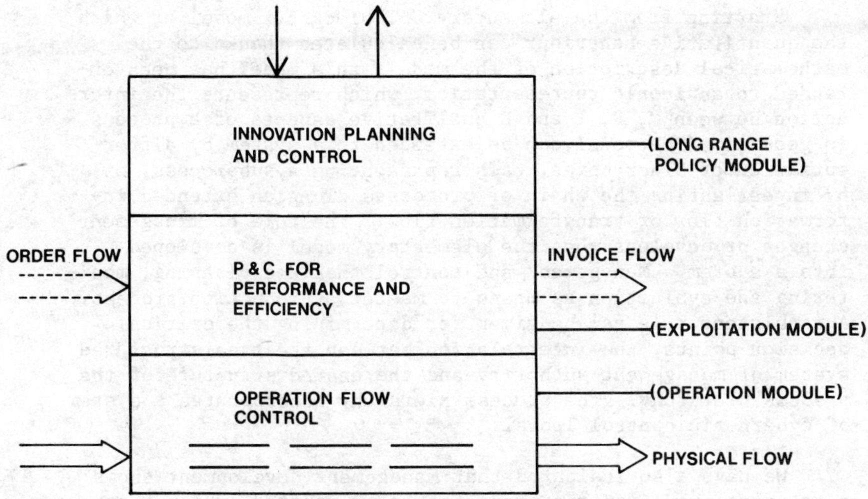

Fig. 5

If we look at a company in practice we detect that we have not been as consistent as we should have been. In fact, we discover that the exploitation module knows also a transformation flow that transforms orders into invoices comparable with the physical flow, where materials are transformed to end-products. In fact, we have found here a clue, where to find interfaces with additional flows of data to be transformed by higher planning and control processes. The model now developed, in this case by a bottom to top approach, will give us guidelines for the development of a M.I.S.

It is clear that as long as the operations flow has not yet reached a certain level of homogeneity, continuity and volume it is no use to predesign much, leading to a degree of standardization in associate procedures to plan, monitor and control the operations flow. If, however, such a degree can be obtained, we can cultivate the predesign in the direction of the two higher planning and control processes, i.e. on the exploitation level and on the innovation level.

The models given can be used to build process-models for quantitative analysis, but also for the development of conceptual models.

Summary

Starting from the elementary GST black box model of which the quantitative behaviour can be calculated thanks to the mathematical description of the model, this model has been extended to an iconic representation, which represents the interaction between M, P, I and E qualitative aspects of a process in general. The model can be extended to a system by differentiation of black boxes, each representing a subprocess, or by investigating the chain of processes along an extended information flow or transformation flow. The role of management changes or develops when the elementary model is developed into a system. Management and control then use planning, monitoring and evaluation as means to master a production process. A consistent rule can be given for determining the critical decision points, the interrelation between the tree-structured system of management authority and the nested structure of the process hierarchy. The process hierarchy incorporates a system of cybernetic control loops.

We have also indicated that management development shows a trend to predesign the processes to be managed, which then are ripe for automation. Automation itself gives more certainty that the execution is exactly according to plan. Moreover, economic rationalization tends to create the continuity, the homogeneity and, by expansion, the volume that makes the predesign of processes and the automation economic acceptable. All these activities find a *common objective* in reshaping the entreprise *processes* to obtain better management and the benefits of automation and rationalization. Although on a fundamental level quite a number of aspects are now related to each other in an integrated system, there are some more aspects to deal with.

SYSTEM DYNAMICS RELATED TO TECHNICAL, ECONOMIC AND SOCIAL ASPECTS

It is known that one of the greatest problems managers have to face nowadays is to adapt for change and to keep pace with the ever accelerated rate of change in society. Besides that there is the question how and what is the contribution of technical, economic and social sciences to the state of art in company organization, e.g. there is a growing social pressure of customers to get better and cheaper products, better service and from the workers to get better working conditions, better tools, permanent education etc. Hence, management needs guidelines for building a dynamic and balanced multi-disciplinary system, in contrast to the conventional one-sided static structures used today.

To deal with the multi-disciplinary and the dynamic aspects of process systems we start from the same elementary process model. For the iconic representation of our thoughts, however, the model of Fig. 6 is better suited.

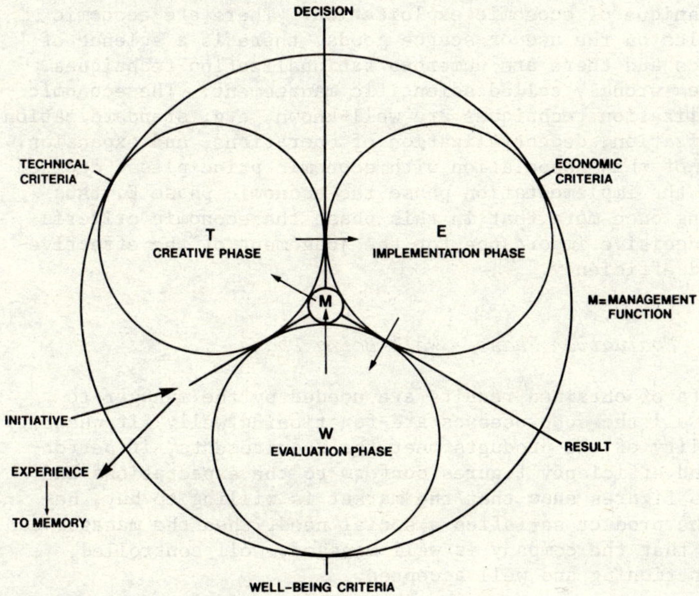

Fig. 6. Elementary process

Basic Pattern

A process consists of three phases, a creative phase, an implementation phase and an evaluation phase. A process as a whole is managed, i.e. is started, stimulated, controlled and maintained by a management function.

In the P phase a plan has to be created to give shape to the implementation. The activity to give shape to an idea is above all a technical matter. The science that provides the necessary knowledge for this purpose is a technical science. As the technical state of art reaches a higher level, more ambitious plans, e.g. space flights or the realization of very complex systems, can be carried out. As in this phase the technical criteria are of decisive importance, it will be called the T-phase from now on. The impetus of this phase is the pursuit of perfection.

a. Implementation Phase - Economic Exploitation Phase

The aim of implementation phase is to make as much profit as possible by the economic exploitation of the idea realized in the T-phase. For many years society has been familiar with the technique of economic exploitation. There are economic principles on the use of scarce goods, there is a science of economics and there are numerous rationalization techniques, sometimes wrongly called scientific management. The economic rationalization techniques are well-known, e.g. standardization, specialization, decentralization of operations, and expansion. Because of this association with economic principles I decided to call the implementation phase the economic phase E, thus stressing once more that in this phase the economic criteria are of decisive importance for the judgement of the effectiveness and efficiency.

b. Evaluation Phase - Well-Being Phase

Data of obtained results are needed by the manager to know if all the subprocesses are functioning well. If quantity and quality of the products meet the requirements, if performance and efficiency figures conform to the expectations and if sales figures show that the market is willing to buy, because the product satisfies a social need, then the manager can be sure that the company is well managed, well controlled, well functioning and well accepted.

It is difficult to find an English term for the concept "to be in form", that expresses the well-status of the abovementioned aspects. So I created the word "*Well-Being*" which includes the concept of well-being, but is not restricted to human feelings. The Science of *Well-Being* is the collection of disciplines studying the objectives and conditions to be realized in order to master the *Well-Being* in the whole field, that is the company and its environment.

c. Multi-Disciplinary Approach

As said before, ever more voices are raised in favour of a multi-disciplinary approach of a problem. However, in my opinion such an approach should not mean that a number of experts with various scientific backgrounds are brought together into one team and that all start on the problem at the same time.

The model I have introduced clearly shows that in the creative phase the problems to be solved are mostly technical problems. And not until some experience has been gained with the technical aspects, will the product be ready for large-scale manufacturing and exploitation. As soon as the exploitation is running well, the next step should be to examine whether there are still "social" criteria (*Well-Being*) to be met or, what is more often the case, whether the economic rationalization has violated the living and working environment. A well-known example of the latter is environmental pollution. The development of a process is not completed until sufficient attention has been paid to all criteria, the technical, economic, and social criteria.

The greater stress that is put on the multi-disciplinary approach of problems nowadays can be explained by the enormous increase of speed with which industrial processes develop. It used to be possible to think in eithertechnical or economic terms for years on end, but this is not any longer the case.

Besides the T, E, W and M criteria there are more aspects to discuss and to study, resulting in many existing theories and techniques, each dedicated to a special aspect. We will call this mono-disciplines. To unite or even to discuss these aspects *all at once* is impossible. However, there is a common objective in each enterprise that can always be discussed. It is *to work and operate efficiently* on every level, ranging from a single operation up to the functioning of the whole enterprise.

d. Conclusion

If there exists a basic and general system theory applicable to an enterprise, this has to be a *process* systems theory. Every technique, method or theory useful to improve the performance and efficiency of an enterprise has to be based on the typical character of a subprocess or on an aspect of such a process. So, if there is a gap, difference between two ways of looking at problems in the enterprise, a common interface between these two different disciplines can be detected at the base, i.e. the common and actual process that should be served by the two conflicting disciplines. A process-system theory is the only philosophy which can unite already existing disciplines and other philosophies provided that these philosophies are pragmatically oriented and so stem from a common starting point.

It is my sincere belief that any other approach will result in endless discussions without communication. *Communication* can only be established on a *common* subject. Cultivation of a balanced multi-disciplinary approach will result in a concentrated effort to analyse and design more sophisticated processes, which makes the enterprise ripe for wide-scale automation too.

Systemstructures of Processes

Applying the principle of structuring, which says that each sub-process shows the same basic pattern as a complete process, we obtain Fig. 7.

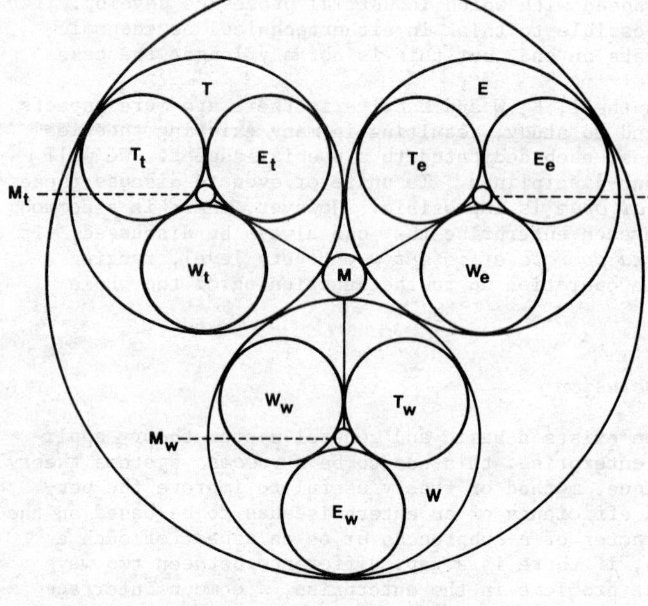

Fig. 7. Two level hierarchy of processes with two management levels.

From this model a number of dedicated sub-models can be derived, e.g. a model for a decision-making process for innovation. It is represented by the T circle and contains T_t = orientation and thinking, E_t = giving shape to possible solutions and W_t = evaluation for judgement and the selection of the most satisfying solution.

The Implementation Model

The implementation model as presented in Fig. 8 is most commonly used. It corresponds closely with the model of Fig. 1, which is generally used by automation experts. Although in the planning (T) and evaluation phases (W) the subphases are not indicated, these phases really exist but not as distinguished subprocesses, delegated to different people. Because concrete implementation requires planning in detail, the implementation cycles are differentiated one or more steps further. The names in practice given to the subprocesses are:

T_1 = policy planning
T_2 = capacity planning
T_3 = scheduling

W_1 = evaluation for innovation control
W_2 = evaluation for performance and efficiency control
W_3 = evaluation for monitoring and quality control

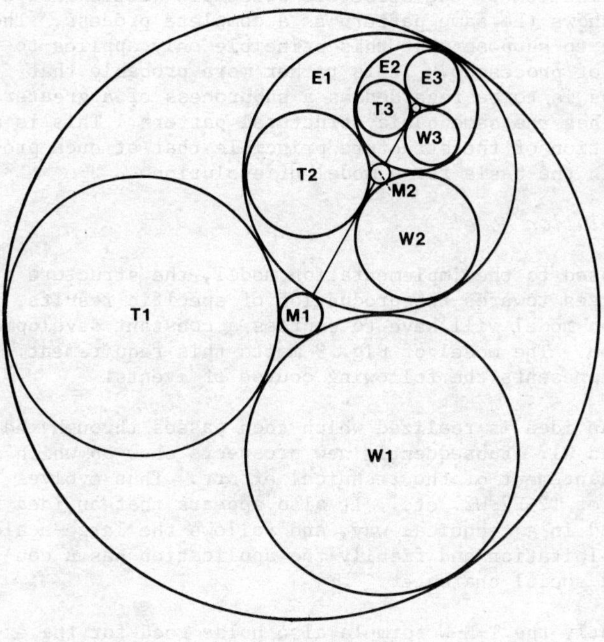

Fig. 8. Implementation model

As a matter of fact, the terms capacity planning and efficiency control belong not to the process of implementation of a new project but to the exploitation of existing designs. To be precise it is better to separate, at least to distinguish between implementation and exploitation. Implementation is focussed on the implementation of something new; we can call it a "top to bottom" approach. Exploitation is based on the optimization of the flow of operations (physical flow) and therefore requires a "bottom to top" approach.

This economic representation form expresses clearly the "nested" structure of a process hierarchy which is different from the "tree" structure of authority (Management). In the implementation model the two structures are combined. Even this very simple model compels us to be more precise in presenting concepts than we usually do.

Evolution

The definition of the structure principle states that a subprocess shows the same pattern as a complete process. There is no reason to suppose that this principle only applies to the subdivision of processes. It is rather more probable that every process is to be regarded as a subprocess of a greater entity that has the same basic structural pattern. This is a wider definition of the structure principle that at once provides us with the basis for a model of evolution.

The Evolution Model

As opposed to the implementation model, the structure of which converges towards the production of specific results, the evolution model will have to express a constant development and expansion. The model of Fig. 9 meets this requirement. The model represents the following course of events.

In T1 an idea is realized which then passes through the phases E1 and W1. Subsequently new prospects show up which require an enhancement of the technical effort. Thus evolves the process of T2-E2-W2. etc. It also appears that an idea is first applied in a technical way, and follows the large-scale economic exploitation and fianlly the application has a controlling and social character.

Apparently the T-E-W formula also holds good for the expansion of an idea, i.e. the fields of application. This can be illustrated with the evolution of the objectives of a business enterprise. At first a new product is created, then follows the exploitation and profit-making, and finally comes the wish to continue in favourable conditions and to provide permanent employment.

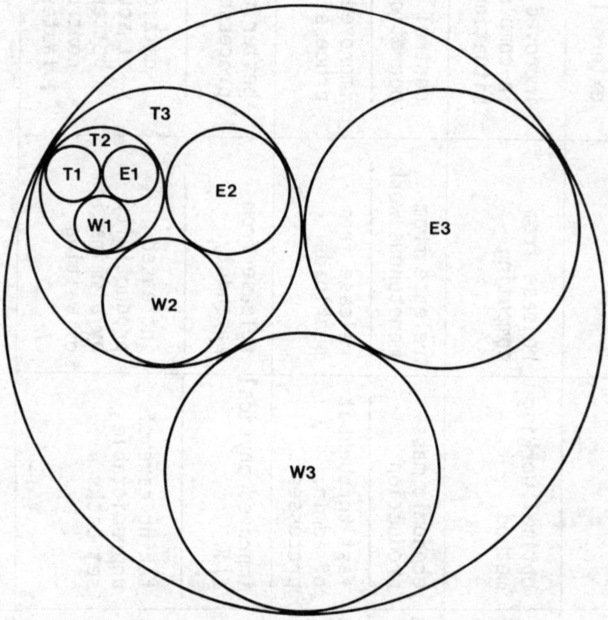

Fig. 9. General evolution model

I will give you one more example of what we find in reality and which should prove the validity of the model. The development of the computer applications lends itself quire well for this purpose. Fig. 10 gives a concise survey of this development.

At first the computer was used purely as a calculating machine to find optimum solutions to very complex problems. Next the computer was furnished with fast input/output equipment and thus made profitable for administrative data processing (which originally used the punch cards technique). This application utilizes the computer as being an automatic process. As the computer became equipped with disc stores, it became possible to process all consequences of one input data in one complete run. The individual data processing enables continuous processing of orders with this method, as the necessary administrative operations take very little time. An

ASPECTS / PHASE ↓	T	E	W	
	computer used as	economic benefit	human (life-work)	company (internal, external control)
Innovation control	automatic computing machine	optimal working method	release from computing	improved control in complex situations
Performance and efficiency control	automatic dataprocess (parts of process	economic mass-production	release from monotonous work	control of mass operation
	total process	fast throughput of admin. processes	release from peakloads	improved order-processing flow
Operation flow control	process-control-process	improved physical flow	release from watchduty	better managed processes
	multi-access man-machine dialogue	taking care of unpredictable set backs	increased productivity by elimination of waiting	. data collecting at source . better operation control . faster research

Fig. 10. Development of automation

extra advantage of this method is the improvement of the working conditions for the employees as they are confronted with a continuous flow or work, instead of being forced to have either too little or too much work to do as is often the case with other mass processing methods. The short interval of time between the input and output of data makes it feasible to use the computer for the control of operational processes. When the computer is equipped with data transmission networks and has multi-accessibility, it becomes possible to control geographically dispersed operations of an enterprise and to solve the problems of operational control and data collection.

The control of the physical flow offers the right basis for the enlargement of a Management Information System that also controls the flow of data for the management and decision making processes.

Development of the State of Art

We have characterized a subprocess by the first letter of the name of the scientific discipline that solves the problems of the design of this subprocess. Each scientific discipline is still in development. It is surprising to note that this development process follows a trend that corresponds with the T.E.W. formula.

Let me give you an example. The design of the motor of a car was first a pure technical problem. When this technique was mastered the development was directed to design an economical motor making more revolutions per second. Nowadays we are more interested in an automatic controlled transmission of the power and a clean motor, which are W features.

System Dynamics

The system model shows a cyclic pattern of at least three steps respectively, T.E.W. On the development level we should add, after technical, economical and well-being improvements have been implemented, the step of management system improvement. If the development is fast the cycle time has to be shortened. One way of shortening cycle time is to make the steps small in analogy what we do with mechanical parts in mechanics and electrical components in electro-dynamics. It is self-evident that the dimensions of the different T.E.W.M. development steps sould be tuned mutually, i.e. should be of the same dimension. Briefly, *dynamic change requires a balanced multi-disciplinary approach with small steps to allow for a high cycle time*. We do that e.g. when applying heuristic methods and also when shooting down a fast moving object with a guided missile instead of missing it with one well prepared gunshot.

Resistance to Change

Likewise you have to apply force to get a physical object to move and again force to stop it or change the direction of its movement; human beings are slow to start, slow to stop and resist change in the kind of thinking familiar to them. By nature a human mind is static, and only by education and cultivation it can become versatile and dynamic. That is why an expert is a perfectionist regardless of whether he is a technician, an economist or an expert in some other discipline. In the past when a phase in evolution lasted for a generation we could identify change by growth, i.e. expansion without significant change in aspect.

When the rate of change accelerates and the T.E.W. and M. steps should be kept deliberately small and tuned to the same level, the danger of an overshoot in one aspect, i.e. overdone perfection, becomes more and more relevant. Every development activity shows the characteristic pattern of a slow start, then the slope of the curve rises when the take-off of success emerges. In the past this was an encouragement to proceed along the same lines, nowadays it is a warning signal to start with the next step in the development, which has a completely different character that is determined by the T.E.W.M. formula. Instead of falling into the trap of overdone perfection we have to control for balanced multi-disciplinary development, which also means that mono-disciplinary extrapolation of trends is very dangers (Fig. 11).

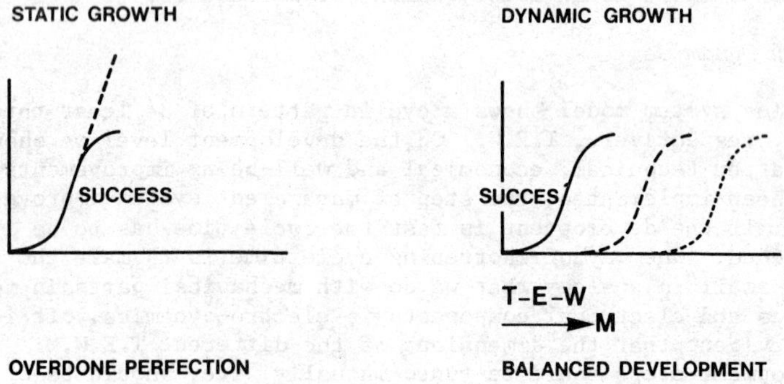

Fig. 11. Overdone perfection versus balanced development

Computer manufacturers, who sell today a solution for the problems of the future, should know the kind of development that is coming. On the other hand, it is also not wise to offer a customer a system which is two steps ahead of his development level; it cannot be implemented. The art of developing is not to be too early and not to be too late with modernization. Once the automation manager of a bank asked my opinion about the direction for improvement. Should he plan for the new concept of applying terminals and direct-access to speed up the operations flow or should he improve the existing batch processing by optical character reading as his competitor does? Well, that was exactly the difference between development and perfection. In a rapidly changing world it is wiser to look for development than for perfection.

CONCLUSION

It is not my intention to present just another systems theory, but to give a systems approach to unite existing system approaches. My object is to clarify with the help of a simple model what is happening in the Real World in which we live and work.

UNDP (United Nations Development Programme) learned its lesson a couple of years ago. Development of a country is not a matter of pouring in expert knowledge, but to teach the people of that country the art of balanced development of their own production processes. Today we accept that the survival of the world does not depend any longer on progress in technical ability or on economic growth, but on world-wide planning and control.

What is happening on the macro-level is also valid on the micro-level of automation policy. Third generation automation policy is, therefore, oriented towards planning and control systems. MIS is not wishful thinking but a must. The model presented is just a map for orientation purposes. It offers guidelines both on a micro-level and on a macro-level. On the micro-level of a process it is pointing towards the acceleration of flow by sophisticated automatic planning and control systems. On the development level, acceleration is promoted by balanced multi-disciplinary development instead of a mono-disciplinary drive for perfection. The development model can help to classify the phase and level of an enterprise and then to determine the kind of tools needed to improve that business. It specifies the kind of scientific discipline to call to assistance. It helps to set a course between a too pessimistic realism and a too optimistic Utopism, when introducing new control systems. To conclude, it is an aid to master the situation when promoting progress in development.

THE MANAGEMENT OF RISK IN SYSTEMS DEVELOPMENT

R.E. SHANNON

Industrial and Systems Engineering, University of Alabama in Huntsville, P.O. Box 1247, Huntsville, Alabama 35807, U.S.A.

SUMMARY

The domain of technical management has the three dimensions of time, resources and performance. In systems development, each of these dimensions present risks which management must avert or overcome if the development is to be successful. These are, the risk of cost overruns, the risk of schedule or timing delays, and the risk of unsatisfactory system performance. The advantages of innovative organizational structures (such as the matrix concept) for bringing the expertise of various technical specialists to bear on the systems problems is discussed as well as a closed-loop systems approach to the design of information and reporting systems.

INTRODUCTION

The task of technical management has become increasingly difficult as the man-organized and designed systems of our society have become more complex. A very real question facing us today is whether we have the managerial skills and know-how required to control the current technological explosion and bend it to mankinds benefit. The goal of management in any systems development is to turn the resources of materials, facilities, time, funds and people into a system with the desired performance for a reasonable cost and within a reasonable schedule. Thus the managerial domains of interest to us are cost, schedule and performance.

Each of these domains present risks to management which must be averted or overcome if the system development is to be successful. These risks are those of cost overruns, schedule delays and inadequate system performance. It cannot be stressed too strongly that success depends upon averting all three types of risk. If we are developing a system and the final performance meets our initial specifications and goals, it may still be a dismal failure if the development costs far exceeded our initial estimates. Likewise, it may be a failure from an overall viewpoint, if the time for development was so long that the end product has been made obsolete or the market taken over by a competitor. Considering only the three dimensions of cost, performance and schedule, there are eight possible outcomes of a development project, only one of which constitutes success (see Table I). Thus, if we assume equal probabilities for each of the outcomes, the odds are 7 to 1 against success without even considering whether management made the correct decisions in the beginning. The problem to be addressed in this paper is how we might change those odds.

TABLE I. Possible Outcomes of a Project

COST	PERFORMANCE	SCHEDULE	RESULT
controlled	adequate	on-time	success
overrun	adequate	on-time	failure
controlled	inadequate	on-time	failure
overrun	inadequate	on-time	failure
controlled	adequate	too-late	failure
overrun	adequate	too-late	failure
controlled	inadequate	too-late	failure
overrun	inadequate	too-late	failure

Usually, cost overruns, schedule slippages and inadequate performance can be traced directly to the fact that we overlooked certain technical aspects until they suddenly created or presented serious problems in product or system performance. We are then forced into crash programs of redesign, additional testing, and retro-fits. This, in turn leads to cost overruns, schedule delays and oftentimes compromise trade-offs of performance. Since hindsight is always perfect, we find when we look back at projects which were less than total successes, that almost without exception, these failures can be traced to one of three causes. These are:

1) Failure to seek the help of appropriate specialists.

2) Failure to ask the specialists the right questions at the right times.

3) Failure to heed the advice of the specialist after it is given.

TABLE II. Aspects of Risk Aversion

DISCIPLINE	GOALS
Program Control	Management visibility into what is really happening regarding costs and schedules and what to do about it
Design Engineering	Designing of hardware and equipment that will meet the mission or system requirements
Systems Engineering	Assurance that everything is being done technically that needs to be done
Interface Control	Assurance that hardware designed and/or built by different groups will fit and work together
Configuration Management	Knowing what the hardware looks like and when and how to introduce changes
Logistics	Getting the right thing to the right place at the right time
Production and Value	Assurance that the designs are converted to hardware at the lowest cost
Reliability and Safety	Knowing it is built right, will work right, and will be safe

Thus, we can see that one of the most significant aspects of management risk aversion is that of trying to insure that the proper specialists are asked the right questions at the right time and that their advice is heeded when given. Over the years, a number of specialist disciplines have grown up and developed powerful tools to aide management in risk aversion. Several of these are shown in Table II. The diffculty is that too often these disciplines and specialists are ignored until a problem is already out of hand and the project in trouble. Their proper input should be in avoiding the problems before they arise, not in solving or fixing them after the damage has been done. The question is, how best to help insure that these specialists are properly used to aide management in risk aversion.

Since the advent of the space program in the United States, there has been great interest in possible technological spinoffs and the application of the knowledge and experience gained to other sectors. It may very well turn out that the most valuable spinoff will be our improved knowledge of how to plan, coordinate, monitor, and control multitudinous disciplines, and organizational segments working to accomplish complex undertakings. At its peak, the Apollo/Saturn Program entailed the management and coordination of a government headquarters; several widely dispersed government laboratories and centers; some 20,000 industrial contractor, subcontractor and supplier organizations; faculty and students at 200 universities and colleges; and the efforts of almost 400,000 non-governmental workers. In terms of technological and managerial complexity, it has certainly been a unique experience from which much can hopefully be learned. The managerial problems of the large, multi-plant, multi-product industrial organization differ from the Apollo/Saturn management problems only in magnitude and scope, not in complexity. With this thought in mind, several studies of the Apollo/Saturn Program management system have been conducted [1,2].

Perhaps one of the most striking of these investigations was the discovery of the amazingly wide and extensive use of the so-called "Matrix Management Structure" throughout NASA and its major contractors [3]. At the beginning of the space program, the organization of the NASA Headquarters, field centers, and industrial contractors was based upon the traditional hierarchial pyramid. Some were decentralized or organized along product or project lines, and others along functional lines. But as the program progressed, each of the NASA centers and major industrial contractors evolved into basically the same organizational pattern. It is important to note that this structure was not imposed upon them by higher authority or the government, but, rather, derived from their own experiences and internal needs. Since the adaptation of the matrix organization was universal among the NASA agencies and major contractors, the questions naturally arise as to why did they go that way, and would such an untraditional structure be beneficial to other organizations?

One of the key mechanisms through which management strives to achieve its goals is the organization structure itself. The purpose of organizational structure is to:

1) Specialize executive activity.

2) Simplify the tasks of management.

3) Group employees for the purpose of direction and control.

4) Provide the formal channels of communication and co-ordination.

Thus, the organizational structure is one of the most important means by which management brings its precious resources to bear upon problems. Before we look at the matrix concept of organizing, it would perhaps be well to take a look at the tradional hierarchial pyramid structure to see why it was inadequate during the space program, and why it does not lend itself to the rapid responses required of the closed loop management process of systems development.

THE PYRAMID

We might first consider what are the strengths and weaknesses of the pyramidal structure which has served us so well. It originally came into being because of its efficiency in the military sphere. As a command structure it enables the commander to give instructions to thousands of troops in just a few easy steps. The commander tells ten senior officers what he wants done. Within minutes, each of these tells ten junior officers each of whom in turn tells ten non-commissioned officers. Each NCO then tells ten soldiers what is to be done and we have given directions to 10,000 troops in four easy stages. The pyramid is at its best when it is squat, allowing rapid communication both up and down.

Clearly, such a structure has tremendous power as an instrument of command. So long as each executive can control ten subordinates (certainly not an unreasonable span of control) an organization of 10,000 people could theoretically consist of only four hierarchial levels. But how many large organizations do you know with such a compact structure? They are more likely to have ten levels or more and one might wonder why. The answer is that at each level, only half are actually line executives and the other half, advisors or staff specialists. The distinction is between those who are doing something and those who are commenting upon how something should or is being done. The end result is that each executive is directing an average of five doers rather than ten and the hierarchial levels proliferate. Unfortunately, as the number of managerial levels increase, so do the communications problems. It is now a well documented fact that some of the content is lost each time a message is re-transmitted. Thus, as the number of expert advisors rises in proportion to the number of line executives (a trend that is very evident, see reference 4) the number of hierarchial levels will also increase bringing with it a decrease in the speed and efficiency of executive control.

One very important requirement for any organization engaged in the development of technical systems, is that it be capable of adding and dropping technical skills as required. In the pyramidal structure, we find that the ability to do this depends to some extent upon the basis of the authority structure. Traditionally, the most common basis of organization has been to group together activities dealing with a common product, customer, geographic area, function (engineering, manufacturing, marketing, etc.) or process. If the pyramidal structure is based upon function (i.e. skills) it makes it much easier to recruit the specialist skills we need. We can hire an electro-mechanical engineer and an electronic engineer rather than two generalist electrical engineers. It also minimizes the number of people we need in each skill as well as expensive equipment, test facilities, etc. because we can pool resources and time share them across products or projects. On the other hand, if the basic pyramidal structure is project or product oriented, it makes the hiring, utlization and retention of specialists much more difficult. If there are two projects, each requiring a half time electro-mechanical engineer and a half time electronics engineer, the pure project organization must either hire one generalist electrical engineer for each project, thus reducing specialization, or hire four engineers (two in each specialty). This results because the pyramidal, project structure makes it difficult if not impossible to share people between projects. Experience suggests that once a specialist is assigned to a particular branch of the pyramid structure, he tends to become reserved by that branch for its sole use. Traditionally, if a man is needed in an area where he is not permanently employed, his supervisor will resist even his temporary transfer for fear of losing a good employee.

One of the common difficulties with the functional type organization is that since each of the sub-groupings is usually based upon common academic background or skills, there is a tendency for each to become a sort of intellectual ghetto or closed shop and develop very parochial interests. Thus the integration of the various technical skills into the pursuit of a common purpose or goal becomes a difficult task when the organization is pursuing several different projects or product lines simultaneously. In order to get the different disciplines to work together when they are in separate organizational groups requires either fantastic amounts of information or long lead times for task completion. The end result is that we usually find a proliferation of ad hoc task teams, appointment of numerous liaison men and large amounts of time spent in coordination meetings.

The product or project form of organization, on the other hand, has almost the exact opposite set of costs and benefits. The greater the diversity among product lines or project types and the greater the importance of rapid response, the greater are the pressures to move toward a structure based upon product or project lines. This facilitates coordination among the specialties, on-time completion, and staying within the budgetary constraints. It allows quick reaction time to tackle problems that develop and everyone involved is dedicated to a single goal or purpose. From a negative viewpoint, as already mentioned, it makes the hiring, utilization and retention of specialists much more difficult.

Additional drawbacks of the project type of organization derive from the reluctance of personnel to become associated with risky projects. If a certain project appears to be relatively risky and many people don't think it will fly, then the process of recruiting staff in this area becomes very difficult. People realize that despite assurances to the contrary, that in the project type structure, the success or failure of their project can make or break their careers. They know all too well, that they can disappear when the particular job does. Specialists also recognize that in the project type organization, no one is responsible for the long-run technical development of the specialties and that they can very rapidly become technically obsolete. Thus each form of organization has its own advantages and disadvantages. A similar analysis could be applied to geographical or client-based structures.

One other important shortcoming of the pyramid-type structure is the lack of flexibility. Most jobs are staffed for the peak workloads. Thus the organization functions very well during that period, but problems arise when the scope of the work changes and an imbalance of skills begins to occur. For example, if you don't have enough engineers in a particular area, the impact is clear — the job doesn't get done. If you have too many engineers, the impact is not so obvious. The thing that happens is that the engineers begin to "make" work. The excess of engineers in a department which has no work, accounts in part for the fact that it is very difficult to move a project out of research and development into production. The engineers keep inventing. Since they can always present cogent technical reasons for what they are doing, it is almost impossible for the manager to know when it is legitimate and when it is merely to protect their jobs.

THE MATRIX CONCEPT

The basic concept of matrix management is to try to achieve the advantages of two different bases of organization by setting up an interplay of checks and balances or "controlled conflict" between a group of managers who have specific product, program or project responsibilities and another group of executives who have specific functional responsibilities. The concept is essentially a derivative of the well-known task force approach that has been modified, improved and refined to meet the complex management needs of today. Figure 1 illustrates the fundamental structure of the matrix management organization as adapted to, or rather, superimposed on the conventional functionally oriented organization. Obviously, the titles of the program managers and also the functional lines of responsibility will vary from organization to organization. Likewise, the determination of whether the program managers or the functional managers are the vertical or horizontal segments varies. The important aspect is the formal specialization of management responsibilities from the two viewpoints (project and function) and the establishment of built-in checks and balances between the different responsibilities.

The object of this superimposed configuration is to allow projects to be born, mature and finally terminate in an orderly manner. Each project manager has direct access to the specific manpower expertise required for his project for a planned time duration and finally rapid release of surplus manpower as project needs decrease. By controlling manpower in such a manner, the Project Manager has a vital cost control weapon; in that, he can expand and contract his project organization as dictated by budget and technical needs without the need for layoffs or new hires.

In a company with management basically decentralized and organized around product line responsibilities, the functional executive provides a unifying force which crosses the boundaries of the various product-line organizations to establish and maintain high standards of technical performance; to transfer the latest techniques and practices throughout the company; to insure that certain important technical aspects are not being overlooked; and to assure that experienced personnel are retained and developed.

In the company that is organized primarily along functional lines, the program or project executives provide the unifying coordination to insure that their project or program is getting the appropriate attention and required level of effort from each of the functional areas. In addition, the project manager

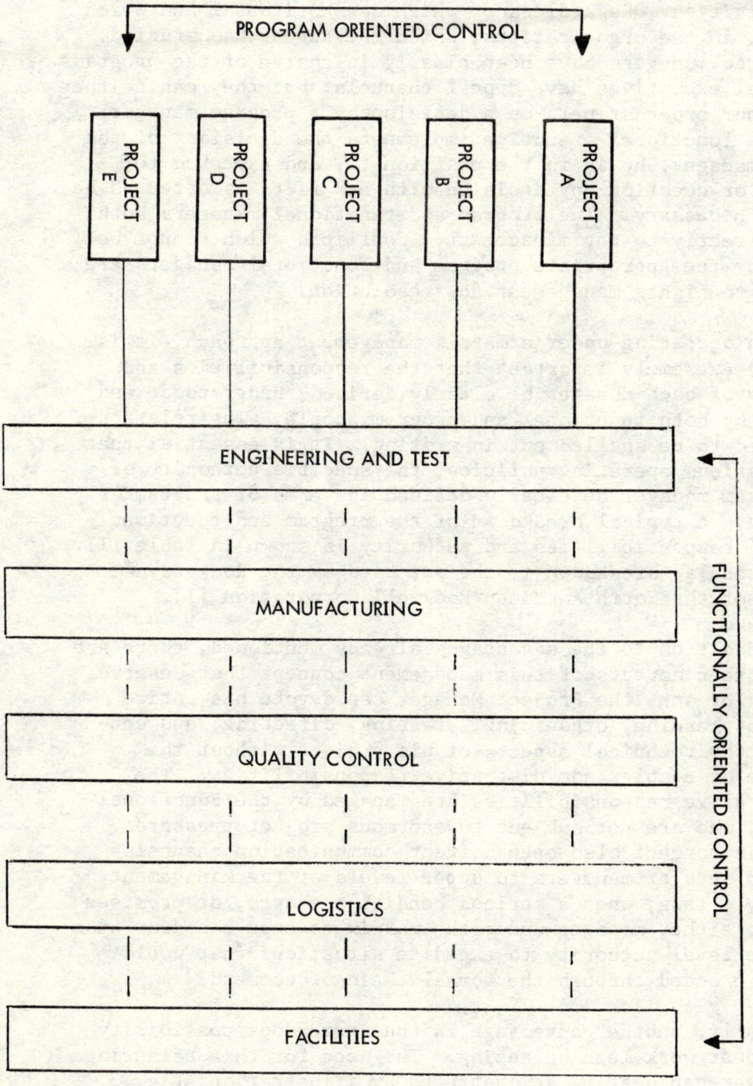

Fig. 1. Matrix management structure

continuously monitors the status of costs, schedules, and performance; provides the technical integration; defines requirements; and provides the prime contact with the customer for program activities. Regardless of which was horizontal and which vertical, in the organizations, which the author has studied, the program managers have been clearly in charge of the programs. Functional executives have appeal channels, but they can neither irgnore nor procrastinate on a decision by a program manager. While the functional executive implements the decisions of the program manager, he is in the position to, and expected to, re-raise or question any decision with new facts as often as he feels it necessary. The program and functional managers both report directly to top management. Conflicts which cannot be settled by the appropriate program and functional managers are referred to higher management for resolution.

When operating under a matrix management approach, it is obviously extremely important that the responsibilities and authority of each manager be clearly defined, understood, and accepted by both functional and program people. The relationships need to be spelled out in writing. It is essential that in the various operating policies, the specific authority of the program manager be clearly defined in terms of program direction. A typical breakdown of the program and functional managers' responsibilities and authority is shown in Table III. This particular breakdown is the one used by the Rocketdyne Division of the North American Rockwell Corporation [1].

In addition to the advantages already mentioned, there are several other aspects of this management concept that deserve noting. For one, the Project Manager can devote his entire effort to planning, organizing, staffing, directing, and controlling the technical aspects of his project without the hindrance of complex administrative responsibilities. The administrative responsibilities are managed by the Functional Managers, who are not subject to enormous project pressures. The matrix concept also opens direct communication channels from both sets of managers to upper levels of the management hierarchy. Thus, when a serious condition erupts, or promises to erupt, either manager under the matrix concept can draw upon executive level authority to expedite situations that would normally proceed through the formal chain of command.

Finally, another advantage is the tremendous possibility for manpower work load balancing. The need for this balancing of manpower can best be demonstrated by illustration, Fig. 2. It will be noted that manpower requirements for each project grow slowly at first, rise rapidly to a peak, and finally trail off with time. By programming manpower needs and time phasing

TABLE III. Program and Functional Manager's Responsibilities

PROGRAM MANAGER	FUNCTIONAL MANAGER
Program Direction	*Operational Direction*
Directs and controls company functional organization and subcontractor activity to achieve program objectives	Determines *who* will perform detailed tasks *where* they will be done, and *how* they are to be accomplished
Develops master program plans	Provides a stable base for the development of talent and skills to assure the maintenance of technical capability
Determines and issues the work breakdown structure and related work statements, budgets, and schedules which define *what* effort will be accomplished, *when* it will be performed, and *who* will have accountability	Provides necessary facilities and services to support program requirements
Assures the attainment of the technical, schedule, and cost objectives of the program	*Operational Control*
Program Control	Responsible for the technical excellence and quality requirements of assigned tasks
Monitors cost, schedule, and technical results against master program plans	Assures that all tasks are accomplished in accordance with technical specifications, on schedule, and within budget
Replans and rebudgets as necessary to assure accomplishment of program objectives	*Administration*
Monitors contractual reporting	Performs administrative services in support of personnel assigned to a program
Configuration Management	Initiates merit increases for all personnel within his organization
Controls changes and assures configuration accountability affecting the program	
Customer Coordination	
Provides the prime contact with the customer for program activities	
Administration	
Approves the assignment and concurs in merit increases of key functional personnel assigned to the program	

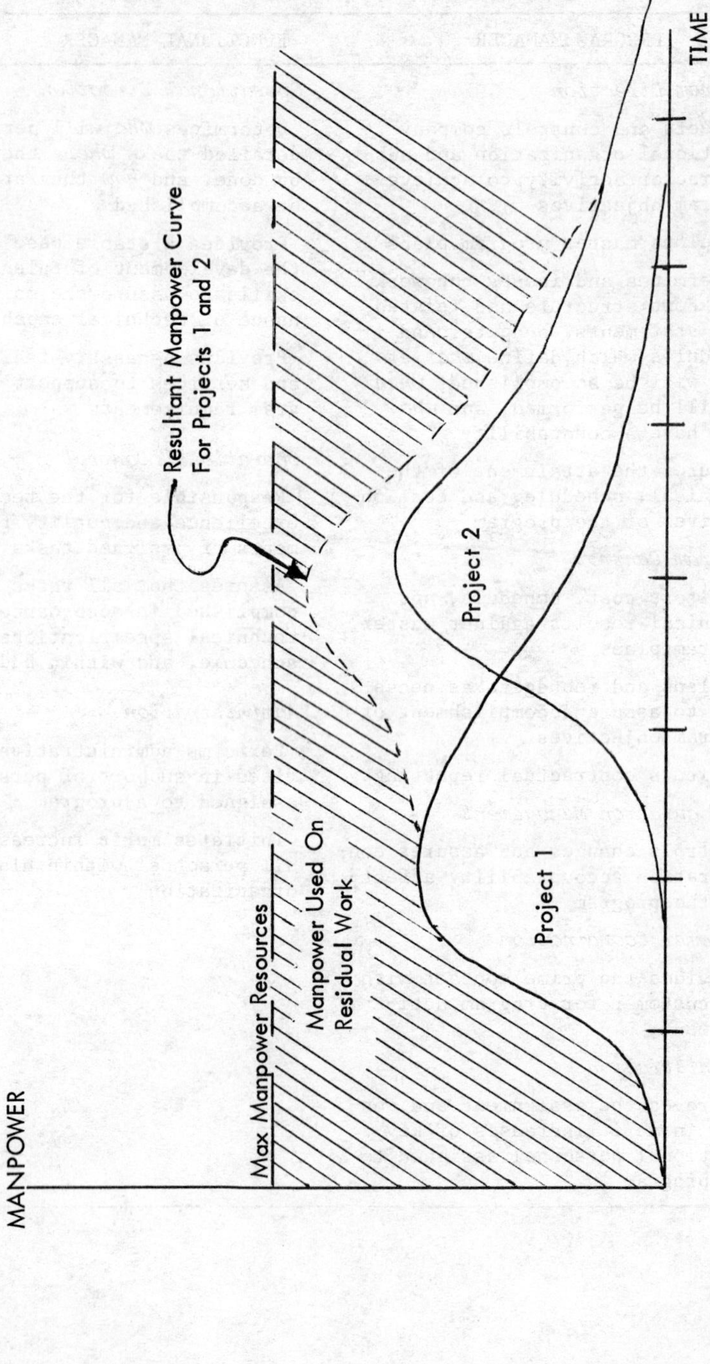

Fig. 2. Manpower utilization curves

projects, it is possible to overlay projects in such a manner as to not exceed available manpower resources. Residual work provided by low priority functional tasks handled in the normal organizational fashion may be used to "absorb" excess manpower (crossed area under upper manpower resources line) that may remain after the superposition of project manpower load curves. With diligent long range planning and careful time phasing of projects, the ultimate in manpower work load balancing may be achieved.

ADVANTAGES AND DRAWBACKS

Whenever there is such an ample supply of obvious advantages to any scheme or organization, there is usually some equally obvious draw-backs. A student of the classical management school will immediately detect an apparent serious flaw in the matrix management approach; that is, Fayol's second principle of management, "Unity of Command", has been violated [5]. The conviction that the very foundation of good management rests upon this principle of unity of command (i.e. that no one can work under two bosses at the same time) is so deeply rooted in popular mythology that many managers will cringe at the very thought of the matrix concept.

On examination, however, this apparent shortcoming may not be as serious as it at first appears. The casual observer may fail to recognize that almost every organization today already contains elements of the matrix philosophy although camouflaged under the guise of line and staff. In an earlier article [4], we have suggested that a blurring of line and staff relationships and the concept of unity of command has already taken place and it is expected that this trend will grow in the future. *Business Week* has also detected this prevailing tendency to violate the unity of command principle and the crumbling of other old management maxims [6]. They pointed out that it is not at all uncommon today for mid-level executives and staff men to report to half a dozen different bosses during the course of some project. Furthermore, whenever you have a situation in which the quality control department can reject a batch of parts and perhaps shut down a production line; when the scheduling department can tell the plant what to make and when to make it; when the engineering department tells the plant how to make something and how long it should take to do it, you no longer have unity of command. Traditionalists will argue that all the commands are coming through the supervisor but they are confusing semantics with reality. The crucial question is who makes the decisions not what mechanisms are used for transmittal of the information.

The violation of this important unity of command principle cannot be disregarded or taken lightly. Due to the psychological and sociological implications, management must be constantly on the alert to head off or solve personnel problems promptly. It is interesting to note, however, that in those organizations which have adopted the matrix concept, the major personnel problems have derived from conflicts arising amongst the managers rather than amongst the workers.

Looking at the matrix concept from the non-managerial employees' viewpoint, there are several distinct advantages. First of all, the multi-boss situation allows him to gain far greater visibility, because of working with and for a number of different managers. It also means that he will be working with a larger number of different people and be able to establish a more satisfactory array of personal relationships. It gives him the chance to avoid the sort of boredom and stagnation that often comes from doing the same job, at the same desk, with the same people for an indefinite period of time. The matrix concept allows an employee dissatisfied with his job, to change it more radically with less upheaval than in a typical pyramidal organization. Without forcing a show-down with his boss, the employee in the matrix organization can usually explore different job areas. He need not request a formal transfer, nor need he make a long-range commitment if he wants to try something new. He no longer needs to change companies in order to change activity. The matrix organization requires a greater number of personal transitions, but all of them keep him actively involved in his area of expertise.

In addition, the employee will quickly learn to appreciate the fact that he has gained a check and balance type performance review, one from the project manager, and one from his functional manager. Thus his future salary and advancement opportunities will not be totally dependent upon the judgement or whims of a single individual. This dual evaluation will give the competent employee a greater sense of security and a greater assurance of fair treatment. Finally, the rather quick pace of most project oriented assignments has a very definite tendency to smother concerns about split-boss allegiance. Employees engaged as integrated members of a project work team, tend to become engrossed in their assignments and develop great enthusiasm toward meeting project goals.

A much more fertile area for people problems are those related to the interactions between the managers. Both the strength and weakness of the matrix concept is that we are deliberately setting up a system of check and balances and controlled conflict. The key word in the preceeding sentence is *controlled*. We must carefully guard against the manager developing an attitude or feeling that his authority is being usurped by someone else. We need to maintain a balance of power between the project managers and the functional managers so that decisions are made on the merits of the case and not on the basis of power relationships. While the exact balance of power is an unachievable goal, a reasonable balance can be obtained by careful definition of functions and through enforced collaboration on budgets, salaries, reporting systems and dual authority relations. The authority and responsibilities of each manager must be carefully detailed in job descriptions and the formal communication paths carefully planned.

With the matrix type of organization, the problem of communication is of greater significance than with the conventional hierarchial arrangement. Communications are more difficult, more costly, and generate a great deal more paper. Obviously, the problems of keeping tabs on all employees for scheduling purposes, as well as job and cost control can become an enormous problem. More people have to be continuously appraised of what is going on all of the time. Fortunately, the computer provides us with a powerful tool. By careful design of the management control system, reports related to budgeting, job cost control and technical progress reports can be prepared for as many different levels of detail as needed.

PROGRAM CONTROL

Closely tied into the matrix concept of organization (as applied in the space progra) has been the use of the "work package" management control system. The underlying philosophy of the work package system is the concept of management by objectives and decentralization of accountability. Implementation of the system requires that a work breakdown structure or tree be constructed. This is done by dividing the overall task by project or product subsystems (hardware, software, and services) and then further breaking down the product oriented elements into functional work packages. Each work package is basically a performance control element. Each work package is negotiated with and assigned to a specific manager. This work package manager agrees to a specific objective (which is measurable), detailed task descriptions, specifications, schedule task milestones, and a time phased budget in both dollars and manpower for his work package. He is then held fully and personally responsible for that work package in terms of technical, schedule and cost performance by both the program and functional managers. All program tracking and accounting for

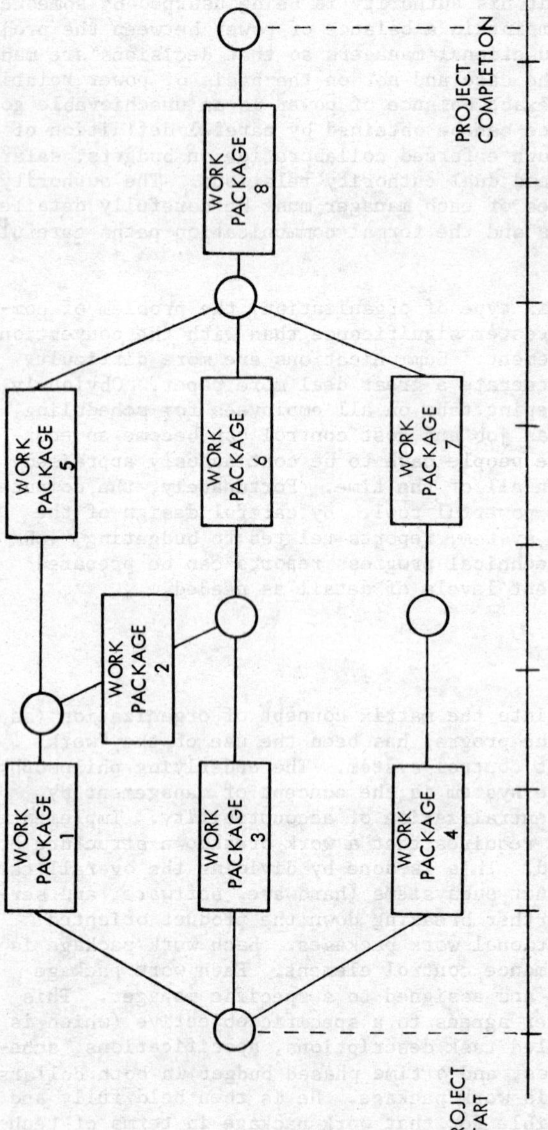

Fig. 3. Work package scheduling

control purposes is done by work packages, utilizing some appropriate scheduling system (see Fig. 3) such as the Critical Path Method (CPM) or Program Evaluative and Review Technique (PERT). Summary reports are furnished to both the program and functional management structure as appropriate.

The combination of the use of the matrix concept of organization and the work package control system provides several vital benefits for risk aversion. First of all, the very process of establishing the work breakdown structure or tree, provides an orderly procedure to insure that all of the needed specialist skills are brought to bear on the problem. Since each of the functional managers participates in establishing this breakdown, he has an opportunity to see that the project manager recognizes and provides for the input of each of the specialist areas. In addition, when the work packages are negotiated and scheduled, each functional manager can insure that the inputs of the specialists under his control will have their input at the appropriate points in time rather than as an afterthought when the project is already in trouble. The matrix organization structure allows the necessary skilled manpower to be deployed and retracted as needed for each work package. If this was not possible without hiring and firing, cost over-runs would be almost sure to occur due to the people making work. The matrix concept makes it possible to bring each specialist's skill to bear on the problem at precisely the time it is needed and only for as long as required.

Earlier we said that another cause of problems in system development was the ignoring of expert advice after it was given. A second advantage to the matrix concept is that it helps to preclude this possibility. If a specialist's advice is to be ignored, that decision must be concurred in by at least two different managers (the project manager and the appropriate functional manager). This is what we mean by the built-in check and balance of the matrix concept. If a specialist raises a question about some aspect of the project and the two managers concerned cannot agree as to what should be done about it, then the conflict must be resolved by a higher level of management. This still will not insure that a correct decision will be made, but at least the issue will have been thoroughly aired and everyone will be aware of a potential problem area.

Management awareness and control requires a continuous monitoring and evaluation of all program aspects in terms of cost, schedule and technical performance. In order to achieve this, we need to consider the management process or system from a feedback control viewpoint. Being deeply involved in technical

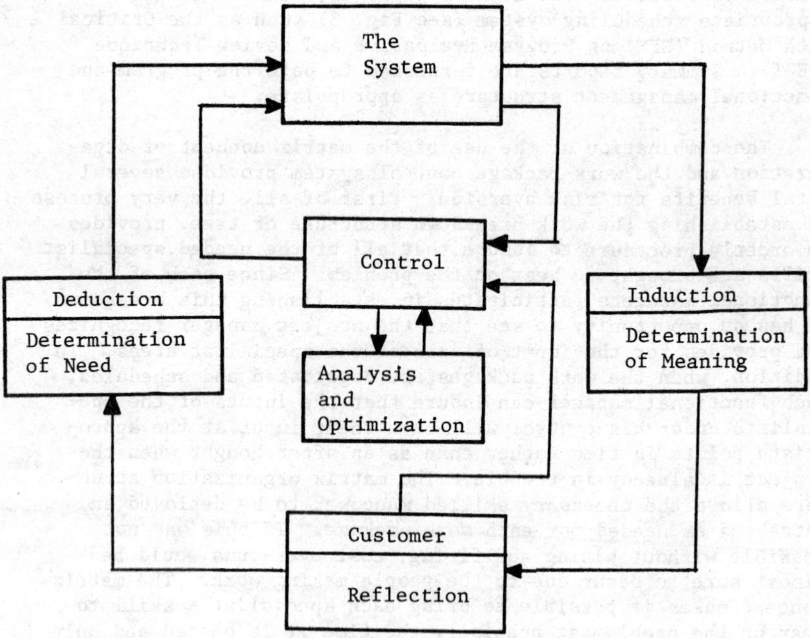

Fig. 4. Closed-loop systems control

problems, this was a very natural way for the aero-space executives to view their managerial problems, and it is not surprising to find the process thus depicted [1]. In a very interesting paper, Bartee [7] discusses the process of solution synthesis and control as a closed loop system (see Fig. 4). He argues very cogently, that we must consider the user of the system as an integral part of the process if we are to succeed. It is interesting to note that almost all of the aerospace companies this author has studied, do in fact depict their management process as a closed loop system. A typical example is shown in Fig. 5 from Sperry-Rand Corporation briefing charts, in which the customer is an integral part of the system. Note that there are two feeback loops as suggested by Bartee. In the aero-space industry the government representatives are considered to be the customer. In an industrial situation the marketing, manufacturing and/or operations people of the company might serve in the same capacity. It is very important when you wish to develop and deploy complex technical systems, that there be early and continuous inputs from the operational people in the design phases. Very early in the planning and design process, you must impose certain constraints to ensure proper operational and system efficiency characteristics of the end product. This can best be done by the operational people.

In order for such a closed loop, feedback control system to operate efficiently, the organizational system must be capable of rapidly responding to the changes required. As we have tried to show, the traditional pyramid is incapable of this rapid response. Too many people have too many vested interests and the organization is designed for static not dynamic operation. The matrix organization, on the other hand, is designed specifically to provide for rapid change without disruption or lengthy delays. The work package system becomes the mechanism for implementation and control as well as the basic unit of the management information system.

The management visibility of the status of the programs, which was developed at all levels in the Apollo/Saturn program was based upon detailed monitoring and auditing systems that allowed the flow of information both vertically and horizontally throughout the program. The ability of management to anticipate and correct problems and deficiencies in the program prior to their assuming large proportions was mandatory. Periodic technical and management reviews were a critical feature.

One important feature of the Apollo/Saturn management system was the conception and development of a joint contractor/government panel or working group structure. These technical working groups were organized according to technical disciplines and/or sub-systems to manage technical interfaces and to provide in-depth visibility support to the program manager. All of these working groups had one thing in common — they were real-time decision-making boards. Problems were identified and solutions decided upon. People were stuck with the decisions they made at those meetings. The decisions were recorded and they became binding on the parties involved in the meeting.

These working groups were most useful in identifying problems and making decisions of a technical and hardware nature during the research and development phases. As the designs were hardened and the manufacturing and operational aspects came into the forefront, most of the technical working groups, having served their purpose, were discontinued. These technical working groups played an important role from several viewpoints. First, they exposed the problems at the various interfaces for everyone to see. Second, they forced face to face communication of the various organizational segments thus reinforcing the team concept. Third, visibility and flexibility

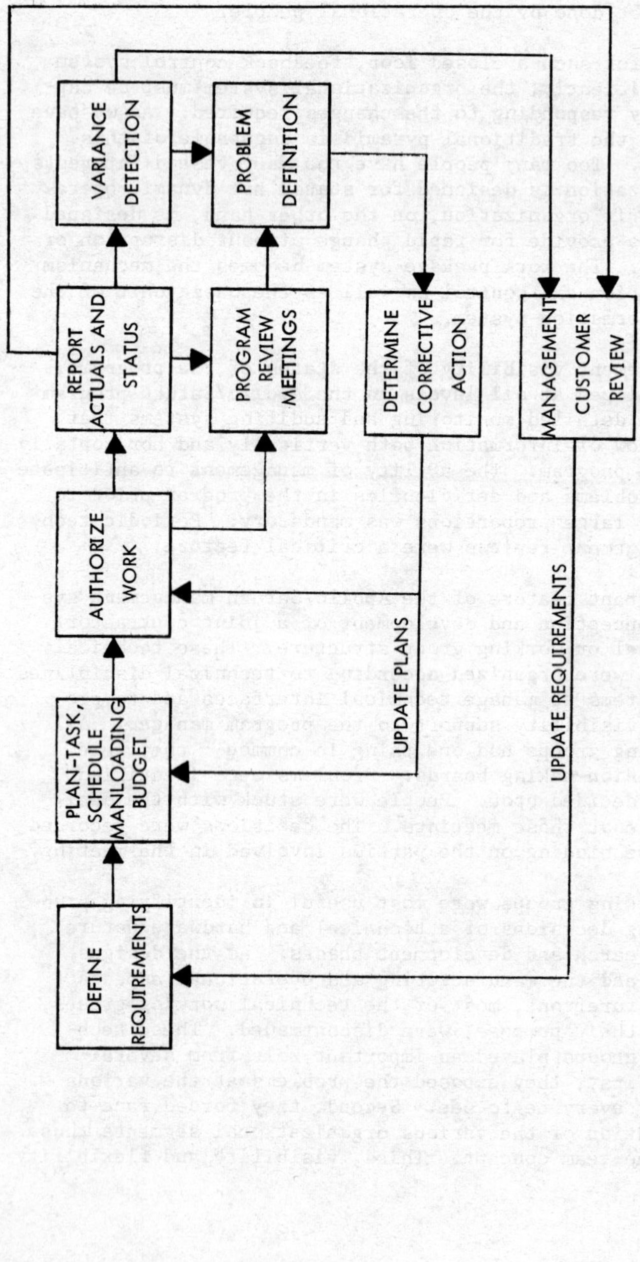

Fig. 5. Closed loop management flow diagram

requires a knowledgeable decision point close to the work and most of the various group members were working level engineers or managers. Fourth, they provided an interchange of technical information and allowed the different organizations to learn from each other and to profit from each other's mistakes. Finally, it forced each organization to defend its decisions before a group of technical peers, knowledgeable in the disciple under discussion. It is the authors opinion that the same concept would prove very beneficial in an industrial situation where the working group team members are drawn from the different functional groups and the role of customer is played by manufacturing, marketing, etc.

In addition to the working groups, periodic program reviews were held with top management in which *both* program managers and functional managers presented progress reports and problem analysis regarding technical performance, costs and schedule. Significant problems were often exposed in these management review meetings, when the project manager and a functional manager gave conflicting reports of a situation. Neither set of managers could hide their problems because they would most likely be exposed by the other, again demonstrating the desirability of built-in checks and balances.

CONCLUSIONS

The task of organizing and managing the Apollo/Saturn program has been almost as complicated and demanding as overcoming the attendant technical difficulties. It is important to note that the development of the management systems and techniques used in the Apollo/Saturn program was a dynamic and ever-changing undertaking. That is, the management system developed was evolutionary not revolutionary. It was derived and evolved from prior military, industrial experience and does not represent any brand new management panaceas. However, portions of the management system which evolved should be applicable to the management of ther technological and systems development programs.

In order to successfully avoid the risks of poor technical performance, slipped schedules and cost over-runs, management must develop program visibility at all levels of a systems development. Furthermore, it must provide the mechanisms for early problem detection and rapid, flexible processes for recovery from anomalies and failures. The obvious success of NASA suggests that the key concepts of the matrix organization, the use of the work package breakdown structure, and cross-organizational technical working panels provides this visibility and flexibility. These concepts offer any organization engaged in systems development:

1) Specialization of management skills

2) Built-in checks and balances

3) Rapid transference of technical know-how between programs or projects

4) Greater flexibility of skilled man-power utilization

5) Reduction of duplication of effort and thus reduced costs.

REFERENCES

1. "Apollo program management" *Staff Study for the Committee on Science and Astronautics, U.S. House of Representatives* (U.S. Government Printing Office, Washington, D.C., July 1969).

2. R.E. SHANNON, "Apollo/Saturn program management" Chapter 3 *Sourcebook of Saturn Benefits* (UARI Report, University of Alabama in Huntsville, Research Institute, December 1970).

3. R.E. SHANNON, "Matrix management structures" *Industrial Engineering 4*, No. 3 (March 1972).

4. J.P. IGNIZIO and R.E. SHANNON, "Organization structures in the 1980's" *Industrial Engineering 3*, No. 9 (September 1971).

5. H. FAYOL, *General and Industrial Management*, translated from French by C. STORRS (Pitman Publishing Corp. New York, 1949).

6. "The new management finally takes over" *Business Week* (August 23, 1969).

7. E.M. BARTEE, "On the methodology of solution synthesis" *Management Science 17*, No. 6 (February 1971).

INFORMATION THEORY AND MANAGEMENT DECISIONS

N.S. TZANNES

School of Electrical Engineering, University of Oklahoma, Norman, Oklahoma 73069, U.S.A.

SUMMARY

In many statistical models of management problems (inventory, manpower, product marketing, expansion, etc.), the final decision must be based on limited prior data, which is often obtained with error margins. The author has recently formulated a theory of prior probability models for such problems which involve limited prior data. This theory is based on Shannon's information theory and more specifically on "rate distortion theory". A principle is formulated, called the Mutual Information Principle (MIP), which can pick a prior probability model based on the available data for the random variables, even when the data is obtained with error. In this paper, the MIP is used in a problem of management production decisions, in the presence of constraints imposed on the company by environmental protection agencies. The final decision is based on MIP models and is thus "optimum" in the information theory sense.

INTRODUCTION

Most management decisions have to be based on limited prior data, often obtained with error margins. In this paper we will show that under certain conditions such problems can be solved, using a theory whose foundations are the concepts of information theory.

The idea that information theory has application in management decisions is not new. E.T. Jaynes [1] was the first to recognize that the concept of entropy can be used in problems of decision making in the face of uncertainty, and Tribus [2] later applied Jaynes' Maximum Entropy Principle (MEP) to the field of management decisions. The author has recently [3] extended the basic theory to the case when the prior data is obtained with errors, and to continuous random variables. In this paper, after a brief review of the theory, a problem in management decision making is presented, and solved. The problem is intended as a typical case of the wide applicability of the theory. The main contribution of this paper is the demonstration that the extended theory [3] can be used to model decisions for problems for which the prior information is obtained with errors.

The first part of the paper is devoted to a discussion of the production problem for which an optimum decision must be rendered. Next, the theoretical background necessary for the formulation of the problem is discussed. Finally, the production problem is modeled using the theory, and the "optimum" decision is found in the information theory sense.

TYPICAL MANAGEMENT PROBLEM

In this section we consider a problem which is typical of the type that can be solved using the propose theory. In the fourth section, we shall return to this problem, and solve it using material discussed in the next section.

A chemical plant produces three chemicals A, B, and C. The wastes are dumped in a nearby river. An environmental agency has investigated the pollution in the river, and has concluded that the production of the chemicals must be reduced to a quantity D per day, considerably less than is presently being produced.

A new management is installed at the company, and it is immediately realized that it is no longer economical to produce all three chemicals every day in small quantities. Instead, only one chemical must be produced on a given working day.

The new management is now faced with the following decision: which chemical should they produce on a given day, so that their losses are minimized, and at the same time they comply with the demands of the environmental agency?

The decision on what to produce on a given day, is dependent on the availability of prior information such as inventory, type of possible orders etc. which are available to the management on that day. We shall assume for simplicity that the profit per pound of each chemical is the same (non-uniform profits can easily be included), and that the quantity D (amount of pounds to be produced per day) is 10. We further assume that on the day in question the management uncovers from the records the following prior data:

(i) The inventory of chemicals:

Chemical A: 10 lbs.

Chemical B: 15 lbs.

Chemical C: 20 lbs.

(ii) The records also show that the daily order for the chemicals never exceeded 49 lbs., and that "average daily orders" for the chemicals in the past have been:

Average daily order for A: 4 lbs.

" " " " B: 12 lbs.

" " " " C: 18 lbs.

However, the above averages were computed on incomplete records, and thus the above averages are in error by amounts a,b,c on an average absolute value error basis.

How can the management use all this information in a "wise" sense to arrive at some "optimum" decision on what to make that day?

III. THE THEORY

It is assumed here that the reader is familiar with the notions of Entropy and Mutual Information, two fundamental concepts in Information Theory.

The Maximum Entropy Principle (MEP) due to Jaynes [1] is also important for the development of the theory presented here. The MEP is a method for assigning prior probability models to discrete random variables when the prior data is taken without errors. Briefly stated, the MEP picks the probability mass function (p.m.f.) $p(x_i)$ which maximizes the informational Entropy of the random variable X.

$$H = -\sum_i p(x_i) \ln p(x_i) \tag{1}$$

subject to the constraint,

$$\sum_i p(x_i) = 1 \tag{2}$$

and to other constraints which reflect all prior knowledge about X. The interested reader is referred to the recent book by

Tribus [2] for details and examples of this method.

We now take up the case of errors. We shall develop the subject for the discrete random variable (r.v.) case. The theory can be extended to continuous r.v.'s but the final solution is difficult.

Let us assume that we are interested in modeling a discrete random variable X, but that we are unable to observe X due to errors in the measuring instrument. In actuality then, we are able to observe another random variable Y (the distorted form of X), where X and Y are related by some error criterion. The situation is illustrated further by referring to Fig. 4.1. The r.v. X is the one

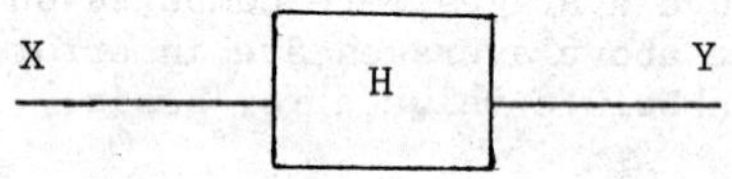

Fig. 1. Actual and observed r.v.'s

whose model is desired, whereas Y is the output of the instrument H, which is actually observed. Now viewed in this manner, the prior information is really based on Y, and as such it is information about Y. This being the case, the MEP can be used to find the prior model of Y. Once this is done, the prior model of X can be found by the method described below, which will be called the Mutual Information Principle (MIP).

First, let us assume that the error involved in observing X through Y, is mathematically described by

$$E\{d(X,Y)\} \leq \varepsilon \quad (3)$$

where ε is assumed known, and $d(X,Y)$ is some known error function as for example $|X - Y|$ or $(X - Y)^2$.

Denoting now the p.m.f. of Y by $q(y_k)$ the conditional p.m.f. of X given Y by $p(x_i/y_k)$ and the desired p.m.f. of X by $w(x_i)$, the MIP has the following steps.

a) The p.m.f. of Y is found first using the MEP, in conjunction with all prior information given *a priori* about Y. This step has already been mentioned.

b) The conditional p.m.f.'s

$$p(x_i/y_k) \quad \text{for all } k \quad (4)$$

are found by minimizing the mutual information functional

$$I(X,Y) = \sum_i \sum_k q(y_k) p(x_i/y_k) \ln \frac{p(x_i/y_k)}{w(x_i)} \quad (5)$$

with respect to these conditional p.m.f.'s and subject to the constraints,

$$\sum_i p(x_i/y_k) = 1 \quad \text{for all } k \quad (6)$$

$$E\,\{d(X,Y)\} \leq \varepsilon \quad (7)$$

In the above expression (5)

$$w(x_i) = \sum_k q(y_k)\; p(x_i/y_k) \quad (8)$$

c) The desired p.m.f. $w(x_i)$ is found by (8) using the now known $q(y_k)$ and $p(x_i/y_k)$.

The MIP is based on minimizing the mutual information between Y and X, a quantity which is interpreted as average amount of information that one obtains about X by observing Y. The mutual information I(X,Y) reduces to the Entropy of X when X = Y i.e. when X is observed errorlessly and thus, the MIP reduces to the MEP in that case.

The minimization of I(X,Y) indicates that the chosen $w(x_i)$ is a pessimistic choice, a choice when nature is playing the worst adversary.

It should be noted that the ranges of X and Y may not be the same. The main difficulty of the MIP approach is the assumption that the functional form of d(X,Y) must be known. This is usually impossible in practice, and thus one must usually assume some reasonable form. Better yet, one may try to solve the problem for two different types of forms and see how the results vary. In fact, this would be an interesting problem for investigation, namely how the form of d(X,Y) effects the final solution of the minimization.

The formulation of the MIP was given using the interpretation of Fig. 1. Naturally, in many practical problems, no actual instrument is involved.

It should be noted that the mathematical formulation presented above is identical to the one used in the problem of coding a source with a fidelity criterion (rate distortion theory). The interpretation of the problem and its solution, are quite different, however. Nevertheless, the similarity enables us to borrow a lot of the mathematical theory developed already for such problems.

Returning now to step (b), we proceed with the refinement of the variational problem, a problem which seldom enjoys a closed form solution.

Introducing Lagrangian multipliers for the constraints (6) and (7) the problem is reduced to minimizing,

$$R(\rho,P,f) = \sum_i \sum_k q(y_k)\, p(x_i/y_k) \left[\ln \frac{p(x_i/y_k)}{w(x_i)} + \rho d(x_i,y_k) - \ln \frac{f_k}{q(y_k)} \right] \tag{9}$$

where ρ is the Lagrangian multiplies of (7), and where the k Lagrangian multiplies for (6) have been denoted by

$$- q(y_k) \ln \left[\frac{f_k}{q(y_k)} \right] \tag{10}$$

as in Gallagher [4]. The f_k's are constants.

Differentiating R with respect to the conditionals and setting it equal to zero, we obtain

$$p(x_i/y_k) = \frac{w(x_i)}{q(y_k)} f_k \exp\{- \rho\, d(x_i,y_k)\} \text{ all for } x_i,y_k \tag{11}$$

If we now multiply both sides by $q(y_k)$ and sum over k, we have

$$\sum_k f_k \exp\{- \rho\, d(x_i,y_k)\} = 1 \text{ all } i \tag{12}$$

If we also sum (11) over x_i and using the constraints

$$\sum_i p(x_i/y_k) = 1$$

$$\frac{f_k}{q(y_k)} \sum_i w(x_i) \exp\{- \rho\, d(x_i,y_k)\} = 1 \text{ all } k \tag{13}$$

We can solve equations (12) for the f_k's and then (13) can provide us with the desired $w(x_i)$. However, in the above formulation we have not constrained the solution for the $p(x_i/y_k)$ to be

$$p(x_i/y_k) \geq 0 \text{ all } x_i, y_k \tag{14}$$

as we should for it to be an acceptable p.m.f. For this reason we must pursue the matter even further.

Let us restrict attention to only those $p(w_i, y_k)$ which obey the condition (14). Then the following theorem has been established whose proof can be found in Gallagher [4].

Theorem: If the entropy of Y is H(Y), let

$$R_0\ (\rho,P) = \sum_i \sum_k q(y_k)\ p(x_i/y_k) \left[\ln \frac{p(x_i/y_k)}{w(x_i)} + \rho d(x_i,y_k) \right] \tag{15}$$

Then for any $\rho > 0$,

$$\min_P R_0(\rho,P) = H(Y) + \max_f \sum_k q(y_k) \ln f_k \tag{16}$$

where the maximization is over $f = (f_0,\ldots f_{K-1})$ with non-negative components satisfying the constraints

$$\sum_k f_k e^{-\rho d(x_i,y_k)} \leq 1 \quad 0 \leq i \leq I - 1 \tag{17}$$

Necessary and sufficient conditions on f to achieve the maximum in (16) are that a set of non-negative numbers $w(x_0)$ ... $w(J-1)$ exist, which satisfy (13), and that (17) is satisfied with equality for each x_i with $w(x_i) > 0$. In terms of this f and w, $p(i/k)$ as given by (11) minimizes $R_0(\rho,P)$.

The main part of interest is the latter part which gives necessary and sufficient conditions on the f's. It should also be noted that the final evaluation of ρ will come from constraint (7).

There exist a number of other theorems which can be developed for the above variational problem. The interested reader is referred to Berger [5] where this topic is developed for rate distortion theory. We have discussed the topic here only up to the point where our solution to our problem can be sufficiently understood.

THE APPLICATION

We now return to our problem mentioned in the second section.

We denote the random variable "Total daily order for chemical A" by X_1 and the total daily orders for B and C by X_2 and X_3 respectively. Our first concern will be the assignment of a prior joint probability model for the vector r.v. (X_1,X_2,X_3).

We shall assume that these random variables (r.v.) are discrete with ranges 0.1,...,49, the upper limit imposed due to the knowledge available *a priori*. The above assumption also means that all orders are quoted in integer number of pounds.

We denote the observed r.v.'s by Y_1,Y_2,Y_3 respectively. Their range is the same as for the X's. The first concern of the application of the MIP, is to apply the MEP to the vector r.v. (Y_1,Y_2,Y_3) and calculate the joint p.m.f. of this r.v. subject to the condition of known means M_1,M_2,M_3, given on p. 00.

It can be shown [6] that when no prior joint information is given about the r.v.'s (for example the correlation matrix) then the r.v.'s are statistically independent. Thus, we concentrate on say Y_1 and X_1, and the rest of the models follow using the same method.

The model of Y_1, denoted by $q_1(y_k)$ is found using the MEP.

The prior information about Y_1 is:

(i) Range is 0,1,...49

(ii) Mean of Y_1 is $M_1 = 4$

We must maximize

$$H(Y_1) = -\sum_{k=0}^{49} q_1(y_k) \ln q_1(y_k) \tag{18}$$

subject to the constraints

$$\sum_k q_1(y_k) = 1 \tag{19}$$

$$\sum_k y_i\, q_1(y_k) = M_1 \tag{20}$$

The solution is

$$q_1(y_k) = \exp\{-\lambda_0 - \lambda_1 y_k\} \tag{21}$$

where λ_0, λ_1 are Lagrangian multipliers associated with (19) and (20) respectively. The values of λ_0, λ_1 must be found by substituting equation (21) into (19) and (20) and by solving them simultaneously. The solutions can not be obtained in close form. If M_1 is small with respect to the middle of the range of Y_1 (as it is the case for Y_1 and Y_2) an approximate solution is [6],

$$q_1(y_k) = e^{-\lambda_0} \left[\frac{M_1+1}{M_1}\right]^{-y_k} = e^{-\lambda_0} \left(\frac{5}{4}\right)^{-y_k} \tag{22}$$

where $d^{+\lambda_0} = \sum_0^{49} \frac{5}{4}^{-y_k}$

Now that $q_1(y_k)$ has been found, we must proceed with the minimization of expression (6) subject, of course, to the appropriate constraints. At this stage we must establish the nature of $d(x_i, y_k)$ and of the values of the average error a. Let us assume that

$$d(x_i, y_k) = \left| x_i - y_k \right| \text{ all } i, k.$$

and that $E\{\left| x_i - y_k \right|\} = 0.74$

i.e. that $a = 0.74$

The variational problem was solved in the IBM 360 and the results for $p_1(x_i)$ are shown in Table I.

A similar procedure leads to the p.m.f. $p_2(x_i)$ shown in Table II. The error function was taken to be of the same form, with $b = 0.80$. The model $p_3(x_i)$ was also found in the same manner, with $c = 0.83$, and it is given in Table III. The only difference is that the approximation (22) is not applicable for $q_3(y_k)$ and thus it had to be found numerically.

At this point, we are in a position to set up the problem so that an "optimum" decision can be made in the *information theory sense*.

The optimum decision is the one which will result in minimum average loss for the day. It will be assumed that orders which are not filled the same day they are received are lost to the company. This is an assumption which simplified the solution.

TABLE I. The P.M.F. of X_1

Value	Probability	Value	Probability	Value	Probability
0	0.16909050	21	0.00175979	42	0.00001623
1	0.22037790	22	0.00140783	43	0.00001298
2	0.12211000	23	0.00112627	44	0.00001039
3	0.09768765	24	0.00090101	45	0.00000831
4	0.07815033	25	0.00072081	46	0.00000665
5	0.06252003	26	0.00057665	47	0.00000532
6	0.05001589	27	0.00046132	48	0.00000545
7	0.04001302	28	0.00036905	49	0.00000154
8	0.03201039	29	0.00029524		
9	0.02560835	30	0.00023619		
10	0.02048665	31	0.00018895		
11	0.01638934	32	0.00015116		
12	0.01311146	33	0.00012093		
13	0.01048915	34	0.00009675		
14	0.00839134	35	0.00007740		
15	0.00671308	36	0.00006192		
16	0.00537043	37	0.00004953		
17	0.00429635	38	0.00003963		
18	0.00343707	39	0.00003170		
19	0.00274968	40	0.00002536		
20	0.00219974	41	0.00002029		

TABLE II. The P.M.F. of X_2

Value	Probability	Value	Probability	Value	Probability
0	0.05736529	21	0.01450422	42	0.00270080
1	0.09843910	22	0.01338852	43	0.00249305
2	0.06636995	23	0.01235865	44	0.00230128
3	0.06126435	24	0.01140794	45	0.00212426
4	0.05655191	25	0.01053046	46	0.00196085
5	0.05220157	26	0.00972040	47	0.00181002
6	0.04818628	27	0.00897269	48	0.00219625
7	0.04447927	28	0.00828247	49	0.00090693
8	0.04105832	29	0.00764536		
9	0.03789993	30	0.00705726		
10	0.03498453	31	0.00651439		
11	0.03229345	32	0.00601329		
12	0.02980931	33	0.00555071		
13	0.02751635	34	0.00512375		
14	0.02539975	35	0.00472962		
15	0.02344590	36	0.00436579		
16	0.02164237	37	0.00402997		
17	0.01997761	38	0.00371997		
18	0.01844085	39	0.00343383		
19	0.01702232	40	0.00316969		
20	0.01571292	41	0.00292586		

TABLE III. The P.M.F. of X_3

Value	Probability	Value	Probability	Value	Probability
0	0.02754016	21	0.02009881	42	0.01014269
1	0.05205372	22	0.01945476	43	0.00981770
2	0.03731626	23	0.01883139	44	0.00950311
3	0.03612051	24	0.01822794	45	0.00919862
4	0.03496320	25	0.01764396	46	0.00890388
5	0.03384297	26	0.01707854	47	0.00861856
6	0.03275844	27	0.01653132	48	0.01108009
7	0.03170880	28	0.01600160	49	0.00509896
8	0.03069277	29	0.01548889		
9	0.02970925	30	0.01499259		
10	0.02875738	31	0.01451219		
11	0.02783597	32	0.01404718		
12	0.02694397	33	0.01359710		
13	0.02608074	34	0.01316138		
14	0.02524493	35	0.01273967		
15	0.02443611	36	0.01233145		
16	0.02365304	37	0.01193634		
17	0.02289517	38	0.01155385		
18	0.02216157	39	0.01118367		
19	0.02145148	40	0.01082528		
20	0.02076406	41	0.01047846		

If it is removed, the management may wish to take into account possible actions for the following day, and the day after that. All such possibilities can be included in the formulation of the decision problem.

With the above assumption, the average loss to the company if the decision is made to produce chemical A will be

Total average loss = (Losses from unfilled orders of A) +
(" " " " of B) +
(" " " " of C) +

If A is made there will be 20 lbs of A for the day, whereas the inventory for B and C will remain the same at 15 and 20 respectively. Since the profit is assumed unity per lb., the Total Average Loss (TAL) will be,

$$TAL = \sum_{21}^{49} p_1(x_i) + \sum_{16}^{49} p_2(x_i) + \sum_{21}^{49} p_3(x_i)$$

In a similar manner the TAL for the other two possible decisions can be calculated. The results are tabulated in Table IV.

TABLE IV. Decisions and Total Average Losses

Decision	Loss from A	Loss from B	Loss from C	Total Average Losses (TAL)
Make A	0.00878463	0.26273340	0.38307940	0.65459743
Make B	0.08193129	0.10774800	0.38307940	0.57275869
Make C	0.08193129	0.26273340	0.20872980	0.55339449

The optimum decision is obviously to make chemical C on the given day. The new management will immediately begin to take new data and use it to improve on the estimates of the models. The ranges may increase, variances may be calculated, and even correlation coefficients may start to show up in the orders for the three chemicals. All these new prior data will improve the joint model of the three chemicals and thus improve the estimation of average losses.

REFERENCES

1. E.T. JAYNES, "Prior probabilities" *IEEE Trans. on Systems Science and Cybernetics SSC-4*, No. 3 (Sept. 1968).

2. M. TRIBUS, "Rational descriptions, decisions and designs" (Pergamon Press, New York, N.Y. 1969).

3. N.S. TZANNES, "The mutual information principle and some applications" *Proceedings of the International Conference on Systems, Computers and Networks* (Jan. 1971, Oaxtepec, Mexico) pp. 858-862.

4. R.G. GALLAGHER, "Information theory and reliable communication" (Wiley, New York, 1969) Chapter 9.

5. T. BURGER, "Rate distortion theory" (Prentice-Hall, Englewood Cliffs, N.J., 1971) Chapter 2.

6. J.P. NOONAN, "The maximum entropy principle" *Master's Thesis*, (Tufts University, Medford, Mass., 1969).

A MODEL OF BEHAVIOUR

E. GOLDSMITH

Unified Science Institute, 73 Kew Green, Richmond, Surrey, U.K.

SUMMARY

The object of this paper is to provide the basis of a model permitting the prediction of change in behavioural systems, and in particular human social systems, in the process of disintegration.

STABILITY

The law of economy appears to be the basic law of behaviour. Things take the line of least resistance and move thereby to positions where free energy is reduced to a minimum, i.e. equilibrium. Since positions of unstable equilibrium are, by their very nature, unlikely to be maintained for long without external or asystemic intervention, changes will be towards stable equilibrium or stability.

We can regard this teleonomic behaviour as passive in pre-life forms and increasingly active as life develops.

Stability is normally regarded as the ability of a system to return to its point of departure after a disturbance. A behavioural system as opposed to a man-made incomplete system cannot return to its exact point of departure, but to that which involves the minimum change compatible with the maintenance of a stable relationship with a changing environment and hence with the internal stability of the corresponding supra-system*.

Systems can be more or less stable. The more stable, the smaller will be the disequilibria occurring between them and

---

*For this reason, C.H. Waddington suggests the use of the term *homeorhesos* (from the Greek: rhesos, to flow) rather than *homeostasis*, to describe the negative feedback behaviour of behavioural systems as opposed to that of incomplete man-made systems. The term "system" in this paper will be used to refer to the former.

their respective environments, and the corresponding corrections. A system whose stability is increasing is referred to as "damped"; one which is out of control as "runaway".

The behaviour pattern of a system can be represented by a series of oscillations corresponding to disequilibria and their corrections. Thus in a stable system oscillations are small and in an unstable one large. A damped system is one in which they are diminishing, while in a runaway system they are increasing (see Fig. 1).

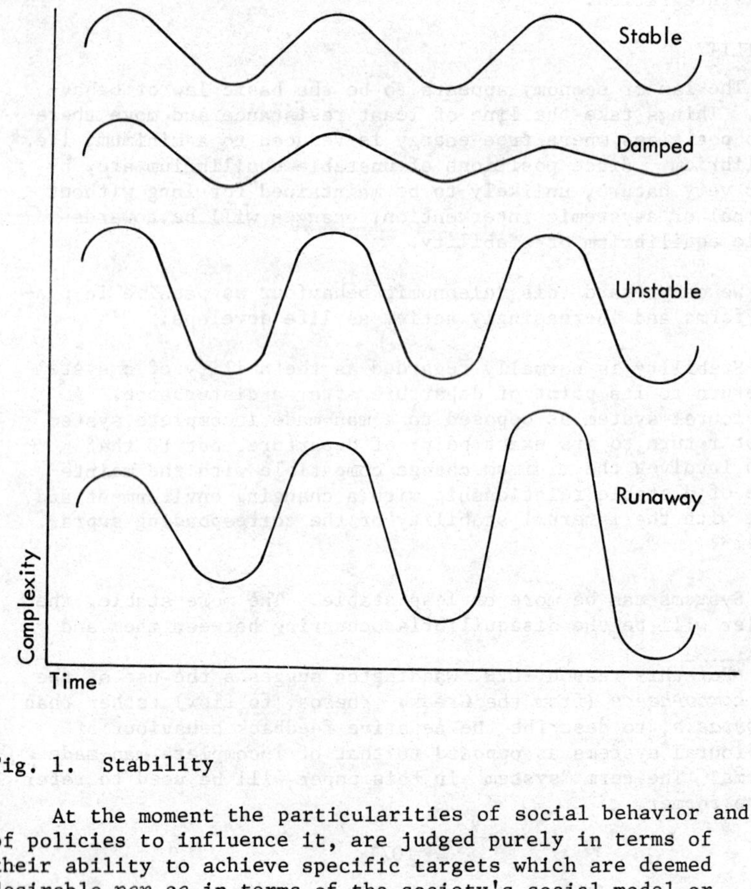

Fig. 1. Stability

At the moment the particularities of social behavior and of policies to influence it, are judged purely in terms of their ability to achieve specific targets which are deemed desirable *per se* in terms of the society's social model or "weltanschauung". Attempts to question the desirability of achieving these targets are regarded as unscientific, unobjective and falling within the category of value judgements. Once we accept that stability is the goal of behaviour, then we have at our disposal a precise criterion, an objective measuring rod for judging the desirability of behavioural trends regardless of the level of organisation at which they occur, and of their degree of generality.

CONTROL

A system is defined as a unit of behaviour, and is composed of a control mechanism plus that part of the environment that it controls.

The control mechanism is fundamentally the same at all levels of organisation. Relevant data are detected, transduced into the appropriate informational medium, and organized, or interpreted, in the light of the system's model, not of its environment but of its relationship with its environment. The responses mediated are those which appear the most adaptive in the light of the model. This adaptiveness must depend on the quality of the model. Relevant to this are the number of elements, their degree of organisation, and the time-lag between detection and the mediation of the appropriate response (See Fig. 2).

The role of the model in the determination of responses is more evident in the case of behaviour at a low level of organisation, for instance during protein synthesis; but it is equally important in a human society. The latter's behaviour pattern can, in fact, be regarded as determined by its model, world-view, or *weltanschauung*, interacting with its environment both internal and external. Institutionalised external controls, except superficially and in the short-term, are ineffective in counter-acting behavioural tendencies associated with a given model or world view.

ENVIRONMENTAL PARAMETERS

Evolution is a feedback process between a system and its environment. Seen slightly differently, the system evolves to fulfil a specific function within a larger system. The rate and extent of possible changes in the latter, as in all systems, must be limited by a number of different factors. For instance, in order to maintain its basic structure, the total rate of change must be limited by that of its slowest changing subsystem.

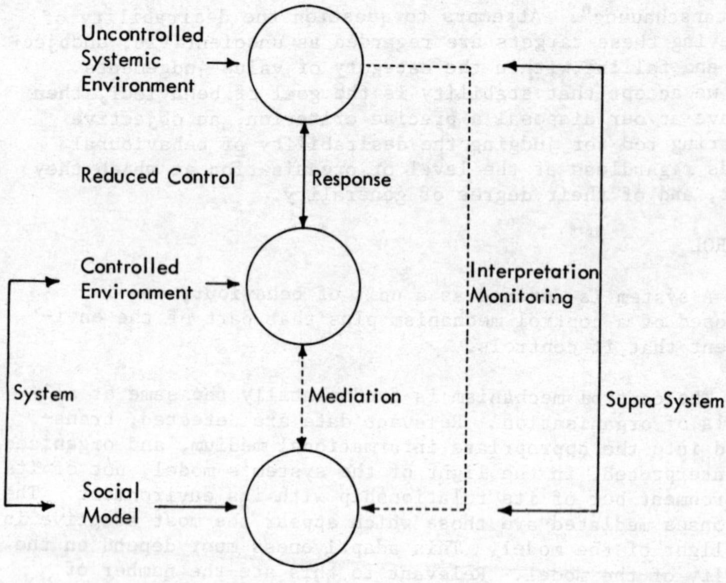

Fig. 2. A self-regulating system.

Hence environmental changes are only tolerable within certain limits. I shall use the term "environmental parameters" to refer to the minimum and maximum values of the variables, in terms of which the supra-system is described, to which the system is hand capable of adaptive responses, Disequilibria caused by changes in which these values are exceeded are referred to as asystemic.

Behavioural processes proceed from the general to the particular by differentiation. As the system differentiates, as a unicell, for instance, evolves into a complex metazoa, or as a foetus develops into an adult, so it becomes capable of dealing with ever more serious environmental challenges. This means that the values will increase. One can draw a graph to illustrate this (See Fig. 3).

In Fig. 3, seriousness of environmental challenges is illustrated along the vertical axis, time along the horizontal axis; the curve shows the development of the ability to cope with environmental challenges with time, and the two dotted lines indicate the parameters, or limits within which systemic changes can occur. It is to be noted that the curve does not rise in linear fashion, but by a series of jumps; this is

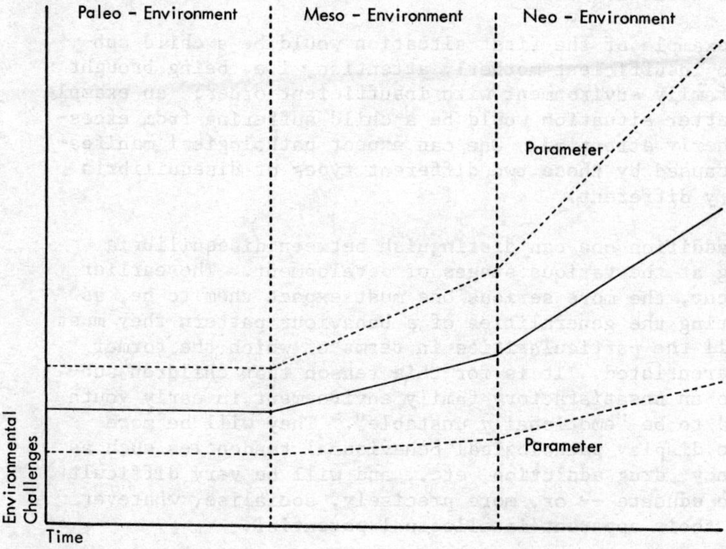

Fig. 3. Environmental parameters.

because, during phylogeny, different critical points or levels of organisation are reached. When this happens, new behavioural principles enter into operation permitting greater behavioural possibilities. During ontogeny there are critical moments, such as birth when a child is suddenly removed from the highly ordered environment of the mother's womb and subjected to a considerably less ordered environment: That of a family unit. Puberty marks another important environmental change, as at this point in a stable society the child enters into the still less ordered environment of the community as a whole. It is significant that in most stable societies these critical moments in a child's life are marked with festivities often involving some traumatic experience (circumcision, for instance), which has a similar effect to shock treatment in helping destroy a now obsolete behaviour pattern and introducing those conditions most favouring the rapid inculcation of a new one. In Fig. 3, the periods lying between these critical points have been separated and labelled. The labels used, paleo-, and neo-, are purely tentative and the number of divisions arbitrary. It is possible to distinguish two different types of disequilibria: those in which the maximum and those in which the minimum values have been exceeded. The former situation can be referred to as *deprivation*, and the latter as *saturation*.

Again the terms are tentative.

An example of the first situation would be a child subjected to insufficient motherly attention, i.e. being brought up in a family environment with insufficient order; an example of the latter situation would be a child suffering from excessive motherly attention. One can expect pathological manifestations caused by these two different types of disequilibria to be very different.

In addition one can distinguish between disequilibria occurring at the various stages of development. The earlier these occur, the more serious one must expect them to be, as by affecting the generalities of a behaviour pattern they must colour all the particularities in terms of which the former are differentiated. It is for this reason that children subjected to an unsatisfactory family environment in early youth will tend to be "emotionally unstable". They will be more likely to display pathological behavioural tendencies such as delinquency, drug addiction, etc., and will be very difficult indeed to educate -- or, more precisely, socialise, whatever might be their apparent intellectual potential.

It is, therefore, one of the conditions of stability that a system be able to develop from the very start in the appropriate environmental conditions.

Responses to asystemic environmental changes will not only themselves be asystemic but, if occurring in the early part of development, will prevent the system from being able to respond systemically to any changes at all.

It is suggested that this might provide a means for classifying disequilibria, and then corrections, systemic and asystemic. This is particularly necessary in a field such as psychology where the classifications used: psychoses, neuroses, etc., are non-functional, and mainly refer to symptoms. It should also prove useful in classifying social disequilibria.

RESPONSES

A system can develop in two ways: firstly, it can increase its capacity to cope with environmental challenges and modify the environment in such a way that such challenges become both less severe and less likely to occur.

To a large extent it is by doing the former that it succeeds in achieving the latter. To increase its capacity to deal with environmental challenges it must build up its model so as to improve its ability to interpret and predict environmental changes. At the same time it must increase its control over environment both in space and in time. This means expanding by destroying and assimilating systems otherwise organised. As a system does this, so by the same token it increases its capacity for dealing with environmental challenges and hence for further expansion. This process cannot go on indefinitely, and one must expect a hierarchy of negative feedback loops to be operative. In a social system some of these are likely to be of a cultural nature.

In the final instance, the law of economy provides the final such negative feedback: if we assume that responses occur in answer to a challenge present, predicted or imaginary, then expansion must ultimately reduce such challenges to a point where they are no longer sufficient to trigger off further expansion.

ENTROPY

Clearly, in the first stages of development when few predictions can be made regarding environmental change, the most adaptive organisation must be one of disorder or entropy. When the number of elements is maximal and order is minimal, the range of possible reactions to unpredictable environmental changes is maximised.

VARIETY

As the environment builds up, and with it one's capacity for prediction, so more effective responses can be mediated towards different possible challenges. In such conditions a corresponding number of somewhat more complex reactions must be made possible -- Variety can be said to be replacing entropy. For reasons of economy, there must be a limit to the number of such challenges to which a system can respond adaptively. The higher the probability of the challenge that can be predicted, the more the system must be capable of reacting adaptively to it. Therefore, the greater a system's variety, the higher the improbability of the challenge to which it can adapt. What is taken for redundancy (animal populations, neuron populations, etc.) in a stable system is, in fact, variety.

COMPLEXITY

Normally variety and complexity are used interchangeably. I prefer to distinguish between them. When it is possible to predict the occurrence of environmental challenges in a particular spatio-temporal pattern, the system gives rise to a correspondingly complex response. In this way it becomes specialised in dealing with a specific environmental situation, one that can be predicted as being highly probable. This gives rise to a *damped* system so long as unforeseen challenges can be prevented from occurring.

CENTRALISATION

In communication theory, it is assumed that the recipient is interested in a message if it conveys sufficient information, i.e. if its improbability is sufficiently low. In a behavioural context this is not necessarily so, as a signal must also be important, i.e. relevant to the recipient's behaviour pattern or general to it. The more general it is, the greater must be that proportion of the system affected by it. That organisation favouring the detection of such signals and the mediation of the correct responses must display a high level of centralisation.

COMPROMISE BETWEEN THE SATISFACTION OF THESE REQUIREMENTS

Centralisation means reducing the variety of possible responses that can be mediated by sub-systems at a lower echelon of control. As a system becomes more complex so also is its variety reduced, since it is committing itself to a specific environment, thereby reducing the possible range of environmental changes to which it can react adaptively. Also as a system becomes more complex, and hence more specialised, so is it likely to become less centralised, so that responses can be mediated as much as possible by the increasingly specialised sub-system more intimately in touch with their respective equally specialised environmental situations.

It must follow that the response mediated by a system, and the organisation it will display, must be a compromise, that which in the light of its model can be predicted as likely to give rise to the most adaptive behaviour.

DISRUPTION OF THE SYSTEM

A system breaks down when the self-regulatory mechanism essential for ensuring adaptation ceases to be operative. In such conditions, there is no means of maintaining the level of variety, complexity and centralisation that would enable it to meet environmental challenges. The system, no longer under control, becomes progressively less stable until it collapses.

ALIEN SUB-SYSTEMS

What is likely to cause disruption of this sort? Geophysical changes can bring about serious upheavals. They can lead to ecological invasions by alien sub-systems. Since these were not developed to fulfil specific functions within the system, it is likely that they would not have developed the capacity for ritualising their behaviour, thereby limiting its impact on the new environment. Also, it is likely that the latter would not provide the necessary controls for keeping their population in check, enabling them to proliferate and destroy the system.

Therefore, it is not surprising to find systems at all levels of organisation equipped with rejection mechanisms to exclude elements alien to it. Whether one likes it or not, such mechanisms are operative at the level of a human society, so long as it remains capable of self-regulation and hence of adaptation.

When such mechanisms break down, the introduction of alien sub-systems in any quantity could lead to an increase in randomness or in a reduction in order. This can be counteracted by incorporating these new sub-systems into the system's basic structure, which can be done at different levels of organisation. Immigrants can be assimilated at the level of the individual, assuming that their cultural pattern can first be broken down, or foreign groups can be incorporated in a cultural symbiotic relationship (as has occurred with the spread of Hindu civilisation). However, this can only occur in specific cultural conditions.

SURPLUS ENERGY

We who live in a society that equates progress with increasing energy consumption should consider that there is an optimum amount of energy required for operation of any system. Plants only exploit a minute fraction of available solar energy, not because they are inefficient, but because, if they were to photosynthesize more, the nutrients in the soil would be exhausted and the environment would cease to be capable of supporting them.

It is significant that stable societies appear to exploit various strategies for channelling surplus energy into those uses that will result in the minimum supra-systemic disruption. I shall refer to this as the "ritualisation of economic behaviour". It means providing a maximum outlet for surplus energy with the minimum use of natural resources in such a way as to cause the minimum social disruption.

Thus in many societies we find a large proportion of the society's resources being channelled into feasts and other forms of ostentatious spending. The best known example being the Potlatch of the Kwakiutl and other Indians of the American North West coast. The production of subtle and highly contrived human artefacts, and indeed artistic activities in general, can also be regarded as ritualisations. Artisans spending their life in carving a cathedral door will use considerably less resources and cause correspondingly less pollution than if they were employed in an automated ball-bearing factory. Also the finished products of their activity do not interfere with the optimum function of their society, as do the utilitarian consumer products manufactured by modern industry.

It must be remembered that the family, a *sine qua non* of a stable society, is an economic as well as a biological unit, and it is difficult to see it surviving in a society in which food, clothing, and other basic requirements normally produced at a family level, are manufactured by some vast company and are available in the local supermarket. Nor can it survive when the functions normally fulfilled by the father have been usurped by the government's social services: (education, welfare, health, etc.).

The same is true of the small community whose survival is menaced by the ever greater centralisation of industrial activity required to fully exploit the so-called economics of scale which manifest themselves as production becomes increasingly capital-intensive. In such conditions a small community is either deprived of its livelihood or forced to commit itself to the production of a specific commodity which must seriously affect its basic social structure as well as rendering it

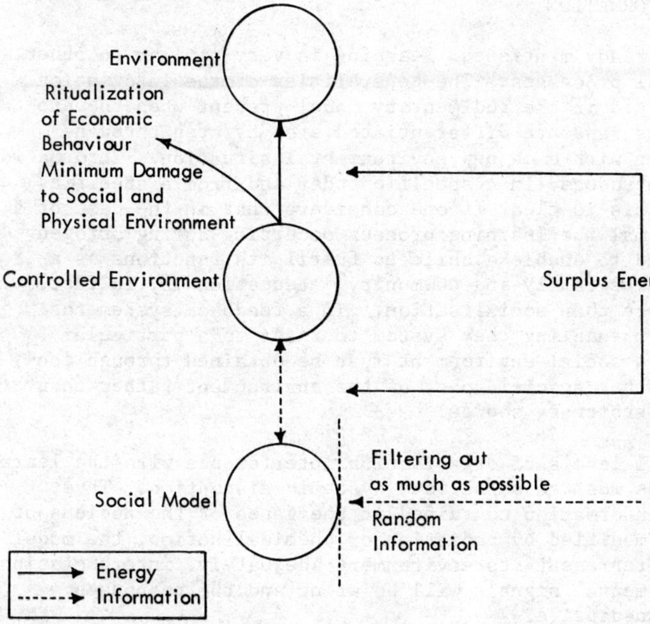

Fig. 4. Dealing with surplus energy and random information

particularly vulnerable to changes likely to alter the demand for the commodity in question.

On the other hand, economic activity geared to the production of non-utilitarian commodities, such as works of art have no adverse effect on social structures. If anything they are likely to reinforce them by causing the society to concentrate on those religious and artistic activities that distinguish the society from its neighbours, and that provides it with the pride that will lead them to divert ever more energy and ingenuity towards its preservation.

We are thus led to the paradoxical conclusion that to preserve stability and thereby ensure the survival of a social system, energy should be channelled from the production of utilitarian products to that of non-utilitarian ones.

RANDOM INFORMATION

As already mentioned, learning is very similar to other behavioural processes. The generalities of the information are contained in the rudimentary model present when the process starts, and are differentiated step by step through interaction with each new environmental situation. Information must be introduced in a specific order and from a specific source. This is clear if one considers that in the case of a social animal the learning process occurring during ontogeny is designed to enable a child to fulfil its functions as a member of its family and community. Education is, in fact, nothing more than socialisation. In a feedback system the information enabling they system to react to a particular part of its social environment must be obtained through contact with that specific part of the environment rather than from some arbitrary source.

At all levels of organisation interference with the learning process must cause serious systemic disruption. Thus when the information contained in the genes or the nucleus of a cell is modified by radiation or chemical action, the model ceases to represent its environment adequately, interpretations of environmental signals will be wrong and the responses mediated unadaptive.

If any of the feedback loops linking the systems to its environment are severed, if behaviour becomes "institutionalised" as in the case of modern government, then behaviour can no longer be influenced by environmental requirements and from the point of view of the supra-system it must become random.

The introduction of random information into the system must have a similar effect. Unfortunately, as our society "progresses" so its inhabitants tend to be bombarded with ever greater quantities of it. Obvious sources are television personalities, newspapers, and, unfortunately, one must include to an ever greater degree our educational system which is increasingly institutionalised and centralised, and hence ever less capable of fulfilling its basic function: that of providing that information which will enable people to fulfil their functions as members of their (now defunct) family and community.

A system will only tend to detect and interpret signals that are relevant to its behaviour pattern, i.e. will affect the value of the variables used. This means that random information which is irrelevant to a man's behaviour pattern, is likely to be filtered out. However, as the environment changes, and the signals become more relevant they are more likely to be detected. It is more difficult to filter out random data in childhood. A child's brain is not designed to encounter random data, normally excluded as much as possible from the protective family environment. Also in the child's case it will do more damage by affecting the generalities of the learning process, which will colour the subsequently developed particularities of his world-view.

THE GROWTH OF INSTABILITY

Once changes occur beyond the system's environmental parameters, it is no longer possible to deal systemically with its challenges. Some of these the system will not even have the means of detecting. Thus we are not provided with mechanisms for detecting the 3,000 or so chemical additives which are systematically introduced into our food, nor, for that matter, the pollutants, such as heavy metals, pesticide residues, and radio-isotopes which also find their way into it, and into the water we drink and the air we breathe. We thus have no means of behaving adaptively towards them.

Even when we are capable of detecting the presence of asystemic elements, the tendency is to mistake them for outwardly similar elements of which we have some phylogenetic and ontogenetic experience. In this way dangerous pollutants such as strontium 90, for instance, are introduced into our life-processes. Stephen Boyden refers to such reactions as *pseudo-adaptations*. They tend towards an equilibrium position, but one in which stability is reduced rather than increased. This must be so because they are designed to satisfy a single supra-systemic requirement, rather than to provide the optimum compromise between the various supra-systemic requirements, thereby leading to increased stability. They must, by their very nature, create further disequilibria, each giving rise to further pseudo-adaptations, leading to further disequilibria, etc., hence causing the system to proceed ever more rapidly towards inevitable breakdown.

I prefer to refer to such reactions as *asystemic*. Practically all the behaviour of our industrial society falls within this category. The mechanism whereby asystemic response are mediated at a higher level of complexity, i.e. at the level of a human society, is an interesting one.

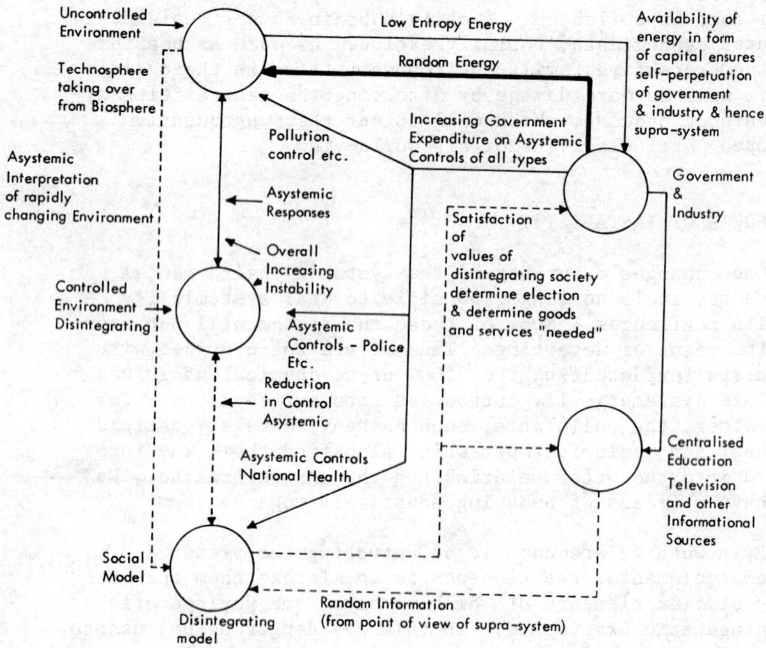

Fig. 5. A model of a modern society.

It is known that perception is not an objective means of acquiring information. The perceiver tends to see what he expects to see, i.e. what in the terms of his particular model he can predict is likely to be there. Extremely unpleasant situations whose correct interpretation would be intolerable to him, i.e. would lead to the breakdown of his mental equilibrium or personal control system, he will tend to re-interpret in such a way as to render them tolerable. What is true of individuals is also true of society. A society will tend to interpret asystemic situations so as to render them acceptable. Thus any information whose correct interpretation would lead one to cast doubt on the basic tenets underlying the society's model or world-view is almost certain to be interpreted in such a way as to ensure their reconciliation.

THE RUNAWAY SOCIAL SYSTEM

Unfortunately the system's instability will increase by positive feedback. This means that the asystemic corrections required restore, however precariously, the environmental conditions in which the system can function must become of an ever more radical nature, causing ever greater disruption, and hence still further increasing instability. Thus in our industrial society, measures required to bridge the widening gap between population and food supply are becoming ever more desperate and ever more destructive of the soil's food-producing capacity. It is no coincidence that 4 billion acres of desert have been created in the last 70 years.

As measures become increasingly desperate, so they tend to become ever more dependent on advanced technology and capital-intensive, highly centralised industry, putting an ever greater stress on natural resources and generating an ever greater amount of pollution. Human activity will also become increasingly utilitarian to the point where ritualised behaviour will tend to be regarded as anti-social and unethical in that it does not contribute towards providing the temporary relief of increasing human misery.

Unfortunately, the system's instability will increase by inevitably be caught up in this process, and introduce further positive feedback into the system. The process continues until the disequilibria are so serious that no expedients are available to prevent collapse.

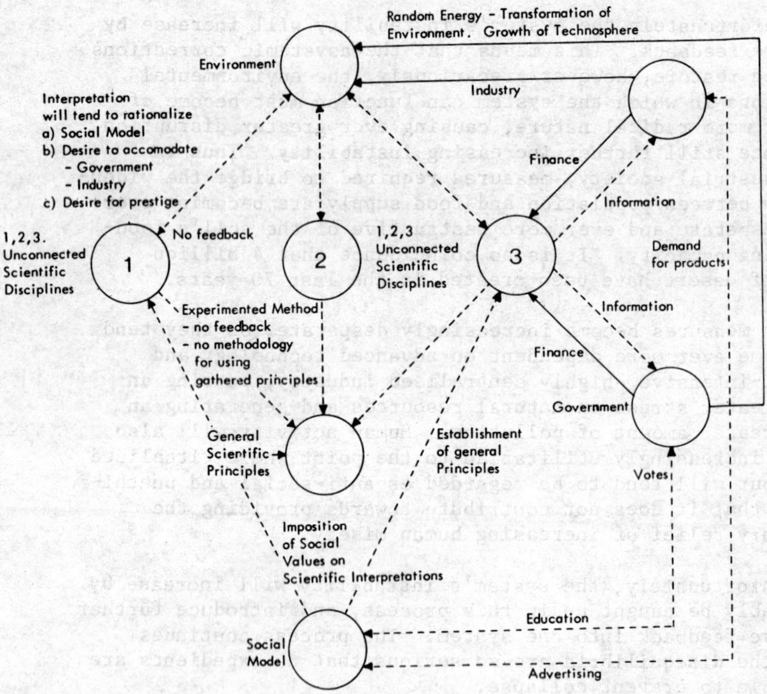

Fig. 6. A model of science.

PLANNING DECISION AND CONTROL IN SOCIAL SYSTEMS

C.G. SOUMELIS

Directorate for Scientific Affairs, O.E.C.D.,
2, rue André Pascal, Paris 16e, France

SUMMARY

The paper attempts to reconsider the functions of planning, decision-making and control of social systems in the light of General Systems Theory making use of cybernetic concepts. It presents a conceptual construct which can easily be applied to concrete social systems and their components (systems in themselves). At the same time, it is also applicable at the various hierarchial echelons of a social system, should it be organised in echelons. It may also suggest ways by which the effectiveness and efficiency of the existing planning and control subsystems could be improved, e.g. by restructuring and/or expanding the capacity of the means by which the decision-making system is enabled to receive, store, process and retrieve information.

INTRODUCTION

The subject* at hand has been, either in its entirety, or separately in its three parts, extensively discussed in the literature. It has been covered under Management Science, Decision and Control Theory, Systems Analysis, Economic Planning, P.P.B.S., Educational Planning, Urban and Regional Planning, etc.

I decided to re-discuss the subjects because of an uncomfortable feeling I always had when dealing with planning and management in general. The dispute among academicians and among field personnel sounded to me unreasonable. It is obvious that

*Some of my ideas have been influenced by Dr. Alex Weilenmann to whom I am also indebted for reading and commenting on an early version of my paper.

all of them are, at the same time, right and wrong, because decision-making, control, and especially planning have received many connotations, usually not even free of ideological preoccupations. There are dozens of examples of definitions for planning; so many that communication among field personnel and/or among academicians coming from various disciplines becomes impossible.

It may be that this situation is due to the fact that a supporting conceptual framework (not necessarily a theory) is lacking. The lack of such a framework gave rise to partial approaches, and the emphasis was placed on the techniques rather than on the conceptualization of the problem. And, the general problem, in its entirety, remains unsolved, while operational problems have been adequately attacked and solved.

One of the messages, perhaps the only serious one, that the recent book, *The Limits of Growth*, conveyed to me was that despite planning and control which is supposed to be exercised on human activities at various levels, the direction toward which the world as a whole moves, seems to be undesirable to man himself. This manifests at least a lack of overall coordination and control of human activities which may prove disastrous, if the necessary measures are not taken in the immediate future.

SYSTEMS

The above are basically the major reasons that compelled me to deal with this subject. And, I have chosen this forum for two reasons: *First*, because of my conviction that General Systems Theory and Cybernetics could provide the necessary concepts for the construction of the needed conceptual framework; and *secondly*, because general systems theorists and cyberneticians are perhaps the only ones capable of elevating themselves above disciplinary boundaries and barriers to see the problem in its generality and approach it in a fresh manner.

I shall assume that we can visualize a world situation as consisting of well-defined systems, each of which is, at the same time, a supra-system and a sub-system. The delineation, i.e., the definition, of these systems is left to us.

We will be concerned here with human social systems composed of elementary units which are human beings. These, in turn, are systems in themselves. We will also be concerned with the performance of the system, i.e., its behaviour. We will attempt to question the *way* a system behaves and *why* it behaves in such a way and not differently.

The overall behaviour of a system is certainly a function of the behaviour of its parts. Thinking in this way, we can descend all the way to the individuals, i.e., to the elementary parts of the system. This compels us to study the system's overall behaviour, vis-à-vis, the individual's one. Historically, we can detect that in some types of social systems and at different time periods, the behaviour of these systems was influenced more by some of their elements than by others. It will also be necessary to study what type of mechanisms a system has or can develop which could allow it to perform predictably enough irrespective of the type of individuals it contains. This could be, for example, a net of constraints and/or particular structural arrangements which could constrain and shape individual behaviour as desired.

In everyday life we do see that individuals' behaviour is very much constrained by some norms — of a general or specific nature — that prevail. These norms — expressed in *oughts* or *shouldn'ts* — are set at every systemic level within which a particular individual has to operate. An individual, on the other hand, may belong, at the same time, to more than one system. We could distinguish norms set through the overall cultural system and norms (laws) set by the political or administrative system as rules of behaviour. Also, each system develops its own norms — i.e., own culture. The difference between norms and laws is that laws can be changed fairly easily whereas cultural norms, especially of the supra-cultural system, by their very nature, are not amenable to immediate change. They have been internalized by the individual gradually while living within the system, and we may say that they make up his "consciousness". They also differ from laws from the point of view of the compliance means they employ.

Both norms and laws, however, operate as control instruments of the individual's acts — implicit or explicit policies of behaviour — that force the individual to conform, more or less accurately, to some desired behaviour. They condition his acts — his decisions.

The individual's acts, of course, are the result of decisions which, when taken, lead to a certain course of action — immediate or future. The setting of norms being an act in itself is a result of a set of decisions. This obviously leads us to a circular process of a rather vicious nature, as it is shown below:

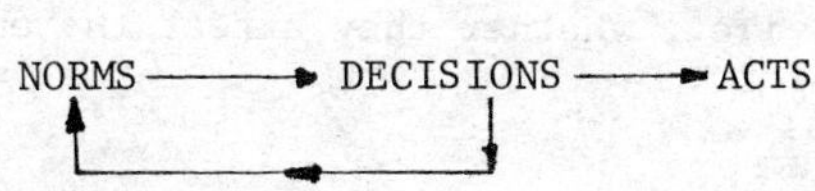

THE DECIDING PROCESS

We can, however, distinguish a decision-making system whose purpose is to make whatever decisions are necessary — decisions about the norms and decisions about all other acts. The taking of decisions, on the other hand, implies the existence of other processes such as "*thinking*". Without going into the psychological details of the thinking process — which would be necessary for the better understanding of how the entire procedure works — it may suffice to indicate that *thinking* is considered as the most important activity for the individual's decision. It is an activity which precedes the decision-making. It is very difficult — almost impossible — to distinguish decisions that are taken without thinking. In the case of an automatic or habitual act, for example, decision and thinking had already taken place at some point in the past, and the act, after continuous repetition, became automatic. (We do not deal here with pathological situations). Especially obvious, however, is the thinking activity in non-automatic (voluntary) acts particularly of a problem-solving nature. In these cases, the individual must discover *what* he should do, *how* and *when* he should do it. This implies consideration of (a) his control norms which, to a large extent, condition his will, i.e., his objectives; (b) the importance of the goal to be met vis-a-vis other possible goals; (c) other constraints that might prevail such as financial or technological ones; and (d) the implications of a possible course of action which usually conditions future acts. In other words, the individual considers, before deciding on a particular act, both the utlity of his goal and the probabilities of meeting the goal with the resources available.

These various steps involved in the thinking process — before deciding — can be presented as shown [1] in Fig. 1.

The figure is self-explanatory, but some qualifications are necessary as to the terms "goals" and "norms".

Goals, in general, are states that the individual attempts to reach through a particular course of action. It is the cause of his behaviour. The reverse should also be true in non-pathological cases, of course: that a particular course of action implies the existence of a goal. It is obvious that we here are discussing purposive behaviour. The goals, however, that an individual attempts to fulfil can be classified in terms of order of importance for the survival and welfare of the individual, i.e., whether they affect the entire system or some parts of it.

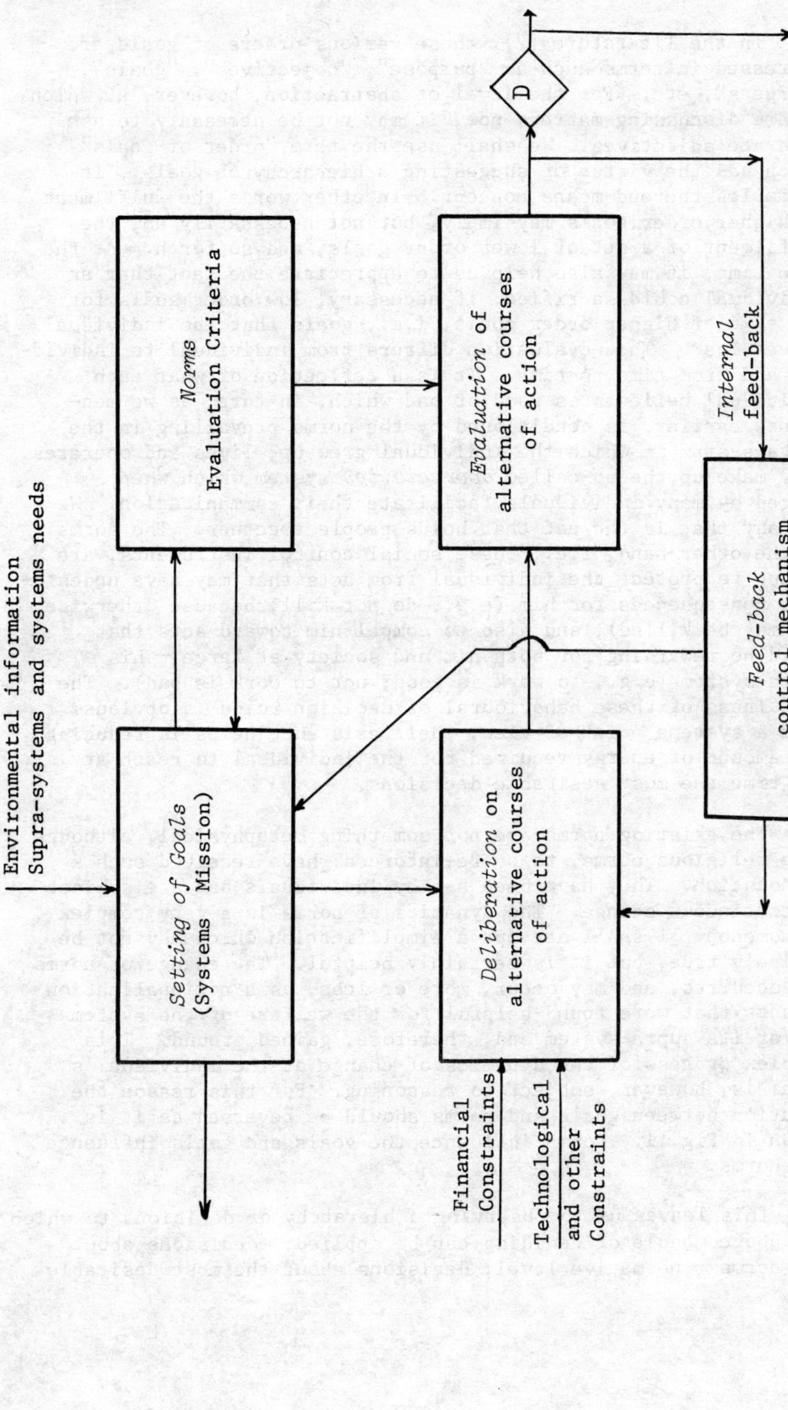

Fig. 1. The deciding module

In the literature [2], these various orders of goals are expressed in terms such as "purpose", "objectives", "goals", "targets", etc. For the level of abstraction, however, at which we are discussing matters now, it may not be necessary to use separate adjectives. We shall use the term "order of goals" which has the virtue of suggesting a hierarchy of goals. It resembles the end-means concept. In other words the fulfilment of higher order goals may imply, but not necessarily so, the fulfilment of a set of lower order goals, and so forth. At the same time, it may also help us to appreciate the fact that an individual could sacrifice, if necessary, low order goals for the sake of higher order goals, i.e., goals that the individual values most. This evaluation differs from individual to individual and from time to time. It is a reflection of what each individual believes as good or bad which, in turn, as we mentioned earlier, is conditioned by the norms prevailing in the supra-system in which the individual grew up, lives and operates. They make up the so-called *appreciative* system which when shared by many individuals facilitate their communication. We can say that is the net that holds people together. The norms, on the other hand, i.e., these social control instruments, are set up to protect the individual from acts that may have undesirable consequences for him (e.g., do not kill, because otherwise you may be killed), and also to compel him toward acts that would be rewarding for both him and society at large — his supra-system (e.g., to work is good; not to work is bad). The usefulness of these behavioural or decision rules is obvious. From a systems point of view, their existence helps in reducing the amount of energy required for the individual to reach at any time the most desirable decisions.

The existing norms are not something metaphysical, although some religious norms, to be re-inforced, have received such a connotation. They have been set by individuals and are subject to continuous change. The dynamics of norms is a very complex phenomenon. I shall attempt a simplification which may not be entirely true, but it is certainly helpful. The change of norms has occurred, and may occur, more or less, as a rationalization of acts that were found helpful for the welfare of the system and/or its supra-system and, therefore, gained ground. This complex process of the dynamics of change at the individual's level is, however, subject to reasoning. For this reason the relation between goals and norms should be reversed as it is shown in Fig. 1. Norms influence the goals and goals influence the norms.

This leaves us to observing a hierarchy of decisions to which the above module of deciding can be applied: decisions about the norms — normative level; decisions about the most desirable

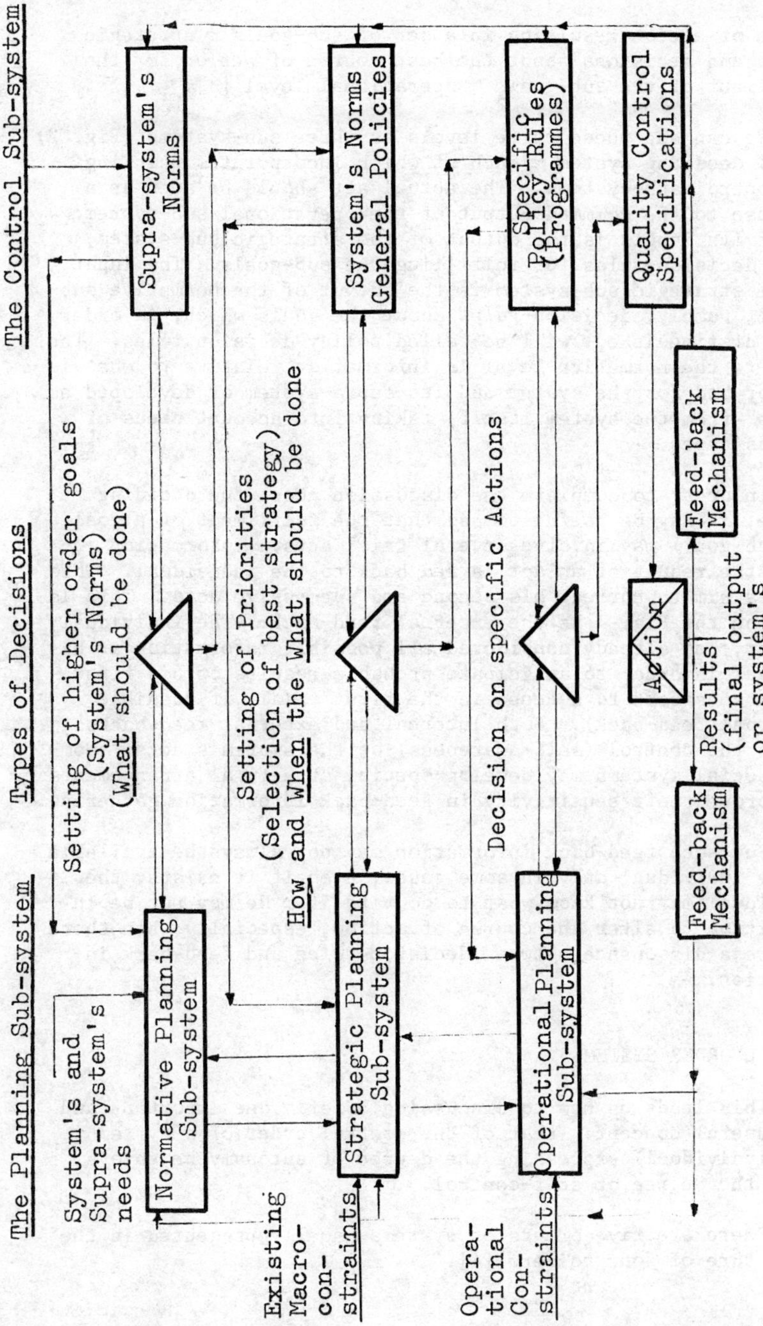

Fig. 2. The decision-making system

course of action resulting in a set of sub-goals — strategic level; and decisions about the best course of action for the fulfilment of the sub-goals — operational level [3].

We can see these three levels as three sub-systems (Fig. 2) of the deciding system — each of which incorporates thinking and control sub-systems. The actual act should be seen as a response to the command output of the operational sub-system; one of its inputs is the output of the strategic sub-system, i.e., decision-rules for fulfilling the sub-goals. The input to the strategic sub-system is the output of the normative sub-system, namely, decision-rules about the goals which, in order to be distinguished, will be called policy-decision rules. The input to the normative level is information relative to what is good or bad for the system and its supra-system or developed as "wills" from the system itself, taking into account needs of various types.

In order to complete the discussion about the deciding module, it may be useful to add that the fulfilment of a goal (or sub-goal) may involve several trial acts. Information about the result of an act is fed back to the individual. This enables him to correct his second and successive acts. This is noted on the Fig. 1 as the external feed-back. The individual, however, has already considered all possible information at his disposal in order to anticipate probable results of his first act in an effort to succeed in the first trial, if possible (internal feed-back). Both internal and external feed-backs add to the control (self-awareness) of the system's acts. Complex social systems may develop special structural arrangements to improve their sensitivity in feed-back information gathering.

But such feed-back information may not always be available to the individual and, in some cases, even if it exists, the individual may not know what to do with it. He may not be in a position to alter the course of action, especially when there will be a dissonance between decision-rules and feed-back information.

CONTROL ORDER SYSTEMS

This leads us now to discussing briefly one important and very useful concept: that of the control order of a system — (the individual) expressing the degree of autonomy he enjoys, i.e., the degree of self-control.

There are five orders of systems usually presented in the literature of four to zero [4].

(a) A *fourth-order* system is the system which has reached the highest level of autonomy. It has the ability to learn and, as a result, consciously develops, selects and implements new and improved goals.

(b) A *third-order* system can develop new decisions but based only on a pre-determined set of goals.

(c) A *second-order* system has only one goal but can act on a wide, although limited, scale of different input conditions.

(d) When the system has only one goal but cannot act on different input conditions, it is said to be of *first-order*.

(e) A *zero-order* system is the one which does not know what to do with the information received about its output and is, therefore, unable to correct it.

Fourth-order control systems are not easily detectable. The individual by his very nature has all the pre-requisites to be a fourth-order system — an entirely free and autonomous system. By the conditions of his life, however, his actual autonomy may be reduced from fourth to third or even to zero order. There have been attempts for classifying the individuals within an organization according to their functions [5]:

SYSTEM ORDER	INDUSTRIAL ORGANIZATION	MILITARY ORGANIZATION
0	Production workers	Troops
1	Foremen	Sergeants
2	Executive Vice Pres.	Company Commander
3	President and Staff	General and Staff
4	Board of Directors	General Staff

The above is indicative of the reduction of autonomy to which the individual is subjected by the supra-system considering, of course, the organization's goals. It may not, however, be true that production workers and the troops are zero orders. They are definitely not zero order in emergency situations. And, it may not also be entirely true that the Board of Directors or the General Staff are fourth-order systems. They are also subjected to the norms of their supra-system.

But the most important thing to be noted is that an individual while, e.g., a zero-order within a particular supra-system, can be a fourth-order in another system at the same time (for instance, a production worker within his family), and in any case, because of his human nature he may not be always prepared to see his autonomy reduced below a certain limit.

So far we have restricted our discussion to the elementary sub-system of a social system, namely, the human being. In so doing we did not have to mention "*planning*" and have also not distinguished decisions in terms of their time effect.

In order to complete our discussion, however, it is necessary that we now proceed to a higher level of analysis. The difficulty involved in this further step is minimized by the fact that the models we have presented previously hold almost in their entirety at any system's level.

The decisions in a larger system are taken by individuals on behalf of the system. The system, through time, develops its own norms, culture, and some more specific decision-rules to guide individuals in their decisions so that they can decide and act according to what is "good" for the system — the organization. The individuals, however, being parts of other systems — cultural, political, etc. — at the same time carry in their minds the norms of these other systems as well. Which norms now will most influence the individual's decision in relation to any of the various systems in which he is a part depend mostly on the degree he has internalized the various norms. A striking example could be the enormous preoccupation of recent western societies against "communists" and of eastern societies against the "capitalists" which was a result of the competition between western and eastern worlds. This pre-occupation has influenced, and still is influencing, individual decision irrespective of whether such a factor has any relevance whatsoever for the decision at hand. We can also draw examples with norms that have been enforced by the church. Killing is not good, but killing your enemy in battle is good. This socially accepted operational dissonance many times proved non-existent. In other words, individuals with strong "not to kill" pre-occupation refused to kill even during a combat, accepting the fact that this may course their lives. We can say that the norm "not to kill" as a goal of behaviour has been elevated to a higher order goal than the survival goal.

An additional example would be the internalization by the individuals of the protestant ethic — as a norm of behaviour — which gave rise to capitalism. Development economists and sociologists dealing with the development of less-developed countries have early enough realized the need for new cultural norms to be internalized by the members of these societies which could work as driving forces toward the goal of development.

Similar and other examples are numerous in the literature. In the above examples, however, one of the norms was much more profound than the others. In everyday life, however, we must expect that more than one norm affecting a decision bear the same or much the same wieght, and also that system preference, i.e., goals, may contradict the individual's norms, as they are affected by other systems. It becomes clear now that the setting of systems objectives requires a deliberation which may not necessarily be entrusted to one member of the system and may invite more members of the system into this deliberation. The same applies to many other classes of decisions, especially those that affect the entire system.

PLANNING AND CONTROL

It may be necessary now to relate this deliberation to the concept of thinking which, as it was previously discussed, is preceding the taking of a decision. It is exactly this deliberation or systems thinking that I wish to call "*planning*". I was compelled to this general definition of planning because I do not see what else really is planning and also because after defining planning in this way, it would be easy to speak of planning that is necessary for various classes of decisions. The process will always remain the same. It would be the means and the techniques at the disposal to any decision point that would vary: they can range from the individual responsible for taking decision, making use only of his personal memory and general intelligence and/or his files, his experts and committees, to more well-structured arrangements like "planning" or "intelligence", offices that undertake the task of collecting and processing all information relevant to the decision or problem at hand. The use now of any of the various possible available information systems is perhaps a matter of culture: *first*, overall, i.e., that of the supra-system, and *secondly*, that of the specific system, indicating what means the system considers as good. In this consideration, of course, all possible constraints, including cost, are or should be taken into account.

We can observe in the real world a variety of such planning means being used for the same classes of decisions. And the temptation always was to attempt to prescribe for the various types of decisions the best way for arriving at such decisions. This idea appeals tremendously to the technically-minded. I would avoid entirely dealing with this question here, because it definitely requires a specific focus, i.e., a specific system with its environment.

What is, however, of general interest is a discussion of the relationships between the sub-systems of the deciding system mentioned previously, namely, that of planning (thinking) and control.

We have said that planning and control are sub-systems of the deciding system which, in turn, is one of the sub-systems of a social human system.

In the human being case, the process of thinking and that of control, i.e., this which makes the individual aware of the probable and/or actual success of his acts, vis-a-vis his goals, go hand in hand. The actual decisions are the natural end result of both these processes. It is absolutely necessary to remember this natural co-operation that exists between these two processes whenever dealing with planning and control at any system's level. But this does not happen always. When developing structures for carrying out planning and control activities, there is a tendency to keep them separate and loosely linked to the actual decision point. Because of their internal dynamics, planning and control sub-systems tend to develop their own goals and they rapidly show an increased autonomy, vis-a-vis their supra-system. The end result of this is that the elementary elements of the deciding system, i.e., the individual who is entrusted with decision-making authority, because of his feeling remote to the planning and control sub-systems, develops a mistrust toward them which leads him either to rely solely upon his own human thinking and control abilities and/or to develop his very personal consultative bodies on questions of planning and control.

In actual life, the above led to the debate as to who is the real decision maker in a social system: is it the planner or the person officially entrusted with the decision-making authority? The debate is based on false assumptions. According to us, the decision is the end result of the co-operation of these processes and it is expressed through an authorized channel — the *effector*. It is impossible, therefore, at least conceptually, to make the distinction as to who is the real decision maker and who is not. The problem in reality arises from personality conflicts. Various people are competing for the credit of a particular decision and the power that a particular decision point may hold. This unfortunate debate had tremendous implications for the effective development of the necesary structural arrangement for planning and control. This becomes more important in large and complex social systems where high order decisions and especially those with long-term effects require the collection and processing of a large amount of information. In these situations the development of specialized structures for carrying out the functions of planning and control are essential, but very careful design of both the structural arrangements and the behavioural rules to guide the behaviour of these sub-systems are necessary. During the last decade when organized planning activities were recognized as something "good", many social systems, e.g., business, governments, etc., have developed planning stuctures. But this was in many cases done as a response to a fashion rather than from the recognized need by the system itself of the necessity of these structures. This resulted in a careless design of such structures that were kept outside the traditional decision process. This led to two extreme developments: either these structures died gradually, usually because of the elimination of the necessary matter-energy inputs after awhile; or they grew to para-decision systems competing with the actual decision system. There were, of course, in-between cases and also some attempts for re-designing the arrangements, but the end result was loss of energy and, in very few cases, especially in business, did contribute to the improvement of decision making. The above described situation has continuously been used as an argument against planning. This is again unfortunate because it neglects the very fact that planning is taking place continuously, with or without organized structures, since decisions never stop being made.

What is at stake, however, is not planning; it is the *quality* — the correctness of the decisions: the decisions on *what* to do, *how* to do it, and *when* to do it. And, it is unfortunate to see people rely mainly on the trial and error technique for problem solving and learning; unfortunate because the information about the error in the most crucial decisions for the survival and welfare of the large social system and, ultimately, mankind, is either never received or if it is received, the time lag is so big that the information is useless since, in the meantime, the environmental and systemic situations would have certainly changed. This change is usually uncontrolled and is the result of unco-ordinated low-level decisions.

One of the necessities that we are emphasizing here is the necessity to increase the "intelligence", if you like, of social systems and make them capable of greater insight and foresight abilities.

The direct implication of this is two-fold: on the one hand, to improve planning and control mechanisms at all system levels, considering all these as sub-systems of a supra-planning and control system. On the other hand, to pay increased attention to the elements of the social system — the human being — and attempt to fill in the most crucial decision points with individuals that their appreciative system is free of pre-occupations of any type and who could reason freely about the goals and policy-decisions that their system should have.

REFERENCES

1. LOCKHEED INTERNATIONAL, *Systems Analysis of Sudan Transportation System* (Los Angeles, 1966).

2. H. OZBEKHAN, "Toward a general theory of planning" In: E. JANTSCH (ed.) *Perspectives of Planning* (O.E.C.D., Paris, 1969) p. 125.

3. *Ibid.*, p. 135.

4. VAN COURT HARE, Jr., *Systems Analysis: a Diagnostic Approach* (Harcourt, Brace and World, Inc., New York, 1967) pp. 127-128.

5. *Ibid.*, p. 129.

A STUDY OF SOCIAL SYSTEMS

V.H. BRIX and R.L. CLARKE

The Pantiles, Churchland Lane, Sedlescombe, Sussex, England

SUMMARY

Cybernetics and Systems Analysis can only progress if there is clear thinking and mutual understanding of the concepts and terms which are used. This paper is a suggested taxonomy for a "new" social science which is based on a cybernetic model of the human being. The basic parameters of social situations then appear to be reducible to a minimum, i.e., information, time, and a bio-dynamic tension within the human being. Attempts are made to apply the taxonomy to groups, conflict and coercion. This leads to meaningful concepts of bureaucracy, nationalism, etc., and also suggests ways in which political movements can be analysed and defined.

INTRODUCTION

Little has been published to bring cybernetics to the aid of social science. The aim of this paper is to suggest an interpretation of social conflict in engineering terms so that its causes may be simply explained and its issues extrapolated. The shortcomings of a hypothesis based on observation rather than experiment are acknowledged. It is put forward only to stimulate those people with deeper knowledge to apply more rigorous treatment.

GENERAL SYSTEMS

The first need is to evolve a set of definitions and accept them universally. The taxonomy of social systems must be compatible with that already in use for general systems.

The basic unit of observation at a given degree of resolution is commonly called the ELEMENT. The element is indivisible in the context of the system in question, and is distinct from other elements.

If the behaviour* of one element has some degree of predictability with respect to the behaviour of another element, (i.e. there is some corellation), there is said to be a RELATIONSHIP between them.

RELATIONSHIP implies an observed probability of behaviour of one element contingent on the behaviour of another.

A SYSTEM consists of two or more elements joined by a relationship. It is self-contained and distinguishable from the environment even though elements may be shared with other systems.

An element may be resolved as being itself a system at the next level down. For instance the human being is an element at the level of the social group, although it is a system at the physiological level.

SYSTEMS OF DIFFERENT TYPES

Solid systems consist of elements with fixed relative spatial arrangements within the time scale in which behaviour is observed. *Mechanical systems*, on a higher level of resolution, consist of elements which themselves are solid systems. The relationship between elements in a simple mechanism shows a probability of behaviour of unity. *Adaptive systems*, like automatically controlled machinery, react to the environment to maintain their stability. The stability is derived from the behaviour differences between the disturbed and undisturbed states as in "servo" systems. The undisturbed state is a *goal* [6]. The adaptive system is goal seeking, i.e. it acts homeostatically.

Organic systems are adaptive systems which can acquire the additional power of (a) stimulating self-growth, and (b) controlling their environment. We associate their active as against their passive reaction with the phenomenon of life. Growth is achieved by acquiring new elements or by increasing the number the depth of the relationships between existing elements (complexity).

Survival of an organic system means homeostasis, and we identify this as the primary goal of an organic system, attained by optimisation of homeostatic operation. This entails adequate information input, decision-making capacity exercised to the full, rapid feedback and general smooth functioning. The homeostat

---

*Behaviour, in cybernetics, is defined as a succession of states identifiable by changes in one or more parameters [6].

reacts to internal and external disturbances (uncertainties), the effect of these being annulled by the energy derived from bio-dynamic tension putting into effect various programmes carried out by the effector organs [2]. Dealing with the human being (referred to as the "element") this primary goal can be broken down into two sub-goals as follows:

1) The seeking of optimum control over environment through self-growth, i.e. increasing its own structure or complexity, or the handling of increasing power or energy resources.

2) The seeking of full feedback coupling with other elements of the same kind to build larger systems of such elements, and in this manner, to reduce environmental uncertainty (threat).

We bring these two concepts into line with conventional social theory by denoting the first as "H", which refers to the self-centred, individualistic drives of human beings which formed the basis of Hobbes political theory. The second drive goal is labelled as "L", in honour of the political philosopher Locke, who emphasised the gregarious or socialising nature of human beings.

It might be recognised that some of our greatest problems today are those of choosing the best relative proportions of "H" and "L" to secure optimum overall survival probability of elements at the human systemic level.

Note that "H" deals mostly with rapid responses obtained through the element itself, whereas "L" deals with interaction with other elements, a slow process. The difference in response time between H and L is very important and is referred to below.

SOCIAL SYSTEMS

The following propositions are made on the basis, at present, of being reasonable assumptions for a socio-cybernetic model:

1) Systems built up of human beings as elements show similar homeostasis on their levels as the elements. Thus a system composed of elements, each having its own "H" and "L", evinces a new "H_s" and "L_s" at systemic level. These systems, in turn, can be regarded as elements, forming "super"-systems at a higher level. These, again, react homeostatically to survive.

2) A necessary condition for optimum homeostatic working of human elements (i.e. working with minimum tension) is for

optimum homeostasis of systems of elements, super-systems of systems and so on, indefinitely, at each systemic level.

3) There is a good deal of ambiguity with regard to the range where the self-interest H overlaps the socialising drive L. Note that the "L" drive bringing elements together at one level, becomes an "H" drive for the system, when viewed as an element at the higher systemic level. The predominance of H goals in the case of systems at the level of nation-states is obvious at the present time.*

4) An element begins to socialise, i.e. replace the H by L by accepting constraints on its behaviour. These constraints, perceived by the elements, are termed *"roles"*, and as such, form functions of the system.

BUILDING THE SOCIAL STRUCTURE

In cybernetics the human being is modelled on the basis of a servo system. (Miller, Klir & Valach, etc.). Information from the perceptors (the input) is compared with an internal conceptual model which is closely coupled with the memory subsystem. Differences, i.e. mismatches, between the input signals and the model arouse bio-dynamic tension (Sokolov). Thus feedback from the environment (1) is sensed and activates transfer functions, manifest as apprehension, anxiety, etc, the effect of which is to unlock decision programmes to annul the mismatches, just like the voltage feedback signals correcting mechanical servos.

The dynamics of this homeostatic mechanism are so powerful that, failing other means of dispelling the mismatch, for instance, by acting on the environment to remove the disturbance, the internal model itself may become distorted. The element then loses realism in its percept of the environment. Unresolvable anxieties lead to psycho-somatic disorders.

We now examine the interaction between two such elements to form the simplest system, the two-person social system. We are examining the "L" process.

When two such elements, say A and B, both strangers, come within social distance, they will both be faced with the decision of how to constrain their "H" behaviours and socialise

*Most animals exhibit the "L" process. They perform rituals which define "territoriality" (Robert Ardrey, "The Social Contract").

(L behaviour). The elements can do this by developing, gradually, similar percepts of their new systemic, A-B relationship. This is a bargaining process [2] whereby information is exchanged in small packets between A and B until a common percept emerges. Whilst there is mismatch between A's percept of the new system and B's percept of the same system, disturbing signals are received by both, and the internal tension will seek to annul the errors. The final equilibrium state, where mismatch is annulled, is a new A-B system, in which A and B have certain roles, and bear a certain status relationship to each other, equally perceived by both.

The relationship between A and B in a given system may develop either from the reciprocal transfer of a small amount, or, a large amount, of information. In the former case we have a shallow relationship, in the latter a deep relationship. Where there is great environmental threat, for instance in the face of an emergency like a flood, or accident, people will form shallow systems to fulfill immediate goals. The system collapses as soon as the goals are met, usually before the people even get to know each other. Marriages are examples of deep relationships, for the marital dyad only forms after prolonged periods of courtship (reciprocal information transfer).

In the deeper relationships the process of bargaining can take a long time. The time is considerably cut down by the existence of agreed norms and folkways. This is common structural information shared by the elements forming the system, and is referred to as a *culture*.

STRUCTURAL DEFINITIONS

The simplest system at the level of human society is that formed between two people. It can be shallow or deep.

When more than two elements (people at this level) form a system, however, everyone may or may not form a relationship with every other. In the former case there are $n(n-1)/2$ linkages for n elements. A system with $n(n-1)/2$ linkages is termed fully COHERENT.

Systems are rarely fully COHERENT however. For instance systems are often structured in two ways;

1) the STAR, with one element linked centrally to several other, mutually unrelated, elements.

2) the RING with every element linked to two others [8]. The Star structure is the least coherent, it has only (n-1) links. Feedback is difficult because the central element becomes overloaded, and this limits the homeostasis, and therefore viability, of this type of system. It is useful for the execution of commands rapidly from a central point and forms the basis for bureaucracies and military systems.

The RING structure is more sensitive to the environment, but slower in taking action. Unless executive roles can be developed by mutual agreement, action may indeed be impossible.

A combination of these structures is usually evolved where a discussion group elects an executive.

In ref. (1), it was shown that every element within a system should share a common, coincident, percept of the role structure of the system including itself, otherwise structural ambiguity may lead to breakdown and internal conflict. A system where there is such a coincident percept shared by all is referred to as FULLY CONGRUOUS. So many factories and business organisations today lack such full congruity, and this leads to much misunderstanding and quarrelling between different levels within the hierarchy.

INFORMATION

The exchange of information between elements is a vital part of establishing a relationship. It is a cautious process because the element which gives information without receiving information in exchange makes a concession, and this is not consistent with the elements individual drive "H". A strong need to socialise (L) should be perceived as worth while.

There are two types of information, namely, what to say and how to say it. The first relates to the element, and is called SPECIALIST INFORMATION. The second type of information is how to deal with specialist information, i.e. when to make use of it, how, and what priority to assign to it. This is STRUCTURAL INFORMATION.

Structural information is, or should be, shared by all elements in a system. This can be done if it is fully congruous, and coherent. Specialist information is one of the inputs to a cybernetic system. Specialist information has to be supplied by separate elements because there is far too much for one to carry.

A committee, with its chairman, treasurer and members should work cybernetically. Each member is a source of specialist information. The way in which the specialist information is used in order to make joint decisions is structural information. The precedence of the members, i.e. status, is also structural information. There should be no perceptual mismatch on these matters. If mismatches occur, and there is inadequate time or information to annul them, there may be polarisation and conflict. The system then splits up. A committee should work as a perceptual homeostat.

VARIOUS APPLICATIONS OF THE MODEL

Bureaucracies and current hierarchical organisations follow the "star" pattern described. Roughly speaking they consist of two parts, a decision-making part, i.e. an elite, managerial board etc., and the effector part, where people just carry out orders.

The former enjoy considerable homeostatic operation, being primarily decision-makers; the latter suffer deprivation of homeostatic operation as their decision making machinery* is by-passed [7]. Such systems therefore have much frustration built into them (Argyris, et al.). The people in them tend to develop informal sub-systems which are more congruent. The elite, who suffer less from frustrations than those lower in the hierarchies, are however continually plagued by anxieties about the stability of the system as a whole. They therefore seek other methods of control, for instance by coercion**. The coercion may be economic, psychological or even physical, as in the case of a police state. Such systems also require "loyalty" from subordinates, i.e. concessions from their lower members to keep them in being.

Bureaucracies of this kind are frequently so unstable that external hostility has to be fostered so that the external threats will keep the members together, for their relationships are very shallow. We see this phenomenon manifest in organisations which contain various departments, each of which is a

---

*It is not possible to discuss these points in detail within the compass of this paper. The significance of decision-making within organisations has been fully discussed by Brown [3] and Jaques [9].

**Coercion has been dealt with in [1]. A coerces B when he replaces direct feedback exchange of information by manipulating B's environment so as to increase B's uncertainty and make him alter his goal in the direction of A's. It is a "secondary loop control".

pyramidal hierarchy. The departments usually find reasons for conflict and are at odds with one another.

On a national scale, internal congruence has to be fostered by mythologies, i.e. slanted historical indoctrination, so as to distort the models. Incidents outside the systems (nations) have to be perceived as hostile to maintain internal stability (more appropriately — meta-stability [4,5]).

Conflict can be modelled in an interesting way. We have pre-supposed that an "L" drive always exists. Elements and systems *want* to co-exist in harmony. However, the L homeostasis, for reasons such as inadequate information, inadequate time, or other dysfunctions, may not be effective, and the "H" drive of each system predominates by default. The relationships between the elements and systems are then determined by signals which cannot be matched with realistic internal models. They become positive feedbacks, which only escalate the fears and anxieties on both sides. These, in turn, can only be discharged by internal models which become increasingly distorted in frantic efforts to annul the ever-growing mismatches. The escalation, so elegantly described by Richardson, has mechanical analogies in the form of runaway oscillations, whirling shafts, etc.

REFERENCES

1. V.H. BRIX, "Cybernetics and social structure" In: *Progress in Cybernetics* (Gordon and Breach, London 1969) p. 1107.

2. V.H. BRIX, *Cybernetics and Everyday Affairs* (Rendel, London, 1968); also, *You are a Computer* (Emerson, New York, 1970); also, *Alles ist Kybernetik* (Akadem. Verlag, Berlin, 1971); also, *La Cibernetica nella vita d'ogni Giorno* (Mursia, 1972).

3. W. BROWN, "Organization" (Heinemann, London, 1971).

4. J.W. BURTON, *Systems States Diplomacy & Rules* (Cambridge U.P., 1968).

5. K.W. DEUTSCH, "The nerves of government" (Free Press, London, 1966).

6. W.R. ASHBY, "Design for a brain" (Chapman & Hall, London, 1960).

7. V.H. BRIX, "Human relations: an engineers approach" *Paper presented to Institution of Production Engineers, U.K.* (London, 18 Nov. 1971).

8. J. KLEIN, *The Study of Groups* (Routledge & Kegan Paul, London).

9. E. JAQUES, *Equitable Payment* (Heinemann, London, 1961).

CYBERNETIC CONCEPTS AND TECHNIQUES IN THE PROGNOSIS OF THE SOCIAL AND ECONOMIC DEVELOPMENT OF ROMANIA

MANEA MĂNESCU

The Academy of Economic Studies, Bucharest, and President of the Centre of Economic Computation and Economic Cybernetic, Bucharest, Romania

SUMMARY

The fundamental idea of the paper is that forecasting of future development of a national economy can be studied by means of a simulation process of the subsystems of which it is made up, one of these subsystems being the macro-economic subsystem of forming and allocating national income which has the important role of system control. The paper defines the main stages in forming and allocating national income, the connection among productive effectory macro-systems (industry, agriculture, science and technology, circulation etc.) and systems of population, education, social culture etc. It integrates the main forecasting elements of Romania's development into a complex cybernetics structure. Some forecasts for the next 2 or 3 decades are given.

PROGNOSIS - A FUNDAMENTAL INSTRUMENT OF ECONOMIC AND SOCIAL MANAGEMENT

The economic and social transformations which are taking place in the world today, make it more necessary than ever the drawing up of long-term strategies of development and the prognosis of economic and social phenomena, which have become so very urgent and complex, with a view to substantiating the decisions of economic policy. One of the defining features of our epoch lies in the rapid, quantitative and qualitative change in all the aspects of social production.

The ampleness and intensity of the unfolding of the contemporary technical and scientific revolution, the requirements for an ever more rational use of the material and human resources, the intensification of economic relations among states, the necessity of using the advantages offered by the international division of labour show an important need for a prognosis of the economic and social development.

In this context, a trend that is making its way into the science of prognosis consists in the development of long term research. The estimation of the distant effects of the decisions taken at present, especially the investigation of and change in these decisions in keeping with the foreseeable action of the economic and social factors, have become fundamental imperatives of the management of society. By obtaining knowledge of events in the future, by exploring the alternatives of development and by detaching the tendencies of evolution, conditions are being created for social management factors to draw up decisions in keeping with the needs for progress of society.

As it is known, a decision is always "a penetration" into the future. It requires a consideration of mobility, structural transformations proper to contemporary economy, which are permanently creating new situations, and problems with which the empirical decisions can no longer cope. Continuous changes in economy have become a positive aspect of progress which management has to take into consideration in the making of decisions. In consequence, prognoses must be available when decisions are being taken.

Prognosis represents the necessary stage of long term planning, offering it the main landmarks in the planning of economic and social development, which are important elements in choosing options of economic policy.

In the conditions of the socialist system, the prognosis is not only necessary but it is also acquiring an ever larger field of action, due to the unitary character of the economy. On the basis of the socialist ownership of the means of production, an organic unity between prognosis and planning can be ensured.

In Romania, prognosis has been transformed into a constituent element of management, as a part and parcel of the development program of society. By means of long term prognoses the alternatives for the political decisions of a strategic character will be established and the guiding lines for the creation of an extensively developed socialist society will be delineated.

To further ensure an accelerated rhythm of the economic, scientific and cultural development, and a continuous rise in our people's living standards for a longer period of time, measures have been established for the organization and unfolding of the activity of drawing up prognoses until 1990, and for some problems and sectors until the year 2,000. The entire activity of prognosis and planned economic and social development of Romania is led by the leader of our state, the President Nicolae Ceausescu.

CYBERNETICS AND ECONOMIC PROGNOSIS

Considered from the point of view of cybernetics, economy (from the single enterprise to the whole) appears as an extremely complex, controlled system. We can consider the national economy, the branch or enterprise economy - taken separately or as a whole - as being a cybernetic system adjusted by control parameters, which define the proportions and the main technical and economic indicators of their functioning. The national economy being conceived as a cybernetic system, made up of a very big number of subsystems coupled between them by feedback, allows the scientific explanation of extremely complex phenomena which are taking place in the system. The mechanism of adjustment of an economic cybernetic system must ensure the permanent correction of the best evolution, taking into consideration both the changes and malfunctions occuring inside the system and those deriving from its sphere of action.

This principle, deriving from the general peculiarity of the cybernetic systems of containing self-adjustment factors in their intrinsic structure (structure of transformation), is of particular importance for the activity of economic and social management. An essential element, which qualitatively differentiates the economic cybernetic systems from other systems, is that the part of the structure of transformation pertaining to the function of control and adjustment is always achieved through the direct and conscious presence of man. Consequently, in a macro-economy, for example, the social and political organ, aiming at the best evolution of the system for a period of several years, is drawing up prognosis studies based on figures, it establishes the best solutions and is continuously following its evolution by carrying out the function of adjustment and control.

It is known, from the theory of systems, that an oriented system may be presented by the relation

$$Y = Ax$$

where x stands for the system access, Y for the system feedback, and A is the structure of transformation. Generally, $x = x(t)$, $y = y(t)$, $A = A(t)$, and in economy the time is considered as quantized in calendar units.

Economy, conceived as a cybernetic system, allows us to attach an efficiency function to its subsystems of the type

$$\psi = \psi(t)$$

$$\psi(t) = \frac{||A(t_i)|| - ||A(t_{i-1})||}{t_i - t_{i-1}}$$

Also, we may state a rate of the economic development by the relation

$$r(t) = \frac{||A(t_i)|| - ||A(t_{i-1})||}{||A(t_{i-1})|| - ||A(t_{i-2})||}$$

as well as a speed of rate growth:

$$V_r = \frac{r(t_i) - r(t_{i-1})}{t_i - t_{i-1}}$$

From the cybernetic point of view, economic and social prognosis on a national scale should comprise in its sphere of interest both the development of the executive cybernetic macro-systems of society (population, production, transport, circulation of goods, science and technology, etc.) and the direct and inverse connections among these macro-systems.

The most complex problem is to establish the inverse connections which, in our opinion, must compulsorily contain parameters of social control as well; this is attempted in the next section of this paper.

A MODEL OF CYBERNETIC PROGNOSIS CONCERNING THE ECONOMIC AND SOCIAL DEVELOPMENT OF ROMANIA

In our opinion, the formulation of cybernetic notions on economic and social management implies a harmonious integration both of the objectives of the present activity and of those regarding the long-term prognosis of the future into the general interests of the leading social and political body. In this

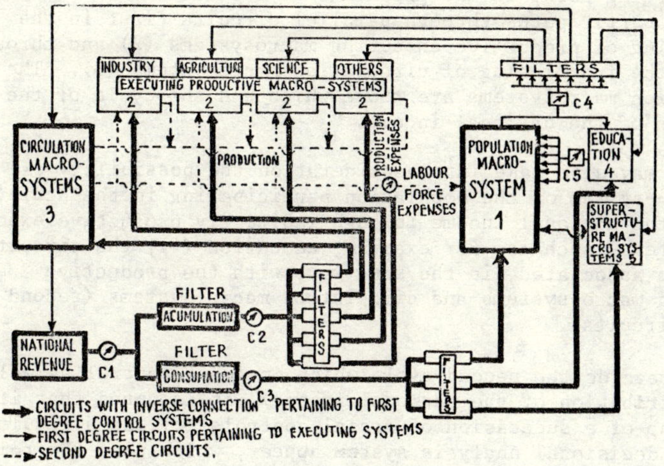

Fig. 1. General representation of cybernetic connections in the national economy

context, in the prognosis of the future development of Romania, it was considered possible that the interconnection among the economic and social macro-systems should be simulated through the national income.

This concept has an important consequence that the formation and distribution of the national income becomes, in its turn, a macro-system through which not only social control but also mutual influences are being exerted; this is the fundamental requirement of cybernetics as regards inverse connections among systems.

As shown by the diagram presented in Fig. 1,* the executing macro-systems of the national economy are participating, as part of the first cycle, in the achievement of the national income, generating a set of parallel connections, which are finally mediated (transformed) through other systems.

---

*It is stressed, that this diagram does not pretend to give an exhaustive presentation of all systems.

Thus, the macro-system of the population (1), the development of which from multiple political and social points of view is a starting point in the prognosis of the future of the country, participates through parallel circuits first in the functioning of productive executing macrosystems (2) and through them in the functioning of circulation macrosystems (3). The circulation macrosystems are those which end the cycle of the formation of the national income.

One may also take into consideration the possibility of the macro-system of the population participating in the achievementoof the national income through inditectly productive executing systems, such as, for example, education (4), the circuits of which are associated, in the same way, with the productive executing macro-systems and circulation macro-systems (second degree circuits).

As regards the second cycle which includes control as well (the distribution of the national income), it is noted that it is made up of a succession of social controls (c), as a result of which decisional analysis system appear, which play the role of filters with a limited flowing capacity, the size of which is established by the political and social authority. First, the size of the two filters is established: accumulation and consumption for which social control C1 is given. Then social control C2 and C3 follow, which establish the distribution of the accumulation fund to the productive executing macro-systems and of the consumption fund to the consuming systems.

As a rule, a necessary but insufficient cybernetic connection is thus being achieved. First of all, mention should be made of the fact that there are a number of circuits between the economic and social macro-systems which achieve inverse connections through operations entering their decisional capacity. At the same time, as we speak of economic and social macro-management, the three social controls cannot ensure the functioning, with maximum efficiency, of the system. Sometimes the placing of filters is necessary, which should allow the adequate guidance of feedback from other systems.

In this way, the introduction of a social control is possible on the feedback of the macro-system of the population (C4) for ensuring an adequate guidance of labour force, on the feedback of the macro-system of education (C5) for ensuring specialized staff, on the feedback of productive macro-systems for guiding the correlations among them, or on the feedback of the circulation system for establishing the share of material expenses and the link with other systems.

In order not to overload the diagram, such social controls appear only in the macro-systems of population (C4) and education (C5) which, as a matter of fact, are included in the prognosis objectives of our country as well.

Conventionally, we shall consider the first two circuits of the primary distribution of the national income and the decisions pertaining to them, as first degree circuit and controls, namely without their existence the functioning of the system is practically, impossible. We shall consider the other circuits and controls to be of second degree (self-adjusting).

In our opinion, taking into consideration that the first degree circuits and controls pertaining to them constitute, in essence, the attributes of the economic and social policy of a country, it follows that the more actively the state intervenes for integrating the entire economy into these circuits and decisions, the more powerful its leading functions will be carried out.

Worth mentioning in this connection is that the socialist economy has great possibilities for including in the sphere of first degree decisions almost the entire economic and social activity. The instrument by which this integration is being achieved is the state plan, the substantiation of which is to be found again to an ever greater extent in the study of the prognosis of the future.

In accordance with Fig. 1, the work on prognosis in our country is being conceived as a systematic effort having the character of scientific research; it aims at estimating the probable-quantitative and qualitative-evolution for a longer period of time of the main processes of social and economic development, stress being laid in various variants on the levels of five-year periods.

On a cybernetic plane, it is considered that the economic and social systems of Romania, functioning according to the above-mentioned concept, create the need that prognosis in various economic fields should reflect at least the development of the macro-systems introduced in the scheme: Population, industrial production, agriculture, science, technology, education, circulation and the national income.

Figure 2 presents schematically the correlation between the plan and prognosis according to cybernetic concept on the use of prognoses in economic and social management.

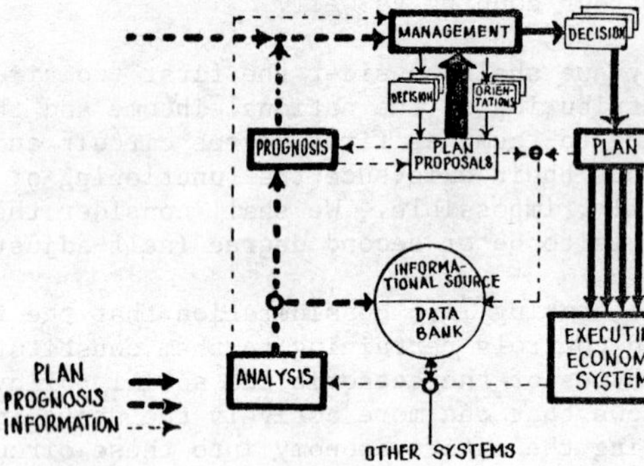

Fig. 2

Based on internal economic and foreign information systems, the political and social leading body is drawing up prognosis and decision variants which are going to be turned into plans. The plans are being established and transmitted to the executive bodies, an improved management of the entire national economy being thus achieved. As can be noticed, the economic information system is playing an important role in this scheme.

In the conditions of the accelerated rate of raising production and because of the huge amounts of economic information, one of the fundamental targets of cybernetics and informatics is to elaborate the economic information and decisional system, capable of contributing to improving the mechanism of management of the economy.

By achieving a decisional information system on the scale of the whole economy and having the capacity of forecasting the dynamic picture of economy, in general, and of its component forces, we consider that the cybernetic management system can be applied with efficient results in the mechanism of guidance of economic life.

COORDINATES OF ROMANIA'S DEVELOPMENT

To estimate the probable quantitative evolution and the qualitative changes which will take place in each branch, 28 prognosis commissions on branches have been set up in Romania, as follows: Basis of raw materials and materials, energetics, metallurgy, the machine-building industry, the chemical industry, the light industry, the food industry, agriculture and silviculture, transport and telecommunications, etc.

Also, district commissions have been set up for elaborating prognoses, which will have to contribute to the justification of the policy of territorial distribution of capacities and productive forces.

Prognosis studies concern the following fields: Rapid and multilateral development with maximum efficiency of the productive forces in the branches of material production as an essential factor of the large increase of national income and of the progress of the whole of society; continuous modernization of productive activity, the wide-scale introduction of mechanization, automation and cybernetics, the steady improvement of technologies; growth and continuous improvement of the labour force and the rapid increase of social labour productivity; rational organization and better systematization of the country's territory, the creation of new town centres and the organization on scientific bases of the life of the villages so as to ensure a gradual approach of the village to the town; creation of a just relation between the accumulation and consumption funds, which should ensure systematically and continuously rising socialist production, parallel with the continuous rise in the people's living standards, through a rapid increase in the consumption fund and its distribution in the spirit of socialist equity; improvement of the organization, management and planning of the entire activity, ensuring an ever more active participation of the working class and of the entire people in the management of society; improvement of relations of production and relations among the members of our socialist society; raising of living standards of the entire people, creation of conditions for the ever fuller satisfaction of the requirements of all the members of society; a powerful increase in the cultural and educational level of the citizens and a considerable reduction of the differences between physical and intellectual work.

By applying the previously presented model a rough calculation has led to the following data regarding Romania's development until the year 1990:

	M.U.	1938	1972	1975	1990
Generation of electricity	Thousand million kWh	1.1	40.9	60.6	180-200
Steel output	Thousand tons	284	370	9700	20.000-25.000
National income per annum	Dollars/inhabitant	70-80	500-600	1000-1100	2500-3000
Mean age of population (longivity)	Per inhabitant	42	68	69	72-75

All these prognoses will determine the main directions of the growth of productive forces and will define the fundamental co-ordinates of economic development. At the same time, the prognoses will have to envisage the transformations which will take place in the structure and organization of society and to establish material, social and cultural conditions for a fuller satisfaction of requirements of all the citizens of our country.

A prognosis on the rise in material and cultural living standards considers the evolution of incomes and consumption of the population and the changes which will take place in the structure of demands for goods and services. Prognosis studies will have to outline solutions in connection with the extension of education and cultural, artistic, entertaining, tourist and health protection activities, housing, administrative and household work, individual and public transport, the extension of the commercial network, social and cultural constructions and complex problems of the environment as part of the urbanization and systematization of the territory.

The transition to a large and systematic activity in the elaboration of economic and social prognoses marks an important stage in the improvement of management and planning systems, based on the application of cybernetic methods.

In conclusion, in the prognosis of the social and economic development of Romania cybernetic concepts are called to play an essential role. The model presented represents the sketch of a pattern which has the advantage that, different from other models and due to its cybernetic character, allows us to obtain a realistic picture as true as possible and, at the same time, to ensure an improvement of the economic and social development of Romania.

RESOURCE ALLOCATION IN ECONOMIC CYBERNETIC SYSTEMS

STEFAN BÎRLEA

Centre of Economic Computation and Economic Cybernetics, Piata Romana No. 6, Bucharest, Romania

SUMMARY

The purpose of this paper is to present some properties of interconnected systems. Any cybernetic system receives resources produced by the other systems in the network. The outputs of any productive system are resources for consumer systems and can provide - through the transformation structure of these systems - the necessary resources for the initial productive system. In this framework it is possible to give a cybernetic specification of the whole process with models on four decision levels. The paper presents a mathematical description for formalizing these statements and an application to a cybernetic system in the field of science and technology.

GENERAL STRUCTURE OF THE MODEL

Interactions between cybernetics and modelling are increasing and becoming more significant. What can be affirmed already by now is, in our opinion, that econometric modelling with the aid of continual functions will refer in the future to systems with a very high aggregation degree, as a rule, at the level of the national economy. For industrial systems (enterprises, head offices and even branches) preponderant modelling will probably be that based on discrete variables.

The most adequate mathematical methods for measuring the scope of their activity are, in our view, those based on the utilization of ranged and polygonal functions. Likewise, the most appropriate measure unit is the value one, although in some cases it is more advantageous to work with physical units as well. Without claiming to make an exhaustive presentation, the model elaborated for the development of science and technology in the S.R. of Romania also comprises a practical demonstration of this idea.

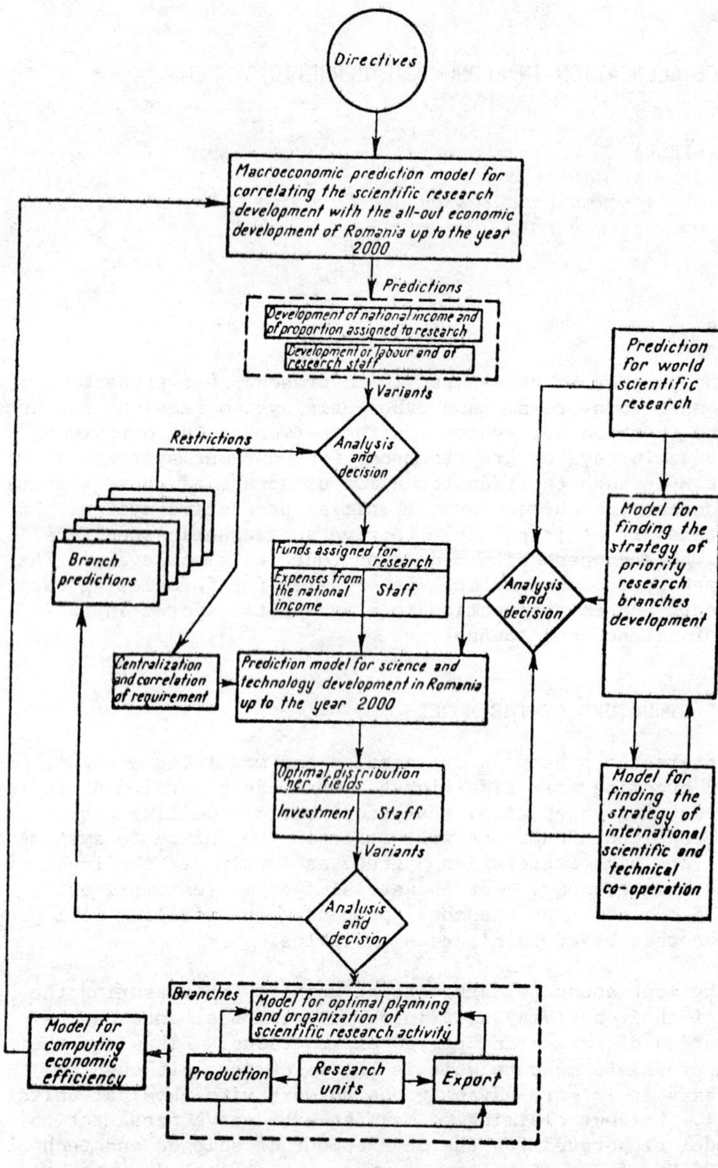
Directives
Macroeconomic prediction model for correlating the scientific research development with the all-out economic development of Romania up to the year 2000
Predictions
Development of national income and of proportion assigned to research
Development or labour and of research staff
Variants
Restrictions
Analysis and decision
Prediction for world scientific research
Model for finding the strategy of priority research branches development
Branch predictions
Funds assigned for research
Expenses from the national income
Staff
Analysis and decision
Centralization and correlation of requirement
Prediction model for science and technology development in Romania up to the year 2000
Optimal distribution per fields
Investment
Staff
Variants
Model for finding the strategy of international scientific and technical co-operation
Analusis and decision
Branches
Model for optimal planning and organization of scientific research activity
Model for computing economic efficiency
Production
Research units
Export

Fig. 1

On analyzing the problems related to the development, prediction and strategies for Romania's scientific research, the author has reached the conclusion that it is essential to draw up a number of cybernetic and economic models closely interconnected. Figure 1 offers a general view of such models, the manner in which they mutually supply information to each other and the way in which the output data of some of them become the input data (restrictions) of some others.

Taking into account the questions to be answered, we have concluded that it is necessary to draw up and study the following extension types of models:

a) Aggregate macro-economic models for correlating scientific research development with the general economic growth in the Socialist Republic of Romania. The author understand such models to be similar to the economic growth models, with the only difference that the branch of science stands out distinctly. These models shall underlie prediction for the development of the proportion of expenses assigned for research within the entire national income (or the final social product), as well as for the research staff in the context of the total labour force.

Denoting by Y_n the final social product created at moment n, we shall assume this to be a function of four variables: The amount of labour existing in economy L_n; the amount of fixed funds (as a rule, only the productive fixed funds shall be considered) K_n; the technological level attained in economy T_n; and the time factor n that stands for the general influence of the technical progress on the economic growth.

As a rule, as pointed out, we draw a distinction between the technological level T_n and the time factor n.

Hence:

$$Y_n = F(L_n, K_n, T_n, n)$$

The structure of the social product, according to its economic assignation, is given by the following relationship:

$$Y_n = A_n + I_n^s + B_n$$

where A_n stands for the funds assigned for production expansion, I_n^s is the expenditure for science, and B_n is the level of total resources assigned for social requirements of consumption.

The equation for the development of fixed funds in the sphere of material production is:

$$K^p_{n+1} = K^p_n - K^p_n \cdot K^p_n + a_n \cdot A_n$$

where ^p_n stands for the coefficient of physical and moral depreciation of the funds in the sphere of material production and a_n stands for the share of investment in productive fixed funds meant for expanding production. We have assumed that the volume of depreciation $_n \cdot K^p_n$ is proportional to the amount of funds.

The law funds evolution in the field of science K^s_p is of the same form, namely:

$$K^s_{n+1} = K^s_n - \lambda^s_n K^s_n + I^s_n$$

We have:

$$K_n = K^p_n + K^s_n$$

In general $\lambda^s_n >> \lambda^p_n$, since wear, particularly moral wear, has a far more intense action in science.

With reference to the technological level T_n, we shall assume it to depend on the level of effective research E_n, which in its turn depends on labour R_n existing in the field of research at moment n, fixed funds existing in the field K^s_n and labour existing in national economy L_n.

Total labour is considered an independent variable of the function of effective research, because the possibilities of selecting better gifted, talented and efficient research workers increase in direct proportion to the volume of L_n.

Consequently, the function of effective research is

$$E_n = G_n(R_n, K^s_n, L_n)$$

In this case, the technological level T_n depends on the level of effective research E_n and on the technological level at moment n-1, n-2, ..., $n-0_n$.

Therefore, the equation of technological level development is:

$$T_{n+1} = H_n(E_n, T_n, T_{n-1}, \ldots, T_{n-0_n})$$

where $H_n(.)$ are increasing functions in variables E and T and concave in variable E; hence:

$$\frac{\partial Hn}{\partial E} > 0; \quad \frac{\partial Hn}{\partial T} > 0; \quad \frac{\partial^2 H}{\partial E^2} < 0$$

and 0_n is a "delay" occuring naturally in the phenomenon.

b) Another class of models of the system contains those constructed for predicting general development of science on a world scale. In such models, one shall make use of all available information related to predictions drawn up in other countries, alongside with an inquiry, a Delphi-type investigation of large numbers of experts in all the fields of science and production.

c) Models for ascertaining strategy in view of developing some priority fields of Romanian science. With the aid of the information achieved through the prediction models described in b), and taking into account the traditions of and the potential to be attained by Romanian science, it will be necessary to predict the priority fields in which Romanian science is to develop.

From the standpoint of economic cybernetics, we think that such a model shall pertain to the class of dynamic games, in which one of the partners is Romanian science, and the other partner is the science of other countries.

d) If we consider the prediction models in the form of some co-operation dynamic games, we shall be able to draw up a number of predictions with regard to the possibilities and advantages of co-operating with other countries in certain fields.

As we can see in Fig. 2, the models described both at point c) and point d) provide information (input data-restrictions) for the model underlying the optimal configuration of Romanian science and technology.

e) Econometric models of prediction for the development of scientific research requirements in each branch of national economy.

By means of a previous deep economic analysis the main factors, which determine the research capacity development in each branch, have been discovered. Such elements, contingent upon the peculiarities of each branch, are production dynamics, investment dynamics (out of which arise investment for new technologies of an original concept), new products (out of which arise new products of an original concept), labour dynamics, and labour productivity dynamics, etc.

Prediction models underlying the minimal and maximal limits of the requirement for scientific research labour in each branch are models of an econometric type.

f) Dynamic models of prediction for science and technology development in Romania. Such models determine the development of an optimal distribution of necessary research staff and investment in fields and branches.

We stress once more that the concept of working out such models is a unitary cybernetic one, so that among all the types of models a permanent information flow will exist, and the alteration of an element in one of the models will enable the automatic correction of the whole system of results. We further describe the concept of the prediction model for the development of research capacity in Romania during 1971-1980, as well as a number of concrete results achieved in agreement with this model.

The main functions of model have as an object the optimization of resources distribution per potential consumers.

Based on the models described in section e, we assume that these consumers and previous development are known, as reflected by various indicators.

For each prediction element, the restrictions shall be generated by the situation that serves as a starting point, the stage attained when the prediction has been drawn and the set of values determined by the probable developments at the ultimate level of prediction, or at various intervals within this field.

A similar diagram for each prediction element and field is available, and with its aid we shall find the set of admissible solutions. It is obvious that for more complex circumstances the set of admissible solutions appears to be an intersection of the spaces pertaining to each prediction element.

The model contemplates the use of several prediction techniques for the correlated factors. In our opinion, this is of particular importance for, given the generally distinct nature of the resources (investment means, labour of different skill, etc.), distinct exploring techniques are required.

WORKING HYPOTHESES

In order to draw up the model we have considered the following working hypotheses:

1. Starting from Romanian experience and taking into account the situation existing in other countries, it has been assumed that the scientific national potential can adequately be expressed through the number of highly qualified staff carrying out scientific research work. Analyses carried through have shown that, owing to the diversity of the research activity, the measurement of the scientific potential by "the number of research workers" or "total number of wage earners" is not sound at present.

2. It has been necessary to make an adequate investigation, contingent upon the characteristic features of each field of science, regarding the proportion of highly qualified staff and other personnel concerned with research activities, as well as the number of highly qualified staff and the degree of provision with fixed funds, particularly with apparatus.

The following hypotheses have been assumed as regards the restrictions related to the way of development of certain branches:

a. The research capacity in each branch of national economy shall be developed in agreement with the assignments laid down in the general Directives of the Romanian Communist Party, the priority research programmes, the surveys carried out recently in order to improve the five year plan, as well as other assignments given to respective fields of activity.

b. The increase in the research activity shall be achieved in a per branch differentiated manner, depending on the properties they have got within the general programme of development of national economy.

c. A two- or threefold increase in the total number of highly qualified staff, as against their number in 1970, shall be achieved in the priority branches of national economy before the end of 1975.

d. Each highly qualified wage earner shall be provided with a certain amount of fixed funds, particularly with apparatus, as well as with assistance personnel (middle-school employees and workers), so as to ensure adequate conditions and employment for the creative capacity of the highly qualified staff.

To this end,,a per branch differentiated ratio between total research personnel and highly qualified research workers has been considered up to 1975; this ratio varies from 1 3 to 5 0, and it was correlated with the suggestions advanced by the ministries and included in the staff training programme for 1971-1980.

3. The prediction has been worked out for 24 branches.

DESCRIPTION OF THE MATHEMATICAL MODEL

After every technical and economic aspect of the problem has been cleared up, a mathematical model is worked out. In broad lines we discern here three essential points: ascertaining the unknowns of the problem; working out the restrictions; and drawing up the objective function.

The unknowns of the problem, in agreement with working hypothesis No. 1, are:

x_i^n stands for the number of highly qualified wage earners in branch i, in the year n

$i = 1,2,\ldots\ldots\ldots\ldots,24$
$n = 1975,\ 1980$

Consequently, for the two prediction levels we have 48 unknowns in all.

Restrictions

Restriction 1. The total number of research wage earners on a national economy scale shall not exceed a level S, ascertained in an exogene manner. This level interfering in the model as a restriction is an output of the economic growth model as described in section a).

Consequently:

$$\sum_{i=1}^{24} \alpha_i^n \chi_{ik}^n \le S_k^n \quad n = 1975,\ 1980 \quad k = 1,2,3,4,$$

were $\overset{n}{i}$ is the total number of research wage earners as against one highly qualified research worker in branch i, and

$$\alpha_i^{1975} = \alpha_i^{1980}$$

We specify that the very element α_i^n is a prediction element.

Restriction 2. Total investment for science shall not exceed level I, as ascertained in an exogene manner; this restriction shall represent an output of the economic growth model.

Consequently, we have restriction;

$$\sum_{i=1}^{24} \beta_{ik}^n \chi_{ik}^n \leq I_k^n \qquad n = 1975, 1980 \quad k = 1,2,\ldots,5$$

where β_i^n is the investment per highly qualified research worder in branch i.

One of the restrictions taken into account when predicting values has been the provision for a technical equipment increase in 10 per cent of fixed funds per highly qualified research worker in 1975 as against 1970. Likewise, based on some predictive calculations, it has been estimated that

$$\beta_i^{1980} = 1 \cdot 3\beta_i^{1975}$$

Restriction 3. Investment in apparatus shall represent at least level $_1^n$. The simulation variants of solutions have been similar to those for restriction 2, where

$$I_{1,k}^n = 0.6\ I_k^n (k = 1,2,\ldots,5;\ n = 1975,\ 1980)$$

was assumed.

We have the following restrictions:

$$I_{1k}^n \leq \sum_{i=1}^{24} \gamma_i^n \chi_{ik}^n \leq I_k^n \qquad n = 1975, 1980 \quad k = 1,2,\ldots,5$$

where: γ_i^n is the investment in apparatus per highly qualified research worker in branch i.

When working out prediction for indicators i the provision has to be considered for an increase in at least 0.20 per cent of apparatus equipment per highly qualified research worker as against the year 1970.

We have:

$$\gamma_i^{1980} = 1.4\ \gamma^{1975}$$

Restriction 4. The research equipment with import devices shall be effected within the limits of the fund assigned for this purpose: V^n

The following variants have been considered:

Variant 1: $V_{1,k}^n = 0.5\ I_{1,k}^n$ $\quad n = 1975, 1980$

Variant 2: $V_{2,k}^n = 0.65\ I_{1,k}^n$ $\quad k = 1,2,\ldots,5$

The restriction is:

$$\sum_{i=1}^{24} \delta_i^n\ \chi_{ik}^n \leq Vek \qquad \begin{array}{l} n = 1975,\ 1980 \\ e = 1,2;\ k = 1,2,\ldots,5 \end{array}$$

where δ_i^n is the equipment with imported devices per highly qualified research worker in branch i.

We have the following variants:

$$\delta_i^{1980} = 2\delta_i^{1975}$$

$$\delta_i^{1980} = 1.5\delta_i^{1975}$$

$$v^{1980} = 4v^{1975}$$

Restriction 5. These restrictions concern the minimal (respectively maximal) level to be attained (respectively not to be exceeded) by scientific research in each branch.

Consequently:

$$A_i^n \leq X_i^n \leq B_i^n \qquad \begin{array}{l} i = 1,2,\ldots,24 \\ n = 1975,\ 1980 \end{array}$$

Values A_i^n and B_i^n have been found with the aid of prediction models similar to those described under section e).

We stress that a most accurate ascertainment of these two levels is of particular importance, for they play an essential part in finding the space within which solutions can be simulated. As a rule, the most frequent situations in which these values have been found in different variants have been:

For the year 1975:

$$E^{1970} \leq A_i^{1975}$$

$$1.1E^{1970} \leq B_i^{1975} \leq 3E^{1970}$$

where: E^{1970} stands for the existing staff at the level of the year 1970.

Objective Functions

For this mathematical model several types of objective functions have been considered, taking into account various economic criteria, as well as a number of aggregate objective functions.

Objective function I. The branches of national economy whose activity (production) increases more quickly have a priority in the assignment of scientific research staff.

Consequently, the objective functions is:

$$\max \sum_{i=1}^{24} p_i^n X_i^n \quad n = 1975, 1980$$

where p_i^{1975} is the production increase of branch i as against 1970; and p_i^{1980} has a similar meaning.

Objective function II. The branches of national economy developing more quickly (involving higher investments) have a priority in the assignment of scientific research staff.

Consequently:

$$\max \sum_{i=1}^{24} q_i^n X_i^n \quad n = 1975, 1980$$

where q_i is the absolute value in units of the investment.

Objective function III. The branches of national economy in which new products, made on the basis of an original national concept, attain higher values, have a priority in the assignment of scientific research staff.

Consequently:

$$\max \sum_{i=1}^{24} \lambda_i^n X_i^n \qquad n = 1975,\ 1980$$

where λ_i is the absolute value in units (thousands of lei) of the new products made during the five-year period.

Objective function IV. The branches of national economy in which the total number of wage earners has a higher proportion have a priority in the assignment of scientic staff.

Consequently:

$$\max \sum_{i=1}^{24} r_i^n X_i^n \qquad n = 1975,\ 1980$$

where r_i^{1975} is the wage earners growth index in 1975 as against 1960.

r_i^{1980} has a similar meaning.

Objective function v. The branches of national economy in which productivity must increase at quicker rates have a priority in the assignment of scientific research staff.

Consequently:

$$\max \sum_{i=1}^{24} t_i^n X_i^n \qquad n = 1975,\ 1980$$

where t_i^{1975} is the labour productivity growth index at the level of the year 1975 as against 1970, and t_i^{1980} has a similar meaning.

Objective function VI. The branches of national economy in which commodity-output expenses per 1,000 lei must decrease more sharply have a priority in the assignment of scientific research staff.

Consequently:

$$\min \sum_{i=1}^{24} z_i^n X_i^n \quad n = 1975, 1980$$

where Z_i^{1975} is the absolute value (in lei) of the expenses made per 1,000 lei of commodity-output at the level of the year 1975, and Z_i^{1980} has a similar meaning.

Beside the solutions reached on the basis of these objective functions, a number of solutions making use of aggregate objective functions of the form:

$$\max \sum_{j=i}^{6} C_j F_j$$

have also been simulated, writing $F_1,\ldots,F$ for the objective-functions, described above, whereas proportions C_j have been ascertained, in different variants, based on some inquiries carried out among specialists in various fields and organizations.

As an illustration, we give further three estimates for such proportions.

Proportions of the Objective Functions

	I	II	III
1. Gross output	0.5	0.7	0.8
2. Investment in agreement with new technologies of an original national conception	0.3	0.9	1.0
3. New products made in agreement with an original national conception	0.2	0.9	1.0
4. Total number of wage earners per central body	0.6	1.0	0.7
5. Labour productivity	0.1	0.8	0.8
6. Expenses per 1,000 lei of commodity output	0.4	0.5	0.7

All this clearly illustrates the tremendous number of variants in which the model has been worked out. In order to shorten the performance time on the computer, a L.P.S. (Linear Programming System of the I.B.M. programs library at the

Computation Centre of the Economic Cybernetics Department, the Academy of Economic Studies) has been used to simulate the different prediction variants.

All the details of the problem, the different variants for the model parameters, as well as the optimal solution are stored on magnetic discs in index cards that can be pe⁻manently analyzed. When considering a new variant, this shall be computed starting from the previous optimal variant by updating it, without resuming the whole operation from the very beginning.

A particular advantage offered by the L.P.S. program is related to the variety and abundance of information provided by the post-optimal linear programming analysis, which is obtained by request. This post-optimal analysis enables a through investigation of the behaviour of the solution around the optimal point, when some of the parameters of the problem are altered, as well as the finding of the variation limits of these parameters, on condition that the optimal solution is hot altered.

CONCLUSIONS

By solving the models described in this paper, valuable information regarding the trends of scientific research capacity development during 1971-1980 has been obtained. The experience accumulated so far has once more stressed the efficiency that can be achieved by making use of economic cybernetic methods and of computation techniques in working out long-term predictions. Likewise, the necessity of simulating a great many variants has become apparent, out which the decision-making factors will choose the most efficacious variants.

We have to add that with aid of such models it was possible to substantiate at a higher level the provisions of the five-year plan concerning the research capacity growth, closely related to the assignments contained in the framework of national economy growth.

THE STABILIZING RATE OF ECONOMIC GROWTH AND PROSPECTS FOR ITS ACHIEVEMENT — THE YUGOSLAV CASE

N. ČOBELJIĆ

Dept. of Economics, University of Belgrade, Belgrade, Yugoslavia

SUMMARY

This paper deals with the problem of how to achieve stability as a precondition of an optimal development of the big economic system, with Yugoslavia as an example. While considering the direct prospects for the achievement of the stabilizing rate of economic growth, the author also deals with the main constraints in the Yugoslav economy. These constraints fall into three groups: a) Constraints arising from the amount of new investments; b) constraints due to structural disproportions and, finally, c) those connected with foreign trade. The author then examines the main goals of development of a big economic system vis-a-vis the most important management parameters for their achievement under specific Yugoslav conditions, in the light of stability of the system.

INTRODUCTION

If we follow the system approach to economic development, then the optimization of this development ought to be our main self-managing goal. As far as the rate of economic growth is concerned, this would imply that the partial optimal growth rates of various sectors should be coordinated in the first place. The next step is the correction of the growth rate of the whole economy, as originally envisaged. It is only in this way that we obtain the optimal rate of economic growth, which unites in itself the interests of both the whole and its parts, whereby the primacy of the whole must be borne in mind, while the interests of its parts must be likewise given due consideration.

However, such an optimal rate of economic growth cannot yet be determined in practice for reasons connected with our inadequate knowledge of optimization of large economic system.

It is a matter of common knowledge that the calculation of the optimal rate is impeded by three main reasons. These are: a) The immeasurability of a large number of influential factors; b) the inability to determine precisely the degree of certainty or uncertainty of factors, and c) under-developed methods by means of which we calculate the degree of their limitation. However, these methods are one of the main conditions of any optimization.

Being unable to determine directly the optimal rate of economic growth, we have decided to deal in this paper with the stabilizing growth rate and prospects for its achievement under the present conditions of the Yugoslav economy. We shall try to determine it by means of the main variables underlying a stable economic development, which have been verified in practice. The stabilizing rate of economic growth will be derived from the development of the Yugoslav economy to date as well as from various conditions which call for the achievement of such a rate of economic growth for the future period. It will be best if we determine right now the rates of economic growth we bear in mind; we maintain that this growth rate ought to amount to 7-8 percent. It may be explained on the ground of the corresponding growth rate of employment (l) and of the growth rate of labour productivity (p), that is:

$$r = l + p = /3 \div 3.5/ + /4 \div 4.5/ = 7 - 8\%$$

Of course, such a rate of economic growth presupposes also a corresponding rate of gross fixed investments, which we obtain in the following way:

$$l + p = \frac{i}{k} ,$$

where i is the rate of gross fixed investments in the economy and k the capital coefficient. It follows that

$$i = k/l + p/ = 3[\ /3 \div 3.5/ + /4 \div 4.5/\ ] = 21 - 24\%$$

We have assumed that the capital coefficient will be 3. This is to what it amounts approximately today. Present conditions in the Yugoslav economy are such that we cannot rely upon a more favourable capital coefficient. They suggest rather that it is likely to increase, which might result in corresponding changes in the assumed rate of gross fixed investments. The rate of investments which would provide for the corresponding rate of employment would be:

$$i_1 = k.l = 3./3 \div 3.5/ = 9 - 10.5\%,$$

while the rate of investments which enables the increase of labour productivity, i.e. the necessary rate of technical progress, ought to be:

$$i_2 = k.p = 3\ ./4 \div 4.5/ = 12 - 13.5\%$$

I maintain that such a qualification of the rate of economic growth is very close to what the Yugoslav economists bear in mind and that there would be no major differences of opinion in this respect. Economists know very well how valuable high growth rates are. Following Peter Wiles [1], I would only like to add that rapid economic growth is the best thing for any country, particularly if an underdeveloped country like Yugoslavia is involved.

I shall explain in brief the above-mentioned qualification of the rate of economic growth in order to define it or to show what it really means to the Yugoslav economy.

The growth rate of 7-8 percent per annum provides for a minimum rate of employment under Yugoslav conditions, that is for such a rate of employment which enables only the absorption of the current increment of the active population, without touching upon and without decreasing the large reserve of labour which is to be found in the agrarian overpopulation. A lower rate of employment would imply a further increase of the present number of unemployed workers and an unaltered emigration of the labour force abroad. It would bring about high internal tension and limit possibilities and perspectives for the employment of a new educated personnel. It would jeopardize the political and for that matter also the economic stability of the system.

A similar statement can be made also for the assumed growth rate of productivity. Its achievement seems to be indispensable if we want to keep pace with the contemporary technical progress to some extent at least. A lower rate of productivity would imply technical stagnation and lower economic efficiency of economic development. It would aggravate the unenviable position of Yugoslavia as small and underdeveloped country in the world competition and would act as a destabilizing factor of the social system.

Finally, a considerable deviation from the above mentioned stabilizing rate of economic growth would aggravate possibilities for the gradual approach of Yugoslavia to developed countries. The distance between it and developed countries of the world would remain unchanged. Of course, such a situation would favour neither the socio-political nor the economic stabilization of the system.

We are able now to qualify the above mentioned rate of economic growth of 7-8% more properly. Under present Yugoslav conditions it plays the role of a *homeostat*. The role of a stabilizer of the Yugoslav economic system. The system cannot reckon upon a considerable stabilization unless this rate is reached.

ECONOMIC GROWTH

Let us concern ourselves for a while with the rates of economic growth which were achieved in Yugoslavia throughout the last decade, particularly in recent years. These were the following rates: during the period 1959-1964 the growth rate amounted to 9.4 percent, for the whole decade from 1961 until 1970 it was 6.6 percent, while it fell to 5.5 percent during the last six years (1965-1970).

Before explaining why the decline in the growth rate meant a certain destabilization of the Yugoslav economy, we have to make two important statements. First, not even under conditions of a highly stable economy can we expect that the growth rate will accelerate or be maintained on a high level over a longer period of its development. It is altogether normal for the rate of economic growth to fluctuate from time to time and to slow down at higher levels of development. Second, the increase of social welfare cannot be identified with the pace at which the material production is growing. Bearing in mind these two remarks, we shall consider the recent decline of the growth rate of the Yugoslav economy, trying to find out how to keep it stable. We mean thereby the fuller utilization of its productive factors, particularly of large reserves of labour force and of existing natural resources, as well as of all the potential sources of accumulation for new fixed investments.

We are sticking therefore to considerations which indicate that a growth rate of 5.5 percent, which we were having during the last six years, cannot help us to solve the key problems of our economic and social development. Such a growth rate has brought about a high level of unemployment in the country, while many workers emigrated abroad. Yugoslavia faced thus cumulative effects of unemployment as well as the fact that problems involved in the employment of the labour force have become *more important* than they were in any period of the post war development.

The adverse effects of the lower rate of employment (this rate amounted on the average to 1.1 percent in the period

1965-1970) could not be, under the given circumstances, offset by a more rapid increase of labour productivity; the rate of productivity did not accelerate. Namely, a low growth rate does not enable an increase of the productive and technical efficiency of the economy. All the three interrelated circumstances, i.e. the fall of the growth rate, the fall in the rate of employment and the inadequate increase of labour productivity, stemmed mainly, even though not solely, from the rapid decline of the rate of fixed investments in the economy.

Economic repercussions involved in the decline of the rate of investments have been considerable, particularly in the area of structural relations in material production. The slowdown of the rate of investments frustrated attempts which were to smooth out the deep structural disproportion between the production of raw materials and manufacturing industries. Much valuable time was lost in this way, during which essential changes could be made. Namely, not only was the disproportion not smoothed out, but it even increased towards the end of the sixties. The production of raw materials plays a many-sided role in the system of inter-industry relations. Lagging behind others, it caused tremendous dislocations in the whole network of interrelated sectors of production. These dislocations manifest themselves in the under-employment of existing facilities, in the *immobilization* of a considerable portion of the social capital, which is not used in production.

This deeper structural disproportion is the main obstacle in the way of the expansion of our export and the main cause of the rapid growth of the import. The domestic production is highly dependent on the import of raw materials and other means for present manufacturing activity, since it abounds in structural defects. A *new cycle aggravating* our balance of trade and payment has been launched in this way, which is characterized by a rapid increase of the divergence between the commodity export and import.

Our above-mentioned data on under-employment and on the aggravation of the balance of payment should be explained more fully. Talking about under-employment we have to say that the above-mentioned stabilizing rate of economic growth would enable us to absorb the whole surplus labour force in the near future. This is impractical since the agrarian overpopulation is still considerable in Yugoslavia. In addition to this, it adopted the principle of the altogether free movement of the labour force, which implies that it may abandon agriculture freely and settle in town. What the stabilizing rate ought to solve in this area is the employment of the current increment of the active population. As far as the aggravation of the balance of payment is concerned, it must be mentioned that small countries cannot easily avoid it, if the growth is to be a relatively stable one. This follows from statistical data for small countries in the stage of their accelerated industrial development; Yugoslavia is just in the middle of such a stage. However, in like manner as with employment, we have to explain in greater detail what we have to expect from a stabilizing rate of economic growth. It ought to prevent, in the main, a more rapid increase of the deficit in the balance of payment than the rate of economic growth and development in the opposite direction.

LIMITING FACTORS OF GROWTH

The question in which we are interested now has to do with prospects for the achievement of the above-mentioned stabilizing rate of economic growth. In other words, did we already pass through a very unstable period and is it finally over? Unfortunately, we cannot give a positive answer to this question. Structural problems of production and some vital questions involved in the functioning of the Yugoslav system have not yet been solved, so that they will be a serious *limiting factor* of economic growth in the years to come. I shall try to indicate briefly some most important limiting factors.

1. *The rate of necessary investments* is likely to be one of the limiting factors. What is at stake is not any rate of investments, but a rate which could increase the employment and help to smooth out the existing material disporportions and add to the necessary gradual technical and technological tramsformation of the economy. One of the general and vital preconditions to this is that the growth of real income of the population be kept approximately within limits of the rise in labour productivity, so that the *difference* between the overall rate of economic growth and the rate of the increase in productivity might secure sufficient sources for the financing of economic development.

The situation which prevailed up to the present time was abnormal in this respect. Personal incomes were rising more rapidly than labour productivity and the national production, accumulation used to be transferred into consumption, while the deficit in the balance of payment served in large part not the needs of development but to finance current consumption. All this happened under conditions of a high level of unemployment, when a considerable percentage of the work force left the country to find jobs abroad. Some main economic variables rose in the following order during the period 1965-1970: the real incomes of the population rose at the rate of 6.5

percent, the social product at the rate of 5.5 percent, the labour productivity rose by 4.4 percent and that of employment by 1.1 percent [2]. Such a movement indicates undoubtedly an altogether formulated policy of development and particularly a lack of coordination of the main factors of economic growth.

There are various observations which make us doubt that the rate of investments in the economy will be high enough in the years to come:

a) There are no corresponding rules of behaviour and instruments in our system which would direct the economic subjects to a socially rational distribution of newly created values. It is impossible to achieve the desired results if the rate of investments is formed only on the basis of free actions of economic units. What we are most concerned about is the fact that there are ample possibilities in our country for the transfer of accumulation from the economy into the private sector and into the population sector, where it is spent for non-productive purposes. Namely, the population buys real estate or articles of luxury, which do not match the development level of the country. The non-liquidity in the economy has been much discussed. What has been altogether ignored here is the fact that one stratum of the population has in its possession a larger stock of liquid assets than the whole Yugoslav economy. The bad organization of flows of accumulation and the low efficiency of the social control over them have resulted in the formation and expansion of those channels through which accumulation flows from the economic sphere into the sphere of consumption and of private activities.

b) Consumer psychosis and the year-long habit that more is spent than it is produced do not favour the formation of accumulation and a rapid economic growth. What threatens the Yugoslav society is a danger that it will become a consumption-oriented society without the corresponding material basis. The Yugoslav economist Cveta Mlakar said in one of her recent writings that the Yugoslav economy and society have behaved for several years already as fanatic consumers [3].

c) The limiting factor in the formation of the necessary rate of investments will be, among others, existing material disproportions in the composition of production. These disproportions are the reason why the natural composition of accumulation will be characterized by a heavy scarcity of many products which are essential for investments (equipment and chief raw materials). It will be more and more difficult for Yugoslavia to overcome them because of the already mentioned appreciable deficit in the balance of payment.

d) Disturbances may also be expected because of some opinions underrating the overall economic significance of accumulation in the economic development. An extremely objectivistic laisser-faire point of view is opposed, in fact, to any other socially efficient settlement of relations between accumulation and consumption. The echo of these opinions may be found, unfortunately, also in the writings of some leading economists, who suggest the idea that it is possible to achieve a high growth rate of production also with a lower rate of accumulation, thanks to the efficient functioning of the market mechanism [4]. To talk under present conditions about a lower rate of accumulation when there is a high level of unemployment in the country alongside of large structural disturbances would imply that we are ignoring the actual problems of the Yugoslav economy.

2. *Structural disproportions* in material production will be, in addition to the rate of investments, the next problem which cannot be easily overcome. These disproportions are characterized by a growing deficit in the production of raw materials and products for the current manufacture in general. It is because of them that the Yugoslav development has been characterized throughout a whole decade by an under-employment of manufacturing facilities, which fluctuates between 45 and 60 percent in some industries. The level of unemployed facilities indicates that funds of production are rather passive and that there are, on the other hand, latent possibilities for the growth of industrial production and of the national income. It sounds like a paradox at first sight that in a country which has got ample resources of labour force there exist, at the same time, under-employed though available productive facilities. If we add thereto the former statement on the inadequate domestic accumulation, then this under-employment of facilities is still less tolerable.

It is impossible to achieve high growth rates of industrial production as well as a fuller employment of productive factors unless this disproportion between primary and manufacturing industries is overcome. Yugoslavia will not be able to create more stable conditions for the employment of its working population until these productive potentials are made use of. The problem is not a new one; it became evident a long time ago, but it was not included into the economic policy. The system did simply not find corresponding methods to solve it in an organized and decisive way. There are no clear indications for the time being as to the way in which the new development plan and economic policy will treat it during the years to come. We know, however, that any further ignorance of these material disproportions would breed more and more critical situations in the Yugoslav economy and keepen the sources of its instability.

3. *Foreign trade* is another equally serious limiting factor impeding the achievement of the stabilizing rate of economic growth. The expansion of the industrial development is becoming more and more dependent on the import of raw materials and semi-finished products. The growth of industrial output of 10 percent was accompanied by a proportional growth of import during the fifties. The coefficients of the flexibility of import rose sharply towards the end of the sixties. Given a growth rate of output in industry of 10 per cent, the import of products for manufacture is more than twice as large. We may derive thereof *the firm limits* with which any higher growth rate of industrial output will meet. Such a pressure on the import can obviously not last long in view of the present amount of deficit in the balance of trade and the high indebtedness of Yugoslavia abroad.

The above-mentioned weak points concerning the composition of the Yugoslav output in the sphere of foreign trade have brought about the formation of a vicious circle, with which small countries are very well acquainted. In order to expand production more rapidly, we have to import more raw materials. Greater import calls for greater export, since import is in the last instance a function of the revenue from export. However, a greater export is possible if output is expanding and if it is expanding rapidly, which depends, again, on the heavier import of raw materials. Of course, this closed circle may be interrupted only if the domestic production of primary and semi-finished products is growing. This would enable a fuller utilization of manufacturing facilities and their heavier export. The heavier export would, on its part, bring about a heavier import. The fuller utilization of facilities would result not only in the growth of production and export but also in the reduction of unit costs of production, which would very much improve the competitive power of the Yugoslav export.

We have only mentioned the most important limiting factors which the Yugoslav economic development has faced and is still going to face in years to come. However, there are more of them and they are more complex. But even if we present them in a succinct form, they do highlight the seriousness of the economic position and its inevitable repercussions on the future rate of the Yugoslav development.

CONCLUSIONS

The policy of development and solutions in the system of the functioning of the economy ought to be *aimed uniquely* at the maximum moderation of effects of the above-mentioned limiting factors. If these solutions are conceived independently of the above-mentioned pressing problems of the economy, then they will not bring us closer to stability, but rather farther away from it.

We can reckon neither upon the liberalization of the domestic market nor upon the liberalization of the foreign trade, nor even upon the desired higher degree of independence of the enterprise until the Yugoslav economy has solved the existing problems involved in its composition. Under conditions of large disturbances and instability in the composition it is impossible to build up and to promote a reasonable system of business activities, since the main criteria for a reasonable behaviour have got lost under such an inadequately settled development. Market methods of business activity may only function successfully if the composition of production is more balanced and if the economy has reached a higher level of stability.

We shall try to be optimistic at this moment; we shall assume that the Yugoslav system will be strong enough to solve efficiently problems involved in the formation of the necessary rate of investments. We also assume that the investment policy will solve the vital problems associated with the composition of production. We make these assumptions even though we are perhaps not justified to do so if we bear in mind the economic development throughout the last decade. The question that now arises is whether we may even under these assumptions reckon upon a considerable acceleration of the Yugoslav economic growth throughout the next few years or whether the above-mentioned stabilizing rate is likely to be achieved.

It is, of course, not easy to give a positive answer to such a question. Errors of the past, which were present for a whole decade, cannot pass unpunished. Problems connected to the composition of production are no *short-term problems* and they cannot be solved through short-term measures. It takes, of course, a somewhat longer time period to settle them because of the nature of disproportions, which can be overcome neither easily nor rapidly. What is involved are new productive facilities, whose up-building calls for a high concentration of resources and for a longer time of activization. The cycle throughout which they will be constructed and after which they will be able to yield full effects lasts for 5-6 years. The Yugoslav economy will come across large difficulties during this time period, a scarcity of essential products for investments and for current manufacture, an inadequate utilization of productive facilities, which is the main factor limiting the more rapid industrial uprise.

We are driven, therefore, to the conclusion that Yugoslav development will be still affected by *destabilizing elements* throughout the next few years. They will manifest themselves in the under-employment of productive factors, in an economic growth which will not correspond to Yugoslav requirements, and in a considerable deficit in the balance of foreign trade. A reasonable policy of development could undoubtedly shorten this critical period. However, if the existing weak points in the composition of production are not overcome systematically, then will the Yugoslav economy soon be in serious economic trouble and it will have to make much greater efforts in order to achieve a stable economic growth.

REFERENCES

1. P. WILES, "Growth versus choice", *Economic Journal 266*, 244 (June, 1956).

2. *Statistical Yearbook of Yugoslavia* 98-99 and 112 (1971).

3. C. MLAKAR, "The commodity character of business activity under the self-managing socialist economic system", *Self-Managing Socialist Economic System* (Belgrade, 1971), p.20.

4. J. SIROTKOVIĆ, "Theoretical problems involved in the economic system of the Yugoslav self-managing society", *Ibid.*, p.34.

TOWARDS PROCESSES OF DECISION MAKING FOR CONSUMPTION

H. ABELE

Institut fuer Wirtschafts- und Sozialpolitik (Department of Economics)

P.P. SINT

Interfakultaeres Rechenzentrum (Computer Centre), University of Vienna, Austria

SUMMARY

Traditionally the consumption behaviour of an individual unit is viewed as a problem of maximizing a given static utility function with respect to several constraints. We try, however, to center our interest on the process of arriving at a consumption decision. The stimulating factors in the regulation of this decision process are studied in their dynamic interaction. As a special feature of our approach we try to remove the classical constraint of a fixed consumption space and study one possibility to introduce new goods in the economic system. We use simulation technique to scrutinize the model.

INTRODUCTION

Recent research has shown that the explanation of consumer behaviour may be fruitfully given by various disciplines [2]. The long dominating approach of economic theory has become more and more questionable and, therefore, a number of scholars have attempted to replace this narrow view by a general concept including psychological, sociological, and economic elements alike. In a similar way the focus of interest has broadened. Economic theory tries to explain budget decisions as being an allocation of scarce resources, income and money, to the given ends represented by a utility function or a preference ordering. Besides the income allocation a number of studies have given explanations of brand choices, purchases, information acquisition, and so on [6]. As a consequence, the decision process of the consumer, be it an individual or a household, becomes more and more complex. The great advantage of a utility function, its conceptual simplicity and elegance, cannot suffice for the process of selecting consumption goods any further. It is interesting to note, however, that in modern theory the role of the utility function is nothing more than to serve as a *choice* function, whereas the complexity of the decision process brings us back to the ancient concepts of utility being a concept with material content, eventually a complicated multidimensional measure.

Given the need to replace the utility approach by a more realistic concept one faces great difficulties. Obviously there are a great number of interactions of the individual and his environment which consists of goods and other individuals as well. Hence one is led to conclude that information plays an important role in several respects in the consumer's decision process [3,6,8]. A seminal approach is to view the individual consumer as part of a larger system, the economy, and information as one of the links between the subsystem and its embedding. The requirement of a certain degree of "connectedness" of the system accompanies thus even an extreme micro-oriented research strategy. In a comparable manner proofs of the existence of general economic equilibrium have to make use of macro-economic features of the economic system.

Such a piecemeal strategy brings along some problems concerning identification of various parts and validation of the model. On the one hand, it may be easier to estimate parameters on the micro-level, but on the other hand this advantage may turn out to be mere illusion, because one has ignored the "disturbing" feedbacks of the system. In any case we think that the difficulties do not look unsurmountable and we believe that it should be possible to build a macro-model of an economy based on an elaborated decision process model of economic agents at the micro-level, the consumer's decisions serving as a starting point.

THEORETICAL CONCEPT

In order to prepare an adequate framework for the consumer's decision process one should consequently rely on the progress achieved in the study of *Artificial Intelligence* and other branches of Computer Sciences. Since our intellectual capacity turned out to be rather limited, however, we decided to concentrate on the economic aspects first and to reduce the considerations of other influences and processes as far as possible. Thus one may regard our study as an attempt to enrich the traditional view of economic theory and to give a progress report.

"Economic theory has been primarily concerned with the exchange process, with little explicit interest in looking beyond the point of sale" [9], but we have worked hard to remedy the serious defect of traditional theory "that time is not important, whereas it may very well be that time is of the essence " [5]. In our view the consumer's decision process involves time in several respects, giving rise to a separation of the decision into two dimensions. One is concerned with the allocation of financial resources to desired acquisitions in the form of a purchase plan — this should include the explanation of the distribution of purchases over time, and the other is dedicated to the flow aspect of the use of goods itself. The consumer manages thus his consumption stream in a way similar to the decisions of a producer, although the processes appear fundamentally different at first sight.

Another important feature of our approach is the distinction between goods and attributes [7]. All goods have attributes, which the consumer chooses and then tries to find goods matching this desire. The consumption plan of the consumer, therefore, does not consist of single separated items but of a mental image, a "*Gestalt*".

The organization of the decision process corresponds to the hierarchical structure of the selection problem. One mainly finds three levels allowing for feedbacks and dynamic influences. The top level is a description of the state of satisfaction of the consumer where we distinguish four different fundamental needs: Nutrition, housing, clothing, and social needs. The consumer tries to achieve a balanced level of satisfaction of these needs. The dynamic nature of the problem is represented by both experiences and expectations playing a role in the performance indicator.

Attributes provide contributions to satisfaction which decrease along with the additional amount of the attribute used. It should be noted, however, that one cannot consume attributes without goods to which they are tied. As the next step it is necessary to search for goods on the basis of the desired attributes in order to achieve the desired ratio of the levels of satisfaction of the fundamental needs. Both relations, between fundamental needs and attributes, and between attributes and goods, are dependent on subjective factors of the individual and may be conceived as uncertain and subject to learning; here basically cognitive activities and memory processes enter the scene. We introduce only a limited amount of learning in the form of a post choice process, because we assume that the consumer has correct information about the attributes of a good after he has used the good.

A further complication arises because of the different relations among goods. We assume goods to be grouped in 'bundles' in accordance with their attributes. If the goods are complementary, it is necessary to have both goods for use to gain satisfaction at all. Substitutive goods point to an easy replacement of one by the other in the purchase plan helping to save deliberation effort and time.

Monetary variables, income and prices, have a twofold influence on the decisions. They are subject of an accounting routine which adapts the stock of wealth according to inflow and outflow of financial resources, and they govern the composition of the purchase plan and the replacement of goods on the list. We assume in the present version both income and prices to be constant, although this must be regarded as not too realistic nowadays.

A number of serious theoretical problems especially concerning the performance measure of the individual consumer, have been solved in a pragmatic way. We are experimenting with alternative solutions and hope to improve these aspects according to the explicit inclusion of cognitive elements by further research.

THE MODEL

The art of model building is identical with the ability to retain as much as possible of an almost too ambitious research programme, when one's ideas are translated into a set of assumptions and hypotheses for deriving conclusions. We face the same difficulties in our work, even more because we decided to write a program and to use the computer for experiments. Our compromise has been to take, we admit, simple versions of the relevant elements, but to develop a general framework which is open for further implementations. Thus the present outlay of the model has several deficiencies we are aware of, but which are used because of simplicity.

The central point of the model is the shopping list and the process of arriving at an updated version of this list. Those goods which have turned out to be unsuccessful in the past, e.g. if goods have other attributes than thought, are changed. Another cause for revision of the shopping list is the appearance of new promising alternatives [1,4]. New goods may be added to the 'general' list during each period. Their probability to become known is higher than that for goods already in the market, portraying the greater effort to make them better known. 'Old' goods may get the label new as well indicating e.g. a special campaign promoting the good.

Naturally the probability of getting wrong information is higher as well.

As we already mentioned the process of choice is handled by means of an intermediate factor, namely the attributes. It is clear, however, that the price of the 'superior' good may be inhibiting, so that no switch to another good takes place. As in reality time is scarce and thus the updating of the shopping list may be terminated before the optimum composition is reached.

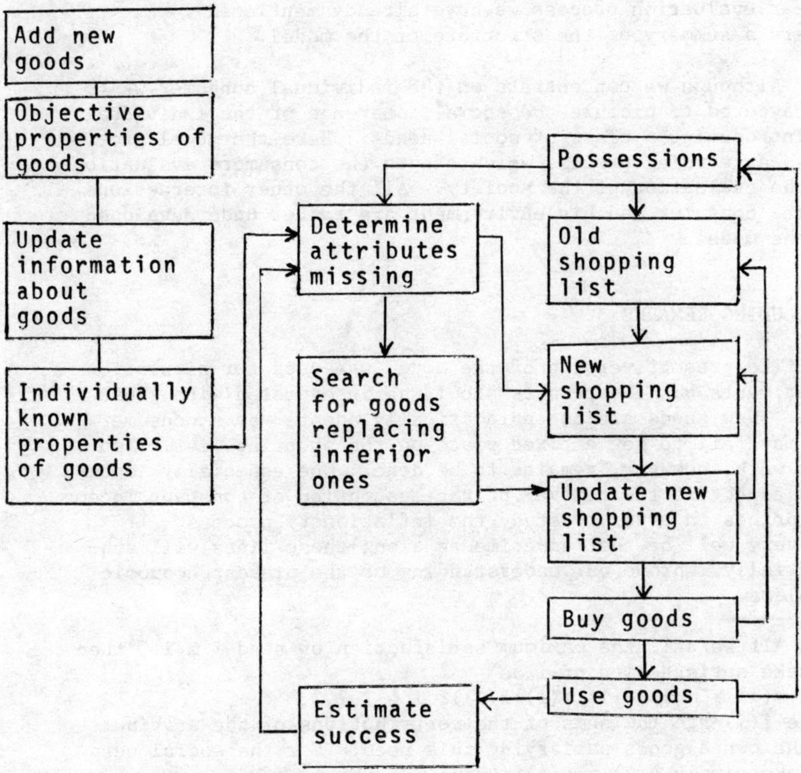

Fig. 1. Logical network of structure underlying the model

The present version of the model does not contain separate decisions on the intensity of use of the goods. In other words, what is needed is a more elaborated depreciation process instead of a depreciation depending on a fixed lifetime.

However, the goods in the market consist of nondurables and durables which have a lifetime of one or two periods, respectively. Hence we assume that durables are used with equal intensity over time, one half this period, the other half next period. The consequence of the possession of durable goods becomes evident in the performance indicator, since a durable bought last period will continue to give satisfaction next period and thus influence the estimate of the future state of fundamental needs. This forecast and the prediction of goods' possession based on the provisional shopping list give rise to the search process of wanted attributes making use of the non linear evaluation process we have already mentioned*. Fig. 1 offers a summary of the structure of the model.

Although we concentrate on the individual consumer we endeavoured to picture the social coherence of the individual by introducing a class of social needs. Here the model provides a learning process which adapts the consumers evaluation to the evaluation of the society. All the other interactions of the consumer and his environment are rather underdeveloped in the model.

CONCLUDING REMARKS

The present version of the model was used for simulation experiments but the results should be interpreted with great care. New goods are not automatically adopted by a consumer and may fail to get a fixed place on the shopping list. Important work, however, remains to be done. One especially important aspect is the removal of the assumption of constant income and prices in order to study the inflationary process. It may very well be that experiments along these lines will substantially improve our understanding of the present economic problems.

---

*If we call the maximum satisfaction of need i m(i), then we take satisfaction of i as

$$s(i) = m(i)f(i)/(m(i)+f(i)),\ i = 1,2,3,$$

where f(i) are the sums of the contributions of the attributes of the owned goods satisfying this need. For the social need we take simply $s(4) = c(4)f(4)$.

The overall satisfaction is given by the expression $s = smin + \Sigma_i\ a(i)d(i)smin/(1+d(i))$, where smin is the minimum satisfaction and d(i) the excess of the satisfaction of the other needs above this one. d(i) is a measure of the distance: $d(i) = s(i) - smin$, $i = 1,2,3,4$. c(i) and a are constants.

REFERENCES

1. J. ARNDT (ed.), *Insights into Consumer Behavior* (Boston, Mass., 1968).

2. M.C. BURK, *Consumption Economics: A Multidisciplinary Approach* (New York, Sidney, London, 1968).

3. J.F. ENGEL, D.T. KOLLAT and R.D. BLACKWELL, *Consumer Behavior* (New York, Chicago, San Francisco, Atlanta, Dallas, Montreal, Toronto, London, 1968).

4. D.S. IRONMONGER, *New Commodities and Consumer Behaviour* (Cambridge, 1972).

5. G.H. HAINES, Jr., *Consumer Behavior. Learning Models of Purchasing* (New York, 1969), p. 12.

6. F. HANSEN, *Consumer Choice Behavior. A Cognitive Theory* Table 19.1 (New York, 1972).

7. K.J. LANCASTER, "A new approach to consumer theory" *J. Polit. Econ. 74*, 132-157 (April 1966).

8. F.M. NICOSIA, *Consumer Decision Processes. Marketing and Advertising Implications* (Englewood Cliffs, N.J. 1966).

9. P.B. SCHARY, "Consumption and the problem of time" *J. Market. 35*, 50-55 (April, 1971).

THE STRATEGY OF ECONOMIC DEVELOPMENT IN A SMALL SOCIALIST COUNTRY OF A SELF-MANAGING TYPE — THE YUGOSLAV EXPERIENCE

R. STOJANOVIĆ

Faculty of Economics, University of Belgrade, Belgrade, Yugoslavia

SUMMARY

The choice of optimal strategies of economic development is specific for a small country. A small country cannot be identified with a big country on a reduced scale; it is an altogether different social and economic system. The author deals in her paper with some specific problems of a small country in its choice of development strategy as well as with possible strategy types.

INTRODUCTION

The choice of an optimal strategy of economic development is a highly complex task. It is necessary to establish criteria of optimization, to set goals and priorities of development, to fix the list of social needs and their intensity in order of importance, to indicate all the important factors of growth (economic and noneconomic factors, factors which can be measured and those which cannot), the different degrees of limitation of material factors and different possibilities for their substitution as well as the corresponding price policy; it is necessary, further, to set the direction of the future development of the management system, particularly to find the optimal decision-making system and the like. All this is a very complex area, which has not been sufficiently investigated and highlighted. Even though spectacular results have been achieved in this field of economics during recent years, even though the optimization theory has made huge progress, yet many of these results are still in their "laboratory phase" (the measurement of the needs priority, the calculation of the factors limitation, the contribution of numerous unmeasurable and, particularly, noneconomic factors to the rate of economic growth, e.g. the influence of the political system in a given country etc.).

Without underrating some of the highly important contributions of various small countries it must be stated that the major part of the above-mentioned scientific results has been achieved, quite logically, in big and developed countries of the world. This is where a problem arises which is typical of all small countries: To what extent is it possible to use the scientific achievements and the practical experiences of big and developed countries in the choice of the strategy of economic development in a small and still under-developed country? And further: to what extent can a small country develop a sufficiently strong own "defence system" against big and developed countries? We mean, thereby, protection against the penetration of new scientific achievements in the choice of the growth strategy, as well as the protection against the penetration of new products, new technology and management system which are not relevant to a small country or call for considerable adjustments. A rigorous selection and inventive adjustments are extraordinarily complex jobs, requiring a very high degree of professional knowledge on the part of those who perform them, and are becoming more and more important for a small country. To what extent can such a small country perform them successfully?

It was quite a long time ago that economic theory started to spell out clearly various specificities of economic development of small countries. International economic meetings were likewise devoted to this question [1], there have been many studies [2] and different comparative analyses. However, it was but recently that conclusions could be reached which are a serious warning to small countries, since their specificities are remarkable and numerous if compared to big countries.

This paper is devoted to some of these outstanding specificities of a small country in the choice of an optimal strategy of economic development. We shall focus our attention here on what is particularly typical of a small country like Yugoslavia, i.e. of a small socialist country of a self-managing type in the medium stage of development, in which the supply of the labour force is unlimited.

SOME SPECIFIC PROBLEMS OF A SMALL COUNTRY IN ITS CHOICE OF DEVELOPMENT STRATEGY

A small country cannot be identified with a big country on a reduced scale; it is an altogether different social and economic system. This difference is so great that principles and criteria which hold for big countries do not hold for small ones at all. Even if some of them do hold, then they have got a different meaning.

a. Let us start with *priority* in the economic development. Firstly, what is involved in the case of big countries is ordinarily only a different place on the list of priority, namely, what we are concerned with is the question whether some social need, some area of economic life, some branch or some region will be in advance of or after others. In such a case everything is important, but the priorities are different. Possible errors connected to the setting of priority cannot be so big, neither is it difficult to overcome them. Such a type of disproportion can be always corrected in the course of time. In the case of a small country we are concerned simultaneously with priorities and selections, the latter being very strong ones. If an error is made in the choice, i.e. in the selection, then will such a wrong decision bring about consequences which are much more severe; in other words, what is involved is a long-run misinvestment and not a contemporary disproportion.

Secondly, the order of priority is the more different the bigger the country to which it is being compared to a small one. The first priority, the most important for every small country, is its foreign trade. The growth rate of a small country depends so much on foreign trade that effects of the export and the anti-import policy are its chief concern. However, Yugoslavia has also an unlimited supply of labour force. These two facts are not only its two main priorities but also its profound contradictions: What stimulates the export most is often not the best solution for the increase of employment.

b. General criteria of *efficiency* and criteria for the *distribution of new investment* by industries used to be transferred from big countries into small ones without being properly investigated as to the importance they have got for a small country. What is most important for a small country is to find the variable minimizing the import during the given period, i.e.

$$\beta(I_t \cdot x_t) + (L_t \cdot y_t) = \text{min.}$$

and maximizing, at the same time, the share of export (P_{ext}) in the total production (P_t), i.e.

$$\frac{P_{ext}}{P_t} = \text{max.}$$

(β = parameter of regulation, equal for all industries; I_t = total investments in the given variant excluding the labour force; x_t = coefficient of the share of foreign exchanges per unit of total investments; L_t = investments into the labour force; y_t = coefficient of the share of imported consumption goods in the total consumption per employed worker according to the given variable).

If there is an unlimited supply of labour force, as it happens to be the case in Yugoslavia, then we have to concern ourselves with another essential criterion, as soon as this first effect of foreign trade has been achieved. This is the coefficient of absorption of the labour force per unit of new investments.

These two main investment criteria in a small country are usually, as we have already indicated, opposite to each other: the strategy which favours the foreign-trade variable does not favour, as a rule, the increase of employment and vice versa. Of course, this statement holds, generally speaking, also for a big country which is underdeveloped and overpopulated, but to a much smaller extent. In a big country, which is rich in natural raw materials and energy, the foreign-trade variable rests on anti-import measures rather than on the increased export in order to keep control over the balance of payment; if the production is oriented in a greater part to the domestic market (inward-looking strategy), the foreign-trade variable comes much closer to the employment-favouring variable of economic development, than in the case of a small country in which the lack of resources (of raw materials and equipment, in the first place) forces it to resort to specialization and for that matter to a constant increase of exports (outward-looking strategy).

It is, therefore, quite possible that altogether wrong decisions will be made if either the coefficient of the relative efficiency of new investments will be the main criterion for the choice of investments, which happens to be the case with Soviet economists (the so-called "srok okupaemosti"), or the marginal capital coefficient, which is to be found in many Western economists. This does not imply that these main criteria of big countries are of no value in a small country, but they must relinquish their priority position in favour of the maximization of exports and of employment. The order of criteria will change.

c. The lack of the so-called *critical mass* for the upbuilding and further development of a large and rising number of industries is also a distinguished feature of a small country. The amount of "the critical mass" increases continuously as modern techniques of production develop, so that the number of countries unable to develop various industries rises more and more rapidly in the contemporary world. The complete monopoly of the biggest and most developed countries stands out already in some areas of electronics (e.g. electronic computers), in machine-building (e.g. the airplane and the automobile industry) or in the chemical industry, not to talk about some gigantic and very expensive scientific researches or even flights into space.

What holds for the area of production holds to a greater extent also for the area of scientific research or for the education of sicentific workers and experts of different types with quite narrow fields of specialization.

This continuous accelerated loss of "the critical mass" and of material and human resources necessary for the own independent development of various industries forces a small country to establish a closer productive cooperation with other countries. Firstly, licenses for new products are bought; people go abroad for purposes of specialization; later on, small countries take over whole technological procedures and methods of management from the biggest and developed countries; finally, through various forms of productive cooperation small countries become more and more dependent on the big ones until domestic enterprises may be said to have become parts of foreign enterprises.

This process of "satellization", as it has been termed by Prof. Francois Perroux, cannot be avoided by a small country, but it can be made more favourable so as to impair less the scope of the own "manoeuvre space" in the policy of economic development or in the main guidelines regarding the choice of the economy and society which we would like to achieve. The penetration of foreign technology is not naive at all. These technological methods have been adjusted to big countries in the first place as well as to forms of management in them; this may bring about many disturbances in a small country. The intensity of these disturbances will depend, in a great measure, on the degree of development of the own "defence system", i.e. on the organized way in which the society prepares and accepts the cooperation with big countries.

d. A small country feels the vicinity of the *zero point* in all its important decisions. All its investments and all its efforts become quickly exhausted, so that the falling curve of total benefits and the rising curve of total costs intersect on a much lower level of results achieved. The transition over this borderline, at which costs are equal to benefits, brings about the ascendancy of negative effects, the decline of the total rate of economic growth. This vicinity of the zero point in a small country may be depicted graphically most simply in the following way (Fig. 1):

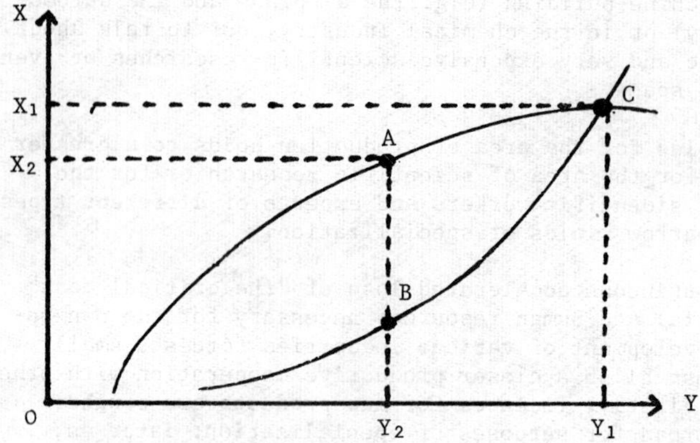

Fig. 1. The vicinity of the zero point

C is the zero point, i.e. $X_1 - Y_1$ is the marginal case, whereas $X_2 - Y_2$ is the optimal case because of the biggest distance between the curve of investments and the curve of results (the distance A — B). Every positive result in every economy has got a falling and every investment a rising function. Thus, there is no large economic system (national economy) which has not got its numerous limitations. Every country must, therefore, reckon with the zero point. What is important for small countries is their restricted scope, the fact that the zero point is very close and that it may be reached rapidly in all the areas of economic life. This is why these countries must often resort not to the optimal foreign-trade effect (in foreign trade as a rule, which may be depicted graphically as the longest distance between the curve of additional investments in exports or anti-imports and the curve of results in terms of the rise of the national income) but to any positive effect which is close to the zero point. A small country would have a lower efficiency rate of foreign trade even if the position of small countries in the international trade were not unfavourable and if the maximum consideration were given to principles of exchange which are deprived of any discrimination. That means that a small country has to choose not the optimum ($X_2 - Y_2$) in this area, but has to move away from it consciously, since it is the total positive effect of foreign trade that matters to it. This is the first element underlying its further economic development.

e. In connection with this vicinity of the zero point in a small country and with the simultaneous urgent need to come almost up to it for the purpose of maximizing the total positive effect (regardless of whether we are concerned with the influence of foreign trade, employment or some other economic magnitude on the total rate of economic growth), there arises another phenomenon, which stands out particularly in a small country of a self-managing type. Namely, real possibilities for the *approach of individual to social interests* or, to be more precise, possibilities for the coordination of interests on lower and those on higher levels of the large economic system, then appear in a special light. The main goal function of enterprises in self-managing countries is the maximization of income per worker employed, which implies that all their decisions tend to move around the optimal relationship between their investments and the results achieved by virtue of them. The country as a whole maximizes the total results by crossing this borderline, particularly if it has got an unlimited supply of labour force. The highest rate of total economic growth and the highest income per worker on the level of every individual enterprise will apparently not coincide in this case. It is difficult for enterprises to grasp the effects of the so-called external economy ("costs involved in effects of the feed-back couplings", in the terminology of Novozhilov and Kantorovich). All this calls for a more complex economic policy and for a much more advanced system of regulating parameters.

We shall illustrate this conflict between individual and social criteria in decision-making on an example which is very frequent in Yugoslav circumstances. Yugoslavia is undoubtedly confronted with the problem of an accelerated technical modernization of many industries. This process is important particularly for export industries, whose competitive power must be kept continuously on the necessary level. Enterprises will, of course, make decisions on modernization in the frames of resources which they have at hand. Starting from the maximization of income per worker employed in the given organization, they will consider which volume of modernization will suit them best and when. We shall express the results of modernization as a certain increase of fixed funds (f_k) and as a certain increase of labour productivity per worker employed (p). We shall thus depict on a graph (Fig. 2) the different possible effects of modernization on total employment in the country (r_z):

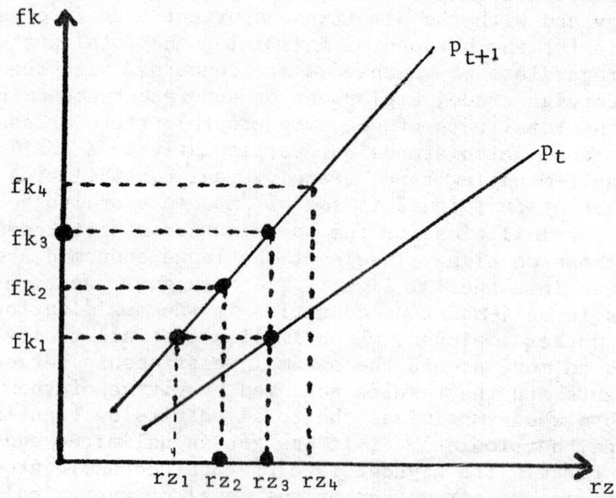

Fig. 2. The effects of modernization on the total employment

At a given level of techniques, which will raise the labour productivity from level p_t to level p_{t+1} in a country with an unlimited supply of labour force, which happens to be the case in Yugoslavia, the absolutely lowest admissible total level of modernization for the whole economy will be $f_{k_3} - r_{z_3}$. Thus, even though the fixed funds will rise from f_{k_1} to f_{k_3}, employment will not increase (the former relationship was $f_{k_1} - r_{z_3}$), but it will at least remain constant on the same level, which may be likewise only a very short-run and an extraordinary policy. The rise of f_k from the level f_{k_1} to the level f_{k_2} would bring about an increase of unemployment (the difference between r_{z_3} and r_{z_2}), while employment would start rising, which must be borne in mind to some extent, at least when the level of new investments in fixed funds has surpassed the borderline f_{k_3}(the case $f_{k_4} - r_{z_4}$ in our graph).

Enterprises can have no knowledge of this socially admissible borderline, but it is necessary to calculate and to enter it into intermediate-range plans of economic development of the national economy. This will call for an advance analysis, which will indicate in which areas it is socially worthwhile to carry out the modernization and in which it is not, i.e. where some of its objective borders are to be found with regard to employment. Practically this calls for an elaborate national program of modernization* with an emphasis on priority industries whose survival in the international market is dependent on this very process. Of course, the program of modernization must comprise also industries which ought to be subordinate to another essential priority (employment in the case of Yugoslavia). Individual decisions of the enterprise might easily conflict with the interests of the whole without such a national program and they might affect adversely the total rate of economic growth, not to mention how they can jeopardize the social solidarity, which is no less important.

f. No matter which division of theoretically possible growth strategies we have chosen, i.e. which division into forms of so-called pure strategies, we always encounter in the practice *mixed strategies*, which are composed of elements of the following pure strategies: The strategy of the balanced and the strategy of the unbalanced (accelerated) growth; consumption-oriented growth strategy or accumulation-oriented growth strategy; the strategy of extensive or the strategy of intensive growth; the inward-looking or the outward-looking strategy [3]; the strategy over finite or the strategy over infinite time, i.e. the strategy which solves or which does not solve the generation problem, or in the terminology of Inagaki: The UMIT-strategy (Utility Maximization over Infinite Time) or the MUEFT-strategy (Marginal Utility Equilibrium over Finite Time)[4].

Even though only a mixed strategy is possible in social systems with many levels and many goals (these are typical multi-level multi-goal systems), i.e. with different interests and goals of various social groups, various branches and various regions, yet the final form of strategy depends, among other things, also on the size of the country. The size of the country affects not only the choice of the structure of production in dependence of available factors of production, as it has been often emphasized. Moreover, the size of the country determines, in large measure, how many elements of a given form of a possible pure strategy will be represented in

*In the absence of an elaborate program of modernization of the whole production, Yugoslav enterprises do what they can. Since they do not want to leave their workers without jobs, they establish often various small enterprises and various new departments in the frames of existing enterprises, even if they are not closely connected with them. Without concerning ourselves with the rationality of such decisions, we have to emphasize that they can only prevent the critical borderline from falling when unemployment rises. However, the problem of new employment is relevant to the whole process of modernization.

the mixed strategy that has been chosen. The predominant importance of foreign trade in Yugoslavia in the present stage of self-management necessitates an outward-looking strategy, i.e. a strategy of intensive development, whereby modern techniques should concentrate on the most important export industries. It necessitates, further, the MUEFT-strategy as well as the consumption-oriented strategy of development. However, the unlimited supply of labour force calls for a large share of elements of the inward-looking strategy, i.e. the strategy of extensive development, as well as of elements of the UMIT-strategy and the accumualtion-oriented growth strategy. The heterogeneity in the orientation of production diminishes the final effects very much, but the same effects may be also diminished in a small country, if it tends too much towards a specialization which would prevent it from using many natural resources, particularly the abundant labour force. The optimal strategy of development may be, therefore, apparently only such a mixed strategy which will avoid both extremes as much as possible, selecting thereby branches and regions and stimulating in them various elements of one form of pure strategy, as well as branches and regions in which there will prevail elements of other forms of pure strategy. Consequently, we shall be able to achieve the greatest results in the national economy of Yugoslavia as a whole. It would be altogether wrong to insist on elements of only one form of pure strategy for the country; this would not even be feasible in practical life. Two central Yugoslav problems and, at the same time, two central priorities in its development policy - foreign trade and employment - are so outstanding that they have assumed the character of fixed goals which have to be accepted and from which one cannot deviate. As distinguished from small and undeveloped countries, big and developed countries can never have so strong priorities which dominate others.

We have mentioned only some specificities of small and undeveloped countries, by which they differ from big and developed ones as regards the choice of growth strategy. As a matter of fact, we have strayed from the main characteristics of Yugoslavia.

As it has been stated at the beginning, all the specificities of small countries have been known so far. However, they have not received the necessary consideration. Real economic life forced us to deviate from the experience of big countries, while the theory of economic policy was not explicit enough in this matter.

In order to get a better insight into the growth strategy of a small and self-managing socialist country, we shall make some further observations regarding the choice of the main priorities.

THE CHOICE OF THE MAIN PRIORITIES IN GROWTH STRATEGY

If we had to fix in order of importance the main priorities of a small country with all the basic characteristics of Yugoslavia, then it would be, undoubtedly, the following:

a. *Foreign trade,* which affects directly the rate of economic growth, since every economic growth is associated, more or less, with the import of raw materials and most often of the whole equipment; there is no increased manufacture without imports, and the precondition to the continuous rise in imports must be the continuous rise in exports.

b. *New employment* as the main economic and social problem in a country with an unlimited supply of labour force; this is the combination of the main element of social solidarity with the most important factor involved in the rise of living standard and with the very important criterion of the utilization of production factors, the latter being important particularly when decisions are made on the substitution of the labour force by new techniques.

c. Closely connected to employment is *the factor substitution policy and the factor price policy;* what is most important in countries with an absolute surplus of the labour force is the substitution of labour by techniques and, consequently, the relationship between the price of the labour force as factor in unlimited supply and the price of capital as a highly limited factor.

d. *External economies* in the broadest sense, i.e. as the increase of all the favourable effects and as the reduction of all the adverse ones thanks to the functioning of the whole system of important (characteristic) feedback couplings of the national economy.

e. *Professional cadre* as vital element in the continuous process of selection and adjustment to scientific and technical achievements of big countries as well as in the continuous adjustment to changes coming from the very large environment of a small country.

f. *The functioning of the so-called alarm system,* which is extraordinarily important for the self-managing and democratic socialism, for the observation of critical points in the whole society and for the making of crucial national decisions in due time. Any delay in this decision-making may either jeopardize seriously social solidarity or cause strong disturbances in economic development.

Each of the above-mentioned priorities in the growth strategy of a small country needs to be explained much more fully but that would exceed the scope of this paper. We shall deal, therefore, only with three priorities which have got special features in a small country. However, we shall highlight only some of their aspects which ought to receive more attention in the future policy of development in every small country. These are external economics, the professional cadre and the alarm system.

(i) The time is past when *external economies** used to be connected to: 1. Branches such as transport or the electrical energy, which are associated technologically with all the other branches. This is why "bottlenecks" in them may bring about the insufficient utilization of facilities in these branches or higher costs of production; and vice versa, they may bring about additional savings in them because of the subsequent better utilization of facilities which have not been utilized so far; and, 2. to the relationship of the enterprise to the market, whereby changes in costs and prices of some enterprises may affect favourably or adversely costs of production and the prices of products of other enterprises. The most important effects of external economies today is not the fall or rise of direct costs of production in some branches under the influence of others (even though costs of the natural environment, which are part of direct costs, are rising very much because of the pollution of air and water). Effects of external economies mostly depend on the functioning of the system of characteristic feedback couplings in the national economy. This holds particularly for feedback couplings in the area of regulation of the economic development. Some of these are: Feedback coupling information — decision-making, and the feedback coupling plan — market.

The most important of these feedback couplings is the feedback coupling information — decision-making. Thus, its influence on external economies is very appreciable. It goes, therefore, without saying that all the advanced countries of

---

*External economies have been termed altogether differently: "external economy" (this term dates back to Alfred Marshall), "external effects" or just "externalities". The same thing has been termed "zatraty obratnoi svyazi" by Novozhilov, i.e. costs caused by effects of the feedback couplings, which may be a positive, a negative (diseconomies) or a zero magnitude depending on whether changes in the "environmental sector" have brought about additional savings or additional costs in some system or whether the situation has remained unchanged.

the world expect in this area, the largest savings.* This is the result of a higher general efficiency of the national economy, which may be achieved through the optimization of the whole system of management and of its main subsystems, among which the system of decision-making and the information system are the most important. The central problem in the system of decision-making is connected undoubtedly to the level on which decisions can be made in the best way and in the shortest time. We mean thereby, in the first place, strategic decisions regarding the future economic development. Every type of decision has got its optimal level (there is "set of levels" in Jan Tinbergen terminology), i.e. the level on which it can be made over the shortest time period and with the greatest exactitude. These huge effects of external economies could not be achieved in any other way. Closely connected to the decision-making system is the information system, taking information as a basis of any type of decision-making. The significance of an organized, fast growing information system is altogether evident in a country of a self-managing type, which is, in addition, small. Working collectives cannot make the proper decisions in time without a highly developed system of information. On each level of decision-making there must be available the corresponding information. Its share is so significant that many reputable economists and computer scientists all over the world have attributed the greatest effects of external economies to the information system.

Even though the potential effects of external economies are great, yet the extraordinary significance of the information system in a small socialist country of a self-managing type is coupled with the fact that the success of self-management, particularly of decision-making in enterprises, depends very much on the efficient functioning of the information system. In fact, levels of decision-making could be lower if costs in collecting, in processing and in the distribution of information were not so high as they usually are, if the unlimited expansion of this system were worthwhile. The costs of every bit of information have to be examined in advance to prevent its price from exceeding its useful effect (its value in use).

The degree of democracy and freedom, being inevitable integral elements of a self-managing society, depends in a greater part on the character of the information system. Democracy and freedom cannot be achieved unless the citizens

---

*All the socialist countries, inclusive of Yugoslavia, focussed their attention for a long time on the reduction of direct costs of production. Later on they realized that the largest reserves are to be found in savings which are due to a better system of management.

take part in decision-making and unless they are so well informed as to make the proper decisions. Available information are an extraordinarily important question of every democratization step under socialism. It is a matter of common knowledge that centres of power have been established both in capitalist and socialist countries, on the basis of control over information systems as a whole, that is over all kinds of information. In our time, information system is a threatening dangerous form of monopoly. This is why the struggle against bureaucracy under socialism must not only be limited to the ownership of the main means of production nor to the decentralization in decision-making. The battleground must include also the information system; it must be coordinated with the decision-making system not only because of the quality of decisions which are made by working collectives, but also for the sake of destroying centres of power with the monopoly of information underlying them.

(ii) The importance of the *professional cadre* cannot be overemphasized in the case of a small country which has entered the new stage of development of a socialist society.

Firstly, the professional cadre is the most important part of the whole "social capital" of a small country. It is the part of its production factors which can help it to keep pace with the most developed countries. Also the professional cadre is the main element of its "defence system" against the domination of big and developed countries. A small country must make huge efforts to select innovations from all over the world and to adjust them to its needs. To this purpose it must engage the whole of its own professional cadre. Experts from big and developed countries cannot offer much help. They are adapted to another "system of standards" for all the social and particularly for economic magnitudes, to other scales of priority or to put it into brief terms, they are adapted to reason under altogether different social systems. They usually disregard magnitudes to which attention is paid in small countries, which try to make use of them. If such foreign experts come from countries with a very limited supply of labour, then they cannot appraise properly where the labour force should be replaced by machines and where not, what are the branches in which many operations can be performed by manual labour and the like [5]. This is why small countries are practically left to themselves in as a sensitive process as is the adjustment of scientific and technical achievements in all the areas of the social life and not only in the economy; this is left to its people, to their knowledge and to their good solutions. There cannot be many people able to do this in a small country, notable if experts are free to go and work abroad. Finally, people who have got a developed sense for the specificities of a small country can be trained abroad only in part, while every country has to train the majority of its cadre alone. Consequently, nothing can be obtained from abroad in an altogether ready form: neither techniques of production, nor methods of management, nor the professional cadre.

Another matter which is connected with the professional cadre and the educational system as a whole, lies in the area of social solidarity. Socialism cannot, particularly during its first stages of development, offer a solid material basis for many forms in which the equality of people stands out. However, it seems that it ought to do more in one area than in all the others, namely at the beginning of their career young people must have the same opportunity to qualify for some sort of social activity. In a country which educates self-managers, this training would enable the working collectives to realize and to understand their problems, being an integral part of a large socio-economic system. This would be a step towards the understanding of the main directions of development, the main characteristics and priorities of such a society and a step towards the incorporation of these insights into development programs of enterprises, branches and regions.

The training of people for highly complex processes of adjustment, of people who will be qualified to take part in decision-making, i.e. in the self-management on various levels, and who will help to maximize effects of external economies and, finally, the strengthening of the social solidarity in the most sensitive area, i.e. in the gradual equalization of young people at the beginning of their career — these are the reasons why the problem of a professional cadre is very important in a small socialist country of a self-managing type. This is why standards regarding the professional structure of the employed in some other countries have no relevance for our country, the more so since these countries do not have the Yugoslav type of the socio-economic system, namely, the increasing participation of working people in the process of decision-making.

(iii) Finally, the functioning of the so-called *alarm system*, being the most important part of the information system, attracts more and more the attention of economists not only of one type of countries, but of the whole world. The shortcomings of this system are very important in the modern society for two reasons: Firstly, it is difficult to choose proper signals which will warn us in time of the increasing destabilization of the large economic system; the second reason is the monopoly of information and even its availability as a state secret. The alarm system has proved to be still one of the weakest points also of the socialist world. Many economic, social or political perturbations seemed to be unexpected, and the society was altogether unprepared to meet them since the alarm system was not adequate.

There are many signals, of which we would like to single out those which indicate clearly destabilization. Of the signals coming from the market it is necessary to stress the following: The movement of market prices, changes in stocks, the increase of unemployment and the changes in imports and exports. However, small countries face likewise some difficulties in the utilization of these market signals. The lack of the sufficient number of producers of some products, various monopoly positions, subventions granted to some export industries as well as continuous inflationary trends curb, in a great measure, the role of prices as signals of the real position in the economy. Signals coming directly from production or from the development of the national economy are by far more reliable and for a longer duration, particularly when they are combined with signals from the environment, notably with those which have to do with scientific and technical discoveries, with new forms of management, with deeper structural changes in the world economy, with the appearance of new professions, new specialities, and with different concepts of the socio-economic development.

The environment affects small countries very much, since they depend, in a greater part, on foreign trade. Their abilities to pile up various stocks, the availability of resources and their "defence power" are not such as to enable them to go through profound changes without any former longer preparations. This is why the proper functioning of this part of the alarm system is extraordinarily important for a small country. It may experience a profound destabilization of the economy if it is not aware of the development of new branches which jeopardize its existing export branches, if the technology of production changes vitally or if conditions for the sale in the foreign market change without being registered by the alarm system. Instruments which are used to measure such appearances must be extraordinarily precise.

The registration of outstanding signals in the development of the domestic economy is no less important. These signals do not come from the market (or if they do, then they come very late), but from banks, chambers, associations of enterprises etc. We think particularly of investments. If we find out too late that the investment credit has been exceeded, that the distribution of national income was wrong or the like, then we may derive the conclusion that there is no developed alarm system which would signal immediately the relevant phenomenon.

Yugoslavia has not yet sufficiently developed its feedback couplings in the alarm system which is based in a greater part on the upward movement of signals. This is one kind of absurdity for a self-managing country, which weakens thereby its ability to fight against destabilization, while it supports, on the other hand, some governmental institutions no longer justified.

Having entered the new phase of the further development of the socialist society prior to other countries, Yugoslavia has reached a position which is historically very specific and very responsible, indeed; namely, it has to pave the way and to precede other countries in new solutions. Being a small, multinational and still undeveloped country, it has encountered numerous difficulties in this attempt. These difficulties have manifested themselves particularly in the possibility of choosing optimal strategy of future development. Out of this broad area we have singled out only one aspect, which is always present in everyday life, but which has not been highlighted enough; these are specific problems connected with the choice of the optimal strategy in a small country.

REFERENCES

1. E.A.G. ROBINSON (ed.), "The consequences of the size of nations" *Procs. Conf. held by the Int. Econ. Assoc.* (London, 1963).

2. S. KUZNETS, "La croissance économique des petites nations" *Economie Appliquée* No. 1-2 (1959).

3. D.N. KEESING, "Outward-looking policies and economic development" *Econ. J.* (June, 1967); B. BALASSA, "Growth strategy in semi-industrial countries" *Quart. J. Econ.* No. 1 (1970).

4. M. INAGALKI, *Optimal Economic Growth - Shifting Finite versus Infinite Time Horizon* (Amsterdam, London, 1970).

5. P.N. ROSENSTEIN-RODAN, "The modernization of industry" In: M. WEINER (ed.), *Modernization — The Dynamics of Growth* (New York, 1966).

THE RELATION OF FEEDBACK TO THE CONCEPT OF AUTHORITY

Sister STELLA MARY

St. Dominic's Priory, Carisbrooke, Newport, Isle of Wight, United Kingdom

SUMMARY

This paper is concerned with feedback as related to the concept of authority. It owes much to an inherited bent towards engineering but carries a basic knowledge of feedback into the area where authority confronts a major challenge today. With the intention of stimulating thought and encouraging discussion, the suggestion is put forward that inordinate fear, whether conscious or not, is the greatest obstacle to that adequate use of feedback which makes for enlightened authority in control of the human element in any system inclusive of intelligent beings. The conquest of fear is the preliminary to the development of productive brotherly love, without which the human relationships inherent in the concept of authority become barren and unreal.

INTRODUCTION

In every sector of life today authority meets with a major challenge, a challenge that calls for courage to accept or reject change. However unpalatable to the taste of those reared in another social environment or a different regional culture some changes may be, their open-minded acceptance places authority in an unassailable position as a recognized and esteemed source of unity, security and peace. Nevertheless, if an atmosphere of respect and confidence is to be maintained, and without respect and confidence communications break down, there must be no weak compromise but courageous rejection of change that is not developmental and hopefully directed towards healthy growth.

Healthy growth presupposes that every sub-system in the system is fulfilling its proper function and consequently contributing its share towards the co-ordinated life of the whole. Without change there can be no growth but, unless it is controlled by a competent authority, change may outrun the strength of the system in which it takes place. Today there is such an acceleration of change in every environment where it operates that authority, left breathless in the attempt to adapt its customary methods to new demands, is tempted to put up a resistance to change. When the entrenchment of management in its fixed beliefs is attacked by those whose concept of authority is hostile to such beliefs, a conflict ensues and there is no likelihood of settlement until satisfactory lines of communication are opened up. This is where feedback is found to be in close relation to the concept of authority and where fear may be detected as the main cause of blockage.

UPROOTING A ROOT

One translation of the Book of Job tells us that:

> '. . . a tree hath hope,
> If it be cut down, it will sprout again
> And its shoots will not cease' [1].

From Job's time backwards and onward experimental knowledge has proved that it is not easy to obliterate all traces of an old tree; unless the stump is completely eradicated, it will continue to burgeon hopefully from year to year. One way of destroying the stump is to burn it out but that takes time and, if the slow-fire is not expertly managed, may cause a conflagration. Of course, we may resort to chemical warfare against the residue of lumber but most ecologists will agree with the author of 'Silent Spring' [2] that chemical action may be a menace to man himself and upset the balance of his environment. (This is not a new warning indeed; Wiener was among the first to give timely warning of danger from the assaults of technology) [3]. Fortunately, long before the chemical invasion an alternative to incineration had been found and, with modernized equipment, it is used today.

This paper is not a period piece; nevertheless, a flashback to the earlier years of this century may show up the passage from the arbitrary and self-assured position of the 19th century, when the universe was seen as a place where everything happened precisely according to physical laws verifiable down to the last decimal, to the more open frame of mind that gradually broke down the rigid divisions of society. Cybernetics was not yet presented to the world as 'the science of control and communication in living beings and machines' [4] but communication and control and the use of feedback, if not its name, was the concern of men who explored and experimented, especially in the realms of mathematics and engineering, whether as a gentleman's hobby or professionally. Let us then go back to the autumn of 1910 and watch a root extraction through the eyes of one onlooker, then a child.

A giant tree had recently been felled and the trunk, stripped of its branches, carried off on a timber carriage. Now the removal of the stump is taking place.

An engine is brought up (probably an Aveling-Porter) and one end of a chain cable attached to it. The other end of the chain encircles the tree-stump and this iron girdle is securely fastened with spikes driven into the wood. When all is ready, someone calls out:

'Right-O, Guv'nor!'

At a word of command from the Guv'nor, the engine driver sets to work. Backwards and forwards he drives with such control of his engine that there is immediate response to every fresh directive. When he stops, men with picks and shovels remove some loosened earth, the Guv'nor shouts a warning to the on-lookers to keep out of the way and the final tug is given. With an almost human groan out comes the tree-stump in a shower of soil. Men with axes reduce its bulk to pieces fit for stowing in a waiting wagon.

Operation Tree-stump has been successfully carried out. The next piece of business arising is the replacement of the tree and, after free discussion on every suggestion, the Guv'nor decides to order a scarlet oak. Then, before the assembly breaks up, he pulls some papers from his pocket and introduces the subject of a motor-plough he saw at a recent agricultural show and for which he has booked a trial demonstration. Eager hands grasp booklets and leaflets and when the meeting dissolves everyone is ready to accept the innovation, except one who always walks 'in the way of tenacity' [5], acting as a human brake on a rush of enthusiasm.

GOVERNORS

Allowing for tricks of memory and the effects of 'anno-dominitis', that word-picture introduces a pattern of thought that began to take shape in the mind of a future cybernetician — a pattern that was to take shape or had already taken shape in more powerful and influential minds in many parts of the world. The keyword to the pattern was not 'authority' or 'feedback' but 'governor', a word that in the context of this pattern conveyed two meanings:

(a) governor — someone in authority who controls the affairs and activity of others,

(b) governor — a self-acting device for controlling a machine.

The human governor controlling Operation Tree-stump, by choice both engineer and farmer, fitted naturally into his place. The men who worked for and with him in the iron-works or on the land had grown up with him in the same village and identified themselves with him as co-sharers in the fruits of his superior education and engineering expertise. Their happy relationship with him was unusual at that period, especially in the freedom with which they voiced their opinions and discussed all that led to the decision ultimately his; nevertheless, it indicated an upthrust of new growth that was gradually introducing a pattern of change that involved change in the pattern of society. Within that society the concept of authority must also change as the pattern of authority was more generally recognized as a pattern of service.

The other kind of governor, a contrivance controlling the engine, was a development of the Watt's governor, more elaborate in design and more efficient in its functioning yet simple enough for a child to understand. The word 'feedback' had yet to be added to one's working vocabulary but the pattern of feedback was recognizable not only in the engine extracting the tree-stump but also in such things as the giant windmill with its fantail device that was a distinguishing feature of the landscape.

That early picture of two kinds of governor operating in an ideal agricultural environment must be modified by wider experience in human relationships involving both men and machines in various urbanized settings. Not all masters and men made up groups of people who had grown up together, spoke the same language even the same dialect, shared the same interests and welcomed innovations after free discussion among themselves. Even in that English countryside the spread of mechanization of farming had repercussions causing disquietude similar to that caused by the intrusion of cybernetics into the world of business and industry today.

AUTHORITY CHALLENGED

Since those comparatively peaceful times two World Wars have forced the pace of scientific endeavour and we find ourselves in the full spate of technological development. Silently and under cover of excitement and clamour about new discoveries a revolution has taken place and nowhere is this turn of events more evident than in every field where authority is operative. Authority like so much else that formerly met with unquestioning acceptance and was rarely discussed critically, is now confronted with a challenge. Where the challenge is taken up and authority is willing to admit investigation into its own proceedings while showing readiness to investigate the claims and grievances of its challengers, problems are quickly resolved; but too often there is a chasm between authority and its opposition that seems unbridgeable. A confrontation may take place but those on either side speak different languages and contain themselves within their own hostile encampments disposed for battle.

Basically the problems of management in business and industry seem surprisingly familiar to those who have studied the progressive history of the great religious orders. The age-old problem of 'inaccessible prelacy' [6] is easily recognizable in the pattern of government in institutions remote from religious organizations. The human element in any system inclusive of intelligent beings requires some kind of governor or equivalent authority if any goal is to be attained; but when the controlling authority ignores the feeback response from subordinate levels and communication always takes the form of command coming from the top downwards the stage is set for an ultimate explosion. If those on the lower levels are strong enough to rebel intelligently and control the force of the explosion, the system survives with renewed health and developmental capacity; if the explosive element is suppressed, the lower ranks in the system feed on whatever dole of information is allowed to them till ultimately the concentrated dissatisfaction leads to an outburst that may shatter the system irreparably.

We cannot do without authority (even while we may admire some anarchic personalities, like Ammon Hennacy [7], and concede to them their special rôle as prophets); but authority exercised exclusively on an authoritarian basis with a total disregard for feedback leads to the overthrow of government. Admittedly, in times of crisis, the only way of saving the situation may be the authoritarian way but it should be only a temporary measure to be abandoned when the crisis is over.

If, as I think, fear is the main cause of blockage of communication in any system involving human relationships in a master/man context, then the solution of most of our managerial problems lies in the conquest of fear by love. At this point we must be careful that we are using the words 'fear' and 'love' meaningfully and in their real full-blooded sense.

Fear is not bad when expressed in love-generated reverence; it is bad when expressed in awe that is terror-stricken. Love is not love, in the sense in which we use it here, if it does not involve an attitude of will. Intellectual attempts to rationalize love are as far from love as emotional outbursts of something mistaken for love. The love that breaks down the beaver-dams of fear is something visceral; it springs forth from the bowels of human compassion; it has the guts to take a risk, the guts that with creative imagination and the gift of spontaneous laughter clears the smog of long-standing misunderstanding and distrust. It is easy to pontificate about 'having a sense of humour' or about 'seeing the funny side of things'; that attitude may be far remote from wholesome, happy laughter. As Karl Rahner has said: 'Only the person who has also a gift for affection can have a true sense of humour. A good laugh is a sign of love' [8].

Fear of the world in which we live because it seems to be slipping human control; fear of the vast store of accumulated information that crushes us under the weight of our own ignorance; fear of the efficiency of our own systems of communication that are as much a threat as an aid to our security — these are some of the fears we all share but, because we are looking at them from very different viewpoints and never examine and discuss them on the same level, they may deepen and widen divisions among us where they might have helped to unify. Shared fears can lead to shared love and shared understanding of the new age that is already born and awaiting our acceptance. When we attain to that acceptance we shall bring to this frightened world of ours a fresh concept of human liberty that is recognized by authority set in a pattern of service that meets reciprocation in willed and willing acceptance of authority.

Looking back to that day in the past when Operation Tree-stump took place, we see an example of authority in service meeting reciprocal service and all the human beings concerned breathing in an atmosphere of freedom. In contrast to that are powerful super-organizations where genuine human needs and rightful freedoms are sacrified to the demands of an impersonal 'Something'. According to Aristotle 'Love consists in wanting good for someone' [9]. Obviously there can be no love if we do not recognize a 'someone', if human beings are treated as 'hands', 'bods' or cogs in a machine. Neither can there be any really effective and lasting authority unless there is 'someone' in whom authority is vested, someone to be loved with the love that is reinforced with a wholesome kind of reverential fear.

It is right that we should concern ourselves about the material needs of our fellow men: just wages, good living conditions, educational opportunity, medical care, adequate facilities for recreation are things that must be provided; but our responsibility and accountability does not end there. 'People trouble' can and does occur in situations where the material environment leaves little to be desired. At the roots of the trouble is a secret fear of being depersonalized and that fear can only be exorcised by a love that shares not only the material goods of life but those things that belong to the deeps of man's nature and that alone satisfy his secret yearnings for what he cannot define but knows he lacks.

ACCEPTING A DISCIPLINE

In this age of technology we find ourselves obliged to accept new disciplines. They are often imposed upon us and materially inescapable. There is, however, a discipline we are always free to accept or reject; it is one which gives the key to fruitful, real and emotionally satisfying human relationships, opening the way to unity of mind and purpose. It conquers fear, releases a stream of goodwill that ensures the productivity of brotherly love and outstrips the carefully measured provisions of our calculating prudence.

This discipline may be called the Discipline of Love or Charity — not the charity of flag-days and alms-dishes and highly organized appeals. It is a dynamic love, ever in a state of evolution, growing stronger and better from generation to generation and manifesting its power of controlling the turbulent forces of human passions and of breaking down the fear-rigged barriers that separate men from their brother men.

Like every other worthwhile discipline that which fosters brotherly love cannot be mastered in a moment. It is largely a gift; but such a gift requires cultivation and cultivation requires patience which is, after all, the pith and marrow of charity. Wherever authority is faced with a major challenge today there is need for steadfast men, and women too, of whom it can be said that they are 'commended for the gift of discipline' [10] and specialists in the discipline of love.

REFERENCES

1. E.J. KISSANE, *The Book of Job* (Brown and Nolan, Dublin, 1939).

2. R. CARSON, *Silent Spring* (Hamish Hamilton, London, 1963). cf. F. FRASER DARLING, *Reith Lecture (1969)* No. 3.

3. N. WIENER, *The Human Use of Human Beings* (Eyre and Spottiswoode, London, 1954).

4. N. WIENER, *Cybernetics or Control and Communication in the Animal and the Machine*, 2nd ed. (M.I.T. Press, Mass., 1961); *id.*, *God and Golem Inc.* (M.I.T. Press, Mass., 1964).

5. S. BEER, *Decision and Control* (Wiley, New York, 1966) Ch. 2.

6. J. MICHAEL of COUTANCE, *Carthusian Spiritual Exercises*, (c.1594). (English Trans., London, 1912).

7. A. HENNACY, *Book of Ammon* (Published privately by his widow, U.S.A., 1970).

8. K. RAHNER, *Alltägliche Dinge* (Benziger-Verlag, Einsideln, 1964). English Trans. *Everyday Things* (Sheed and Ward, London, 1965).

9. ARISTOTLE, *Rhetoric II, 4*. 1380635.

10. *BIBLE*, O.T., Wisdom, Chapter, 7, Verse 14.

MAN: NEW ARCHITECT OF THE ENVIRONMENT

F.R. BAHR

Department of Management, University of Southern California, University Park, Los Angeles, California 90007, U.S.A.

SUMMARY

The Industrial Revolution nurtured to reality the prospect of inducing massive changes into the orderly evolution of the planet Earth.

Man, the leader of that revolution, has gained the power to become literally the architect of his own environment. This unique opportunity offers both vistas of promise and a host of new problems. Paradoxically, the characteristics which come under negative scrutiny (i.e. nature of man) are the very factors which propelled him into species superiority. They stem from patterns of behaviour which became progressively dominated by responses to situational opportunism. Ultimately, this type of self-serving activity must come into direct confrontation with global demands for logic, order, and balance.

SOMETHING OLD — SOMETHING NEW

Heraclitus' Children

Two major philosophical approaches can be isolated in scholarly attempts to characterize man and his environment, in this the twenty-first century. Each seeks to introduce a different rationale as the cornerstone in the explanation process. Both can be identified, initially, in the writings of the Greek philosophers Parmenides and Heraclitus.

For the first of these scholars, stability was the only reality. The state of being was continuous and on-going. Change, in the form of creative acts, was inherently contradictory and therefore illusionary. In contrast, Heraclitus saw change as the only reality. Stability was viewed as a myth perpetuated to mask concern and fear for the future.

There have been conflict and oscillation between these two

divergent views throughout the period that has marked the development of modern man. The Parmenidean influence has sought to channel human endeavor by: (1) recognizing the constraint of universal laws and properties of nature, (2) requiring allegiance to on-going social institutions, and (3) reinforcing those values which appear to be crucial to the continuance of existing structures and activities.

Over and over again the struggle has been to establish "things as they really are". During periods when this philosophy of human activity has been dominant, the potential of progress and improvement has given way to the promise of stagnation and ultimate degradation.

Fortunately the nature of man is such that the dynamic of change is a personal imperative. It highlights the central mystery of man, his persistent restlessness. It is the cause of discontent, the force behind the call for technical, social, and finally cultural change. More importantly, this kinetic-like activity has resulted in: (1) a surplus of material goods, (2) and a release of excess energy. It has been said that "only in a civilized society can man contemplate his inability to live on bread alone, and dream of better ways of living" [1].

Advocates of the Heraclitan approach to life appear to have gained the advantage in shaping the destiny of those nations who aspire to be free-enterprise, industrial powers. Collectively they represent a "society that . . . views its institutions as man-made for human purposes . . . that welcomes variety and change instead of enforcing rigid conformity, and accordingly provides its members with personal opportunities and responsibilities beyond mere obedience. It is Athens as opposed to Sparta" [2].

Springboard to Dominance

With the exception of man, all living forms have only one method to secure their survival: they learn to adapt to environmental change. "In fact, the interaction of the organism with its environment is a phenomenon of universal significance. If the environment has changed due to the specific acitivities of other species, it has been purely accidental and obviously unplanned."[3] Man, alone has been able to alter the environment to suit himself.

This unique capability for self-determination has led some scholars to confer on man the distinction of being a "thinking" or "rational animal". However, a sense of awareness coupled with the ability to form abstract ideas does not seem to be exclusively a human prerogative.

> There is one trait which is uniquely and typically human, it is the making of tools. From the dawn of civilization to the present, tools or "facilitators of increased productivity" have been indispensable for human survival and growth. They have been the catalyst in bringing about the formation of society. They have had, indeed, a unique and lasting impact on every aspect of human life [4].

Homo sapiens has not experienced radical biological change for perhaps thirty thousand years. During this period of human evolution, his thrust to specie dominance "has taken the form of using hand and eyes and brains to construct all manner of devices which take the place of the slowly evolved adaptations of all the rest of the animal kingdom . . . Man has made tool after tool until now his largest ones are factories that cover square miles of territory" [5].

The Morality of Choice

Scholars have looked to all forms of society, both primitive and advanced, to discover what human nature is in its "pure" state. We have not found such a universal form or model. Instead we have been confronted with "a fantastic diversity in designs for living, with often an outrageous disregard of the reputed laws of human nature" [6].

The answer, then, appears to be associated with a process not a prototype. The key to any evolutionary activity, whether in biology or in society, lies in a set of related phenomena involving teaching, learning, and most importantly some form of documentation. As we proceed higher and higher in the animal order, instinct is dramatically reduced as activity incorporates more and more cultivated responses. In man, it represents a maximum of learning and a minimum of impulse.

The complete human faculty for induced action includes the ability to anticipate cause and effect relationships through the use of mental images. This capability, in turn, is based on the ability to form symbols and store them for future use.

However, Heraclitus' children are also Cain's off-spring. For instance, it is difficult to describe the development of nuclear weapons as anything but the union of native aggression with growing intelligence. As a specialized implement, it represents the irresistible drive to specie superiority. We are still creatures with both residual animal instincts and the sapient powers to mask their presence and ignore their implications. This contradiction is confronting man with choices of action of the gravest consequences.

This mixture of perplexity and promise was alluded to by one author when he pointed out that:

> Physical and biological technologies have alleviated pestilence and famine and many painful, dangerous, and exhausting features of daily life, and behavioral technology can begin to alleviate other kinds of ills. In the analysis of human behavior it is just possible that we are slightly beyond Newton's position in the analysis of light [7].

In any event, we do have the power not only to conceive but to visualize ourselves in future situations. Whether this expanded capacity for self-awareness will impose new conditions of self-control is still conjectural. In the past, when human consciousness of potential disaster has come into conflict with instincts of animal origin, our reaction has been to desert reason.

However, "no creature who began as a mathematical improbability, who was selected through millions of years of unprecedented environmental hardship and change for ruggedness, ruthlessness, cunning and adaptability . . . may be regarded as a creature without promise" [8]. The measure of freedom that he has gained during the ten thousand years of what we may call civilization has not only permitted abuses of freedom but has heightened the awareness of the limits to that freedom. Having learned his strengths, man is having to rediscover his weaknesses.

A METAPHOR IN THE MAKING

Proximity and Dependency

The segment of human history that we have been describing can be summed up in two main statements. First, it has been advancing persistently for thousands of years. Second, the rate of march has varied from time to time and from place to place. Even the most backward of people have made some progress along the lines of the most advanced.

In all cases, tools have tended to increase in number and complexity. There also has been a growing capability to use natural resources. Lastly, increases in the density of population have led to more complex forms of government and society. In effect, man ". . . has learned to accommodate himself to a world increasingly organized. The trend toward more explicit and consciously drawn relationships is profound and sweeping; it is marked by depth no less than by extension" [9].

These transitions have already changed much of the world

from rural-agricultural forms to those based on technology and representing urban-industrial activity. The result has been an increase in the proximity and the dependency of people. As conditions of the new social order, they represent new threats of human conflict and new uncertainties over the nature of modern social structure.

It is important to point out that these organizational forms are:

> . . . not the product of creative 'group mind' or the expression of a 'general will'. No society began with a social contract, no economic system with the idea of barter or wages, no family structure with an insight into the advantages of cohabitation. A culture evolves when new practices further the survival of those who practice them [10].

The sources of discord are present, to some degree, in all societies from the most primitive to the most modern. They become factors of critical concern when the very survival of a society rests on the maintenance of highly intricate and delicately balanced forms of human collaboration. The civilization that we have created depends upon the preservation of just such an equilibrium of human activity.

The Ultimate Tool

Industrial nations, particularly those of European extract, have been characterized as being "organizational societies" and its working population as being "organizational men" [11]. It is also true that evolving nations use organizations as major tools in the development of their political, economic, social, and military systems. While these observations may convey negative as well as positive consequences, they are descriptively accurate. We do live in a world surrounded by and made up of organizations.

These groupments, of course, take many forms and represent a myriad of value systems. During periods of social transition, they can be both collective instrumentalities advocating change as well as activities resisting that effort. They are, in themselves, sources of societal discord.

The ambivalent view of organizations is often rejected as a matter of definitional inconsistency. In these cases, the term "organization" is being confused with the broader term, "social organization". Within this more liberal context, they are "networks of social relations between individuals and groups, and. . . a system of shared beliefs and orientations, which serve as standards for human conduct" [12]. Thus, social organizations emerge as the broader set of relationships and processes of which organizations are a part.

While the term social organization contributes significantly to our understanding of the total interactional process in society, it fails to give character and identity to the formal structure of organizations. Through the initiative action of their human components, these structures have the potential to act and react within the "networks of social relations" and "system of shared beliefs" noted above. As such, they become the ultimate in man-made tools — they become life-like in their responses.

The Human Dilemma

Advances in technology require changes in social institutions; at the same time evolving social institutions call for technological improvements. "We cannot say in any simple way that one change produces the other, only that they are enormously interrelated and both aspects of human life change together" [13]. One generalization can be risked: these change phenomena are mutually reinforcing and feed upon each other. They propel us into a more complex and interrelated environment.

In contrast, it appears that physical evolution has come to an end in man. "Biologically the people of today are not superior and may be inferior to those of two thousand or even twenty thousand years ago" [14]. With the present limitation on anatomical inheritance as a positive force in cultural advancement, increased emphasis is placed on the quality of physical environment and on cultural endowment.

The challenge is formidable. While the majority of the peoples of the world struggle to break the grip of privation and want, the industrialized nations are attempting to cope with the physical and cultural problems of affluence. The conflict between these two levels of aspiration cannot be minimized. Together they have created "a number of traps which . . . may either prevent man and his planet earth from making the transition altogether or delay it for many generations or even thousands of years" [15]. Boulding isolates four such pitfalls:

1) The most obvious trap is that of war. It is now theoretically possible for man to build devices which will eliminate life from the earth.

2) The next obstacle is a tremendous upsurge in the rate of population. Alleviating human misery and suffering through advancements in medicine, without a concomitant decrease in

birth rate, may result in enormous insoluble problems in the future.

3) The third possible trap is technology itself. We may not be able to develop a genuinely stable, high-level technology which is independent of existing physical resources.

4) The last pitfall may be the very nature of man itself. "If the dangers and difficulties which now beset man are eliminated. . . will not his creativity be diminished and may not he dissipate his energies in a vast ennui and boredom?" [16]

THE GREAT LEAP FORWARD

An Accelerated Thrust

More than a century of accelerated technological growth has forced the nations of the world into a global embrace which has diminished both space and time. We are approaching a phase of cultural advancement where the "creative process of knowing" will be collectively and corporately extended to the whole of the human race [17]. It gives further cause to question the inevitability of events and the orderly unfolding of the future.

The dynamics of technology have allowed most of the Western world to achieve the miracle of material wealth and surplus power. As a result, these nations have moved steadily to a time and space posture where action and reaction occur almost at the same time. Communications and travel media have created opportunities for shared political, social, and economic self-consciousness. In a sense, it represents a closing-in of history for the Western world, but more importantly it has signalled "an opening-out of history for most of the people of the world" [18].

The coexistence of two worlds, one active and one passive, is disappearing or has already vanished. A transformation of history is taking place with enormous rapidity. The forces which began to re-orient the activities of Western man three centuries ago is now having its impact throughout the world. The revolutionary concept of a meaningful future has finally penetrated to the corners of the earth. Until recently these regions existed silently and inertly alongside the ferment of the West.

Paradise Gained or Paradise Lost

While the twentieth century has not seen the resolution of the world's economic and related social problems, it has brought the Western world to levels of unparalleled affluence.

America, most of the nations of Europe, and other countries who have emulated our cultural pre-occupation with increases in industrial productivity, have reaped a rich harvest of physical goods and services.

One might expect the social outcome of these material blessings to parallel if not exceed the satisfaction of physical need. Precisely the opposite has taken place:

> With gratification of biological needs, reduction of tensions, education and conditioning with scientific techniques, there was an unprecedented increase in mental illness, juvenile delinquency, crime not for want but fun, the serious problem of leisure in an automated society, and the appearance of new forms of mental disorder diagnosed as existential disease, malignant boredom, suicidal retirement, neurosis and the like — in fact, all the symptoms of a sick society [19].

The inability to predict as well as to respond to these serious social conditions, suggests, among other problems, the presence of a dangerous Narcissus complex. Homo Sapiens is faced with an identity crisis, because "the traditional conception of man is flattering; it confers reinforcing privileges. It is therefore easily defended and can be changed only with difficulty" [20].

As we grope for the true nature of modern man, we are confronted with behavioral characteristics which reflect what Ardrey calls "the mysterious strength of a pre-historic, bad-weather animal" [21]. The contrast is significant. While we exhibit massive enlargement of the cerebral cortex as well as the specialized centers of the neocortex, we show little development of "the old brain, the paleoncephalon — the site, in humans, of primitive functions, drives, instincts, emotions, the primeval depth personality" [22].

> The sudden addition of the enlarged brain to the equipment of an armed already-successful predatory animal created not only the human being but also the human predicament . . . . The final foundation on which we stand has a strange cement . . . . The deposit was laid down in a time of stress. It is no mere rubble of courage and cunning. City and foundation alike are compacted by a mortar of mysterious strength, the capacity to survive . . . . The quality of the mortar may hold future significance far exceeding that of the material it binds [23].

Changing Role Relationships

Operating the colossal social structure of our time with the ethical orientation of a nomadic bronze-age society has brought us to the brink of chaos. Homo Sapiens has become entangled, controlled, even governed by impersonal and often inhuman social forces of his own making. The hunting primate free from his forest prison, now finds himself a captive of a new and more threatening milieu — the urban-industrial complex.

Autonomous man is a creature of the past; modern man is a function of his environment, "but it is an environment which is almost wholly of his own making" [24]. This new threat will represent the severest test to date of man's capacity to survive.

KNOWLEDGE AND SELF-CONTROL

New Conceptual Imperatives

The movement to greater complexity has paralleled a trend to more elaborate organizations. The condition of greater complexity represents changes in the nature of the environment; organizations, as pools of resources with the potential of response, reflect those environmental changes. The two phenomena are mutually reinforcing. Together they characterize the new demands for understanding as well as adaptation that are being made upon man.

Traditional views of organizations are grossly inadequate under these pressures for change. They can no longer be defined as "collectives . . . that have been established for the pursuit of relatively specific objectives on a more or less continuous basis" [25].

The recognition of additional, essential characteristics, such as: relatively fixed boundaries, a normative order, authority ranks, a communication network, and an incentive system, can be viewed as a response to increased technological and social pressures [26]. However, they do little to relieve the tension. In fact, taken by themselves, they introduce greater rigidity and therefore less potential response to environmental change.

This attempted update in design and functional capacity also ignores an essential change in the corporate nature of organization — they now have the capacity for indefinite life-expectancy. Through the planned replacement of essential components, organizations can effectively become non-entropic in nature. Man remains a terminal entity. The paradox is cruel but evident. By his own organizational handiwork, man's dream of immortality has become an envied reality to be used but not to be shared.

Operational Implications

The implications of this essential change in potential organizational life-span are profound.

First, this change exposes a radical cleavage between the life strategies of man and his creation — organizations. The certainty of growing incapacity and ultimate death shapes man's actions and conditions his allocation of resources and energies. They provide the ultimate parameters to his struggle for survival. For organizations, neither decay nor death are now necessary or pre-destined. The significance of this fact cannot be overemphasized. The whole concept of organizational accommodation and adaptation is altered with the elimination of these constraints.

Second, this condition of indefiniteness creates problems in the availability of conventional materials and energies that have been heretofore ignored. "In terms of man's own history, at present rates of consumption the known reserves will be largely exhausted in a mere matter of centuries" [27]. This could be speeded up dramatically if the balance of the world join the present industrial nations in the accelerated production of goods and services.

To continue the use of this sophisticated and productive tool, man may well be required to sustain himself through the circulation of a closed cycle of materials. While we cannot conceive of a closed cycle in the economic use of energy, this does not appear to be a problem. Supplemental sources of nuclear and solar power are available if we can learn effectively and safely to harness their use.

Third, it has encouraged an increase in the use of symbolic language. Without this method of expressing relationships, we would have insurmountable gaps between the antimate and inanimate, the simple and the complex, and lastly natural and induced relationships. Symbols have become the building blocks of logic and the facilitators of action in man's attempt to fulfill his role as the architect of his own environment.

Katz and Kahn have suggested four additional characteristics in response to these changes in man-organization relationships.

1) Organizations should be differentiated by the nature of their "through-put". The distinction that is being sought is between activities that are transforming objects and those that are "transforming" people, or those directed to accomplish both.

2) Organizations should be viewed as having both expressive and instrumental orientations. Expressive orientations characterize activities in which members participate for some intrinsic satisfaction while an instrumental orientation is one in which participation is for the purpose of receiving physical reward.

3) The next basis of differentiation is the nature of the organizational structure itself. Three sub-properties gain importance in this analysis: (a) the degree of boundary openness or permeability, (b) the degree of structural elaboration, (c) and the nature of reward allocation.

4) The final basis of additional characterization is the manner in which organizations attempt to conserve the energy or resources at their disposal [28].

Collectively these four additional characteristics confer on organizations the capacity to react as a living organism, "within the framework of its general structure and the limitations of its resources . . . continuously [responding] to the vagaries of the environment and its own internal demands for change" [29].

The New Stewardship

In summary, man's current demise has been brought about by:

> eating from the tree of knowledge; that is, in modern parlance, invention of symbolic universes. This made man both better and worse than other species with their inbuilt drives and controls . . . Man became the enormously dangerous beast he is precisely by the clash between [his] instinctual and symbolic worlds, by using techniques of symbolic manipulation for aggression [30].

How that contest is decided may well determine the fate of the world. Man has the power to reshape society into an instrument of unshakable tyranny and unspeakable corruption. It would appear that he also has the tools, techniques, and resources to support a sustained program of physical and social change. The goal would be a society in which the major sources of human misery would have been eliminated.

The result in either case will be restraint, perhaps constraint, of human activity. Even the movement toward an enlightened society will require the voluntary surrender of unfettered, individual freedom of action. Renouncing this, the first gift of the predatory way of life, will be particularly symbolic. Failure to act could lead to a lethal cultural mutation.

Because of their role in monitoring the activities of complex organizations, "symbolic systems may become more potent than man, their creator . . . . Symbolic entities . . . may govern man and his behavior more strongly than biological reality or organismic drives" [31]. The contest will be fierce, for man's nature represents the union of a new and growing intelligence with a predatory instinct that reaches back ions into the past.

It is ironic that we may well be aware of the outcome of this struggle before its conclusion. The use of symbolic universes, which characterizes man's rise to intellectual dominance, also allows him to view the future and anticipate its consequences. Homo Sapiens will be afforded ample opportunity to savor his successful conversion to a creature of constraint and disciplined action. If he fails, he will also have time to sit in self-indictment. This is a condition that is unique to man. Is it not fitting for the creature chosen to be the new architect of the environment?

REFERENCES

1. H.J. MULLER, *The Uses of the Past: Profiles of Former Societies* (Oxford University Press, Oxford, England, 1952) p. 53.

2. *Ibid.*, p. 75.

3. F.R. BAHR, "Man-machine symbiosis" *Kybernetes 1*, No. 1, 169-174 (1972).

4. *Ibid.*

5. E. HUNTINGTON, *Mainsprings of Civilization* (Mentor Books, New York, 1959) p. 44.

6. H.J. MULLER, *op. cit.* p. 50.

7. B.F. SKINNER, *Beyond Freedom and Dignity* (Alfred A. Knopf, New York, 1972) pp. 213-214.

8. R. ARDREY, *African Genesis: A Personal Investigation into the Animal Origins and Nature of Man* (Atheneum, New York, 1970) p. 348.

9. R. SEIDENBERG, *Post-Historic Man* (Beacon Press, Boston, 1951) p. 1.

10. B.F. SKINNER, *op. cit.* pp. 133-134.

11. R. PRESTHUS, *The Organizational Society*)Alfred A. Knopf, New York, 1962) and W.H. WHYTE, Jr., *The Organization Man* (Simon & Schuster, New York, 1956).

12. P.M. BLAU and W.R. SCOTT, *Formal Organizations: A Comparative Approach* (Chandler Publishing Company, San Francisco, 1962) p. 4.

13. K.E. BOULDING, *The Meaning of the Twentieth Century: The Great Transition* (Harper & Row, New York, 1964) p. 9.

14. E. HUNTINGTON, *op. cit.* p. 43.

15. K.E. BOULDING, *op. cit.* p. 24.

16. *Ibid.* pp. 24-26.

17. M. McLUHAN, *Understanding Media: The Extension of Man* McGraw-Hill Book Company, New York, 1964) pp. 3-4.

18. R.L. HEIBRONER, *The Future as History* (Harper & Row, New York, 1960) p. 93.

19. L. von BERTALANFFY, *Robots, Men and Minds: Psychology in the Modern World* (George Braziller, New York, 1967). p. 17.

20. B.F. SKINNER, *loc. cit.* p. 213.

21. R. ANDREY, *loc. cit.* p. 317.

22. L. von BERTALANFFY, *loc. cit.* p. 24.

23. R. ARDREY, *loc. cit.* p. 316.

24. B.F. SKINNER, *loc. cit.* p. 205.

25. W.R. SCOTT, "Theory of organizations" In: *Handbook of Modern Sociology*, (ed.) R.E.L. FARIS (Paul McNally and Co., Chicago, 1964) p. 488.

26. *Ibid.*

27. K.E. BOULDING, *loc. cit.* p. 142.

28. D. KATZ and R. KAHN, *The Social Psychology of Organizations* (John Wiley & Sons, New York, 1966) pp. 111-128.

29. F.R. BAHR, *loc. cit.*

30. L. von BERTALANFFY, *loc. cit.* p. 44.

31. *Ibid.* p. 3.